K_d	Cost of debt
K_e	Cost of equity capital
K_j	Required rate of return on investment *j*
K_M	Rate of return on the market portfolio
K_p	Cost of preferred stock
K_r	Cost of retained earnings
n	Number of periods (usually years)
N	Number of shares outstanding
NOI	Net operating income
NPV	Net present value
p	Selling price per unit
P	Price or value
PV	Present value
PVIF	Present value interest factor
PVIFA	Present value interest factor of an annuity
r	Rate of return
R_F	Risk-free rate of return
RRR	Required rate of return (also designated by *K*)
σ (sigma)	Standard deviation
t	Time period
T	Marginal income tax rate
v	Variable costs per unit
V	Value (also designated by *P*)
VC	Total variable costs

This modern text is designed to prepare you for your future professional career. While theories, ideas, techniques, and data are dynamic, the information contained in this volume will provide you a quick and useful reference as well as a guide for future learning for many years to come. Your familiarity with the contents of this book will make it an important volume in your professional library.

EX LIBRIS

Principles of Financial Management

Principles of Financial Management

Burton A. Kolb

University of Colorado, Boulder

1983

BUSINESS PUBLICATIONS, INC.
Plano, Texas 75075

ISBN 0-256-02879-6

Library of Congress Catalog Card No. 82–72371

Printed in the United States of America

1 2 3 4 5 6 7 8 9 0 K 0 9 8 7 6 5 4 3

This textbook is accompanied by a Student Workbook/Study Guide, published by Business Publications, Inc. and available through your college bookstore. The Study Guide is designed to enhance your learning experience in this course by offering additional supplementary material and review questions for self-examination or extra credit work. If the bookstore does not have the Study Guide in stock, please ask your bookstore manager to order a copy for you.

To my wife, *Eleanor*

Preface

This text is designed to provide an understanding of the financial considerations, analyses, and decisions pertinent to the management of a business firm. The fact that financial management is inseparably related to the other functional and ancillary areas of business management is recognized. Therefore, we emphasize such interrelationships throughout, rather than treat financial management as an isolated function. The general philosophy of the text is pragmatic and practical. Substantial development of financial theory is incorporated, but abstractions are avoided where possible and theory is treated in terms of its practical application to managerial problems.

Principles of Financial Management is intended primarily for use in the undergraduate core course in business finance. While providing a sound base for advanced study of finance, it is relevant to *all* students of business administration. The text also may be used to advantage in a core finance course for MBA students whose undergraduate work is either remote or in a field other than business administration. It also may be appropriately used in conjunction with case-method instruction in MBA or management development programs.

Objectives

An overriding pedagogical objective is that the text be *understandable* and therefore teachable. To accomplish this, the book begins on a relatively simple plane. Complexity gradually increases at a pace that the student can readily absorb. For example, valuation is introduced (in admittedly oversimplified form) in the first chapter, then revisited at various appropriate points throughout the text, each time in a more complete and complex fashion. Similarly, operating and financial leverage are introduced in Chapter 3 and treated in full detail in Chapter 17. This technique enables the student to develop throughout the course, rather than being frightened or lost in the early stages and perhaps bored with some of the material presented later.

The writing style emphasizes *readability*. Great care is exercised to define the terms, spell out the logic of each model, and walk the reader through realistic examples illustrating the use of each analytical tool.

A major educational objective is to provide *balanced* coverage of both appropriate quantitative analysis and the nonquantifiable factors that influence financial decisions. The text does not sacrifice essential information relative to institutional constraints or nonquantifiable implications in favor of elaborate development of esoteric models having little or no practical application.

Organization

Principles of Financial Management focuses upon the objective of maximizing value of the owners' equity of the firm (wealth of the common stockholders). It is organized largely in a balance sheet format because this approach both provides a direct linkage to the student's background in accounting and enhances teachability by allowing gradual development from relatively simple and familiar concepts to new and more complex ones.

Part One consists of three chapters providing an introduction to the field, basic organizational and tax information, and an overview of operating and financial considerations pertinent to managerial finance.

Part Two treats the accounting-related tools of financial analysis and short-term planning and control in two chapters.

Part Three deals extensively with working capital management, devoting one chapter to working capital policy, two chapters to current asset management, and two to short-term financing.

Part Four, consisting of five chapters, covers capital investment decisions (capital budgeting) and related subjects. The first chapter provides the background of the mathematics of finance, and the second develops the analytical methods. The third chapter deals with estimating relevant cash flows, and the fourth treats risk differentials and strategic considerations. The final chapter develops the cost of capital.

Part Five includes seven chapters dealing with raising funds in the capital markets, capital structure planning and policy, the use of long-term debt, convertible and equity securities, leasing, and dividend policy.

Part Six, on expansion and contraction, consists of a chapter on mergers and acquisitions and one treating failure, reorganization, and bankruptcy.

Part Seven discusses the unique financial considerations relative to international trade and management of the multinational firm.

Each chapter includes an extensive set of questions and problems. Present-value tables are provided both on the accompanying laminated card and in the Appendix of the text. A Glossary also is provided at the end of the text.

Instructors wishing to cover topics in a different order from that of the text may do so with little loss of continuity. For example, Part Three, on working capital management, may be used in the latter part of the course, if desired. Or Chapter 22, dealing with dividend policy, may be shifted to an earlier position—say, following Chapter 15, on the cost of capital. Portfolio theory and the capital asset pricing model (CAPM) are incorporated only in portions of Chapters 14 and 15. These may be omitted at the instructor's discretion. Appendixes following several chapters also may be omitted.

Accompanying materials

A Study Guide to Accompany Principles of Financial Management, coauthored with Adrian C. Edwards of Western Michigan University, is available to aid students in studying the text.

An *Instructor's Manual,* a *Transparencies Kit,* and a *Test Bank* are available to adopting professors. The instructor's manual includes teaching suggestions for each chapter, complete answers to chapter-end questions, and fully developed solutions to all problems. In addition, cases contained in J. Keith Butters, William E. Fruhan, Jr., David W. Mullins, and Thomas R. Piper, *Case Problems in Finance,* 8th ed. (Homewood, Ill.: Richard D. Irwin, 1981), and George N. Engler and John A. Boquist, *Cases in Managerial Finance* (Plano, Tex.: Business Publications, 1982), are identified for use in connection with appropriate chapters of this text. The transparencies kit contains acetates for overhead projection of all key illustrations. The extensive test bank provides true-false and multiple-choice test questions.

Acknowledgments

I gratefully acknowledge my debt to the many professors, business executives, and students who have indirectly contributed to this text by sharing their wisdom and experiences with me. Specifically, I thank Professors Verlyn D. Richards of Kansas State University; Adrian C. Edwards of Western Michigan University; J. Kenton Zumwalt of the University of Illinois, Champaign-Urbana; Joseph Messina of San Francisco State University; and Charles Barngrover of the University of Cincinnati for their constructive reviews of the manuscript and very helpful suggestions. Additional thanks are due to Adrian C. Edwards for his excellent work on the study guide. I am also especially indebted to Sally Carpenter for her diligence in typing the manuscript. Finally, I wish to express appreciation to my wife, Eleanor, to whom this book is dedicated, for her patience and encouragement and for doing most of the things I should have done while I was writing this text.

Burton A. Kolb

Contents

Part One
Introduction

Part Two
Analysis, Planning, and Control

Contents

Part Three
Working Capital Management

Part Four
Capital Investment Decisions

Contents

Principles of Financial Management

Part One
Introduction

Chapter 1
The Function of Financial Management

What is finance? What is financial management? Who is responsible for financial management? How does finance relate to the welfare of the whole firm and its various parts? In order to familiarize ourselves with the finance function and to try to find some answers to these questions, let us examine a few of the problems that might confront the management of a business (our business):

1. The production vice president wants to renovate our St. Louis branch plant, doubling its capacity by replacing "obsolete" equipment with new equipment employing the latest and "most efficient" technology.
2. The controller thinks he needs a new computer and accompanying peripheral equipment. These could be either purchased outright or leased.
3. The purchasing agent wants to buy in larger quantities to take advantage of quantity discounts and to maintain larger safety stocks to avoid frequent expediting and occasional stock-outs.
4. The marketing vice president insists that one of our product lines be redesigned and manufactured in a greater variety of models and colors. The production vice president is equally insistent that this is unnecessary. The director of distribution doesn't think much of the idea either, because this would greatly increase the cost and difficulty of maintaining inventories in our 4 factory warehouses and 12 regional warehouses.
5. The sales manager believes that the company's credit policy is too restrictive. Three of the last 10 orders obtained by one of our salespeople have been refused by the credit department because the risk of nonpayment was considered too high. One of our important customers also has complained about the nasty tone of a letter received from us pressing for collection of an overdue account and has threatened to seek another supplier.
6. Our forecast indicates we will accumulate a seasonal excess of cash during the next three months, and the treasurer is trying to decide what to do with it.

The above list could go on almost endlessly, but we have enough here to learn how the finance function relates to the management of the firm. Although these problems originate in various areas of the organization (marketing, production, finance, purchasing, and accounting), they all include financial considerations. Decisions that must be made will have financial implications. What do they have in common? Each involves the commitment to spend or invest funds and/or the expectation of receiving funds. Directly related to these funds flows, each decision entails the bearing of risk. These things are what finance is about—committing funds, obtaining funds, and weighing the risks to be borne in doing so.

Almost everything done in a business organization involves financial considerations. The salespeople perceive their association with the marketing function, but from a financial point of view they are spending funds—their salaries and expenses—with the expectation that they will sell our product, thus creating accounts receivable that will be collected in cash. The purchasing agents are buying raw material inventories, which create accounts payable that will have to be paid in cash. These inventories will be processed by the production people, who in turn expect that the finished goods inventories will be sold by the salespeople, etc. Nearly everyone in the organization is committing funds with the expectation that funds will be obtained in the future. Each person also is committing the company to bear risks that the anticipated funds flows will not materialize.

Financial perspective of the firm

Figure 1–1 is a somewhat simplified diagram of the flow of funds within the firm. When the firm is organized, the owners (equity holders) invest their cash into the cash pot. At this point, the firm is completely liquid. Its funds may be obtained dollar for dollar in cash at any time, and it does not owe anybody anything. It is subject only to the risks of failure of the bank in which the cash is deposited (accompanied by failure of a government agency, the Federal Deposit Insurance Corporation, to make good on its insurance commitment) and, of course, the inflation risk that the purchasing power of the dollars when later withdrawn from the bank might be less than when they were invested in the firm. The only trouble with this firm is that at this point its expected rate of return is zero.

Next, as the management people get to work, they invest the funds in fixed assets (land, buildings, and equipment) and raw materials. They hire people, including themselves, to work in the offices, in the plant, and on the sales force. They commit the company to pay these people wages, salaries, and fringe benefits. To do this they pay out cash, lowering the content of the cash pot.[1] Notice that in this process the liquid asset, cash, is being "frozen" to varying degrees. The fixed assets are frozen for the longest time. The plant asset, land, is a frozen value usually as long as it is owned by the firm. Buildings and equipment values are frozen, to be "thawed" via depreciation charges into work in process over the useful lives of these assets. Raw materials inventories are frozen for a much shorter period of time until

[1]This is oversimplified in that part of the fixed assets and most of the raw materials probably have been purchased on credit terms and the employees are not paid each hour as they work. Therefore, the downward flow of funds would be delayed for the short period that these costs would be lodged in accounts payable and accrued liability accounts.

Figure 1–1 **Flow of funds**
A financial perspective of the firm

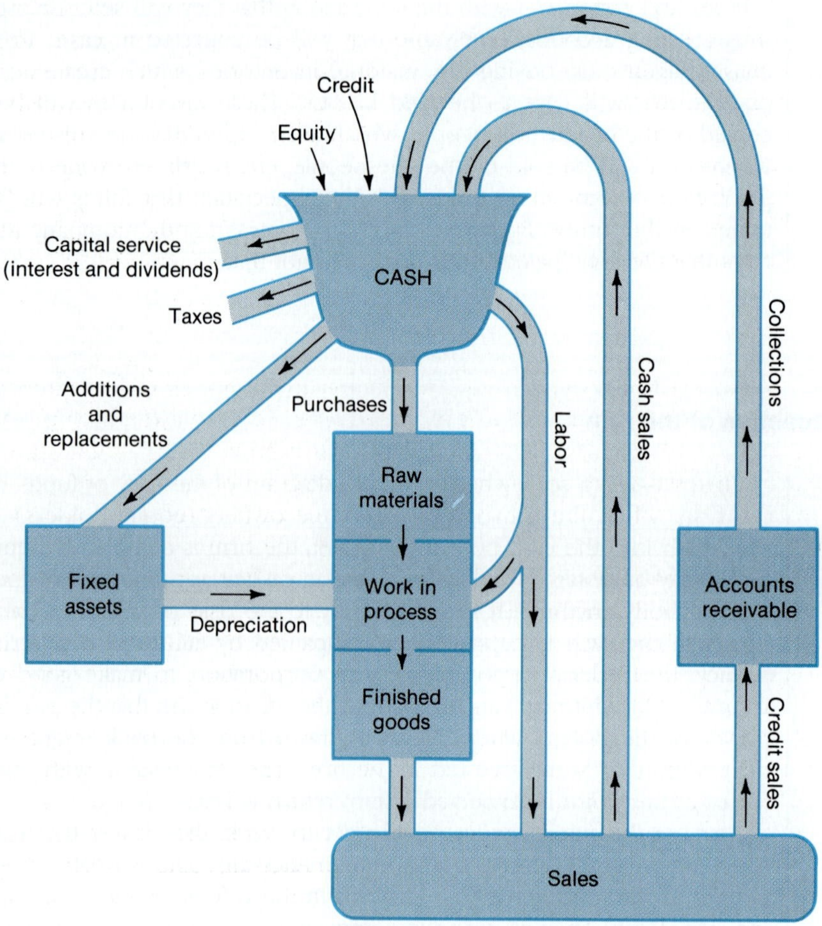

they move into work in process. Plant labor costs are accumulated in work in process inventory. Then, as production is completed, work in process is transferred to finished goods inventory, where it will remain frozen in the warehouse until sold.

To this point the system has operated more or less as if under the law of gravity, with funds flowing quite easily downward out of cash into the assets which are frozen or illiquid to varying degrees. The cash pot is now nearly empty. It may have been necessary to replenish it by obtaining credit externally—say, by a loan from the bank.

As the finished goods are sold, these assets are either thawed immediately and pumped into cash or converted to accounts receivable, one step closer to cash. As the accounts receivable are collected, they are turned into cash, which is pumped back into the cash pot.

If the firm has operated successfully, sales will have been made at a profit, and income taxes will have to be paid to the government out of the cash pot. If the firm has borrowed, it will have to service this debt by paying interest and repaying the principal according to the terms of the loans. Also, if operations have been profitable and the need for funds to pay expenses, replenish inventories, and invest in additions and replacements of fixed assets has not required all of the cash in the pot, management (or the board of directors if the firm is organized as a corporation) might use some of the cash to service the equity capital by distributing cash dividends.

Monitoring investment in assets

Financial management involves continual monitoring of this "money machine." One of the principal concerns is the level of investment in each of the asset "tanks."[2] Some of the problems encountered in connection with the investment in fixed assets were illustrated by items (1) and (2) in our initial list of problems on p. 6. Let us examine them in the context of Figure 1–1:

In Problem 1, the production vice president wants to renovate the St. Louis plant, replacing "obsolete" equipment with new machinery employing the latest and "most efficient" technology. This is expected to double the capacity of that plant. This proposal is going to have to stand examination to prove (1) whether or not the equipment is in fact obsolete from an *economic* standpoint, (2) whether or not the use of new equipment is in fact the most efficient from an *economic* standpoint, and (3) whether we can *economically* utilize the doubled capacity of this plant at this time. In other words, can this proposal be accepted on the basis of cost-benefit analysis, or should it be rejected or modified? After all, some production people have a natural tendency to "gold-plate" the plant (they appreciate technology, and that is the reason they are there).

In Problem 2, the controller thinks he needs a new computer and accompanying peripheral equipment. This is the same kind of problem as (1). It should be subjected to the same scrutiny. In addition, the choice between leasing and buying must be resolved by financial analysis.

Similarly, the levels of investment in the inventory "tanks" in Figure 1–1 must be continually monitored. Regarding Problem 3, the life of the purchasing agent will be most pleasant if we maintain stocks of all items in the raw material inventory at such high levels that we never come close to

[2]Financial management is also concerned with the level of liabilities such as accounts payable, notes payable, long-term debt, accrued wages and taxes, etc., which are not shown in the simplified Figure 1–1.

running out of any individual item. Then he or she never will have to do any expediting (hunting around trying to find an emergency supply of some item because continued production will be jeopardized tomorrow if we don't have it). A policy that would allow this might improve the health of our purchasing agent because more afternoons would be free for playing golf. But it could be costly from a financial management viewpoint because it might tie up an excessive amount of funds in the inventory account. Thus, financial considerations will induce us to seek optimal levels of inventory.

Problem 4 illustrates additional financial considerations relative to the level of raw materials, work-in-process, and especially finished goods inventories. The marketing vice-president insists that one of our product lines be redesigned and broadened to offer a greater variety of models and colors. From a strictly marketing viewpoint, this would be advantageous in that it would enable us to compete more effectively for sales. But from a production standpoint, the proposal is opposed because the redesign, changeover of production processes, and shorter production runs of a greater variety of models and colors would increase costs. From an inventory standpoint, this strategy would involve somewhat greater investment in raw materials and work-in-process inventories and a substantially higher investment in finished goods inventories. We would have to maintain much larger stocks to be able to ship orders of any of the wider variety of models and colors. (Perhaps it was this sort of proposal that induced Henry Ford, Sr., to state, "They can have any color they want as long as it is black.") Financial management considerations involve weighing the expected additional returns from greater sales against the additional costs of production and investment required to carry the additional inventories. Also the increased risk of inventory obsolescence must be evaluated. The decision on this proposal must eventually be based upon such financial analysis.

Financial management also is concerned with monitoring the level of investment in accounts receivable. Our Problem 5 illustrates this. The sales manager is complaining that our credit and collection policies are too tight. From a strictly marketing point of view, a sale is a sale whether or not we ever collect for it. From a financial point of view, however, we must consider eventual benefits to be obtained from the sales in terms of cash collected from receivables created by the sales. Maybe the credit and collection policy *is* too tight and we are turning away too many potential sales that would result in satisfactory collection. This whole matter must be weighed in financial terms of costs, benefits, investment in receivables, and risk of bad-debt losses.

Finally and most directly, financial management is concerned with the level of cash. Too much cash on hand at any time is costly in terms of what the funds could be earning if they were employed rather than lying idle in the bank account (our treasurer's problem—number 6). The treasurer would be even more concerned with any foreseen shortage of cash. Inability to raise cash to cover maturing obligations would cause acute financial embarrassment, which—at the limit—might throw the firm into bankruptcy. A major reason for financial management's concern about the levels of funds invested in all of the other assets of the business (and the amounts and maturities of the liabilities) is this direct responsibility for maintaining such a relationship between the cash inflows and outflows that he or she always is able to write checks that do not "bounce".

Monitoring flow of funds

Another area of concern of financial management is the rate of flow through the tubes from each asset tank to the next. Impediment of the normal flow of funds at any point in the system that is not fully compensated by adjustment of the flows at preceding points will cause a build-up in the investment in the asset tank(s) upstream, delaying the eventual flow into cash. For example, failure of sales to materialize at the expected rate would result in accumulation of finished goods inventory. Likewise, a delay in collection of accounts receivable would result in a build-up of receivables beyond the expected level and a corresponding reduction of cash inflow.

An additional concern of financial management is the security (in both physical and economic senses) of the funds-flow system. Holes have a way of developing in the tanks and tubes of this system, resulting in leakages of funds.

At the plant gate a worker is leaving with a lunchbox containing $150 worth of parts. One night last week someone failed to lock the gate; an unidentified truck entered our warehouse and departed with several thousand dollars worth of our finished goods inventory. Several thousand dollars worth of manufactured parts are being scrapped because they were rejected at the inspection station. Last year an explosion in the boiler room caused several hundred thousand dollars worth of damage and resulted in the plant's being closed for a month for repairs; an insurance policy covered the damage, but we did not have any business interruption insurance. In the finished goods warehouse a huge pile of obsolete models of our product is covered by a heavy layer of dust. We have $100,000 invested in that pile and will be lucky to get $200 for it from the junk dealer.

In the marketing offices a map with a lot of little red-headed pins in it identifies the whereabouts of each of our salespeople. It is January, and we notice a concentration of pins at Miami Beach. We turn out to be wrong on this one; the sales manager explains that the annual convention of the buyers of our product is being held this week in Miami Beach.

Perhaps we have exaggerated a little, but maybe you are starting to develop a financial awareness of the operations of a firm. The financial viewpoint involves an understanding of, and an involvement in, each of the following:

1. The amount of funds employed in each asset owned.
2. The rate of flow of funds from cash through each successive type of asset and back to cash.
3. Obtaining cash externally when needed but not produced from operations.
4. The disposition of excess cash when available.
5. Control of leakages of funds.

But understanding and being involved with the decision-making and control processes of the firm are not enough. They do not tell us what we are trying to accomplish as we go about our business. To this point we have dealt with financial considerations in such general terms as *economic justification* and *cost-benefit trade-offs*. We must develop an understanding of the ultimate *goal* of the firm. In other words, we must answer the question, "What is our target as we make or influence decisions?"

The goals of the firm

Business firms are conceived by one or more persons, the owners, who invest their funds (in cash or perhaps other assets) with the hope of making enough money to justify employment of the funds they have invested. Even if the founders were not strictly "moneygrubbers" (as might erroneously be inferred from the above statement) the firm will have to be financially nurtured through either the internal generation of funds or entering the money and capital markets. There potential suppliers of funds must be induced to part with their savings in exchange for the expectation of returns sufficient to justify the risk entailed in the employment of their funds.

If a viable combination of internal and external financing cannot be obtained, the firm will wither and die. This may seem (at this stage of our discussion) very cold, but it is true in the framework of the relatively free enterprise, capitalistic economic system in which the firm must live (or die). A business firm either makes money or it doesn't, and it retains part or all of these funds to finance itself internally or it doesn't. The alternative of external financing through the money and capital markets involves trading a piece of paper (say, a note, a bond, or a stock certificate) for money. The provider of that money can hardly be expected to part with it for whatever esthetic pleasure he or she may get from admiring the engraving on the paper. The inducement must exist in terms of the *value of the expected future return* of money in the form of interest or dividend income and the proceeds from redemption or sale of the paper to someone else in the future.

Returning to the interest of the owners (the providers of the equity capital) of the firm, we see that the goal of the firm is to maximize the *value* of the owners' equity. This may be stated another way as maximizing the *wealth* of the stockholders. To be more precise, if we are considering a corporation, *the goal of the firm is to maximize the value per share of the common stock in the long run.*[3]

There are *two elements* that influence the value of the equity of the firm: (1) *the expectation of returns* and (2) *the risk to which the investment is exposed.* We shall have much more to say about these later in this chapter and the rest of the book. But first, let us clear up some misconceptions regarding the central goal of the firm.

Some misconceptions

Many people misunderstand the goal of the firm because of biases of perspective, misconceptions, or just plain fuzzy thinking. We shall try to identify these misunderstandings and clarify them.

Maximization of size Perhaps it has been part of our cultural development to equate bigness with goodness. Increasing size, however, does not *per se* translate into increased value. Thus, maximizing sales volume alone (or other measures of size, such as total assets or number of employees) does not directly increase the value per share of the common stock. At the extreme, we could follow the old saw of "losing money on every sale but making up for it on the volume," which obviously would lead the firm to bankruptcy. Although it may be true in some situations that increased size will result in greater returns and/or lower risk, maximization of size alone is an incomplete statement of the goal of the firm.

Maximization of earnings The maximization of earnings (or earnings per share of common stock) also is an incomplete goal because it ignores the risk that may be borne in quest of the increased earnings. If we were to accept simple maximization of earnings as a goal, we would take the corporate treasury to the nearest race track and bet it on the horse with the highest odds. The point is that seeking increased earnings does not translate directly to increased value unless the degree of risk is unchanged by the means through which increased earnings are pursued. This rarely will be true because opportunities to make higher earnings usually are accompanied by greater risk of loss (just as in gambling odds).

[3]This precision is necessary because (1) the company could have outstanding other types of stock, such as preferred stock, which did not belong to the residual equity holders (the common stockholders) and (2) a managerial action might create a sufficiently large number of additional shares relative to the value of the assets obtained that the value *per share* would be reduced. (If this is confusing, do not worry about it, as it is a bit premature at this stage of our work.)

Another factor diminishing the validity of this goal is that reported earnings are a function of an accounting process that yields a highly imperfect determination of *economic* earnings. (This will be discussed in Appendix A of Chapter 3.)

Minimizing risk The goal of minimizing risk simply overemphasizes the other side of the coin in examining the risk-versus-return trade-off. As was pointed out earlier in relating the financial perspective of the firm, the minimization-of-risk goal would lead us at the extreme simply to leave the funds invested in the bank account. We would have minimum risk and little or no expected return except that of the original investment.

Constraints on the firm It must be understood that the firm does not operate in a vacuum: it exists in *an environment of social, political and moral constraints.* Management pursues the value-maximization goal within the limits imposed by that environment. In rather crude terms, this means that management is expected to play the game according to the rules. The legislative branch of government makes the rules, the executive enforces them, and the courts interpret them. Ultimately, the court of public opinion influences the three branches of government to establish and enforce such rules regarding the behavior of business firms as are deemed to be in the public interest. Thus, under a properly functioning system of government, pursuit of the value-maximization goal is not by any means a dirty, no-holds-barred fight to grab all one can for the stockholders. Rather it is simply doing one's job in a socio-economic-political system that, although admittedly imperfect, is probably the most satisfactory means of satisfying the needs of people that civilization has yet devised.

Those who have serious moral or ethical objections to the way in which pursuit of the value-maximization goal by the management of a firm works out in practice must, in all reasonableness, press their claims through the mechanisms of government to improve the system in such a way as to remove the imperfections or inequities that they believe exist. The faults, and we all probably perceive some, do not lie with the firm's goal of value maximization but rather with the ways in which some management personnel may be allowed by the legal mechanisms to pursue it. Furthermore, if you as a manager have moral or ethical standards of conduct that you feel are higher than those imposed by law and public opinion, you surely are quite free to adhere to those standards and pursue the value-maximization goal within such additional constraints. Many managers successfully do so.

Individual goals versus firm goals Probably one of the most prevalent and serious misunderstandings regarding the goal of the firm is the confusion of that goal with the much more complex goals of life of the person. It should be clear at the outset that the goal of the firm is not to be confused with the goal of an individual living his or her life. It relates only to that portion of a person's activity involved in the business decision-making process. I sincerely hope that your overall life goals are on a different and more lofty plane. There is no reason that the goals of the firm and your personal goals should be incompatible if the constraints on the firm indicated above are fully recognized and if your life is broader than just your job.

What is value?

The value of the common stock of a firm, which we are seeking to maximize, is a function of two elements, return and risk. *Return* is that benefit (normally in terms of dollars) expected to accrue in the future to the holders of the stock. *Risk* relates to the degree of uncertainty as to whether those benefits will materialize as expected. For an introductory (and grossly oversimplified) illustration, let us assume that you own a share of X Manufacturing Corporation stock. You expect average returns of $2 per year into perpetuity to accrue to you as a result of your ownership of this share. You could, alternatively, invest in a riskless security that would yield a return each year of 5 percent of the amount invested. This 5 percent *pure (or risk-free) interest rate* is simply the compensation for foregoing the use of the money.

But this share of stock you own is not riskless. Although you *expect average* annual returns of $2, these returns may be higher in some years and lower in others, and the average may or may not turn out to be $2. Also, rather than being certain of the amount that you will receive if and when you sell this security, you may receive more or you may have to take less than the amount that you paid for it when you sell. Owning this stock requires you to bear risk as well as simply forego the use of the money you have invested in it.

As you perceive the magnitude of this risk, you require, say, 5 percent to compensate for bearing the risk in addition to the 5 percent that you could get on the riskless investment. Thus, you *value* this stock at

$$\text{Value} = \frac{\text{Expected annual returns}}{\text{Pure interest rate} + \text{Premium for risk}} = \frac{\$2}{.05 + .05} = \$20.$$

You would be willing to hold the stock if the market price were about $20. If the market price were less than $20, you might be willing to buy some more of this stock, and if it were more than $20, you would consider selling this stock. Thus, *if* all of the participants in the market perceive the expected return and risk as you do, the market price of the stock should tend to hover about $20.

Assume that you are considering buying the stock of another company, Y

Manufacturing. You again estimate the expected average annual return to be \$2 per share, but you perceive the risk to be twice as great. You would value that stock at

$$\text{Value } (V) = \frac{\$2}{.05 + .10} = \$13.33$$

Similarly, if you were considering the stock of a third company, Z Manufacturing, for which you estimate the future average annual return to be \$2.50 and you perceive the risk to be equal to that of the first company, X Manufacturing, you would value that stock at

$$V = \frac{\$2.50}{.05 + .05} = \$25.$$

Thus, we see that the value of the stock of the firm is (1) directly related to the expected average return anticipated in the future by the investor and (2) inversely related to the risk borne. The logic is essentially the same when management considers a policy decision of the firm. If it is striving to maximize the value of the common stock, it must consider both the expected future returns and the risk to be borne as a result of that decision. Each individual decision will affect the total return-risk combination of the common stock and thus influence the stock's value.

Subgoals and strategic policies

Maximization of the value of the common stock is the common economic goal of firms and provides a general criterion for policy decisions. But it does not provide specific direction and guidelines for maintaining the necessary coordination of management efforts. For this reason, the top management of most large firms and the owner-managers of smaller ones establish more specific subgoals and voluntary constraints that define "what kind of company we shall strive to be." These usually relate to the perceived competences of the firm in terms of technological know-how, marketing organization, production capability, financial resources, etc., and the recognized weaknesses or limitations of the firm. On the basis of such an appraisal, management establishes subgoals that are believed to be attainable with the resources available.

For example, a large international conglomerate firm—say, ITT—might seek to acquire almost any business firm in any industry anywhere in the world that it is financially capable of acquiring and that appears to meet the general criterion of increasing the value of its common stock. On the other hand, a firm such as Procter & Gamble, with a great deal of know-how in the mass marketing of consumer products through retail supermarket channels, might establish a voluntary constraint limiting its operations to the manufacture of products that can be marketed through these channels only. Or a firm with an outstanding electronic research staff might have a subgoal of pioneering in the development of highly sophisticated electronic measurement and communication devices. Another firm in this industry, strong in production and cost control capability but weak in research talent, might have a policy of letting others do the inventing and concentrating its efforts on the subgoal of lowering prices by mass-producing electronic products at the lower end of the technology spectrum.

In essence, each of these subgoals represents an effort to reach the general goal of value maximization for the individual firms, with each taking a different route to that goal. One firm may intentionally assume increasing risks in an attempt to more than compensate by increasing expectation of return. Another might seek to limit or reduce its risks even though this may be partially offset by limitation or reduction of expected return.

Then a firm will establish strategic policies that have to do with the means by which it seeks to attain the subgoals and ultimately the value-maximization goal. For example, the mass-producer of low-technology electronic equipment may have a strategic policy of placing heavy emphasis on cost reduction via simplified product design and tight cost control of the production process, competing largely on a price basis.

Finally, these subgoals and strategic policies, all relating eventually to the general goal of value maximization, tend to specify and clarify the criteria or guidelines for the decision-making process. Thus, in making a particular decision, the executive can better understand the relationship of the specific decision to the efficient functioning of the whole firm.

The goals of financial management

The goals of financial management are intimately related to the goals of the firm. Within the framework of subgoals, voluntary constraints, and strategic policies, financial management seeks to accomplish the general goal of the firm, the maximization of value of the common stock. Thus it plays its vital role in the allocation of resources among each of the various types of assets of the firm. It is concerned both with the acquisition of assets and the flows from one asset to another, as discussed earlier in connection with the flow of funds.

Moving to the other side of the balance sheet we find financial management responsible for the acquisition of funds by utilizing various liabilities, such as accounts payable, notes payable to banks, and bonds, and by raising equity funds when necessary. It must coordinate the use of these liability and equity sources of funds in such a way that the firm is always able to meet its obligations under the contracts by which funds have been obtained. Thus an important subgoal of financial management is to maintain adequate liquidity so that the firm can pay its bills when due.

Responsibility for financial management

Who is responsible for financial management?

To this point we have not mentioned the term *financial manager* because, in one way or another, financial management is the responsibility and concern of almost everybody in the business organization. It is not by any means the sole responsibility of the chief financial officer or the people in the department commonly recognized as being the finance end of the business.

At the beginning of this chapter we listed six problems that involved financial considerations. Two of them originated in the marketing department, one involving interrelationships of marketing and finance and another involving the marketing, production, and distribution departments. One each came from executives in production, accounting, and purchasing. The remaining problem lay entirely in the finance area. This was done to make a point, that financial management is involved in any action anywhere in the firm that will influence future returns, incur costs, expose the firm to risks, or affect allocation of resources, internal flow of funds, or external acquisition or investment of funds.

Almost any action, ranging from building a new plant to the janitor spilling a bottle of floor wax, involves financial management (or mismanagement). Whether you are going into marketing, production, law, labor relations, accounting, transportation, engineering, or even finance, you are going to be involved with financial considerations. The higher you go in management, the more important these financial considerations will be. Finally, if you become the chief executive officer of the firm, you will be very heavily involved with financial management. Perhaps this explains why an increasing proportion of chief executive officers of major firms have developed through the financial route.

The financial manager

In most middle-size and large firms, the chief financial officer is the vice-president for finance. Directly responsible to this person are the controller and the treasurer. The controller is responsible for the internal accounting and auditing functions. The treasurer is responsible for management of cash and marketable securities; raising funds from external sources such as the commercial banks, the commercial paper and bond markets; and usually the operation of the credit department. A recent development is the creation of a planning department (or strategic planning department) responsible for coordinating forecasting and the staff work for long-range strategic planning. Sometimes insurance, office management, merger and acquisition activities, the legal department, and regulatory matters also are responsibilities of the vice president for finance. In any particular company the specific organization is a function of the firm's operations and the capabilities of its people.

What does the financial manager do? The financial manager and his or her staff have sole responsibility for the performance of some financial management functions. These usually include such things as managing the cash, maintaining the banking relationship, investing excess cash, and dealing with investment bankers and/or institutional lenders in connection with long-term financing. In more general terms, the financial manager is directly responsible for handling the relationship of the firm with the money and capital markets. These functions plus the accounting functions performed by the controller's office usually account for more than half of the time and energy expended in the department but less than half of the financial officer's personal activity.

In handling some of the functions, the finance department serves as a funnel through which information is gathered from the rest of the organization and relayed to higher management, the chief executive officer and/or the board of directors, or to committees of top management, such as the executive, forecasting (or budget), finance, long-range planning, or capital investment (budgeting) committees. Usually the chief financial officer, as a member of these committees and of the board of directors, participates in the formulation of major policies and decisions of the firm.

Much of the power of the financial manager is informal. For example, the financial manager usually does not *make* either the capital investment policies or the decisions regarding major capital expenditures. But he or she has a great deal of *influence* upon them because the proposals are funneled through the finance office, analyzed by its staff, and reported to the capital investment committee. In that committee's deliberations, the financial manager often has a major influence. Depending upon the magnitude and importance of such proposals, they may, after approval by the capital investment committee, move up the line to the executive committee and/or the board of directors. In these committees, again, the financial officer may present the proposals and exert considerable influence on the deliberations.

Another way in which the financial manager and his or her staff influence the performance of the finance function in the firm is purely *informal*. This involves discussion—between the financial manager and such other officers as the vice presidents for marketing, production, or labor relations—of the financial implications of problems and policies that are under their jurisdictions. In these sessions the financial officer ensures consideration of the financial implications.

In summary, much of the performance of the financial management function is not by any means solely under the direct jurisdiction of the financial manager. Some of the decisions are his or hers to make, but many of them are made by other people in the management organization who are influenced formally or informally by the financial manager or staff.

What financial management is not

You, as a student embarking upon a course in financial management (or business finance or corporation finance), might have some misconceptions regarding this subject. If so, we would like to dispel them right now.

Financial management is not another course in accounting. The two fields, however, are closely related. In financial management we almost constantly use a background knowledge of accounting and the data developed by the accounting process. But there is a distinction. We use accounting as our data base. To us, accounting is not an end in itself but rather a source of information that we analyze to see what the figures tell us in relation to problems that require decisions. In essence, financial management involves decision-making, doing things. We push a lot of numbers as means to decisional ends.

Neither is financial management a review of mathematics. From time to time we employ mathematical formulas or models in order to clarify our thinking as to how various data relate to each other in a meaningful fashion. For example, we have already employed an oversimplified valuation model in this introductory chapter. But at least this author does not see any sense in running you over the mathematical coals of complex derivation of models for intellectual exercise. We shall try to deal with the real and imprecise world without, for the sake of abstract theoretical precision, overly complicating such mathematical analyses as are necessary.

Financial management also is not a branch of statistics. Again, statistical concepts are employed to analyze financial data as means to making decisions. But we shall try to keep our analyses on a practical, useful level.

Financial management can be fun. It is not abstract but a highly practical pursuit. It is relevant in that nearly every person in business is involved in activity to which financial considerations are pertinent. And it is interesting because it relates to such a wide variety of activity in all areas of the business enterprise, not just to itself. At the risk of overselling, we think financial management is where it all comes together.

Organization of this book

This textbook is organized into seven parts, generally following a balance sheet approach:

Part One. Introduction
Part Two. Analysis, Planning, and Control
Part Three. Working Capital Management
Part Four. Capital Investment Decisions
Part Five. Long-Term Financing
Part Six. Expansion and Contraction
Part Seven. International Financial Management

Each of these parts is briefly discussed below to provide an overview of this book and the nature of business finance.

Part One. Introduction

Part One begins with the orientation of the financial management function. The purpose is to establish a financial overview of the firm and to describe the performance of the financial management function in a business organization. Chapter 2 develops the major legal forms of business organization and provides background regarding the tax environment essential to financial decision-making. Chapter 3 provides an operating and financial overview by reviewing the principal financial statements and analyzing operating characteristics of the firm. Operating and financial leverage concepts are introduced.

Part Two. Analysis, Planning, and Control

Part Two, which consists of Chapters 4 and 5, develops some of the accounting-based tools of financial analysis, planning, and control. These include ratio analysis, analysis of balance sheet changes, sources and uses of funds statements, cash forecasts, and pro forma financial statements. These tools are widely used in financial analysis and decision-making.

Part Three. Working Capital Management

Here the balance sheet orientation of the text begins. Chapter 6 considers overall working capital policy. Chapters 7 and 8 focus on the management of the current assets. Chapters 9 and 10 deal with the short-term financing of these assets through current liabilities.

Part Four. Capital Investment Decisions

The focus shifts to the management of fixed assets. Part Four begins with Chapter 11, presenting the compound interest and discount concepts necessary to analyze, in a cost-benefit framework, capital investment (budgeting) proposals. Chapters 12 and 13 deal with the rationale and techniques of capital investment analysis under simple assumptions. Then, in Chapter 14, the simple assumptions are lifted and capital investment is considered under perceived differences in uncertainty of project results. Estimating cost of capital is treated in Chapter 15.

Part Five. Long-Term Financing

Long-term debt and equity financing (the capital structure) are considered in Part Five. Chapter 16 introduces the capital markets, the sources of long-term funds, and the institutional mechanisms through which they are reached. Chapter 17 deals with long-range financial forecasting, operating and financial leverage, the various theories related to minimizing the cost of capital, and the development of target capital structure proportions. Chapter 18 describes term loans and bonds, and Chapter 19 deals with the financing alternative of leasing capital assets. Common and preferred stock financing are discussed in Chapter 20. Warrants and convertible securities are treated in Chapter 21. Retained earnings and its counterpart, dividend policy, are discussed in Chapter 22.

Part Six. Expansion and Contraction

Part Six begins with Chapter 23, which deals with financial analysis of external expansion through mergers and acquisitions. Chapter 24 discusses varying degrees of financial difficulty and alternative remedies, including bankruptcy and reorganization.

Part Seven. International Financial Management

In the final part of this text, Chapter 25 deals with the financial considerations relative to foreign transactions by primarily domestic firms and with topics specific to the financial management of the multinational firm.

Summary

This chapter provides an introduction to the financial management function by showing how it relates to the overall management and achievement of appropriate goals of the business enterprise.

A financial perspective of the firm is developed through the use of a simplified flow-of-funds diagram to demonstrate how liquid funds (cash) are "frozen" to varying degrees into fixed assets and inventories, then "thawed" through sales back into cash or temporarily lodged in accounts receivable until collection in cash. Financial management involves continual monitoring of these flows and the asset investments of the firm in an effort to assure that the asset investments are economically efficient and that the flow into cash is sufficient to provide for payment of obligations when due.

When operating cash flows are not sufficient, financial management must arrange external financing to provide the necessary funds on terms that the firm can live with. Conversely, when cash flows exceed operating needs, financial management arranges the disposition of excess cash by investing externally, retiring debt, paying dividends to stockholders, etc.

If the business firm, as an economic organism, is to function efficiently it must have a goal and appropriate strategies for accomplishing that goal. The general goal of the firm, and of financial management as a functional part, is the maximization of value of the common stock (or the wealth of the common stockholders) in the long run. This value, in turn, is a function of (1) the expectation of returns and (2) the risk to which the stockholders' investment is exposed. In pursuing the general value-maximization goal, management must in turn develop subgoals and strategic policies that establish more specific direction and constraints to guide the decision making of its executives.

The responsibility for financial management rests to some degree on nearly all the people in a business organization. The financial manager is solely responsible for some functions, such as managing the cash, maintaining relationships with the money and capital markets, and (usually) supervising the accounting functions. He or she is also responsible for collecting and analyzing financial data and communicating this information to various other managers, stockholders, government agencies, etc. The financial manager engages in many activities of a more subtle and indirect nature in working—sometimes formally and often informally—with various management committees and peers in other functional areas, influencing decisions and actions that have financial implications.

Financial management is closely related to accounting, mathematics, and statistics in that it utilizes the accounting system to provide data and mathematical and statistical methods to analyze those data. But it differs from these fields in that it focuses primarily on making decisions, doing things, taking action, considering nonquantifiable information as well, rather than pushing numbers as ends in themselves.

Questions

1. What financial considerations might influence the following decisions made by nonfinancial managers?
   a. The purchasing agent's choice of buying a given part direct from the manufacturer in carload lots or from a local distributor in smaller quantities.
   b. The production manager's decision to invest in a new machine to perform an assembly operation presently done by hand.
   c. The marketing manager's choice of distributing our product through wholesalers or establishing our own sales force.
   d. The labor-relations manager's decision to risk a strike rather than give in to a union demand.

2. Why is the financial manager more concerned with cash flows than the accountant?

3. Why is financial management concerned with:
   a. The amount of funds invested in each asset?
   b. The rates of flow of funds from each asset to the next?
   c. "Leakages" of funds?

4. What is the general goal of the firm?

5. Why is maximization of earnings *not* a satisfactory general goal of the firm?

6. How do expected returns, the pure interest rate (risk-free rate), and perceived risk relate to the value of the stock of a firm?

7. Who is responsible for financial management of a firm?

8. Why are a large proportion of a chief financial officer's activities informal?

Chapter 2 Organization and Environment of the Firm

A business firm operates in a complex environment of legal, economic, political, and social forces that continually influence its actions. This chapter introduces two legal and economic aspects of this environment that are particularly pertinent to financial management. These are (1) the alternative legal forms of organization of the firm and (2) the taxes to which the business is subject. Only a brief overview of each subject can be provided here. The serious student of finance should take at least a course each in business law and income tax accounting or law to provide a sufficient background in these subjects to enter the field of business financial management.

Forms of business organization

Three major forms of business organization are in general use in the United States, the *proprietorship* (sometimes called the sole proprietorship), the *partnership* (sometimes called copartnership), and the *corporation*. The largest number of firms are proprietorships, but these account for only a minor portion of total business activity as measured by volume of sales or assets employed. The corporation is a far more important factor in our economy, accounting for more than 80 percent of total business activity.

The proprietorship

A *proprietorship* is simply *a natural person engaging in business*. There is no legal distinction between the owner as a person and the business unit. If John Jones wishes to establish the Jones Drug Store as a proprietorship, from an organizational standpoint he simply starts doing business retailing drugs and allied lines. (He will, however, have to register and obtain several licenses from local, state, and federal authorities to operate as a drugstore.) Legal title to the assets of Jones Drug rests in John Jones, the liabilities of the store are his personal liabilities, and the owner's equity of Jones Drug is part of John Jones's net worth.

If anyone should file a legal claim growing out of the operation of the store, the lawsuit would be brought against John Jones. Thus, the proprietor *owns all* and *risks all*. Liability is unlimited; creditors of the business may look to all assets of the proprietor, whether or not these assets are connected with the business, for satisfaction of their claims.

Unlimited liability may or may not be significant to our proprietor, John Jones. It would be insignificant if substantially everything he has is invested in the drugstore. But it would be highly significant if he were wealthy, the investment in the drugstore representing only a small fraction of his net worth. In the latter case, organizing the drugstore as a proprietorship would place all of his other assets within reach of creditors of the business. This fact would greatly enhance the credit (ability to borrow funds) of the business, but, on the other hand, it would so increase the owner's personal risk that the risk-return trade-off would not be attractive. Therefore, use of the proprietorship usually is limited to the firm owned by an individual who has little wealth outside the business.

As the business grows, the only practical means of increasing its equity are the reinvestment of earnings or departing from the proprietorship form by establishing a partnership or a corporation to raise funds externally. All earnings of the firm and any earnings the proprietor may have from other sources are taxable as personal income to the owner. Reinvestment of earnings is limited to the amount available after the proprietor's living expenses and personal income taxes have been paid.

A proprietorship is extinguished if the business is sold or ceases operations. If the proprietor as an individual goes through bankruptcy, the assets of the firm as well as his personal assets are seized by the court and may be liquidated to satisfy the claims of creditors.[1] If the proprietor dies, the firm terminates because it was never separate from the proprietor as a natural person. This does not imply that the business necessarily will cease operations. The assets of the business become part of the proprietor's estate and the liabilities of the business also are those of the estate. Continued existence of the firm will depend upon the settlement among the heirs. The business might be continued in operation as a proprietorship by an heir, continued as a partnership of several heirs, or incorporated, with stock in the succeeding firm being distributed among several heirs. Or the business might be sold by the estate and the proceeds distributed among the heirs.

The significant shortcomings of the proprietorship as presented above explain why many firms, begun as proprietorships, switch to other organizational forms (usually corporations) as they grow in size, earning power, and asset requirements. They simply cannot otherwise attract sufficient equity capital to finance their growth. Still, the proprietorship has its place in business organization, namely, the situation where an individual of relatively small means invests most of his or her capital in a business that either is not growing significantly or can support relatively large growth in sales volume with only a modest increase in equity capital employed. This includes a great many small businesses, particularly those in the service industries.

The partnership

The *general partnership* (sometimes called the copartnership) is simply *two or more natural persons engaging jointly in a business enterprise* un-

[1]This seizure and liquidation of assets is subject to exemptions incorporated in the federal bankruptcy statutes, detailed explanation of which is beyond the scope of this text.

der an agreement (written or oral) among the partners.[2] The partnership agreement, called the "articles of copartnership," usually states the terms under which the partners are to contribute their capital and energies to the business. It also should define the partners' understanding on such matters as the nature of the business, division of profits or losses, limitation of withdrawals, powers and duties of each partner, admission of additional partners, and terms of dissolution.[3]

Partners are *jointly and severally liable* for the debts of the partnership. Thus each partner potentially risks his or her entire net worth. Although the partnership agreement often states the manner in which liability for losses is to be divided among the partners, it has no force with regard to outside creditors. It relates only to partners' claims among each other. Inability to attract external capital, mentioned earlier as a limitation of sole proprietorship, applies with even greater force to the partnership. Each partner not only bears unlimited liability for debts he contracted but also for those contracted by other partners in the name of the firm. Financing growth internally also is difficult due to the income tax status of the partnership. Each partner's portion of the income of the business, regardless of how much has been withdrawn, is fully taxable to that person as individual income.[4] If earnings are high, the large withdrawals necessary to pay the partners' personal income taxes will limit retention of earnings.

Lack of permanence is another deterrent to the attraction of capital in a partnership. Although one's risk might be reduced by the right to withdraw and force dissolution of a partnership, the other partners' right to do the same increases the risk that a partner's withdrawal might force liquidation at an inopportune time.

Likewise, death of a partner may either force liquidation or lead to the admission of an undesirable partner. This risk, however, may be limited by a prearranged buy-out agreement and/or shifted through a life insurance policy under which the maturing policy will make available funds to satisfy the claim of the deceased partner's estate.

The partnership and proprietorship suffer from similar limitations. Many small businesses begun as partnerships change to the corporate form as the firm expands to significant size. Still, the partnership may be appropriate where two or a few people are engaged in a business in which relatively little capital is required, earnings are of such magnitude that the tax advantage lies with the unincorporated business, most of the earnings are withdrawn, the partners are able to get along with each other, and the investment in the business represents the major portion of the net worth of each

[2]The term *partnership* will be used to denote general partnership unless preceded by *limited.*
[3]Competent legal counsel should be employed to draw the partnership agreement.
[4]The partnership must file a federal income tax return, but this is only informational to show the income that must be reported on the individual tax returns of each partner.

partner. This is particularly true if the personal services of the partners are vitally important to operation of the firm.

Some professional practices, particularly law and accounting, have traditionally been conducted under either proprietorship or partnership forms. Others, including medicine, dentistry, and engineering, formerly were so organized. As many states have provided for the professional corporation, however, the trend has been toward incorporation of these professional practices.

The laws of many states provide for the *limited partnership*. Such a firm must have one or more general partners, who have unlimited liability and the power to transact business, and one or more limited partners, whose liability is limited to the amount of capital contributed and who cannot transact business for the firm. A limited partnership interest usually is transferable without consent of the other partners.

The limited partnership is used widely in industries such as oil, gas, and other mineral exploration; apartment houses, shopping centers, and other real estate ventures; theatrical productions and cattle-feeding operations. The promoter and operator of the firm is the general partner and limited partnership interests are sold to investors seeking tax shelters. As the firm is not subject to corporate income tax, the individual investors can utilize, in proportion to their partnership interests, the expenses and write-offs of the business on their personal income tax returns.

The corporation

Any form of business organization fundamentally is a vehicle used to attract, hold, and control capital dedicated to a business purpose. When a corporation is formed, *a separate legal entity* is created by the state.[5] This separate existence as "an artificial being" greatly enhances the corporation's effectiveness in attracting, holding, and controlling capital. An individual or group wishing to form a corporation files *articles of incorporation* with the designated official, usually the secretary of state. If this document complies with the state corporation act and is accompanied by payment of the required fees, this official is obliged to endorse the articles, which are then recorded and constitute the *charter* of the corporation.[6]

Then, at the first meeting of stockholders, the *bylaws* are adopted, providing the set of rules regarding stockholders' meetings, election of directors,

[5]Although nearly all corporations are chartered by the individual states, some are federally chartered. These include all national banks (which are chartered by the Controller of Currency), the Communications Satellite Corporation (COMSAT), and the Federal National Mortgage Association ("Fannie Mae"), which are chartered by Congress.

[6]In a broader sense the charter includes the articles of incorporation, the state corporation law, and the body of judicial decisions interpreting it.

directors' meetings, appointment of officers, selection of standing committees of the board, issue and transfer of stock, etc. The initial capital contributions are paid into the corporation, and the stock is issued.[7] When a large corporation is formed, the incorporators usually purchase only a portion of the shares, the remaining shares being offered for public sale.

An important advantage of the corporate form is that the *liability* of stockholders *is limited* to the amount originally invested in the firm. If the corporation should fail, its creditors can look only to the assets of the firm to satisfy their claims. If the value of these assets is not sufficient, the creditors cannot proceed against the individual stockholders to collect the balance.[8]

Other financial advantages relate to the fact that the equity is divided into a number of shares of stock, which are transferable. The firm's ability to raise additional equity capital is enhanced because the equity is more marketable and the longevity of the firm is increased. Upon death, a stockholder's shares may be sold or transferred from the estate to the heirs. Control of the firm also is improved by the corporation's orderly mechanism for election of its directors by the stockholders and appointment of its officers by the board of directors.

Income of the corporation normally is subject to the corporate income tax. Dividends paid by the corporation to its stockholders are, in turn, subject to personal income tax. Depending on individual circumstances, taxation of income at the corporate level could be either an advantage or disadvantage. The corporate form may provide a tax advantage to the owners of an expanding firm in which a large portion of the earnings are retained. In a firm with stable equity capital requirements where most of the earnings are paid out in dividends, the corporate form may be a significant disadvantage because of double taxation. Under certain circumstances, however, small, closely-held corporations may elect to be taxed as if they were partnerships, thus eliminating the corporate income tax but subjecting the stockholders to personal tax on the income of the firm. These tax matters will be discussed in more detail in the next section.

The only disadvantages of the corporate form are the usually nominal legal expenses and filing fees required to obtain the charter and, in some cases, the income tax status. For the great majority of firms of significant size, the corporation is the most appropriate form of business organization. In fact, the formation of capital to produce the goods and services required by our economy would be impossible without it (unless there were revo-

[7]Although three or more incorporators usually are required, in effect a one-person corporation can be created by authorizing and issuing, say, 50,000 shares: 49,998 shares are issued to the one person and one share each issued to two other people who immediately endorse those shares and assign all rights thereunder to the first person.

[8]In practice, however, when lending to small, closely-held corporations, banks often will require the principal stockholder(s) to sign the note in addition to the corporation. In this way they eliminate the limitation of liability as it relates to this borrowing.

lutionary changes in our economic system). Because the corporation is the dominant form of business organization, it will be assumed throughout this book.

Tax environment

Everyone has heard the old saw about the certainty of death and taxes. As this book deals with financial management rather than mortuary science our principal concern is with the latter. Taxes influence almost all major financial decisions. Our multilayered government imposes taxes at the federal, state, and local levels. State and local taxes may include those on income, personal and real property, excise taxes on certain items, and sales taxes. As these vary widely among states, counties, cities, school districts, and other governmental units, we shall confine our discussion to the federal income tax system. The reader, however, should be aware that some state and local taxes, particularly those on income, may significantly affect many financial decisions, and their effects should be included in related analyses.

A corporation is subject to federal income taxation at rates ranging from 15 percent on the first $25,000 of taxable income to 46 percent on all taxable income over $100,000. Individuals are subject to federal income taxes at progressive rates ranging up to 50 percent of taxable income. With a minor exception, dividends received by individual stockholders are fully taxable. Thus, "double taxation" affects most business income, which is first taxed at the corporate level and then is subject to individual income tax when distributed in dividends to stockholders.

Income tax is an extremely complex subject that requires the professional services of specialized accountants and lawyers where substantial amounts are involved. It also is subject to change whenever the Congress changes tax laws, the tax courts issue decisions interpreting them, and/or the Internal Revenue Service (IRS) issues interpretive rulings. Here we shall introduce only the fundamental elements most pertinent to business financial management.[9]

The income tax system of the United States was drastically altered by the Economic Recovery Tax Act of 1981, which provided for major reduction in individual income tax rates in steps from October 1, 1981, through 1984. Corporate income tax rates were slightly modified, and methods of determination of taxable income were significantly changed. Unless indicated

[9]For additional information regarding federal income taxation, see either *Federal Tax Course* (New York: Commerce Clearing House) or *Federal Tax Course* (Englewood Cliffs, N.J., Prentice-Hall), both published annually.

otherwise, all tax information in this book will be based on the rates and procedures applicable to 1983 as legislated in the Tax Act of 1981.[10]

Individual (personal) income tax

Taxation of individual income is the largest single source of revenues of the U.S. government. Laws and regulations relative to its computation also tend to be the most complex. This section will provide a brief outline of the individual income tax, emphasizing the aspects that are business related.

Individual income tax rates are highly *progressive,* that is, they ascend steeply upward from 0 percent on very low incomes to a maximum of 50 percent of taxable income over $215,400 on a joint return. Applicable tax rates also depend upon the individual's filing status: single, married filing a joint return, married filing separate returns, or unmarried head of household.

Filing an annual individual income tax return involves listing first all income by source, such as salaries and wages, interest and dividends received, rents, royalties, etc. Then, allowable adjustments such as moving and employee business expenses are subtracted to determine *adjusted gross income. Exemptions* of $1,000 each are allowed for the taxpayer, spouse, and each dependent. Additional exemptions are allowed for those who are blind or 65 years old or older. Next, allowable *deductions* may be itemized (medical expense in excess of 5 percent of adjusted gross income, state and local taxes, interest expense, charitable contributions, some casualty or theft losses, and miscellaneous deductions). Alternatively, the taxpayer may elect to take the "zero-bracket amount," which is a standard deduction of $2,300 for a single individual or $3,400 for a married couple filing jointly. Exemptions and allowable deductions are subtracted from adjusted gross income to determine *taxable income.* The *tax* is determined from tax tables developed by the IRS on the basis of progressively graduated tax rates or, in some cases, computed using a tax rate schedule.[11]

Taxable income may be classified as ordinary income or capital gain, the latter being subject to special tax treatment.

Ordinary income Income from nearly all sources, such as wages and salaries, interest and dividends received, business income, farm income, pensions, rents, royalties, etc., is considered to be *ordinary* income. Note that all income from operating a proprietorship and/or the proportionate share of income from a partnership is ordinary income. Interest and dividend

[10]As this goes to press, the Tax Equity and Fiscal Responsibility Act of 1982 provides for some modification of the Tax Act of 1981. Significant changes are incorporated in the text.

[11]The 1981 Tax Act provides that, beginning in 1985, individual income tax brackets, personal exemptions, and zero-bracket amounts (standard deductions) will be adjusted annually for inflation by the change in the consumer price index.

income of $200 for an individual or $400 on a joint return is excluded; otherwise, dividend income is fully taxable. Interest income received on obligations of states or political subdivisions (cities, school districts, etc.) is exempt.[12] With these and other minor exceptions, all ordinary income is fully taxable.

Individual capital gains and losses *Capital gains* result from the sale of capital assets, such as stocks, bonds, or real estate, where the net proceeds exceed the original cost. A *long-term capital gain* results if the asset has been held for more than one year; otherwise, it is a *short-term capital gain.* Only 40 percent of a net long-term capital gain is subject to tax at the individual's ordinary tax rate. Thus, if the individual were subject to a 30 percent marginal (incremental) tax rate on ordinary income, a long-term capital gain would be taxed at only 12 percent (.40 × .30). As the maximum individual tax rate is 50 percent, the maximum taxation of a long-term capital gain is 20 percent (.40 × .50). Short-term capital gains are fully taxable at the individual's marginal rate.

This special tax status of long-term capital gains is an important factor in the use of the corporate form of organization, in determining capital structure policy, and in several other financial management considerations. It also may influence dividend policy. For example, a corporation owned by stockholders in high income tax brackets usually will pay small dividends, if any. Dividends would be taxed at the stockholders' marginal rates. If retaining earnings increase the market value of the stock, the stockholders can eventually sell their stock at long-term capital gains, only 40 percent of which will be taxable at their marginal rates.

When a capital asset is sold at less than its original cost (or unrecovered capital cost, which will be discussed later), a *capital loss* results. This capital loss is either long-term or short-term, depending on whether the asset has been held for more than one year. In determining *net* long-term capital gains, long-term capital losses are subtracted. Net short-term capital losses, up to $3,000 each year, may be subtracted from ordinary income. Forty percent of net long-term losses, up to $7,500 per year, may be applied to reduce ordinary income by up to $3,000 (.40 × $7,500).

Tax payments Taxes are paid largely on a "pay-as-you-go" basis. Individual income taxes on wages and salaries are withheld and remitted by the employer to the IRS. Self-employed persons and those with significant income from sources other than salaries and wages file a declaration of estimated tax for the current year on or before April 15 and make quarterly payments to the IRS on April 15, June 15, and September 15 of that year and on January 15 of the following year. Then, when the income tax return is filed by the taxpayer on or before April 15 of the following year, any excess of

[12]Beginning in 1985, 15 percent of net interest income, up to a maximum of $450 on a single return or $900 on a joint return, will be tax exempt.

withholding and/or estimated tax payments over the total tax bill may be refunded or applied against the current year's tax obligation. If payments are less than the tax liability, the taxpayer must enclose the balance due with the return. Interest or penalties may be assessed if the shortfall is too great.

Corporate income tax

As mentioned earlier, corporations, as separate legal entities, are subject to federal income tax. The corporate income tax rate is progressive, but only up to the first $100,000 of taxable income. Corporate income tax rates effective 1983 and thereafter are:

Taxable income	Tax rate
$0 to $25,000	15%
$25,000 to $50,000	18
$50,000 to $75,000	30
$75,000 to $100,000	40
Over $100,000	46

Thus, if a corporation had taxable income of $150,000, it would be taxed $48,750, calculated as follows:

1st $25,000 @ 15%	$ 3,750
2d $25,000 @ 18%	4,500
3d $25,000 @ 30%	7,500
4th $25,000 @ 40%	10,000
Tax on 1st $100,000	$25,750
Additional $50,000 @ 46%	23,000
Total tax	$48,750

Note that this corporation's *average* tax rate is 32.5 percent ($48,750/ $150,000), and its *marginal* (or incremental) tax rate is 46 percent.

A large corporation with taxable income of $50,000,000 would be subject to tax of $25,750 on the first $100,000 of income and $22,954,000 on the remainder (.46 × $49,900,000), totaling $22,979,750. Its average tax rate would be 45.96 percent and its marginal rate 46 percent.

Interest and dividends received by a corporation Interest received by a corporation (except on obligations of a state or political subdivision) is fully taxable as ordinary income. However, 85 percent of *dividends received* by a corporation is tax exempt. As only 15 percent of dividends received are taxable as ordinary income, the effective marginal tax rate is 6.9 percent (.15 × .46). The tax relief provided by the 85 percent dividend exemption might influence a corporation to invest in high-grade preferred stock, with dividends subject to a 6.9 percent tax rate, in comparison to a similar quality bond with interest taxed at 46 percent.

This special treatment reflects an effort by Congress to minimize *triple* taxation through (1) the corporate tax on income of the dividend-paying firm, (2) the corporate tax on the firm that receives the dividend, and (3) the individual income tax on the recipient of dividends from the second corporation.

If Corporation A owns 80 percent or more of the common stock of Corporation B, it may file a *consolidated* income tax return. As the consolidation process eliminates intercompany transactions, no taxes would be paid on dividends received by Corporation A from Corporation B if a consolidated tax return were filed.

Interest and dividends paid by a corporation When a corporation finances by borrowing—say, through a loan from a bank or by selling bonds to investors—it must pay interest on these obligations. *Interest paid* by the corporation is an allowable expense (deduction) in calculating its taxable income. Therefore the *after-tax* interest cost of borrowing funds is reduced by this tax deduction (called a tax shield). For example, if a firm borrows $1 million for a year at an interest rate of 15 percent, it pays the lender $150,000 interest. But this payment reduces the firm's taxable income by $150,000, therefore its federal income taxes will be $69,000 (.46 × $150,000) less than otherwise. In effect, its after-tax interest cost on the borrowing is $81,000 ($150,000 interest less $69,000 tax shield), or 8.1 percent ($81,000/$1,000,000).

Dividends paid by a corporation to its stockholders are *not* deductible for tax purposes. They are considered as distributions of income rather than expenses. The tax deductibility of interest on debt compared to the nondeductibility of dividends on stock is an important consideration in the choice between financing by borrowing or selling additional stock.

Improper accumulation of earnings The tax code provides that a corporation may be subject to an additional penalty tax if it accumulates earnings for the purpose of avoiding personal income tax payments by its stockholders. The accumulation of $250,000 in retained earnings is fully exempt from this provision. Beyond that accumulation, a corporation may retain earnings for any legitimate reason such as financing its growth of operating assets, paying off debt, or providing reasonable liquidity to cover future cash needs. In general, the IRS levies the penalty tax only when a closely-held corporation is obviously and unjustifiably retaining earnings for the sole purpose of avoiding personal income tax of its stockholders.

For example, if a manufacturing company whose stock was owned by one or a few individuals accumulated a portfolio of investment securities and real estate not related to its operations, it would run a serious risk that a penalty tax would be levied by the IRS. The reasoning would be that the corporation was using its earnings to accumulate investments for the benefit of the stockholders, rather than paying these earnings out in dividends to the stockholders, who would pay taxes on the dividends and invest the remainder in the securities and real estate.

Payment of taxes Corporate, like individual, income taxes are on a pay-as-you-go basis. The corporation files an estimated tax form on or before April 15 and must pay at least 90 percent of the year's estimated tax in equal installments on April 15, June 15, September 15, and December 15. Additional taxes or refunds of overpayments must be settled when the annual tax return is filed. Penalties equal to the average prime rate charged by banks during September may be levied for underpayment.

Capital cost recovery

Ordinary taxable income is determined by subtracting from gross income all operating and financial costs and expenses, such as materials, labor, selling, administrative and general expenses, interest expenses, and depreciation expense. In essence, *depreciation expense* is the *recovery of that portion of capital outlays previously made that are attributable to operations of the current year.* Fixed assets acquired prior to January 1, 1981, usually are depreciated for tax purposes over their estimated useful lives using an accelerated method, either the double-declining balance method or the sum-of-the-years'-digits method. Either of these accelerated depreciation methods provides larger tax deductible depreciation expense than straight-line depreciation during the early years of the asset's useful life. When the unrecovered cost (original cost less accumulated depreciation) of an asset declines to the point that straight-line depreciation will provide a larger tax deduction, the firm is allowed to switch to the straight-line method.

The 1981 Tax Act provides a new and more beneficial tax treatment of capital cost recovery. The act replaces the previous concept of depreciation based on useful life of the asset with the *accelerated cost recovery system* (ACRS). This system employs standard recovery percentages for each year over predetermined periods. The recovery periods gênerally are shorter than the assets' useful lives and ignore salvage values. Property placed in service after January 1, 1981, may be depreciated for tax purposes under the ACRS.

The ACRS classifies tangible property and assigns *capital cost recovery periods* on the following basis:

Three-year property consisting of automobiles, light-duty trucks, research and development equipment, and some other relatively short-lived personal property.

Five-year property includes most other machinery and equipment except long-lived public utility property.

Ten-year property consists of public utility property with useful lives between 18 and 25 years, railroad tank cars, and some relatively short-lived buildings.

Table 2–1 ACRS Standard recovery percentages
Property placed in service during 1981 through 1984

Recovery year	Property class: 3-year	5-year	10-year	15-year public utility†
1*	25%*	15%*	8%*	5%*†
2	38	22	14	10
3	37	21	12	9
4		21	10	8
5		21	10	7
6			10	7
7			9	6
8			9	6
9			9	6
10			9	6
11				6
12				6
13				6
14				6
15				6

*Taxpayer is also entitled to investment tax credit in the first year.
†The schedule applicable to real estate is slightly different. It provides a considerably larger first-year recovery because most real property investment does not qualify for the investment tax credit.

Fifteen-year property includes most buildings and some longer-lived public utility property.

Each of the above classes of property placed in service from 1981 through 1984 may be depreciated for tax purposes according to the ACRS *standard recovery percentages* shown in Table 2–1. Property placed in service during 1985 may be depreciated according to the standard recovery percentages shown in Table 2–2. For property placed in service in 1981 or 1982, the full cost may be depreciated by the percentages indicated. Beginning in 1983, one half the investment tax credit (ITC) must be deducted from the cost of the asset to determine the amount subject to ACRS depreciation. In general, the ACRS provides larger tax deductions related to capital cost recovery by shortening the period and accelerating the allowable depreciation expense. While ACRS is used for tax purposes, depreciation on the basis of estimated useful life is still used for regular accounting purposes.

The increase in tax deductions for depreciation (capital cost recovery) provided by ACRS has important implications relative to the capital investment decisions of the firm (treated in Part IV, Chapters 11–15 of this book). By decreasing tax outlays in the early years of a capital asset's useful life, ACRS increases the attractiveness of replacing old fixed assets with new, more efficient ones. The broad economic goal is to increase productivity of

Table 2–2 ACRS Standard recovery percentages
Property placed in service in 1985

Recovery year	Property class: 3-year	5-year	10-year	15-year public utility†
1*	29%*	18%*	9%*	6%*†
2	47	33	19	12
3	24	25	16	12
4		16	14	11
5		8	12	10
6			10	9
7			8	8
8			6	7
9			4	6
10			2	5
11				4
12				4
13				3
14				2
15				1

*Taxpayer is also entitled to investment tax credit in the first year.
†The schedule applicable to real estate is slightly different. It provides a considerably larger first-year recovery because most real property investment does not qualify for the investment tax credit.

American industry by providing an incentive to increase production efficiency through plant modernization.

Tax effects of inventory valuation methods

Income taxes also may be affected by the method of valuation of the firm's inventory. The two most widely used inventory valuation methods are first-in, first-out (FIFO) and last-in, first-out (LIFO). In an inflationary period, the use of FIFO causes cost of goods sold to be charged with inventory valued at the lowest cost (because it was acquired at the earliest date). This results in charging lower costs against revenues of the period; therefore taxable income is higher and higher taxes must be paid. For this reason, most firms use the LIFO method of inventory valuation for tax purposes, transferring into cost of goods sold the costs of the inventories last acquired (at higher prices). This results in higher costs being charged against revenues; therefore taxable income is reduced (compared to FIFO), and taxes are minimized.

Corporate capital gains and losses

Corporations as well as individuals receive special tax treatment of net long-term capital gains. A long-term capital gain occurs when a capital asset that has been held for longer than one year is sold at a price in excess of its original cost. A short-term capital gain is taxed as ordinary income, but a long-term capital gain by a corporation is taxed at only a 20 percent rate. If a small corporation is subject to an ordinary tax rate of less than 20 percent, it may elect to declare the long-term capital gain as ordinary income subject to tax at the lower rate.

The technical definition of a capital asset is very complex, but usually capital assets held by corporations are either securities (notes, bonds, or stocks) or fixed assets (machinery, equipment, or real estate).[13]

When a firm sells a depreciable asset, such as a building or a piece of equipment, at a price higher than its unrecovered cost (original cost less accumulated depreciation) but lower than its original cost, the gain is *not a capital gain* but rather is considered to be a *recapture of depreciation.* Recaptured depreciation is ordinary income subject to taxation at the firm's regular tax rate. The IRS considers that this gain reflects excess capital cost recovery (depreciation) during the period that the asset has been held, and it taxes the recapture as ordinary income to recover the excessive tax deductions that were previously allowed. However, if the sale price of a capital asset exceeds its original cost, that portion in excess of original cost is taxed as a capital gain.

To illustrate, assume that a firm sells for $50,000 a machine that had been purchased two years previously for $40,000 and had been depreciated 15 percent in the first year and 22 percent in the second, under ACRS for a five-year asset. Its unrecovered cost would be $25,200, that is, $40,000 (1.00 − .37). Recaptured depreciation of $14,800 ($40,000 original cost less $25,200 unrecovered cost) would be taxed as ordinary income. If the firm were subject to a 46 percent marginal tax rate, the tax on the recaptured depreciation would be $6,808 (.46 × $14,800). The long-term capital gain of $10,000 ($50,000 selling price less $40,000 original cost) would be taxed at only a 20 percent rate, or $2,000 (.20 × $10,000). If the machine were sold for only $35,000, the excess of the sale price over unrecovered cost of $9,800 ($35,000 − $25,200) would be taxed as recaptured depreciation at 46 percent, or $4,508 (.46 × $9,800).

If a firm sells a depreciable asset, such as a building or a machine, at *less than* its unrecovered cost, the entire loss may be deducted from ordinary taxable income of the period. Thus if the machine discussed above were sold for $20,000, the firm would incur a capital loss of $5,200 ($25,200 unrecovered cost less $20,000 sale price). This $5,200 loss could be deducted from ordinary income, creating a tax shield (saving) of $2,392 (.46 × $5,200).

[13]Technically, real and depreciable properties used in business, such as buildings, machinery, and equipment, are not defined by the Internal Revenue Code as capital assets. Net proceeds from sale of such property in excess of original cost, however, are treated as capital gains.

A capital loss resulting from sale of a nondepreciable asset not used in trade or business, such as a debt security or stock in another firm held as an investment by the corporation, can be used *only* to offset capital gains. Such a loss, however, may be carried back to prior years or forward to future ones, as we shall see presently.

Tax loss carry-backs and carry-forwards

To provide equitable taxation for "feast or famine" businesses, the tax code allows losses to be applied to offset taxable income of previous and future years. Operating losses may be carried back 3 years and forward up to 15 years to offset taxable operating income. Capital losses may be carried back 3 years and forward up to 5 years to offset capital gains. A loss in a given year must first be applied to offset income of the third previous year. Taxes for that year are recomputed, giving effect to the loss carry-back, and the firm is then eligible for a refund of taxes paid in that year. If the loss carry-back is not exhausted, the remainder is applied to offset taxable income of the second previous year, then the preceding year, and progressively into future years until the loss carry-forward is exhausted.

For example, if Apex Corporation had taxable income of $1 million each year from 1980 through 1982, then suffered an operating loss of $5 million in 1983, it could carry back $3 million of the 1983 loss to obtain refunds of all taxes paid on 1980 through 1982 income. Then it would have a tax loss carry-forward of $2 million. If its taxable income in 1984 were $700,000, it would be offset by applying that amount of the carry-forward, and Apex would pay no taxes that year. If 1985 taxable income were $1,500,000, the balance of the carry-forward, $1,300,000, would be applied, reducing the taxable 1985 income to $200,000. In the unlikely event that Apex's profitability were not sufficient to utilize the carry-forward by the end of 1998, it would expire.

Tax credits

A *tax credit* is a direct dollar-for-dollar reduction of tax liability. Tax credits have been enacted by Congress at various times to induce certain types of expenditures. They are available to either corporations or individuals.

Investment tax credits The *investment tax credit* (ITC) is designed to induce business firms to invest in machinery and equipment. Depending upon economic conditions, Congress has from time to time provided or repealed such credits. Presently an investment tax credit of 6 percent of the purchase price is allowed for acquisition of 3-year property and 10 percent for 5-, 10-, or 15-year property. Nearly all new property except real estate and personal property with a useful life of less than 3 years is eligible for the credit. Eligible used property is limited to $125,000 per year in 1981–84 and $150,000 in 1985. The credit is allowable in the year in which the asset is placed in service.[14]

If the asset is sold prior to the expiration of its cost recovery period, the IRS may recapture an appropriate proportion of the tax credit. For example, if a 5-year asset were sold during the second year after its acquisition, 80 percent of the tax credit may be recaptured; if sold during the fourth year, 40 percent may be recaptured.

If a firm's investment tax credits exceed its tax liability in a given year, the credits may be carried back or forward in a manner similar to that applied to operating losses. This provision is particularly valuable to young, rapidly growing firms that may accumulate large investment tax credits but have little or no taxable income in their early stages of development.[15]

The cost that may be recovered through depreciation (ACRS) must be reduced by one-half the amount of the investment tax credit. Thus if a firm acquires a depreciable asset for $100,000 and receives a $10,000 investment tax credit, it can recover $95,000 through depreciation (accelerated cost recovery).

Research and development tax credit The 1981 Tax Act provides a special credit to induce increase in research and development (R&D) expenditures. Effective from mid-1981 through 1986, a tax credit equal to 25 percent of the annual *increase* in expenditures for R&D materials and supplies over the average of the three previous years' R&D expenditures is allowed. For example, if Apex Corporation had average annual R&D expenditures from 1980 through 1982 of $100,000, but spent $150,000 on R&D in 1983, it would be eligible for an R&D tax credit of $12,500, that is, .25($150,000 − $100,000) on its 1983 income tax. This credit also may be carried back or forward if it exceeds the current year's tax.

Other tax credits Direct tax credits also are allowed for rehabilitating old buildings, taxes paid to foreign governments, and for expenditures in connection with certain job-training and employment programs.

Subchapter S corporations

Subchapter S of the Internal Revenue Code provides that a corporation with 25 or fewer stockholders (all of which must be individuals or qualifying trusts) *may elect that its earnings be taxed as if it were a proprietorship or partnership.* If this election is made, the firm is known as a *Subchapter S corporation.* The corporation then is not subject to any corporate income

[14]Progress payments made during the period of construction are eligible if the normal construction period is two years or longer.

[15]An additional special benefit to small businesses is an election to expense (rather than capitalize and depreciate) limited investments in depreciable business assets. The annual expense limit is $5,000 for 1982–83, $7,500 for 1984–85, and $10,000 for 1986 and thereafter.

tax, but rather its annual earnings are apportioned on a ratable (share for share) basis to its stockholders, who are subject to individual income taxes on their proportionate shares of the earnings.

A Subchapter S election may be beneficial if the firm pays out nearly all of its earnings to the stockholders because it avoids double taxation. It also may be appropriate if the firm is incurring tax losses and/or is eligible for significant depreciation (accelerated cost recovery) allowances or investment tax credits that cannot be utilized by the corporation but that would be valuable to its stockholders in reducing their individual income taxes.

In many cases in which the corporate form would be disadvantageous from an income tax standpoint but advantageous for other reasons, such as limited liability, transferability of shares, or longevity, the firm should be incorporated and immediately make a Subchapter S election. If this action is considered, competent tax counsel should be obtained.

Summary

This chapter dealt with two of the important environmental factors influencing financial management: legal aspects of business organization and the taxation system. There are three major forms of business organization in the United States, the proprietorship, the partnership, and the corporation. Although proprietorships and partnerships are simpler to form and outnumber corporations, their disadvantages of unlimited liability and direct taxation of the principals limit their use in attracting sufficient equity capital to finance growth. The corporation, as a separate legal entity, is more effective in attracting, holding, and controlling capital. Its advantages of limited liability, division of equity into transferrable shares, and orderly control mechanism have led to its becoming the dominant form of business organization. Although usually taxed separately, some closely-held corporations may elect under Subchapter S to be taxed as if they were proprietorships or partnerships.

Taxes influence almost all major financial decisions. Tax law is extremely complex, but all business managers should be aware of the fundamental elements of the federal income tax system and the various taxes imposed by the governments of states and localities where their firms operate. Federal income taxes are imposed at both the corporate and individual levels. Individual income tax rates are highly progressive, ranging from 0 to 50 percent as income increases. Ordinary income, including that from proprietorships and partnerships, is fully taxable, but 60 percent of net long-term capital gains are exempt. All interest and dividends (subject to a small exclusion) are fully taxable.

Corporate income taxes are progressive only up to the first $100,000 of income at rates ranging from 15 to 46 percent. Interest received is fully taxable, whereas 85 percent of dividends received by corporations is exempt. Interest paid is deductible, but dividends paid are not. Capital cost recovery (depreciation) is an allowable expense. Depreciable assets acquired prior to January 1, 1981, usually are depreciated for tax purposes using an accelerated method for the early years and later converting to straight line. Assets acquired after January 1, 1981, may be depreciated under the accelerated cost recovery system (ACRS), which employs standard recovery percentages over predetermined periods. This system departs from traditional depreciation over useful lives of the assets, providing substantial tax benefits during relatively short cost recovery periods.

Net long-term capital gains of corporations are taxed at a 20 percent rate. Recapture of depreciation is fully taxable. Most capital losses on depreciable property may be deducted from ordinary income. Operating and capital losses may be carried back and forward to offset income in past and future years, subject to time limitations. Tax credits encourage certain types of expenditures; the most important is the investment tax credit (ITC).

Questions

1. *a.* What are the three most prominent forms of business organization used in the United States?
   b. Define each.
   c. Which is economically the most important?
2. Define and indicate the organizational form(s) associated with each:
   a. Unlimited liability
   b. Joint and several liability
   c. Limited liability
3. Indicate the major advantages of the corporation and possible disadvantages.
4. Why is the corporate form of organization vital to our economic system?
5. Why might an individual in a high tax bracket prefer investing in a limited partnership engaged in certain types of business—say, shopping centers or apartment complexes—to investing in stock of a corporation?
6. In what sense does "double taxation" of corporate income occur?
7. *a.* Explain, in a general way, how the taxable ordinary income of an individual is determined.
   b. How are individual capital gains determined, and how does their tax treatment differ from that of ordinary income?
   c. When are individual income taxes paid?

8. How are interest and dividends *received* by a corporation treated for tax purposes?

9. How are interest and dividends *paid* by a corporation treated for tax purposes?

10. Explain how losses may be carried back and forward.

11. How does allowable depreciation (capital cost recovery) affect a firm's income taxes?

12. *a.* What is the difference between a capital gain and a recapture of depreciation on a depreciable asset?
    b. What are the tax implications?

13. What is a Subchapter S corporation? How is it taxed?

14. What is an investment tax credit (ITC)? How does it differ from an allowable deduction?

Problems

1. Mary Kelly and George Jefferson are equal general partners in Margeor Company. Mary has net personal assets of $100,000 (outside the firm) and George has $5,000 (outside the firm). Mary and George each have invested $8,000 in Margeor. Margeor fails, with assets liquidating at $6,000 and liabilities of $25,000. Creditors have become impatient and are filing lawsuits to collect the amounts owed to them.
    a. Against whom do the creditors file their claims?
    b. From whom will they collect?
    c. How will Mary come out after all settlements are made?
    d. How would Mary's position differ if Margeor had been a corporation?

2. Corporation A has net taxable ordinary income of $42,000 and Corporation B, $1,000,000.
    a. What is the *marginal* federal income tax rate of each?
    b. How much income tax would each have to pay?
    c. What is the *average* tax rate of each?

3. The Hodding Corporation has net income from operations of $500,000, interest income of $100,000, and dividend income of $200,000.
    a. What is its marginal tax rate on interest income?
    b. What is its marginal tax rate on dividend income?
    c. What is its total tax?
    d. What is its average tax rate on net income?

4. Exar Corporation has net operating income of $800,000, *paid* interest of $100,000, and *paid* dividends of $200,000.

   a. How much income tax must it pay?

   b. What is its average tax rate on net income?

5. Milon Corporation, which has taxable income well over $100,000, bought and installed a new machine on January 1, 1982, for $100,000. The machine is classed as 5-year property under ACRS.

   a. What depreciation (cost recovery) can be charged for 1982 for this machine?

   b. What investment tax credit (ITC) can be taken against 1982 income tax?

   c. What is the total tax saving in 1982 resulting from this purchase?

   d. What depreciation (cost recovery) can be charged in 1983 for this machine?

   e. What tax saving in 1983 will result?

6. Milon Corporation sold another machine in 1982, receiving net proceeds of $65,000 from it. This machine had been purchased in 1978 for $60,000 and at the date of sale had an unrecovered cost (depreciated book value) of $20,000.

   a. What recapture of depreciation occurred?

   b. What was the tax on this?

   c. What, if any, capital gain occurred?

   d. What was the tax on this?

   e. What was the total tax effect of the sale?

7. The Utam Corporation sold in 1983 its 20 percent stockholdings in the Mehr Company for $3,800,000. This stock had been purchased in 1958 at a cost of $900,000. Utam also sold in that year a small holding of Luxor stock for $200,000. This stock had been purchased for $310,000 in 1972.

   a. What was Utam's net long-term capital gain on these stock transactions?

   b. What was its tax resulting from these transactions?

8. Volatile Skicorp had taxable ordinary income of $800,000 in 1979, $1,900,000 in 1980, and $300,000 in 1981. In 1982 it did not snow in Volatile's area, and the corporation suffered an operating loss of $2,800,000.

   a. What can Volatile Skicorp do (besides considering buying snow-making machines)?

   b. About how much can it get in tax refunds from the IRS?

9. What income tax would an individual in a 34 percent marginal tax bracket pay in 1983 as a result of each of the following transactions? (Consider each item separately.)

a. A gain of $1,000 on sale of stock held for five years.
b. Receipt of $220 in dividends.
c. Receipt of $300 interest from a savings account.
d. A gain of $500 on sale of a stock held for four months.
e. Receipt of $120 interest on a bond issued by the State of New Jersey.

Chapter 3
Operating and Financial Overview

In Chapter 1 we used a flow-of-funds diagram (Figure 1–1) to illustrate a financial perspective of the firm. There are other useful ways of viewing the operations and financing of the firm that aid in controlling operations and providing appropriate funds to finance these operations. First we must understand the operating characteristics of the firm. Since operations provide the earnings and cash flows to support and service the financial arrangements, we must understand the effects of changes in levels of operations upon earnings and cash flows.

Analysis of operating characteristics and operating leverage will disclose the fluctuation in earning power that may result from changes in volume of operations. Then the effects of various alternative financial arrangements upon the returns to and risks borne by the stockholders may be developed through financial leverage analysis. These returns and risks determine the value of the stock. Our goal is to maximize this value.

The financial manager derives much information from the financial statements of the firm, the balance sheet and income statement. A guide to the interpretation of these statements is provided in Appendix A of this chapter.

Operating characteristics perspective

The production engineer looks at a firm's operating characteristics in terms of the people and machines that perform various operations to create the product and the transfer of product from one production stage to another. The marketing person views operations as organizing the channels of distribution, transporting and warehousing the product to make it available to the market and conducting the advertising, sales promotion, and market research activities required to penetrate the market. From a financial viewpoint, operating characteristics are entirely different from these more or less physical considerations. They involve anything that influences the rate of return on the investment in assets of the firm.

The fundamental operating characteristics of the firm from a financial manager's point of view are listed in Table 3–1. We have already mentioned that financial management does not exist in a vacuum. In a normal going concern, operations ultimately must provide every dollar of profit that will attract investment in the firm and every dollar of cash flow that can be used to meet the firm's obligations, including the satisfactory servicing of the capital invested. Analysis of operating characteristics begins with (1) sales, works down to (2) the operating profit margin, the number of cents the firm can make on a dollar of sales, then to (3) the relationship between sales and the funds invested to get those sales (operating asset turnover), and finally to (4) the degree of control that management has over costs related to changes in the sales volume. A financial manager, before considering almost any specific financial decision, must understand the operating characteristics of the firm as a profit-making and cash-generating organism.

Table 3–1 Fundamental operating characteristics
Influencing (1) Rate of return
(2) Variation in return

1. Sales volume
   Physical volume fluctuation
   Price fluctuation
2. Operating profit margin
3. Operating asset turnover
4. Control of costs
   Fixed versus variable

Sales volume

Because every dollar of operating profits and/or cash inflow begins with sales (or gross operating revenues), the financial manager must have a working knowledge of the nature of the market for the goods or services offered by the firm. By picking the brains of the marketing people and the company economist (if there is one), the financial manager seeks to estimate future sales revenues.

Dollar sales fluctuate as a function of two elements, (1) the physical or unit volume of sales and (2) price. Is the company engaged in a "feast or famine" industry, such as copper mining or heavy machinery manufacturing, or a relatively stable industry, such as the soft drink industry (and is the company Coca-Cola or the Fizz Pop Company)? Are prices in the industry subject to violent fluctuation caused by "dog-eat-dog" price competition or are they relatively stable, perhaps under the influence of price leadership of one or a few very large firms? What is the past record of sales volume fluctuation in the industry and of this particular firm in relation to the industry?

There are a myriad of economic factors that influence the potential fluctuation in dollar sales volume. No one can fully comprehend all of them, but the financial manager must understand the major ones well enough to make at least a crude estimate of (1) the percentage fluctuation in dollar sales volume that might occur in the future and (2) the period of time over which this change might take place. The rest of the analysis of operating characteristics attempts to identify what would happen to the firm's rate of return on the assets employed if and when such a fluctuation should occur.

Operating profit margin

The operating profit margin tells us how many cents are left from a dollar of sales after covering the *operating* costs and expenses. It is computed by dividing the net operating income (before taxes) by sales (gross revenues):

$$\text{Operating profit margin} = \frac{\text{Net operating income (before taxes)}}{\text{Sales}}$$

Acme Manufacturing Company's income statement (Table 3–2) shows net profit before taxes of $23 million. All nonoperating income and expenses must be eliminated from this figure because we are interested only in the results of operations. In this case, the financial expense, interest of $4 million, must be added to that figure. Income is computed prior to the deduction for interest expense because interest results from the choice of means of financing, namely debt. Here we are trying to understand operations as they influence rate of return, without regard for the means by which these operations were financed.

Table 3–2

ACME MANUFACTURING COMPANY
Income Statement
Year ended December 31, 1982
($000)

Sales	$360,000
Cost of goods sold (including depreciation of $10,000)	280,000
Gross profit	80,000
Expenses:	
Selling, general and administrative expenses	53,000
Interest expense	4,000
Net profit before taxes	23,000
Income taxes (federal and state)	11,500
Net profit after taxes	$ 11,500

If Acme had earned income from sources other than its normal operations, such as interest or dividends from investments in other firms or rent from a piece of real estate not used in its regular operations, such income should be eliminated in determining net operating income. Likewise, if it had incurred nonoperating expenses other than the interest charges indicated above, such as amortization of securities-issuance expenses, they should also be excluded. We are using net operating income before taxes because income taxes are to some degree a function of the financing method used. Sales are net of returns and allowances. The operating profit margin of Acme Manufacturing Company in 1982 was

$$\text{Operating profit margin} = \frac{\$27\text{ million}}{\$360\text{ million}} = 7.5\%$$

The importance of this figure is that it tells how much sales could drop with no change in operating costs and expenses before this would become a nonprofit business (even though it wasn't intended to be that way). Viewed another way, it tells us the approximate percentage by which the operating costs and expenses could increase with no increase in sales before the profits would be wiped out. In other words, this is the margin that will absorb adverse fluctuations of either sales or costs and expenses. If other things were equal (which they rarely are, as we shall see later), the greater the operating profit margin, the *less* the risk to which the investment in the firm is exposed.

Operating asset turnover

The operating asset turnover shows the relationship between annual sales volume and the net tangible operating assets that are employed to achieve these sales. It is computed by dividing sales by the net tangible operating assets.

$$\text{Operating asset turnover} = \frac{\text{Sales}}{\text{Net tangible operating assets}}$$

The sales figure to be used here is the same as that discussed above. Calculation of the net tangible assets figure requires deducting from total assets any nonoperating assets, such as investments in other firms or real estate not used in operations, and intangibles such as goodwill, patents, or trademarks. Acme Manufacturing Company's balance sheet, shown in Table 3–3, shows total assets of $185 million. From this we subtract investments (nonoperating assets) of $1 million and goodwill (an intangible) of $5 million to calculate the net tangible operating assets of $179 million. The operating asset turnover of Acme is

$$\text{Operating asset turnover} = \frac{\$360\text{ million}}{\$179\text{ million}} = 2.0\text{ (times)}$$

This figure gives us a relative measure of the *capital intensity* of the firm. A company with high capital intensity (reflecting large investments in durable fixed assets compared to sales volume) will have a low operating asset turnover, often less than one. A firm with low capital intensity (employing a large proportion of labor as compared to capital) will have a high operating asset turnover, perhaps five or six times per year. The importance of this figure is that any change in the operating profit margin is magnified in its effect upon operating rate of return by the operating asset turnover. Other

Table 3–3

ACME MANUFACTURING COMPANY
Balance Sheet
December 31, 1982
($000)

Assets	
Current assets:	
Cash	$ 20,000
Marketable securities	6,000
Accounts receivable	24,000
Inventories	30,000
Total current assets	80,000
Fixed assets (at cost)	179,000
Less: Depreciation	80,000
Total fixed assets	99,000
Investments	1,000
Goodwill	5,000
Total assets	$185,000
Liabilities and Net Worth	
Current liabilities:	
Accounts payable	$ 18,000
Accrued taxes	6,000
Other accruals	16,000
Total current liabilities	40,000
Long-term debt	45,000
Total liabilities	85,000
Stockholders' equity:	
Common stock	40,000
Retained earnings	60,000
Total stockholders' equity	100,000
Total liabilities and net worth	$185,000

things being equal, the greater the operating asset turnover, the *greater* the risk to which the investment is exposed.

Operating rate of return

The operating profit margin multiplied by the operating asset turnover yields the operating rate of return:

$$\text{Rate of return} = \text{Margin} \times \text{Turnover}$$

For Acme Manufacturing Company this is

$$\text{Rate of return} = 7.5\% \times 2.0 = 15.0\%$$

(Note that in the above formula the terms have been slightly simplified for brevity.)

Of course, the rate of return may be calculated directly by dividing net operating income by net tangible operating assets:

$$\text{Rate of return} = \frac{\text{Net operating income}}{\text{Net tangible operating assets}}$$

$$\text{Rate of return (Acme)} = \frac{\$27 \text{ million}}{\$179 \text{ million}} = 15.1\%$$

(The difference from 15.0 percent is due to rounding.) The long way of calculating return (margin × turnover) is more useful because it separates the rate of return into its functional components. If the rate of return of the firm has declined, management and investors will ask why. Was it because margin slipped and, if so, was that the result of declining sales or rising costs? Or has turnover declined? If so, was this the result of sales decline or has the company perhaps overinvested in operating assets? To carry this line of analysis further, the Du Pont system of operating analysis was developed. It has made a significant contribution to the control of operations of that company and many others that have copied it.

The Du Pont system An application of the Du Pont system to Acme Manufacturing Company (Tables 3–1 and 3–2) is shown in Figure 3–1. Using this tool, usually accompanied by parenthetically showing the corresponding figures from the previous accounting period, top management can move from left to right to answer the questions posed above and raise others as to what has happened to the operations of the firm. Operating rate of return (sometimes called return on investment, ROI) is the most important single measure of operating performance. What is its level and did it rise or decline? Then, moving across the exhibit, the components of each column are shown in the next column. The principal items of the income statement and the asset side of the balance sheet are brought together into relationships that will identify the sources of change in margin and turnover.

This type of analysis answers some questions as to what happened and why. It raises other questions, which can be sent down the line seeking answers as to why the change occurred and what can be done about it. For example, if rate of return is down from the previous period, this decrease may be traced to a decline in margin, which in turn resulted from an increase in operating expenses with no change in sales. The breakdown of operating expenses may indicate a rise in selling, general, and administrative expenses. Now management can ask for the detailed accounts comprising this total and compare the trends of these figures for recent periods to get down to the "nitty-gritty" of what happened where, who is responsible, and what can be done about it.

This sort of analytical device does not run a firm, but it helps people to run it by calling attention to where the problems are and getting the processes rolling to do something about them. Rate-of-return analysis is partic-

Figure 3–1 Du Pont system applied to Acme Manufacturing Company*

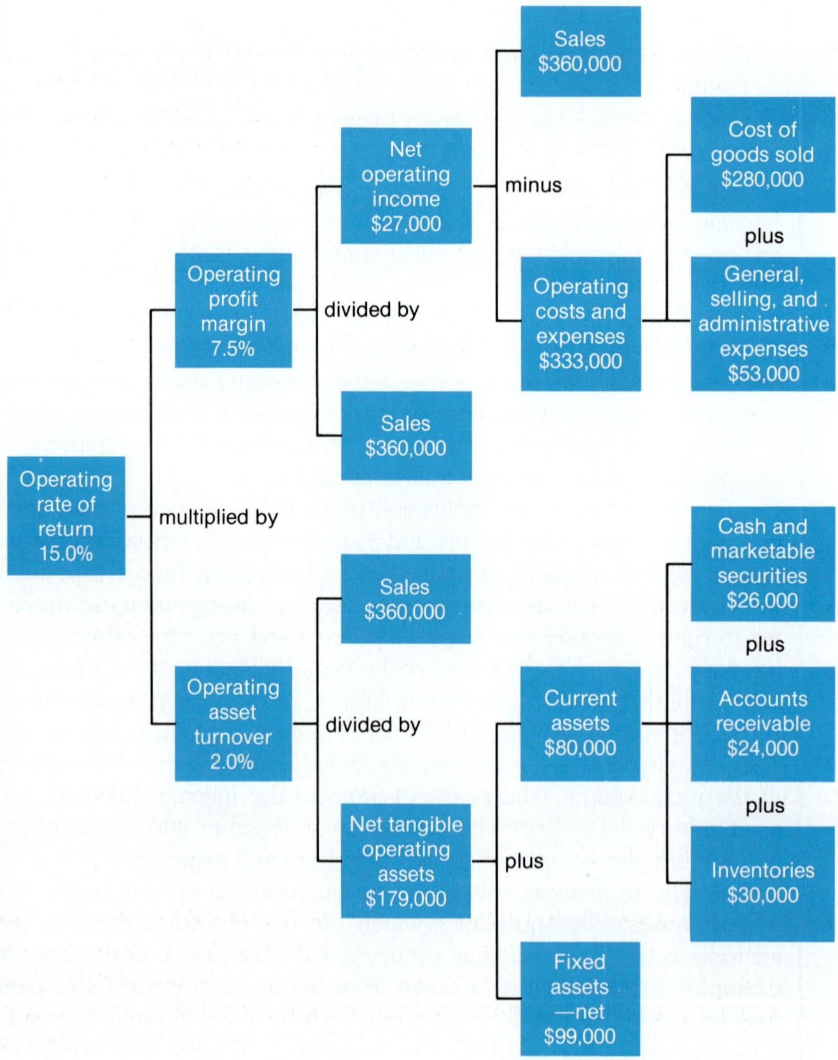

*Dollar figures in thousands.

ularly useful for review of operations by top management of large corporations that are, in turn, divided into several divisions, subsidiaries, or profit centers, each of which is responsible for the rate of return on the capital allocated to it. A small group of corporate executives, meeting periodically with the officer in charge of each division, can examine the Du Pont type of chart for that division and obtain the background and explanatory information necessary to control its operations.

Risk implications of margin and turnover

Margins and turnovers of different firms vary widely. It might be useful at this point to compare a supermarket chain, a low-margin, high-turnover type of business, to an electric utility, a high-margin, low-turnover business (Table 3–4). The supermarket chain showed net operating income before taxes of only $15 million on sales of $459 million, resulting in an operating profit margin of only 3.3 percent. (This reflects neither a poor year nor an inefficient firm; it is normal for such a business to operate on a pretax profit margin of 2 to 4 percent.) The electric utility company shows net operating income before taxes of $108 million on sales volume (gross revenues) of $494 million, or an operating profit margin of 21.9 percent.

Table 3–4 **Margin and turnover analysis**
($ millions)

	Supermarket chain		Electric utility	
	Amount	Percent	Amount	Percent
Sales	$459	100.0%	$494	100.0%
Operating costs and expenses	444	96.7	386	78.1
Net operating income before taxes	$ 15		$108	
Operating profit margin		3.3%		21.9%
Net tangible operating assets	$ 93		$1,206	
Operating asset turnover		4.9x		.41x
Operating rate of return (M × T)		16.2%		9.0%

But the supermarket chain required an investment in assets of only $93 million to achieve its sales volume of $459 million, whereas the electric utility required an investment of $1,206 million to achieve the only slightly larger sales volume of $494 million. Thus, the operating asset turnover of the supermarket chain was 4.9 times whereas the turnover of the electric utility was only .41 time. As a result, the 3.3 percent margin of the supermarket chain was magnified 4.9 times to yield an operating rate of return of over 16 percent. The thick margin of 21.9 percent of the electric utility was multiplied by a turnover of only .41 time yielding a rate of return of 9 percent. (You can think of this loosely in terms of a Monopoly game, with the supermarket collecting 3.3 percent each time it passes "Go" but it goes around the board about five times a year; the electric utility collects 21.9 percent each time it passes "Go," but it takes it about 2½ years to get around the board.)

For illustrative purposes, we might make an admittedly unreasonable assumption that all of the costs and expenses of each of these firms are fixed, that is, they do not vary with a change in sales volume. If we further assume a 4 percent drop in sales volume of each firm next year, the operating result of these two firms would be as shown in Table 3–5. The supermarket chain's margin has been wiped out, changing to −.8 percent which is magnified by the slightly reduced turnover of 4.7 times to yield a negative rate of return of 3.8 percent. The thick margin of the electric utility has been reduced from 21.9 percent to 18.6 percent. This is multiplied by a turnover of .39 time to reduce the rate of return from 9.0 percent to 7.3 percent. From this we see that, other things being equal, the *greater* the margin and *lower* the turnover, the *lower the risk* (or vulnerability) of the rate of return if sales should drop. The same would be true if we assume stable sales but an increase in cost and expenses (a cost squeeze). Part of this results from the change in the margin and the other part from the magnification of that change by a turnover greater than one, or conversely the demagnification of the margin change by a turnover of less than one. (Think, if you wish, of the change in margin passing through a convex or concave lens.)

Table 3–5 Margin and turnover analysis
With 4 percent drop in sales and all costs and expenses fixed ($ millions)

	Supermarket chain		Electric utility	
	Amount	Percent	Amount	Percent
Sales (down 4%)	$440.6	100.0%	$474.2	100.0%
Operating costs and expenses	444.0	100.8	386.0	81.4
Net operating income before taxes	$ −3.4		$ 88.2	
Operating profit margin		−0.8%		18.6%
Net tangible operating assets	$ 93.0		$1,206.0	
Operating asset turnover		4.7×		.39×
Operating rate of return (M × T)		−3.8%		7.3%
(Percent decline)		(123%)		(18.9%)

Control of margin and turnover

Management more or less continually seeks to increase the operating rate of return (within the constraints of risk considerations) by increasing margin and/or turnover. Management action may also be defensive in trying to maintain margin and/or turnover in the light of adverse developments.

Take the supermarket chain we just examined. Almost every sales promotion it undertakes, ranging from "Super Duper Bingo" to "7 cents off on Brand X beans," is an attempt to increase turnover by increasing sales volume relative to the fairly stable asset investment in a store. By analyzing the rate of sale of each brand, size, and product of the merchandise offered on its shelves relative to the profit margin on the item, management is almost continually weeding out items showing a low margin-turnover combination and adding others that show promise of increasing the rate of return. The same process goes on as low-return stores are closed and high-return ones are expanded. Almost all of the nongrocery items such as drugs, housewares, and notions are in the store because they yield higher margins than groceries.

Similarly, our electric utility company has been fighting a defensive battle trying to maintain its margin and turnover in the face of both rising costs and expenses and increasing investment required in operating assets. Its rates (prices) are regulated by the state public utilities commission. Every rate case it has fought in recent years has involved efforts to document the deterioration in margin (reflecting increases in operating costs) and the increases in investment in operating assets (which is called the "rate base") to support the contention that increased rates are required to yield a reasonable rate of return on its rate base.

These are just a few examples of ways the managements of these two firms are continually seeking to control their margins and turnovers and thus their rates of return. (If you have a few minutes it would be worth your time to think about a particular business with which you are familiar in terms of how it might seek to increase or at least maintain its margin, its turnover, and its resulting rate of return.)

Control of costs

In our discussion of margin and turnover analysis, we admitted an unrealistic assumption that all costs and expenses were fixed even though sales volume changed. This assumption was made to isolate the risk implications of different margins and turnovers. The real world is not that simple. Almost any firm will have some costs that remain the same regardless of the level of sales volume. These are *fixed costs*. Other costs will vary directly with sales volume. If sales increase by 10 percent, these *variable costs* will likewise increase by 10 percent.

Information as to the relative magnitude of fixed and variable costs may be used to refine our analysis of what might happen to the rate of return, given a change in sales volume. This information is generated by the firm's cost accounting system. The cost accountant should be able to provide financial management with at least a useful approximation of the percentages of total costs that are fixed and variable at a given sales volume. This again involves some simplification. Cost analysis is not an exact science, and all particular items of cost are not purely fixed or variable. Some are "semivariable" in that they follow a stair-step pattern as volume moves from zero toward full-capacity operations. But at least within a range of volumes of sales, varying by, say, 10 or 20 percent, useful approximations should be available.

Usually there is an inverse relationship between the percentage of costs that is fixed and the operating asset turnover. In other words, a more capital-intensive business will have a greater percentage of fixed costs. Heavy investment in fixed assets tends to result in high, largely fixed costs of depreciation, maintenance, and property taxes. In some cases, labor costs also may be largely fixed because the operators of highly specialized heavy equipment cannot as a practical matter be discharged or hired at will. On the other hand, firms with high operating asset turnovers (low capital intensity) will tend to have highly variable costs. Most of their costs—for raw materials and labor—can be readily adjusted to changes in sales volume.

For example, let us look again at our supermarket chain and electric utility. Over 80 percent of the supermarket chain's costs reflect the cost of merchandise sold, clearly variable. In addition, much of the labor cost is variable as the number of stockers, checkers, and other workers can be adjusted to changes in the volume of sales. In an effort to live with its thin profit margin, management seeks to make as many costs as possible variable. Management personnel are paid relatively low base salaries, and the remainder of their compensation is based on a percentage of sales. Most of the stores are leased, with rents based upon a percentage of sales subject to a minimum rent expected to be less than that based on sales. Much of their equipment, such as cash registers, refrigerator cases, and trucks, is leased. If sales should drop so much that the equipment is not needed, it can be returned to the lessor. The result is that up to 90 percent of the costs may be variable.

A considerably larger proportion of our electric utility company's costs is fixed. Depreciation, maintenance, property taxes, and almost all labor costs are fixed. These amount to about 40 percent of total costs. The remaining 60 percent, largely fuel cost and the cost of electricity purchased from other utilities on the power grid, are variable.

Assume that the cost structure of our supermarket chain is 10 percent fixed and 90 percent variable and that of our electric utility is 40 percent fixed and 60 percent variable. Let us go back to the margin and turnover analysis to see what would happen to their rates of return when these differences in cost structures are incorporated. In Table 3–6 we again assume a 4 percent drop in sales for each firm, but we make a more realistic assumption about the nature of costs. The operating profit margin of the supermarket chain is not wiped out (as it was in Table 3–5 under the extreme assumption of all cost being fixed) but is reduced from 3.3 percent to 2.9 percent. The margin of the electric utility is reduced from 21.9 percent to 20.6 percent. Operating asset turnovers remain the same as in Table 3–5. Multiplying each firm's profit margin by its turnover, we see that the rate of return of the supermarket chain is reduced from 16.2 percent to 13.6 percent (a decline of 16 percent) and that of the electric utility is reduced from 9 percent to 8.1 percent (a decline of 10 percent).

Table 3–6 Margin and turnover analysis
With 4 percent drop in sales; fixed and variable costs as indicated ($ millions)

	Supermarket chain		Electric utility	
	Amount	Percent	Amount	Percent
Sales (down 4%)	$440.6	100.0%	$474.2	100.0%
Operating costs and expenses				
Fixed	44.4 (10%)		154.4 (40%)	
Variable	383.6 (90%)		222.3 (60%)	
	428.0	97.1	376.7	79.4
Net operating income before taxes	$ 12.6		$ 97.5	
Operating profit margin		2.9%		20.6%
Net tangible operating assets	$ 93.0		$1,206.0	
Operating asset turnover		4.7×		.39×
Operating rate of return (M × T)		13.6%		8.1%
(Percent decline)		(16.0%)		(10.0%)

Large differences in risk (as measured by potential change in the rate of return) indicated by analysis of margins and turnovers in isolation (that is, assuming everything else to be equal) are partially offset by differences in cost structures of the two firms. The percentage decline in rate of return of the supermarket chain was greater than that of the electric utility (16 percent versus 10 percent) but the difference was not nearly as great as we found in Table 3–5 using the same 4 percent drop in sales but assuming the cost structures of each to be equal and fixed. The illustration in Table 3–6 reflects more closely the normal relationship of cost structures to differences in margins and turnovers.

Summary—operating characteristics

To understand the operating characteristics of a firm, financial management first must understand the market for its product(s) and the potential sensitivity of its dollar sales volume to future adverse conditions. Second, the operating profit margin and operating asset turnover must be calculated. Multiplying the margin by the turnover yields the operating rate of return. Third, the cost structure (fixed versus variable) existing within the range of possible change in sales volume must be estimated. Fourth, these factors can be integrated by analyzing what would happen to sales, margin, turnover, and rate of return under such adverse conditions. With this background understanding of the financial implications of operations, management can more intelligently approach the problems involving assumption of financial obligations in the future.

Introduction to leverage

Leverage is simply the magnification of change. If you had a plank set up on a fulcrum so that when you moved one end one foot the other end moved three feet, you would have a degree of mechanical leverage of three times. In financial management we are interested in operating leverage and financial leverage, which work the same way in their effects upon profits.

Operating leverage

Operating leverage is the relationship between the rate of change that takes place in sales and the resulting rate of change in net operating income. In other words, *the degree of operating leverage indicates the magnification of a change in sales upon the resulting change in net operating income:*

$$\text{Degree of operating leverage} = \frac{\text{\% Change in net operating income}}{\text{\% Change in sales}}$$

In Table 3–6, compared to Table 3–4, a 4 percent decline in sales of the supermarket chain resulted in a 16 percent decline in its net operating income ($15 million to $12.6 million). The degree of operating leverage was 4 times (16% ÷ 4% = 4). The same 4 percent drop in sales (gross revenues) of the electric utility resulted in a drop of net operating income of 9.7 percent ($108 million to $97.5 million); thus its degree of operating leverage was 2.4 times (9.7% ÷ 4% = 2.4).

Operating leverage *results from the existence of fixed operating costs.* If all operating costs were variable, a given drop in sales—say, 4 percent—would result in the same relative drop in net operating income, 4 percent. Therefore the degree of operating leverage would be one. But it is hard to conceive of a business firm having all variable and no fixed costs. In general, the higher the proportion of operating costs that is fixed, the greater will be the degree of operating leverage.[1] (This is an oversimplification; we shall analyze operating leverage with greater precision in Chapter 17.) In any case, only after the leverage related to operations is fully understood

[1]This generalization is oversimplified in that it assumes that the nature of costs (fixed versus variable) is the *only* pertinent variable (everything else is equal). This assumption is *not* true in the example used above.

should financial management consider the creation of additional leverage affecting the owners of the firm through the use of financial arrangements involving fixed financial costs.

Financial leverage

Financial leverage further magnifies the effect of change in net operating income of the firm upon income of its owners. If all operating assets of a business were financed by the owners' equity and thus there were no fixed financial costs, the degree of financial leverage would be one. A given change in the net operating income would result in the same relative change in income of the owners. However, part of the asset requirement may be financed by borrowing, committing the firm to pay fixed interest charges, or by issuing preferred stock, incurring a limited obligation to pay dividends. These fixed (or limited) financial commitments will result in a magnification of the effect of change in net operating income upon the return that finally comes down to the owners.

For a simple illustration of financial leverage, assume that you and your roommate have $1,000 each and an idea that you can make some money by buying a number of used refrigerators and renting them to your fellow students to equip their rooms and apartments. This would require the investment of $2,000 in the refrigerators. You estimate that after all costs of repairs and maintenance, collecting the rent and the occasional loss of a refrigerator (that refrigerator and the student renting it having departed for parts unknown), you can make a net profit on this operation of $400 a year.

As a business student, you are the entrepreneurial type and quite willing to assume risk. You put your $1,000 into this venture on an equity basis, that is, you will be the proprietor. Your roommate is averse to risk and does not want to invest as a partner, but is willing to lend you $1,000 at 10 percent annual interest. Your roommate's investment (your debt) will be subject to less risk than yours because, if the venture does not work as well as planned, you will still be under the obligation to pay $100 per year interest and to pay back the $1,000.

In financial jargon, you are *trading on the equity*. You are in a sense pledging your $1,000 equity—and any other net assets that you may have—to support the loan. All of your investment may be lost before your roommate will lose anything. The other side of this coin is that if the operating profit of the business should turn out to be as high as expected, or even higher, you are committed only to pay $100 per year interest to your roommate and the rest of the profit is yours.

Consider three possible results of your venture, Hardknocks U. Refrigerator Rentals, as shown in Table 3–7. If operations turn out as expected, the net operating profit will be $400. You will pay $100 to your roommate as interest and $300 will be left for you, a 30 percent return on your $1,000 investment. It is your choice as to what portion of this you wish to withdraw and what portion you will leave in the business to buy more refrigerators or perhaps diversify into hi-fi equipment or television sets.

Table 3–7 Financial leverage
Hardknocks U. Refrigerator Rentals

Investment:	
Roommate—loan @ 10% interest	$1,000
Self—owner's equity	1,000
Total	$2,000

Results:	Expected	Bonanza	Flop
Net operating profit (loss)	$400	$1,000	($ 900)
Roommate's interest	(100)	(100)	(100)
Self—net profits (loss)	$300	$ 900	($1,000)
Return on investment:			
Total investment	20%	50%	(45%)
Roommate (creditor)	10%	10%	10%
Self (owner)	30%	90%	(100%)
Return on owner's investment / Return on total investment	30% / 20% = 1.5×	90% / 50% = 1.8×	(100%) / (45%) = 2.2×
Financial leverage	Favorable	Favorable	Unfavorable

Note that if you had not traded on the equity, that is, you had invested all of the $2,000 requirement yourself, or if your roommate had invested the $1,000 on an equity basis rather than debt, the profits to the owner(s) would have been $400 on $2,000 total investment, or 20 percent. The additional 10 percent profit that you made was not a windfall but rather the result of your taking the additional risk of entering into a fixed financial contract with your roommate to pay $100 per year interest and the principal of $1,000 at maturity. Thus, in essence, you made a 20 percent return as compensation for taking the operational risks of the refrigerator rental business and an additional 10 percent for taking the *financial risk* related to the obligations of the debt you assumed.

What would happen if this firm turned out to be a real bonanza? As operations began, you discovered that the demand was considerably greater than you had expected, so you increased rental rates; repairs, maintenance, and collection costs were lower than expected, and nobody ran off with any of the refrigerators. As a result of this favorable operating experience, the net operating profit was $1,000 per year. You paid $100 to your roommate (who at this point was sorry that he or she had not taken the risk and joined you as a partner) and earned a profit of $900 for yourself. Thus, the rate of return on your equity investment was 90 percent. The operating rate of return ($1,000 on $2,000 total investment in operating assets) was 50 percent and you earned an additional 40 percent as compensation for assuming the financial risk of the debt contract.

In both the "Expected" and "Bonanza" cases, the financial leverage has been favorable to you. This *favorable leverage* resulted because the operating rate of return you achieved was greater than the interest rate you had to pay on the debt. Financial leverage will always be favorable as long as you are able to make an operating rate of return (before taxes) greater than the rate of interest paid on the debt.

There is, however, another side to the financial leverage coin. This is shown in the column headed "Flop" in Table 3–7. Operations did not work out as expected. The student housing authorities at Hardknocks University vigorously enforced a rule prohibiting unauthorized appliances in dormitory rooms, and fraternities, sororities, and many rooming houses did the same. As a result, you had to take back a large number of refrigerators you thought you had rented. On those that were still rented, the repair and maintenance costs were considerably larger than expected, collection of rents turned out to be a big problem, two of your refrigerators (uninsured) were burned in a rooming house fire, and three others disappeared along with their lessees who flunked out of the university. The net result of all this bad fortune was that you incurred a net operating loss of $900. You still have to pay your roommate $100 interest and you owe the $1,000 principal of the loan at maturity. The net loss of $1,000 to the owner has completely wiped out your equity investment in the firm. The rate of loss for you has been 100 percent.

If you are lucky enough to sell the refrigerators you have left for $1,000, you will be able to pay off the $1,000 loan, and you will have to consider the loss of the $1,000 that you invested as tuition for learning a very hard lesson about financial leverage. The lesson you have learned is about *unfavorable financial leverage.* The operating loss of $900 on a $2,000 investment in operating assets was 45 percent. But this has been magnified to a 100 percent loss of your equity investment.

As a general observation, you note that at any operating rate of return less than the 10 percent you have contracted to pay in interest on the debt, your rate of return would be diminished (and eventually your rate of loss would be increased) as a result of your trading on the equity. If you wish to test this observation, assume that net operating profits are $200 (10 percent of the investment in operating assets) and run through the calculations as in Table 3–7. You will find that the rate of return on owner's equity will also be 10 percent, so the degree of financial leverage would be 1.

Effect of income taxes The skeptical reader may have noticed that the previous illustration was oversimplified by ignoring income taxes. Chapter 2 pointed out that interest is an expense for income tax purposes and that the

Table 3–8 Financial leverage

Giant Refrigerator Manufacturing Corporation ($ millions)

Investment:	
A. Common stockholders' equity	$2,000
B. 10% bonds	$1,000
Common stockholders' equity	1,000
Total	$2,000

Results:

	Expected		Bonanza		Flop	
	A	B	A	B	A	B
Net operating profit (loss)	$400	$400	$1,000	$1,000	($900)	($900)
Bond interest	—	(100)	—	(100)	—	(100)
Net profit (loss) before taxes	$400	$300	$1,000	$ 900	($900)	($1,000)
Income taxes @ 46%	(184)	(138)	(460)	(414)	414	460
Net profit (loss) after taxes	$216	$162	$ 540	$ 486	($486)	($540)
Return on investment:						
Bondholders	—	10.0%	—	10.0%	—	10.0%
Stockholders	10.8%	16.2%	27.0%	48.6%	(24.3%)	(54.0%)
Return on B stockholders' investment / Return on A stockholders' investment		16.2% / 10.8% = 1.5×		48.6% / 27.0% = 1.8×		(54.0%) / (24.3%) = 2.2×
Financial leverage		Favorable		Favorable		Unfavorable

payment of interest thus creates a *tax shield.* With a maximum corporate tax rate of 46 percent on incremental income, our skeptic might think that the effects of financial leverage have been misrepresented. To test this, let us assume in Table 3–8 that the business is the Giant Refrigerator Manufacturing Corporation, put all our dollar figures in millions, and consider the tax effects. To demonstrate the relationship between aftertax returns on investment and financial leverage, we shall here compare results obtained under two different capital structures: A, the corporation has an all-common-stock capital structure, and B, one-half of the investment is financed by 10-percent bonds and the other half is financed by common stockholders' equity.

Table 3–8 shows that the *financial leverage* in each of the outcomes is the same after considering corporate income tax as it was in Table 3–7, in which taxes were ignored. The magnification factor remains the same. However, what is being magnified, now the *aftertax equivalent* of the operating rate of return (as indicated by the return on the common stockholders' equity in the "A" columns), is changed substantially by the application of corporate income taxes. These aftertax equivalent results of operations are substantially lowered by income taxes equal to 46 percent of the pretax operating profits; therefore, the rates of return (or loss) on investment of the stockholders of both A and B are commensurately lower. The most notable result of the application of income taxes is that in the last column (Flop "B"), Giant Refrigerator stockholders suffer a loss of 54 percent of their investment, compared to 100 percent in our previous illustration (ignoring income taxes). If Giant Refrigerator had paid income taxes exceeding $460 million during previous eligible periods, a tax refund claim of $460 million, which could be pressed against the Internal Revenue Service, would save the company from a total loss of its stockholders' investment.

Degree of financial leverage Strictly speaking, the Hardknocks U. Refrigerator Rentals and Giant Refrigerator Manufacturing Corporation illustrations do not precisely determine the *degree of financial leverage.* This, like the degree of operating leverage, is an *incremental* concept. The degree of financial leverage is the magnification of the effect of a *change* in net operating income (or EBIT, earnings before interest and taxes) on the *change* in the total or per share earnings to to the residual owners attributable to fixed financial costs:

$$\text{Degree of financial leverage} = \frac{\%\ \text{Change in earnings to residual owners}}{\%\ \text{Change in net operating income}} \text{ or } \frac{\Delta EAT}{\Delta EBIT}$$

(Note: Our mathematical friends designate an incremental change with the symbol Δ(delta).)

Now, if we go back to our electric utility illustration (Tables 3–4 through 3–6), we can develop the degree of financial leverage. Assume that our electric utility is financed by $724 million in bonds bearing interest at 7 percent and $482 million of common stock equity. It is subject to a 46 percent income tax rate. As shown in Table 3–9, the decline of 9.7 percent in net operating income results in a decline of 18.1 percent in the earnings to the residual owners (the common stockholders). This difference is a function of the fixed return of 7 percent ($50.7 million) that must be paid to the bondholders. The degree of financial leverage is

$$\frac{\Delta\ EAT}{\Delta\ EBIT} = \frac{18.1\%}{9.7\%} = 1.9\times$$

Thus a change in net operating income will be magnified 1.9 times in its effect upon the earnings to the common stockholders.

Table 3–9 Degree of financial leverage
Electric utility ($ millions)

	Table 3–4	Table 3–6	Decline
Net operating income (before taxes)	$108.0	$97.5	9.7%
Bond interest ($724 × .07)	50.7	50.7	
Earnings before taxes	$ 57.3	$46.8	
Taxes (@ .46)	26.4	21.5	
Earnings to residual owners	$ 30.9	$25.3	18.1%
Degree of financial leverage		$\frac{18.1\%}{9.7\%} = 1.9\times$	

Total leverage

We have seen how operating leverage magnifies the effect of changes in the volume of operations upon net operating income. We have also seen how financial leverage magnifies the effect of changes in net operating income upon the income to owners. How do these two types of leverage relate to each other? They work just like two lenses in a simple telescope. The first lens, operating leverage, magnifies the effect of change in sales volume the net operating income. Then the second lens, financial leverage, further magnifies that change in its effect upon the income to the owners. Therefore,

$$\text{Total leverage} = \text{Operating leverage} \times \text{Financial leverage}$$

Thus, in our electric utility example, a 4 percent change in sales (gross revenues) resulted in a 9.7 percent change in net operating income, reflecting operating leverage of 2.4 times. This change was magnified again by financial leverage of 1.9 times, as the net operating income change of 9.7 percent resulted in a change of 18.1 percent in earnings to the residual owners. Total leverage was

$$2.4 \times 1.9 = 4.6$$

Therefore, for each 1 percent change in sales volume, income to the common stockholders will change 4.6 percent.

If the degree of operating leverage is relatively high, the owners of a firm may not wish to further magnify the effect of fluctuation in sales volume by multiplying it through the use of financial leverage. Conversely, if the degree of operating leverage is low, the owners might wish to seek higher returns through favorable financial leverage by obtaining a considerable portion of the required funds through fixed (or limited) return financing arrangements such as debt. Basically, decisions relating to both operating leverage and financial leverage involve weighing the risks versus the expected returns in seeking to maximize the *value* of the owner's equity.

While this treatment of leverage is only introductory, it will get us started in understanding financial management. Operating and financial leverage will be treated in considerably more detail in Chapter 17 in connection with managerial policy regarding capital structure.

Summary

This chapter provides an overview and illustrated demonstration of the operating characteristics of the firm and an introduction to the concepts of operating and financial leverage.

The financial manager is concerned with the operating characteristics of the firm because he or she must (1) monitor the operations to influence control of them and (2) thoroughly understand their effects upon operating rate of return and its influence on the ability to service financial obligations.

As all operating profits begin with sales, the market for the firm's products must be studied with a view to estimating volatility of sales volume. Sales are then translated into operating profits through the operating profit margin. This margin, in turn, is magnified by the operating asset turnover to yield the operating rate of return (or return on investment). Causes of changes in margin and turnover may be identified through the use of the Du Pont system. In addition, the operating risk of the firm may be crudely (but incompletely) understood through margin and turnover analysis.

The control of costs may be understood through analysis of the relationship between fixed and variable costs to see the effects of fluctuation in sales volume upon margins and turnovers, and thus upon operating rates of return.

We approached analysis of operations another way: by introducing operating leverage. This is the magnification of change in sales upon change in operating income resulting from fixed operating costs. Finally, the effect of financial leverage upon changes in net income to owners was demonstrated. Financial leverage results from fixed financial costs. Total leverage, the cumulative effect of changes in sales volume upon the earnings to the owners of the firm, was then shown to be the product of operating leverage times financial leverage.

Questions

1. How do operating profit margin and operating asset turnover influence
   a. Magnitude of operating rate of return?
   b. Variations in operating rate of return?
2. Why is the financial manager interested in the operations of the firm?
3. Why must a capital-intensive firm (one with a low operating asset turnover) have a high operating profit margin to survive?
4. What factors might you wish to examine if your firm's operating profit margin were declining?
5. Explain how a discount store with an operating profit margin of 5 percent might achieve a higher operating rate of return than a steel company with an operating profit margin of 20 percent.
6. Usually a firm with a low operating asset turnover also will have a high percentage of fixed costs.
   a. Explain why this statement is true.
   b. What is the effect of this relationship on variation of operating rates of return?
7. What set of operating characteristics would typify a "feast or famine" business?
8. What is
   a. Leverage?
   b. Operating leverage?
   c. Financial leverage?
9. What causes
   a. Operating leverage?
   b. Financial leverage?
10. What is indicated by
    a. A degree of operating leverage of 2?
    b. A degree of financial leverage of 1.5?

11. *a.* What does the expression "trading on the equity" mean?
    b. Why would a management decide to trade on the equity?

12. What is
    a. Favorable financial leverage?
    b. Unfavorable financial leverage?

13. What is total leverage? How does it relate to operating and financial leverage?

Problems

1. Vital Corporation had net sales of $8,200,000 and total operating costs and expenses of $7,600,000 in 1981. Its December 31, 1981, balance sheet indicates total assets of $5,000,000, including investments of $500,000 and goodwill of $300,000. Calculate Vital's
    a. Operating profit margin.
    b. Operating asset turnover.
    c. Operating rate of return.

2. In 1982, Vital Corporation (see 1981 data above) increased net sales by $700,000, incurred additional operating costs and expenses of $500,000, and invested an additional $200,000 in net tangible operating assets. In 1982, what was its
    a. Operating profit margin?
    b. Operating asset turnover?
    c. Operating rate of return?
    d. Degree of operating leverage (as reflected by 1982 experience versus 1981)?

Problems 3 through 6 are based upon the financial statements of the Sample Company (see next page).

3. Compute
    a. The operating asset turnover.
    b. The operating profit margin.
    c. The operating rate of return.

4. Was financial leverage favorable or unfavorable last year? (Show your figures.)

5. What was the rate of return (after taxes) on stockholders' equity?

6. *a.* If the bonds had an interest rate of 16 percent (rather than 8 percent), what would have been the rate of return (after taxes) on stockholders' equity?
    b. Would financial leverage have been favorable or unfavorable? (Show figures.)

SAMPLE COMPANY
Income Statement
Last Year
(000s omitted)

Sales		$940,000
Less: Returns and allowances		40,000
Net sales		900,000
Cost of goods sold		700,000
Gross profit		200,000
Expenses:		
Selling, general, and administrative expense	$100,000	
Interest expense	8,000	108,000
Net income before taxes		92,000
Income taxes (@ 50 percent)		46,000
Net income after taxes		$ 46,000

SAMPLE COMPANY
Balance Sheet
December 31, Last Year
(000s omitted)

Cash	$ 40,000	Current liabilities	$ 50,000
Accounts receivable	50,000	8% bonds due in 10 years	100,000
Inventories	100,000	Common stock	200,000
Fixed assets (net)	260,000	Retained earnings	100,000
Total assets	$450,000	Total liabilities and capital	$450,000

7. What would be the effect of an *increase* in the price of a firm's product *not* offset by a decrease in physical volume of sales or any change in operating costs
   a. Upon its operating profit margin?
   b. Upon its operating asset turnover?
   c. Upon its operating rate of return?

8. Typically, business firms with high operating asset turnovers have low operating profit margins. Consider a supermarket with a turnover of 8 times. What operating profit margin will it need to achieve an operating rate of return of 20 percent?

9. Elmwood Corporation has the following capital structure:

12% bonds	$10 million
Common stock	12 million
Retained earnings	6 million
Total	$28 million

Its earnings before interest and taxes (EBIT) were:

Year	EBIT
1980	$3.1 million
1981	6.7 million
1982	5.9 million

Assuming that the income tax rate is 50 percent and that all earnings are paid out in dividends, determine the following:

a. Rate of return (before taxes) on total capital structure for each year.

b. Rate of return (after taxes) on common stock equity for each year.

c. Whether financial leverage was favorable or unfavorable each year. (Show figures.)

d. The degree of financial leverage from 1980 to 1981 and from 1981 to 1982.

10. Companies A and B are identical except for their capital structures, which are:

	Company A	Company B
10% bonds	—	$10 million
Common stock	$15 million	5 million
Retained earnings	5 million	5 million
Total	$20 million	$20 million

a. Assuming, for convenience, a 50 percent tax rate, what is the rate of return on the common stock equity of each company when earnings before interest and taxes (EBIT) are (1) $4 million? (2) $2 million? (3) $1 million?

b. How do you explain the differences in the rates of return on the common stock equity of the two companies in each case?

c. Why is the common stock of Company B riskier than that of Company A?

Appendix 3–A—Financial statement perspectives

The balance sheet shown in Table 3A–1 may be viewed as a "still picture" as of a stated moment in time—midnight, December 31, 1982—of Acme Manufacturing Company. The income statement presented in Table 3A–2 may be viewed as a "moving picture" showing what happened at Acme

Manufacturing Company during the year 1982. These statements evolved from the accounting process, following accepted doctrine, principles, and procedures of the accounting profession. That is not an unmixed blessing in terms of information value unless the financial manager fully understands the nature of the accounting process and the doctrine, principles, and procedures that have been applied. (For this reason, accounting usually is a prerequisite to the study of financial management.)

Table 3A–1

ACME MANUFACTURING COMPANY
Balance Sheet
December 31, 1982
($000)

Assets	
Current assets:	
Cash	$ 20,000
Marketable securities	6,000
Accounts receivable	24,000
Inventories	30,000
Total current assets	80,000
Fixed assets (at cost)	179,000
Less: Depreciation	80,000
Total fixed assets	$ 99,000
Investments	1,000
Goodwill	5,000
Total assets	$185,000
Liabilities and Net Worth	
Current liabilities:	
Accounts payable	$ 18,000
Accrued taxes	6,000
Other accruals	16,000
Total current liabilities	40,000
Long-term debt	45,000
Total liabilities	85,000
Stockholders' equity:	
Common stock	40,000
Retained earnings	60,000
Total stockholders' equity	100,000
Total liabilities and net worth	$185,000

In general, the long-term trend in accounting doctrine has been directed toward making the income statement more meaningful. In the process, however, the usefulness of the balance sheet as an indicator of values has suffered. Therefore the financial analyst must understand rather precisely what the balance sheet and the income statement purport to show and what they cannot and do not show.

Table 3A–2

ACME MANUFACTURING COMPANY
Income Statement
For the Year Ended December 31, 1982
($000)

Sales		$360,000
Cost of goods sold (including depreciation of $10,000)		280,000
Gross profit		80,000
Expenses:		
Selling, general, and administrative expenses	$53,000	
Interest expense	4,000	57,000
Net profit before taxes		23,000
Income taxes (federal and state)		11,500
Net profit after taxes		$ 11,500

The balance sheet

Assets

The balance sheet begins with a listing of the firm's assets, in other words, "what we own," generally in order of the liquidity (nearness to cash) of these assets. Often the financial analyst is most interested in the *current economic value of the assets,* whereas the accounting process emphasizes a *book value* concept dominated by considerations of meaningful income determination. The net result is that, as we descend the list of assets, the value of each tends to become less meaningful in relation to current economic value.

Cash and marketable securities The value of cash gives the financial analyst little difficulty. If the auditing process is adequate and the banks in which the cash is deposited are sound, then the value of cash reported on the balance sheet truly represents current economic value in dollars, although not necessarily in future purchasing power. Likewise, the value of marketable securities should be subject to little question if the criteria by which these securities have been selected are sound (these will be discussed in Chapter 7) and if any securities of questionable value have been identified by footnote.

Accounts receivable Although accounts receivable are just one step (the collection) away from cash, in some cases that step may be over the Grand

Canyon. Qualitative appraisal of the receivables (to be discussed in Chapter 8) may disclose overvaluation in that the collectibility of some of these receivables may be remote. On the other hand, the accounts receivable may be undervalued. Hidden values may exist because accounts receivable normally are stated net of allowance for doubtful accounts, and the latter may be excessive.

Inventories There often is a great discrepancy between book value and current economic value of the inventories. As discussed briefly in Chapter 2, income tax regulations allow the selection of either LIFO (last-in, first-out) or FIFO (first-in, first-out) inventory valuation. The book value resulting from the accounting process usually will be the same as that used in income determination for tax purposes. If FIFO has been used, the residual inventory will be valued fairly close to its current costs. But if LIFO has been used, the inventory value may be greatly understated. Some inventory may be valued at cost tracing back many years to the date when the LIFO method was adopted. This inventory will be valued at only a small fraction of its current cost if significant inflation has occurred since that time. In such cases, the analyst may wish to revalue the inventory on the basis of an estimate of its economic value at current price levels.

Fixed assets If inflation has occurred, the value of fixed assets on the balance sheet rarely bears any significant relation to current economic value. Accounting and economic value will be close only if a major portion of the fixed assets was acquired very recently. There are several reasons for this. First, land is valued at its cost when acquired by the firm. Land acquired 20, 30, or 40 years ago may have a book value that is meaningless compared to current value. (In theory, if the Dutch company that bought Manhattan Island from the Indians for approximately $24 worth of beads still held that property, it would be valued on the balance sheet at $24.) The valuation error may also work the other way if land were acquired when it was in the most valuable heart of the city but it is now in a slum.

Second, the gross value of buildings and equipment usually is based on historical cost and subject to the same problem we have just discussed. To arrive at net value, accumulated depreciation is deducted. Net book value therefore is subject to question as to what depreciation methods, estimated useful lives, and assumed salvage values have been used. Usually the straight-line method of depreciation is used for book purposes even though an accelerated method is utilized for tax purposes. Although net book values may be either understated or overstated, in an inflationary period they usually are understated relative to current value.

Large corporations which are required to file form 10-K reports with the Securities and Exchange Commission must include in those reports estimates of replacement cost of inventories and productive capacity investments. These data usually are not included in their published annual reports, however. If the financial analyst is interested in current values of inventories and/or net fixed assets, the balance sheet may be recast by substituting replacement cost estimates for the stated book values. If replacement cost information is not available, crude estimates, perhaps based upon such information as appraised values for property tax purposes, insured values, or even "seat of the pants" estimates, may be used.

Investments Investments might be in nonconsolidated subsidiaries, such as a captive finance company or a separate corporation holding real estate used by the firm. These investments usually are valued at the amounts directly invested plus the retained earnings of the subsidiary. Where the investments are external to the firm, such as Internorth's holding of a large block of stock in Mobil Corporation, the book value usually is stated at original cost and the current market value indicated parenthetically or by footnote. In such cases, the analyst might wish to substitute current market value in recasting the statement.

Intangibles Intangibles, such as goodwill, patents, formulas, trademarks, and copyrights, may be grossly misvalued. Treatment of intangibles largely reflects the degree of conservatism of the accounting policies rather than real economic values. For example, although the Coca-Cola Company reports over $100 million book value of intangibles, nearly all of this reflects purchased goodwill, that is, the unamortized excess of purchase price of acquired companies over the net tangible asset values transferred to the books in connection with those acquisitions. The book value of the Coca-Cola formula and trademark, surely the greatest assets of the firm, is one dollar. In theory, goodwill represents the excess of the intrinsic value of a going concern over the book values of its tangible parts. In practice, however, there is a common expression that "those who have it don't book it and those who don't have it do." Therefore, the financial analyst often proceeds on the basis of net *tangible* assets, simply ignoring the book values of intangible items.

Liabilities

The liabilities owed by a firm to its creditors, such as notes payable, accounts payable, accrued taxes, salaries and wages, advances from customers, and long-term debt, usually do not create significant valuation problems for the financial analyst.

However, one item, deferred income taxes, is a bit troublesome. (This account does not appear in Table 3A–1, to avoid confusion.) Deferred income taxes are in a sense a quasi-liability rather than a pure one. The account is created when a firm uses an accelerated depreciation (cost recovery) method for income tax purposes but straight-line depreciation for book purposes. If the majority of assets are in the earlier years of their cost recovery periods, this results in payment of lower income taxes for the current year than if straight-line depreciation had been used for both tax and book purposes. If straight-line is used on the books, this tax saving does not "flow through" to income. Instead, income taxes are divided on the income statement into a current amount that must be paid for the given year's income and a deferred component representing the difference between the amount that has to be paid and the amount that would have been paid if straight-line depreciation had been used in the tax computation.

Deferred income taxes are transferred to the balance sheet and accumulated in the deferred income tax liability account. These deferred taxes will have to be paid only if and when the firm eventually declines and its net buildings and equipment account falls toward zero as a result of depreciation of the assets without replacement. If the firm's fixed assets are growing or remaining stable, the time of this eventual payment and the resulting decline of the deferred income tax account is delayed into the unforeseeable future. Thus the account may be viewed as an interest-free loan from the government in the backhanded sense that the government did not collect the taxes that would have been due it in the absence of accelerated depreciation, with an indefinite maturity. Further, in event of bankruptcy, the government would have no claim upon this account. If these attributes are understood by the analyst, then the account may be considered as a liability. In many cases, however, misunderstanding of the nature of this account might lead one to an erroneous conclusion that liabilities were out-of-line on the high side, when from a practical standpoint they were not.

Net worth or equity capital

The net worth, or equity capital (the terms will be used interchangeably), represents the net value of the assets after all liabilities to creditors have been covered. Net worth includes (1) the preferred stock account(s), (2) the common (capital) stock account, (3) capital (paid-in) surplus, and (4) retained earnings (variously labeled reinvested earnings or earned surplus). If proprietary reserves such as reserves for contingencies have been established, they should be added to net worth.

The total of all of the above accounts reflects the book value of the investment of the owners in the firm. Preferred stock would be subtracted from this total to get the common stock equity. Capital surplus normally reflects the excess cash paid in by the common stockholders over the amount booked as common stock. If common stock with a par or stated value of $10 per share were sold for $35 per share, $10 per share would be added to the common stock account and the remaining $25 per share added to the capital surplus account.

All earnings after preferred stock dividends (if any) belong to the common stockholders. If a company earned $4 per common share in a given year and paid a dividend of $2.50 per share, the remaining $1.50 per share would be reinvested in the business and would remain in the retained earnings account. This $1.50 is just as much a part of the common stockholders' investment in the firm as amounts that were paid in when the stock was first issued. In effect, through action by the board of directors who were elected by them, the common stockholders have indirectly chosen to reinvest $1.50 per share in the equity of the firm.

If the analyst adjusts the book value of the assets to reach a more useful approximation of current economic value, the total liabilities should be deducted from the adjusted total assets to arrive at an approximation of the current value of the net worth in a net assets value sense. It is important to recognize that the current values of assets and net worth so determined are based entirely upon the summation of piecemeal values of the individual parts of the firm. The intrinsic value would equal the estimated current value so determined if and only if the firm were considered to be worth more dead than alive. This provides a "floor" value.

In most cases, a going concern will be worth more than this because the firm will be more valuable alive than dead. The value of the firm as a going concern will not be based upon balance sheet values or adjustments of them to current values, but rather upon the concept introduced in Chapter 1, the estimated future benefits to the owners related to the risk borne by them.

The income statement

The income statement tells what has happened to the firm during a period of time, usually the previous year, according to the doctrine, principles, and procedures incorporated in the accounting system. Inasmuch as the trend in accounting development has emphasized more meaningful income determination, the financial analyst may not have as many problems in interpreting this statement as the balance sheet.

The fundamental basis of accrual accounting is the matching of costs with revenues. The income statement begins with sales (or gross revenues), deducts from sales the operating and financial costs allocated to these sales, and ends with net profit attributable to the period's business activities. The principal problems of interpretation arise from the fact that all cost allocations ultimately are based upon past dollar outlays, while the primary focus of financial management is on the present and future. For example, cost allocation for the depreciation of a machine based upon an investment of $20,000 several years ago may not be fully meaningful to a manager who knows that this machine will have to be replaced next year at an investment in excess of $35,000. Therefore, from a going-concern viewpoint of maintaining the productive capability of the firm, depreciation charged to operations of the period may have to be adjusted upward to reflect the inflated replacement cost.

Conversely, the doctrine of realization requires the accountant to recognize income only when the sale of an asset takes place (with certain exceptions, such as installment sales and franchise sales). In an inflationary period, substantial increases in value of inventories and/or fixed assets may have taken place during an accounting period without being shown on the income statement. Sometimes the analyst must add these unrealized profits to see the income more realistically in the sense of economic improvement during the period.

This is not to criticize the accounting profession; they are doing exactly what they purport to do, accounting for what *has happened* in the past. They do not and should not speculate as to the future. But financial managers are obligated to look to the future, hazy as the view might be. Financial managers must prepare the firm, by influencing operating decisions, capital allocation, and financial arrangements, to live with the future. Thus, it may be necessary to adjust the income statement, at least in a rough fashion, to understand what net profits would have been if present and sometimes future costs and values were taken into consideration.

Some information useful in coping with this problem is provided by large companies required to make form 10-K reports to the Securities and Exchange Commission. The 10-K form requires disclosure of the approximate effect that replacement costs of fixed assets and inventories would have had on the cost of sales and depreciation expense for the period. This information, although not necessarily incorporated into the financial statements, may be useful in making crude adjustments to the income statement for analytical purposes.

The accounting profession also has been making progress toward the ultimate development of price-level adjusted accounting systems. The first materialization of this effort is incorporated in Statement 33 of the Financial Accounting Standards Board.[1] Under this statement certain large publicly held corporations must report supplementary financial data disclosing the effect upon reported earnings (under historical cost information) of adjustments for general inflation. This is done by adjusting inventory and depreciation data using the consumer price index for all urban consumers (CPI-U). While this is a useful first step, it is very crude and requires much further modification by the financial analyst to estimate true "economic" earnings.

[1]The Financial Accounting Standards Board (FASB) is the standard-setting board of the accounting profession.

In summary, financial management requires a continual use of accounting statements, particularly the balance sheet and the income statement. These are not considered as ends in themselves, but rather as information bases for further analysis. The better your background in accounting theory, the clearer your interpretation of these statements will be. Then you will recognize where, when, and how they may be used and modified to relate to particular financial problems at hand.

Profits versus cash flows

Income accounting deals with the determination of *profits,* not cash flows. The principal reason for the existence of the accrual system of accounting is that management and investors would be grossly misled if they considered the net cash flows for a given period to be the earnings (profits) for that period.

However, for financial planning purposes, management may be concerned directly with *cash flows* rather than profits. The financial manager must be in a position to pay in cash the obligations of the firm as they come due. Also, when the more sophisticated methods of capital investment analysis are used, estimates of future cash flows are pertinent in appraising the expected return from investments in capital projects. Therefore, in many financial analyses it is necessary either to deal with cash flows directly or to convert crudely the profits as determined by the income statement to cash flows.

Net profits from the income statement can be adjusted to a crude estimate of cash flows by adding back any noncash charges that were considered as costs in that statement. Adjustments are required for costs such as depreciation, depletion, or amortization that have been properly charged against income but did not involve the paying out of cash during the period. Thus, taking the income statement for Acme Manufacturing Company (Table 3A–2), we convert as follows:

Net profit after taxes	$11,500,000
Plus depreciation	10,000,000
Net cash inflow	$21,500,000

This adjustment is crude because it assumes that, except for depreciation and net worth, the balance sheet remains stable from the beginning to the end of the accounting period. It is, however, useful as a starting point, particularly in long-range financial planning. For short-term planning, where more precision is required, a more detailed cash forecast may be developed. This tool will be discussed in Chapter 5.

Summary

The balance sheet is a "still picture" of the firm, listing and valuing its assets (what is owns), its liabilities (what it owes), and the owners' equity (what is left) as of a given moment of time. The crux of the problem regarding financial interpretation of the balance sheet is that the book values of the assets (other than cash and marketable securities) are residual values resulting from an accounting process dominated by considerations of meaningful income determination. These values, based largely on historical costs, might or might not be useful to the financial analyst.

If the analysis seeks current economic values, it may be necessary to recast the balance sheet by substituting estimates of current values of assets for the stated book values. This is particularly true regarding inventories, if LIFO valuation has been used, and fixed assets, if significant inflation has taken place since their acquisition. Investments may have to be restated at current market value, and intangibles often must be eliminated. Valuation of liabilities presents few problems, but the quasi-liability nature of deferred income taxes must be clearly understood. If the asset values have been adjusted, then the value of the equity capital must be adjusted to reflect these changes.

The income statement may also require interpretation and/or adjustment because of the use of historical costs and the doctrine of realization. This is particularly true regarding depreciation charges and, sometimes, inventory appreciation. Considerable progress is being made by the accounting profession in reporting supplementary asset valuation and income data for large publicly held corporations, recognizing both replacement values and price level changes.

Questions

1. In general, why is there often a substantial difference between the book values of assets on the balance sheet and the current economic values of these assets?

2. Specifically, how and why might the book values of the following assets vary from current economic values:
    a. Accounts receivable?
    b. Inventories, where LIFO valuation has been used?

c. Land?
d. Buildings and equipment?
e. Investments?

3. If, for certain analytical purposes, asset values on the left side of the balance sheet are adjusted to reflect current economic values, how is the right side of the balance sheet adjusted?

4. Why is the financial manager interested in cash flows as well as accounting income?

Part Two
Analysis, Planning, and Control

Chapter 4 Financial Analysis

Analysis is the prelude to intelligent decision making. You do it every time you cross a busy, uncontrolled intersection. You stop, look one way, see what is approaching and assess its speed, look the other way, do the same thing, relate what you have observed in each direction, then decide whether or not to cross and whether to walk or run. If you fail to do this, you will not be around very long to make such decisions. In financial management, you are engaging in the same sort of process for the same reason. Although the data you observe, assess, and relate usually are more complex, the basic procedure is essentially the same.

Before making a decision, management must first *gather and assess the relevant facts.* These facts often take the form of accounting or statistical data, such as contained in the balance sheets and income statements discussed in Chapter 3 and its Appendix A. The *initial assessment* involves either *accepting* a given piece of information, such as the valuation of inventories as stated on the balance sheet, or *modifying* that information, perhaps by adjusting it from the stated (book) value to an estimate of the current value. In short, you are trying to focus on the data to eliminate distortions so that the most meaningful information available is used for the purpose at hand.

The next phase of analysis involves *relating the data to each other* in such a fashion as to enhance the relevance to the problem at hand. Then, and only then, are you in a position to proceed with the decision. Thus, analysis is the necessary homework of the decision-making process. If it is not done in a logical and meaningful fashion, just as in the decision-making process of crossing busy intersections, you simply will not be around much longer to engage in this process.

We actually began our study of financial analysis in the preceding chapter. As we developed margin and turnover analysis and introduced operating and financial leverage concepts, we were relating various pieces of information to each other in such a way as to make them more meaningful than they were in isolation. Identifying these key relationships enhanced our understanding of the operations and financing of the firm. Such analyses could then be used by management for planning and controlling future activities.

In this chapter and throughout the rest of the book, we shall develop additional analytical tools and relate their appropriate uses in connection with financial planning, decision making, and control.

Before proceeding to examine specific analytical tools, we must first understand that no analysis is done for its own sake. Analysis in general, or any specific analytical tool, is only of value as a logical means of assembling, evaluating, and/or relating specific pieces of information. The objective is to produce new information that is more valuable than the individual raw data. The tools selected to enhance the value of information must be related to the specific task or problem at hand. Thus, one or several analytical tools might be applicable to management of cash, while a different tool (or tools) would be useful in appraising and controlling accounts receivable, and a still different set of tools would be meaningful in appraising opportunities to invest in additional fixed assets. Our kit of tools is somewhat like that of a plumber, whose kit contains such things as various sized pipe wrenches, pipe cutters, a soldering torch, soldering iron, and pipe threader. Each is useful in connection with one or more particular tasks but useless for others. The plumber's skill lies not only in knowing his tools and how to use them, but in knowing which particular tool(s) to use in doing a given task. Likewise, to understand financial management, you must not only understand the analytical tools, but learn how to apply each tool appropriately to particular tasks and problems.

Viewpoint of the analyst

The four major types of parties who have financial interests in a business firm are the short-term creditors, long-term creditors, stockholders, and management. The viewpoint of each differs because the nature of the financial relationship to the firm is different. Only by examining these differences can we understand the perspective of each and recognize the lines of analysis that are meaningful to each. The managers of the firm must understand all three of the external viewpoints if they are to attract and hold sufficient funds to operate the business.

Short-term creditors

A short-term creditor, such as a commercial bank that has loaned money to the firm on a short-term note or a supplier that has sold raw materials or merchandise to the firm on trade credit terms, is interested primarily in *liquidity*. The immediate concern is that cash will be generated to pay off the obligation when it is due. Thus, the most pertinent analysis relates to the current assets as compared to the current liabilities and the timing of funds flows from inventories through receivables into cash.

If liquidity analysis indicates significant doubt as to the firm's ability to generate sufficient cash to pay its obligation when due, then the short-term creditor also becomes interested in the ultimate *solvency* of the firm. If the debt is not paid, will this creditor and others still be adequately protected by the total value of assets in excess of total liabilities? Or is there substantial risk that creditors might lose all or part of their investment?

Note that the short-term creditor usually is not primarily interested in the profits of the firm. Of course, any bank or trade supplier would rather have a profitable customer than an unprofitable one because profitable operations enhance the probability and magnitude of future business with the customer. But the bank or trade supplier does not participate directly in profits; the bank receives only its fixed interest charges and the trade creditor only its profits on sales to the customer. These parties want their money back in a relatively short period of time and are immediately concerned with the risk that they will not get it. Most short-term credit analysis is focused upon the question, "Will the obligation be paid even in the absence of profits?"

Long-term creditors

Long-term creditors, including bondholders or term lenders such as pension funds or life insurance companies making loans extending over several years, also are interested in short-term liquidity because they would be in trouble along with everybody else involved in the firm's financing if current obligations could not be met. But they probably would not have bought the bonds or made the term loan if significant liquidity risk were perceived at the time. They usually are more interested in *solvency,* the excess of value of total assets over total liabilities (including the obligations they hold). Finally, and perhaps most importantly, they realize that in order to meet its obligations to pay interest and principal on long-term debt, the firm must maintain its *profitability* in the long run. Thus, they require additional analysis of the firm's estimated future earnings and cash flows over many years as compared to future interest and principal payment requirements under long-term debt obligations. They are particularly interested in the expected stability of profits over the period to maturity of the obligations they hold.

Stockholders

The stockholders (or proprietors or partners in unincorporated firms) are, of course, interested in liquidity, solvency, and the relationship of future profits and cash flows to the obligations to service long-term debt. Since they are in a residual position to benefit directly from the profitability of the firm, they are most interested in *profits* and the *risks* related to whether or not such profits will materialize in the future. As discussed in Chapter 1, the value of their stock is a direct function of expected future profits (or, theoretically more correct, cash flows) and the risks to which their capital is exposed. Thus the stockholders' analysis focuses upon expectations of future profits and views short-term liquidity and ability to service long-term credit obligations from the standpoint of the risk borne by the stockholders.

Management

Management, recognizing its objective of maximizing the value of the stockholders' equity, should maintain essentially the same viewpoint as the stockholders. However, stockholders also hold management responsible for maintaining sufficient liquidity to satisfy obligations to creditors and for raising sufficient capital from both debt and equity sources. Therefore, management also is involved in analysis relating to the viewpoints of the short- and long-term creditors. They must understand the creditors' viewpoints from the other side of the desk.

Ratio analysis

Of all the tools of financial analysis, ratio analysis is perhaps the most widely used, overused, and misused. A ratio is simply the relationship between one number and another number. Any item or combination of items on the balance sheet and/or income statement could be divided by any other to produce a financial ratio. But that surely does not mean that the resulting ratio would assist an analyst by enhancing understanding of the firm's financial condition. The analyst is interested only in those ratios that are *relevant* to particular financial problems or decisions. One must be selective, using only the ratios drawn from balance sheet and income statement data that yield more pertinent information than that contained in the raw data. The overuse of ratio analysis results from ignoring this test.

The misuse of ratio analysis usually results from reading too much meaning into a given ratio. It is naive to conclude from any given ratio that a firm's liquidity is satisfactory or unsatisfactory, that its capital structure is sound or unsound, or that the ratio is too high or too low. Remember that a given ratio simply reflects the relationship between two numbers. The ratio may be symptomatic of a problem, but further analysis is required to determine the cause or to draw conclusions of a qualitative nature.

The great advantage of ratio analysis is that it reduces raw data of widely varying magnitude to a common comparative basis. Thus, ratio analysis is the most meaningful way to compare financial information regarding a given firm to that of other firms that are larger or smaller, or to a composite of other firms, such as an industry. The value of this will be evident as we proceed.

Comparisons

Because the principal use of ratio analysis is in making meaningful comparisons, we must be satisfied that the comparisons are valid.

Absolute standards Absolute standards, such as "a current ratio (current assets/current liabilities) of 2 to 1 or higher indicates that a firm's liquidity is satisfactory," or "a firm with a current ratio of less than 1 to 1 will not be able to meet its current obligations," are absolutely *false* and *misleading*. They may be summarily dismissed for the simple reason that every firm is a unique entity. Any given ratio within reason could be fully adequate for one firm and inadequate for another. The ultimate test of adequacy is the ability of a firm to live and prosper. With regard to the current ratio, the ultimate test of adequate liquidity is the ability of the firm to pay its bills on time. For one firm this may require a current ratio of 3 to 1, whereas for another, .8 to 1 may be adequate. (Many financially sound electric utility companies in the United States regularly report current ratios of less than 1 to 1.)

Similar businesses The analyst seeks to compare ratios of a given firm to those of other businesses having essentially the same characteristics. Thus, a banker considering a loan application from a hardware store might compare pertinent ratios for that store to those of several other hardware stores among the bank's customers that are reasonably comparable in terms of their markets, merchandise offered for sale, and credit terms. The ratio comparisons can then be evaluated in terms of the bank's experience in lending to the comparative stores to guide its judgment regarding the feasibility of a loan to this particular firm. Even with this familiarity with comparable firms, due allowances must be made for differences both in accounting methods used and in the nature of operations. For example, some firms may value inventories on FIFO and others on LIFO. One comparative store may do a larger proportion of its business with building contractors and another a larger proportion in "big ticket" items such as major appliances. Even hardware stores differ from each other all the way from the hardware supermarket to the small neighborhood store.

Industry data Subject to the cautions indicated above, pertinent ratios for a given firm may be compared to those of the industry in which it operates. Industry average ratios are published regularly by Dun & Bradstreet, Robert Morris Associates, and the Federal Trade Commission. In addition, trade associations for many industries compile average ratios for their particular industries and make them available to their members either through trade journals or bulletins.

Dun & Bradstreet, the largest mercantile credit agency, annually publishes ratio information for a large number of industries based upon samples of firms on which it furnishes credit reports. Dun & Bradstreet compiles 14 ratios for each standard industrial classification category, showing the median and upper and lower quartile ratios from the sample.

The annual *Statement Studies* published by Robert Morris Associates, the national association of bank credit and loan officers, contains 11 average ratios for each of over 150 industries. These ratios are based upon financial statements of firms in each industry that have been submitted to the banks that are members of the association.

The Federal Trade Commission publishes extensive quarterly balance sheet and income statement data developed from a large sample of corporations reporting to the commission. These data, reported by standard industrial classifications, may be reduced to ratios for comparative purposes.

Industry ratios obtained from any of these sources are useful for comparative purposes, but two additional cautions are necessary. Because such data are broadly based, they may or may not be truly comparable to those of any given business. For example, an average ratio for the soft drink industry will be derived from statements of companies as diverse as Coca-Cola on one hand and small regional or local soft drink producers on the other. Some only make the syrup or concentrate, while others also bottle and distribute the beverages. They have little in common. The average may not be very useful for comparison to either Coca-Cola or the Fizz Pop Company.

A second problem in using industry ratios derives from the fact that many firms formerly engaged almost entirely in a single industry have diversified extensively during recent years. While they are still identified as members of a given industry, their operations now involve a complex mixture of activities in numerous different industries. Thus, the "purity" of industry data has been significantly diluted.

Historical comparisons Ratio analysis is widely used in comparing ratios from the current statements of a firm to those of previous years. Such comparisons are particularly valuable in identifying trends. By spreading the pertinent ratios for several years across an analysis sheet or by graphing the time series, either independently or in comparison to industry ratios, the analyst may discern trends. Trends may be useful to creditors, stockholders, or management for identifying improvement or deterioration in operating efficiency or financial condition. Care must be used to distinguish a trend resulting from a change in operating policy, such as a change in the credit terms of sale or the manufacture of parts that formerly were purchased from suppliers, from a change produced by a true increase or decrease in efficiency.

Types of ratios

The four major types of ratios that will be discussed are those related to liquidity, debt, coverage of obligations, and profitability. Comparative balance sheets and income statements of the Smith Mercantile Company shown in Tables 4–1 and 4–2 will be used to illustrate these ratios.

Table 4–1

SMITH MERCANTILE COMPANY
Balance Sheet

	December 31, 1981	December 31, 1982
Assets		
Current assets:		
Cash and marketable securities	$ 10,000	$ 26,000
Accounts receivable—trade	22,000	24,000
Inventories	29,000	30,000
Total current assets	61,000	80,000
Fixed assets—net	88,000	90,000
Total assets	$149,000	$170,000
Liabilities and Net Worth		
Current liabilities:		
Accounts payable	$ 15,000	$ 23,000
Accrued taxes	3,000	6,000
Other accrued liabilities	10,000	16,000
Total current liabilities	28,000	45,000
First mortgage bonds, 9-1/8%, due in 1991	55,000	55,000
Total liabilities	83,000	100,000
Common stock (4,000 shares)	40,000	40,000
Retained earnings	26,000	30,000
Net worth	66,000	70,000
Total liabilities and net worth	$149,000	$170,000

Liquidity ratios

Liquidity ratios are of primary interest to short-term creditors because they *collectively* will provide insight as to the ability of the firm to pay its current obligations. The *static* liquidity ratios, which relate to the current asset coverage of current liabilities, are derived solely from the firm's balance sheet.

Table 4–2

SMITH MERCANTILE COMPANY
Income Statements

	Years ended December 31	
	1981	1982
Net sales	$300,000	$360,000
Cost of goods sold	240,000	280,000
Gross profit	60,000	80,000
Expenses:		
Selling, general, and administrative expenses	41,000	55,000
Interest expense	5,000	5,000
Total expenses	46,000	60,000
Net profit before taxes	14,000	20,000
Income taxes (federal and state)	7,000	10,000
Net profit after taxes	$ 7,000	$ 10,000

Current ratio The current ratio is probably the most widely used measure of liquidity. It is calculated by dividing total current assets by total current liabilities. The current ratio for the Smith Mercantile Company on December 31, 1982 is calculated as follows:

$$\text{Current ratio} = \frac{\text{Current assets}}{\text{Current liabilities}} = \frac{\$80{,}000}{\$45{,}000} = 1.8$$

This compares with 2.2 at the end of 1981. If nothing else were known, this decline might be symptomatic of some deterioration in liquidity, that is, some weakening in the ability of Smith to meet its current obligations. But such an interpretation might be erroneous because these ratios (1.8 versus 2.2) do not tell us anything about (1) the composition of the current assets, (2) the time frame within which the noncash current assets may be expected to turn into cash, and (3) the maturity distribution of the current liabilities. Thus, all we can say with confidence is that at the end of 1982, Smith had $1.80 of current assets to cover each dollar of current liabilities compared to $2.20 at the end of 1981.

To strengthen this point of caution, we make an admittedly exaggerated comparison in Table 4–3. Company A shows a current ratio of 3.0 whereas company B's ratio is only 1.5. But company A is out of cash, has only nominal receivables, and substantially all the current assets are inventories. If these inventories just happened to be toys and the date of the balance sheet is December 31, there is little possibility that company A will be able to pay its current liabilities when they mature, particularly if they are due in a short period of time. Company B, which shows a current ratio of only 1.5 times, is, in fact, too liquid. From a creditor's standpoint, there could be almost no question as to its ability to pay because its current liabilities are covered dollar for dollar by cash in the bank. This example is extreme, but the point is made that one cannot draw conclusions regarding the soundness of the current position from a single ratio, particularly the current ratio. The principal reason for this is that the numerator of the ratio is a combination of several different items and the ratio itself does not disclose either the proportions or the quality of the different components.

Table 4–3 Current ratio comparison

	Company A	Company B
Current ratio	3.0	1.5
Current assets:		
Cash	-0-	$10,000
Accounts receivable	$ 1,000	3,000
Inventories	29,000	2,000
Total current assets	$30,000	$15,000
Current liabilities	10,000	10,000

Nonetheless, the current ratio is a useful starting point in liquidity analysis, particularly when it is compared historically and to that of other firms engaged in similar operations.

Quick ratio The quick ratio (sometimes called the *"acid test" ratio*) allows one to focus on a more immediate measure of liquidity by removing inventories from the numerator of the fraction. Inventories are the furthest removed from cash. They must be sold before they turn into either cash or accounts receivable and, in the latter case, the receivables must be collected before the firm obtains cash. Sales are indefinite; they may be at prices greater than, equal to, or less than cost (the book value); possibly, they will not occur at all. By eliminating inventories, the analyst is in effect determining that, even in the absence of future operations, there will be so many dollars of cash, marketable securities, and receivables to cover each dollar of current liabilities.

The quick ratio for Smith Mercantile Company at the end of 1982 is computed as follows:

$$\text{Quick ratio} = \frac{\text{Current assets} - \text{Inventories}}{\text{Current liabilities}}$$

$$= \frac{\$50{,}000}{\$45{,}000} = 1.1$$

This compares to 1.1 at the end of 1981; thus there has been no material change. This ratio says that Smith has approximately $1.10 in the total of cash, marketable securities, and accounts receivable to cover each dollar of current liabilities. If the cash balance is accurate and the marketable securities are high-quality short-term securities worth very close to their book value, only two questions are left: (1) Is the quality of the accounts receivable sufficiently high that they are worth approximately their book value? (2) Can they be collected in time to add sufficient amounts to the existing cash to pay the current liabilities as they mature? If these questions can be answered positively, one may conclude that the liquidity of the firm is sound. Sometimes, however, receivables prove to be worth much less than their book value and/or they may be due in installments stretching over a considerable period of time.

Calculating the quick ratios from our extreme comparison in Table 4–3, we find that of company A to be .1, in contrast to company B's quick ratio of 1.3. This shows the fallacy of jumping to a conclusion after examining only the current ratio by pointing out that the liquidity position of company A is extremely poor, whereas that of company B is excellent.

Cash position ratio The cash position ratio (which is used less than the two above) goes one step closer to pure liquidity by eliminating the receivables. This recognizes that receivables, although closer to cash than inventories and not dependent upon future operation of the business, are still one step removed from cash. Sometimes, unfortunately, that step is an insurmountable one. This ratio is computed for Smith Mercantile Company as of December 31, 1982, as follows:

$$\text{Cash position ratio} = \frac{\text{Cash + Marketable securities}}{\text{Current liabilities}}$$

$$= \frac{\$26{,}000}{\$45{,}000} = .6$$

This compares to .4 at the end of the previous year.

Inasmuch as marketable securities normally are only a telephone call away from cash and worth approximately their book value, for practical purposes the cash position ratio tells us that Smith has approximately 60 cents in cash available to cover each dollar of its current liabilities and that this position has improved substantially from the end of the previous year.

Although the cash position ratio is of considerable use to trade creditors in analyzing the liquidity of their customers, it is not particularly useful to a commercial bank in appraising loan applications. Usually a bank's customer would not be applying for a loan if its cash position were greater than nominal. Banks do find it of some use in connection with periodic analyses relative to the renewal of lines of credit.

To this point we have examined only static ratios derived from the balance sheet, which depict financial relationships at a given point of time. Unless these were extremely favorable or unfavorable, we still would not be in a position to draw conclusions regarding the adequacy of a firm's liquidity. We have not yet considered the rates at which funds can be expected to flow upward from inventories into receivables or from receivables into cash. To perceive these we must examine *dynamic* liquidity ratios, which are derived from income statement data in relation to balance sheet data. These are sometimes called *activity* ratios, because they disclose rates of movement or flow of funds in the firm.

Inventory turnover The inventory turnover ratio shows the rate of upward flow from inventories into receivables or directly into cash, if the firm sells on a cash basis. It is calculated for Smith Mercantile Company for the year 1982 as follows:

$$\text{Inventory turnover} = \frac{\text{Cost of goods sold}}{\text{Average inventory}}$$

$$= \frac{\$280{,}000}{\dfrac{\$29{,}000 + \$30{,}000}{2}} = 9.5 \text{ times}$$

If we assume that normal inventory levels were reflected in the year-end figures, then Smith, which sells entirely on a credit basis, turned its inventories into accounts receivable 9.5 times during the year.

If you find it more meaningful, you can divide this 9.5 into 365 days to determine that on the average Smith's inventory turned over every 38 days. Thus, if past experience is repeated, sale of Smith's year-end inventory of $30,000 should result in the generation of accounts receivable of that amount plus the gross profit on those sales by about February 7 of the next year. To put this still another way, about 30/38 (or .79) of $30,000, or $23,700, of inventory plus the gross profit thereon should turn into receivables each month.

In the calulation of inventory turnover, *cost of goods sold* is properly used as the numerator, because the inventories are valued at cost. To use sales (valued at selling prices) would be comparing apples with oranges. Nonetheless, some comparative industry data, including the ratios compiled by Dun & Bradstreet, use sales. Therefore, for such a comparison you must do likewise.

Average inventory should be obtained from the best data available. In our calculation, we had only beginning and ending inventories for the year. If we had quarterly balance sheets, we would average the four quarter-end inventory figures. Internal analysts may have access to monthly (or possibly even weekly or daily) inventories, in which cases these more detailed data should be averaged. If the analyst is concerned that the current inventory may be out of line, the current figure (rather than an average) might be used to test this. In summary, the theoretically correct inventory turnover is calculated by dividing cost of goods sold by average inventory, but there is nothing hard and fast about this where either data limitations force the use of something less than ideal or where the purpose of the analysis may dictate otherwise. Consistency, however, must always be maintained in comparing inventory turnover (or any other) ratios.

Receivables turnover The receivables turnover ratio is used to estimate the rate of cash flow expected from the collection of accounts receivable. This ratio for Smith Mercantile Company for the year 1982 is calculated as follows:

$$\text{Receivables turnover} = \frac{\text{Net credit sales}}{\text{Average accounts receivable}}$$

$$= \frac{\$360{,}000}{\dfrac{\$22{,}000 + \$24{,}000}{2}} = 15.7 \text{ times}$$

Another way of measuring cash flow from the collection of receivables is to convert the receivables turnover ratio to an *average collection period.* This may be done by taking the reciprocal of the receivables turnover (1/RT) and multiplying it by the number of days in a year (365). For Smith Mercantile this would give

$$\text{Average collection period} = \frac{1}{\text{Receivables turnover}} \times 365$$

$$= \frac{1}{15.7} \times 365 = 23 \text{ days}$$

The direct formula for calculating the average collection period is

$$\frac{\text{Average accounts receivable}}{\text{Credit sales/365}} = \frac{\$23{,}000}{\$360{,}000/365} = \frac{\$23{,}000}{\$986.30} = 23 \text{ days}$$

This formula involves calculating the average credit sales per day (the denominator) and dividing that into the average accounts receivable.[1]

The analyst sometimes has difficulty obtaining sufficient data to compute either the receivables turnover ratio or the average collection period exactly as indicated above. Net *credit* sales should be used, that is, credit sales net of returns and allowances. But often only net sales are available, without any breakdown of the portion of sales that were made on credit versus those made for cash. The use of net sales, rather than net credit sales, generally is appropriate for manufacturers and wholesalers as most of their sales are on credit. But one would get a rather ridiculous and meaningless

[1]An alternative formula for calculating the average collection period is

$$\frac{\text{Average accounts receivable} \times 365}{\text{Credit sales}} = \frac{\$23{,}000 \times 365}{\$360{,}000} = \frac{\$8{,}395{,}000}{\$360{,}000} = 23 \text{ days}$$

ratio if net sales of a grocery chain were used, because it is well known that the great majority of its sales are for cash.

Another problem relates to the use of *average* receivables and is exactly the same as discussed above regarding average inventories. It should be handled in the same fashion.

Receivables turnover ratios (or average collection periods), in addition to their value for historical and industry comparisons, may also be useful for comparison to the terms of sale. For example, if Smith Mercantile sold its merchandise on net 10 day terms, the average collection period of 23 days would appear to be very long and suggests that (1) collection policies might be lax, (2) some of the customers were poor credit risks, or (3) perhaps some of the accounts receivable were worthless. At the other extreme, if its selling terms were net 30 days, the average collection period of 23 days would indicate exceptionally high receivables turnover, and the analyst would only ask why Smith's customers were so nice to them. Caution must be exercised, however, in comparing collection periods to terms of sale, because in some cases the stated terms of sale are only nominal, that is, neither buyer nor seller really expects that the bills will be paid on time according to the terms stated on the invoices. If this is understood, comparison to terms of sale is not very useful, and the analyst should rely on historical and industry comparisons.

Integrated liquidity analysis

No individual ratio provides enough information to judge whether or not a firm can pay its maturing current liabilities on time. However, the five ratios may be related to each other in such a way that one may confidently draw such a conclusion. The cash position ratio of .6 showed that Smith Mercantile Company had 60 cents in cash and marketable securities to cover each dollar of current liabilities. The quick ratio of 1.1 showed that it had another 50 cents ($1.10 − .60) in receivables per dollar of current liabilities. With a receivables turnover of 15.7, that 50 cents should be collected over a period of 23 days, the average collection period. Thus, the existing cash and marketable securities plus the collection of receivables should provide $1.10 within 23 days to pay off maturing current liabilities and leave 10 cents to spare. If, for example, we knew that none of the current liabilities were overdue and that they matured rather evenly over the next two months or a longer period of time, we could conclude that the company's liquidity position was sound.

In addition, the current ratio of 1.8 revealed that inventories are equal to 70 cents per dollar of current liabilities ($1.80 − $1.10). The inventory turnover of 9.5 times per year (.79 per month) tells us that each month, accounts receivable of 55 cents (.79 × 70 cents) plus the gross profit will be generated to replenish the receivables. This will start in motion the cycle which, approximately 23 days after the sales, will result in the generation of more cash to pay future maturing current liabilities.[2]

This type of integrated liquidity ratio analysis provides significant information in addition to comparison of liquidity ratios to historical ratios and those of the industry or similar firms. Such analysis, although somewhat indirect, may be valuable to outsiders, such as credit analysts of suppliers or banks, who must rely on balance sheet and income statement data. Within the firm, greater data availability usually will facilitate the forecasting of short-term cash availability by using a much more precise tool, the cash forecast, discussed in Chapter 5.

Debt ratios

Debt ratios are *static* ratios that relate total debt or particular types of debt to either total assets or owners' equity in the firm. They measure *solvency* by showing how much deterioration in value of assets could take place as the result of operating losses or direct losses in asset value before the owners' equity would be wiped out and the creditors' claims would be impaired. They are useful to short-term creditors if liquidity analysis indicates significant risk of nonpayment of their claims when due, to long-term creditors in appraising the risks that their claims might be impaired, and to stockholders in that they are crude measures of financial leverage.

Inasmuch as debt ratios are partially based upon the value of fixed assets as well as current assets, the analyst must exercise particular caution in accepting asset values as stated on the balance sheet. As discussed in Chapter 3, Appendix A, book values of net fixed assets often bear little resemblance to current values. If they do not, estimated current values should be substituted before proceeding with debt ratio analysis.

Another accounting-related problem concerns the treatment of deferred income taxes that may exist on the liabilities side of the balance sheet (also discussed in Chapter 3, Appendix A). Some analysts consider these to be liabilities, while others consider them as part of the owners' equity earmarked for future income tax payments. The trend is toward the latter treatment. Other analysts simply eliminate this item and deduct an equivalent amount from the total assets. There is no clearly right or wrong treatment; the important thing is to maintain consistency when comparing debt ratios.

Still another concern relates to subordinated debt and preferred stock. Although from a legal standpoint, subordinated debt is debt and preferred stock is a type of owners' equity, they both are inferior to senior creditors' claims. Therefore, they both should be considered as equity in an analysis

[2]A more complete liquidity analysis of this type is developed in Verlyn D. Richards and Eugene J. Laughlin, "A Cash Conversion Approach to Liquidity Analysis," *Financial Management,* Spring 1980, pp. 32–38.

from the standpoint of senior creditors. But, from the viewpoint of residual owners, the common stockholders, preferred stock may be considered a quasi-debt because it must be serviced before the common stockholders may receive anything. If the analysis is for the use of common stockholders or management (who represent their interests), both subordinated debt and preferred stock may be included with debt.

Debt to total assets The ratio of debt to total assets shows the percentage of the tangible assets that has been financed by creditors. In other words, it shows how many cents of "other people's money" have been used to finance each dollar of tangible assets of the firm. For Smith Mercantile Company on December 31, 1982, this ratio is calculated as follows:

$$\text{Debt to total assets} = \frac{\text{Total liabilities}}{\text{Total tangible assets}} = \frac{\$100{,}000}{\$170{,}000} = .59 \text{ or } 59\%$$

This compares to .56 at the end of the previous year.

Note that the debt in this ratio includes all current liabilities ($45,000) as well as long-term debt ($55,000). Intangible assets, such as goodwill, patents, copyrights, and organization expenses, are deducted from the total assets, because this ratio is essentially a measure of creditors' protection in the event of cessation of operations. The value of intangible assets tends to relate to continued operation, so the value would be, at best, questionable in liquidation. Of course, if the analyst has confidence in the value of a given intangible—say, that of a patent that could be sold to another company—that value may be included.

This ratio tells us that the creditors of Smith Mercantile Company have furnished 59 percent of the financing of its tangible assets, whereas the stockholders have furnished 41 percent. The company could suffer a 41 percent direct or indirect loss of asset values before the creditors would stand to lose anything. With this in mind, the analyst must use some imagination to estimate what might happen to the value of the assets in the event of unfavorable developments (such as general business recession, loss of important customers, or obsolescence of inventories or fixed assets) to make a judgment as to the probability that the equity cushion might be wiped out.[3]

Debt to equity The debt to equity (or debt to net worth) ratio is calculated by dividing the total liabilities (both current and long-term) by the owners'

[3]The highly sophisticated analyst might develop scenarios of various combinations of unfavorable events and employ simulation techniques to forecast the effects of the various events upon asset values to discover what combinations of events would eliminate the 41 percent equity cushion and thus impair creditors' claims. This elaboration of analysis is beyond the scope of our discussion.

equity (normally less any intangible assets). The debt to equity ratio for Smith Mercantile Company on December 31, 1982, was

$$\text{Debt to equity} = \frac{\text{Total liabilities}}{\text{Owners' equity} - \text{Intangibles}} = \frac{\$100,000}{\$\ 70,000} = 1.43 \text{ or } 143\%$$

This compares to 1.26 at the end of the previous year.

This ratio measures essentially the same thing as the debt to total assets ratio but does so more vividly. the total debt (liabilities) is divided by only the owners' equity rather than the total tangible assets. Here it indicates that Smith is using $1.43 of other people's money for each dollar of investment by the owners. A high debt to equity ratio in relation to similar firms is a symptom that the company may be running out of borrowing power, that is, creditors may be reluctant to furnish additional debt capital unless the equity cushion is reinforced.

The soundness of any given debt to equity ratio is dependent upon the stability of asset values and earning power. A commercial bank or finance company, whose principal assets are the debt obligations of other firms or individuals and whose earnings tend to be relatively stable, can safely be financed by debt equal to several times its equity. In contrast, a highly specialized electronics company, whose assets might be rendered obsolete by rapidly changing technology and whose earnings may fluctuate violently, can safely be financed by debt equal to only a small portion of its owners' equity.

Long-term debt to total capital structure This ratio ignores the current liabilities and focuses only upon the capital structure of the firm, that is, the long-term debt and the owners' equity. It is computed by dividing the long-term debt by the total capital structure (normally less intangibles). This ratio for Smith Mercantile on December 31, 1982, is calculated as follows:

$$\text{Long-term debt to total capital structure} = \frac{\text{Long-term debt}}{\text{Total capital structure} - \text{Intangibles}} = \frac{\$\ 55,000}{\$125,000} = .44, \text{ or } 44\%$$

This compares to .45 at the end of the previous year.

This ratio may or may not be meaningful for some manufacturing or marketing firms. Their current liabilities may be relatively large and more important than long-term liabilities. However, the long-term debt ratio tends to be more important in highly capital-intensive industries, such as public utilities, where the great majority of debt financing is long-term.

Long-term debt to equity This ratio measures essentially the same thing as the above ratio, but does so more vividly by comparing the long-term debt to only the owners' equity. It is computed as follows:

$$\text{Long-term debt to equity} = \frac{\text{Long-term debt}}{\text{Owners' equity} - \text{Intangibles}} = \frac{\$55{,}000}{\$70{,}000} = .79, \text{ or } 79\%$$

This compares to .83 at the end of the previous year.

Coverage ratios

In addition to the static debt ratios discussed above, long-term creditors are also concerned with dynamic coverage ratios reflecting a firm's ability to maintain sufficient earnings and cash flows to service the obligations they hold.

Interest coverage The interest coverage ratio, sometimes called *times interest earned,* reflects a firm's ability to make sufficient earnings to meet interest obligations on its long-term debt. The ratio is calculated by dividing the earnings before interest and taxes by the interest requirement. For Smith Mercantile in 1982, the ratio would be

$$\text{Interest coverage ratio} = \frac{\text{Earnings before interest and taxes}}{\text{Interest requirement}} = \frac{\$20{,}000 + \$5{,}000}{\$5{,}000} = 5 \text{ times}$$

This compares to 3.8 times for the previous year.

Earnings *before taxes* should be used because interest is an expense for tax purposes. We must add interest back to the numerator to compute a true *coverage* ratio. The ratio tells us that if Smith's earnings from operations fell to one fifth of their 1982 level, the firm would still earn enough to pay the interest on its long-term debt. The next analytical step would be to estimate the volatility of earnings from operations (discussed in Chapter 3) to assess the probability that earnings might fall to less than one fifth of their 1982 level during the next nine years that this debt will be outstanding.

The major securities services, Standard & Poor's and Moody's, report interest coverage on both before-tax and aftertax bases. From the creditors' standpoint, the before-tax basis should be used. From stockholder and management viewpoints, it may also be useful to examine this ratio on an aftertax basis, recognizing that income taxes are essential costs of doing business.

Although highly useful, the interest coverage ratio has three shortcomings. The first is that the service of long-term debt may not be the only fixed financial requirement that must be met. The second is that service of long-term debt may require not only periodic interest payments but also mandatory payments on the principal. The third is that fixed financial service requirements are paid in cash, the generation of which may not coincide with earnings. These shortcomings are largely overcome through the use of other coverage ratios discussed below.

Fixed charge coverage Many firms acquire the use of fixed assets by leasing as well as by borrowing the money to buy them. When assets are leased on a long-term basis, the company incurs fixed or minimum rental payment requirements. In this case we must include required rental payments in our calculation of *fixed charge coverage* by adding rental payments to both the numerator and the denominator of the interest coverage ratio as follows:

$$\text{Fixed charge coverage} = \frac{\text{Earnings before interest and taxes} + \text{Rental payments}}{\text{Interest charges} + \text{Rental payments}}$$

As in our interpretation of the interest coverage ratio, the reciprocal of the fixed charge coverage ratio indicates the decline that could take place in earnings from operations before earnings would be insufficient to cover interest and rental payment obligations.

Smith Mercantile Company does not lease assets, but for illustrative purposes let us assume that it does and that the required rental payments are $4,000 per year. If so, we calculate its fixed charge coverage in 1982 as follows:

$$\text{Fixed charge coverage} = \frac{\$20{,}000 + \$5{,}000 + \$4{,}000}{\$5{,}000 + \$4{,}000} = 3.2 \text{ times}$$

Thus, Smith's earnings from operations available to cover fixed financial charges could decline to a little less than one third of their 1982 level before earnings would be insufficient to pay them.

Burden coverage We have not yet coped with the fact that many long-term debt contracts require not only the periodic payment of interest but also mandatory periodic payments on the principal. The principal payments may be installment payments on a term loan or sinking-fund payments required by a bond contract. (These will be discussed in detail in Chapter 18.) Periodic payments on principal are not expenses for either accounting or income tax purposes, but rather represent repayment to the lenders of funds originally provided to the firm. But they do constitute cash flow requirements because they must be paid or the lenders may take legal action. To take this financial requirement into account, we calculate a *burden coverage* ratio, that is, the ratio of approximate cash generation to fixed cash outflow requirements.

Inasmuch as depreciation is a charge against income but does not involve a cash outflow, we add it to numerator of the ratio to convert reported earnings to cash flows available to service financial obligations. This admittedly crude way of estimating net cash flows from operations assumes that no replacements or additions to fixed assets occur and that net working capital (current assets less current liabilities) remains stable. Nonetheless it is an approximation that is useful in long-term financial analysis.

We must also add to the denominator the required annual principal payments on debt adjusted to a before-tax basis. If the required annual principal payment is $5,000 and the income tax rate is, for simplicity, assumed to be 50 percent, then $10,000 of before-tax income would be required to pay $5,000 of income taxes and have $5,000 left to make the principal payment.

To illustrate the computation of the burden coverage ratio, let us assume that Smith Mercantile Company is required under the terms of its long-term debt to repay $5,000 of the principal each year and that its effective income tax rate is 50 percent. Depreciation charges are $8,000 per year. The computation for 1982 is as follows:

$$\text{Burden coverage} = \frac{\text{Earnings before taxes} + \text{Interest} + \text{Rental payments} + \text{Depreciation}}{\text{Interest} + \text{Principal payment } [1/(1 - \text{Tax rate})] + \text{Rental payments}}$$

$$= \frac{\$20{,}000 + \$5{,}000 + \$4{,}000 + \$8{,}000}{\$5{,}000 + \$5{,}000\ (2) + \$4{,}000} = \frac{\$37{,}000}{\$19{,}000} = 1.9 \text{ times}$$

This tells us that the annual cash flow before taxes, interest, and rental payments was 1.9 times the cash requirement to service all fixed financial obligations including the principal payments. Or, to put it another way, the annual cash flow from operations could fall to a little over one-half its 1982 level before the company would fail to generate sufficient cash to meet its long-term financial obligations (assuming that net working capital remains stable and it does not make any replacements or additions to fixed assets).

The burden coverage ratio may seem a bit complicated to calculate, but it is very informative in appraising the ability of a firm to cover its financial obligations. In practice this line of analysis is often followed even further to include coverage of the before-tax equivalents of preferred stock dividends (if any) and of common stock dividends that management feels a strong obligation to maintain at a given level. If a company is committed to a long-term program of capital expenditure (such as an electric utility with generating plants under construction), these requirements should also be included in this type of analysis.

Profitability ratios

Chapter 3 covered perhaps the most important profitability ratio analysis in an overview of the operating characteristics of the firm. There you learned how to calculate and interpret the operating profit margin ratio and to combine it with the operating asset turnover ratio to determine the operating rate of return ratio. This analysis of profitability from operations can then be expanded by use of the Du Pont system to analyze, through ratios, the various factors that influence operating profit margin and asset turnover. There are a few other profitability ratios with which you should be familiar.

Gross profit margin The gross profit is net sales less the cost of goods sold. The *gross profit margin* is the gross profit divided by net sales. This ratio for Smith Mercantile Company in 1982 is

$$\text{Gross profit margin} = \frac{\text{Gross profit}}{\text{Net sales}} = \frac{\$\ 80{,}000}{\$360{,}000} = 22\%$$

This compares to 20 percent in 1981.

In a marketing firm such as a wholesaler or retailer, the gross profit margin is watched very closely, because any deterioration in it may indicate the beginning of a "profit squeeze." This may, in turn, initiate efforts to reduce cost of goods sold by shopping suppliers to obtain lower prices, increase selling prices, or adjust the sales mix (pushing the higher profit-margin items). In a manufacturing concern, in addition to the above indications, a declining gross profit margin might indicate inefficiency in the manufacturing processes.

The net operating profit margin (before taxes) has been discussed in Chapter 3. A net operating profit margin that has declined while the gross profit margin has remained stable or increased may indicate that selling, general, and administrative expenses are getting out of line and that the efficiency in these areas should be improved. Further analysis requires breaking these expenses down into their components, studying the trends, and scrutinizing the expenditures that have disproportionately increased.

In addition to these ratios, management and stockholders are interested in the net operating profit margin *after taxes,* recognizing the fact that taxes are a part of the cost of doing business and that perhaps they may be reduced by judicious operating and financial decisions.

Rate of return on common stock equity Naturally, the stockholders are most interested in the rate of return on their investment. This ratio is calculated by dividing the net profit after taxes (less preferred stock dividends, if any) by the common stock equity (usually the sum of the common stock, paid-in or capital surplus, and retained earnings). The ratio is sometimes called the *rate of return on net worth,* which is appropriate for firms having no preferred stock. For Smith Mercantile Company in 1982, the ratio is calculated as follows:

$$\begin{aligned}&\text{Rate of return on common stock equity}\\&= \frac{\text{Net profit after taxes less preferred stock dividends}}{\text{Net worth less preferred stock}}\\&= \frac{\$10{,}000}{\$70{,}000} = 14.3\%\end{aligned}$$

This compares to 10.6 percent in 1981. This ratio indicates the final rate of return on the book investment of the residual owners of the firm.

Earnings per share The ratio most important to the common stockholder, earnings per common share, is calculated by dividing the net profit after taxes (and preferred dividends, if any) by the average number of common shares outstanding during the period. It is the ultimate measure of profitability in relation to his or her position in the firm. This ratio is calculated for Smith Mercantile Company in 1982 as follows:

$$\text{Earnings per share} = \frac{\text{Net profit after taxes and preferred dividends}}{\text{Average number of common shares outstanding}}$$

$$= \frac{\$10{,}000}{4{,}000 \text{ shares}} = \$2.50 \text{ per share}$$

This compares to $1.75 per share the previous year; the increase should make the stockholders happy.

Direct analysis of financial change

Chapter 1 introduced the concept of a business enterprise as a system of funds flows. At that stage the discussion was oversimplified, but the point was made that nearly all actions of management, operational or financial, influence the flow of funds in relation to the various asset, liability, and stockholders' equity accounts on the balance sheet. The transactions involved number in the thousands or millions, and any attempt to analyze them individually would result in our failure to see the forest because we were looking at too many trees. We shall now develop some analytical tools through which the net flows of funds between two points of time may be summarized to enhance our understanding of the effects of these flows on the financial condition of the firm.

Analysis of Balance Sheet Changes

Assume you were approached by the management of a company and asked to lend or invest money to participate in the financing of that firm. Your first question probably would be, "Where has this company's money come from and what has been done with it?" You would ask the same question if you had just been hired or transferred to participate in the financial management of the company. To get an approximate answer you should analyze the changes in the balance sheet accounts over an appropriate period of time in the manner shown in Table 4–4. First, simply list the balance sheet accounts as of the beginning and end of the period you wish to re-

Table 4–4

JACKSON WHOLESALE SPORTING GOODS COMPANY
Analysis of Balance Sheet Changes
($000)

	Year 1	Year 4	Sources	Uses
Assets				
Current assets:				
Cash	$ 13	3	$ 10	
Accounts receivable	115	255		$140
Inventories	130	242		112
Other current assets	5	1	4	
Fixed assets (net)	11	16		5
Total assets	$274	$517		
Liabilities and Owners' Equity				
Liabilities:				
Notes payable—bank	$ 9	$ 36	$ 27	
Accounts payable	57	228	171	
Accrued liabilities	8	13	5	
Long-term liabilities	20	14		$ 6
Owner's equity:				
Common stock	80	80		
Retained earnings	100	146	46	
Total liabilities and owners' equity	$274	$517	$263	$263
Sales	$772	$1,590		

Note: Comparative sales are not part of this analysis, but are shown here for reference.

view. Then calculate the changes in each, identifying as *sources of funds* any:

1. Decrease in assets.
2. Increase in liabilities.
3. Increase in owners' equity.

and as *uses of funds* any:

1. Increase in assets.
2. Decrease in liabilities.
3. Decrease in owners' equity.

Although this analysis does not attempt to show detailed historical flow of funds, it is very useful because it allows the analyst (1) to identify the important sources and uses of funds and (2) to ask the right questions, leading to further analysis to identify problems in either asset management or financing of the funds requirements.

Reviewing the uses of funds in Table 4–4 with an analytical eye, we readily see that accounts receivable have more than doubled during the three-year period, absorbing $140,000, and that expansion of inventories has used $112,000. This sharpens our curiosity to analyze these accounts further through the use of ratio analysis or other tools to appraise the efficiency of management of these current asset accounts. For example, noting that sales have approximately doubled, whereas accounts receivable have considerably more than doubled, we should calculate the receivables turnover or average collection period and perhaps utilize other analytical tools to discover whether Jackson has an accounts receivable management problem.

In Jackson's case, expansion of net fixed assets was not important. However, in some cases a large expansion of this account may have drained working capital. This fact should in turn lead us to examine the detail of gross expenditures for fixed assets, depreciation, retirement of fixed assets, and the appropriateness of the financing of the net increase.

Examination of Jackson's sources of funds indicates that the bank has furnished $27,000 and trade creditors (accounts payable) have provided $171,000 of the total $263,000; the owners have provided only $46,000 of the required funds through the retention of earnings. The relationship here—over $4 of other people's money for each dollar provided by the owners to finance roughly doubling the volume of business—appears to be out of line. It should lead the analyst to check the debt ratios and the age of the accounts payable to determine whether the firm is exhausting its credit sources.

If this analysis were made in connection with an application by Jackson for an increase in the bank loan, the bank, after carrying out the additional analysis indicated, probably would refuse unless the owners of the company were willing to provide additional equity financing or contract the volume of the firm's operations.

Note that the analysis of balance sheet changes by itself usually does not provide definite answers as to soundness of management of operations or financing, but rather furnishes the overall insight to encourage meaningful further investigation. By so doing, it avoids superfluous analysis in unfruitful areas.

To this point we have used the term *funds* rather loosely. The purist who defines funds as *cash* might take issue with Table 4–4, our Analysis of Balance Sheet Changes, showing the decrease of cash of $10,000 as a source of funds. It is a resource available to pay obligations in the sense that if you have $5 in your wallet and use $3 of it to buy your lunch, the reduction of your cash from $5 to $2 has paid for your lunch. But if funds are defined as cash, then the net change in cash that has occurred must be explained by identifying the sources and uses of this particular resource.

Sources and Uses of Funds Statement

By defining funds as *cash* and using more detailed accounting information, we can develop a more formal Sources and Uses of Funds Statement.

The Analysis of Balance Sheet Changes (Table 4–4) disclosed changes in three accounts—fixed assets (net), long-term liabilities, and retained earnings—which can be broken down further to supply additional information as follows:

(1) Change in fixed assets (net)	$ 5,000
Additions to fixed assets	$10,000
Proceeds from sale of fixed assets	(1,000)
Depreciation charges	(4,000)
(2) Change in long-term liabilities	($ 6,000)
Additional long-term borrowings	$ 3,000
Repayment of long-term debt	(9,000)
(3) Change in retained earnings	$46,000
Net profit from operations	$82,000
Dividends paid	(36,000)

Depreciation is employed as a source of funds only in the sense that it is charged against income but does not involve a cash outlay, as discussed earlier in this chapter under "burden coverage."

The Sources and Uses of Funds Statement for Jackson Wholesale Sporting Goods Company is shown in Table 4–5. The net decrease in cash of $10,000 is explained by identifying the current account changes that increased or decreased net working capital (excluding cash) and the detailed changes in long-term accounts. This additional detail sorts out the net funds flows provided from (1) operations, in the form of net profits and depreciation charges, (2) changes in net working capital, (3) the fixed assets account, in the form of gross additions and proceeds from sales, (4) dividends paid to stockholders, and (5) changes in long-term liabilities in terms of borrowings and repayments. To illustrate the usefulness of additional detail regarding changes on long-term accounts, recall our earlier concern that retained earnings increased only $46,000 over the three-year period. Now we see that net profits were $82,000 but $36,000 of these profits were paid to the stockholders in dividends. These facts (in addition to information on the owner-officers' salaries and expense accounts) would be of considerable value to a loan officer considering an application for an increase in the bank loan.

The particular form used in Table 4–5 is not the only one that may be utilized in organizing a statement of sources and uses of funds. Others might organize the data by long-term and current accounts, and still others might list the increases and decreases in current assets and liabilities without relating them to their effects on net working capital. The form really does not make much difference as long as the analyst understands the information.

Another definition of *funds,* often used by accountants, considers funds to be *net working capital.* Where this definition is used, the Sources and Uses of Funds Statement (sometimes called "Statement of Changes in Working Capital") starts with the beginning net working capital, then traces

Table 4–5

JACKSON WHOLESALE SPORTING GOODS COMPANY
Sources and Uses of Funds Statement
Year 1 to Year 4
($000)

Sources		
Funds provided from operations:		
Net profits	$ 82	
Depreciation charges	4	
Total funds from operations		$ 86
Decrease in net working capital (excluding cash):		
Decrease in other current assets	4	
Increase in notes payable—bank	27	
Increase in accounts payable	171	
Increase in accrued liabilities	5	
Total decrease in working capital		207
Proceeds from sale of fixed assets		1
Long-term borrowings		3
Total sources of funds		$297
Uses		
Additions to fixed assets		$ 10
Dividends paid		$ 36
Increases in net working capital (excluding cash):		
Increase in accounts receivable	$140	
Increase in inventories	112	
Total increase in net working capital		252
Repayment of long-term debt		9
Total uses of funds		$307
Excess of (uses) over sources		($ 10)
Net (decrease) in cash		($ 10)

through all details of the changes in long-term accounts, and ends with ending net working capital. The analyst concerned with utility companies and other capital-intensive firms finds such a statement useful because most assets and liabilities are long-term, therefore the changes in individual current asset and current liability accounts usually are of less importance. The emphasis may be quite the opposite in many manufacturing and marketing firms. In analyzing these, statements that do not reveal the changes in current asset and liability accounts might hide the most important information regarding changes in financial condition.

Statement of Changes in Financial Position

A type of sources and uses of funds statement, titled Statement of Changes in Financial Position, is included in the financial statements published by most major corporations in their annual reports. Such a statement for the Coca-Cola Company is reproduced in Table 4–6. This statement identifies

Table 4–6

THE COCA-COLA COMPANY AND SUBSIDIARIES
Consolidated Statements of Changes in Financial Position
($000)

	Year Ended December 31		
	1980	1979	1978
Source of working capital:			
From operations:			
Net income	$ 422,108	$ 420,120	$ 374,692
Add charges not requiring outlay of working capital during the year:			
Depreciation	133,807	112,939	94,024
Deferred income taxes	33,104	12,298	19,070
Other (principally amortization of goodwill and container adjustments)	38,084	29,546	19,549
Total from operations	627,103	574,903	507,335
Increase in long-term debt	99,415	7,234	—
Disposals of property, plant and equipment	77,053	25,041	17,127
Proceeds from exercise of stock options and appreciation rights	726	921	1,228
Tax benefit from optioned shares sold	128	212	318
Total sources of working capital	804,425	608,311	526,008
Application of working capital:			
Cash dividends:			
The Coca-Cola Company	266,928	242,159	214,344
Presto Products, Incorporated	—	—	298
Additions to property, plant and equipment	287,186	329,559	306,022
Acquisitions of purchased companies excluding net current assets:			
Property, plant and equipment—net	5,885	51,842	—
Other assets including goodwill, net of other liabilities	7,593	23,456	—
Increase in investments and other assets	95,254	25,223	16,277
Decrease in long-term debt	—	—	72
Other	2,348	7,147	3,696
Total applications of working capital	665,194	679,386	540,709
Increase (decrease) in working capital	$ 139,231	$ (71,075)	$ (14,701)
Increase (decrease) in working capital by component:			
Cash	$ 22,799	$ (49,265)	$ 6,780
Marketable securities	59,716	(123,655)	(34,879)
Trade accounts receivable	88,044	96,788	58,440
Inventories	140,621	131,353	96,747
Prepaid expenses	5,470	13,820	5,956
Notes payable	16,229	(55,573)	(10,962)
Current maturities of long-term debt	(3,144)	1,283	(947)
Accounts payable and accrued expenses	(156,161)	(66,830)	(113,759)
Accrued taxes—including income taxes	(34,343)	(18,996)	(22,077)
Increase (decrease) in working capital	$ 139,231	$ (71,075)	$ (14,701)

the sources and applications of working capital. Then it lists the increase (or decrease) in working capital by individual current accounts but does not identify these changes as to sources or uses. The Statement of Changes in Financial Position provides adequate information as to sources and uses of funds (defined as cash), but it is a little more difficult to read and analyze, particularly regarding current accounts, than the statement we have used in Table 4–5.[4]

Summary

Analysis is the necessary homework of the decision-making process. This chapter deals with ratio analysis and direct analysis of financial change. In essence, analysis is the gathering, assessing, and assembling of pertinent information in a fashion relevant to a specific problem or decision. The analysis that is appropriate depends upon the viewpoint of the analyst (short-term creditor, long-term creditor, stockholder, or manager) and the problem or decision at hand.

Ratio analysis simply involves the relationship of one number to another number. Care must be taken to be sure that such a relationship is pertinent and that one does not jump to unwarranted conclusions from one or a few ratios. The principal value of ratios is that they facilitate comparisons both to past periods for the same firm, to deduce trends, and to other similar firms or the industry, to note differences. In making these comparisons, careful interpretation must be made of differences in accounting methods and in the nature of operations.

Four major types of ratios were discussed—those related to (1) liquidity, (2) debt, (3) coverage of obligations, and (4) profitability. Liquidity ratios, which are of primary use to short-term creditors and management, collectively provide information as to the ability of a firm to pay its bills as they come due. The static liquidity ratios—the current ratio, quick (or acid test) ratio, and cash position ratio—show the relationship of various current assets to current liabilities. Dynamic liquidity ratios (activity ratios)—the inventory turnover and receivables turnover (which may be converted to average collection period)—provide measures of the rate of conversion of inventories into receivables (or cash) and receivables into cash.

Debt ratios, which measure the relationship between debt and equity fi-

[4]At this writing (December 1981) the Financial Accounting Standards Board (FASB) has appointed a committee to consider requiring that a cash-based Sources and Applications of Funds Statement, along the lines of the statement shown in Table 4–5, be included in firms' annual reports rather than the Statement of Changes in Financial Position, as shown in Table 4–6.

nancing, provide information relative to the solvency of the firm. These static ratios are sometimes important to short-term creditors and always to long-term creditors, stockholders, and management. The most comprehensive debt ratios are debt to total assets and debt to equity. In some analyses, where one wishes to focus upon only the capital structure (excluding short-term liabilities), the ratio of long-term debt to total capital structure or of long-term debt to equity may be used.

Coverage ratios relate to the firm's ability to maintain sufficient earnings and cash flows to service financial obligations. The most widely used coverage ratio, the interest coverage ratio, shows how many times interest charges have been earned during the period. If the firm leases some of its property, the fixed charge coverage ratio may be more useful, as it relates available earnings to both interest and rental payment obligations. To extend the analysis to cover obligations to make periodic payments on principal as well as interest and rental payments, the burden coverage ratio would be appropriate. This type of analysis also may be extended to include coverage of any cash outlays that management feels obligated to make, such as common stock dividends or committed capital expenditures.

Profitability ratios, which are of greatest interest to stockholders and management, were introduced in Chapter 3 and expanded here to include the gross profit margin, rate of return on common stock equity, and earnings per share.

Another useful type of financial analysis is to identify directly in dollars the sources and uses of funds during a period of time. The simplest approach to this is the analysis of balance sheet changes, classifying the changes as sources or uses of funds. If greater detail of changes in fixed assets, long-term liabilities, and retained earnings is desired, a formal sources and uses of funds statement may be developed. A variation of this tool is the statement of changes in financial position.

Questions

1. What is analysis? Why must financial analysis be related to a specific objective?

2. *a.* Briefly describe the viewpoints of (1) short-term creditors, (2) long-term creditors, (3) stockholders, and (4) management, relative to the financial condition of a firm.
   b. Indicate the financial ratios in which each type of party would be primarily interested.

3. What is a ratio? What is a current ratio? What does the current ratio tell you? How might it be misused?

4. Why is it invalid to compare a given financial ratio of a firm to an *absolute* standard?

5. What ratio *comparisons* are useful for internal financial analysis?

6. How do the quick ratio and cash position ratio narrow the focus upon liquidity from that disclosed by the current ratio?

7. How do receivables turnover (or average collection period) and inventory turnover relate to the generation of cash?

8. How does the use of averages in computing turnover ratios improve the validity of such ratios?

9. *a.* Why, in analyzing the *solvency* of a manufacturing or marketing firm, might the ratio of debt to total assets be more informative than the ratio of long-term debt to total capital structure?
   b. Why might the above *not* be true in analyzing the solvency of most public utility firms?

10. From a long-term creditor's viewpoint, why is the interest coverage ratio more meaningful when calculated by using earnings before taxes than when earnings after taxes are used?

11. If a firm leases a significant portion of its fixed assets, its fixed charge coverage ratio may be more meaningful than its interest coverage ratio. Why?

12. How does a burden coverage ratio add to the knowledge of a long-term creditor regarding the ability of a firm to meet its debt obligations?

13. How does the gross profit margin differ from the net operating profit margin?

14. Why is the rate of return on common stock equity sometimes referred to as "the bottom line"?

15. How does an analysis of balance sheet changes provide a crude but useful disclosure of the sources and uses of funds during the period between two balance sheet dates?

16. How might a crude analysis of balance sheet changes be refined into a formal sources and uses of funds statement?

Problems

1. Annecy Corporation has current assets of $500,000 and current liabilities of $200,000. Considering each transaction *independently,* indicate the effect of each of the following transactions upon Annecy's current ratio.

a. $10,000 of accounts payable are paid off with cash.
b. A delivery truck valued at $5,000 is sold for $5,000 cash.
c. Inventories of $50,000 are purchased on credit.
d. A short-term bank loan of $40,000 is obtained, and the proceeds are credited to the firm's deposit account.
e. Additional common stock is sold for $50,000 cash.
f. A long-term loan of $80,000 is obtained, and the proceeds are invested in a new machine in the plant.
g. Accounts receivable of $20,000 are collected in cash.

2. Geoffry Corporation had credit sales of $2 million last year. Its average accounts receivable balance was $210,000.

a. What was its accounts receivable turnover?
b. What was its average collection period?

3. Xenon Corporation's financial statements for last year are shown below:

XENON CORPORATION
Balance Sheet
December 31, 198-
($000)

Assets		*Liabilities and Capital*	
Cash	$ 26,000	Accounts payable	$ 18,000
Trade accounts payable	24,000	Accrued income taxes	6,000
Inventories	30,000	Other accruals	16,000
Fixed assets (net)	90,000	20-year 10% bonds	60,000
Total assets	$170,000	Common stock	40,000
		Retained earnings	30,000
		Total liabilities and capital	$170,000

XENON CORPORATION
Income Statement
Year ended December 198-
($000)

Sales		$365,000
Cost of goods sold		285,000
Gross profit		80,000
Expenses:		
Selling, general and administrative expenses	$54,000	
Interest expense	6,000	
Total expenses		60,000
Net profit before taxes		20,000
Income taxes		10,000
Net profit after taxes		$ 10,000

Compute the following:

a. Current ratio.
b. Quick ratio ("acid test" ratio).
c. Cash position ratio.
d. Average collection period (assume all sales on credit).
e. Inventory turnover ratio.
f. Debt to total assets ratio.
g. Debt to equity ratio.
h. Long-term debt to total capital structure ratio.
i. Interest coverage ratio (times interest earned; before tax).
j. Gross profit margin.
k. Rate of return on common stock equity.

4. Kalipso Company had earnings before interest and taxes (EBIT) last year of $8,360,000. Expenses included depreciation of $2,500,000. Kalipso's $20,000,000 of 12 percent bonds require periodic payment of principal of $1,000,000 per year. The firm leases part of its machinery and equipment. The leases require annual rental payments of $400,000. Its income tax rate is 46 percent. Compute the following coverage ratios:

a. Interest coverage (times interest earned; before tax).
b. Fixed charge coverage.
c. Burden coverage.

5. Financial statements of the Jeffco Corporation are shown below.

JEFFCO CORPORATION
Balance Sheet
End of Last Year

Cash	$ 40,000	Current liabilities	$ 40,000
Accounts receivable	50,000	8% bonds due in ten years	110,000
Inventories	100,000	Common stock	200,000
Fixed assets (net)	260,000	Retained earnings	100,000
Total assets	$450,000	Total liabilities and capital	$450,000

JEFFCO CORPORATION
Income Statement
Last Year

Net sales (all credit)		$900,000
Cost of goods sold		700,000
Gross profit		200,000
Expenses		
Selling, general, and administrative expenses	$100,000	
Interest expense	8,000	
Total expenses		108,000
Net profit before taxes		92,000
Income taxes		46,000
Net profit after taxes		$ 46,000

Compute the following ratios:

a. Current ratio.
b. Quick ratio ("acid test" ratio).
c. Accounts receivable turnover.
d. Inventory turnover.
e. Debt to total assets.
f. Long-term debt to equity.
g. Interest coverage (before taxes).
h. Rate of return on common stock equity.

6. The Yale Unlock Company, a manufacturer of keys, has current liabilities of $1,000,000 and fixed assets equal to current assets. It is subject to a 50 percent income tax rate. All sales are on credit. Yale shows the following ratios:

Current ratio = 3.
Quick ratio = 1.
Cash position ratio = .5.
Receivables turnover = 10×.
Inventory turnover = 5×.
Debt to total assets = .5.
Net operating profit margin (before tax) = 10%.
Rate of return on common equity = 15%.

Construct Yale's balance sheet and income statement.

7. Indicate which of the following changes in balance sheet accounts are sources or uses of funds (in the cash sense).

		Change			Change
a.	Accounts receivable	−	*f.*	Long-term liabilities	−
b.	Inventories	+	*g.*	Fixed assets	+
c.	Accounts payable	−	*h.*	Investments	−
d.	Accrued tax liabilities	+	*i.*	Notes payable—bank	+
e.	Retained earnings	+	*j.*	Common stock	+

(Note: Problems 8 and 9 are a series.)

8. *a.* Using the following comparative balance sheets for the Donner Corporation, develop an analysis of balance sheet changes (crude sources and uses of funds analysis).
b. Interpret the analysis of balance sheet changes you have made.
c. Has the financial condition of the Donner Corporation improved or declined over the period from December 31, 1979, through December 31, 1982?

9. *a.* Given the following additional information, construct a formal sources and uses of funds statement for Donner Corporation from December 31, 1979, through December 31, 1982 (see Problem 8 above).

Additions to fixed assets	$51,000
Proceeds from sale of fixed assets	5,000
Depreciation charges	10,000
Net profit from operations	29,000
Dividends paid on common stock	20,000

b. Interpret the additional information provided by the formal sources and uses of funds statement.

For Problem 8*a*.

DONNER CORPORATION
Comparative Balance Sheets

	Years Ended December 31	
Assets	1979	1982
Cash	$ 10,000	$ 4,000
Marketable securities	8,000	—
Accounts receivable	24,000	35,000
Inventories	30,000	42,000
Fixed assets (net)	35,000	71,000
Total assets	$107,000	$152,000
Liabilities and Capital		
Accounts payable	$ 21,000	$ 30,000
Notes payable—bank	12,000	33,000
Accrued tax liabilities	10,000	11,000
Long-term debt	25,000	20,000
Preferred stock	—	10,000
Common stock	25,00	25,000
Retained earnings	14,000	23,000
Total liabilities and capital	$107,000	$152,000

Chapter 5
Short-Term Financial Planning and Control

Planning is simply thinking ahead—forecasting or estimating what will take place in the future. Nearly everyone finds it necessary to plan; otherwise one's actions would be aimless, uncoordinated, and unrelated to the circumstances. To manage a firm, it usually is necessary to formalize the planning process into written documents, putting numbers on planned actions in terms of units and dollars, and to control subsequent actions by comparing what has been done to what was planned to be done. This is basically what a system of planning and control is all about.

A planning and control system provides a mechanism to help people direct actions of the firm toward accomplishment of its goals. The plan recognizes the limitations imposed and opportunities presented by the firm's human, physical, and financial resources and its economic, technological, social, and political environment. The plan should be the servant of the people to help in management of the firm, rather than the people being servants of the plan. In all too many cases, unduly rigid use of the plan as a control device has had the effect of defeating its purpose by limiting the actions of people to the detriment of the firm.[1]

A plan is properly used as a set of guidelines or expectations, with full recognition that changing circumstances and conditions frequently require deviation from or modification of the plan. A firm's operating or financial plan is similar to the course plotted by a ship's captain at the outset of a voyage. If during the voyage a hurricane is reported to be obstructing his planned course, he would be foolhardy to continue to follow his plan and head right into the storm. Rather, he must adjust his course to attempt to avoid the storm and, when it is past, replot the course to reach the intended port. The same is true of business management. When unforeseen changes in the environment, such as competitive changes in the market, are perceived, the manager would be foolhardy to continue slavishly following the plan. Management must depart from the plan by taking appropriate action to cope with the changed circumstances and adjusting the plan in the light of these changes.

The planning process is not by any means the sole responsibility of the financial manager and the departments immediately under his or her control. Rather, the entire management organization is involved in developing a firm's plans. As shown in Figure 5–1, this process is initiated by developing a series of operating forecasts in various departments of the business. These operating forecasts are then used by financial managers to develop a

[1]The planning process is often called *budgeting,* the forecasts called *budgets,* and the utilization of them as control devices referred to as *budgetary control.* The change in terminology in many business organizations to *planning* or *forecasting* has largely been due to negative connotations of the term *budget.* Such connotations usually are the results of unpleasant experiences with past overuse and misuse of budgets as control devices. The term *fuss-budget* reflects this problem. Therefore, the term *budget* will be avoided where possible in this book. The terms *plan* and *forecast* will be used synonymously.

Figure 5–1 The planning process

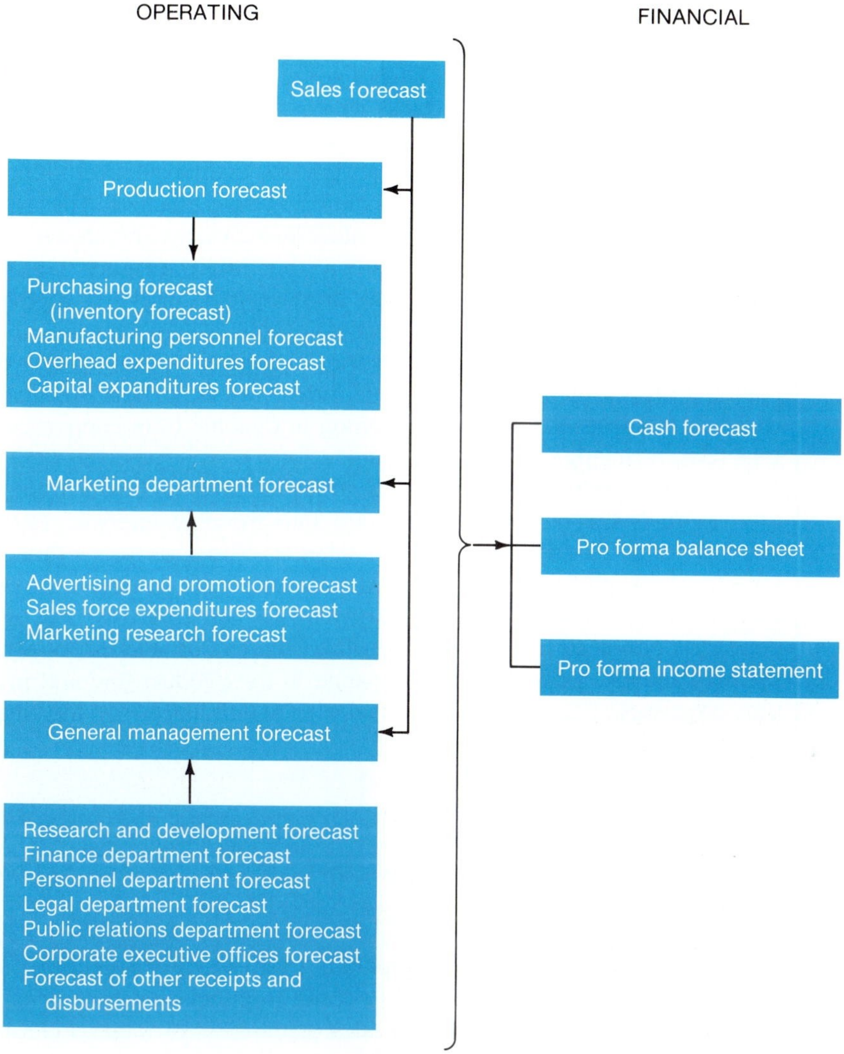

cash forecast and the pro forma financial statements that are identified specifically with the finance function. Inasmuch as the financial forecasts are based upon operating forecasts, an important responsibility of financial management is to work with the operating people to guide, advise, and coordinate their development of the several operating forecasts. In large firms, a planning department, which usually reports to the chief financial officer, is charged with overseeing and coordinating development of the various forecasts.

Business plans are formulated in two or more distinct time-frames. *Long-range planning* is done in a time frame of some three to five years and may even be extended to ten years. This planning involves assessment by top management of economic, social, and political trends as they are expected to influence the markets in which the firm deals. Such things as research requirements, capital asset additions, working capital requirements, and long-term financing requirements over a relatively long time span are forecasted. This type of planning is only tentative. The forecasts require at least annual adaptation to unforeseen changes and are recognized to be increasingly rough as they look further into the future. Long-range planning is of great value, however, because it induces management to broaden its outlook and develop corporate policies and strategies to cope with and benefit from a changing world. This level and time-frame of the planning process is beyond the scope of the present chapter. We shall deal with some aspects of long-range planning in Chapter 17 in connection with long-term financing.

We are presently concerned with *short-term planning,* in which the usual time-frame is the coming year divided into monthly intervals. However, there is nothing sacrosanct about the calendar. The appropriate time-frame for short-term planning is that period over which the management people feel they have a high degree of confidence in their forecasts. This in turn depends upon such factors as the relative volatility of markets, operational stability, and rate of technological change in the product line and production processes.[2] The planning interval also is influenced by the financial strength of the firm.

The short-term operating plan

Development of the short-term operating plan requires forecasting all actions of the firm that are expected to result in either an inflow or outflow of cash. Some actions, such as cash sales or payment of wages and salaries, will result in immediate cash flows. Others, such as credit sales or purchases of raw materials on credit terms, will create changes in noncash balance sheet items that later will be collected or paid in cash. We must start with the sales forecast and then project production, marketing, and general management staff activities that will be required to support the forecasted sales volume. This operating planning process is outlined in Figure 5–1.

[2]For an extreme example, the author recently was told by a consultant that one of his extremely dynamic client firms had a short-range planning horizon of one week and considered three months to be long range.

The sales forecast

It is of vital importance that the sales forecast be as reasonable and accurate as possible because all subsequent operating and financial plans are based upon it and can be only as strong as it is. If the sales forecast rests upon guesses pulled out of thin air, the entire plan may be more misleading than informative. At the extreme, an inappropriate sales forecast can lead to actions that are detrimental to the general goal of maximizing the value of the firm or that even threaten its continued existence. For this reason, it usually is advisable to draw from both internal and external sources and to utilize a small committee of people with differing viewpoints to prevent domination of the whole plan by one person whose perception may be biased.

In building the information base for this forecast, the sales department will have a major input. To obtain useful information from as close to the action as possible, the salespersons in each territory will be asked to estimate their sales for the period (say, the next year by months). District sales managers will review these estimates, modifying them in light of their knowledge of the salespersons' abilities to perceive the market and their individual optimistic or pessimistic biases. These modified forecasts will then be consolidated at the district level and passed on up to the general sales manager, who repeats the process and passes the consolidated forecast to the chief marketing officer. Then, on the basis of additional knowledge of plans for the introduction of new products, sales support activities such as advertising and sales promotion campaigns, and simply seasoned judgment, the marketing department's sales forecast is finalized.

In many firms, marketing department forecasts cannot necessarily be accepted as the basis for the entire short-term plan. Marketing people, particularly successful ones who rise from the field to become sales managers and marketing vice presidents, tend to be optimists. The modification process, designed to reduce bias, may in practice increase it as the forecasts move up through channels. This can result in a final marketing department sales forecast that is unrealistically high. Another problem, counter to this one, becomes apparent in firms where the sales forecast is used later as a control device upon which to base bonuses, promotions, or other awards to the sales organization for their performance. Here we find a natural bias toward pessimistic forecasts induced by the salespersons' attempts to establish quotas that they think they can exceed. The result may be that the reviewer of the marketing department's final forecast is in a quandary, never knowing which of the potential biases dominates the forecast.

For the above reasons, in addition to the inherent value of macroeconomic statistical information obtained from unbiased sources, external input usually is valuable. If the firm is large enough, its economist or economic research department develops this external input. The forecasting process may employ such approaches as establishing a statistical relationship between changes in the Gross National Product (GNP) and sales in the industry through regression analysis. Then, if industry sales can be predicted, trends in the firm's share of industry sales (developed from such sources as the Nielsen services in the grocery and drug industries) may be related to the industry forecast to derive a sales forecast for the firm.

In addition, management must estimate not only unit sales but also the product market prices that are expected to prevail during the period. In view of inflationary pressures and other economic influences upon prices in recent years, this is no small task.

The final sales forecast probably should be prepared by a small committee including representation from at least the marketing department, economic research staff, and the chief executive's office. This committee can weigh the evidence brought forth from internal and external sources, develop a final forecast that the firm can depend on, and lend credibility to the sales forecast in the minds of people throughout the management who are going to use the forecast as the basis of their planning.

Production forecast

The production forecast must then be developed to make available the products required to meet the sales forecast. Although this will be the primary responsiblity of the production vice president, some input and liaison will be required from the personnel, inventory, and financial managers. As shown in Figure 5–1, the production forecast subsequently must be translated into the purchasing forecast. From this, along with the sales and production forecasts, the various inventory forecasts for raw materials, work in process, and finished goods can be projected. The production forecast also will involve estimating labor and overhead costs related to operation of the plant.

The production forecast must be related to the capital expenditures forecast, as sufficient plant capacity must be available to fulfill the planned production requirements. These capital expenditure requirements will be assumed in this chapter. This very important and rather complex subject will be treated later in Chapters 12–14.

Marketing department forecast

Expenditure forecasts by the marketing department for advertising and promotion, sales force salaries, bonuses and expenses, marketing research, and the like will be developed in conjunction with the sales forecast. These are interrelated in that marketing support activities will influence the volume of sales and sales volume will, in turn, affect the cost of some of these activities.

General management forecast

Forecasts of other expenditures and receipts in the ensuing period are developed by various staff departments shown in Figure 5–1 under the heading General Management Forecast. Although organization of staff functions varies considerably among different firms, the forecast usually will include expenditures to operate the research and development, finance, legal, and public relations departments. In addition, salaries and bonuses of the corporate executives, their personal staffs, and related overhead expenses must be forecasted. Various other expected funds flows, such as dividends to be received from stock held in other corporations, rental payments on leased property, interest to be paid on outstanding debt, and royalties on patents licensed to others also will be included in this forecast.

Sales, production, marketing, and general management forecasts provide the basis for the financial forecasts. It may appear that we have wandered somewhat astray from financial management in relating the development of the operating forecasts. This digression is justified for the simple reason that financial management does not operate in a vacuum. In the case of short-term financial forecasting, most problems, shortcomings, and difficulties of executing the financial plans derive from the use of faulty input from the operating plans. Careful and laborious monitoring, often in an informal fashion, of the development of operating plans yields a great return in the confidence that can be placed in the financial plans.

The short-term financial plans

The three major short-term financial plans or forecasts are the cash forecast (often called the cash budget or cash flow forecast), the pro forma income statement, and the pro forma balance sheet. *Pro forma* financial statement simply means the forecast or estimate of what the statement will be in the future, such as the income statement for given future months or the coming year and the balance sheet at the end of those periods.

The cash forecast

In essence, the cash forecast is the estimate of what will happen to the firm's bank account as a result of planned activities. Cash forecasting starts with the cash balance, the bank account, at the beginning of the period. Then all cash inflows (deposits to that bank account) expected during the period are added to the initial cash balance to estimate the total cash available. From this all cash outflows (checks written on the account) expected during the period are subtracted to yield the tentative ending cash balance.[3]

On the basis of this tentative cash balance, the financial manager can plan either the borrowing that will be necessary to maintain a reasonable minimum cash balance or the investment of excess cash. A reasonable minimum cash balance is determined by the larger of either (1) the minimum balance required by the bank in connection with the firm's account activity and borrowing arrangements or (2) an amount sufficient to cover the lack of coincidence of cash inflows and outflows during the period and the degree of uncertainty of the estimates. Minimum cash balance requirements will be treated in detail in Chapter 7.

The following cash forecast illustration is somewhat simplified to clarify the methodology and to avoid getting bogged down in detail. We shall develop the cash forecast for a firm having relatively simple operations, discussing briefly as we go along the complications encountered if operations are more complex. Although most cash forecasting is done by months over the ensuing year, our example will cover only the last six months of the year.

The Conmore Corporation manufactures a single product with a selling price of $100 per unit. Its sales forecast indicates expected sales of 36,000 units ($3,600,000) over the full year 1982. Demand for the product varies seasonally, with approximately 60 percent of sales expected in the last six months of the year and nearly one third of annual sales concentrated in September and October. Management has decided on level production throughout the year. Thus the firm has been producing at 3,000 units per month during the first six months and has built up some inventory in anticipation of the coming selling season.

Cash inflows from operations Our first task is to estimate the cash inflows that will result from sales. Please note that here, as in all cash budgeting, we are interested *only in the anticipated flows of cash,* as differentiated from income and costs in the accounting sense. As shown in Table 5–1, 10 percent of Conmore's sales are usually on a cash basis and 90 percent on credit terms. Analysis of past collection experience indicates that collection of 20 percent of credit sales may be expected in the month of sale and 80 percent in the month after the sale. We must project the credit sales to the months in which cash will be collected. At the beginning of July, Conmore has accounts receivable of $160,000 (80 percent of $200,000 credit sales in

[3]Cash forecasts may utilize different formats. Another widely used approach lists the forecasted cash inflows and subtracts the outflows to estimate the net cash flow for each period. This is then added to the beginning cash. The minimum cash balance is then subtracted to estimate the cash surplus or deficit.

June) that are expected to be collected in July. Of the $250,000 sales expected in July, $25,000 will be received from cash sales. Of the $225,000 credit sales, $45,000 are expected to be collected in July and $180,000 will rest in accounts receivable with collection anticipated in August. This breakdown by terms of sale and anticipated collection pattern provides the cash receipts information to be incorporated in the cash forecast.

Table 5–1

CONMORE CORPORATION
Worksheet—Collection of Sales Revenues
Last Half, 1982
($000)

	June	July	Aug.	Sept.	Oct.	Nov.	Dec.
Sales:		250	300	500	600	300	200
Cash (10%)		25	30	50	60	30	20
Credit (90%)	200	225	270	450	540	270	180
Collections:							
Month of sale (20%)		45	54	90	108	54	36
Month after sale (80%)		160	180	216	360	432	216
Total collections		205	234	306	468	486	252

So far, the possible oversimplifications are that (1) Conmore sells only one product at a standard price, (2) the cash versus credit sales mix is anticipated to be the same each month, (3) the receivables collection pattern will be the same each month, and (4) all accounts receivable will be collected, that is, there will be no bad debt losses. To illustrate the complications in a more complex business, take a department store that sells alternatively for cash, on regular 30-day charge accounts, and offers 6- to 18-month installment terms on "big ticket" items such as furs, jewelry, furniture, and major appliances. Such a firm will experience month-by-month differences in the cash versus credit sales mix and in the collection experience on its credit sales. A larger percentage of sales will be on credit in the pre-Christmas months of November and December, and the collection period on these credit sales will be stretched out more than on the credit sales of, say, August. Thus, the task of projecting the cash receipts anticipated from sales in such a business is a much more complicated job than indicated by our simple illustration in Table 5–1.

The monthly cash forecasts for Conmore Corporation during the last half of 1982 are shown in Table 5–2. The cash inflows have been taken from the worksheet (Table 5–1). All of Conmore's cash inflows result from sales.

The June 30 balance sheet shows a cash balance of $100,000, which is assumed to be the minimum that management estimates to be necessary. This is a month-end target figure and does not imply that Conmore will keep $100,000 on deposit with its bank at all times. The balance will fluc-

Table 5–2

CONMORE CORPORATION
Cash Forecast
Last Half, 1982
($000)

	July	Aug.	Sept.	Oct.	Nov.	Dec.
Beginning cash	$100	$100	$100	$100	$100	$100
Cash inflows:						
Cash sales	25	30	50	60	30	20
Collection of receivables	205	234	306	468	486	252
Total cash inflows	230	264	356	528	516	272
Cash available	330	364	456	628	616	372
Cash outflows:						
Payment of accounts payable	144	144	144	144	144	144
Wages and salary payments	60	60	60	60	60	60
Payment of overhead expenses	26	26	26	26	26	26
Payment of selling expenses	28	30	40	43	30	25
Payment of general and administrative expenses	15	15	15	15	15	15
Payment for new machine	—	—	40	—	—	—
Payment of income taxes	—	—	19	—	—	19
Principal payment—term loan	—	—	—	—	—	30
Interest payment—term loan	—	—	—	—	—	27
Payment of dividends	—	—	25	—	—	25
Total cash outflows	273	275	369	288	275	371
Tentative ending cash balance	57	89	87	340	341	1
Less minimum cash balance	100	100	100	100	100	100
Borrowing required (repayment)	43	11	13	(240)	(27)	—
Cumulative loan balance (beginning $200)	243	254	267	27	—	—
Cash available for temporary investment	—	—	—	—	214	115

tuate each day. Some days after large payments have been made, it may be close to zero.

Nonoperating cash inflows In a more complex firm, cash flows from sources other than the sales-receivables-collection cycle may be anticipated. Nonoperating cash inflows may reflect such items as rent to be received from a building that is owned but not used in the business, royalties from patents licensed to others, interest or dividends from investments, proceeds from a contemplated issue of stock or bonds, or tax refunds. By adding the total cash inflows forecasted to the beginning balances we estimate the cash that is expected to be available each month.

Cash outflows from operations Cash outflows from current operations (the first five items in the outflow section of the cash forecast) are based upon operating forecasts developed by the various departments of the business. Inasmuch as Conmore plans to produce 3,000 units per month and raw material costs are forecasted at $48 per unit, $144,000 worth of raw materials will be put into production each month. If we assume that the company plans to maintain a stable level of raw materials inventory and that these raw materials are purchased in relatively small lots (such as the quantity sufficient to support one or two weeks' production), then the purchasing agent will be buying about $144,000 in raw materials each month. If Conmore buys from its suppliers on 30-day terms and pays its bills on time, the treasurer will be writing checks to pay $144,000 of accounts payable to suppliers each month.

With level production and assuming no projected increase during the period in salaries, wages, and fringe benefits, the payroll is expected to be $60,000 per month. Payments of overhead expenses, such as heat, light and power, insurance, telephone bills, and rental payments, are forecasted to be $26,000 per month.

Cash outlays to cover selling expenses are forecasted to vary in the different months. About half of these expenses, $15,000 per month, are fixed (they must be paid each month regardless of sales volume); for example, the sales manager's salary and the expenses in connection with his office. The remaining selling expenses—for example, commissions to the salespeople and delivery expenses—will vary directly with sales volume at a rate of $5 per unit of sales. Therefore, the July selling expenses will be $28,000, of which $15,000 will be fixed expenses and $12,500 (rounded to $13,000) will be variable expenses. This variable expense estimate reflects 2,500 units of forecasted sales times $5 variable selling expenses per unit.

Payment of general and administrative expenses for operating the various executive and staff departments indicated in Figure 5–1 has been forecasted at $15,000 per month regardless of sales volume.

Again, we have simplified a great deal to avoid getting bogged down in detail. If the production schedule had incorporated month-to-month variations in forecasted production levels, as it would in many cases, forecasting the first three cash outflow items would have been much more complex. Purchases would vary in different months; therefore, the required payments of accounts payable would lag one month after the date of purchase. The labor forecast might include payment of temporary labor, overtime, or second-shift rates. Part of the overhead costs would have been fixed and part variable with the changing volume of production. One would have to estimate the variation in these outlays as we did in forecasting the selling expenses.

In addition, Conmore buys all of its raw materials on the same credit terms and pays for them in the month following purchase. If this were, say, a canning firm, fruits and vegetables would be purchased on a COD (cash on delivery) basis, cans or jars on one set of credit terms, sugar on another, spices on a third, and some of the terms would include a discount for early payment while others would not. In short, projection of the month of payment from the detailed purchasing forecast is a complex process. Fortunately, a computer can be programmed to forecast these lagged payments.

The forecast of cash outflow items was further simplified by assuming that monthly payments would be exactly the same as the expenses. For example, wage and salary payments are considered to be stable at $60,000 per month. This would be true if all of the employees were paid semimonthly or monthly. However, if some of the employees were paid weekly, we would have to check to see which months had four paydays in them and which had five and then adjust the monthly forecast accordingly. The same problem might be encountered in connection with salaries and wages included in the selling, general, and administrative expenses. Rarely in practice would one expect the evenness of operating cash flows implied by this example.

Note that we have been careful to exclude from the cash forecast those expenses that do not require current cash outlays. An example of a noncash expense is the $10,000 monthly depreciation charge included in Conmore's overhead costs of $36,000 per month. The $10,000 depreciation charge is properly included in the accounting process transferring the value of goods produced into finished goods inventory and subsequently charging this value against sales. But it does *not* involve any current cash outlay. It is simply an allocation reflecting the using up of value of fixed assets that were bought and paid for during earlier periods. Therefore, $10,000 is deducted from the $36,000 total overhead costs to get the $26,000 forecasted *payment* of overhead expenses each month.

Nonoperating cash outflows Conmore has ordered a new machine costing $40,000, which is scheduled for delivery in August. As the supplier's terms are net 30 days, a $40,000 cash outflow is forecasted in September to pay for it.

On the basis of its estimated $163,000 income before taxes for the year, Conmore is obligated to pay estimated taxes of $75,000 in four quarterly installments. Thus, income tax payments of $19,000 each are forecasted to be made in September and December.

A $30,000 installment payment on the principal of a $300,000 term loan is due on December 31. In addition, interest of $27,000 (9 percent of the $300,000) is payable at that date. Conmore also plans to pay quarterly dividends of $25,000 each to its stockholders on September 15 and December 15.

These are all of Conmore's forecasted cash outflows. In a more complex business there might be others, such as progress payments on a plant under construction, rental payments under leases, royalties on patients licensed from others, or prepayment deposits with suppliers.

The next step in Table 5–2 is to subtract the forecasted cash outflows from the cash available each month to obtain the tentative cash balance. This tentative balance is compared to the minimum cash balance requirement to forecast the *borrowing required* each month or the cash expected to be available for repayment of short-term loans. Conmore estimates that required borrowings during the period July through September will add $67,000 to its bank loans of $200,000 at the beginning of the period. Thus it forecasts a total debt to its bank of $267,000 by the end of September. Then the heavy cash inflows during October and November, resulting largely from the collection of receivables generated by peak sales in September and October, are expected to provide cash to repay $240,000 of the bank loan in October. The remaining $27,000 should be paid off early in November.[4] During the remainder of November, Conmore will develop over $200,000 excess cash available for temporary investment in marketable securities. However, subsequent cash drains required in December to pay income taxes, principal and interest on the term loan, and the quarterly dividend will require cashing in nearly $100,000 of these temporary investments during December.

Uses of the cash forecast The most obvious use of the cash forecast is to arrange sufficient credits to finance the firm's requirements in the short-term future. Normally the financial manager arranges a line(s) of credit with the company's bank(s) for the ensuing year at the time the financial statements for the past year become available. Conmore's cash budget indicates that this line of credit must be somewhat over $267,000, or management cannot proceed according to plan. For example, if the financial manager finds that the maximum available bank line is $250,000, plans must be changed to reduce the forecasted borrowing requirement. Perhaps delivery of the new machine can be rescheduled for September, and payment delayed until October, and/or the dividend proposed to be paid on September 15 can be delayed one month. The financial manager would still not be quite out of the woods because the forecast of cumulative loan require-

[4]Note: The interest on short-term borrowing has been ignored because the amount of borrowing (therefore the amount of interest) was not known as the forecast was developed. In practice, when the forecast is finalized, this interest should be estimated and added to the cash outflows.

ments for August is slightly over $250,000 and July's requirement is nearly equal to this loan limit. Thus some other changes would have to be made in order to proceed safely.

To take a more extreme example, the bank might not be willing to lend over $200,000 and no other lender could be found willing to do so. Management of Conmore would have to revise operating plans drastically, perhaps by changing their level production schedule to one varying somewhat with seasonal fluctuation in sales, cutting back planned scale of operations or increasing equity through the sale of additional stock. The point is that the cash forecast indicates future financial requirements. By forewarning management of possible financial problems, the cash forecast provides management the opportunity to revise plans to bring them into line with the firm's financing capability.

The cash forecast also assists in planning the temporary investment of excess cash in marketable securities by indicating approximately when funds will be available for such temporary investment, the amount, and the approximate length of time until these funds will again be required for use in the firm. Conmore's cash forecast in Table 5–2 indicates that some $214,000 should become available in November, but that nearly $100,000 of this will have to be liquidated in December. If we had forecasted cash flows over the succeeding three or four months, we would see when the rest of these securities would have to be liquidated. Efficiency in the management of the marketable securities portfolio is increased by investing in securities maturing on or near the dates when funds will be needed.

The cash forecast is also useful in connection with evaluating a proposed major change in operating policy or an important change in operations such as accepting a large contract. For example, assume that an automobile parts manufacturer is considering bidding for a large contract to produce shock absorbers for next year's model of a given car in the General Motors line. This contract would involve substantial outlays for additional machinery and tooling, hiring and training additional labor, and carrying larger raw materials and work in process inventories. Before bidding on the contract, the company should compare its existing operating and cash forecasts to revised forecasts including the contract to determine the added financial requirements of this contemplated business, and it should obtain assurance from its bank that the required financing will be made available. If this forecasting were not done before bidding on the contract, it would be quite possible that several months later the company would find itself committed to cash outlays beyond its financial capability and/or unable to meet the delivery requirements of the contract. (Incidentally, General Motors' purchasing department would be doing some financial forecasting along the same lines before accepting the bid to protect itself regarding this contingency.)

The preceding applications of cash forecasts relate to planning and decision making. In addition, operating and cash forecasts are used as control devices. In this connection, forecasted and actual figures are compared to determine the variances. These variances are classified as controllable—determined to result from actions of the manager in charge of the activity and thus that person's responsibility—and uncontrollable—those over which the given manager had no control. It is particularly important in doing this classifying, and in the personal reviews based upon it, that changed conditions be fully recognized and that individual initiative not be stifled by rigid insistence on conforming to the plan. On the other hand, of course, too lax control of costs and cash outlays can defeat the purpose of the forecast and result in a lack of control and coordination that may lead to financial ruin. Additional discussion of this aspect of the forecasting process will be left to experts in management and organizational behavior.

Recognition of changing conditions and uncertainty One of the biggest problems encountered in using any forecast is the deceptive appearance of certainty. In reviewing Table 5–2, one might think that the peak borrowing will be $267,000 on September 30, or that the company will have $100,000 on deposit with its bank on December 31, and $115,000 invested in marketable securities. Those things just won't happen. The sales for any given month will not be exactly those indicated in the worksheet; the cash-credit mix will not be the same as forecasted; and the collection of receivables will not materialize exactly as expected. Likewise, the payroll will not be exactly $60,000 each month, nor the payment of general and administrative expenses exactly $15,000. Conmore Corporation exists in an uncertain world and, even though its management people have been both wise and careful in developing their forecasts, conditions will change from those assumed and the results will be different from those forecasted.

The first requirement upon recognizing these facts of life is to revise the forecasts either on a systematic basis, such as monthly or quarterly, or whenever it is apparent that conditions have so changed as to make the original forecast materially obsolete.

The second requirement is to allow for uncertainty in interpreting the forecasts, either informally or by incorporating more complex means of dealing with uncertainty.

The informal approach, which is most widely utilized particularly in small and middle-sized firms, involves simply realizing that each figure in the operating forecasts and the resulting cash forecast is the central or most probable estimate of what management believes might happen. The sales forecasting committee estimate September sales at $500,000 (5,000 units at a price of $100 per unit). They are in fact saying that this is the mean of a subconsciously estimated probability distribution that, in detail, looks something like Figure 5–2. This distribution indicates their opinion that it is more likely than not that September sales will be between $450,000 and $550,000 and that it is highly unlikely that they will be as low as $350,000 or as high

Figure 5–2 Conmore Corporation Sales forecast—September 1982

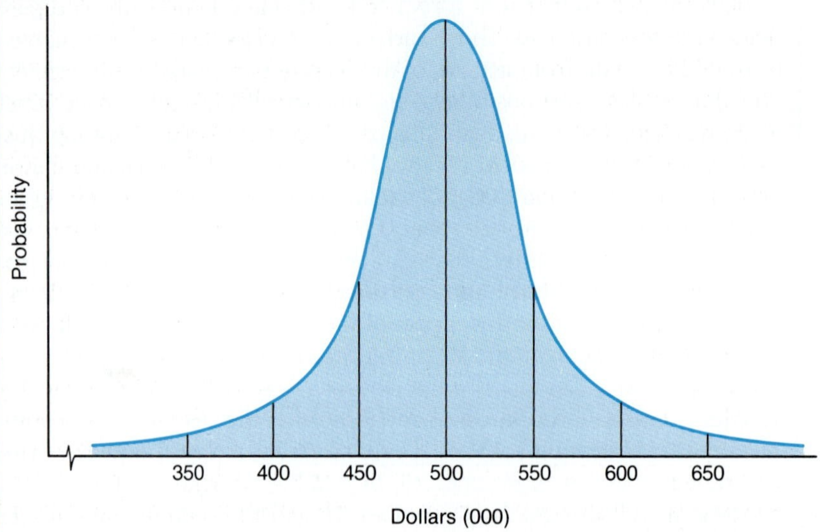

as $650,000. In other words, while the forecasters do not by any means *know* that sales will be $500,000, that figure is the central tendency of their subjective probability estimates. This distribution in turn is a composite of two other probability distributions, one of unit sales volume and another of selling price. And so it goes all the way through the operating forecasts, such as the purchasing forecast or the estimate of payments of general and administrative expenses.

These subjective probability curves may have different shapes. For example, if Conmore employs its production workers under a union contract that runs through the end of the year, the curve would be bell-shaped and very narrow, indicating little uncertainty about the forecasted labor expenses. On the other hand, the curve showing the probabilities of less certain general and administrative expenses may be broader and flatter, depending upon how much the president might fly around in the company airplane. A few of the outflow items are practically certain, such as the payment for the new machine (if it has been purchased on a firm fixed-price contract) and the interest and principal payments on the term loan.

If the user of the forecast (1) recognizes, largely on the basis of experience, that the forecast represents only central tendency estimates and (2) comprehends the degree of subjectivity that went into the estimates (everything from pure guesses to almost certain facts), then uncertainty may be handled by thinking in terms of safety margins. For example, the financial manager of Conmore may view the $270,000 peak loan requirement forecasted at the end of September as indicating that he must have a line of credit of at least $300,000 (or perhaps $350,000) in order to feel safe in going along with the plan. This position would reflect experience as to how far actual results deviated from forecasts in previous years.

A more formal means of recognizing uncertainty is to use multiple forecasts, sometimes called "minimax" forecasts. This technique involves the development of three forecasts, with one—incorporating the central tendency estimates as we have done above—designated the "most probable" forecast. The other two forecasts are a "minimum" forecast, incorporating the least favorable estimates, and a "maximum" forecast, incorporating the most favorable estimates.[5]

This technique refines the thinking of the various operating people in developing forecasts and the communication of that thinking up the line. However, in practice, there are problems at the operating level in understanding what is meant by minimum and maximum. The cumulative effect on the minimum forecast of lowest cash inflows and highest cash outflows may yield financial requirements far beyond the firm's financing capability. Conversely, the maximum forecast, incorporating highest cash inflows and lowest cash outflows, may indicate that the firm would have extremely large amounts of excess cash available. The result is that management tends to fall back on the most probable forecast, informally incorporates a safety margin, and more or less ignores the minimax forecast.

Another, still more sophisticated, technique for coping with uncertainty is the use of computer simulation. The essential idea is to incorporate a variety of possible operating experience in the operating budgets. For example sales may be forecasted at five different levels. Based on the resulting multiple sales forecasts, the production department develops five different production schedules. In turn, the purchasing department develops five different purchasing schedules, and so on. Each set of forecasts is based upon a different scenario, or set of conditions that might exist in the firm's environment.

An advantage of this technique is that, as conditions in the environment are recognized to be changing, the appropriate set of forecasting data may be supplied to the computer, which quickly generates a revised forecast. Probabilities may be assigned to each of the scenarios and a cash forecast developed in terms of a probability distribution of borrowing requirements and cash available for temporary investment. The financial manager may, at least in theory, then arrange credit accommodation to protect the firm against the degree of risk believed to be prudent. Although this technique has conceptual appeal, it may or may not be cost efficient. When one rec-

[5]Recognizing that the tails on probability curves may go far out in both directions, the terms *minimun* and *maximum* should not be taken literally, but rather they should define the limits of 95 percent probability that experience will be above the minimum or below the maximum forecasted. In statistical language, this is two standard deviations.

ognizes the subjectivity in assigning probabilities to the various scenarios and in the detailed operating forecasts produced by this process, does the resulting information justify the cost of developing it?

Pro forma financial statements

The cash forecast is indeed a necessary and useful tool of financial planning and management, but it has two important limitations. First, it does not provide information regarding the expected future profitability of the firm because it deals only with cash flows, not accounting profits. Second, it yields the expected balances in only three balance sheet accounts—cash, marketable securities, and short-term notes payable. Thus it provides only limited or fragmentary information relative to the future financial condition of the firm.

It usually is worth while to carry the forecasting process further by developing pro forma financial statements (also variously called projected, forecasted, or planned financial statements). These are the *pro forma income statement* and the *pro forma balance sheet.* These statements are based largely upon information already developed in connection with the various operating forecasts and the cash forecast.

Pro forma income statement The pro forma income statement is simply a forecast of the income statement for the planning period. Conmore's pro forma income statement, shown in Table 5–3, starts with the accumulated

Table 5–3

CONMORE CORPORATION
Pro Forma Income Statement
Six Months Ended December 31, 1982
($000)

Sales		$2,150
Cost of goods sold:		
Materials	$1,032	
Labor	430	
Overhead (including depreciation of $60)	258	
Total cost of goods sold		$1,720
Gross profit		$ 430
Expenses:		
Selling expense	$ 196	
General and administrative expenses	90	
Interest expense	13	
Total expenses		$ 299
Net profit before taxes		$ 131
Income taxes		60
Net profit after taxes		$ 71

monthly sales forecasted earlier and shown in our worksheet, Table 5–1. Cost of goods sold is derived from information originating in the production forecast and already used in developing the cash outflow forecast relating to payment of accounts payable, wages and salaries, and overhead expenses.

The production plan indicated that materials costs were $48 per unit. Thus, sales of 21,500 units ($2,150,000 divided by $100 selling price per unit) at a materials cost of $48 per unit yields total materials costs of $1,032,000 for the period. Note that here we are *matching costs with revenues* by determining the materials costs related to 21,500 units of sales. We are not directly concerned with the cost of production during the period.

Labor costs of $720,000 per year ($60,000 per month times 12) amount to 20 percent of the $3,600,000 estimated sales for the year. Therefore, labor costs related to the $2,150,000 sales during the last six months will be $430,000 ($2,150,000 times 20 percent). Overhead costs of $36,000 per month equal 12 percent of sales; therefore, 12 percent of $2,150,000 in sales, or $258,000, is the overhead expense. Note that this overhead expense properly includes depreciation of $60,000. This is allocated as a *cost* but will not involve a cash outlay and therefore did not enter into the cash forecast.

Total cost of goods sold of $1,720,000 yields a forecasted gross profit of $430,000. Against this are charged selling expenses of $196,000, identical to the accumulation of payments indicated in the six-month cash forecast. General and administrative expenses of $15,000 per month will equal $90,000 for the six-month period. Interest expense on the term loan will be $13,000. Although $27,000 interest will be paid in December, this is the interest for the full year and only half of it, $13,500 (rounded to $13,000), is an expense chargeable to the last six months. Subtracting these expenses from the gross profit yields net profit before taxes of $131,000 on which the company will be liable for taxes at a 46 percent rate. Thus, net profit after taxes for the six-month period ended December 31, 1982, is forecasted to be $71,000.

Pro forma balance sheet The starting point for the development of a pro forma balance sheet is, of course, the balance sheet at the end of the preceding period. The balance sheet of Conmore Corporation as of June 30, 1982, is shown in Table 5–4. To develop the pro forma balance sheet as of December 31, 1982, shown in Table 5–5, we start with the $100,000 cash balance indicated by our cash forecast (Table 5–2) and assume that $115,000 indicated as cash available for temporary investment at the end of December will be invested in marketable securities. Accounts receivable will be $144,000, representing 80 percent of credit sales expected to be made in December but not collected until January.

Table 5–4

CONMORE CORPORATION
Balance Sheet
June 30, 1982
($000)

Assets		*Liabilities and Capital*	
Current assets:		Current liabilities:	
Cash	$ 100	Accounts payable	$ 144
Receivables	160	Notes payable—bank	200
Inventories	592	Term loan—current portion	30
Prepaid taxes	22	Accrued interest	14
Total current assets	874	Accrued other liabilities	21
Fixed assets:		Total current liabilities	409
Gross plant	1,200	9% 10-year term loan	270
Less depreciation	400	Total liabilities	679
Net plant	800	Capital:	
Total assets	$1,674	Capital stock	200
		Retained earnings	795
		Total liabilities and capital	$1,674

Table 5–5

CONMORE CORPORATION
Pro Forma Balance Sheet
December 31, 1982
($000)

Assets		*Liabilities and Capital*	
Current assets:		Current liabilities:	
Cash	$ 100	Accounts payable	$ 144
Marketable securities	115	Notes payable—bank	-0-
Receivables	144	Term loan—current portion	30
Inventories	312	Accrued interest	-0-
Prepaid taxes	-0-	Accrued other liabilities	21
Total current assets	671	Total current liabilities	195
Fixed assets:		9% 10-year term loan	240
Gross plant	1,240	Total liabilities	435
Less depreciation	460	Capital:	
Net plant	780	Capital stock	200
Total assets	$1,451	Retained earnings	816
		Total liabilities and capital	$1,451

Inventories are expected to be $312,000, as forecasted by the following calculation:

Beginning inventory	$ 592,000
Plus: Production	1,440,000
Total available inventory	$2,032,000
Less: Cost of goods sold	1,720,000
Ending inventory	$ 312,000

The $1,440,000 total cost of goods produced (from the production forecast and reflected in the cash forecast), is comprised of materials at $144,000 per month, labor at $60,000 per month, and overhead expenses of $36,000 per month ($26,000 in cash outlays indicated by the cash budget and $10,000 per month depreciation, a noncash charge). The cost of goods sold is taken from the pro forma income statement (Table 5–3). Raw materials and work in process inventories are assumed to be stable.

The beginning balance sheet included prepaid taxes of $22,000. Our pro forma income statement (Table 5–3) indicates that income taxes on a $131,000 taxable income in the last six months will be $60,000. However, our income tax payments (from the cash forecast, Table 5–2) will be $19,000 each in September and December, totaling only $38,000. Therefore, the prepaid taxes on the June 30 balance sheet will be absorbed and the balance in that account on December 31, 1982, will be zero.

Gross plant will be increased by $40,000, the price of the machine scheduled for delivery in August.[6] The allowance for accumulated depreciation is increased by the $60,000 projected depreciation charges for the period that were used in developing the pro forma income statement.

On the liabilities and capital side, accounts payable of $144,000 reflects purchases to be made in December and paid for in January. This implicitly assumes that the company intends to continue level production next year at the same rate as in 1982. (Note: The fact that accounts payable and accounts receivable are exactly the same figure, $144,000, is purely coincidental.) Notes payable to bank will be zero, as the cash budget indicates that all bank borrowings will have been paid off in November.

The current portion of the term loan will be $30,000, the payment due December 31, 1983. The long-term portion of this loan will be reduced to $240,000, reflecting the payment to be made December 31, 1982. Accrued interest on the term loan will be reduced to zero when the interest payment of $27,000 is made on December 31, 1982. Accrued other liabilities are assumed to be the same as at the beginning of the period.

[6]We are assuming this to be an additional machine. If it were a replacement for an existing machine, we would have to account here for the elimination of the gross value and the depreciation related to the retired machine. The cash forecast would include an inflow, the net proceeds expected to be received from the sale of the retired machine. We would account for the net gain or loss on this transaction as an adjustment to retained earnings.

Capital stock remains the same, as no issue or redemption is contemplated. Retained earnings, beginning at $795,000, are expected to be increased by $71,000 (net profit after taxes) and decreased by $50,000 (paid in dividends), leaving $816,000.

In developing the pro forma balance sheet, any one of the accounts could have been used as a "plug figure"—a figure that will make the balance sheet balance. However, refraining from using this shortcut provides a check upon the mathematical accuracy of all three financial forecasts—the cash budget, the pro forma income statement, and the pro forma balance sheet. They all tie together.[7]

Uses of pro forma financial statements The firm is in business to make money. Although an oversimplification, that is reason enough to develop a pro forma income statement. Often, however, there are additional reasons. If, for example, a company had maintained an enviable record of earnings growth for a number of years and the pro forma income statement for next year indicated a slight decline, management would make great efforts to prevent that happening. Reevaluation of operating policies and strategies underlying the operating forecasts might lead to revision that would increase the expected sales revenues or reduce costs. "Belts would be tightened"; marginally productive personnel would be let go. In some manner, management would adjust operations to avoid an expected decrease in earnings.

Sometimes, to be sure, such action may be "penny wise and pound foolish"; a preoccupation with maintaining a rising earnings curve may induce managerial actions with detrimental long-run consequences. This detriment has in some instances manifested itself in later years in precipitous declines in earnings and stock prices. Nonetheless, the temptation is great to do something about a forecasted decline in earnings, and in many cases action so induced is constructive in both the short and long run.

Or perhaps management is considering a change in operating policy, such as a change in the pricing of its product(s), development of additional markets, or selling some of its plant assets and buying the items produced by them from subcontractors. Development of operating forecasts and pro forma income statements that indicate the expected effects of such changes may provide valuable insight relative to such decisions.

When considering a proposed acquisition of another firm, management almost always would run off pro forma income statements to indicate earnings per share if the acquired firm had been merged in the past and future

[7]There are other methods of estimating pro forma financial statements. These relate the various expense and balance sheet items directly to sales volume. As these methods are more appropriately used in long-term forecasting, they are discussed in Chapter 17.

earnings per share expected to result from the acquisition. These would be compared to the past and pro forma income statements of the firm without the acquisition. Although not the only analyses appropriate to an acquisition consideration, these pro forma income statements would be useful. (Mergers and acquisitions will be considered in much greater detail in Chapter 23.)

Pro forma balance sheets are of particular value when they reveal expected deterioration in the financial soundness of the firm. Reappraisal of policies and strategies may result in changes designed to prevent such deterioration.

In addition, a pro forma balance sheet will be developed to show the *immediate* effect of a proposed acquisition or a major long-term financial transaction, such as a company's repurchasing some of its stock, selling additional stock, or issuing additional bonds. The pro forma balance sheet will allow before and after comparison and, in turn, provide data for the development of pertinent financial ratios that relate to the soundness of the transaction. Not only will management develop these statements for their own use, but also the Securities and Exchange Commission will require that they be included in required filings and in the prospectus issued to prospective securities holders in connection with the proposed transactions.

Although our present interest is largely in the use of financial forecasts for internal management purposes, outside parties are sometimes interested in them. For an additional example, a bank loan officer considering an application for a line of credit or an individual bank loan might wish to analyze pro forma balance sheets as of the dates that loans are expected to be outstanding to the applicant. In the case of Conmore Corporation the banker would want to see pro forma balance sheets for at least August 30 and September 30, the dates when bank loans are expected to peak and the risk exposure of the bank would be the greatest.

Summary

The planning system is a means by which management assesses the environmental factors expected to influence the firm in the future and directs its activities to cope with them. This requires a coordinated effort by nearly all management personnel. Although planning may be done over any time span, this chapter covered only the short term, usually one year divided into months. All short-term planning begins with the operating plans, which, in turn, start with the sales forecast. Because the sales forecast influences all subsequent plans, both operating and financial, it is important that it be realistic and based upon both internal and external input.

The three major financial plans, the cash forecast, the pro forma income statement, and the pro forma balance sheet, are developed almost entirely from data contained in the operating plans. The cash forecast provides estimates of the cash that will be available or required at the end of each period. It begins with the initial cash balance, adds expected cash inflows, and subtracts estimated cash outflows to provide a tentative cash balance at the end of the period. Then the minimum cash required is subtracted to show the excess cash available for investment or the external financing required. The forecasted cash position forewarns the financial officer of borrowings that must be arranged or of availability of funds to be invested. If sufficient funds will not be available, operating plans must be changed before financial difficulties arise. The cash forecast also is a useful device in evaluating contemplated changes in operating policy.

The pro forma financial statements (income statement and balance sheet) estimate the effects of future operations upon the income and financial condition of the firm. The pro forma income statement is useful in forewarning management of the effect on income of contemplated operating actions, perhaps leading to revision in operating plans. Similarly, the pro forma balance sheet provides useful information regarding changes in financial conditions expected to result from contemplated operations. These pro forma statements also will be of value to bankers (or other lenders) in appraising applications for loans or lines of credit to finance future operations. A specialized use of pro forma financial statements is in connection with analysis of proposed acquisitions.

Two major problems may be encountered in using a planning system. The first arises from the appearance of certainty of the various forecasts although in fact nearly every estimate simply reflects the central tendency of a subjective probability distribution of possible outcomes. An informal way of coping with this is education of the personnel using forecasts regarding uncertainties implicit in the forecasting process. This should be accompanied by revision of forecasts whenever changes in the environment warrant. Formal methods include the use of minimax forecasts and computer simulation of varying possible operating experience to provide flexible forecasts that are changed as operating experience unfolds.

The other problem relates to the use of plans as control devices. Some managers may fail to recognize that changed circumstances require adjustment of operating action regardless of the initial plan. Therefore, it is important that management personnel at all levels understand that a plan is a tool to help them manage but not an inflexible master of their destiny.

Questions

1. Why is the sales forecast of prime importance to the entire planning process of a firm?

2. Why is external input to the sales forecast in addition to input from the marketing department desirable?

3. "A planning and control system is a tool to aid management in directing actions of the firm toward accomplishing its goals. The system should be the servant of the people rather than people being servants of the system." Discuss.

4. What are the principal uses of the cash forecast?

5. List and briefly discuss some of the ways by which changing conditions and uncertainty may be recognized in the planning and control process.

6. Explain how collection patterns and purchasing terms are incorporated into the cash forecasting process.

7. Indicate the nature and uses of pro forma financial statements for internal management purposes.

8. *a.* Specifically, why might a banker or other lender be interested in a firm's pro forma balance sheet?
   b. Why would a firm contemplating merger or acquisition be interested in pro forma financial statements?

Problems

1. Marin Corporation's sales were $120,000 in May and $110,000 in June. Its forecasted sales for the last half of the year are:

Month	Sales
July	$100,000
August	125,000
September	140,000
October	135,000
November	120,000
December	105,000

Ten percent of each month's sales are for cash. The remaining 90 percent of sales are on credit. Experience shows that 20 percent of credit sales are collected in the month of sale, 65 percent in the following month, and 15 percent in the second month following sale. Bad debt losses are negligible. Prepare a worksheet to estimate the cash inflows from operations of Marin Corporation for each month, July through December.

2. Sencorp forecasts sales for the next seven months as follows:

July	$70,000
August	60,000
September	75,000
October	80,000
November	85,000
December	72,000
January	67,000

Raw material costs equal 40 percent of sales; the materials are purchased on credit one month in advance of sales. Thirty percent of purchases are paid for in the month of purchase and the remaining 70 percent are paid in the following month. Prepare a forecast of cash outflows reflecting the payment of trade accounts payable for the months of July through December.

(Note: Problems 3 and 4 are a series.)

3. Mentor Manufacturing Corporation forecasts *unit* sales for the next eight months as follows:

July	1,000 units
August	1,300
September	1,600
October	1,700
November	1,900
December	1,100
January	900
February	900

The firm maintains a finished goods inventory equal to the next two months' estimated sales. The finished goods inventory at the end of June is 2,300 units, representing 1,000 units produced in May and 1,300 units produced in June.

Raw materials are purchased one month prior to completion of production, cost $10 per unit, and are paid for in the month following purchase.

Direct labor costs are $5 per unit and are paid in the month incurred. Manufacturing overhead costs (supervisory labor, heat, light and power, etc.) are $4,000 per month and paid in the month incurred. Selling expenses are $2,000 per month plus $1 per unit sold. General and administrative expenses are $2,000 per month.

Mentor is obligated to pay $3,000 interest on its long-term debt in December. It also plans to pay $4,000 in quarterly dividends to its stockholders in September and December. Quarterly tax payments of $6,000 each are due in September and December.

Prepare a production schedule and forecast the cash outflows for the months of July through December.

4. Mentor Manufacturing Corporation (Problem 3) sells its product at $26 per unit. All sales are on credit. Sales were $28,600 (1,100 units) in May and $31,200 (1,200 units) in June. Its estimated collection pattern is: *(a)* 20 percent in the month of sale, *(b)* 70 percent in the month following sale, and *(c)* 8 percent in the second month following sale. The remaining 2 percent of sales are expected to become bad debt losses.

a. Develop a worksheet forecasting collection of accounts receivable.

b. Combine this receivables collection forecast with the forecast of cash outflows (from Problem 3) to produce a cash forecast. Mentor expects no other cash inflows. (Note: Summary figures are sufficient.) Mentor has no short-term loans outstanding and has a cash balance of $20,000 at the end of June. This is considered to be its minimum cash balance requirement.

c. In essence, what does this cash forecast tell the financial manager of Mentor?

(Note: Problems 5, 6, and 7 are a series.)

5. On the basis of the following information, prepare a cash forecast for Louran Stores for the first six months of 1983.

a. Sales, actual and forecasted:

December 1982	$64,000 (actual)
January 1983	72,000 (forecasted)
February 1983	58,000
March 1983	69,000
April 1983	74,000
May 1983	56,000
June 1983	61,000

Seventy-five percent of sales are for cash. All credit sales are expected to be collected in the month following sale.

b. Purchases of merchandise, actual and forecasted:

December 1982	$40,000 (actual)
January 1983	45,000 (forecasted)
February 1983	37,000
March 1983	43,000
April 1983	47,000
May 1983	35,000
June 1983	38,000

All trade accounts payable are paid in the month following purchase.

c. Wages and salaries, forecasted:

January 1983	$15,000
February 1983	12,000
March 1983	14,000
April 1983	15,000
May 1983	13,000
June 1983	13,000

All wages and salaries are paid in the month the costs are incurred.

d. Rent is $1,800 per month.

e. Other general and administrative expenses are estimated at $2,000 per month and are paid in the month incurred.

f. A tax payment of $17,000 is due in April, 1983.

g. The cash balance on December 31, 1982, is $50,000, which is the minimum required level of cash for planning purposes.

6. Using the following information and that developed in Problem 5, develop a pro forma income statement for the first six months of 1983 for Louran Stores.

a. Depreciation is $1,000 per month.

b. The tax rate is 40 percent.

c. Cost of goods sold is 63 percent of sales.

7. Using the following balance sheet at December 31, 1982, and the information developed in Problems 5 and 6, develop a pro forma balance sheet for Louran Stores at June 30, 1983.

LOURAN STORES
Balance Sheet
December 31, 1982

Assets		*Liabilities and Equity*	
Cash	$ 50,000	Accounts payable	$ 40,000
Accounts receivable	16,000	Accrued income taxes	10,000
Inventories	134,000	Long-term debt	60,000
		Common stock	100,000
Fixed assets—net	80,000	Retained earnings	70,000
	$280,000		$280,000

Part Three
Working Capital Management

Chapter 6
Working Capital Policy

Working capital is the investment of the firm in short-term or current assets, which include cash, marketable securities, accounts receivable, short-term notes receivable, inventories, and, in some firms, expense prepayments. Current assets are limited by accounting convention to those that are expected to be converted into cash within a year. *Gross working capital* is the total of current assets. A portion of the investment in current assets is financed by current liabilities, such as accounts payable, short-term notes payable to banks, accrued wages, income tax liabilities, and, in some cases, advances by customers. Current liabilities are defined as those obligations due within one year. *Net working capital* is the current assets less the current liabilities. In other words, net working capital is that portion of the current assets financed by long-term debt and equity sources. These concepts are illustrated in Figure 6–1.

Working capital management encompasses the administration and control of current assets, utilization of short-term financing via various current

Figure 6–1 Schematic balance sheet

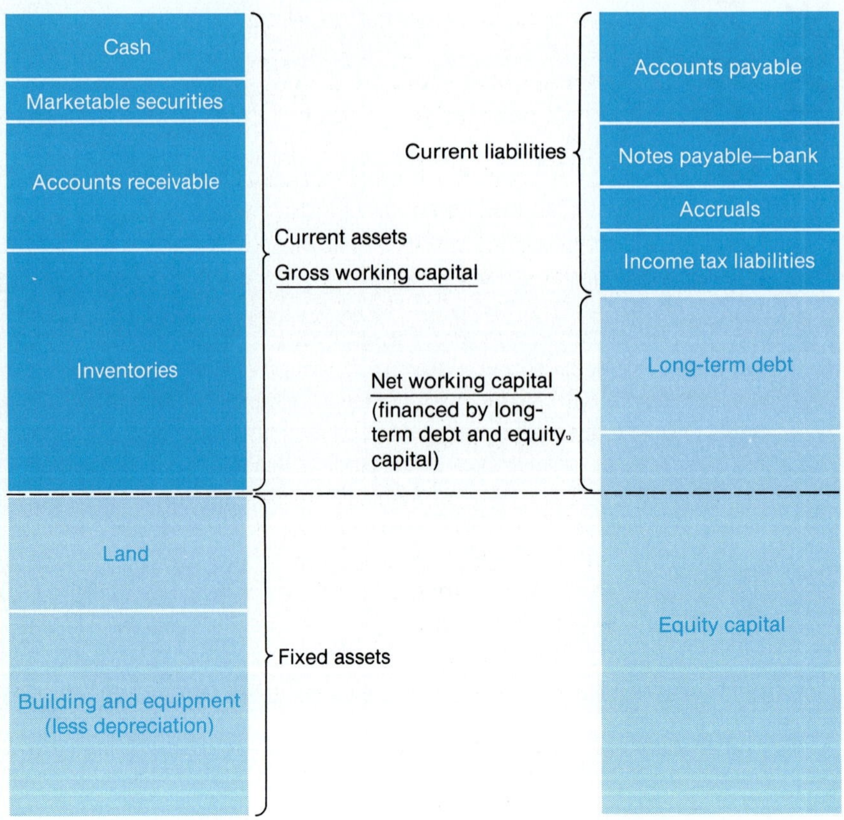

liability sources, and control of the amount of net working capital. The specific objectives of working capital management are to:

1. Contribute to the firm's goal of value maximization by managing the current assets so that the marginal return on investment in these assets is equal to or greater than the cost of capital utilized to finance them.
2. Minimize—over the long run—the cost of capital employed in financing the current assets.
3. Control the flow of funds upward through the current assets and the availability of funds from debt sources in such a way that the firm always is able to meet its financial obligations when due.

Importance of working capital management

The third goal indicated above has to do with maintaining sufficient liquidity. Thus working capital management is sometimes referred to as liquidity management. *Liquidity* relates to the ability to pay in cash the obligations that are due in cash. If sufficient liquidity is not maintained to do this, the firm is *technically insolvent* and at least faces the financial embarrassment of renegotiating its obligations to its creditors. At worst, it faces elimination through bankruptcy.[1]

The importance of working capital management cannot be overemphasized. Regardless of excellent products, effective marketing, efficient production, and wise fixed asset management, many a management has lost control of its firm because a liquidity crisis resulted in takeover by creditors, forced merger, or bankruptcy. An excellent long-run outlook for a business becomes immaterial if control is lost in the short run. In other words, if short-run liquidity fails, there is no long run.

In addition to this basic fact, there are several other reasons working capital management is important. First, in the majority of manufacturing and marketing firms, current assets constitute well over half of total assets. These current assets, particularly accounts receivable and inventories, are relatively volatile. Their magnitude changes greatly with fluctuation in sales volume. Thus they may get out of line unless continually monitored and controlled.

This is particularly true in small firms and in larger ones that are growing rapidly. Because their access to long-term capital markets is limited, small firms often have a larger proportion of their total assets invested in current assets, leasing rather than owning their buildings and a large portion of

[1]In a legal bankruptcy sense, insolvency exists when the value of the assets of a firm is less than its total liabilities. Technical insolvency exists when the firm is unable to meet its obligations to pay cash.

their equipment. In rapidly growing firms, regardless of size, requirements to finance additional accounts receivable and increased inventories often heavily tax their financial capability. In addition, expansion of fixed assets to increase production capacity in line with expanding sales of growing firms may drain net working capital to the point that liquidity is impaired. Thus many apparently successful, rapidly growing firms develop serious working capital management problems.

Working capital management also is important because of the sheer amount of time spent on it. Well over half of the financial manager's time and that of other personnel in the finance department usually is devoted to working capital management. There are two reasons for this. First, with the exception of inventory management, the various areas of working capital management are centered in the finance department. Second, the management of cash, marketable securities, and accounts receivable; the payment of accounts payable, wages, and taxes; and maintaining relations with the firm's banks are largely day-to-day, week-in-and-week-out jobs. In contrast, matters relating to capital allocation, dividend policy, long-term financing, mergers, and acquisitions, although very important, occur less frequently.

Working capital requirements

At first glance, it would appear that the gross working capital requirement would simply be the sum of amounts needed to maintain adequate inventories, to carry the receivables generated by sales, and to maintain sufficient cash balances to cover the discrepancies in day-to-day cash inflows and outflows and satisfy requirements of the firm's bankers. Determination of these amounts will be dealt with in Chapters 7 and 8. The short-term financing of this gross working capital requirement would, in turn, be a function of the amount of current liabilities that arise in the normal course of business through purchasing on credit terms, paying for the services of employees periodically rather than each hour that they work, and paying taxes periodically rather than as each dollar of taxable income is generated. These short-term financing sources are called *spontaneous* current liabilities and will be treated in Chapter 9. The remaining current asset financing requirement would be the *net* working capital investment, which, along with the fixed assets, would be financed by long/term debt and/or equity.

In most firms, however, this view would be a gross oversimplification because there would be temporary fluctuations in gross working capital requirements resulting from seasonal variations in production and/or sales volume and from cyclical fluctuations in volume of business activity. Thus, the working capital requirement breaks down into two categories, *tempo-*

rary and *permanent.* These fluctuations give rise to *working capital policy,* that is, an area where management discretion must be exercised as to the amount of *net* working capital that the firm will maintain relative to its *temporary,* as well as *permanent,* gross working capital requirements.

This point is illustrated by Figure 6–2. In a firm that is neither growing nor declining through a period of years, the fixed assets and the *permanent* current assets will tend to remain stable. Permanent current assets represent the minimum levels of cash, accounts receivable, and inventories required during each annual period. Additional investment in current assets is required to cover seasonal increases in inventories and/or accounts receivable up to the peak level indicated by the vertical broken line labeled "*temporary* current assets." These additional amounts are worked off during the downtrend of the seasonal cycle until the total asset requirement returns to the permanent level. Note that some of the current asset requirements will be financed by spontaneous current liabilities. This spontaneous financing

Figure 6–2 Asset requirements of a stable firm
(All current asset requirements are shown less spontaneous liabilities.)

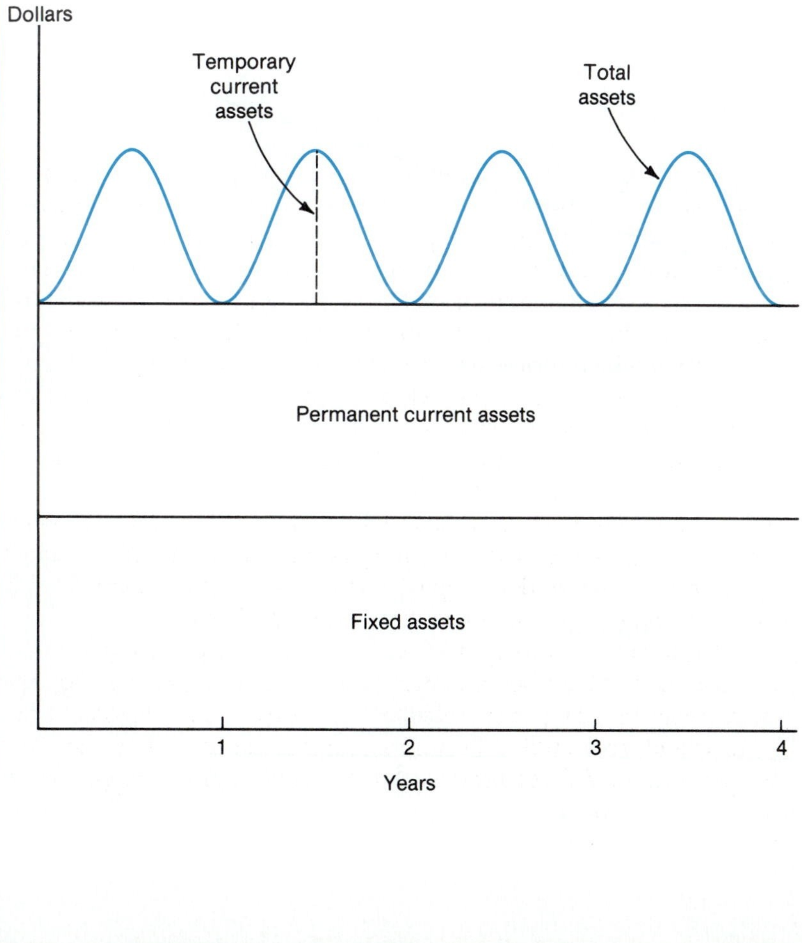

has been subtracted from the asset requirements shown in Figures 6–2 through 6–7 for simplicity of illustration.

The asset requirements (less those financed by spontaneous liabilities) of a steadily growing firm are depicted in Figure 6–3. Here, in addition to the temporary current asset financing requirement, management also is obliged to finance increasing investments in fixed assets and permanent current assets.

In comparing these two graphic illustrations, the astute reader should question the validity of Figure 6–2 in a world of inflation. This graph purports to show the asset requirements of a stable firm. But if that means stable in terms of physical volume of operations in a period during which the prices of raw materials, labor, plant and equipment replacements, and

Figure 6–3 Asset requirements of a growing firm
(All current asset requirements are shown less spontaneous liabilities.)

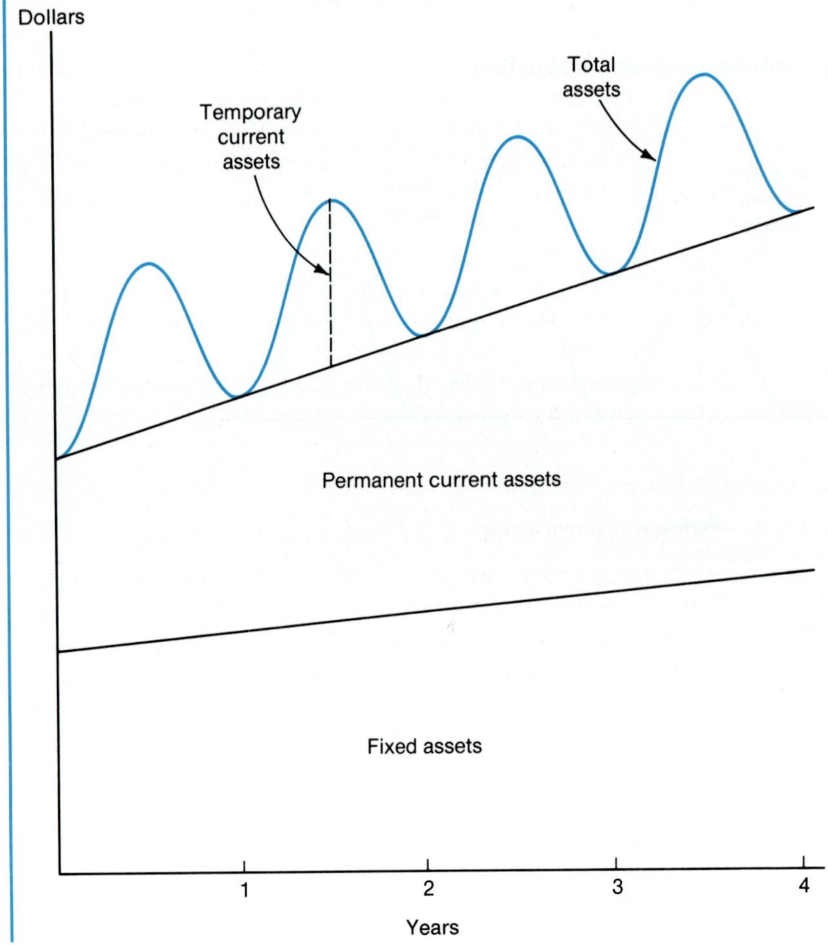

the firm's selling prices to its customers are increasing, then the asset requirements of such a firm in dollars will increase, being more like those shown in Figure 6–3. The asset requirements of a growing firm, if the growth is in physical volume as well as inflation, ascend at an even higher rate than shown in Figure 6–3. This effect of inflation must be recognized by financial management. It has been a major factor responsible for the financial difficulties encountered by many firms during the highly inflationary periods of the 1970s and so far in the 80s.

Financing working capital requirements

What sources should be utilized to finance working capital requirements? First, a portion of both temporary and permanent requirements will be financed more or less automatically by spontaneous current liabilities, particularly by accounts payable resulting from the normal terms of purchase of inventories, by the accrual of wages and fringe benefits, and by tax liabilities related to payment terms under the tax laws. (Funds provided from these sources have been abstracted from the asset requirements shown in Figures 6–2 through 6–7.) Second, the remaining permanent and temporary current assets must be financed by utilizing a combination of short-term or long-term sources of funds.

The use of nonspontaneous sources, which entail direct financing costs, is at least to some degree at the discretion of management and therefore raises a policy question. The usual sources of such short-term financing are loans from commercial banks, the sale of commercial paper, or, in some cases, loans from finance companies. (Details regarding these borrowing arrangements will be discussed in Chapters 9 and 10.) The long-term sources include both long-term debt and equity. (These will be discussed in Chapters 18 through 22.) The policy considerations here relate only to the maturity, risk, and cost of the financing. Short-term financing adds to the current liabilities and thereby reduces net working capital, while long-term debt or equity financing provides net working capital. Therefore, the policy question may be stated another way. What is the appropriate level of net working capital that a firm should maintain?

Appropriate level of net working capital

There are basically four policy options available to management in deciding the appropriate level of working capital to maintain or, in other words, the proportion of current asset requirements to be financed from short-term versus long-term sources.

The options

These options are (1) to follow the "self-liquidating" principle, (2) to adopt a "conservative" policy requiring financing of all assets (except those financed by spontaneous liabilities) from long-term sources, (3) to follow an "aggressive" policy by financing both temporary and part of the permanent current asset requirements from short-term sources, and (4) to follow a "balanced" policy by financing a portion (say half) of the temporary current assets from short-term sources and the remainder from long-term sources. These options, their risk versus return implications, and the factors to be analyzed in deciding which option to adopt will now be discussed.

The self-liquidating principle The self-liquidating principle, sometimes called the "hedging" or "matching" principle, emphasizes the temporary nature of increases in current asset requirements related to seasonal patterns of operating activity. For example, a department store would substantially increase its investment in inventories in anticipation of the pre-Christmas selling season. These inventories subsequently would be reduced during the holiday selling season and an expansion in accounts receivable would result from the increased sales. In January and February, the collection of receivables should generate an increase in cash that could, in turn, be used to pay off short-term borrowings created previously in financing the buildup of inventories. Thus, the bank would consider the short-term loan required for this financing to be a self-liquidating loan.

From this concept, the self-liquidating principle depicted in Figure 6–4 emerges. It simply holds that *temporary current asset requirements should be financed from short-term sources* and that the total of permanent current asset and fixed asset requirements should be financed from long-term sources. (Note: This, and all succeeding discussion in this chapter, assumes that spontaneous liabilities are utilized as available to finance part of the current asset requirements.)

This principle seems logical as a basis for working capital policy and might be recommended *if* management and the firm's creditors knew that the asset requirements indicated in Figure 6–3 were correct, that is, if the firm operated in a world of certainty. But the principle is oversimplistic and subject to question because we live in an uncertain world. Its adoption as a policy entails risks resulting from four factors, all related to uncertainty:

1. The temporary expansion in current assets might be greater than forecasted.
2. The subsequent contraction of these assets might not be as great as forecasted, resulting in a larger permanent current asset requirement than expected.

Figure 6–4 Financing asset requirements—Self-liquidating principle

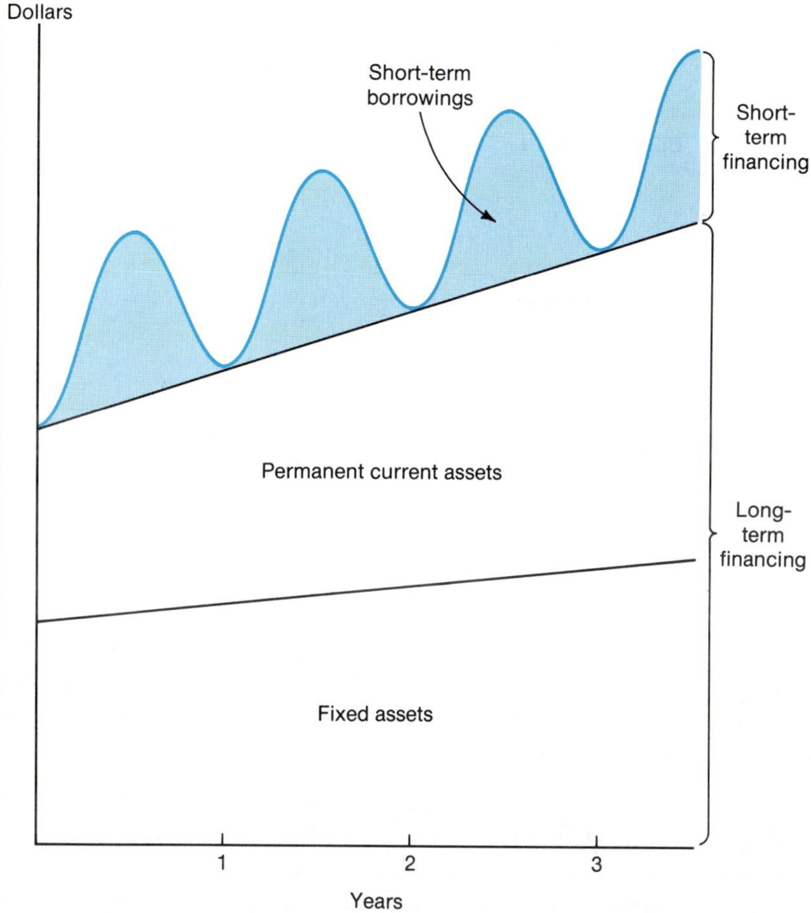

3. The interest cost on the short-term borrowing required is unknown and subject to great fluctuation.
4. At the extreme, sufficient short-term credit might not be available when required.

The self-liquidating principle, by assuming certainty, leaves little margin for error. In a marginal case with adverse experience compared to the forecast, following this principle could result in loss of financial viability. Nevertheless it provides a useful conceptual benchmark for comparison with other policy alternatives.

Conservative policy The most conservative policy would be to finance *all asset requirements,* temporary as well as permanent, from long-term sources, as depicted by Figure 6–5. If this policy were adopted, expected peak seasonal requirements would be financed by funds that had previously

Figure 6–5 Financing asset requirements—Conservative policy

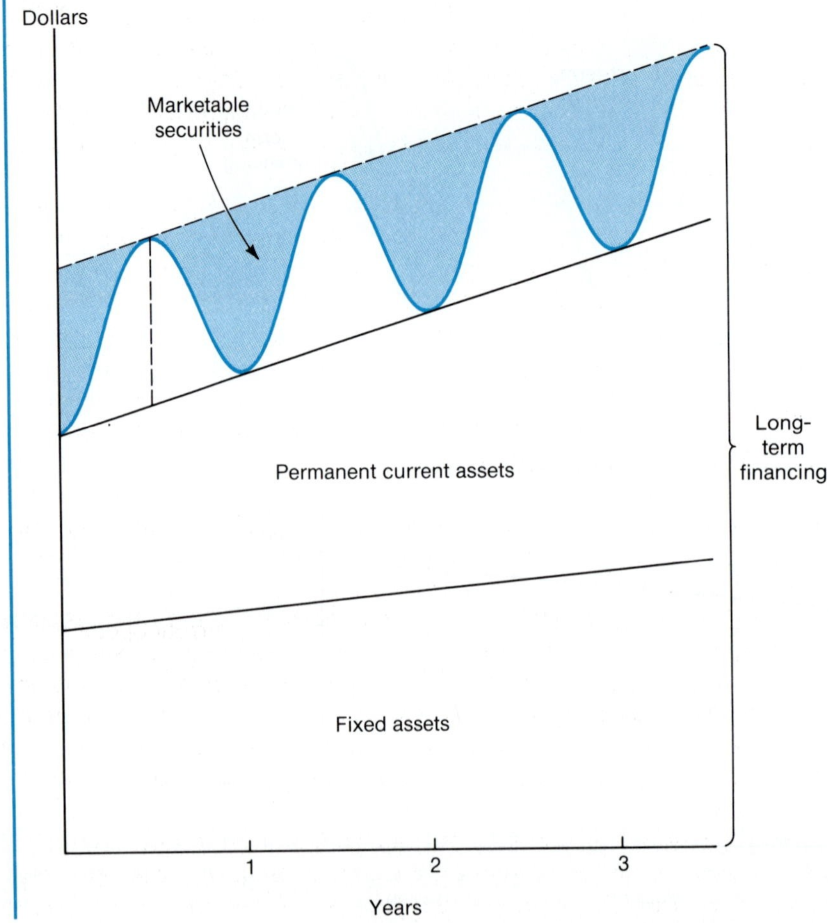

been raised from long-term sources. During the off-peak season, the excess of funds over those required by operations would be invested in short-term marketable securities.

This policy has the obvious advantage of reducing risk since the firm is, in effect, its own banker. It is not subject to the risk of higher-than-expected short-term interest rates or, at the extreme, unavailability of short-term funds in a "credit crunch." Furthermore, assuming that we are comparing firms with identical credit worthiness, the firm would have unused short-term lines of credit available if temporary seasonal needs turned out to exceed those forecasted. It also would not be in an embarrassing position if inventories or receivables failed to contract as expected, thus increasing permanent current asset requirements. Such requirements would already have been financed on a long-term basis; therefore, the firm would not be subject to banker pressure to liquidate assets to pay off maturing loans.

This policy may appear to be almost utopian, and the reader might question why it is so seldom adopted in practice. There are two important reasons limiting its use. First, as a practical matter it is available only to financially strong and usually large firms that have sufficient access to the capital markets to raise the required amount of long-term funds. Most small firms and many larger ones simply do not have the credit standing in the long-term markets to raise the required funds.

A second and more complex consideration relates to the cost of executing such a policy. In the past, this conservative policy has generally been associated with a higher financing cost than other alternatives. That higher financing cost has been based upon the assumptions that (1) the cost of short-term borrowing was less than that of long-term borrowing and (2) this cost differential was not offset by the returns available on short-term marketable securities investments during the off-season. The validity of these assumptions will be considered thoroughly later in this chapter. At this point it is sufficient to question whether the premises will be true in the future. If they will be, then consideration of adopting this policy comes down to a risk-return tradeoff analysis. If they will not, this conservative policy is clearly the superior alternative for firms that have the financial strength to carry it out.

Aggressive policy A firm following the aggressive policy would utilize short-term borrowings to finance not only temporary current asset requirements, as advocated by the self-liquidating principle, but also a portion of its permanent current assets, as shown in Figure 6–6. Assuming short-term borrowing costs to be less than long-term, this policy has been called aggressive because it seeks to increase the rate of return on the equity investment by reducing the cost of debt capital.

It entails greater risk than the self-liquidating principle because the firm is repeatedly required to renew or refinance maturing short-term loans. Cash is not available from normal operations of the business to retire the debt. Either unfavorable developments within the firm that reduce its credit worthiness or tight money conditions in the financial markets may result in financial embarrassment. At worst, inability to refinance the maturing short-term debt may result in bankruptcy. This policy sacrifices liquidity in an attempt to increase profitability to the owners.

The profitability advantage of the aggressive policy depends entirely on short-term interest rates being lower than long-term. If that differential ceases to exist, the policy is clearly disadvantageous because the added risk is not compensated by greater profits. This interest-rate differential will be further considered later in this chapter.

One must bear in mind that, regardless of the owners' propensity to bear risk and the profit motive, many firms, particularly growing, small to middle-sized ones, follow this policy because no viable alternative is available. They simply lack sufficient access to the long-term capital markets. Other firms, even with no growth, are financed in this way not because manage-

Figure 6–6 Financing asset requirements—Aggressive policy

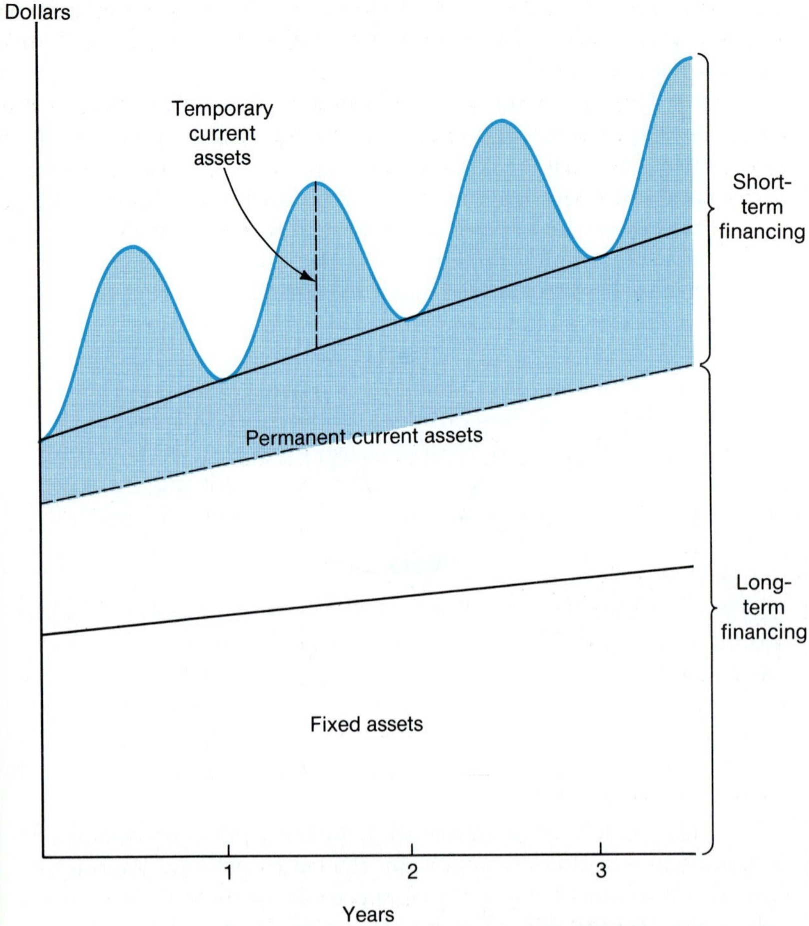

ment wants them to be but rather as a result of short-term borrowings that were expected to be self-liquidating but just didn't turn out that way. Unforeseen changes in business conditions obstructed expected current-asset liquidation.

Balanced policy Now that we understand the self-liquidating principle and have reviewed the purported advantages, disadvantages, and practical limitations of the two extremes of working capital policy, conservative and aggressive, we might come down to a suitable compromise. We shall tentatively accept at this point the traditional expectation that short-term interest rates will be lower than long-term rates. We shall also assume that at any given time this cost advantage of short-term borrowing will not be fully offset by the interest income available on short-term investment of excess funds in marketable securities. In addition, we shall assume that the firm has ready access to either short- or long-term financial markets. We probably would then decide, as many firms have, to adopt a balanced policy as illustrated in Figure 6–7.

If we, the management, are risk averters (as most accepted economic theory holds), we would recognize that the "aggressive" policy would entail too much risk in relation to the profit expectation and that the conservative policy appears to be super-safe at the expense of reduction of profit potential.[2] To follow the self-liquidating principle assumes a degree of certainty

Figure 6–7 Financing asset requirements—Balanced policy

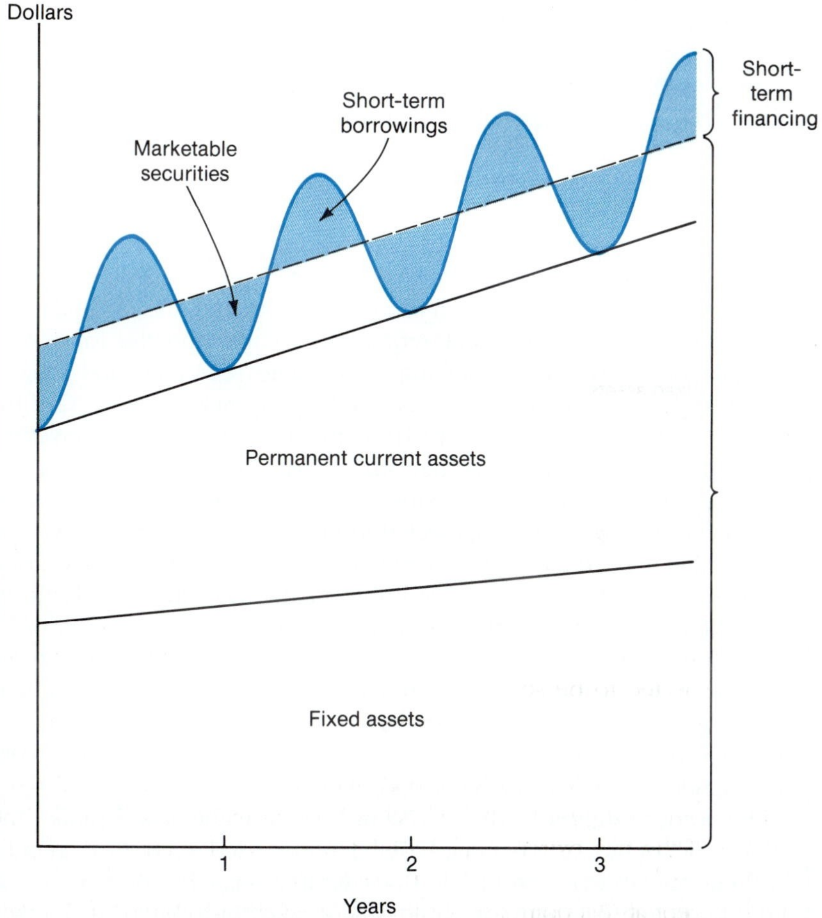

[2]Risk aversion is a low propensity to bear risk. A risk averter dislikes risk and therefore requires an increased potential of return to be willing to assume an added increment of risk.

that cannot be relied upon in an uncertain environment. Therefore, we decide upon a compromise between the self-liquidating principle and the conservative policy.

Under this balanced policy we maintain sufficient net working capital and associated long-term financing to cover the permanent current assets and a portion of the temporary current asset requirement. We borrow short-term funds to cover part of our peak seasonal working capital needs but do not fully utilize the short-term credit available to us. As seasonal requirements are reduced, we pay off the short-term borrowings and then, during the period of low seasonal requirements, invest the excess funds in short-term marketable securities.

This policy provides a safety factor to cover excess peak seasonal needs over those forecasted by utilizing the short-term borrowing power we had not planned to use. If current-asset liquidation should not turn out to be as great as expected, we would still be able to pay off our short-term loans but would have less funds available for investment in marketable securities. If a credit crunch should occur, we shall have to pay higher-than-expected interest rates on the short-term borrowing, but we run little risk that required short-term credit will not be available.

We must recognize that the balanced policy depicted in Figure 6–7 is merely illustrative and somewhat oversimplified. In any particular case, detailed analysis would be necessary to take into account the particular shape of the temporary current asset requirement curve and the interest rates available on short-term borrowing, marketable securities, and long-term borrowing. For how many months would how much money have to be borrowed at what expected rate? How much money could be invested in marketable securities for what periods of time and at what interest yields? What are our forecasts relative to the differential, if any, between short-term and long-term interest rates expected to prevail in the future? Other factors to consider are estimates of how much above forecast our temporary current asset requirement might turn out to be and how much under forecast the liquidation of temporary current assets might be.

Depending on these variables, the dashed line indicating long-term financing might be raised or lowered from a level nearly reaching that of forecasted peak temporary requirements to a level approaching the trough of temporary requirements. But somewhere in this range we should arrive at a sound working capital financing policy.

The reader might ask why we do not use a mathematical model incorporating all of the variables that have been discussed to arrive at an optimal working capital financing policy. Considerable work has been done along these lines, and you may sometime wish to attempt to build such a model. The problems are that (1) there are so many variables that would have to be reduced to subjective probability distributions and (2) so many of these distributions, particularly relative to future interest rates, would be little more than guesses. Consequently, to date such models have not proved widely acceptable in practical working capital policy determination. Sometime in the future they may do so.

Cost considerations

The importance of the differential between short-term and long-term interest rates in deciding among alternative working capital financing policies is apparent from the above discussion. We shall now focus upon these costs to gain some insight on interest rate differentials that might be expected in the future.

Yield curves The term structure of interest rates at any given time is depicted by a *yield curve,* sometimes called a "yield to maturity" or a "term structure of interest rates" chart. Figure 6–8 shows three possible shapes of the yield curve. The upward-sloping curve, labeled A, traditionally has been accepted as the predominant shape of the yield curve. It indicates that short-term interest rates are the lowest available in the market and that interest rates rise rather rapidly as the maturity of debt increases from, say, 90 days to a year or two. As maturity is extended, the rate of increase in interest rates moderates and the yield curve approaches a zero slope.

The flat or horizontal yield curve, labeled B, indicates interest rates that are the same regardless of the maturity of the debt. The declining yield curve, labeled C, depicts a market in which short-term interest rates are higher than long-term, with the rate of decrease through time similar to the rate of increase in A, the traditional yield curve.

Figure 6–8 Yield curves

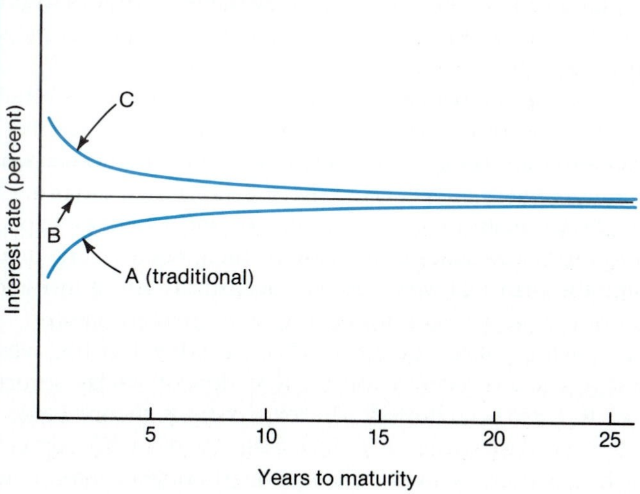

These yield curves are hypothetical and for discussion purposes only. In the real world, the slopes of such curves may vary greatly and sometimes are even bumpy or humped. Any given yield curve relates only to the state of the financial markets at a given time. It is a still picture of a cross section of these markets organized by time to maturity. A particular yield curve applies only to debt securities of the same issuer or risk class.

Theoretical rationale Interest theory explains the yield curve with three lines of reasoning: (1) the liquidity preference theory, (2) the expectations theory, and (3) the market segmentation theory.

The *liquidity preference theory* explains the traditional upward-sloping yield curve. The logic is that lenders are willing to accept the lowest rate of interest only on the lowest-risk debt securities. They will require additional increments of interest to compensate for bearing higher risks. Two types of risk increase with time to maturity: interest rate risk and default risk.

Interest rate risk is the possibility of a decline in liquidation value during the period a debt security is held. If the market rate of interest rises, the current liquidation value of a debt security bearing a fixed rate of interest will decline. It can be sold only at a discounted price that will yield to the buyer the higher current market rate of interest to maturity. The longer the time to maturity, the greater that discount will be. Therefore, the holder of a short-term debt security will bear less interest rate risk and be willing to accept a lower rate of return than the holder of a long-term debt security.

Default risk is the possibility that the issuer will be unable to pay the interest and principal when due. Inasmuch as the possibility of unfavorable change in financial condition of the issuer is to some extent a function of time—today is more certain than tomorrow, next month is more certain than next year, and so on—default risk also increases with time to maturity. Therefore, the required interest rate should increase. Either interest rate risk or default risk considerations, or both, should cause investors to prefer liquidity; therefore, they should be willing to accept lower interest rates on short-term than on long-term debt.

The *expectations theory* holds that the long-term interest rate required by the market is an average of the series of short-term interest rates that are expected to prevail in the market during the longer period. In other words, the long rate is an average of the expected short rates. Thus, if the prevailing interest rate on 90-day maturities were 6 percent and investors expected rates on such short-term securities to increase by increments of one-quarter percent each time the principal were received at maturity and reinvested in new 90-day securities, the investor would require 7 percent interest on a two-year security paying interest quarterly. This would reflect the average interest rate that would be received on a succession of 90-day securities investments over the two-year period. The expectations theory could explain any of the three basic types of yield curves (A, B, or C) depending upon collective perceptions of future changes in short-term interest rates by participants in the debt markets.

The *market segmentation theory* recognizes that various types of investors, having different investment objectives, prefer to invest in debt securities of different maturities. For example, commercial banks and nonfinancial corporations investing temporarily in their marketable securities portfolios tend to prefer short-term debt securities, whereas life insurance companies and pension fund managers prefer long-term debt securities. On the other side of the market, business firms borrowing to finance temporary increases in working capital enter the short-term market while utility companies, real estate buyers, and governmental bodies usually prefer to raise funds on a long-term basis. Thus the debt market is not by any means a single homogeneous market, but rather is made up of different segments with supply and demand in each segment determining a price (interest rate) for borrowed funds at any given time. Of course, there is some overlapping and movement of both investors and borrowers from one segment to another. Although markets are not totally segmented, there is a general tendency towards segmentation by time to maturity. The market segmentation theory holds that at any given time differences in supply-demand relationships existing in the different market segments account for yield curves varying from upward sloping (A) through horizontal (B) to downward sloping (C).

Therefore, other things being equal, liquidity preference theory supports an upward-sloping yield curve while expectations theory and market segmentation theory could at any particular time support a yield curve bending up to horizontal or moving still further to a downward slope.

History of yield curves Figure 6–9 plots on an average annual basis the general pattern of short-term and long-term interest rates prevailing from 1911 to 1980. An attempt has been made to maintain comparability of credit quality by using interest rates on prime commercial paper (four to six months maturities) to reflect the short-term rate applicable to large corporations with very high credit standing and the yield on Standard & Poor's AAA rated corporate bonds to reflect the long-term interest rate applicable to corporations of similarly high credit standing. The vertical distance of the short-term line below the long-term line indicates the degree of upward slope of the yield curve (A). The yield curve is flat (B) wherever the two lines intersect. The degree of downward slope (C) is indicated by the vertical distance of the short-term line above the long-term line.

First, note that short-term rates have tended to fluctuate much more than long-term rates and that these fluctuations have been particularly great during periods of generally high interest rates. Next, and most important, note that this period of 70 years rather clearly breaks into three sub-periods: 1911–29, 1930–65, and the period since 1966. During the 1910s and 1920s, a period of general economic growth, prosperity, and high interest rates, there was no predominant pattern of yield curves. Rather, the curve changed frequently from an upward slope to flat to downward slope and back again. This seems to indicate that some combination of expectation of change in short-term interest rates and market segmentation tended to off-

Figure 6–9 Long- and short-term interest rates

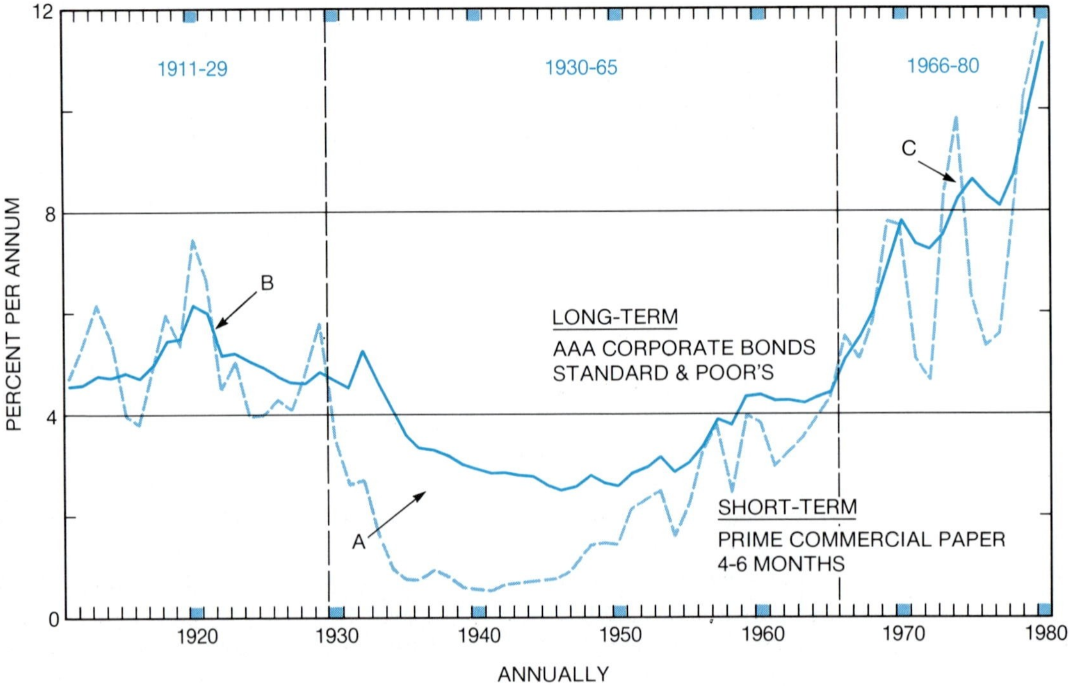

set liquidity preference in influencing the yield curves on several occasions during that period.

The upward-sloping yield curve (A) came to be recognized as "traditional" as a result of observations covering the period 1930 through 1965. With the single exception of a brief period occurring in 1956 and 1957, the traditional upward-sloping yield curve prevailed. Explanation of this necessarily involves over-simplification and conjecture. We note, however, that during most of this period covering the great depression of the 1930s, World War II, and the relatively prosperous growth period from 1946 through 1965, the predominant monetary and fiscal policy of the United States was oriented toward maintaining historically low general interest rates and extremely low short term-rates. Stimulative economic policy, particularly monetary policy as exercised by the Federal Reserve System, tends to have greater suppressive influence upon short-term interest rates than on long-term rates.

The period beginning in 1966 reflects a different pattern of interest rates, characterized by a steep general upward trend in interest rates and extreme fluctuations in short-term rates. Especially in the latter part of this period, after the oil embargo of 1973, the economy became lethargic. The acute awareness of inflationary pressures and related foreign-exchange rate problems made it virtually impossible to stimulate the economy through expansionary fiscal and monetary measures that had been used over the past four decades. The necessary changes in national economic policy, particularly the "bite the bullet" change in monetary policy, which allowed an extreme rise of the prime short-term interest rate (from 13.5 percent at the beginning of October 1979 to 20 percent in April 1980), and assessment of the basic reasons for such changes, lead us to seriously question the assumption that the traditional upward-sloping yield curve will tend to prevail in the foreseeable future.

Future working capital financing policy In light of the foregoing theoretical and historical analysis of yield curves, what working capital financing policy would be appropriate for the future? A reasonable expectation might be that the general level of interest rates will tend to be relatively high and that short-term rates will be extremely volatile. Long-term rates will, of course, fluctuate in the same direction as short-term, but considerably less violently. The shape of the yield curve, therefore, would be expected to change frequently and widely from steep upward slope to flat to steep downward slope.

During some periods, monetary actions of the Federal Reserve System in attempting to cope with inflationary pressures and a weakening dollar-exchange rate would result in a downward-sloping yield curve. Tight monetary policy would force short-term rates up more rapidly and to higher levels than long-term rates for two reasons. First, the effect of monetary action on the short-term market is more powerful and direct than on the long-term debt market. Second, the onerous eventual effects of high short-term interest rates on unemployment and the level of economic activity would be perceived to require lowering short-terms rates in the future. Therefore, expectations of that reduction would hold long-term rates at lower levels. Liquidity preference for short-term securities would not be eliminated; it would simply be outweighed by expectations. During other periods, with high unemployment and declining real gross national product, loose monetary policy would result in an upward-sloping yield curve.

The effect of a money-market environment—in which the probability of a downward-sloping yield curve is about equal to that of an upward-sloping curve—upon working capital financing policy would be to negate any alleged risk-return tradeoff advantages of either an aggressive policy or adherence to the self-liquidating principle. Even the balanced policy would be suboptimal. The least risk would be borne under the conservative policy, and there would be no profitability advantage under any alternative to it.

Therefore, the appropriate policy in such a money-market environment for a firm with the financial strength to carry it out would be the conservative policy of financing all working capital requirements, including temporary ones, from long-term sources and investing temporarily excess funds in marketable securities. Those firms with limited credit standing and/or access to the long-term markets should simply strive to come as close to this goal as feasible.

If management wished to pursue a truly aggressive policy of taking higher risks in seeking higher returns, it would not adopt the policy that has been labeled aggressive. Rather, it would attempt to "play the yield curve" by alternating between short- and long-term financing of temporary needs in anticipation of swings in that curve. This would be very difficult to do, particularly switching from long-term financing to short-term, and is not recommended.

Summary

Gross working capital is the total current assets of the firm. Net working capital, current assets less the current liabilities, is that portion of current assets financed from long-term debt and/or equity sources. Working capital management encompasses the administration and control of current assets, utilizing current liability sources to finance part of the required funds and controlling the amount of net working capital. Sound working capital management is vitally important because if the firm's liquidity should become impaired so that it cannot generate cash to pay its obligations when due, it will be financially embarrassed and, at the limit, may become bankrupt.

The permanent portion of a firm's working capital requirements represents the minimum total current assets that must be carried during the year, or other cycle of business activity. An additional temporary working capital requirement arises from seasonal or cyclical fluctuation in total current assets. It represents the difference between the permanent and peak seasonal requirement. Temporary and perhaps part of the permanent working capital requirements could be financed from short- or long-term sources. The working capital policy question concerns the choice between these sources.

There are four basic policy options. The first is to adhere to the self-liquidating principle by financing temporary needs from short-term sources and permanent needs from long-term sources. The second, the conservative policy, would finance both temporary and permanent requirements from long-term sources and invest excess funds temporarily available during the off-peak season in marketable securities. The third, the aggressive policy, would finance not only temporary but also part of the permanent working capital requirements from short-term sources. The fourth, the balanced policy, is a compromise between strict adherence to the self-liquidating principle and the conservative policy. It would finance a part of the temporary requirement from long-term funds and part from short-term sources, investing temporarily excess funds in marketable securities.

Each of these policy options entails bearing a different degree of risk, ranging from conservative (the safest) to aggressive (the most risky).

The appropriate choice among these alternatives depends largely upon the relationship between short- and long-term interest rates, that is, the shape of the yield curve. This shape is influenced by the liquidity preference of investors, expectations as to future short-term rates, and the supply-demand characteristics of the various segments of the money and capital markets. Traditionally, the yield curve has tended to be upward sloping. Assuming that slope, the choice on the basis of the risk-return tradeoff for a risk-averse firm would be a balanced policy. Risk takers might choose the aggressive policy.

Although the yield curve sloped upward during most of the period from 1930 to 1966, great changes in the economy, fiscal policies, and especially monetary policies during the period from 1966 to the present lead us to question the validity of the assumption that this condition will prevail as a basis for determining policy. It appears more probable that the yield curve will fluctuate erratically between upward sloping and downward sloping and that the probability of each is about equal. If so, the risk averter would choose the conservative policy because the return part of the risk-return trade-off would be eliminated.

Questions

1. What are the objectives of working capital management?
2. How does working capital management relate to *(a)* liquidity, *(b)* technical solvency, and *(c)* risk?
3. Why is working capital management important?
4. What is *permanent* working capital?
5. How does inflation affect the working capital requirements of a firm with a stable physical volume? What is the financial implication?
6. *a.* What is the essence of working capital *policy?*
   b. What are the four basic working capital policy options?
7. State and indicate the rationale of the self-liquidating principle.
8. *a.* Contrast the conservative and aggressive working capital policies.
   b. What are the virtues and vices of each?
9. What practical limitation may restrict use of the conservative policy, even under market conditions favorable to its use?

10. What is the rationale underlying a balanced working capital policy?

11. What is a yield curve?

12. How does the liquidity preference theory of interest rates explain an upward-sloping yield curve?

13. Explain the expectations theory of interest rates. What shaped yield curve(s) does it support?

14. What is the market segmentation theory of interest rates? What shaped yield curve(s) does it support?

15. How does the expected shape of yield curves influence the determination of working capital financial policy?

Problems

1. From the current issue of the *Federal Reserve Bulletin* or other source available in your library:
   a. Construct a yield curve for U.S. government securities as of the latest date available.
   b. Construct a yield curve for the same securities as of one year prior to that constructed in *(a)*.
   c. Comment on the changes noted.

2. The Pitkin Corporation forecasts the following investment in current and fixed assets for the next two years:

	Assets ($ millions)	
Date	Fixed (net)	Current
December 31, 19×0 (now)	$25	$28
March 31, 19×1	25	31
June 30, 19×1	28	33
September 30, 19×1	30	38
December 31, 19×1	30	30
March 31, 19×2	30	33
June 30, 19×2	33	35
September 30, 19×2	33	40
December 31, 19×2	33	32

Pitkin's capital structure currently includes $25 million owners' equity and $14 million long-term debt. Spontaneous current liabilities (accounts payable and accruals) finance about one-half of current asset requirements. The firm expects to retain earnings of about $500,000 per quarter. Long-term loans are available in multiples of $500,000. Short-term bank loans are available in multiples of $100,000.

a. Graph Pitkin's fixed asset and working capital (less spontaneous current liabilities) requirements.

b. Develop a financing plan assuming that Pitkin follows the self-liquidating principle.

c. Develop an alternative financing plan, assuming that Pitkin will change to a conservative working capital financing policy.

Chapter 7
Management of Cash and Marketable Securities

The elementary concept of managing cash and marketable securities was introduced in Chapter 1 with a simplified flow-of-funds diagram. We recognized the necessity of continually maintaining sufficient liquidity in the form of cash to pay the bills as they became due. Chapter 5 developed the cash forecast, which provided estimates of the amounts of cash that would have to be raised from external sources and/or the excess cash that would be available for temporary investment in future periods. This cash planning is perhaps the most important part of cash and marketable securities management.

But to this point we have simply assumed the level of working cash balances required; we have not considered the means by which the cash account may be managed efficiently, and we have not dealt with management of the marketable securities portfolio. These matters will be considered in this chapter.

The term *cash,* as used here, will include currency and the checking account (demand deposit) balance(s) in the firm's commercial bank(s). *Marketable securities* will include various temporary investment instruments, such as treasury bills, certificates of deposit, and commercial paper. These are *near-cash* assets that normally can be turned into cash (liquidated) in minutes or hours. Because of their extremely high liquidity, the total of cash and marketable securities will be considered *liquid assets.* Distribution of the liquid assets between cash and marketable securities is influenced by the motives for holding them.

The two principal motives for holding liquid assets are to facilitate transactions and to provide a safety stock to cover unforeseen needs. The *transactions* motive refers to predictable requirements to pay bills to suppliers, to meet periodic payrolls, and to pay obligations to other creditors as they come due. In most firms there is little coincidence of daily or weekly cash inflows and outflows. The differences in timing between the two will result in fluctuating transactions requirements over short periods of time. Therefore, the liquidity necessary to cover day-to-day, week-to-week needs will normally be held in the form of cash. We shall call these "working cash balances." Funds held to satisfy the transactions motive on a longer-term basis, such as excess funds available during the off-peak period of a seasonal working capital cycle, may be invested in marketable securities. These, in turn, may be liquidated to cover transaction needs as temporary working capital requirements ascend toward the peak.

Holding an additional safety stock of liquidity relates to the *precautionary* motive. In essence, this is the "rainy day fund" maintained to cover unforeseen payment requirements or a shortfall of cash inflows. Liquid assets held for this purpose relate to the uncertainty of operational cash flows and opportunities for investment.[1] A large portion of precautionary balances probably would be invested in marketable securities to obtain a return from them.

Cash management

Management of cash involves three elements: (1) determining the level of working cash balances to be maintained, (2) control of cash by expediting collection of cash inflows and timing payment of cash outflows, and (3) maintaining security of cash. We shall deal with the first two, leaving to the accountants the security considerations.

Determinants of working cash requirements

Inasmuch as no return may be made on currency or demand deposits, at first glance it would appear that working cash balances should be held as close to zero as possible. However, there are two considerations that militate against this. First, we frequently would run out of cash and, second, our bank(s) would not like us. This, in turn, would jeopardize our ability to borrow from them or, at the extreme, might result in their closing our account(s). So we seek to maintain working cash balances that will facilitate our transactions without running out of cash and maintain such a relationship with our bank(s) that our operational and financial needs will be served.

Predictable differences between cash inflows and outflows We can get an initial reading of the day-to-day differences between cash inflows and outflows by analyzing past records of daily deposits to the bank account and checks written against it. The fluctuations in deposit balances will provide a rough guide in determining the average working balances required to prevent our running out of cash.

This is very crude because it relates to the bank balances on our books rather than those on the bank's books. The differences between the two may be substantial because the bank pays the checks we have written only after they have worked their way back through the clearing system to be charged against our account. Likewise, the bank considers our deposits to be "available funds" only after the checks we deposit have been collected

[1]Some authors—including John Maynard Keynes, who first identified the motives for holding liquid assets in his classic work, *The General Theory of Employment, Interest and Money,* in 1936—also cite the *speculative* motive. This relates to unforeseen opportunities for investment, which we have included under the precautionary motive.

through the clearing system from the banks on which those checks were written. We can make a much more accurate analysis of working cash balance fluctuations by consulting with our banker(s) to get the bank's analysis of our account(s). The banker usually will provide this information and, as we shall discuss later under "Compensating balance requirements," will bring these data to our attention if the bank is concerned that our account is not profitable.[2]

This analysis will reveal the fluctuations that have taken place in available balances, but it will not tell us either the average balance that should be maintained or the range within which such balances should be allowed to fluctuate.

Safety factor—To cover the unpredictable The degree of certainty of future cash flows varies from such practically certain flows as tax, rental, and bond interest payments to such relatively uncertain payments as legal fees, uninsured property or casualty losses, and travel expenses. Determination of working cash requirements must take into account unpredictable as well as predictable flows. The usual way of handling these is to increase the planned working cash balances by an amount estimated to be sufficient to cover minor adverse experience that might occur on a day-to-day basis.

Coverage of major unpredictable adverse cash-flow experience over a longer time span is provided by holding marketable securities and/or by establishing bank lines of credit in excess of those required to cover predictable needs. This consideration, in our example of cash planning in Chapter 5, led our financial manager to seek a line of credit somewhat larger than the cash forecast indicated would be required.

Safety factors to be incorporated in the planned working cash balance and investment in marketable securities are based largely upon experience and seasoned judgment. Reviews of variances between past forecasted and actual cash and marketable securities balances over a period of several years and recognition of changes in environmental factors, such as frequency of lawsuits and regulatory action influencing the firm, are useful in making these judgments.

Availability of external short-term funds A firm with extremely high short-term credit standing compared to its normal requirements for short-term funds, say IBM or AT&T, can hold working cash balances at comparatively low levels without jeopardizing the relationship with its banks or its ability to obtain required short-term credit. At the other end of the spectrum is the small fledgling firm—say, Joe Smith's Men's Store—that may need every dollar that can be borrowed from its bank to finance seasonal working cap-

[2]Note that a bank's handling of a commercial account involving a sizable number of transactions is vastly different from that of your personal account. These differences include fees charged for services, compensating balance requirements, "collected" or "available funds" balance requirements, and the account analysis related to these matters.

ital requirements. In this case, the firm's short-term credit is limited, long-term credit availability is nil, and funds requirements are equal to or greater than the credit available. Every business enterprise will fall somewhere between these extremes.

On the one hand, prudent financial management of IBM or AT&T would call for great efforts to maintain its working cash balances at the lowest possible levels. Every million-dollar reduction in cash balances and corresponding increase in marketable securities or other disposition of funds will increase net income by many thousands of dollars. Such firms therefore develop elaborate controls to keep dollars from lying idle in their bank accounts. Their bankers, of course, would like to have them leave excess funds in their bank accounts but have little bargaining power.

On the other hand, Joe Smith would be penny-wise and pound-foolish to attempt to minimize his firm's bank balance by drawing it down any time there were a thousand dollars excess in it. Rather, he would be wise to forget about the few dollars interest that might be earned when his working capital requirements were in their off-season troughs and to leave those funds in the bank. The banker is counting earnings on those deposit balances as part of the compensation for seasonal loans made to the firm. If the loan quality is considered to be marginal and money should become tight, the banker might refuse seasonal loan accommodation because the additional compensation derived from its use of excess account balances would not be available. The banker would like those balances left in the bank and has the bargaining power to require this.

Thus, the availability of short-term credit has a significant influence upon cash management. The financial manager must perceive where his firm lies on the spectrum between IBM and Joe Smith's Men's Store and manage cash balances in such a fashion that sufficient short-term credit is always available to satisfy requirements and, at the same time, ensure that potential earnings are not foregone. This, again, is a risk-return trade-off.

Compensating balance requirements Banks perform many services for their commercial customers. Accepting deposits, paying checks, and making loans are services well known to everyone. Less generally recognized services include providing credit information, financing domestic and foreign transactions through letters of credit and drafts, designing cash-control systems, providing wire transfer of funds, handling lock-box collections, buying and selling some marketable securities, and rendering a variety of financial advisory services. Banks must be compensated for the services rendered through specific fees and/or compensating balances. *Compensating balances* may be either minimum or monthly average balances that the bank requires to be maintained in the firm's checking accounts. Compensating balance requirements are designed to assure that the bank will be able to lend or invest these funds at sufficient net interest returns to compensate for services rendered to the customer.

Compensating balances are of two basic types: (1) those related to the activity in the firm's depository account(s), such as the number of checks cleared, the number of deposits processed, and other services rendered for which specific fees have not been charged, and (2) those related to lending arrangements, such as lines of credit and individual loans. For the nonborrowing customer, the banker will analyze the activity in the account and, on this basis, request that the customer maintain certain balances. These usually are expressed in terms of monthly average balances in available (or collected) funds. Such analyses are reviewed periodically and, if either the specified average balances have not been maintained or the activity has so changed that modification is warranted, the financial manager will hear from the banker.

Compensating balances related to lending arrangements vary greatly. For example, a bank might agree to maintain a $1 million line of credit for a customer, stipulating that 5 percent of the unused line and 15 percent of any portion in use (loans outstanding) will be maintained as a compensating balance. In other cases, compensating balances may be required only against loans outstanding. Although the percentages usually refer to monthly average balances, they may refer to absolute minimum balances.

The working cash balance requirement will be the *higher* of (1) an amount determined on the basis of predictable and unpredictable differences between cash inflows and outflows, also considering the availability of external short-term funds, or (2) the amount required as a compensating balance by the firm's banker. In many cases, as financial officers have become more efficient cash managers, they have reached the point where compensating balance requirements have become the predominant concern. The current banking trend is to adjust the pricing of services from requiring compensating balances to charging fees for specific services. This trend, if continued, will shift the emphasis in working cash balance determination from compensating balance requirements back to transactions and precautionary cash needs.

Cash management models

Ideally, we should be able to use mathematical models to determine (1) an optimal average cash balance, (2) a high point (investment point) at which the cash account should be reduced to a predetermined level by withdrawing funds from the bank to purchase marketable securities (or pay off bank loans), and (3) a low point at which the bank account should be replenished to bring it back up to a predetermined level by selling marketable securities (or borrowing from the bank).

Certainty models In theory, if cash flows were certain, such a problem could be solved by applying inventory control models of the type discussed in the next chapter. Cash would be considered as a particular type of inventory. We would seek to establish its optimal level, an "order point" where it should be replenished, an "economic order quantity" (the amount by which it should be replenished), and an "investment point" where it should be reduced to a predetermined level by the purchase of marketable securities. We would thereby seek to minimize the cost of carrying this "inventory" of cash.[3]

Such cash management models recognize two types of costs pertinent to the level of working cash balances—transactions costs and opportunity costs. *Transactions costs* are relatively fixed per transaction in buying or selling marketable securities. They include costs of the financial officer's time and effort in handling the transaction, clerical costs, and brokerage fees or the difference between bid and asked prices of the securities. *Opportunity costs* reflect the interest obtainable from marketable securities (or payable on bank loans).

The concept is illustrated in Figure 7–1. If working cash balances are held very low, the frequency of investment (borrowing) transaction will be so high that, even though opportunity costs will be low, total costs will be high. As working cash balances increase, the frequency of transactions is reduced. Transactions costs fall faster than opportunity costs increase. Total costs decline until an optimal point is reached, at which total costs reach a minimum. Beyond that point, opportunity costs rise faster than transactions costs

Figure 7–1 Optimal working cash balance

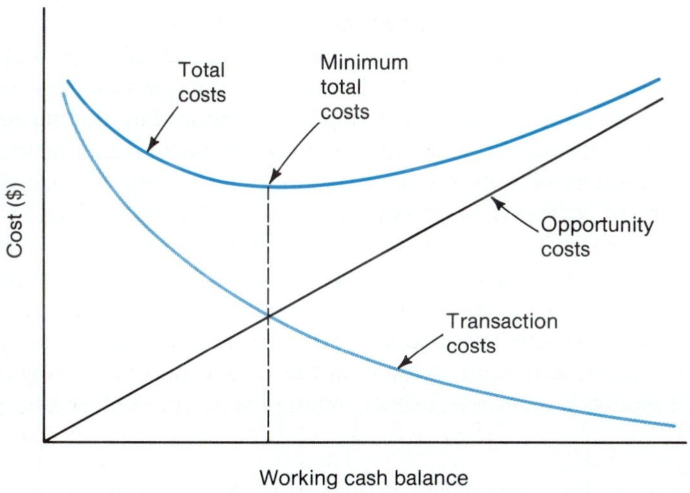

[3]William J. Baumol first applied inventory control theory to the cash management problem in his article, "The Transactions Demand for Cash: an Inventory Theoretic Approach," *Quarterly Journal of Economics,* November 1952, pp. 545–56

fall, and total costs increase. Carrying this concept through by applying inventory models yields the required cash control information.

Such models are useful in sharpening the financial manager's thinking about pertinent cost considerations in determining cash balance requirements. However, their use as mathematical tools to *determine* in practice an appropriate working cash balance, the "order point," and "investment point" has been limited. The deficiencies arise from the models' failure to recognize the influences of uncertainty, availability of external funds, and compensating balance requirements.

Uncertainty models In an effort to eliminate one of the shortcomings of the type of models discussed above—namely, the assumption of certainty—another type of model goes to the other extreme by assuming complete uncertainty of cash flows. These "stochastic" models assume that the differences between cash inflows and outflows will occur on a random basis.[4] Control theory is used to establish maximum and minimum levels within which the cash balances would be allowed to fluctuate, the amount by which cash would be withdrawn for investment in marketable securities at the maximum point, and the amount of securities to be liquidated to replenish the account at the minimum point.

The shortcoming of this approach is that not all cash flows are uncertain. Rather, as indicated earlier, some are certain, some are almost certain, and others are highly uncertain. Thus, the assumption that differences between cash inflows and outflows will fluctuate in a random fashion does not conform to the facts. Nonetheless, these models again are of value in focusing the attention of financial managers upon the element of uncertainty and thereby contribute toward sound cash management.

Considerable work, along both theoretical and practical lines, is being done on cash management models. This may lead to development of approaches that produce useful models of general application. But at present, the average level of working cash balances to be maintained and the specific points and amounts of withdrawal or replenishment of these balances remain matters of seasoned judgment after recognizing the influences that have been discussed. The major current applications of formal cash management models involve control of individual account balances within networks of bank accounts maintained by large corporations in many different locations for a variety of specific purposes. Many large corporations, the major commercial banks, and some consulting firms have developed highly sophisticated models for this purpose that have proved to be valuable in practice.[5]

[4]This type of model, based upon control theory, was introduced by Merton H. Miller and Daniel Orr in their article, "A Model of the Demand for Money by Firms", *Quarterly Journal of Economics,* August 1966, pp. 413–35

[5]These models generally are proprietary information, but even if they were not, their description in this text would be inappropriate because of their complexity and specific application.

Control of cash flows

Chapter 1 introduced the flow-of-funds concept with a simplified chart (Figure 1–1). Now we shall focus upon working capital aspects of the flow of funds to see how control of cash relates to the working capital management process. Figure 7–2 is a time analysis of the *working capital cycle,* alternatively referred to as the "cash cycle" because it relates to the movement of funds from cash back to cash. Raw materials are purchased and are invoiced (billed) to us on the date of shipment. The materials are received, held in raw materials inventories for a short time, processed into finished goods, and sold. In Figure 7–2, this sequence accounts for a period of 60 days during which the goods, along with the values of labor and overhead costs applied to them in the productive process, are in our inventories. The sale converts inventories into accounts receivable, on an average of 18 days later our customers mail their checks to pay the receivables, and 8 days after that the checks will be collected by our bank, thus becoming "available funds."

The elapsed time between the raw material purchases and finished goods sales multiplied by our average daily purchases will determine our investment in inventories.[6] Similarly, the time our customers take to pay their bills times our daily sales will determine our investment in accounts receiv-

Figure 7–2 The working capital cycle
Time analysis

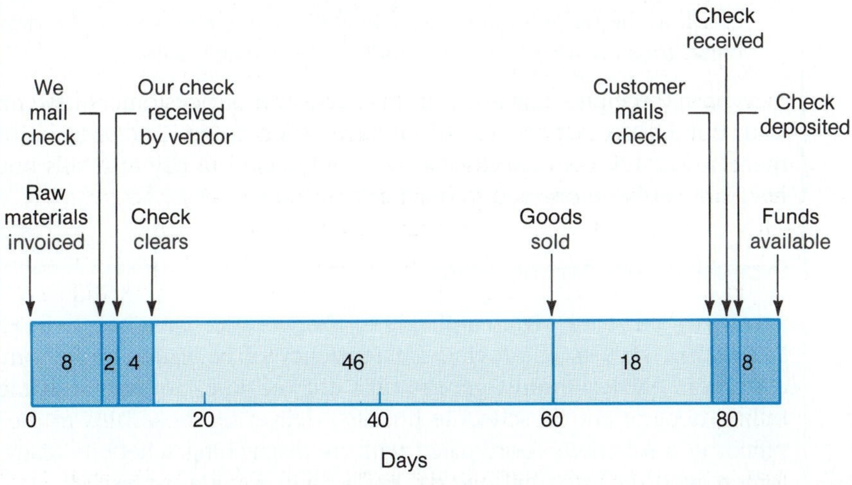

[6]This is not precisely correct as applied to a manufacturing firm because it does not include the labor and overhead costs applied to inventory values. Still, the concept is believed to be of value.

able. The management of accounts receivable and inventories will be treated in the next chapter; at this point we will assume that these assets are managed efficiently. Our concerns regarding the control of cash relate only to the darker shaded areas of Figure 7–2 on each end of the working capital cycle. Initially, 14 days elapse between the date at which purchased raw materials are billed to us and the date on which our check is paid by our bank, thereby reducing our working cash balance. Is there any way we can lengthen this time? At the end of the cycle, eight days elapse between our customers' mailing their checks to us and the checks being collected by our bank, thus becoming available to increase our working cash balance. Is there any way we can reduce this time?

Time is money! Assume we have $1 million average cash flow per day and we can either lengthen the outflow period or reduce the inflow period by one day. If the interest obtainable on marketable securities is 10 percent, we can earn an additional $100,000 per year by so doing. Even one tenth of this would be a very nice raise for our treasurer!

Almost any effort to change these elapsed times will involve changing the "float." *Float* is the amount of funds that have been paid by the drawer of a check but have not yet been collected by the payee's bank. Float may be classified by source into three categories:

1. *Mail float,* which reflects the elapsed time between mailing of a check and its receipt by the payee.
2. *Processing float,* arising from the time lapse between the payee's receiving the check and its deposit in the payee's bank account.
3. *Clearing float,* which reflects the elapsed time between deposit of the check in the payee's bank and collection of that check from the drawer's bank, thus creating available funds in the payee's account.

Incoming (receipts) float arises from checks that our customers have mailed to us but that are not yet available in our bank account. *Outgoing* (disbursements) float refers to checks that we have mailed to pay our bills but that have not yet been charged to our bank account.

Expediting collection of funds

Let us look at the right-hand side of the working capital cycle in Figure 7–2 with a view to improving the efficiency of collecting cash from our customers. First, we must get the bills out on time, not only keeping the billing department on schedule but also delivering those bills to the post office on a schedule coordinated with its dispatching schedule. Many customers who receive a bill one day earlier will pay it a day earlier.

Many firms, particularly those selling to a large number of consumers, such as utility companies, department stores, and oil companies, use cycle-billing procedures to smooth the work load of the billing department. But cycle billing also may be used to attain greater coordination of cash inflows and outflows. For example, if a company's cash outflows are concentrated in the last week of each month, it may bill a larger number of customers in whatever preceding week will result in collection of their payments in the last week of the month. Thus the variation in working cash balances can be reduced.

Concentration banking A large firm doing business over a wide geographical area normally has a large number (perhaps 30, 40 or, in some cases, hundreds) of bank accounts. These accounts are maintained for various purposes, including paying employees and other operating expenses at the firm's plants, conducting transactions in the money markets, and receiving payments from its customers. Here we are concerned only with the latter. The firm usually can improve its control of total working cash balances by collecting its accounts regionally and electronically transfering the fund to one concentration bank, usually located near the corporate offices.

For example, Giant Corporation may have each customer mail payments to the nearest of 15 regional branch sales offices. This considerably reduces the mail float as compared to having all checks mailed to its New York head office.

Each branch office will process the checks and deposit them in a local bank account maintained for that purpose. By handling collections in this way, Giant will reduce the clearing float. If the check is written on a bank located in the same city as the branch office, it can be cleared through the local clearing house that day or the next.[7] Checks that are drawn on banks outside the respective branch-office cities may be cleared either through correspondent banks or through the clearing facilities of the Federal Reserve System.[8] Clearing float is reduced by one or possibly two days through regional collection.

By prearrangement, the regional bank will remit by *wire transfer* to the concentration bank in New York all collected funds in excess of a compensating balance, if any, at the close of each business day.[9] This provides instantaneous availability of funds to Giant for use either to cover checks cleared against it at the concentration bank or to cover its compensating balance requirement. Of course, the regional banks require compensation

[7]A local clearing house is a place where representatives of the local banks meet each day, exchange the checks that are drawn on other member banks of the clearing house association, and settle the balances among each other.

[8]The Federal Reserve System provides clearing facilities for all depository institutions. If the collecting bank and the paying bank are in the same Federal Reserve District (as they almost always would be in this illustration) one-day funds availability is provided. Outside the district, funds are made available in two days.

[9]A wire transfer is an electronic transfer of funds, either over the bank wire network (a system of leased private-line telephone circuits maintained among the larger commercial banks) or the Federal Reserve System's wire network (a service available to all members banks).

for their services in the form of fees for the wire transfers (quite low, $4 or $5 each) and compensating balances or fees based upon activity. If the volume of collections is large, the savings resulting from float reduction may greatly exceed the costs.

Lockbox systems If a firm wishes to take advantage of the float reduction resulting from regional collection but either does not have regional offices or does not want to assume the clerical and bookkeeping functions, it can utilize a lockbox system. Under this arrangement a regional bank maintains a lockbox at the central post office of the city in which it is located, and the firm addresses the envelope furnished with its bill to that lockbox. (If you have an oil company credit card, you probably have noticed the post-office box address on this envelope; the oil company is using a lockbox collection system.) A messenger from the bank collects the mail from the lockbox one or more times a day and takes it to the bank where the collections are recorded. This record is forwarded to the firm's home office by electronic data transmission (or sometimes by mailing the print-outs), and the checks are dispatched in the clearing process.

By prearrangement, collected funds in excess of compensating balances are remitted each day by wire transfer to the firm's concentration bank. Mail and clearing float are reduced, essentially as described in the preceding section, and processing float also may be reduced slightly by the bank's direct pickup and processing of incoming collections. The lockbox bank, of course, is compensated for its services by direct fees and/or compensating balances.

To illustrate the cost-benefit considerations, let us assume that Nation-wide Distributing Company of Cleveland, Ohio, has credit sales of $3,650,000 per year in California. Establishing a lockbox collection system in a San Francisco bank would reduce collection float from five to two days. The San Francisco bank requires a minimum account balance of $10,000 and a service charge of $2,400 per year for handling the collection arrangements. In this case, float would be reduced by $30,000 (3 days × $10,000 per day). Available funds would be increased by $20,000 ($30,000 float reduction less $10,000 minimum balance). If the additional available funds could be invested in marketable securities at 8 percent interest, the interest return would be $1,600 per year. Nation-wide estimates that the San Francisco bank's fee of $2,400 for pickup, clerical, and bookkeeping services would offset $2,000 in expenses it would incur performing these services in its own offices. The net gain per year from establishing the lockbox arrangement would be $1,200 ($1,600 interest less $400 cost differential). Decision: Nation-wide should enter into a lockbox arrangement with the San Francisco bank.

Other collection-expediting arrangements The arrangements described above illustrate only two of several devices for reducing float in collecting accounts receivable. Most large commercial banks, in their role as concentration banks, employ specialists who design banking arrangements to minimize the incoming float of their large commercial customers. Some of these devices are preauthorized checks, depository transfer checks, and even completely automated electronic depository transfer systems. Discussion of these is beyond the scope of this text; your banker can provide much better information than we can.

The trend is clearly in the direction of reducing or eliminating clearing float and considerable reduction of mail and processing float. Electronic funds transfer (EFT) on a mass scale is greatly increasing collection efficiency and soon may practically eliminate float except that connected with processing. In the latter area, electronic data processing (EDP) has greatly reduced this float also. These developments are resulting from both technological progress in the electronics field and pressures on cash management related to high interest rates.

Delaying payment of cash

The other side of cash control is related to the left-hand shaded area of Figure 7–2, the working capital cycle. Here we are concerned with lengthening the period of time between our purchases and the clearing against our bank accounts of checks paying for them. Of course, stalling in paying our bills, that is, stretching our payables, is an obvious way of doing this, but generally not a very wise one. Some firms do it, even on a systematic basis, but they run the risk that in a period of short supply or tight money, their suppliers (creditors) will cut them off. So, for cash management purposes, we shall assume that we pay our bills on time and take cash discounts that are available. (This subject will be discussed in Chapter 9.) We should not pay our bills early. Although credit terms usually relate to the date payment is received by the creditor, some suppliers are quite willing to grant cash discounts (consider payments to be on time) if the postmark date is within the terms. If we learn that this is the case, then mailing the check may be delayed until the close of business on the due date.[10]

Paying on time does not necessarily mean that the date our check will be charged against the bank account is completely inflexible. For this reason we may seek means of increasing the clearing float.

"Playing the float" Our check can be charged against the balance at our bank only after it has been physically transmitted through the bank clearing system. (This will be true only until EFT replaces the clearing system.) Even though the Federal Reserve clearing system guarantees the collecting bank two-day funds availability, that does not mean that our check necessarily will be presented for payment at our bank in two days. Thus, particularly if our

[10]The Internal Revenue Service follows this practice. That is the reason you may see lines at the post office on the evening of April 15.

home office is located in a remote city, drawing our checks upon a bank in that city might increase the clearing time by perhaps several days as compared to drawing them on a major bank in a city having excellent air mail connections. Some firms have even gone so far as to maintain a bank account in a small, remote town for this purpose. It then writes all checks on that account, wire-transferring funds to that bank daily to cover each day's expected clearings.[11] This practice is not recommended, as it antagonizes both suppliers and bankers.

Some firms play the float in a systematic fashion, continually show negative bank balances on their own books while balances on their bank's books are positive. This practice is called "kiting" checks. It is illegal in most states, but if funds are available in the bank account to clear the checks, who is going to file charges?[12] This practice is not recommended on moral and legal grounds, but its widespread use is recognized.

A variation on this theme, particularly in connection with special payroll accounts, is widely used and is considered to be ethical. A company sets up a "zero-balance" account in a bank (often one in which it also maintains a general account) to be used solely for paying its payroll. For example, if the firm has a semimontly payroll of $1,200,000 at a given plant, it could deposit that amount on the morning of the 15th of the month. This would be drawn down over the next week or so to a zero balance as the employees cashed their checks. The original purpose of such an account was to control payroll expenditures.

However, through an analysis of the total amounts cleared against the account each day, the financial manager has learned that withdrawals from this account take place in a regular pattern over an 11-day period. So, rather than depositing the whole $1,200,000 on the 15th, funds are transferred to the account daily to cover only the checks expected to clear against it that day. Thus, $325,000 might be deposited on the 15th, $540,000 on the 16th, $115,000 on the 17th, etc., until a final deposit of $18,000 is made on the 26th to cover the last checks that will clear that day, leaving a zero balance in the account. By utilizing this technique, only a few thousand dollars are ever left in the account overnight and the funds freed are available for use elsewhere. Sometimes arrangements are made under which additional funds will automatically be transferred to this account or overdrafts will be approved if it should ever "run dry."

Payment by draft A draft is an instrument that looks much like a check, but rather than ordering the bank to pay it, the draft is drawn on the issuing

[11] A few years ago one of the major brokerage houses did this, writing all of its checks remitting funds to its New York City customers on a bank located in a small, remote town in California. This practice ceased when some investors threatened lawsuits and the New York Securities Commission ruled that such payments must be made in New York funds.

[12] A friend of the author who is treasurer of a billion-dollar corporation commented on this practice, "If you or I do this in handling our personal accounts, it is 'kiting' and illegal, but if a major corporation does it, it is called 'efficient cash management.' "

firm and names the bank through which it may be collected. When drafts are used to pay bills, the issuing firm transfers funds to the collecting bank only at the close of business on the day that the draft is received through the clearing system and presented for payment. Use of drafts eliminates tying up funds in the bank account while waiting for checks to clear.

Some firms, including AT&T and many insurance companies, by using drafts rather than checks to pay their bills, have greatly reduced their required bank balances. Bankers usually do not like drafts. They charge fees to cover their costs of servicing them and generally discourage their use except in some specialized transactions such as in international trade. But some firms, particularly those with credit so strong that they do not feel the need to maintain large balances with their bankers, find the use of drafts attractive.

The trend toward electronic funds transfer and the resulting "checkless society" are gradually eroding the opportunities to increase efficiency of cash management through increasing payment float.

Marketable securities management

There are three fundamental reasons a firm might maintain a marketable securities portfolio. The first is to temporarily invest excess cash that builds up during the declining period of its seasonal working capital cycle. These funds, according to its cash forecast, will be needed a few months later to replenish declining working cash balances as temporary working capital requirements increase toward the seasonal peak. For example, as a department store increases its cash balances after the Christmas selling season it would invest the excess funds until they are required to cover the increase in inventories for the spring selling season. Or funds required to make future quarterly income tax payments might be temporarily invested until those taxes become due. Marketable securities acquired for such purposes will be liquidated at predictable times in the near future. Such liquid assets are held to satisfy the transactions motive; that is, they will be needed to cover expected future transactions.

The second reason for investing in marketable securities is related to the precautionary motive. Funds so invested are expected to be available to cover unforeseen differences between expected cash flows and those that might occur. In other words, the securities represent a "safety stock" of liquidity to cover the unforeseen. These are the two principal uses of a marketable securities portfolio.

The third reason a firm might invest in marketable securities is simply that cash balances have piled up over a relatively long period of time as cash inflows exceeded operating requirements. These liquid funds usually are expected to be invested internally in operating assets, used to acquire other companies, or paid to stockholders either through dividends or reacquiring some of the outstanding stock. Such funds will be needed in the future, but at unknown dates and for indefinite purposes. Relatively few firms hold marketable securities for this reason.

All three of these motives relate to temporary external investment of excess cash that is expected to be returned to cash in the future for use in accomplishing the firm's objectives. The motives indicated above and this general observation must be kept in mind as we consider the criteria for selection of specific securities to be included in the portfolio.

Criteria for selection of securities

There are three general characteristics of investments: *liquidity, risk,* and *expected return.* Any particular security possesses each of these characteristics to a different degree from another. Marketable securities portfolio management involves, first, determining the degree of each characteristic that best fits the purpose and, second, selecting individual securities that satisfy the appropriate criteria.

Liquidity Liquidity relates to the speed with which a security may be converted to available cash. Convertibility to cash, in turn, depends upon the depth and breadth of the *secondary market* in which outstanding issues of the security are traded. Market *depth* relates to the amount of securities that could be liquidated over a given period of time without materially affecting the price obtained. Thus, if many millions of dollars worth of the securities, say Treasury bills, can be sold at a moment's notice, the depth of that secondary market is great. Conversely, selling a few hundred shares of common stock of a small, closely-held corporation at a reasonable price might require searching for a willing local buyer over a period of perhaps several weeks or months. The secondary market for that security is very shallow.

Breadth of the secondary market refers to how many active buyers and sellers are trading the security. If there are hundreds or thousands of buyers and sellers trading the security every day, the market is broad. At the other end of the spectrum, if the only market for a security, say the bonds of a small town or school district, is one or two local banks or other investors, the market is extremely narrow. Usually the breadth and depth of an over-the-counter market are roughly indicated by the difference between the bid and asked prices and, for a security traded on an organized exchange, by the volume of transactions.

Risk Risk, or more precisely downside risk, is the probability that one might have to sell a security at a lower price than was paid for it. If this should occur, the overall return on the investment would be less than expected or perhaps negative. Although many types of risks could affect investors, we are concerned here particularly with default risk and interest-rate risk, which were introduced in Chapter 6.

Default risk of a debt security relates to the probability that the issuer will fail to meet its obligations to make interest and/or principal payments required by the contract. Default risk ranges from that of U.S. government securities, where it is almost nil as long as monetary mechanisms are available to create money to meet the obligations, through the gamut of corporate and municipal obligations from the highest quality to those that are in default. Default risk is not necessarily synonymous with failure of the issuer. Rather it relates to the perceived probability of failure. Thus, a corporate bond may decline substantially in value in response to a decline in credit worthiness of the issuer, even though actual default does not occur.

Interest-rate risk relates to the probability of fluctuation in market price of a debt security as a result of changes in interest rates during the period that it is held. If the general level of interest rates rises, the market price of an outstanding security will fall so that its yield to maturity will equal that offered by new issues bearing the same default risk and maturing at the same time. The magnitude of decline in price will be a direct function of the time to maturity. (Therefore this risk is sometimes called the "maturity risk".) The closer the maturity, the less the market price fluctuation and the lower will be the interest-rate risk.

Of course, both default and interest-rate risks are two-edged swords. The credit standing of an issuer could improve during the holding period, or market interest rates could decline. Either event would increase the price of the debt security. But here we are concerned mainly with downside risk.

Return An objective in making any investment is to earn a return. Generally, rates of return are inversely related to liquidity and directly related to risk. Efficiency of a market is largely a function of its breadth and depth, which in turn determine liquidity. Therefore one can hardly expect to find a bargain in a marketable security if high liquidity is a prerequisite.

Relation to investment motives Now let us relate the above investment characteristics to the motives for holding marketable securities in order to establish appropriate investment criteria. The motives require that marketable securities may be turned into cash either (1) at a foreseen time in the near future to cover predicted cash needs or (2) at an unforeseen time, to cover uncertain fluctuations in operational cash flows or to seize unpredictable opportunities for internal or external investment. These motives preclude any significant sacrifice of liquidity. Marketable securities are the first line of defense behind the working cash balances required to maintain the firm's liquidity objective of paying its obligations when due.

Not only is liquidity in the marketability sense required, but liquidation must be possible at approximately 100 cents on the dollar. Investment in common stocks or long-term bonds of any issuer, government, municipal or corporate, is ruled out because they are subject to excessive market price fluctuations. In addition, real estate investments and even most short-term municipal securities are eliminated from consideration because their liquidity at full price is impaired by limited marketability. Woe be unto the treasurer who, when notified that so many dollars (or so many millions of dollars) will be needed tomorrow, replies that the market is soft and he or she can produce only a smaller number of dollars, or that it may take several days or weeks to find a buyer of the securities held. There are no excuses! The firm's primary objective relates to its operations, and funds must be available to meet operational objectives. *Rate of return* from temporary investments in marketable securities *is secondary* to the main objectives. Therefore, *liquidity and safety criteria always must predominate,* while greater rates of return are important only when they can be achieved without materially sacrificing these criteria. From a practical standpoint, investments eligible for inclusion in the marketable securities portfolio are limited to money-market instruments.

Investment media

The term *money market* refers collectively to trading in highly liquid, high-quality, short-term debt securities suitable for inclusion in marketable securities portfolios of business firms as well as in secondary reserve portfolios maintained by financial institutions. The term implies very close proximity to cash. Trading in money-market securities is conducted largely by major commercial banks and by securities dealers in New York, such as Goldman Sachs, Salomon Brothers, and Lehman Brothers, Kuhn Loeb. Money-market securities are traded over-the-counter rather than on an organized exchange. Markets are established in terms of bid and asked prices quoted by the major dealers.

Government securities The principal government securities in the money market are U.S. *Treasury bills* (T bills). These bills are auctioned weekly through the Federal Reserve Banks and mature in three months, six months, or one year. They are sold at a discount in denominations from $10,000 to $1 million and are payable at par. The implicit interest rate is determined by the discounted price paid for them. They may be obtained by directly entering the auction at a Federal Reserve Bank or through a commercial bank or securities dealer.

Treasury bills are the premier instrument of the U.S. money market. They offer the highest available liquidity, the lowest interest-rate risk because of their near-term maturity date and, being direct obligations of the U.S. Treasury, a complete absence of default risk. Because the maturity is short and the market so broad and deep (hundreds of millions of dollars worth of them are traded daily), there is virtually no possibility that liquidating them at any time will yield less than the amount paid. Of course, the interest return on T bills is slightly lower than that on other high-quality securities of similar maturity.

Other U.S. Treasury securities that may be suitable for inclusion in marketable securities portfolios are Treasury notes issued with one- to five-year maturities, tax anticipation bills or notes (which are of particular interest because they normally mature one week after income tax payment dates but will be accepted by the IRS at face value for payment of taxes), and U.S. Treasury bonds that originally were issued for longer maturities but currently are within, say, a year of maturity.

Similar, but not of quite as high quality, are federal agency issues, such as debt securities of the Federal Home Loan Banks, Federal National Mortgage Association, Federal Land Banks, or other government-sponsored credit agencies. Although such issues are *not* direct or indirect obligations of the U.S. government, their payment record has been impeccable and their interest rates have been attractively higher than those available on Treasury securities. Of course, only near-term maturities are suitable for marketable securities investment.

Repurchase agreements are instruments whereby a securities dealer sells U.S. Treasury or other high-quality debt securities, agreeing to buy them back at the end of a stipulated short period of time, usually just a few days, at a guaranteed price. The implicit interest is determined by the difference between the selling price and the repurchase price. Such instruments, called "repos," are highly desirable media for marketable securities investment.

Negotiable certificates of deposit Negotiable certificates of deposit (CDs) are issued by commercial banks as transferable receipts for large time deposits. They usually are issued in multiples of $100,000, typically in even millions of dollars, with maturities ranging from 30 days to 18 months. (Do not confuse these instruments with the smaller denomination nonnegotiable CDs issued by banks to individuals. The latter may be redeemed only at substantial interest penalties, and the interest paid on them is regulated by the Federal Reserve.) Large negotiable CDs are regularly traded by the major New York securities dealers. The market, although not as broad as for U.S. Treasury securities, is sufficient to handle many millions of dollars of transactions at relatively narrow bid-asked spreads. Interest rates on highest quality CDs usually are somewhat higher than those on T bills and equal to or slightly higher than the rates available on commercial paper.

Only CDs issured by major banks of unquestioned credit standing, and for which the secondary market is sufficiently broad to absorb one's holdings, should be considered. If this caution is followed, CDs of appropriate maturity to meet portfolio objectives are excellent investment media.

Commercial paper Commercial paper (sometimes called "open-market commercial paper") consists of short-term unsecured notes issued by corporations and payable to bearer at maturity. Some notes are directly placed (that is, sold directly to investors), particularly the paper issued by major finance companies. Others are sold through commercial paper dealers, usually the same firms that deal in secondary markets for other money-market securities. Denominations range from $5,000 to $5 million and maturities from 1 to 270 days. As they are bearer paper, the notes are readily negotiable if the secondary market is sufficiently broad (as it usually will be for high-quality paper of major issuers). Interest rates on prime commercial paper normally are about the same as those on the CDs of major banks. Paper issued by corporations of somewhat lower credit standing may carry slightly higher interest rates.

The same cautions mentioned above in connection with investment in CDs applies to commercial paper. There have been some defaults on commercial paper; undue risks should not be taken. The quality of commercial paper is rated by investment advisory agencies. Many firms limit their portfolios to paper rated in the top or the top two categories.[13]

Other media Other investments in marketable securities might be bankers acceptances, some carefully selected municipal securities, and money-market mutual funds.

Bankers acceptances are short-term debt instruments that usually arise out of international trade transactions. They have short maturities and are backed by the credit of both the importer on whom they are drawn and the accepting bank. Thus they entail very little risk. The volume of bankers acceptances available for purchase is much more limited than for the securities discussed above. Breadth and depth of the market are satisfactory only for acceptances created by major banks. When available and maturities can be correlated with expected funds requirements, they may be excellent investments. Interest rates are usually about the same as those on CDs.

Certain highly selected *municipal securities* might also be considered for inclusion in a marketable securities portfolio. Municipal securities are debt issues of states, counties, cities, school districts, and other governmental bodies below the federal level. Municipal securities are attractive primarily because interest received on them is exempt from federal income taxation. Interest on securities issued by state governments may also be exempt from state income tax for the investor located in that particular state. Of course, the market establishes interest rates on such securities at lower levels than those on taxable securities of similar investment characteristics, largely compensating for the applicable federal corporate income tax rate.

Although municipal securities that qualify under the criteria discussed earlier might be considered for inclusion in the portfolio, the great majority of them do not qualify. Since most municipal securities are of much longer term than would be appropriate for marketable securities investment, the interest-rate risk is too high. Also, many municipals with low default risk—say, those of small, stable midwestern towns or school districts—have such extremely limited marketability as to be ruled out on the liquidity criterion. Many municipal securities having sufficient marketability, such as issues of

[13]Even this precaution is not always adequate. Penn Central's commercial paper held a top rating by one of the advisory agencies the day it filed in bankruptcy. (We all make mistakes.)

large cities, must be eliminated because default risks are far too high. This leaves only a few high-quality, near-maturity issues on which maturity can be correlated with anticipated funds requirements. These may be appropriately included in a marketable securities portfolio. Such issues are hard to find, but a few treasurers find the aftertax interest differential worth the hunt.

Money-market mutual funds are open-end investment companies that sell their shares to investors and, in turn, invest the funds in a diversified portfolio of the money-market instruments discussed above, particularly CDs and commercial paper. Minimum investment in these funds is as low as $1,000, and withdrawals may be made by wire on a few hours notice. The management of such funds usually is compensated by a small fee, ranging from one-quarter to one-half percent of the amount invested.

Although financial managers of large firms would have no interest in these funds, those of small to middle-sized corporations with funds available for temporary investment in marketable securities may find them highly useful. Financial managers of smaller firms usually do not have the time or knowledge to keep informed regarding the money markets on a day-to-day basis and may be investing in smaller amounts than suitable for direct investments in these markets. A well managed money-market mutual fund may provide at least a small differential over the yield available from T bills.

Some multinational firms invest appropriate portions of their excess cash in *Eurodollar deposits*. These are CDs representing deposits of U.S. dollars in foreign banks or foreign branches of U.S. banks. Interest rates may be considerably higher than those on other instruments discussed here, but default risks are also greater because of lack of national or international control over the monetary expansion of Eurodollars. Such firms also invest in money-market securities denominated in foreign currencies such as marks, yen, and Swiss francs. Because of exchange risks, investments in foreign money market securities usually are related to anticipated cash requirements in those currencies. (International financial management will be discussed in Chapter 25.)

Portfolio policy

When the general level of interest rates was relatively low, only financial managers of the largest corporations concerned themselves with aggressive management of marketable securities. Most financial managers simply bought T bills through their banks when excess funds were available and sold them when cash was needed. Differentials in interest yields between T bills and such other money-market instruments as CDs or commercial paper were not worth the time and effort required to keep up with these markets and select the proper securities for inclusion in the portfolio.

Two major changes have taken place in recent years: (1) the general level of interest rates is much higher (largely related to inflation), and (2) the fluctuation in short-term interest rates and differentials sometimes existing between rates on the different types of money-market instruments has become much greater. Because of these changes in the financial environment, policies regarding management of marketable security portfolios have shifted from T bills only to directing much greater efforts toward *managing* the portfolio.

A more aggressive management policy requires that continual attention be given to rapidly changing conditions in the money markets. In a tight market or money crunch, short-term rates will rise rapidly, but rates on different types of securities available will increase at somewhat different rates. Thus, the interest differential between T bills and, say, commercial paper or CDs may increase substantially. This, of course, would call for switching out of T bills and into one of the other investment media. At another time, when the money market is soft and short-term interest rates are declining, these differentials may narrow greatly. This would make it attractive to switch back into T bills.

Table 7–1 compares the interest rates prevailing in the money markets early in December of 1980 and 1981 on selected high-quality short-term securities. In December 1980, when the money market was tightening, the differential of approximately two percentage points between the interest rates obtainable on T bills and CDs probably justified investment in CDs. On the other hand, in December 1981, when interest rates were declining, the negligible differentials among rates available on the various securities probably justified selection of T bills.

The same sort of considerations relate to the particular maturities to be held. When the yield curve is sloping downward, very short maturities are desirable, even though the funds will not be needed at maturity and the

Table 7–1 Interest rate comparison
Selected money market securities (percent)

	Average rates for week ending	
	12/4/81	12/5/80
90-day Treasury bills	10.82%	15.58%
180-day Treasury bills	11.59	15.69
90-day bankers' acceptances	11.25	17.50
90–179-day certificates of deposit*	10.75–11.38	17.25–18.00
90–179-day commercial paper†	11.00–11.25	15.50–17.25
90-day Eurodollar deposits	12.50	18.50

*Corporate money center bank offering rate.
†Directly placed.
Source: Bond Department, Continental Illinois National Bank and Trust Company of Chicago, *Interest Rate Comparisons*, published weekly.

securities must be "rolled over" by investing the proceeds from maturing obligations in similar securities. At another time, when the yield curve has shifted to an upward slope, lengthening the maturity distribution of the portfolio will be called for, even though some of the securities may have to be liquidated in the secondary market rather than held until maturity.

A flexible policy that gives greater attention to management of the marketable securities portfolio relates directly to the observations made in Chapter 6 regarding overall working capital policy. If a firm finds it advantageous to finance a large portion of its temporary working capital requirements at long term, then both the relative magnitude and activity of the marketable securities portfolio justify a more aggressive management policy.

Summary

This chapter dealt with management of a firm's *liquid assets,* cash and marketable securities. The two reasons for holding liquid assets are to facilitate transactions (the transactions motive) and to provide a safety stock of liquidity to cover unforeseen needs (the precautionary motive).

Working *cash* balances are the currency held (minor except in some retail firms) and the balance(s) in bank demand deposit account(s). Four factors influence the working cash balances required. First, they must cover the predictable discrepancies between cash inflows and outflows on a day-to-day, week-to-week basis. Insight regarding the amount required for this purpose may be gained by examining the bank's analysis of daily collected balances. Second, working cash balances should provide a cushion or safety factor to cover unpredictable cash flows that might occur on a day-to-day basis. Third, the availability of external short-term funds will influence the bank balances to be maintained. If a firm is highly dependent upon bank loans to finance operational needs, it must recognize that deposit balances it maintains influence its bank's willingness to make such loans. Fourth (and related to the third factor), compensating balances required by the bank for its servicing of the depository account and credit accommodation must be observed. The working cash balance requirement will then be the higher of that needed for transactions and precautionary purposes or the compensating balance required.

Control of cash flows involves expediting collection and delaying the payment of cash, largely by reducing the incoming float and increasing the outgoing float. The former might be accomplished through concentration banking, lockbox systems, and several other devices to reduce mail, processing, and clearing float. The latter may involve "playing the float" through increasing the time required to clear the firm's checks or by using drafts to pay obligations. Development of electronic funds transfer is gradually eroding the opportunities for such control by eliminating float except that related to processing.

Liquid assets not required for working cash balances may be invested in marketable securities. The reasons for holding marketable securities are (1) to temporarily utilize excess cash inflow during the seasonal decline in working capital until cash is needed to cover net outflows required by subsequent increase in working capital, (2) to cover unpredicted cash requirements exceeding those provided for by precautionary cash balances, and (3) to utilize accumulated funds expected to be needed in the future but at unknown dates and for indefinite uses.

The purposes for which marketable securities are held requires that the portfolio be managed with emphasis upon liquidity and safety, accepting a rate of return commensurate with meeting those criteria. The objective is to be able to liquidate these securities without loss at any time that funds are needed for operational purposes, not to maximize the expected return from such investments. This primary objective limits investment media to high-quality short-term debt securities, such as Treasury bills and other Treasury securities nearing maturity, agency securities with short maturities, negotiable certificates of deposit, commercial paper, repurchase agreements, bankers' acceptances, and other prime money-market instruments.

Questions

1. *a.* What are liquid assets?
   b. Discuss the motives for holding liquid assets.
2. Why might some firms leave sizable balances on deposit with their banks when funds accumulate in the off-season, while others withdraw any excess funds and temporarily invest them in marketable securities?
3. Explain the difference between the bank account balance on a firm's books and the collected or available balance from the bank's viewpoint.
4. What are compensating balances? How do they influence the determination of working cash balance requirements?
5. *a.* What is a cash management model?
   b. What is the basic difference between a "certainty" model and an "uncertainty" model?
   c. What are the practical shortcomings of each in their pure forms?
6. *a.* What is a firm's working capital cycle?
   b. What elements of the working capital cycle relate to cash management?

c. What are the objectives of cash management relative to these elements?

7. a. What is float?
   b. What are the three types or elements of float?
   c. Explain how the trend toward a checkless society is influencing float.

8. How might a firm "play the float"?

9. What are the three basic reasons for investment by a firm in a marketable securities portfolio?

10. a. List in order of priority the criteria for selecting securities to be included in a marketable securities portfolio of a nonfinancial firm.
    b. Explain how this order of priorities relates to the motives for holding a marketable securities portfolio.

11. How do liquidity and risk of a debt security relate to:
    a. The secondary market?
    b. The time to maturity?

12. a. Why are Treasury bills (T bills) the premier instrument of the U.S. money market?
    b. How does this position affect their interest yields compared to other marketable debt securities?

13. Why do federal agency securities usually yield slightly higher interest returns than T bills of similar maturity?

14. a. How do negotiable certificates of deposit differ from the CDs normally available to individuals?
    b. How do these differences affect the suitability of negotiable CDs for inclusion in a firm's marketable securities portfolio?

15. a. What is commercial paper?
    b. Why is high-quality commercial paper suitable for inclusion in a firm's marketable securities portfolio?

Problems

1. The Maclon Company has an inventory turnover of 6 times and receivables turnover of 12 times. All sales are on credit. It purchases inventory in equal amounts daily on 30-day terms, issues checks to vendors 28 days after invoice dates, and experiences an average outgoing (disbursements) float (combined mail, processing, and clearing float) of 8 days. Its clearing float

on checks received from customers averages 3 days. Assuming a 360-day year:

a. What is the elapsed time of its working capital cycle (from collected cash back to available cash)?

b. If Maclon's daily payments are $100,000 and its daily sales $120,000, what are the total funds tied up in working capital at any time?

2. Tastebetter Corporation operates a chain of 300 fast-food restaurants covering a 12-state area. Local restaurant managers have been mailing checks totaling an average of $240,000 daily to the home office in Indianapolis. An average of 2-1/2 days elapses while checks are in the mail, 1-1/2 days while they are being processed in the home office, and 2 days while they are being collected through the bank clearing system. A consultant observes this procedure and recommends that each restaurant manager instruct the local bank to wire transfer receipts to Tastebetter's home office bank, the Indiana National, at 3 P.M. each day.

a. How much money is now tied up in float?

b. What will be the net amount of funds freed for other use if each local bank requires that a minimum compensating balance of $1,000 be maintained at all times after this proposal is adopted?

c. If each bank also charges $5 for each wire transfer, what will be the annual cost (assuming 250 transfers per year from each restaurant, as none can be made on weekends and holidays)?

d. What is the annual percentage cost of the funds freed?

e. If Tastebetter's alternative use of funds would yield 18 percent return (opportunity cost of the funds), what would you, its financial officer, do?

3. Pierre's Parisian Restaurants operates eight restaurants at widely scattered geographic locations. Each manager remits an average of $3,000 daily by check to the home office in Washington, D.C. An average of seven days elapses from the date such checks are issued until Pierre's Washington bank, the Riggs National, collects them. Pierre is considering instructing each restaurant to wire-transfer these remittances daily to the Riggs National Bank in Washington. This would eliminate float related to these remittances.

a. How much money is now tied up in float?

b. What will be the net amount freed if each local bank requires a minimum compensating balance of $1,500 to be maintained at all times after the wire-transfer arrangement is adopted?

c. If each bank charges $5 per wire-transfer, what will be the annual cost (assuming 250 transfers per year for each restaurant)?

d. What is the annual percentage cost of the funds freed?

e. If Pierre's alternative use of funds would yield 18 percent return (opportunity cost), should Pierre's adopt the wire-transfer arrangement?

4. Americo Corporation, located in Detroit, bills its customers and collects all accounts receivable at its home office. Credit sales to customers in the Pacific coast states are $36 million per year. Average elapsed time between the customers' mailing checks to Americo and collection of the checks by its bank, the National Bank of Detroit (NBD) is seven days. The Wells Fargo Bank of San Francisco has offered to set up a lockbox system, collecting checks from Pacific coast customers, electronically transfering the collections daily to NBD and transmitting the record of collections to Americo's computer in the Detroit headquarters. Wells Fargo will require a minimum compensating balance of $30,000 and charge fees of $3,000 per month for this service. Americo's financial officer estimates that clerical and record-keeping costs at the Detroit office will be reduced by $1,200 per month. Elapsed time will be reduced to four days.

a. What will be the net amount of funds freed by this lockbox system? (Use a 360-day year.)

b. What is the net annual cost of the system?

c. What is the net annual percentage cost of the funds freed?

d. If Americo's alternative use of the freed funds is investment in marketable securities to yield 10 percent interest, should the lockbox system be adopted? Why?

e. Would your decision be the same if marketable securities were yielding only 7 percent? Why?

5. Magnum Corporation, headquartered in Chicago, has annual credit sales of $720 million in the United States. It maintains eight regional sales offices. All billings and collections are handled by the Chicago headquarters on a continuous billing system. Magnum is considering a concentration banking system under which collections would be made by the regional sales offices and deposited in their local banks, which would remit daily by wire transfer to the Continental Bank of Chicago, the concentration bank. Magnum estimates that the average elapsed time between customers' mailing checks and funds becoming available to the Continental Bank would be reduced by two days. Compensating balances in the regional banks would be increased by $800,000. Annual service charges and regional office expenses would be $150,000 greater than the office expense reduction in the Chicago headquarters.

a. How much net cash will be freed for other uses if Magnum adopts the concentration banking system? (Use a 360-day year.)

b. What is the net annual percentage cost of the funds freed?

c. If Magnum's alternative use of the funds freed will yield 8 percent, should the concentration banking system be adopted? Why?

6. National Manufacturing Corporation of Philadelphia has always paid its bills by checks drawn upon its principal bank account. A consultant suggests that if it would establish an account in a bank located in a remote town in

the Nevada desert, average clearing time on its checks would be increased by three days. As National issues an average of $1.2 million of checks per day, this tactic appears to be attractive. The Nevada bank would require a minimum compensating balance of $400,000 and charge fees of $280,000 per year for handling the account. National would wire transfer funds from its Philadelphia bank to the Nevada bank daily to cover expected clearings (and maintain the required minimum balance).

a. How much cash would be freed by this arrangement?

b. What would be the annual percentage cost of the funds freed?

c. If National's alternative use of the funds would yield 10 percent, what would be the net rate of return achieved by adoption of this plan?

d. What nonquantifiable factors should be considered in this decision?

e. Should National adopt the consultant's proposal? Why or why not?

7. The Jeffers Company issues 2,000 payroll checks, totaling $2.9 million, at the end of each month. Analysis of the pattern of payment of these checks by Jeffers' bank indicates the following:

Business days after checks are issued	Percent of checks cleared
1	15%
2	32
3	26
4	15
5	8
6	2
>6	2

How would you recommend that Jeffers handle its payroll account?

8. Barlow Corporation issues $500,000 in checks each business day and deducts them from its records of the bank account on the day issued. Its bank clears the checks, on the average, the fifth business day after issue (thus a check issued on Wednesday would clear the following Wednesday). Barlow's $10 million line of credit with its bank requires a compensating balance equal to 10 percent of the line, or $1 million in collected funds. This amount exceeds the balance required for precautionary purposes.

a. If Barlow's collected balance (available funds) currently is $1 million, how much must it deposit daily to maintain this balance? (Assume a stable collection pattern averaging two days of the checks included in Barlow's deposits.)

b. How many dollars of outgoing float does Barlow have at all times?

c. If the bank is to show balances of $1 million on its books, what balance would Barlow show on its record of the bank account?

9. *a.* From the latest available copy of *The Wall Street Journal* (under "Money Rates"), the financial section of a major city newspaper, or

a bank letter such as the Continental Bank's "Interest Rate Comparisons," or the "Weekly Financial Summary" of the Federal Reserve Bank of St. Louis, obtain the current interest rates (yields) on the following 90-day securities: Treasury bills, negotiable certificates of deposit, high-grade commercial paper, and bankers' acceptances.

b. Note the differentials among these rates.

c. If you were a corporate treasurer with $5 million excess funds that are forecasted to be required in 90 days, offhand which type(s) of security would you select? Why? (Note: You would require more detail to select the specific securities.)

Chapter 8
Management of Accounts Receivable and Inventories

The last two chapters assumed that the level of investment in accounts receivable and inventories was appropriate. Now we must deal with the management of these assets, seeking to determine the optimal levels of accounts receivable and inventories and to control the flow of funds through these accounts in an efficient manner.

Unlike cash and marketable securities management, which is the sole responsibility of the financial manager, the management of accounts receivable requires considerable interaction between the sales manager and the financial manager. Sales volume affects the investment in receivables. On the other hand, accounts receivable management policies and actions affect sales volume. Similarly, production and sales requirements influence the levels of inventories that must be carried, and the levels and distribution of inventories have an effect on production and sales volume. Therefore, management of these asset accounts involves a great deal of liaison among the financial, sales, and production managers. Such relationships are not always amicable because the immediate goals of these managers are different. We shall concentrate on the overall goal of the firm, value maximization, as we deal with these subjects.

Accounts receivable management

The management of accounts receivable first requires determination of the firm's policies regarding three variables: (1) the acceptable quality of credit, that is, to whom will we sell on a credit basis, (2) the terms on which we will extend credit to these customers, and (3) the collection methods we will employ if customers do not pay according to these terms. An appropriate credit policy should contribute to maximizing the value of the firm by establishing optimal customer selection standards, terms of sale, and collection policies. Second, we must appraise the credit worthiness of new customers who apply for credit and reappraise from time to time that of existing customers. Third, we must periodically review the aggregate accounts receivable to maintain the desired quality or discover the need for changes in our credit and collection policies.

Credit standards

The tightest credit policy possible would be to require that customers pay "cash on the barrelhead" or take their business elsewhere. In most lines of business, the great majority of them would do the latter. Sales volume would be low, but our credit administration, collection, and bad debt expenses would be nil. A cash-only policy might be highly successful in some lines of business, such as grocery supermarkets or fast-food restaurants, where the customers seem to prefer a low price–no credit package. But it simply would not work in a field such as automobile parts manufacturing, food processing, or steel making.

The point is that a firm markets a package that usually includes not just goods but also a number of services such as promptness of delivery, installation, technical advice, repair service, and *credit.* Since competitive pressures usually require the granting of credit, the question is not whether all sales will be for cash, but rather how liberal the credit-granting policies, terms of sale, and collection policies will be.

At the other extreme, we could grant credit to any customer that placed an order, sell on long terms—say, six months—and allow several months beyond the due date before we really got tough about trying to collect the bill. Such a policy would lead to soaring sales as every "deadbeat" in our trading area would be buying from us. But it would also lead to a horrendous investment in accounts receivable, high collection expenses, and devastating bad debt losses. An appropriate credit policy seeks the optimum level between the two extremes indicated above that will tend to maximize the value of the firm.

Determining acceptable quality standards Visualize the credit worthiness of customers seeking to buy from our firm as falling on a continuum from large prominent firms with highest credit ratings and perfect records of paying their bills to known deadbeats that have established records of default on their obligations and financially are totally unreliable. This continuum is depicted by the line below, with *E* representing the excellent credits and *DB* representing the deadbeats. The question is, "How far should we go from left to right along that line before we say 'no'?" (Or think, if you

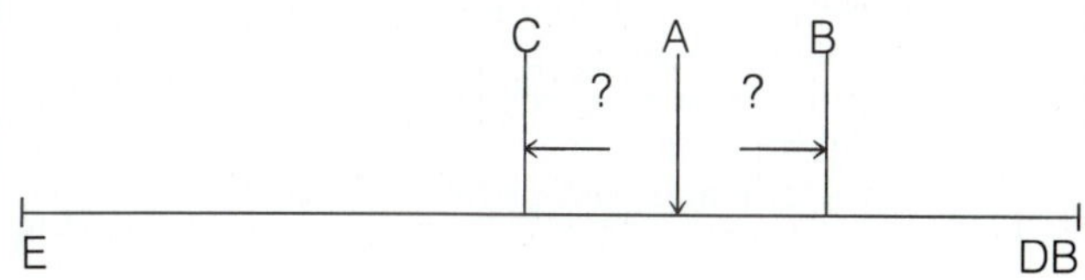

will, of test grades ranging from 100 percent to 0 percent. How low a grade will you consider to be passing?)

Perhaps we are now accepting credits down to point A. Should the credit-granting policy be liberalized by moving on to point B or should it be tightened by pulling back to point C? The answer will depend upon a *marginal* (or *incremental*) *cost-benefit analysis.* We must estimate what would happen if we relaxed our standards, say, from point A to point B. How much would sales increase? How much would costs increase? Would our firm ultimately benefit from the increased volume of business?

Note that we are interested *only* in incremental costs, not total costs. If we are operating below capacity, our fixed costs are irrelevant because they will remain the same. Only the *variable* costs will increase with the increased volume of sales. We must be sure to include, in addition to cost of goods sold and associated incremental operating expenses, the increased costs of credit administration, collection efforts, and bad debt losses that are expected to result from our selling to less creditworthy customers. Subtracting these incremental costs from the incremental revenues will yield the net pretax *change* in profit that would be expected to result from such a policy change.

Next we must question whether or not the expected increase in profits (if there is an increase) justifies the required additional investment in receivables. This involves two factors, the amount of the increased investment and the required rate of return on that investment. If the *expected* rate of return on the additional business created by the change in policy (accepting credits down to point B) is greater than the *required* rate of return on the additional investment, we should so change our policy.

Marginal cost-benefit analysis—Illustration Our sales manager estimates that sales could be increased from their present level of $100 million to $105 million by lowering our quality standards for accepting new accounts (as from point A to point B along the continuum). We will be accepting an additional, or incremental, class of credits that is one notch below our previous cutoff level. Our cost accountants furnish the data contained in Table 8–1, section B, providing a breakdown of operating costs into fixed costs

Table 8–1 Information for a marginal analysis of lowering credit standards

	Fixed	Variable	Total
A. Expected increase in annual sales		$5,000,000	
B. Operating cost data (percent of sales)	Fixed	Variable	Total
Cost of goods sold	—	75.0%	75.0%
Warehousing expenses	2.5%	1.5	4.0
Selling expenses	1.0	2.0	3.0
General and administrative expenses	1.8	.2	2.0
Total	5.3%	78.7%	84.0%
C. Estimated credit department cost increases ($)			
Credit administration		$100,000	
Collections		150,000	
Bad debts		180,000	
Total		$430,000	
D. Estimated turnover—new accounts	6×		
Average collection period—new accounts	60 days		
E. Estimated required rate of return (b/t)—present receivables	22%		
Estimated required rate of return (b/t)—new receivables	25%		

Note: b/t = before taxes.

and variable costs. As we are presently operating at 85 percent of capacity, the added volume can be handled without any increase in fixed costs. Only the *variable costs* (those that would increase directly with increased sales) are meaningful in the marginal (or incremental) analysis we are to make. Excluding credit department costs, the $5 million incremental sales will create additional operating costs of $3,935,000, based on the 78.7 percent variable cost rate.

Then we must estimate the increased credit department costs that would result from accepting this proposal. These estimates are shown in section C of Table 8–1. They include (1) an increase in credit administration costs of $100,000, reflecting largely the addition of credit analysts and increased credit information required to appraise and monitor these lower-quality credits, (2) a $150,000 increase in collection costs associated with the increase in collection efforts required, and (3) an estimated $180,000 of bad debt losses that are expected to be incurred among this additional class of lower-quality credits each year.

Adding estimated marginal credit department costs of $430,000 to $3,935,000 variable operating costs indicates total marginal costs of $4,365,000 as shown in part A of Table 8–2. This yields a marginal profit before taxes of $635,000 on the additional business.

Return on investment Next we must estimate the amount of additional investment attributable to this policy change. The additional accounts receivable will reflect the receivables turnover of the new accounts only. Our

Table 8–2 Marginal analysis of lowering credit standards ($000)

A. Marginal profits		
Marginal sales		$5,000
Marginal operating costs (78.7% × $5,000)	$3,935	
Marginal credit department costs	430	
Total marginal costs		4,365
Net marginal profit (b/t)		$ 635
B. Marginal investment		
Increase in accounts receivable ($5,000 ÷ 6)		$ 833
Marginal investment in operating costs ($833 × 78.7%)		656
Plus credit department expenses invested ($430 ÷ 6)		72
Total marginal investment		$ 728
C. Marginal rate of return (b/t) ($635/728)		87%
D. Required rate of return (b/t) on marginal investment		25%

Note: b/t = before taxes.

present accounts turn over nine times per year. Because of their lower quality, however, we estimate that the new accounts will turn over only six times per year, as indicated in part D of Table 8–1. Expressed another way, we expect the average collection period on these additional accounts to be 60 days, compared to a 40-day collection period on the existing accounts. The $5 million estimated annual sales volume increase divided by the accounts receivable turnover of six times indicates that the balances in these incremental accounts will average about $833.000.

Our investment in incremental receivables balances will be less than $833,000 because the marginal profits included in the receivables will not have required any investment of our funds. To determine the marginal investment associated with operating costs incurred, we multiply the $833,000 by 78.7 percent, the variable (or marginal) operating costs as a percentage of sales. Our investment is $656,000. We should now add the credit department expenses associated with the accounts receivable balances. This would be $430,000 incremental credit department expense per year divided by six, the expected accounts receivable turnover, or $72,000.[1] Thus the marginal investment would be $656,000 plus $72,000, totaling $728,000.[2]

A marginal net profit before taxes of $635,000 on a marginal investment of $728,000 would represent a marginal rate of return (before taxes) of 87 percent per year ($635,000/$728,000) to result from acceptance of the proposed policy change.[3] We then compare this rate of return to the pretax required rate of return on an investment in these lower-quality receivables. Estimating the required rate of return on a particular investment such as this is a rather complicated process that will be dealt with later in Part IV (Chapters 11 through 15). Here we will assume an estimated pretax required rate of return on our present receivables investment at 22 percent. The added receivables will be of poorer quality and our estimates of the credit department costs associated with them were based upon sophisticated guesses rather than actual operating experience. Therefore we estimate the required rate of return on the marginal receivables at 25 percent. The additional 3 percent reflects our estimate of the risk differential between the present and the incremental class of receivables.

[1]We recognize that some of the collection costs and all of the bad debt losses associated with this business would not yet have been incurred on the particular sales associated with the accounts receivable balances at any given time. However as we shall see later, we would have an invalid comparison of expected and required rates of return if we did not include the *normal expectation* of such collection expenses and bad debt losses in the investment figure.

[2]This figure may be determined simply by dividing the total marginal costs, $4,365,000, by the accounts receivable turnover, 6, to yield $728,000. We have calculated it the long way because the detail will be required to demonstrate an alternative method later.

[3]Note that this high rate of return is, to a large degree, a reflection of the high gross margin, 25 percent. If the gross margin were significantly lower, say 15 percent, the expected rate of return would be much lower. Therefore, the gross margin on the product sold to an incremental class of customers may be of great importance in establishing credit standards.

Finally, we compare the 87 percent expected marginal pretax rate of return to the required rate of 25 percent and conclude that the positive differential is quite sufficient to justify our accepting the proposed change in credit standards.

Alternative approach There are two things that might be troublesome about the above analysis. First, although the variable operating costs and the estimated increase in credit administration expenses probably would be fairly reliable, the estimates of additional collection expenses and bad debt losses are highly uncertain, little more than guesses. Second, the inclusion of collection and bad debt expenses in estimating the marginal investment, although theoretically sound, is hard to understand. For these reasons, an alternative approach to the above analysis might be used.

Under this alternative, shown in Table 8–3, only the comparatively solid data are initially incorporated in the cost-benefit analysis. This yields a net pretax marginal profit before taxes of $965,000, as shown in section A, Table 8–3, *before* considering increased collection costs and bad debt expenses.

The marginal investment, again excluding increased collection and bad debt expenses, is calculated to be $673,000, as shown in section B. The $148,000 required pretax return in dollars is calculated in section C as the $673,000 incremental investment multiplied by the 22 percent required rate

Table 8–3 Marginal analysis of lowering credit standards
Alternate method ($000)

A. Marginal profit		
Marginal sales		$5,000
Marginal operating costs (78.7% × $5,000)	$3,935	
Marginal credit administration expense	100	
Total marginal costs		4,035*
Net marginal profit (b/t)		$ 965*
B. Marginal investment		
Increase in accounts receivable ($5,000 ÷ 6)		$ 833
Marginal investment in operating costs ($833 × 78.7%)		656
Plus credit administration expenses invested ($100 ÷ 6)		17
Total marginal investment		$ 673*
C. Required return (b/t) on marginal investment ($673 × 22%†)		$ 148
D. Excess of marginal profit (b/t) over required return (b/t) ($965 − 148)		$ 817*

Note: b/t = before taxes.
*Before consideration of increased collection and bad debt expenses.
†Required rate of return (b/t) on *present* receivables.

of return on present receivables.[4] Subtracting this required return of $148,000 from the net marginal profit estimated at $965,000, we find that the excess marginal profit over required return (both before taxes) is $817,000.

Now we simply ask the question, "Do we believe that the additional annual collection costs and bad debt losses would exceed the $817,000 profit contribution resulting from our taking on the additional marginal accounts? If not, we make a "go" decision; if so, we make a "no-go" decision. Here, as under the initial analysis, it appears that the decision would be "go." If we expect to have a marginal investment of $673,000 in these receivable balances, the accounts could all fail at the end of one year and we would still profit from the incremental business. Of course, if this analysis had yielded an excess return of only $200,000 or $300,000, our decision might be the opposite.

Through the use of marginal cost-benefit analysis, a firm will move in increments toward an optimal credit-granting policy. For example, such analysis might indicate that a loosening to reach point B is advantageous. After that change has been in force for sufficient time to either establish the validity of the estimates or force modification in them, another move further to the right of point B, might be tested. If and when it may be discovered that the policy has become too loose, backtracking will be required. This may be painful in that excessive bad debt losses might be incurred in the process. At any rate, an optimal credit-granting policy may be established in this fashion.

One must realize that the inputs to this type of analysis change through time. For example, when the market for our product is particularly strong, we may reach capacity output and it will be necessary to build a new wing on the plant to increase sales further. At this point the structure of incremental costs changes drastically because the additional costs associated with new plant capacity become incremental costs. This consideration may lead to retracting to a tighter credit-granting policy, cutting off the credit of some marginal customers in order to hold sales volume within currently available capacity to produce.

Terms of sale

Sales may be for cash (cash with order, CWO, or cash on delivery, COD) or on credit terms, such as net payment due 30 days after invoice (n/30). Many credit terms provide a *cash discount* for payment earlier than required at the net payment date. A popular term is 2/10, n/30, providing a 2

[4]We use the required rate of return on *present* receivables here because we are approaching the risk differential of incremental versus present receivables through the collection costs and bad debt losses that could be absorbed, rather than through the required rate of return.

percent cash discount for payment within 10 days of the invoice date, otherwise the full bill is due 30 days after the invoice date. Cash discounts are offered to induce early payment and thus reduce the collection period and the aggregate amount invested in accounts receivable. But, of course, such a reduction is achieved at a cost relating to the percentage of the cash discount and the time differential between the discount date and the final payment date.

Ability to control terms of sale frequently is limited by prevailing customs of the trade. In most lines of business, nearly all suppliers have offered identical terms of sale for many years. For example, drug wholesalers customarily sell to drugstores on terms of 2/10, n/30 EOM (2 percent discount if paid within 10 days of the end of the month of invoice, net due 30 days after the end of that month). Occasionally a firm may deviate from customary stated terms, offering more favorable terms such as a larger cash discount or longer net terms as a competitive weapon to try to increase sales. But this is relatively rare. A more common practice is to deviate from customary terms by informally indicating to customers that it will be all right if their bills are paid, say, 30 days after the final date indicated by the terms printed on the invoice. This usually is done in a buyers' market when sellers are competing vigorously to maintain sales volume.[5] Perhaps more important are changes in collection policies related to differing market conditions that, in effect, alter the real terms of sale.

Appropriate analysis of a contemplated change in terms of sale runs along the same lines as that discussed above relative to credit-granting standards. Analysis of marginal costs, revenues, and investment in receivables yields an expected rate of return. This, in turn, is compared to the required rate of return to reach a decision.

Collection efforts

Collection efforts usually follow a pattern of increasing intensity through time between the point at which a bill becomes overdue and the point at which collection efforts are abandoned and a bad debt loss is recognized. This pattern typically begins with a friendly reminder letter to the effect that perhaps the bill was lost in the mail or through some oversight it has been mislaid. Next comes the inquiry letter, rather politely asking if there is some reason that payment has been delayed and indicating that we hope the goods or services were satisfactory and that we have a pleasant continuing relationship. The gist of the next letter is that "your prompt attention to this matter will be appreciated." The next, and probably last, collection letter

[5]Discriminating in this practice (offering more favorable terms to some customers than to others) is illegal under the Robinson-Patman Act as an unfair trade practice. Enforcement regarding this particular offense, however, is very rare.

might indicate that if the bill is not paid within a stated number of days we shall reluctantly find it necessary to turn the obligation over to a collection agency or our lawyer.

Normally this will be followed by a phone call and/or a personal visit that we might call the confrontation stage. Perhaps at this point the open account will be converted to a promissory note. This (1) provides a document that eliminates argument about the validity of the debt if legal action must be taken, (2) provides for payment of interest, and (3) sometimes reflects an agreement to pay off the debt in definite installments.

As a last resort, if satisfactory arrangements cannot be worked out, the obligation is turned over to a collection agency or to a lawyer. Typically these people first threaten legal action; then, if necessary, they go to court. Legal action is a final resort because (1) the cost is extremely high, often involving a 50–50 split with the lawyer of any collections made, and (2) if the customer is forced into bankruptcy by legal action, the percentage of the obligation recovered probably will be even lower.

Collection policy relates to the time lapse between each of these progressively more severe collection efforts and the general tone of these efforts. Particular care is advised in not getting in any way "nasty" before ascertaining that the customer does not have a just reason for delaying payment, such as defects in the goods or services received or a billing mistake.

Collection policy should be determined through the same type of marginal cost-benefit analysis as recommended in connection with the other credit policy variables. However, the marginal costs are very difficult to estimate because we are concerned not only with costs that are to some degree measurable but also with less predictable costs related to losing the business of antagonized customers. Of course, there comes a time when we have to get tough, recognizing that we are going to lose the customer's future business by so doing. But it is very hard to estimate whether we will also lose business of other customers who pay their bills in a satisfactory manner but may be offended by actions taken against delinquent accounts. For example, we antagonize Joe Smith by aggressive collection tactics; Joe tells his side of the story (we are the villains) to 10 of his friends who are also our customers, they each tell 10 more friends, and we may end up losing a lot of business that had not been contemplated in our analysis. Also, a more direct consideration is that collection efforts are expensive. We must continually guard against spending dollars to recover cents.

Finally, some bad debt losses must be taken. The objective of accounts receivable management clearly is *not* to minimize bad debt losses, but rather to seek optimum policies that will tend to maximize the value of the firm. No credit manager would knowingly approve an individual credit account on which he or she fully expected to incur high collection costs and finally take a bad debt loss. An appropriate credit and collection *policy,* however, incorporates the concept of dealing with *classes of customers* among which will be some individual accounts involving high collection costs and bad debt losses. These costs should be included in the marginal cost-benefit analyses upon which credit and collection policies are based. Extremely low bad debt losses raise a serious question as to whether credit and collection policies have been so tight that the value of the firm is lower than it would be if looser policies resulted in higher bad debt losses.

Appraising the individual credit applicant

In determining credit-granting policy we decided approximately how far along the continuum from excellent credit risks to known deadbeats we were willing to go. If we consider the excellent credit risk to receive a grade of 100 and the deadbeat to receive a grade of 0, we perhaps have decided that we would go down to a 40. Unfortunately, credit applicants do not wear numbers on their backs. We therefore are faced with the job of appraising individual credit applicants and reappraising from time to time our existing credit customers to establish where they fall on this continuum. Is Johnston Hardware a 45 or only a 35? Is Giant Manufacturing a 90 or an 80? Of course, we probably will not use a formal numerical system. In some manner, however, we must make a qualitative appraisal to decide whether or not we will sell to the customer on credit and, if so, what credit limit will be established for that customer. A *credit limit* is a benchmark amount that, if reached, will call for reappraisal and approval or disapproval of shipping the customer additional orders that will create an account receivable balance in excess of the limit.

Sources of credit information Initial information evaluated will be the customer's credit application and our salesperson's comments accompanying it. Credit applications usually are not elaborate, providing only a few background facts regarding the customer, such as location, years in business, previous experience of the principal(s), number of employees, bank of account, and the names of a few trade credit references. Salespersons' comments tend to be notoriously optimistic.

The next step, assuming appraisal of a mercantile (not retail) credit, would be the use of information provided by credit-reporting agencies, such as Dun & Bradstreet, Inc. (D&B). This is the largest mercantile credit-reporting agency, covering several million business firms throughout the United States and Canada. This firm, as well as other specialized credit-reporting agencies, provides services under contract to trade and bank clients. The services include furnishing a periodically updated reference book and individual detailed credit reports. Nearly every credit department subscribes to such services.

The credit rating in the reference book will first be checked and translated to estimated financial strength (equity capital) and credit appraisal using the Key to Ratings reproduced in Figure 8–1. For example, a D&B rating

Figure 8–1 Dun & Bradstreet Key to Ratings

Key to Ratings

ESTIMATED FINANCIAL STRENGTH			COMPOSITE CREDIT APPRAISAL			
			HIGH	GOOD	FAIR	LIMITED
5A	$50,000,000	and over	1	2	3	4
4A	$10,000,000 to	49,999,999	1	2	3	4
3A	1,000,000 to	9,999,999	1	2	3	4
2A	750,000 to	999,999	1	2	3	4
1A	500,000 to	749,999	1	2	3	4
BA	300,000 to	499,999	1	2	3	4
BB	200,000 to	299,999	1	2	3	4
CB	125,000 to	199,999	1	2	3	4
CC	75,000 to	124,999	1	2	3	4
DC	50,000 to	74,999	1	2	3	4
DD	35,000 to	49,999	1	2	3	4
EE	20,000 to	34,999	1	2	3	4
FF	10,000 to	19,999	1	2	3	4
GG	5,000 to	9,999	1	2	3	4
HH	Up to	4,999	1	2	3	4

GENERAL CLASSIFICATION

ESTIMATED FINANCIAL STRENGTH			COMPOSITE CREDIT APPRAISAL		
			GOOD	FAIR	LIMITED
1R	**$125,000**	**and over**	**2**	**3**	**4**
2R	**$50,000 to**	**$124,999**	**2**	**3**	**4**

EXPLANATION
When the designation "**1R**" or "**2R**" appears, followed by a 2, 3 or 4, it is an indication that the Estimated Financial Strength, while not definitely classified, is presumed to be in the range of the ($) figures in the corresponding bracket, and while the Composite Credit Appraisal cannot be judged precisely, it is believed to fall in the general category indicated.

"**INV.**" shown in place of a rating indicates that the report was under investigation at the time of going to press. It has no other significance.

"**FB**" (Foreign Branch). Indicates that the headquarters of this company is located in a foreign country (including Canada). The written report contains the location of the headquarters.

ABSENCE OF RATING, expressed by two hyphens (--), is not to be construed as unfavorable but signifies circumstances difficult to classify within condensed rating symbols. It suggests the advisability of obtaining a report for additional information.

EMPLOYEE RANGE DESIGNATIONS IN REPORTS ON NAMES NOT LISTED IN THE REFERENCE BOOK

Certain businesses do not lend themselves to a Dun & Bradstreet rating and are not listed in the Reference Book. Information on these names, however, continues to be stored and updated in the D&B Business Information File. Reports are available on such businesses and instead of a rating they carry an Employee Range Designation (ER) which is indicative of size in terms of number of employees. No other significance should be attached.

KEY TO EMPLOYEE RANGE DESIGNATIONS

ER 1	1000 or more Employees
ER 2	500 - 999 Employees
ER 3	100 - 499 Employees
ER 4	50 - 99 Employees
ER 5	20 - 49 Employees
ER 6	10 - 19 Employees
ER 7	5 - 9 Employees
ER 8	1 - 4 Employees
ER N	Not Available

of 1A2 indicates estimated equity capital between $500,000 and $749,999 and the credit rating of "good." On the other hand, a rating of HH4 indicates equity capital of less than $5,000 and limited credit worthiness. Credit might be granted to the first customer and probably would be refused to the second on the basis of these ratings.

Up to this point credit applications usually can be handled in a routine fashion at the clerical level. Applicants satisfying certain standards—such as 5 years in business, favorable salespersons' comments, and a D&B letter rating higher than EE with a numerical rating of 1 or 2—will routinely be approved for shipment of initial orders up to $2,000. In any case, if the D&B numerical rating is 4, the customer will be notified that shipment will be made only on a COD basis. If large numbers of credit applicants must be appraised, the principle of management by exception will be applied. Credit requests that appear to fall slightly short of our standard, that is, those considered to be marginal, require individual analysis and judgment by the credit analyst.

Marginal credit applications may justify drawing individual reports, such as that reproduced in Figure 8–2, from the credit agency. A report provides a great deal more information, usually including a recent balance sheet and summary income data, as well as information regarding the customer's banking relationship, history, operatons, law suits, and tax liens. Of particular importance is the trade check indicating the experience of other trade creditors with this prospective customer.

If still undecided or if the credit report is not as up-to-date and thorough as desired, the credit analyst might tap additional sources. These include specialized credit agencies, which cover certain industries in greater depth; reports from the National Credit Interchange System or the National Credit Office (NCO is a subsidiary of D&B); or direct inquiries of other trade suppliers and the customer's bank.

Trade credit analysis Intensive credit analysis is normally performed by trade creditors only with regard to large (or potentially large) accounts, marginal accounts, and those accounts that are in trouble, that is, customers in such financial difficulty that drastic action may be required. Such analysis focuses upon the ability of the customer to generate sufficient cash to pay maturing short-term obligations. Ratio analysis evaluates the current ratio, quick ratio, cash position ratio, and the accounts receivable and inventory turnover ratios. These are integrated to perceive the adequacy of expected cash inflows. If that adequacy is questionable, the debt to net worth ratio (or the debt to equity ratio) becomes important because it provides a measure of the ultimate ability to cover debt obligations if and when liquidity is impaired.

The analyst also is interested in the past record of the customer in paying trade obligations. For an existing account, review of the record of paying our bills is of great importance. Does the customer take discounts, pay on time, or pay late? How late? Has there been a recent tendency to pay slower? What has been the experience of other trade creditors with this account? The trade check in the agency report reveals this information.

Two nonfinancial factors are also important in trade credit analysis. The first is the perceived *character* of the principal(s) of the customer firm. This requires a subjective judgment as to where the individual lies on the

Figure 8–2 A Dun & Bradstreet report

© Dun & Bradstreet, Inc.

This report has been prepared for:

BE SURE NAME, BUSINESS AND ADDRESS MATCH YOUR FILE | ANSWERING INQUIRY | SUBSCRIBER: 008-001042

THIS REPORT MAY NOT BE REPRODUCED IN WHOLE OR IN PART IN ANY MANNER WHATEVER.

CONSOLIDATED REPORT {FULL REVISION}

DUNS: 00-647-3261	DATE PRINTED	SUMMARY
BEAUMONT & HUNT, INC.	OCT 15, 197-	RATING BB1
120 LEMOINE AVE.	DEPARTMENT STORE	STARTED 1956
AUGUSTA, GA. 30901		PAYMENTS DISC-PPT
TEL 404 872-9664	SIC NOS.	SALES $1,600,000
	53 11	WORTH $261,791
DANIEL T. BEAUMONT, PRES.		EMPLOYS 20
		HISTORY CLEAR
		CONDITION STRONG
		TREND UP

SPECIAL EVENTS
09/10/7- Kevin Hunt, Sec/Treas, reported a $3,000 merchandise loss in Sept.8 burglary. Loss is fully insured.

PAYMENTS {Amounts may be rounded to nearest figure in prescribed ranges}

REPORTED	PAYING RECORD	HIGH CREDIT	NOW OWES	PAST DUE	SELLING TERMS	LAST SALE WITHIN
09/7-	Disc	17000	6000	-0-	2 10 30	1 mo.
08/7-	Ppt	6800	300	-0-	30	2 mos.
	Ppt	5000	2500	-0-	30	1 mo.
07/7-	Disc	12000	2500	-0-	30	2-3 mos.
	Ppt	2500	1000	-0-	30	2-3 mos.
	Ppt	1000	-0-	-0-	EOM	2-3 mos.
02/7-	Disc	10000	500	-0-	2 10 30	1 mo.
	Ppt	3000	500	-0-	2 10 30	1 mo.
	Ppt	1500	-0-	-0-	30	2-3 mos.

CHANGES
05/17/7- Subject recently expanded its line of merchandise with the addition of sporting goods.

UPDATE
08/10/7- Aug 10, 197-, Beaumont, Pres. said nine months sales through July 31 were up 10%, profits rising. Concern now employs 20.

FINANCE
02/15/7- Fiscal statement dated October 31, 197-.

Cash	$ 75,000	Accts Pay	$ 140,510
Accts Rec.	110,746	Accruals	48,636
Inventory	285,465	Fed. & other taxes	26,714
Prepaid	1,240		
Current	472,451	Current	215,860
Fixt & Equip	5,200	Capital Stock	50,000
		Retained Earnings	211,791
Total	477,651	Total	477,651

Annual sales $1,600,000; net income $48,000; monthly rent $2,500. Lease expires 198-. Fire insurance on mdse & fixt $300,000. {Above figures from statement provided by Accountant: Fred Mitchell, Augusta, Ga. Prepared from books without audit.}

{CONTINUED}

THIS REPORT, FURNISHED PURSUANT TO CONTRACT FOR THE EXCLUSIVE USE OF THE SUBSCRIBER AS ONE FACTOR TO CONSIDER IN CONNECTION WITH CREDIT, INSURANCE, MARKETING OR OTHER BUSINESS DECISIONS, CONTAINS INFORMATION COMPILED FROM SOURCES WHICH DUN & BRADSTREET, INC. DOES NOT CONTROL AND WHOSE INFORMATION, UNLESS OTHERWISE INDICATED IN THE REPORT, HAS NOT BEEN VERIFIED. IN FURNISHING THIS REPORT, DUN & BRADSTREET, INC. IN NO WAY ASSUMES ANY PART OF THE USER'S BUSINESS RISK, DOES NOT GUARANTEE THE ACCURACY, COMPLETENESS, OR TIMELINESS OF THE INFORMATION PROVIDED, AND SHALL NOT BE LIABLE FOR ANY LOSS OR INJURY WHATEVER RESULTING FROM CONTINGENCIES BEYOND ITS CONTROL OR FROM NEGLIGENCE. 9 R2-25(750320)

Reproduced by permission of Dun & Bradstreet.

continuum between a person of unquestioned integrity and another who has a record of fraud and deceit. The other factor is perception of *economic developments* that will influence the cash-generating ability and eventually, the solvency of credit customers. This is particularly important when the customers are concentrated in a single industry or geographical area. This perception serves as a backcrop to the more formal analysis of the quality of all of the firm's credits. Severe recession in the industry or the locality can cause serious deterioration in the credit worthiness of the customers *en masse,* perhaps with only the strongest and/or most diversified ones surviving.

Appraisal and control of aggregate receivables

Another major responsibility of accounts receivable management is monitoring and controlling the quality of the aggregate accounts receivable.

Ratio analysis Accounts receivable turnover ratios or average collection periods are useful in monitoring receivables, both to identify historical trends and to compare to those of similar firms or industry averages. For example, there is reason for concern if the average collection period of our firm has increased over the past four years from 23 to 25 to 29 to 33 days, while the industry average has remained stable within a 22- to 24-day range and the collection periods of several competitors also have been relatively stable. Perhaps we have consciously been relaxing our credit standards or lengthening our terms of sale on the basis of sound cost-benefit analysis while our competitors have not. But if our credit policy has been unchanged during the period, this trend tells us that the policy has not been followed and remedial administrative action is required.

Aging of receivables To get a more detailed view of what has happened in the receivables account, we may develop an age distribution of the receivables as shown in Table 8–4. The age classifications refer to the number of days elapsed between the invoice date and the present date. In Table 8–4 we compare this age distribution to that of a year ago to note the trends. (This illustration is not intended to be correlated with the collection period data used in illustrating ratio analysis above.) Here we have an indication of great deterioration in the quality of the receivables because 10 percent of them are now greater than 90 days old compared to only 2 percent a year ago.[6] Those invoices over 120 days old must be turning yellow with age! It is highly probable that a large majority of them will be written off as bad debts, and it is somewhat questionable why this has not already been done.

[6]Generally there is an inverse relationship between a receivable's age and its quality. If the credit terms are net 30 days, the receivables in the first age category are not yet due; those in the second are 1 to 30 days overdue; those in the third, 31 to 60 days overdue. The longer the receivable is overdue, the greater the probability that the obligation will not be paid and a bad debt loss will be suffered. This generalization usually is valid with reference to a trend comparison such as this one. However, it is not always valid when applied to comparison of two or more firms whose customers have different paying habits. For example, the U.S. government usually is very slow in paying its bills. This does not indicate high probability that the bills will not be paid, but merely reflects the bureaucratic red tape between the invoice date and the mailing of the check paying the bill.

Table 8–4 Aging of receivables

Age	Amount ($000) Year ago	Amount ($000) Now	Percentage Year ago	Percentage Now
1–30 days	$23,000	$22,500	80%	75%
31–60 days	3,450	3,000	12	10
61–90 days	1,725	1,500	6	5
91–120 days	288	600	1	2
>120 days	287	2,400	1	8
	$28,750	$30,000	100%	100%

Credit rating classification analysis Another method of appraising the quality of aggregate receivables is to classify the account balances according to agency credit ratings (see Figure 8–1 for D&B ratings). Table 8–5 shows a distribution of account balances classified by D&B credit appraisal ratings for the present date and one year previously. It discloses significant deterioration in the quality of receivables. Accounts in the lowest category increased from 1 to 8 percent of total receivables, and those in the top two categories declined from 90 to 83 percent. This, along with the indication of deterioration shown by the aging (Table 8–4), indicates serious decline in the quality of receivables. If no change in credit policy has been made during the year, this deterioration probably would call for the resignation of the credit manager, refusal to ship additional orders to the long overdue customers that are rated "limited", and strenuous efforts to collect the long-overdue receivables.

Table 8–5 Composition of accounts receivable balances by D&B credit appraisal ratings

D&B credit appraisal rating	Amount ($000) Year ago	Amount ($000) Now	Percentage Year ago	Percentage Now
High	$14,375	$13,500	50%	45%
Good	11,500	11,100	40	37
Fair	2,587	3,000	9	10
Limited	288	2,400	1	8
	$28,750	$30,000	100%	100%

Computer applications

The computer has proved useful in handling many of the routine tasks related to accounts receivable management. First, accounts receivable records are put on the computer. Then, by programming the time lapses between routine stages of the collection process, the computer often is utilized to send out appropriate collection letters and to notify the credit person in charge of the account when personal analysis and collection efforts are required. With all detail of each account stored in the computer, appropriate programming will produce the aging of the receivables as was shown in Table 8–4. By also storing with each account the credit agency rating, the composition of accounts receivable distributed by such ratings can be run off at any time. These analyses are useful in appraising the aggregate receivables for control purposes.

Although a good deal of experimentation has taken place, statistical methods utilizing the computer have not been particularly successful in developing credit quality standards, selecting credit applicants, or setting credit limits of mercantile firms. The initial screening of credit applications into thoroughly acceptable or unacceptable categories usually is so simple that assistance of the computer is not required. In analyzing the marginal applications, the factors to be considered and the weights to be given them vary so widely that personal attention of the credit person is required.

The above observations, however, do not apply to the field of retail credit, such as bank credit cards, consumer intallment loans, and the charge accounts of large retailers. Here large numbers of relatively small accounts make it possible to utilize discriminate analysis to identify the pertinent relationships between data supplied on the credit application form and good or bad experience with accounts. By utilizing the computer to run such analyses, firms granting retail credit on a large scale have developed *credit scoring systems* under which, say, having a telephone will be scored one point, owning one's home will get three points, each three years living at the present address will get a point, number of years employed by present and preceding employer will be converted into points, and so on. Then the minimum standard for acceptance of the account and credit limits applicable to it will be established on the basis of given numbers of points.

Because of the large number of accounts, changes in standards may be tested on a sample basis without seriously affecting the quality of the aggregate receivables. It is possible that this type of credit-scoring system might be applied by some very large manufacturers or wholesalers, but the great majority of them cannot successfully utilize such systems because their customers are neither large enough in number nor sufficiently homogeneous for a scoring system to work out in practice.

Inventory management

Unlike accounts receivable management, inventory management usually is not the financial manager's direct responsibility. In a manufacturing firm, inventory management typically will be the responsibility of the production vice president, with purchasing and finished goods inventory management delegated to managers responsible to that officer. In a marketing concern, such as a wholesaler or a retailer, inventories are of such importance that their management may be directly controlled by the chief operating officer or perhaps delegated to the merchandising executive. Whether one is directly engaged in production, marketing, or finance, he or she must understand inventory management. This is an area where the financial officer may have a good deal of input by working in an indirect fashion to influence the policies and decisions of other people on the management team.

Management perspective of inventory

Inventory is an investment in the sense that it is an asset that utilizes funds. If it were not held, funds could be invested in other assets of the business or those funds would not be required to be invested in the business at all. Thus the dollars invested in inventories must be justified in relation to the overall value maximization goal of the firm. This requires that the inventory investment earn its required rate of return or, in other words, that it be justified in terms of cost-benefit tradeoff. Before dealing with the economic justification of inventories, we must understand the functions and types of inventories and the inherent conflicts related to the differences in viewpoints of the various functional executives concerned with inventories.

Functions and types of inventory The basic economic function of inventory is to *uncouple* the stages of production and distribution between the acquisition of raw materials and sale to the ultimate consumer. In theory, if these functions were concurrent in both time and space, no inventory would be required. About the only business we can think of where this is true is that of a market gardener who sells the daily harvest of fruits and vegetables from a roadside stand on the premises.

In a more complex firm—say, a manufacturer of electrical appliances—thousands of raw materials, ranging from nuts and bolts to electric motors and sheets or rolls of steel, must be purchased from geographically scattered suppliers, transported to a plant, and held in raw materials inventories. These are processed into various components and subassemblies that are later brought together for final assembly and held in finished goods inventories at the plant warehouse until transported to various regional distribution warehouses. Finally, the products are sold to wholesalers or retailers. Inventories, both stationary and in transit, at all of these various stages must be carried to facilitate production and distribution. They uncouple each stage from the next one. If efficiently controlled, the investment in inventory at each stage will earn its keep by providing the time and place utility necessary for efficient production and distribution.

The accounting process normally classifies three types of inventories: raw materials, work in process, and finished goods. *Raw materials inventories* uncouple the purchasing and production functions. By investing in such inventories, the firm provides for purchasing in economic quantities, such as carload lots, transporting the goods to the plant, and having them available in sufficient quantities to be put into production at the required time. *Work in process inventories* include all costs transferred to the production process for products that have not been transferred to the finished goods warehouse. Their value includes the cost of not only the transferred raw materials but also the labor and overhead applied in the production process. These inventories uncouple each of the segments of the production process, thereby making possible economic production runs of the various components and subassemblies prior to their final assembly. They also protect against production stoppages that might otherwise result from delays in any of the steps of the production process.

Finished goods inventories uncouple the production and sales functions by making the shipment of products to customers independent of the rate of production. In the case of firms with national distribution of their products, these inventories usually also provide more rapid delivery to customers by transportation to and storage of finished goods inventories in regional distribution warehouses.

The magnitude and fluctuation of inventories vary greatly depending on the nature of the business. For example, a canning company will build up very large finished goods inventories as the seasonally harvested fruits and vegetables are rapidly processed in late summer. Inventories will then be sold throughout the ensuing year. A bathing suit manufacturer, by contrast, may produce at a relatively level rate, gradually building up a large inventory prior to the spring selling season when the inventory is rapidly depleted. A manufacturer of large aircraft or heavy machinery would have large work in process inventories but practically no finished goods inventories because it manufacturers to order and ships immediately upon completion and final testing of the product.

Conflicting viewpoints regarding inventory levels The purchasing agent, the production officer, the sales manager, and the financial manager all have legitimate interests in the levels of inventories. Although each may be well aware of and committed to the overall value maximization goal of the firm, each is a little biased in viewpoint on the levels of inventories to be maintained. Such biases relate to their immediate and direct concerns, goals, bases of remuneration, and methods of ingrafiating themselves with their superiors. The conflicts in these views result from the fact that the operational managers lean toward higher levels of raw materials, work in process, and finished goods inventories, while the financial manager, may lean toward lower levels.

The direct responsibility of the *purchasing agent* to the production officer is oriented toward (1) buying raw materials that comply with established specifications and quality standards at the lowest possible prices and (2) always having them available in sufficient quantities to meet the requirements of production. The temptation of quantity discounts and "special deals" on multiple orders or advance purchases may induce the purchasing agent to buy larger than economic quantities or to buy earlier than necessary, thus increasing the level of raw materials inventories. The bane of a purchasing agent's existence is to be called upon the carpet by the production manager because being out of stock on an item has caused a work stoppage. This not only damages the purchasing agent's record but also may require frantic expediting efforts to obtain the item. The net of all of this is that the purchasing agent's life may be a lot more pleasant if he or she edges up a little on order quantities and safety stocks, which translates to carrying higher raw material inventories than economically required.

The *production officer* naturally seeks to minimize work stoppages at any stage of production, to produce components and subassemblies in long production runs, and to maintain employment and production in the plant as nearly level as possible. All of these tend to minimize production costs for which he or she is responsible. These considerations also tend to increase all inventories, especially the work in process inventories, to higher levels than might be fully justified by economic considerations.

The *sales manager* seeks to maximize sales volume. To lose sales and perhaps to jeopardize customer relations because the finished goods warehouse is out of stock on items for which orders have been obtained is onerous. Thus, the sales manager would like to have all models of all products maintained in stock by all regional warehouses to fill any orders the sales force might obtain. This, however, might lead to the carrying of finished goods inventories at uneconomically high levels.

The *financial manager* should, in theory, focus directly upon the effect of inventory levels upon the value of the stockholders' investment and thereby fulfill the watchdog function of seeing to it that inventories at all levels are economically justified. This, however, may be asking the financial officer to be completely objective when he or she may be under pressures which prevent this. The financial officer is immediately responsible for providing that funds are available to finance the investment in inventories. The dearth of funds may at times induce the financial manager to lean in the direction of reducing inventories to lower than economically justified levels. In short, we are all human!

Inventory management and control techniques

The techniques of management science (operations research) have been applied with great sophistication to the problems of inventory management and control. This is an area in which computerized models (with adequate safeguards providing for human override) have been successful in practical use. Courses in inventory management and numerous textbooks in the management science and production management fields treat this subject in far greater detail than would be possible or appropriate here, so we shall limit our discussion of techniques to establishing the fundamentals of determining economic order quantities, order points, and safety stocks.[7]

Economic order quantity model The economic order quantity (EOQ) model establishes the fundamental concepts upon which most inventory management and control models are based. This model establishes the economic order quantity and average inventory of a particular item under specified idealized assumptions. These assumptions are:

(1) Usage of the item is constant, known with certainty, and independent of the level of inventory,
(2) The carrying costs per unit of inventory per unit of time are constant and known with certainty,
(3) Ordering costs are constant regardless of size of order and are known with certainty,
(4) Orders are filled and delivered instantly.

These assumptions may seem both unrealistic and overly restrictive. They are, but they are necessary at this point to establish some basic concepts. Assumptions will later be relaxed to approximate reality.

Ordering costs are those costs that directly relate to the procurement of an order or batch of inventory. For raw materials, this would include the clerical and communication costs of placing an order and costs of receiving, unpacking, and checking the goods when received. In a manufacturing operation, ordering costs for work in process and finished goods inventories are incurred in scheduling a production run, changing tools and dies, and adjusting machinery to produce a batch of components or finished products. Thus, the ordering costs for different items and types of inventory will vary widely. Only trifling costs may be associated with some raw material purchases, while very high costs may be related to a production run of some work in process inventory components or producing a batch of finished goods inventories.

Carrying costs include the costs of storing, handling, and insuring inventories; spoilage and obsolescence while goods are held in inventories; and the required rate of return on investment in inventories.[8]

[7]For further information, see Richard I. Levin and Charles A. Kirkpatrick, *Quantitative Approaches to Management,* 3d ed. (New York: McGraw-Hill, 1975), chaps. 7 and 8; Lawrence Lapin, *Management Science for Business Decisions* (New York: Harcourt Brace Jovanovich, 1980), chap. 11; or David R. Anderson, Dennis J. Sweeney, and Thomas A. Williams, *An Introduction to Management Science,* 2d ed. (St. Paul, Minn.: West Publishing, 1979), chaps. 12 and 13.

[8]In quantifying the latter items, one must avoid double counting. If the *risks* associated with spoilage and obsolescence are considered in estimating the required rate of return on investment, then spoilage and obsolescence should not be included as separate costs. But if the estimated spoilage and obsolescence losses are included in carrying costs, then the required rate of return on investment should not include recognition of those risks and therefore should be lower.

The general nature of these costs and the logic behind the EOQ model is shown in Figure 8–3. As the order size increases, ordering costs per unit decline as a curvilinear function because these costs per order are assumed to be constant regardless of size of the order. Carrying costs increase as a linear function of order size because they relate to the size and value of inventories carried, which in turn vary directly with order size. Therefore, the total inventory cost curve will be U-shaped. The optimal or *economic order quantity* is that which will minimize total inventory costs. It will be at the point on the horizontal axis directly beneath the lowest point of the total cost curve.

Figure 8–3 Inventory costs

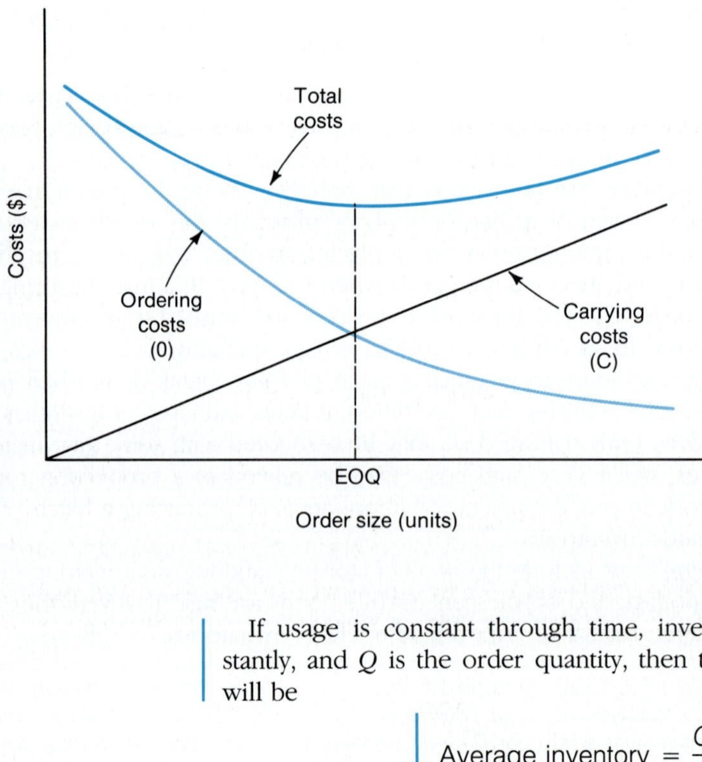

If usage is constant through time, inventories can be replenished instantly, and Q is the order quantity, then the average inventory (in units) will be

$$\text{Average inventory} = \frac{Q}{2} \qquad (8\text{–}1)$$

This relationship is expressed graphically in Figure 8–4.

The EOQ model is developed as follows: Let Q = order quantity (in units); O = ordering cost per order; C = carrying cost per unit per period; and S = total usage (in units) over the planning period. Ordering costs equal the ordering cost per order *(O)* times the number of orders. If total

Figure 8–4 Inventory cycles

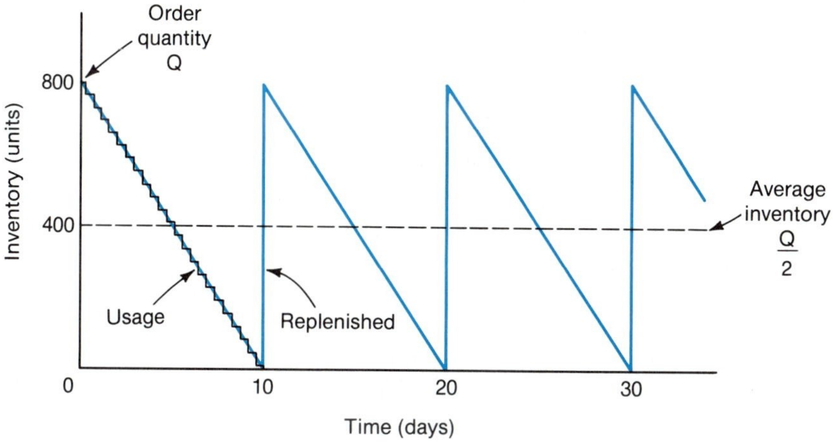

usage over the planning period is S and the order quantity is Q, then S/Q will be the number of orders over the planning period. Therefore,

$$\text{Total ordering costs} = \left(\frac{S}{Q}\right)O \tag{8–2}$$

Carrying costs will be the average inventory times the carrying cost per unit per period, or

$$\text{Total carrying costs} = \left(\frac{Q}{2}\right)C \tag{8–3}$$

Therefore, total costs become

$$\text{Total costs} = \left(\frac{Q}{2}\right)C + \left(\frac{S}{Q}\right)O \tag{8–4}$$

From this equation (8–4), we can obtain the economic (optimal) order quantity, Q^*, by finding the point at which the slope of the total cost curve is zero:[9]

$$Q^* = \sqrt{\frac{2SO}{C}} \tag{8–5}$$

Q^* is the economic order quantity (EOQ). In manufacturing operations it is also known as the economic lot size.

[9]This requires use of the calculus. If you are familiar with it you can derive the EOQ formula by setting the first derivative of total costs with respect to Q equal to zero. Solving this will yield the minimum point on the total cost curve.

For example, assume that ordering costs per order *(O)* is \$40, carrying costs per unit per period of 100 days *(C)* is \$1, and usage over that period *(S)* is 8,000 units. Then the economic order quantity is

$$Q^* = \sqrt{\frac{2(8{,}000)(\$40)}{\$1}} = \sqrt{640{,}000} = 800 \text{ units}$$

With an order quantity of 800 units, orders would be placed every ten days to fulfill the usage requirement of 8,000 units over the 100-day planning period. Average inventory would be 400 units (800/2).

If the firm were to double its usage of this item to 16,000 units each 100 days, the order quantity would be increased to 1,131 units and the average inventory to approximately 566 units. This is an increase of only 41.4 percent, illustrating economies of scale as they apply to inventories. This results, of course, from the square root in the model ($\sqrt{2} = 1.414$).

This model assumes that the price per unit is the same regardless of the quantity ordered. In many cases when raw materials are purchased, quantity discounts are available, such as a lower price when orders are placed for carload lots than for less-than-carload lots. In such situations, the EOQ model serves as the basic framework but is modified to incorporate the quantity discounts, resulting in steps in the cost curves. These modifications are beyond the scope of this text.

Order points and safety stocks In developing the EOQ model above, we assumed instantaneous delivery of orders. Thus orders were placed and delivered simultaneously when stocks were depleted to zero. In practice this would be possible only if your supplier were across the street and an extremely fast worker. Now let us assume that five days are required between the time that an order is placed and the time that the goods are available for our use. This lead time, with reference to raw materials, covers communication of the order to the supplier, filling that order, and delivery of the goods to our warehouse. With reference to components in work in process inventories or to finished goods, such lead time covers planning the production run, setup time, the production period, and transit time to where the goods are needed.

At this point we shall assume that the lead time is known with certainty. We must place the order when inventory of the item is depleted to a five-day supply if the goods are to become available when the inventory is reduced to zero. Thus, in our illustration the *order point* will be 400 units, which is a five-day supply at our assumed steady usage rate, as illustrated in Figure 8–5. When the inventory level of 400 units is reached, an order for 800 units, the EOQ, will be placed. Five days later, when the inventory is depleted to zero, the shipment of goods replenishing the inventory to the 800-unit level will arrive.

But we are still assuming certainty while we live in a world of uncertainty. First, the time lapse, assumed to be five days, between placing the order

Figure 8–5 Order point with certain lead time

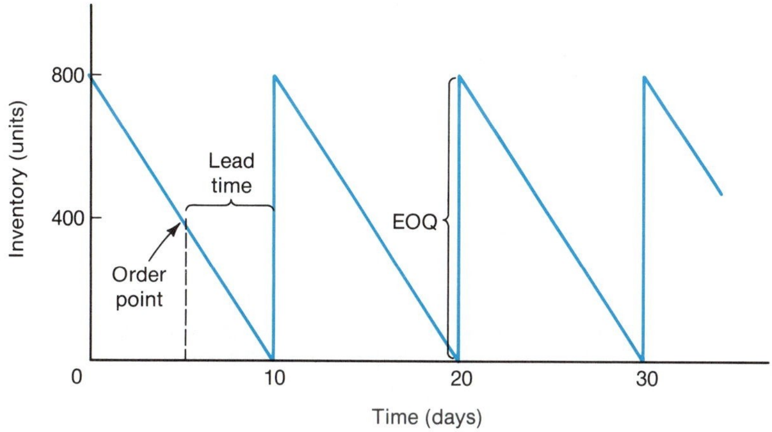

and receipt of the goods is uncertain. If everything connects perfectly, we might receive the goods in only three or four days. If the supplier is temporarily out of stock, the freight car transporting the goods is routed the long way, or any of a number of adverse things happen, we may not receive the goods until a week or 10 days later. Second, we assumed a steady usage rate, but rarely will it be steady. Rather, on some occasions it may be greater than forecasted and on others it will be less.

To protect ourselves regarding these contingencies we will establish a safety stock. This *safety stock* is simply a given amount of inventory in excess of that required by the EOQ formula. The additional inventory provides a cushion to cover perceived uncertainties related to both lead time on orders and rates of usage. Maintenance of a safety stock requires that the order point based upon expected lead time be increased by the amount of the safety stock. The order quantity remains the same. This is illustrated by Figure 8–6, where the order point, formerly 400 units, has been increased to 800 units to provide a safety stock of 400 units.

Uneven usage rates are also shown in Figure 8–6. During the first inventory cycle usage was slightly less than planned, and the order was received slightly early, therefore the replenishing order was received before the safety stock level had been reached. During the second cycle usage was greater than planned and the safety stock was depleted to less than 200 units. This illustrates one use for which the safety stock was intended. In the third cycle, although usage was below the forecasted rate, the safety stock was depleted by about 200 units because shipment of the order was delayed. This illustrates the other function of the safety stock.

Establishing the appropriate safety stock is a complex matter and one to which the solution is not always satisfactory. After all, it is hard to be certain when dealing with uncertainty. In essence, safety stock determination re-

Figure 8–6 Order point with safety stock

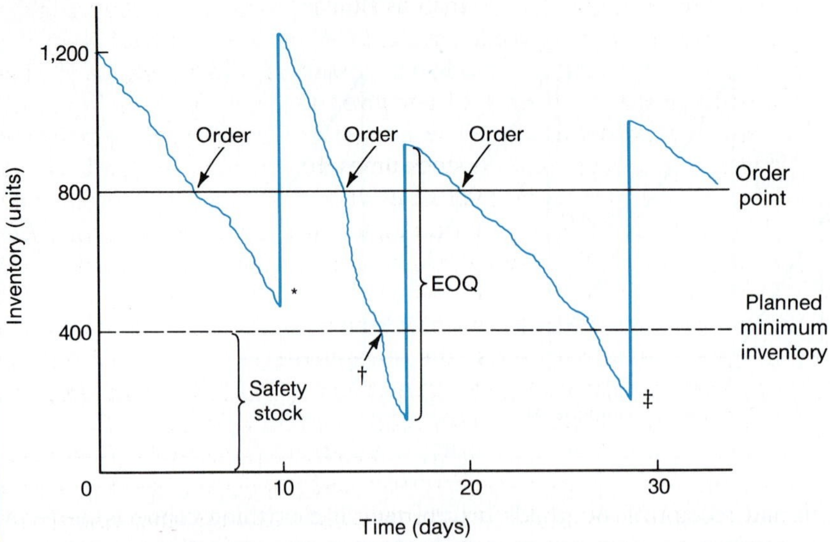

*Order received in four days and usage slightly less than planned.
†Usage this cycle greater than anticipated.
‡Order received in eight days.

quires an attempt to establish the optimal trade-off between the carrying costs of additional inventories and the costs of stockouts. The lower the safety stocks, the lower will be the incremental carrying costs. But the higher will be the probability of stockouts. Rarely if ever are safety stocks established so high that they will completely eliminate stockouts. Rather, they are established to reduce the costs of stockouts to a level equal to the cost of maintaining inventories to prevent them.

The cost of stockouts is the sum of direct out-of-pocket costs and opportunity costs. These relate to such things as work stoppages, production slowdowns, lost sales, and impaired customer relations which may affect future sales. Probabilities of stockouts at different safety stock levels may be fairly reliably estimated through studies of past records of their actual occurrence and those that would have occurred at various safety stock levels. Likewise the direct costs of work stoppages and production delays can be fairly well established. The opportunity costs of lost sales in the past may be estimated by analysis of orders that have been back-ordered and subsequently cancelled. But the indirect costs, such as those related to employee morale in the case of work stoppages or production delays and the future sales that may be lost due to impaired customer relations resulting from stockouts, are extremely difficult to quantify.

If the relevant incremental (marginal) costs can be established with sufficient confidence, then consideration of an additional increment of safety stocks may be viewed as an incremental cost-benefit problem to see whether the incremental net revenues (or savings) justify the additional investment by employing an analysis similar to that demonstrated in connection with establishing credit standards in Tables 8–1 through 8–3.

Optimal investment in inventories Assuming steady usage and sales, the average inventory in units of any given item will be the safety stock plus one-half the order quantity. The average investment in that item of inventory will be the average units in stock times the cost per unit. If a large number of items are carried in inventories and these items are ordered (or produced) at randomly different times, the total investment in inventories will be a function of the safety stocks and order quantities of the various items. Determination of economic (optimal) order quantities and optimal safety stocks of the individual items of inventory results in the *optimal investment* in total inventories. Thus, the value-maximization goal of the firm is achieved through inventory management utilizing economic order quantities and order points based upon optimum safety stocks.

Problems with inventory models In addition to the problems in estimating indirect costs of stockouts, more general problems encountered in using inventory control models are related to inflation and other changes in market conditions. If prices are increasing rapidly, these increases require such frequent changes in both ordering costs and carrying costs that modifications required in the input to the EOQ model may be almost impossible to keep up with. If the EOQs are not based upon current costs, they are no longer optimal. If the inventory consists of several thousand items and many of these costs change every few days, modification may become an impossible task.

Other market changes, particularly those involving shortages of supply of many items, require that orders initiated by the computer executing the order points be overridden. Orders must be manually initiated by the buyers who are keeping abreast of which suppliers are able to ship on order and how much additional delay in receiving shipments must be anticipated. Under such conditions, a well-conceived computerized inventory control system, which functions efficiently in normal markets, may have to be overridden frequently or, at the extreme, shut down entirely.

This simply means that managers must continually be aware that management systems may become inadequate under abnormal market conditions and, when these arise, the system must either be adjusted rapidly to the new conditions or be abandoned in favor of perhaps less sophisticated but more practical human judgement.[10]

[10]An officer of a regional housewares and small appliance wholesaler who had developed a highly sophisticated computerized inventory control system to handle his firm's many thousands of items of inventory informed the author that, during the period of rapid inflation and market shortages created by the oil embargo of 1973, it had become necessary for his buyers to override over 60 percent of the orders generated by the previously smooth-functioning system. This reflected an unusual market condition, but it illustrates the problems discussed.

Finally, a major problem of inventory control that is not directly related to the use of models is a function of erroneous sales forecasts or failure to adjust forecasts to changes in the market for the firm's product(s). When a firm gets into financial difficulty because of excessive inventories, this usually is the result of buying and producing on the basis of a sales forecast that is grossly optimistic. The result is an excessive finished goods inventory that is a glut on the market. Such an error ties up funds in inventories, seriously affecting liquidity because cash is not replenished as rapidly as forecasted. The ensuing liquidity crisis may then force liquidation of excess inventory under unfavorable market conditions, resulting in large losses and sometimes failure of the firm or loss of control by its management.

Summary

Efficient management of accounts receivable and inventories requires establishing policies and procedures that tend to optimize the investment in these accounts by allowing each to expand up to the point that the marginal expected return on investment is equal to the required rate of return.

Management of accounts receivable first requires the determination of policies regarding three variables: (1) the acceptable quality of credit, (2) the credit terms of sale, and (3) the collection procedures that will be used. In each of these considerations, we seek optimal policies by utilizing marginal (incremental) analysis of a proposed change. Marginal costs are subtracted from marginal revenues to yield expected marginal profits. These profits are then divided by the marginal investment to indicate the expected rate of return. The policy decision is then based upon comparison of the expected rate of return to that required by investors. If the comparison is favorable, adoption of the policy would tend to optimize the level of receivables.

The credit worthiness of individual customers must be appraised to determine whether they meet the established credit standards and to establish credit limits. Such appraisal focuses primarily on cash-generating ability and secondarily on solvency.

Finally, the aggregate accounts receivable must be appraised periodically to identify deterioration in quality or deviation from established credit standards. Various techniques—including ratio analysis, aging of receivables, and credit rating classification analysis—are used in this appraisal.

Inventory is a financial concern because it represents an investment that must be justified under the value-maximization criterion. But its management is the direct responsibility of other executives who may view inventory levels differently from the financial manager.

The function of inventory is to uncouple purchasing, production, and sales activities to make possible the performance of these functions independently in an economic fashion. Inventory theory and techniques of control have been developed largley by management science and production people. Their goal is to establish for each item of inventory an optimal order quantity, safety stock, order point, and average level. These will accomplish the goal of value maximization.

The economic order quantity (EOQ) model establishes the optimal order quantity and thus the average inventory by minimizing the total of order costs and carrying costs under idealized assumptions. Optimal safety stocks are then sought to provide protection against perceived uncertainties related to lead time and usage rates. This involves weighing the trade-off between carrying costs of additional inventories and costs of stockouts. The safety stock plus one-half the order quantity will equal the average inventory of the item.

Computerized inventory control systems based upon such models are widely used. Care must be exercised to modify inventory control models or override them when major market changes render obsolete the data upon which they are based.

Questions

1. What are credit standards? How will loosening a firm's credit standards affect *(a)* sales, *(b)* credit administration expenses, *(c)* collection expenses, *(d)* bad debt losses, and *(e)* the investment in receivables?

2. How would you decide whether or not to loosen credit standards? Describe the required analysis.

3. How is a firm's marginal investment in additional receivables determined (In connection with analysis of a proposal to liberalize credit standards)?

4. What, if anything, is wrong with a credit policy of minimizing bad debt losses?

5. If a retailer loosens its credit terms to the point that unreasonably large collection expenses and bad debt losses are incurred, what are the effects upon:

   a. The customer who pays cash for purchases?

   b. The customer who always pays bills on time?

6. Alpha's average collection period is 42 days, while that of its competitor, Beta, is only 34 days. As the financial manager of Alpha, react to this observation.

7. Indicate, in order of cost (from the least expensive upward), some of the major sources of mercantile credit information.

8. Why are informal credit limits often set for accounts?

9. Why do both the financial manager and the sales manager have a legitimate interest in accounts receivable (credit) management? How might their interests conflict?

10. How do terms of sale influence:
    a. The volume of sales?
    b. The investment in accounts receivable?

11. Why does trade credit analysis place primary emphasis upon liquidity and only secondarily consider solvency and profitability?

12. Why would a credit scoring system for appraising credit applicants be useful to Sears Roebuck or J. C. Penney but not to U. S. Steel?

13. A lawn fertilizer manufacturer that operates on a nearly level production schedule is considering selling to its distributors on advanced dating terms under which sales for delivery prior to February 15 will be billed on April 1 (beginning of the selling season) at a 5 percent discount and payable on 30-day terms. This procedure will replace the present terms requiring payment 30 days after shipment. How will this proposal affect the manufacturer's
    a. Investment in finished goods inventories?
    b. Inventory carrying costs?
    c. Investment in accounts receivable?

What might be the net advantage of the change to the manufacturer?

14. Contrast the viewpoints of *(a)* the purchasing agent, *(b)* the production manager, *(c)* the marketing manager, and *(d)* the financial manager regarding appropriate levels of the various types of inventories.

15. Why is the financial manager interested in purchasing-production-oriented inventory control models?

16. Fundamentally, what is the economic function of any inventory?

17. *a.* What is an EOQ?
    b. Draw a crude graph of the simple EOQ model.
    c. What are the assumptions of a simple EOQ model?

18. *a.* What is a safety stock?
    b. Does the safety stock influence the EOQ?
    c. Explain how order lead time and safety stock influence the order point.

19. Under what conditions might it be necessary to override an otherwise satisfactory computerized inventory control model?

20. Why would a fruit and vegetable canning company have a more serious problem of finished goods inventory control than a manufacturer of pencils?

Problems

1. Jackart Corporation has annual credit sales of 16 million and an average collection period of 36 days. The average marginal cost of its products is 72 percent of sales. Management estimates the pretax required return (opportunity cost) on funds invested in accounts receivable to be 22 percent.

   a. What is Jackart's average accounts receivable balance? (Assume a 360-day year.)

   b. What is its average net investment in accounts receivable?

   c. What is the required annual pretax return on investment in accounts receivable in dollars?

2. Boland Manufacturing Corporation currently has annual credit sales of $12 million and an average collection period of 40 days. Its financial manager is considering relaxing credit standards to grant credit to a marginal class of customers. These customers will generate estimated additional annual sales of $1 million. Variable operating costs are 82 percent of sales. Credit administration and collection costs are expected to increase $50,000, and bad debt losses among added customers are estimated at $60,000 per year. The collection period on the additional accounts will be about 60 days. (Assume a 360-day year.)

   a. Estimate the incremental pretax annual profit that will be generated by this additional business.

   b. Estimate the additional investment required.

   c. If the required pretax rate of return on the incremental investment is 25 percent, should the proposal be adopted? Why or why not?

3. Serve-Well Corporation, a wholesaler of small appliances, is considering relaxing credit standards to serve a marginal class of retailers. These customers will generate an estimated $2 million additional sales. Variable operating costs are 88 percent of sales. The collection period on the additional accounts is estimated to be about 54 days. Credit administration and collection cost are expected to increase by $90,000, and bad debt losses among the added accounts are estimated at $110,000 per year.

   a. Estimate the incremental pretax annual profit to be generated by this additional business.

   b. Estimate the additional investment required.

c. If the required pretax rate of return on the incremental business is 25 percent, should the proposal be adopted? Why or why not?

4. Maryann Manufacturing, Inc., is considering relaxing credit standards to sell to a marginal class of customers. These customers will generate an estimated $500,000 additional sales. The collection period on the additional accounts is estimated to be about 40 days, compared to that on present accounts of 35 days. Variable operating costs are 76 percent of sales. Increased credit administration costs are estimated to be $10,000. Required rate of return (before taxes) on present receivables is 21 percent. Using the alternate method of analyzing a proposed change in credit standards, decide whether or not to approve this proposed change. (Use a 360-day year.)

5. Nemora Furniture Company is concerned because its bad debt losses last year were 6 percent of sales. The financial manager believes that if credit standards and collection policies were tightened, these losses could be reduced to 2 percent. Sales, however, would be reduced by 5 percent, from $1,000,000 to $950,000 per year. Nemora's fixed costs are $100,000 per year and its variable operating costs are 60 percent of sales. The change in policy would reduce the average collection period from 72 days to about 45 days. Collection costs would be increased by about $5,000. Although Nemora's overall required pretax rate of return is 20 percent, a larger return, 30 percent, is believed required on the relatively risky receivables that would be eliminated. (Use a 360-day year.)

a. What would be the effect of this policy change upon net pretax profit?

b. What would be the effect upon net investment required to carry receivables?

c. Should the policy change be adopted? Why or why not?

6. The Wellington Corporation is considering installing a computerized inventory control system that is expected to reduce the average investment in inventories by $250,000. Wellington's required pretax rate of return (opportunity cost) is 22 percent. The system will cost $50,000 and require $25,000 per year expenditures to operate. Should Wellington install the system?

7. *a.* If the ordering cost of widgits is $200 per order (regardless of size) and carrying costs are 4 cents per day per widgit, what is the economic order quantity (EOQ) if 400 widgits are used per day in a production process? (Use a 100-day planning period.)

b. How frequently should widgits be ordered?

c. What will be the average inventory of widgits in units and dollars if widgits cost $8 each and a safety stock of 2,000 widgits is maintained?

8. Baxter Corporation uses 2,000 electric motors on a continuous basis each month (30 days). The motors cost $12 each. Ordering cost is fixed at $100 per order and carrying costs are 20 cents per month per motor.

a. Determine the economic order quantity (EOQ).
b. How frequently should orders be placed?
c. If Baxter maintains a safety stock equal to 10 days' usage, what is the average inventory in units and dollars?
d. If carrying costs increase to 30 cents per month per motor because of increased interest rates, how does this change Baxter's optimal average inventory in dollars?

Chapter 9
Short-Term Financing—Spontaneous Credit and Unsecured Borrowings

Now we move to the right side of the balance sheet to examine the current liabilities. These sources finance part of the current assets that have been discussed in the last two chapters. Current liabilities are more or less arbitrarily defined as those obligations that are due within one year. The spontaneous current liabilities, including trade accounts payable, accruals, and customers' advances, will be treated first. Then unsecured short-term financing that must be arranged on a more formal basis—bank loans and commercial paper borrowings—will be discussed. Short-term loans secured by the pledge or assignment of specific assets will be treated in Chapter 10.

Spontaneous sources of short-term financing

Spontaneous credit arises in the normal course of business without any overt action on the part of the user. Such financing becomes available simply by doing business in the customary way. Since it tends to fluctuate with the volume of business operations, more spontaneous credit is available when the volume of operations increases and less when it declines. Although the funds are provided without explicit cost, there usually is some implicit cost and, if alternatives are available, the implicit cost may be high.

The usual spontaneous sources of short-term financing are accounts payable (trade credit); accrued current liabilities, such as accrued taxes, wages, and interest; and such funds as normally may be supplied by customers in the form of advances or deposits.

Accounts payable (Trade credit)

Chapter 8 viewed trade credit transactions from the standpoint of the seller. Now we reverse the viewpoint and study the subject in terms of the credit accommodation we can obtain from our suppliers on the goods and services we purchase.

Nearly all trade credit related to domestic transactions is on *open-book account,* that is, it is represented by an account receivable for the seller and an account payable for the buyer. This form of credit is not documented by a signed financial instrument. It originates informally when the seller ships goods to the buyer and invoices (bills) that shipment.

Occasionally the seller may want documentation of a trade credit. In such cases, either a promissory note or a trade acceptance may be used. If a *promissory note,* the seller will ask the buyer to sign a note promising to pay the buyer so many dollars on a stated or determinable date at a given place. Such a note may or may not be interest-bearing; if it is, it is not spontaneous credit but rather negotiated credit. Promissory notes normally are used in only a very few lines of business. They are, however, more often used by sellers who wish to convert delinquent open-book accounts into formal documents acknowledging these debts. (You may recall our discussing this under "Collection efforts" in Chapter 8.)

If the *trade acceptance* is used, the seller ships the goods and forwards a *draft,* with the bill of lading attached, to the buyer's bank. The buyer must go to his bank and accept the draft in order to get the bill of lading, which must be presented to the carrier to receive the goods. The accepted draft, called a trade acceptance, is then returned to the buyer through the bank clearing system. It may be discounted by the buyer, that is, sold to a financial institution at a discount to obtain cash. Alternatively, it may be held until maturity and then returned to the buyer's bank for collection. Because the use of either promissory notes or trade acceptances is a rigid, awkward, and normally unnecessary procedure, these devices are not widely used. Subsequent discussion of trade credit will refer to the open-book account.

Terms of purchase Terms of sale were discussed in the previous chapter. Now we are looking at the terms through the eyes of the purchaser. There usually is little or no flexibility as to the stated terms of purchase because suppliers probably quote the customary credit terms of the trade. However, buyers should be alert to the possibility that some supplier(s) may deviate from these terms as a competitive device to increase sales. Such deviation usually is informal, that is, the credit terms stated on the invoice are the standard ones, say 2/10, net/30, but the supplier's sales representative orally informs the buyer that if the discount is taken in 15 days it will be considered timely or that if the discount is not taken, the seller will be willing to carry the credit for 60 days.

The probability of more lenient credit terms being available is largely related to the condition of the market. In a sellers' market, strict adherence to stated credit terms probably will be required. However, in a buyers' market, suppliers may informally liberalize credit terms, and a little negotiation on this point may yield still more favorable actual credit terms than those first mentioned. Note that we are suggesting efforts to obtain the best terms available in the market by mutual understanding between the buyer and seller, not unilateral extension of payment beyond the credit terms by the buyer without an understanding with the seller. The latter practice, to be discussed later under "Stretching payables," may be considered both unethical and risky.

There are two types of standard credit terms that have important implications relating to our use of trade credit financing. One is the *net period without discount* term, such as net/30, EOM. This type of term leaves us with no feasible option. We simply utilize the credit by paying the bill at the end of the month following the invoice date. We would be foolish to pay earlier and would run the risk of jeopardizing our credit standing if we paid later. Whatever cost of credit that is implicit in the price of the goods must be paid whether we use that credit or not, so it clearly is wise to use it.

The other type of term, which includes a *net credit period and a cash discount* for earlier payment, such as 2/10, net/30, presents an important option. In a practical sense, 98 percent of the stated price is the real price, and payment to receive that price must be made within 10 days; 2 percent of the stated price is, in effect, a credit charge for the option of paying 20 days later. This option will be discussed later under "Implicit cost."

It is also possible that some purchases may be made under delayed billings. This is called "dating" and is used primarily in selling lines at wholesale where the retail sales are highly seasonal. For example, a manufacturer of garden tools may produce on a relatively level schedule and have inadequate storage facilities and/or financial capability to carry the large buildup of inventory that would result. This supplier may offer to customers who will buy and take delivery in the winter or early spring a dating of April 30 with subsequent terms of 2/10, net/30. The customer, a retailer, can buy and take delivery in February but will not be billed until April 30 and may take the discount by paying on May 10 or pay the net amount due May 30. Where such datings are available and the buyer has unused storage facilities, such terms may be advantageous to both the buyer and seller. The buyer is not obligated to pay until cash is being generated from sale of the goods. The seller benefits from reduction in inventory carrying costs. In many cases, the seller is financing the accounts receivable buildup by borrowing against those receivables (a subject that will be treated in the next chapter).

Availability of trade credit Nearly every firm uses trade credit as a source of financing. Accounts payable constitute about 40 percent of total current liabilities of business corporations and are the largest single source of short-term financing. It is an even more important source for small to middle-sized firms engaged in manufacturing, wholesaling, and retailing.

The availability of trade credit is much broader than for negotiated sources of short-term credit such as bank loans. There are two major reasons for this. First, although the amount of trade payables will vary with seasonal fluctuation in purchases, there will always be some accounts payable on the books of a going concern. These are a continuing source of financing; as some accounts are paid, others are created by new purchases. Short-term bank loans, on the other hand, usually are not rolled over in this fashion but rather are utilized only to cover seasonally high funds requirements.

A second reason for the broader availability of trade credit is that the financial inducement for granting such credit usually is much greater than the incentive related to negotiated credit. In Chapter 8, when we used a marginal cost-benefit analysis in determining acceptable standards for granting trade credit, we discovered that the expected rate of return on an incrementally lower class of credits might be much higher than any reasonable interest rate that a bank or other direct lender would receive. For this reason, the trade supplier often would be pleased to grant credit to a customer whose credit worthiness was below that acceptable to a bank.

This point is illustrated vividly by comparison of marginal profitability of a trade credit versus a bank loan in Table 9–1. Consider a manufacturer appraising the credit of a wholesaler that would buy about $10,000 worth of merchandise each month on 30-day terms versus a bank loan officer appraising the credit of the same wholesaler who has applied for a $10,000 loan for 90 days. The manufacturer has a 10 percent incremental profit margin, not considering incremental collection costs and possible bad debt loss. The bank would lend at an annual rate of, say, 12 percent interest and would estimate its incremental cost of handling this type of loan (again excluding possible collection costs and bad debt losses) at 3 percent per year. If the credit is granted, the manufacturer will make 12 monthly sales of about $10,000 each to the customer, or total annual sales of $120,000, on which it will make marginal profits of 10 percent, or $12,000. Although the banker is considering one 90-day loan to this customer, presumably three other such loans would be made during the year; thus, the bank would make net interest (marginal profits) of $900 per year on such loans.

Table 9–1 Comparison of marginal profitability
Trade credit versus bank loan

	Trade credit	Bank loan
Credit line	$ 10,000*	$10,000
Maximum investment at risk	9,000	10,000
Sales per year	120,000	
Gross loans per year (four 90-day loans)		40,000
Potential marginal profit		
Trade credit @ 10%	12,000	
Bank—12% interest less 3% marginal costs		900
Rate of return on investment at risk	133%	9%

*On terms of sale of n/30 days.

The maximum investment that the manufacturer would have at risk at any time (if the wholesaler pays its bills according to terms) would be $9,000, its incremental investment in the account receivable of $10,000. Its marginal profit of $12,000 on the investment of $9,000 will yield a pretax rate of return of 133 percent per year. This compares with the bank's marginal profit of $900 on an investment at risk of $10,000, or 9 percent.

It is evident that the manufacturer could afford to take substantial risks of collection costs or bad debt losses among such a credit class of wholesalers and still come out with an attractive marginal profit. The bank, on the other hand, could afford to take only slight risks of incurring collection expenses or bad debt losses among the same credit class. If risks materialized in the form of additional costs or bad debt losses, the bank would suffer serious losses on the business. For this reason, there are many firms with insufficient credit standing to justify bank credit that continually obtain trade credit without difficulty.

In addition, major suppliers often are willing to "stake" a new business by informally allowing generous credit terms in order to establish its lines in a promising retail market. For example, assume that Susan Johnston and Betty Jones have several years of good experience in working their way up to assistant managers of retail women's apparel stores. They have become well acquainted with the salespeople representing a number of good lines of sportswear, lingerie, dresses, and accessories, and those people have confidence in Susan and Betty's ability to manage a store. Now Susan and Betty decide to strike out on their own and line up a location in a growing shopping area for their new store, Fashion Boutique, Inc. They have saved a little money, enough to pay a few months' rent and buy the fixtures, but not nearly enough to finance the initial inventory. It is highly probable that they will be able to arrange with their major suppliers to carry their accounts far beyond normal credit terms. These suppliers want their merchandise represented in this outlet and are willing to look quite a way down the road to repeated and growing business as Fashion Boutique develops into a profitable, well established outlet. Only at that point will Susan and Betty probably be able to obtain sufficient bank credit to satisfy their requirements to finance their growing working capital needs.

Implicit cost All credit has a cost. The furnisher of credit must cover the cost of servicing it and provide an adequate rate of return to the investors who supply the capital. Inasmuch as the risk related to trade credit often is relatively high, the cost must be likewise. But the cost of trade credit usually is *implicit,* that is, it is not stated explicitly as an interest charge or a service fee.

Where a single term is quoted, such as net/30, the cost of this credit must be included in the purchase price. If the purchaser had the alternative of buying the same goods for cash, one could easily calculate the implicit credit cost and then choose to buy the goods on either cash or credit terms according to his or her judgment as to the reasonableness of the credit cost. However, if the required goods are available only on such standard credit terms, then, as we mentioned earlier, the buyer would be foolish to pay early and not use the credit being paid for anyway.

Where the terms provide for a net period with a cash discount, such as 2/10, n/30, the buyer has a clear alternative. The buyer may calculate the cost of the additional 20 days' credit available to decide whether to take the cash discount or to utilize the additional credit by paying the net bill in 30 days. If the net bill is $100 and the discount 2 percent, then the real of minimum price is $98 and the minimum credit period 10 days. The credit charge is $2 for the use of $98 for an additional 20 days. Thus the cost of that 20 days' credit is

$$\frac{.02}{.98} \times \frac{365}{20} = 37.2\% \text{ per year}$$

This 37.2 percent per year is a high effective interest rate. The discount term should be taken if the buyer has available funds or can borrow at a lower rate from its bank. Still, there are occasions when the extended credit terms may appropriately be used, such as those in which a highly seasonal business can make a marginal profit considerably in excess of 37 percent by utilizing the full credit period in addition to borrowing all it can from its bank to produce inventories for its peak selling season. Other firms, regardless of seasonal requirements, simply do not have available funds or sufficient bank credit to take advantage of cash discounts and find it feasible to utilize the maximum credit terms.

Another important consideration is that the firm that normally takes cash discounts is, in effect, maintaining a reserve of available credit. This reserve, although expensive, can be used if its bank credit should be restricted in a credit crunch or in event of an unfavorable development affecting the firm's credit standing. Many firms were able to survive the extremely tight bank credit market of late 1979–early 1980 by using all available trade credit.

If the credit terms were 2/10, net/60, then the calculation of effective cost would be

$$\frac{.02}{.98} \times \frac{365}{50} = 14.9\% \text{ per year}$$

which, although it appears high, might be approximately equal to or even below the cost of bank credit to the firm, particularly in a period of tight credit.

The above illustrations assumed that if the firm did not take the available cash discount, it would pay the net bill on the date due. This is not always a correct assumption. Quite often a buyer who does not take discounts also does not pay when bills are due and, either by necessity or design, attempts to stretch its payables, that is, to pay them at a considerably later date.

Stretching payables It must be obvious that stretching payables by paying them later than when they are due reduces the cost of trade credit. For example, in the previous illustration, if the buyer did not take the discount or pay at the end of 60 days, but rather stretched the payable 30 days by paying in 90 days, then the effective cost of the credit would be

$$\frac{.02}{.98} \times \frac{365}{80} = 9.3\% \text{ per year}$$

This is a quite reasonable interest rate. It would be further reduced if the buyer did not pay until 120 days after the invoice date. But this practice entails great risks.

The seller does not have infinite patience. How long a seller is willing to wait beyond a due date before cutting off the customer's credit and refusing to ship except on a cash basis, or before it will take legal action to collect the account, depends upon its credit standards and collection policies as discussed in Chapter 8. These, in turn, reflect the supplier's marginal profit opportunities and, to some extent, the informal customs of the trade. There are some trades in which the stated terms of sale have become nominal; sellers generally do not enforce them but rather expect payments to be substantially past due. But usually the firm that stretches its payables runs a serious risk of losing its sources of supply. Although in a buyers' market suppliers may willingly tolerate slow payments, when market conditions change, supply becomes short, and a sellers' market exists, suppliers naturally cut off the slow-paying accounts first. At this point the firm that has been stretching its payables may be forced out of business.

An additional risk of this practice is the reduction of the firm's credit rating. These ratings, such as those furnished by Dun & Bradstreet, are based to a considerable extent upon the payment record. Slowness in paying trade accounts may lead to downgrading of the firm's credit rating to the point that suppliers generally are not willing to sell to it on a credit basis. For the above reasons, stretching payables clearly is not recommended. It turns out too often to be penny-wise and pound-foolish.

Accruals

Accrual accounts are liabilities representing expenses that have been incurred but not yet paid. The most common accruals are for wages and taxes. Employees are not paid each hour or day they work, but rather receive their paychecks weekly, semimonthly, or monthly. Thus the employer obtains spontaneous short-term financing during the period between the performance of their work and the date they are paid. For example, a firm with a semimonthly payroll of $1.5 million receives about $100,000 labor each day, which is accrued until the $1.5 million is paid to the employees. Therefore it receives an average of $750,000 of spontaneous short-term financing.

The longer the pay period the greater the amount of financing that can be obtained in this way. If the firm could change its payroll to a monthly basis it would increase its average spontaneous financing to $1.5 million. Pay periods, however, are discretionary only to a very limited degree. It is quite improbable that a union would go along with such an increase. Also pay periods often have become so customary for particular types of labor that any attempt to lengthen the pay period might have serious morale implications or even lead some employees to seek employment elsewhere.

In some fields, however, a variation on this theme is quite prevalent. Executive personnel may be paid lower salaries than they otherwise would command but are provided additional compensation in the form of substantial year-end bonuses based upon performance. This practice provides a long accrual of the bonus portion of their compensation as well as some flexibility in the executive compensation structure.

Taxes also provide accrual financing, but this is not discretionary because the taxing authorities set the payment dates. Property taxes levied for a given year usually are payable one half on March 1 and one half on August 1 of the following year (this varies somewhat by state and county). Corporate income taxes are payable quarterly on the estimated taxes for the year. This, in a sense, is not an unmixed financial blessing. The taxpayer is making income on which the tax is levied, and the government is merely foregoing for a time taking its cut from this income. Sales tax and employee withholding tax collections may also provide for some relatively short accruals.

Royalties payable for the use of patents and copyrights sometimes provide spontaneous financing in that they usually are accrued and paid on a quarterly, semiannual, or annual basis. For example, the publishers of your textbooks normally pay royalties to the authors twice a year based upon net sales for the preceding period.

Customers' advances and deposits

In some fields it is customary for the customer to pay in advance, particularly for services. For example, you probably pay for your local telephone service and your room or apartment rent one month in advance, and perhaps you also are required to make a damage deposit with your landlord. These are examples of spontaneous financing available to those who provide such services.[1] Purchasers of heavy custom-built machinery, aircraft, and ships often are required to make deposits with the manufacturers either at the time the orders are placed or the date construction begins. On some occasions substantial advances have been made to oil, gas, coal, and other energy producers to help finance drilling or mining developments in order to secure the right to purchase some of the minerals produced. Such advances are to be paid off in the form of the minerals. Many customers'

[1]The author thought his newspaper deliveryperson was quite bright on this score by collecting a month in advance until his trash collector started billing *three* months in advance. One never knows from whom an education in finance may be obtained!

advances and deposits are spontaneous in the sense that no explicit interest is paid for the use of the funds. However, in some cases interest is paid at an agreed rate, and therefore these may be considered negotiated sources.

Unsecured bank loans

Commercial banks make many different types of loans to their business customers. Such loans may be short- or intermediate-term, unsecured or secured, and on a variety of different contractual bases. To establish some order for our discussion, we shall deal here primarily with short-term unsecured loans. The next chapter will elaborate on secured loans and later, in Chapter 18, longer-term bank lending arrangements will be discussed.

Bank loans, in contrast to the spontaneous current liabilities discussed above, are negotiated credit. They must be arranged by the financial manager of the firm. The amounts, timing, and maturity of such financing are at the discretion of management, subject of course to the willingness of the bank(s). Bank borrowing involves the active acquisition of funds externally as compared to the more or less passive acceptance of financing made available in the normal course of business from spontaneous sources.

Although bank loans constitute a slightly smaller proportion of the current liabilities of all business firms than trade credit, the relationship of a firm with its banker probably is the most important of all external financial relationships. There are three reasons for this. (1) As mentioned earlier, many firms, particularly small fledgling ones, do not have sufficient credit standing to borrow at all from banks. Thus, for the firms that can and do borrow, their bank credit arrangements are more important than disclosed by aggregate figures for all business firms. (2) The firm, unless it is very large, is doing business with one or a few banks, whereas it is purchasing from many, perhaps hundreds, of different suppliers. Therefore, the relationship with any single supplier may be of considerably less importance than the relationship with the bank. (3) The banker, as we shall discuss presently, often not only handles the firm's depository accounts and lends funds to it but also may render many additional services ranging from being its financial "father confessor" to providing advice and aid regarding many other financial matters.

The banking relationship

A strong banking relationship may be one of a firm's greatest intangible assets. Many highly successful corporations figuratively have grown up arm-in-arm with their respective banks.[2] Of course, the greatest element in building a strong banking relationship is the trust that develops through years of dealings in which both the firm and the bank have carefully fulfilled their obligations to each other. Much of this also has to do with the people in both the firm and the bank as they develop understanding of and confidence in each other. Although it is rather hard to put into words that do not sound like excerpts from a sermon, the strength of this relationship is of such importance that in difficult times it may make the difference between survival and the economic death of the firm.

Banks differ a great deal in their attitudes, abilities, and financial circumstances relative to satisfying the borrowing and service requirements of any given business customer. A financial manager should consider the following factors in choosing a commercial bank and in pursuing the development of a banking relationship.

An important variable among banks is the attitude of the banker(s) toward loans, particularly the bearing of risks that loans to your firm will entail. This attitude may vary from an extremely conservative policy of making only super-safe loans to an aggressive policy of seeking out and financing fledgling firms that have the potential for growth but require a great deal of the banker's attention (and sometimes quite a few aspirin tablets) to survive the growing pains. The latter type of loan is called a "development loan."

This attitude may, in turn, be a function of the personal characteristics of the bankers and the major stockholders of the bank and/or the characteristics of the bank's deposit liabilities. The deposit liabilities may be highly volatile as the result of a large percentage of demand deposits compared to time deposits and geographical concentration in an area highly dependent upon one or a few volatile industries. The bank has to adopt a conservative lending policy under these conditions to protect its liquidity. Conversely, a bank that is managed and owned by creative, aggressive people and has a large percentage of time deposits spread over a wide geographical area among either relatively stable or economically widely diversified depositors can be expected to have a relatively liberal lending policy.

Another question to answer is, "Does the banker who will handle (or is handling) your firm's account really understand the nature of your business?" Some smaller banks are rather highly specialized in lending to par-

[2]Some examples of this are the relationships of the Aluminum Company of America (ALCOA) and Gulf Oil with the Mellon National Bank of Pittsburgh, Ford Motor Company with the Manufacturers National Bank of Detroit, General Motors with the National Bank of Detroit, Exxon with the Chase Manhattan Bank, and Coca-Cola with the Trust Company Bank of Georgia. In each case the strong relationship dates back to either the founding of the bank or the early development of the corporation. Some question the propriety of such close relationships. We are not taking sides on that issue here but merely pointing out that such relationships may through the years be of great mutual benefit.

ticular industries. Their lending officers are highly knowledgeable regarding such things as the market for the products of these industries, seasonal borrowing requirements, collateral values of the inventories or receivables, and who the reliable suppliers are. In short, they know how to appraise the risk of loans to firms in those industries. If your firm operates in such an industry, this specialized lending knowledge would be a strong plus factor influencing your decision to choose such a bank. However, if your firm is in a different industry, you would not want to choose such a bank. The risk is too great that the banker would interpret your figures and your actions in the context of an industry with different characteristics.

A number of large banks have organized their lending operations into industry divisions, thereby providing lending officers who are specialists in each major industry represented among their borrowing customers. This may significantly benefit the customer by tending to assure that the loan officer handling the account is knowledgeable regarding the characteristics of the business.

Another factor to consider is the willingness of the banker to provide advice and counsel regarding not only your firm's loan and depository requirements but also concerning other aspects of the financial management of your business. A really good bank officer who is knowledgeable about your business can help you a great deal regarding such diverse matters as control of cash, investment in marketable securities, control of receivables and inventories, and other financial matters. When and if you need long-term financing that is outside the bank's scope, a good banker usually can refer and introduce you to reliable long-term lending institutions or investment bankers to start you along the way in arranging such financing.

A word of caution is in order regarding advice and counsel. It can be of great value if, and only if, the banker really understands your business. If not, it can be a real pain to have a banker repeatedly telling you to do the wrong things because he or she does not understand your business well enough to give sound advice.

Still another factor to investigate is the reputation of the bank regarding its willingness to stand by its borrowing customers through difficult times. This, in part, will relate to the volatility of the bank's deposits and thus its liquidity requirements. Your seek to do business with a bank that will remain loyal to you when and if your firm, or the industry or the economy generally must go through a difficult period. The kiss of death is a banker who will panic and call your loan or refuse to honor your line of credit, forcing either liquidation of assets in an unfavorable market or, at the extreme, bankruptcy.

Finally, you will be interested in the bank's capability of handling your firm's borrowing requirements and depository transactions, its service charges, compensating balance requirements, and interest rates.

Interest rates

The *prime rate* is the rate of interest that a bank charges its most credit worthy customers for short-term loans in large amounts. There are exceptions, particularly in periods of high interest rates, when a bank may lend to an exceptionally good customer at a rate slightly lower than prime. This discount from prime usually is offered to compete with the customer's alternative of borrowing through the sale of commercial paper. All bank short-term lending rates to customers of lower credit standing or those borrowing in smaller amounts are scaled upward from the prime rate.

Prime rates in the United States (and most other major commercial nations) have varied greatly through time. Figure 9–1 indicates that the prime rate in the United States since 1965 has varied from less than 5 percent to about 20 percent. Such wide variations create an additional uncertainty in

Figure 9–1 Short-term interest rates
Prime rate, effective date of change; prime paper, quarterly averages

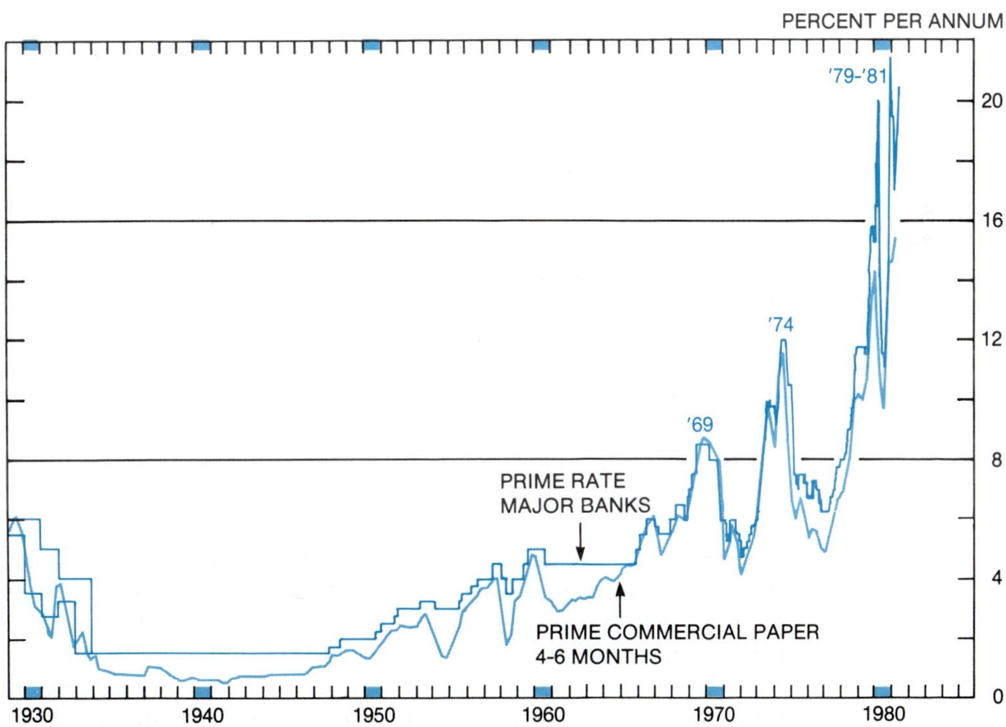

Source: Federal Reserve Chart Book, 1981.

executing a financial policy dependent upon short-term financing, as discussed in Chapter 6. You will also note from Figure 9–1 the close relationship between the prime bank rate and the interest rates on money-market securities as exemplified by the rate on prime commercial paper. During part of this period, from 1971 to 1979, some of the major banks automatically adjusted their prime rates to a fixed differential from the rates on specific money-market instruments.

Any bank may set its own prime rate, but they tend to "follow the leader." Prime rate changes usually are initiated by a major bank. This announcement normally will be followed by several other major banks the next day, and within a few days most banks will have the new rate. If other banks do follow, the initiating bank will be forced by competition to return to the old rate. Thus, the prime rate is determined by competitive forces in the market for bank loans.

Usually a very short-term loan (30 to perhaps 90 days) is made at a fixed interest rate that will equal the prime rate at the time the loan is made plus, say, 2 percent. In light of the great variation in the prime rate indicated above, most banks stipulate on longer-term loans that the interest rate will change periodically, say, monthly, bi-monthly, or quarterly, to reflect changes in the prime. This interest basis, called a *floating rate,* results in loans at, say, 2 percent above floating prime, adjusted monthly.

There are several reasons that banks charge various interest rates scaled upward from prime on loans to particular customers. First, although the prime rate is relatively uniform throughout the country, some regional differences in the supply and demand for funds account for small geographical differences in rates charged. A far more important reason is the difference in perceived credit worthiness among particular borrowers. Thus, one customer whose credit standing is just below that of a bank's best customers may borrow at one half of 1 percent over prime; another, whose credit worthiness is somewhat lower, might borrow on an unsecured basis at 2 percent over prime. Still another, whose credit standing does not justify an unsecured loan, might borrow on a secured basis, assigning accounts receivable or pledging inventories, at 4 percent over prime.

There are other factors that may influence the interest rate charged a particular customer. One is the profitability of other business which that customer does with the bank. For example, a customer that generally maintains relatively large depository balances and/or retains the bank's trust department to manage its pension fund may be charged lower interest rates on its loans than another borrower of equal credit standing. A small corporation, controlling interest of which is held by a family that also controls other larger corporations that are valued customers of the bank, may be charged a lower rate than a similar corporation with no such affiliation. Size of the loan is also a significant factor. It normally costs a bank about as much for credit analysis, loan approval, and accounting costs for a $10,000 loan as for a \$2 million one. But the bank has to make 200 loans of \$10,000 to put \$2 million to work. Therefore, the interest rate charged on a \$10,000 loan must be considerably higher than that on a \$2 million loan if the bank is to make similar marginal rates of return on the funds invested.

The net result of these considerations is that the interest rates charged by a bank on loans to its various business customers range from prime, or perhaps slightly lower than prime, to about 2 or 3 percent over prime on unsecured loans and perhaps up to 5 or 6 percent over prime on some secured loans.

Methods of charging interest Banks usually charge interest on short-term business loans by either requiring that the interest be paid at the time the note is paid off or by discounting the interest. Under *discounting,* interest is deducted from the principal at the time the loan is made and only the net proceeds are transferred to the borrower's account. Under the first method, the nominal or stated interest rate is the same as the *effective* rate. To illustrate, assume that you borrow \$10,000 at 10 percent interest for one year. You are to pay the interest of \$1,000 when you pay off the \$10,000 note at the end of one year. The effective interest rate is

$$\frac{\$\ 1{,}000}{\$10{,}000} = 10.0\%$$

This is the most common method of charging interest and results in no distortion of the effective interest rate. Such a rate may, of course, be subject to adjustment over time on a floating basis.

However, if the interest is discounted when the loan is made, the effective interest rate is not 10 percent, but rather

$$\frac{\$1{,}000}{\$9{,}000} = 11.1\%$$

You receive the use of only \$9,000, the principal less the discounted interest, but you pay interest on \$10,000. Therefore, the effective interest rate is 11.1 percent, or 1.1 percent higher than the nominal rate.

On installment loans, which usually are not short-term, some banks and finance companies charge interest on an *add-on* basis. Interest for the term of the loan is added to the amount paid out to determine the face amount of the installment note. Thus, if you borrowed \$10,000 at 8 percent nominal interest payable in 24 monthly installments, you would sign a note for \$11,600 (\$10,000 plus 8 percent interest on \$10,000 for two years, or \$1,600). Your monthly payments will be \$483.33 (\$11,600/24). The effective interest rate on this loan will be a great deal higher than the nominal rate for two reasons: (1) you will be paying interest on a larger amount than you initially receive and (2) you will not have the use of \$10,000 except during the first month. You will pay off \$483.33 each month and will have the use only of a declining balance through the two-year period. In effect, over the two years you will have on the average only about one half of the initial proceeds. The effective interest rate on this loan is more than double the nominal rate. This method of charging interest is only rarely used in connection with business loans, but is used on many consumer installment loans, for which federal law requires that the lender translate the nominal rate to the effective interest rate and furnish that information in writing to the borrower.

Cost of compensating balances Compensating balances were first discussed in Chapter 7, largely as they related to checking account activity. Here we are concerned with them as they relate to bank borrowing arrangements. Banks usually require compensating balances to be maintained in the checking accounts of their borrowing business customers. These arrangements vary not only among banks and different customers of a given bank but also in relation to changing money-market conditions. They tend to be higher in tight money markets and lower in loose ones.

For a particular borrowing customer with a line of credit at its bank, the requirements might be, say, 10 percent of the total amount of the line that is not in use and 20 percent of the line in use, that is, the current loan balance. If a bank makes available a line of credit of $1 million to Ace Manufacturing Company and Ace is currently borrowing one half of this, or $500,000, it would be required to maintain compensating balances of $150,000 (20 percent of the $500,000 loan balance, or $100,000, plus 10 percent of the $500,000 unused portion of the line, or $50,000).

Banks generally justify compensating balance requirements on the basis that they protect the liquidity of the borrowing customer so that unforeseen cash outflow requirements will not create a liquidity crisis. A bank also takes into consideration that it has the *right of offset.* In the event of bankruptcy or failure of a borrower to pay a matured loan, the bank has the right to transfer that borrower's depository account balance to make payment on the loan. Of course, the bank also considers the income it can make from lending or investing such deposit balances.

The crucial issue from a borrowing cost point of view is whether or not the required compensating balances are greater than, or only equal to, those that would be required otherwise for transactions and precautionary purposes. If compensating balances are only equal to these operating cash requirements, they do not contribute to the cost of borrowing. However, if they are greater than these requirements, the excess contributes to borrowing costs. Ace Manufacturing might have needed deposit balances of only $90,000 but was required to maintain $150,000 in compensating balances. The difference, $60,000, should be considered in calculating its effective borrowing cost. If its bank charges a 10 percent rate of interest payable when the note is repaid, then its $500,000 loan balance provides $440,000 in usable funds ($500,000 less the $60,000 excess cash balance that must be maintained). Thus its effective interest cost is 11.36 percent ($50,000/$440,000).[3]

Where compensating balance requirements refer to *average monthly balances,* as we assumed in the above example, the implicit additional borrowing cost that may be attributed to them usually is small because a large portion of the required balances would be needed anyway for operational purposes. In case the compensating balance requirements refer to *minimum balances* (when used, these usually relate only to loans outstanding), they significantly increase effective interest cost. If the example above referred to a minimum depository balance of 20 percent in relation only to loans outstanding, then Ace's minimum cash balance requirement of $100,000 while borrowing $500,000 would result in an effective borrowing cost of

$$\frac{\$\ 50{,}000}{\$400{,}000} = 12.5\%$$

Credit arrangements

All short-term unsecured bank borrowing is evidenced by promissory notes that are signed by the borrower and indicate the principal amount, the interest rate to be paid, and the time and place that the obligation is due and payable. In the simplest borrowing arrangement, a firm's financial manager applies for a single loan of, say, $25,000 for 90 days. He or she discusses with the loan officer the need for these funds and how the loan can be paid off, fills out a loan application form, and furnishes appropriate financial statements as requested. Usually the application will then be processed and taken to the lending committee for approval. If all goes well, the borrower signs a note and the proceeds are credited to the firm's checking account. As the relationship develops through proper servicing of a few such loans, the financial manager may arrange a line of credit and, somewhere along the way, perhaps a revolving credit.

Line of credit A *line of credit* is an expression of willingness on the part of a bank to lend on an unsecured basis (or on the security of the pledge of specific types of assets) up to a stated maximum amount at a given or determinable interest rate (such as 1 percent over floating prime) during a given period, usually the ensuing year. It nearly always is in the form of a letter addressed to the borrowing customer and signed by the bank loan officer handling the account. Usually that letter will contain a statement to

[3]This example is oversimplified by the assumption that Ace owes $500,000 (and only that amount) throughout the year. A more realistic, but much more complicated, example would reflect the firm's borrowing varying amounts, perhaps up to the maximum $1 million provided by the line, for specific periods of time during the year and being out of its bank's debt during some portion of the year.

the effect that the line is subject to the firm's maintaining its financial condition and an "annual clean-up" provision requiring that the firm be out of the bank's debt for at least a stated number of days during the year. Sometimes it contains other pertinent conditions or provisos.

In an ongoing banking relationship, a line of credit usually is granted after the bank has received and reviewed the firm's financial statements covering the past fiscal year. The banker probably will also wish to discuss the firm's plans for the ensuing year. The cash forecast, pro forma financial statements, and perhaps the supporting operating forecasts may be of great value in such a review.

A line of credit is not a contract, therefore it does not bind the bank to honor promissory notes submitted under it. Rather it is a strong moral commitment on the part of the bank to honor its terms *if* there is no material development in the firm such as deterioration of its financial condition, change of ownership of controlling stock interest, or operational developments that might induce the bank to "pull the line." A reputable bank does not pull a line unless it has very good reason for doing so. Likewise, it does not necessarily rule out granting credit beyond the stated maximum amount, but rather it will require an additional review of the firm's affairs before the maximum may be exceeded. It is assumed that the borrowing firm's financial officer will discuss with the bank's loan officer any material change in the firm's financial condition.

As long as a line of credit is in force, the customer normally can borrow under it within the loan limit by merely submitting a promissory note to the bank's loan officer, who initials it without further review of the firm's credit qualifications. The reason for the annual clean-up provision (usually 30 or 60 days) is to assure that the funds borrowed under the line are used for temporary working capital purposes rather than being frozen into permanent working capital or fixed assets. This annual clean-up assures the bank that the loans under the line are for truly seasonal purposes.[4]

Revolving credit agreement A *revolving credit agreement* is a contract, that is, a legal commitment by the bank to lend up to a stated maximum amount at any time during the period covered by the agreement. A commitment fee, usually one half of 1 percent of the unused credit, must be paid in return for the firm assurance that such funds will be made available. Usually a revolving credit agreement will cover a period of time longer than one year, say three or five years. Because the bank does not have the right to withdraw from such an agreement for a relatively long period of time, the agreement is more complex than a line of credit and stipulates specific conditions relative to maintenance of financial condition of the firm, which

[4]There is an exception to this line of reasoning. If a firm maintains credit lines at more than one bank, it may borrow from one bank to clean up its loans at another. This does not assure the bank that the borrowings are for seasonal purposes, but rather assures it that the firm's credit standing is sufficient to obtain loans from another bank.

must be fulfilled for the agreement to remain in force. Also, the interest rate at which loans will be made is usually tied to the prime rate on a floating basis. The agreement will state that any loans will be made at, say, 1 percent over the bank's prime rate in force at the time and that the interest rate will be adjusted, say monthly or quarterly, as long as such loans are outstanding.

The banker's perspective

The banker looks first to the *function* of the loan under consideration. Basically, there are three major possible functions of a loan: (1) to finance the acquisition of temporary current assets that are expected to be liquidated in the normal course of business, (2) to finance permanent current assets that are not expected to be liquidated in the normal course of business, and (3) to finance the acquisition of fixed assets that are expected to be liquidated only through operations via the depreciation process and retention of earnings.[5] The function of the loan has an important bearing upon the terms appropriate for that loan and the analytical process upon which the decision as to its soundness may be based.

The first type of loan is expected to be *self-liquidating*. This simply means that the transaction(s) giving rise to the need for the loan is expected, as it runs its course, to develop the cash with which the loan will be paid. Such a loan usually will be seasonal. There may be exceptions, such as a construction loan to a contractor to finance a building project that requires more than a year to complete, or a loan to a defense contractor to finance the expansion of inventories and receivables over a three-year period required to complete the contract. The typical self-liquidating loan is exemplified by the now familiar illustration of financing a department store's buildup of its pre-Christmas inventory, which is expected to be worked down in the Christmas selling season, with the cash sales and collection of receivables providing the funds to pay off the loan in January or February.

This type of financing reflects the traditional lending function of the commercial bank and usually is considered by bankers to be the ideal loan. But making only this type of loan would neither satisfy the financing needs of the bank's business customers nor provide sufficient volume to fully utilize the bank's lending capacity. Therefore, banks have expanded the scope of their commercial lending into other types of loans.

The second type, the *net working capital* loan, functionally finances long-term or permanent current asset requirements. But the notes evidencing such loans are of short maturity, often 90 days or 180 days, and are rolled over by renewing each note as it matures. Such loans come into existence in two ways. Some are initially expected to be seasonal self-liquidating loans

[5]There are other possible functions of a loan, such as to pay off another loan, redeem stock, or pay dividends. For simplicity, these functions and related lending considerations will not be discussed here.

but just do not turn out that way. Operational difficulties or market changes obstruct the development of sufficient cash to pay them off, and renewal becomes necessary. Other loans are expected by both the banker and the borrower to be of this type from the start. These loans often are secured by assigned accounts receivable or pledged inventories. Such ongoing arrangements will be discussed in the next chapter.

The third type of bank loan, to finance fixed assets, usually is set up as a *term loan*. Such a loan is documented by a formal term-loan agreement that extends over an intermediate term, three to seven or eight years, with the principal to be paid off in quarterly or semi-annual installments. Cash flows from future profitable operations, and indirectly via depreciation, are expected to provide the repayment. These loans are beyond the scope of our discussion here and will be treated in Chapter 18.

The appropriate analysis relative to the soundness of each of these different types of loans is different.

Liquidity In analyzing the self-liquidating loan, the banker's primary interest is in liquidity, the ability of the firm to throw off cash through normal operations to pay the loan at maturity. The banker is primarily interested in the liquidity ratios, such as the current ratio, quick ratio, receivables turnover (or average collection period), and inventory turnover. He or she is also interested in the cash forecast and the operating assumptions upon which it is based. These analytical tools should provide the basis for an estimate of the probability that the loan can be paid off when due. Such analysis usually looks to payment of the loan even in the absence of profits. Often a self-liquidating loan is justifiable even to a firm that is operating at a loss. For example, a loan may be made to a firm with an excess inventory to buy time to liquidate that inventory if the proceeds of liquidation will provide the funds to repay the loan.

If the probability of payment through self-liquidation appears insufficient, then the banker looks to whether the risk would still be acceptable on the basis of the solvency of the firm or the collateral value of assets that could be pledged as security.

Solvency Solvency is reflected by the excess value of the assets over the total liabilities. Analysis of solvency usually starts with examination of the debt to tangible assets ratio or the debt to equity ratio. Then the assets are revalued in terms of potential net liquidation value if unfavorable developments led to forced liquidation. Recasting the debt ratio on the basis of estimated liquidation values provides the final solvency estimate. This line of analysis is particularly important in the banker's appraisal of a loan that either might turn into a net working capital loan or already is recognized as one. Each time such a loan comes up for renewal, the banker can reappraise its soundness and act accordingly. This is the reason that net working capital loans are made on the basis of short-term notes rather than being recast as term loans; the banker gains control through the reappraisal opportunity at each maturity.

Collateral value If, after appraising both liquidity and solvency, the banker still feels that a loan is too risky to be made on an unsecured basis, he or she then looks to specific assets or types of assets that might be pledged to secure the loan. If adequate security arrangements can be made, the bank might be protected through its right to seize and liquidate specific assets in event of default of the loan. Analysis of collateral values will be treated in the next chapter dealing with secured loans.

Commercial paper

Commercial paper was briefly discussed in Chapter 7 as a medium for investment in marketable securities. Now we shall view it from the standpoint of an issuer obtaining short-term financing by selling commercial paper. Note that only large firms of excellent credit standing generally have access to the commercial paper market.

A commercial paper issue is simply a batch of negotiable unsecured promissory notes payable to bearer at a specified time and place. Maturities range from a few days to nine months and denominations from $5,000 to $5 million, most such notes being for $100,000 and over.

The commercial paper market

This paper is either placed by the issuer directly with investors or sold by the issuer to a commercial paper dealer, who in turn resells it to investors.

Directly placed paper Most of the large and middle-sized finance companies place their paper directly with investors. They are large users of commercial paper because of the magnitude of their financial requirements and the legal limitation of commercial banks to lend no more than 10 percent of their total capital and surplus to any one borrower. Finance companies borrow more or less continually through the use of commercial paper, rolling over maturing paper by issuing more to repay it. By maintaining direct contact with investors, they eliminate the commercial paper dealer's fees. Directly placed issues account for about two thirds of the total volume of commercial paper outstanding.

Open-market paper Nearly all utility, manufacturing, and marketing firms that issue commercial paper sell their notes to a commercial paper dealer, who almost immediately resells them to investors. Most commercial paper is sold through a few dealers in New York. The dealers charge the issuer a fee, which usually is one eighth of 1 percent on large issues and one quarter of 1 percent on smaller issues of lesser known firms.

Secondary market Since most buyers of commercial paper hold it to maturity, the secondary market is not very active or highly developed. But the dealer who sold the paper normally stands ready to repurchase it at the holder's request. Repurchased paper will almost immediately be resold. Thus, the dealer makes a market for outstanding paper.

Investors in commercial paper We have already seen that business firms are substantial investors in commercial paper for inclusion in their marketable securities portfolios. In addition, such paper is held by commercial banks, insurance companies, pension funds, money-market mutual funds, and other institutional investors. The investment motives of all these investors are essentially the same as those discussed in Chapter 7 for the marketable securities portfolios of business corporations.

Impersonal nature—Implications The investor in commercial paper is concerned only that the issuer pays the note at maturity. The relationship to the issuer is completely impersonal. The serious implication of this lack of an ongoing relationship is that there is no loyalty of the lender to the borrower. If the commercial paper market becomes tight, as it sometimes does in a credit crunch, maturing paper must be paid or legal action will ensue. The market may or may not absorb a new issue to roll over this debt.

Therefore, even for a financially strong issuer, relying on commercial paper financing to the detriment of maintenance of the bank relationship may be risky. The bank, by contrast, has a long-standing relationship with its borrowing customer and an obligation to remain loyal in time of crisis either in the money market or in relation to the credit standing of the firm. A safe policy requires the maintenance of bank lines of credit sufficient to cover the firm's short-term financing needs in the event the commercial paper market should become unavailable.

Interest rates

Commercial paper is sold at a discount to mature at the face amount. Thus, as in the case of Treasury bills, the interest rate is the effective yield to maturity that results from the discount. Interest rates on commercial paper usually are lower than banks' prime rates, the differential varying from about one half of 1 percent to as much as 2 or 3 percent under varying money-market conditions.

The principal advantage of using commercial paper is this interest-rate differential. In addition, the borrower may (or may not) avoid compensating balance requirements with its bank(s) relative to commercial paper borrowing. The obvious cost-minimizing short-term borrowing policy would be to use commercial paper when the interest differential is high, then switch back to bank borrowing when the differential is small. The catch to this strategy is that a firm following such a policy might not be welcome when it returns to its bank(s) with its hand out at a time when money markets are tight, the bank's funds are limited, and it may be rationing credit only to its best customers. Such a policy must be tempered with moderation and executed with great care that the banking relationship(s) not be jeopardized.

Back-up lines of credit

Commercial paper dealers and their investor-customers often require documentation that the issuer of commercial paper has a back-up line of credit at its bank(s) sufficient to cover the amount of its commercial paper outstanding plus the new issue. This is to assure the holder of the paper that the issuer can borrow sufficient funds from its bank to pay the notes at maturity even if its operations do not produce such funds or if the commercial paper market should not be able to absorb a roll-over. Banks normally charge a fee of one quarter to one half of 1 percent for back-up lines. In addition, banks sometimes require additional compensating balances equal to 10 percent of the amount of commercial paper outstanding. Such fees and perhaps compensating balances often still do not offset the interest rate advantage of issuing commercial paper over bank borrowing.

Summary

This chapter discussed spontaneous short-term financing and unsecured borrowing through short-term bank loans and issuing commercial paper. Spontaneous credit arises in the normal course of business without overt arrangement by the management of the firm. The largest such sources are accounts payable (trade credit) and accruals of taxes and wages. Other possible sources are accrued royalties, customers' advances, and deposits.

Trade credit arises through purchase on credit terms. Its cost is implicit, and its magnitude tends to fluctuate directly with the volume of business. Only if purchases could alternatively be made for cash or if the credit terms include a cash discount does the purchaser have discretion as to the amount or cost of trade credit. Usually the implicit cost is quite high, favoring taking cash discounts if funds are available or can be borrowed. Trade credit tends to be granted liberally, so many firms that cannot obtain bank loans use it extensively. Stretching trade payables reduces their cost but at the serious risk of lowering credit standing and losing sources of supply in a sellers' market.

Accruals represent expenses that have been incurred but not yet paid. Wage accruals are a function of the length of pay periods. Long pay periods are advantageous to the employer, but are limited by considerations of employee morale and union pressure. Accrued taxes are an important spontaneous source of funds in the sense that funds are available for other uses between the dates that they are accrued and paid. But management has no discretion over these, as payment dates are set by the taxing authorities.

The banking relationship often is the most important external relationship of the firm. Careful selection of the bank—on the basis of ability of its personnel to understand and accommodate the firm's financial needs—and the strengthening of this relationship thorugh years of properly servicing obligations are of utmost importance.

Credit arrangements under which banks provide unsecured short-term loans are individual promissory notes, lines of credit, and revolving credit agreements. A line of credit is not a firm contract to lend funds, but a reputable bank would not cancel a line without good reason, such as serious deterioration of the firm's financial condition. A revolving credit agreement is a firm contract, usually subject to some provisos, that the bank will lend up to a stated amount any time during the given period. A commitment fee is charged on the unused portion, and interest on borrowings usually is based upon the floating prime.

Interest rates on bank loans are scaled upward from the prime rate, the differential depending mainly upon the particular borrower's credit standing, size of the loan, and profitability of the bank's overall business with that customer. In appraising the risk of short-term loans, bankers look first to liquidity, then to solvency, and last to collateral values.

Some large firms of excellent credit standing borrow short-term funds by issuing commercial paper. An issue of commercial paper is a batch of negotiable unsecured promissory notes payable to bearer. These notes may either be sold directly to investors or issued through a commercial paper dealer. Interest rates in the commercial paper market normally are the lowest available to a firm, but this market is somewhat volatile and completely impersonal. Therefore, sound financial policy requires that a firm maintain bank lines sufficient to cover its short-term financing needs in the event the commercial paper market should become unavailable.

Questions

1. *a.* What is the nature of a spontaneous source of funds?
   b. List four spontaneous sources of funds.
   c. Explain how each arises.
2. Explain the following terms of purchase:
   a. COD.
   b. 2/10, n/30.
   c. 3/10, n/60 EOM.
   d. n/30.

3. Explain the implicit cost of not taking a cash discount. How does this cost differ when payment is made at the net due date from that when the payable is stretched?

4. Is there an implicit cost of trade credit when no cash discount is allowed? Explain.

5. Why do accounts payable constitute the largest single source of short-term financing of business firms, especially small firms with limited credit standing?

6. In what sense do accrued wages and income taxes furnish spontaneous short-term financing to a firm? How much control does management have over accrual financing?

7. How does a landlord, a trash collection service, or a magazine publisher obtain spontaneous financing from its customers?

8. In essence, what is the value to a firm of a well established banking relationship? How can such a relationship be developed?

9. What is the prime rate? Why might one firm borrow at prime while another must pay 3 percent over prime? What is a floating interest rate tied to the prime rate?

10. What is a bank line of credit? How does a revolving credit agreement differ from a line of credit?

11. *a.* Why is the effective interest rate on prime commercial paper normally lower than the prime bank rate?
    b. Why might a firm of high credit standing choose to borrow from its bank(s) even though it could issue commercial paper at a lower cost?

12. What are compensating balances in relation to bank loans and lines of credit? How and under what conditions do compensating balance requirements increase a firm's cost of borrowing?

13. How does the *function* of a bank loan relate to the importance of liquidity, solvency, and profitability of the borrower?

Problems

(Note: Problems 1 and 2 are a series.)

1. What is the implicit annual interest cost of foregoing cash discounts under each of the following credit terms, assuming that payment would be made according to net terms? (Use a 365-day year.)
    a. 2/10, n/30.
    b. 3/10, n/60.

c. 1/10, n/30.
d. 2/15, n/45.

2. How would your answers to Problem 1 differ if the buyer were to stretch the payables by 15 days in each case?

3. Sportswear Store, Inc., of Madison, Wisconsin, normally orders swimsuits in April for shipment May 1 on terms of 2/10, n/30. Its buyer is considering an offer from Jansuits Corporation of a 5 percent trade discount if it takes delivery on February 1 of 24 dozen swimsuits wholesale priced at $20 each. The invoice will be seasonally dated May 1 on credit terms of 2/10, n/30. Management estimates storage costs at $2 per month per dozen swimsuits.

a. How many dollars could Sportswear Store save by accepting this offer?
b. What other consideration might influence the decision?

4. Queston Corporation has exhausted its bank credit line and has no funds to take cash discounts under terms of 3/10, n/60 on $50,000 of trade accounts payable. A finance company has offered a loan sufficient to enable Queston to take the discounts at an annual interest rate of 18 percent.

a. If Queston believed it would have to pay these accounts according to terms, should it forego the discounts or borrow from the finance company?
b. Would Queston's decision be the same if it believed that the payables could be stretched by 30 days without any effect upon its relations with suppliers or causing a change in its credit rating?

5. Darley Manufacturing Company purchases 1,000 units per month of a component part on a continual basis. It can buy the component parts from X at $60 each on credit terms of n/30 or identical parts from Y at $60.80 each on terms of 2/10, n/30. Assuming that Darley can borrow funds required to take the discounts at 12 percent from its bank, from which supplier should Darley buy the parts? Why?

6. In negotiations with its employees' union, National Manufacturing Company's labor relations manager is considering a trade-off involving an extra one half of 1 percent wage increase for a change in the firm's payroll period from weekly to every two weeks. Its weekly payroll is $20 million. Assuming that National's pretax opportunity cost of funds is 18 percent, appraise this trade-off.

7. Hayden Corporation requires $1 million for six months. American National Bank offers a loan at a 14 percent interest rate to be discounted. A loan at 14½ percent interest is offered by the Union National Bank, with the interest to be paid at maturity. Compare these two offers and decide from which bank Hayden should borrow (all other considerations being equal).

8. The First National Bank will lend $4 million to the Ill-Mo Corporation at a 13 percent annual interest rate. The bank requires that a compensating

balance of 20 percent of the loan be maintained as an average monthly collected balance. Ill-Mo normally would require an average monthly collected balance of about $500,000 for transactions and precautionary purposes.

a. What is the effective interest cost of usable funds to Ill-Mo Corporation?

b. How would your answer differ if Ill-Mo required an average monthly collected balance of $800,000 for transactions and precautionary purposes?

c. What would your answer be if the First National Bank required a 20 percent compensating balance as a *minimum* collected balance in Ill-Mo's demand deposit account?

9. Kalmia Corporation has the following opportunities to borrow $500,000 for one year:

a. A 12 percent loan on a discount basis with a 15 percent required *minimum* collected funds compensating balance.

b. A 14 percent loan, with interest to be paid at maturity and a 10 percent compensating balance requirement on an *average* monthly balance basis. The compensating balance is equivalent to Kalmia's normal cash requirements for transactions and precautionary purposes.

c. A 13 percent loan on a discount basis with no compensating balance requirement.

Which alternative offers Kalmia the lowest effective interest rate on funds available for its use?

10. Sharon Meyers, treasurer of Loran Corporation, could sell $10 million (face amount) of 180-day commercial paper at an annual discount rate of 10 percent or borrow $10 million for 180 days from Loran's banks at the prime rate of 12 percent. The banks would require compensating balances, on a monthly average collected balance basis, of about $400,000 more than Loran's required operating balances. The commercial paper dealer would charge one quarter of 1 percent for its services. Loran would be required to secure back-up lines of credit from its banks of $10 million to sell the commercial paper. Fees for the back-up lines would be three eights of 1 percent.

a. Which alternative will result in the lowest effective interest cost (annual rate) to Loran? (Use a 360-day year.) How much lower?

b. What other consideration might influence Ms. Meyers' decision?

c. Which alternative should she choose?

Chapter 10
Short-Term Financing—Secured Loans

Both the lender and the borrower would prefer that a short-term loan remain unsecured if that is justified by the credit worthiness of the firm. For the lender this is clean and simple, and for the borrower the loan does not entail any restrictions or encumbrances on its assets. There are, however, two situations that justify requiring that specific assets be pledged to secure a short-term loan. In the first, the firm has reached the limit of its unsecured borrowing capacity, which, in turn, is based upon its general credit standing. If additional credit accommodation that cannot be justified on an unsecured basis is required, the bank may seek the pledge of specific assets to secure a larger loan.

Second, there are many firms, particularly young, growing ones, that are either financially too weak or not sufficiently seasoned to be able to obtain short-term loans on an unsecured basis. Their banks require the pledge of specific assets to secure any loans. Perhaps, if and when the financial condition of such a firm improves and it has established a satisfactory record of servicing loans, security no longer will be required.[1]

As discussed in the previous chapter, the banker looks first for sufficient liquidity, or cash-generating capacity, to pay off the loan when due. If this is questionable, then he or she looks to sufficient solvency that the bank will still be protected even if the loan is not paid when due. If neither liquidity nor solvency appears to be fully sufficient, then the bank looks to the pledge of specific assets that would protect the bank's position (or at least minimize its losses) in case of default. Please understand that no banker makes a loan with the expectation that it will be necessary to seize and liquidate security to repay the loan. But every banker recognizes that the future is uncertain and that, if things do not work out as expected, the bank's interests still must be protected. Our comparison, in the preceding chapter, of the marginal profitability of bank loans compared to trade credits showed that a bank's margin is so thin that it cannot afford to take a high risk of default without protecting its position if that should occur.

[1]There is a third occasion on which secured loans are used, namely, that in which convenient security arises in the normal course of business and it is customary that all loans to firms in that line of business be made on a secured basis. The most prominent example of this is bank loans to securities dealers to carry their inventories of stocks and bonds. Traditionally such loans are secured by pledge of those securities regardless of the credit worthiness of the securities dealer. As a practical matter, the securities might as well be in the bank's portion of its vault as in the securities dealer's box in the same vault. This arrangement is rare in nonfinancial types of businesses.

General considerations

Probably the best way for the business manager to learn about secured borrowing arrangements is to move over to the other side of the desk and look at these loans from the viewpoint of the lender. This furnishes the required perspective to understand the eligibility of collateral that might be provided to secure such loans. The lender looks at three things in assessing the feasibility of a secured loan arrangement: (1) the legal and physical perfection of the lien, (2) the expected net value of the collateral if it had to be seized and liquidated upon default of the loan, and (3) the cost of administering the lending arrangement.

Perfection of the lien

A *lien* is the claim that one party has on the property of another, here the claim of the lender on the property pledged by the borrower to secure a loan. The Uniform Commercial Code, which has been adopted by all states, provides in Article 9 the legal mechanisms through which such liens may be placed against the property of the borrower. In essence, a *security agreement* is drawn, providing a *security interest* in the designated property that is pledged as *collateral* (security), giving the lender the legal right to seize that property in event of default of the loan. This security agreement, usually accompanied by the note or other evidence of the loan, must be recorded in the office designated under state law, variously the clerk of the district court, the county clerk or recorder, or the secretary of state. Because conflicting claims (two liens against the same property) are resolved by giving priority to the earliest claim, it may be necessary for the lender to search the records to assure that there is no prior claim.

Perfection of the lien refers to the degree of assurance the lender has that the assets pledged will be available to it in event of default. Strength of a lien may vary all the way from the physical retention of the pledged property by the lender, through the holding of the property by an independent third party, to a trust receipt making the borrower a trustee of the lender who holds title, to a blanket or a floating lien that allows the borrower full control of the property and is only a "hunting license" that gives the lender the right to seize the property if it can be found. (These legal arrangements will be discussed later in this chapter.)

Other things being equal, the lender will rank the eligibility of collateral offered as security according to the strength of the legal and physical perfection of the lien. Incidentally, if liquidation of the property yields an amount greater than that owed on the loan, the lender must remit the balance to the borrower. Conversely, if the net proceeds of liquidation are less than the amount owed, the lender has an unsecured claim for the amount remaining.[2]

Collateral value

Value of the pledged collateral is the most important determinant of the amount that can safely be loaned against it. Factors that lenders consider are (1) the ease and certainty of the valuation at the time the loan is made, (2) the relative stability of that value, that is, how much downward fluctuation might take place between the time the loan is made and eventual liquidation of the pledged assets if and when default should occur, and (3) the ease and cost of liquidation should it be required. The decisive consideration is an estimate of the net proceeds that could be obtained from sale of the pledged assets after deducting all costs of seizure and liquidation.

Ease and certainty of valuation The nature of the market for the collateral will determine the ease and certainty of its valuation. At the positive extreme, the valuation of a single account receivable from a customer of unquestioned credit standing would require only a phone call to that customer verifying that this obligation was owed to the borrower in the amount as represented. Similarly, the valuation of a commodity, such as 10,000 bushels of No. 2 spring wheat, would require only looking up the quotation of that commodity in the daily newspaper. At the negative extreme, the value of an inventory of many different electronic components, particularly if they were specialized to the requirements of the borrower's product, would be little more than a guess. The lender, of course, could ascertain the cost of these items, but simply would not have the technical knowledge to judge whether or not they were obsolete. Thus, other things being equal, the lender might be willing to lend a very high percentage of the ascertained value of the receivable or the inventory of wheat but might not be at all interested in a loan to be secured by the inventory of electronic components.

Stability of value How much downward fluctuation might take place in the value of the collateral between its appraisal at the time the loan was made and eventual liquidation if required? In the case of the receivable discussed above, a decline in value would require a drastic change in the credit worthiness of a strong firm, which would be highly improbable. The wheat price may change daily (subject perhaps to government price supports), so the wheat would not be as strong collateral unless the lender held a security agreement giving it the right to sell the wheat if its price should fall to the

[2]This discussion relating to the legal perfection of liens under the Uniform Commercial Code reflects a layman's general observations of the law. Competent legal counsel should be utilized in drawing a security agreement or in determining one's rights under such an agreement.

amount of the loan (this is customary on such loans). The inventory of electronic components could become almost valueless in the event of a technological change that made them obsolete. An even greater risk of fluctuation in value would relate to an inventory of perishable goods, such as tomatoes. How would the lender be protected if it were necessary to seize several carloads of rotten tomatoes?

In appraising the stability of value of collateral, the lender must think in terms of what the value might be under conditions that would lead to default of the loan. Such default usually would occur as the result of economic developments unfavorable to sale of the borrowing firm's product(s). Thus, the same economic developments that might lead to default of the loan often also would result in substantial decline in the value of the collateral.

For example, weakness of the end-market for a manufacturer's product might have an unfavorable financial effect upon the firm, resulting in its default of the loan. But that same weakness in the market would affect the cash-generating ability of the firm's customers, so the collectibility of receivables from them would be impaired. Or the introduction of a competitive product that outsells that of the borrowing firm, resulting in default of the loan, probably also would result in a drastic reduction in the value of its finished goods inventory. This is the reason that a lender often takes a more pessimistic view of the value of receivables and inventory collateral than the management of the firm seeking to secure a loan.

Ease and cost of liquidation The lender asks, "How would I dispose of the pledged assets if I had to seize them? How long would it take? Through what channels of distribution could they be liquidated? How much would it cost to dispose of them?" Answers to these questions vary widely. At one extreme, in which listed stocks, bonds, or commodities that are traded daily on an organized exchange are pledged, liquidation would require simply a phone call to a broker and waiting five business days for the settlement to clear. At the other extreme, how is a lender going to dispose of an inventory of toys the day after Christmas, or fireworks on July 5? This liquidation consideration boils down to the marketability of the collateral. It may be such that liquidation is simple and inexpensive, or difficult, expensive, and time consuming, or it may be downright impossible.

Cost of administration

Ultimately, the borrower must pay the cost of administration of any loan arrangement. This cost may be included in the interest charged and/or in additional fees paid to the lender or to other parties, such as a warehousing company's charges for services required to administer the loan. The cost of servicing a loan secured by marketable securities or the assignment of one or a few specific accounts receivable is relatively low. Such a loan may be made at perhaps 0.5 to 2 percent over prime, depending largely on the size of the loan. On the other hand, a loan secured by a large number of receivables that must periodically be confirmed, or one secured by inventory that must be warehoused, may entail substantial cost. A point will be reached at which the cost will be so high that such a loan will not be feasible.

The net result of the considerations discussed above—perfection of the lien, collateral value, and cost of administration—is that some particular forms of collateral are highly desirable, some are acceptable, and some are not suitable from the lender's point of view. Many loans that would not be granted by lenders on an unsecured basis are made possible through the pledge of acceptable collateral. But many borrowers who have approached potential lenders offering security that they thought would adequately secure a loan have been sadly disappointed when they have been turned down because under these criteria the lender found the offered collateral to be unacceptable.

Now let us discuss briefly the sources of secured short-term loans and then proceed to treat in some detail the specific types of security that might be pledged and the appropriate lending arrangements under which secured short-term loans are made.

Sources

Short-term secured loans are made by both commercial banks and finance companies. Usually the higher-quality loans (in terms of both general credit worthiness of the borrowers and desirability of the collateral) are made by commercial banks. When such loans are refused by banks, the potential borrower often turns to a finance company, which might make the loan at a higher interest rate or require larger service fees than those charged by the banks. Even so, such a loan may be a superior alternative to no loan at all. In some states, industrial banks (quite different institutions from commercial banks) also make secured loans to business firms. Their requirements as to acceptable quality are similar to those of finance companies.

Accounts receivable financing

Financing of accounts receivable may be obtained by either assignment of accounts to secure a loan or by factoring receivables, that is, selling the receivables outright to a financial institution. The former method is the most prevalent in most industries.

Assignment of accounts receivable

There are different arrangements under which accounts receivable may be assigned to secure a loan. They all involve the use of a security agreement assigning receivables to the lender and giving the lender the right to collect these receivables in event of default on the loan. Receivables generally are desirable security because they are only one step away from cash in the cyclical flow of funds of a firm. Thus, they have greater liquidity than any other asset that might be pledged except marketable securities (collateral that would only rarely be held by a firm wishing to borrow).

Lender's appraisal of collateral value A potential lender usually appraises receivables offered as collateral in much the same fashion as management does in periodically reviewing its aggregate receivables. You will recall from Chapter 8 the use of such analytical tools as aging the receivables and credit-rating classification analysis in making such an appraisal. In addition, the lender may also review the borrowing firm's collection experience on these accounts over a past period of, say, six months or a year. Based upon such analysis, the lender may then take either of two courses to determine the maximum amount (or percentage of the total amount of the assigned receivables) that will be loaned on this security.

One approach is to select only the acceptable accounts receivable—say, those less than 60 days old, owed by firms with credit-rating classifications in the first two ranks (D&B numerical ratings 1 or 2) from whom the borrower has collected all invoices over the past year within 70 days. Then the maximum percentage that will be loaned against the selected receivables—say, 80 percent—will be determined on the basis of a judgment that, in the event of default, at least 80 percent of these receivables, net of collection costs, could be recovered.

Evaluation of the relevant factors—maximum age, collection experience on the accounts, and credit rating of the customers—will vary according to the lending officer's seasoned judgment, which is in turn based upon experience with similar collateral. In general, the maximum percentage to be loaned will range from perhaps 50 to 90 percent. Bankers rarely make loans when they feel that less than 70 percent is justified. Finance companies may accept the assignment of lower-quality receivables but lend a smaller percentage against them.

Rarely, if ever, will a financial institution lend in excess of 90 percent of the face amount of assigned receivables, even if they should be due from customers of unquestioned credit standing. There are two reasons for this: (1) there always is some possibility that customers of the borrower may have return or allowance claims resulting from the receipt of defective merchandise and would not be fully liable for the total amounts of the invoices or (2) the risk of either erroneous or fraudulent invoices. Any percentage that might be used as a basis for the loan includes consideration of these risk factors as well as those related to difficulty or inability to collect the receivables upon default.

The other course that the lender might take is to array all of the receivables according to a characteristic, such as age, collection experience, or credit rating of the customers. Then, on the basis of a weighted average of such a characteristic, the lender will take an assignment of all of the receivables and lend up to a given percentage of the total amount. This weighted-average approach is illustrated in Table 10–1. In this example, based solely upon aging the receivables (other characteristics may also be used), the lender may be willing to lend 85 percent against receivables less than one month old, 65 percent against those between one and two months old, 40 percent against those two to three months old, and so on. The weighted average of these loan percentages times the percentage of the total receivables that fall in each category yields a weighted average of 70.7 percent. On the basis of this analysis, the lending officer would probably make a loan on a 70 percent basis, or be willing to lend a maximum of about \$60,000 (70.7% × \$85,000) against these receivables. Note that if the second approach is used, the loan percentage generally will be lower than under the first approach, but the total amount of receivables assigned will be larger. The resulting dollar amount of the loan usually will be about the same.

Table 10–1 Appraisal of accounts receivable as loan collateral
Weighted-average approach based upon aging

Age (days)	Receivables $000	Receivables Percent	Loan percentage	Weighted average percentage
0– 30	\$47	55.3%	85%	47.0%
31– 60	25	29.4	65	19.1
61– 90	9	10.6	40	4.2
91–120	3	3.5	10	0.4
>120	1	1.2	-0-	-0-
	\$85	100.0%		70.7%

The lender may or may not formalize the analysis to the degree indicated above. Often an experienced loan officer can approximate the calculation of the maximum loan percentage in his or her head without going through the weighted-averaging process. But the logic indicated above lies behind the lending officer's decision.

General versus specific assignment If the borrower's accounts receivable are relatively few in number and large in individual amounts, such as those of a parts manufacturer selling to the major automobile companies, the acceptable accounts are specifically assigned to the lender. The borrower presents the individual invoices and an accompanying assignment form to the lender under a continuous security agreement and borrows the agreed-upon percentage of the amount of these invoices. The borrower remits all collections on these receivables to a special account set up by the lender. The lender keeps the loan percentage, assumed to be 80 percent here, as payments on the loan and transfers the remaining 20 percent to the borrower's general account. The lender monitors the collateral by verifying invoices with the borrower's customers.

Where the borrower's accounts receivable are large in number and relatively small in individual amounts, a *general assignment* (sometimes called a blanket assignment) of all accounts receivable usually is made. Under this arrangement, the borrower remits all collections to the lender. But individual invoices normally are not submitted to the lender; rather the lender has the right to audit these invoices at any time and usually verifies a sample of them with the borrower's customers. The lender's control over such collateral is considerably less than under the specific assignment of a few large receivables. For this reason, interest and/or service charges tend to be higher under general assignments, and often the loan percentage is lower.

Notification and nonnotification bases The above description of the collection process, in which the borrower receives payments from its customers and remits these to a special account, with the lender retaining the loan percentage as payment on the loan and transferring the remainder to the borrower's general account, illustrates an accounts receivable loan on a *nonnotification* basis. Under this arrangement the borrower's customers are not notified of the assignment of the accounts. They pay their bills as usual to the seller, and the lender's verification of the receivables is handled discreetly, such as by having the self-addressed envelope addressed to "Auditor, P.O. Box 957." Borrowers prefer a nonnotification basis because customers' knowledge of the assignment of accounts receivable may raise questions regarding the firm's future dependability as a supplier. Under such an arrangement, the lender obviously must have faith that the borrower will remit collections as agreed.

If a loan is on a *notification* basis, the borrower's customers are instructed to mail their payments direct to the lender. (This may or may not be camouflaged by use of a post office box.) The lender receives payments of accounts and, as above, usually keeps the loan percentage as a payment on the loan and transfers the balance to the borrower's general account. Usually lenders will not require a notification basis unless they are somewhat apprehensive as to the borrower's reliability in remitting collections.

Ongoing arrangements Some loans secured by the assignment of accounts receivable are simple one-time loans with short maturity, say 90 days. These loans are secured by a batch of receivables assigned when the loan is made, and the loan is collected either through the depository arrangement discussed above or by payment at maturity. Most loans secured by assignment of accounts receivable, however, represent ongoing arrangements whereby the initially assigned receivables are continually replaced by new receivables created through credit sales of the borrower and the existing receivables are continually being paid off by the borrower's remitting collections to the special account.

The lender indicates its intention to lend up to a given percentage, say 80 percent, of the receivables existing at any given time. This commitment is subject, of course, to its continued acceptance of the quality of the receivables and no deterioration in the financial condition of the borrowing firm. Thus, sales creating new receivables will add to the borrowing power of the firm, and collection of previous sales from its customers will simultaneously reduce its borrowing power and pay off the loan percentage based on the amount of collections.

This process may go on month after month and year after year, providing financing equal to the loan percentage (here 80 percent) of the assigned receivables. This ongoing arrangement has the advantage to the borrower of providing flexible financing that will fluctuate in relation to its accounts receivable balances, which, in turn, will fluctuate with changes in sales volume. Technically, this is short-term financing but actually it is a longer-term financing arrangement on a flexible principal basis. Usually a floating interest rate will be set at a given number of percentage points over the prime rate, adjusted periodically, say monthly or bimonthly, as the prime rate changes. This feature may entail substantial risk for the borrower. In a period when credit is tight and the prime rate is rising rapidly, such a loan at, say, 4 percent over prime can become extremely expensive for the borrower to handle.[3]

Costs of borrowing The interest on bank loans secured by the assignment of accounts receivables tends to range between 2 and 5 percent over the prime rate, while on loans from finance companies it may range considerably higher than this. In addition, service fees, usually ranging from 1 to 3 percent of the average loan balance, may be required to cover the costs of monitoring the collateral, such as auditing the invoices and confirming the receivables with the borrower's customers. Both interest rates and service fees may be lower for single loans secured by the assignment of a few specific accounts. As the number of accounts increases and their individual amounts decrease, servicing costs go up and both interest rates and service charges increase to cover them.

To some extent, costs are also a function of the continuing nature of such loan arrangements, repeatedly approving and auditing new receivables and

[3]Near the end of such a tight-money period, a principal of a wholesaling firm told the author, "Last year we worked for the bank. Our sales were very good, but after we paid the interest to the bank on our accounts receivable loans at three over floating prime, there wasn't anything left for my partner and me."

the activity of the collection account. Risk of default, of course, influences the interest differential over prime and, when one recognizes that loans are normally secured only if their risk is considered to be too great for unsecured lending, this differential tends to be rather high.

An indirect cost that is not subject to quantification is the possible reduction in the borrowing firm's credit standing among its trade suppliers. Although assignment of receivables is hardly viewed by them as evidence of a financial crisis, the news that a customer has assigned its receivables, which usually is transmitted by a credit agency, is hardly welcomed with joy by trade creditors. The negative effect upon a firm's credit worthiness as viewed from a trade creditor's standpoint results from the fact that its credits are unsecured while another creditor, the bank or finance company, is now in a preferred position relative to the most liquid asset except cash owned by its customer. The secured lender will henceforth get the first crack at cash generated through the collection of receivables and, in event of default of the loan, can collect the assigned receivables up to the total amount owed to it before the common creditors can obtain any funds from this source. Countering this, perhaps the borrower will be able to use some of the proceeds of the loan to pay off overdue trade credits. If such overdue credits are not paid off, the trade creditors have good reason to be unhappy, and that may be reflected by their unwillingness to continue to supply the borrowing firm and/or to carry overdue accounts.

Factoring receivables

Factoring, unlike borrowing against the assignment of accounts receivable, involves a *sale* of accounts receivable to the factor. Title to the receivables passes to the factor, thereby eliminating these assets from the firm's balance sheet and transferring responsibility for managing the accounts and bearing the risks related to collection and bad debt losses to the factor. This is both good and bad from the firm's standpoint. It is freed from the costs and responsibilities of carrying and managing accounts receivable, but it loses control over its accounts receivable policies. The factor may have a different and tougher attitude regarding collection policies than the firm's management would prefer in consideration of the effect upon marginal sales and profits.

Although factoring is widely used in a few specialized lines of business, particularly the textile and furniture trades, it is used considerably less than borrowing against assigned receivables in most other industries. The financial institutions that provide factoring services include some commercial banks, which offer this service through a subsidiary; factoring subsidiaries of bank holding companies; the same finance companies that lend against assigned receivables; and a few "old-line factors" in New York City whose historical roots are in financing the textile industry.

Procedures When a firm factors its receivables, it usually enters into an agreement running for one year or more with automatic renewal and cancellable only upon stated notice. Its existing receivables are submitted to the factor, who buys all of them except those that may be rejected on the basis of insufficient credit worthiness. Thereafter, each day's orders are submitted to the factor, who buys all accounts it considers credit worthy. If the factor does not accept the order, the firm typically has the option of rejecting it or accepting and carrying that receivable as its own responsibility. In most cases, customers are notified that the receivable is payable direct to the factor. A few factoring arrangements are made on a nonnotification basis: customers pay the firm, which, in turn, is obligated to endorse the checks and remit them to the factor.[4]

The factor remits to the firm, or credits its account, upon collection of receivables and usually is obligated to pay the firm after a given period, say 30 days, whether or not a receivable has been collected at that time. Under this, the most common arrangement, called *nonrecourse,* the factor bears the risk of bad debt losses. Some factoring agreements provide *recourse,* which allows the factor, after an account has been delinquent for a stated number of days, to turn it back to the firm and charge it to the firm's account. In these cases the factor does not assume the risk of bad debt losses.

To this point, a factoring arrangement provides service in handling the selection, administration, and collection of receivables, and, if on a nonrecourse basis, the bearing of the risk of bad debt losses. But no financing has been provided because the firm does not receive any funds until the receivables have either been collected or the payment date has been reached. Financing is provided by allowing the firm to borrow from the factor at an agreed interest rate all or any portion of the uncollected balances in the current accounts receivable less a reserve, usually 5 or 10 percent, which is restricted by the factor to cover cash discounts, returns, or allowances related to the accounts. On the other hand, if the firm wishes to leave collected funds in its account, the factor pays interest (at a lower rate than it charges on advances) on these funds.

There are two principal advantages of factoring receivables. The first is that the firm is relieved of the responsbility and costs of selecting, administering, and collecting receivables, and, if the factor has no recourse, the firm avoids bad debt losses. It is assured of cash flow at the end of the stipulated period. The second advantage is that it is assured of a source of credit equal to the uncollected receivable balances less the reserve. The principal disadvantages to the firm are (1) loss of control of its credit policies,

[4]Factors usually consider nonnotification arrangements to be too risky, as they may be "frauds waiting to happen."

(2) possible deterioration of its credit standing with trade suppliers because under factoring the entire receivables account is removed from the assets of the firm, and (3) the relatively high costs, which will now be discussed.

Costs The costs of factoring receivables take two forms: (1) the factor's fees for servicing and collecting the receivables and bearing the risk of bad debt losses and (2) interest charges on advances. Factor's fees usually range from 1 to 3 percent of all receivables purchased. Note that these fees relate to the volume of accounts factored, not to financing obtained. The particular fee charged a given firm will be based upon (1) the volume of purchased receivables contemplated, (2) the size of the individual orders to be processed and accounts receivable balances to be administered, and (3) the perceived credit worthiness of the firm's customers, which, in turn, relates to contemplated collection costs and bad debt losses. Of course, if the agreement is with recourse, the fact that the factor is not assuming bad debt losses and is limiting collection costs will, other things being equal, reduce the fee charged.

The interest charged on advances usually will range from 2 to 4 percent over prime. Inasmuch as such advances are, in effect, secured by the uncollected accounts receivable, the rate charged will be a function of the firm's general credit worthiness and the quality of the receivables. The interest rate that the firm may receive on available balances left with the factor normally will be less than or about equal to that which it could obtain if it invested such funds in marketable securities. Therefore, interest received from the factor should not be considered as an offset to the interest paid on advances.

Example To illustrate a factoring agreement and its costs, assume that General Manufacturing Company has a sales volume of $1,200,000 a year. Its accounts receivable turnover is 12 times (average collection period 30 days). Sales are not seasonal, therefore its total accounts receivable are about $100,000 throughout the year. General factors its receivables under an agreement requiring 2 percent factor's fees. The factor provides advances at 1 percent per month (12 percent annual rate), subject to a 10 percent reserve, with interest to be charged on a discount basis. First its annual factor's fees will be $24,000 (2% × $1,200,000). General estimates its credit department costs, including bad debts, to be about 1.5 percent of sales, or $18,000 annually. Since the factoring agreement is on a nonrecourse basis, it will eliminate these expenses, thus the net incremental cost attributable to factor's fees will be $6,000 ($24,000 − $18,000).

General intends to utilize all advances available. With uncollected receivables balances of $100,000 subject to a 10 percent reserve, it can roll over monthly advances of $90,000. At an interest rate of 1 percent per month, a $900 discount will be deducted on advances, and General will receive net advances of $89,100. Its annual interest cost on these advances will be $10,800 ($90,000 × 12%).

Adding the $6,000 net incremental factoring fees to interest costs of $10,800, the total annual incremental costs to General of this arrangement will be $16,800. This will allow it to gain $89,100 of incremental financing at a cost of 18.9 percent ($16,800/$89,100). If the 12 percent annual interest rate on advances were based upon prime plus 2 percent, then this financing will be obtained at approximately prime plus 9 percent. This is a rather high cost of funds. The feasibility of General's entering into this factoring arrangement will depend, of course, upon how badly it needs the financing, what financing alternatives, if any, are available to it, and upon the incremental profit it contemplates from using these funds.

Note that a significant portion of the cost in the above example was the differential between the factor's fees, $24,000, and the firm's estimated cost of servicing its receivables, $18,000. In some cases, there may be no differential, or the factor's fees may be lower than the firm's costs. Particularly where the latter is true, factoring may be quite advantageous from a cost standpoint.

The arrangement under which many retail merchants accept bank credit cards (MasterCard or Visa) is very similar to factoring. The credit card issuer (usually a bank) sets up a line of credit for the retail customer. When the customer charges a purchase from the merchant, that merchant deposits the charge slip with its bank and receives the amount of the charge less a discount. The discount ranges from about 2 to 4 percent, depending on the volume and desirability of the merchant's account. The merchant's bank then collects from the card-issuing bank through the clearing system operated by the bank card organization. For the merchant, this arrangement has about the same effect as factoring in that, for the discount fee, it is relieved of managing accounts receivable, financing them, and absorbing bad debt losses. Its cash flow is accelerated as if the credit card sale were for cash.

Inventory financing

A firm may be able to borrow against the pledge of part or all of its inventories. Feasibility will depend upon practical considerations relative to the legal and physical perfection of the lien, the estimated net liquidation value of the pledged inventories in event of default, and the contemplated costs of administering such a loan and its supporting collateral. Financial institutions that make such loans are the same as those that lend against assigned accounts receivable, that is, commercial banks and finance companies. The means of collateralizing such loans include floating or blanket liens, trust receipts that make the borrower a trustee of the lender-owner, or storage of the pledged inventory in either public or field warehouses and furnishing the warehouse receipts to the lender.

Floating or blanket liens

The use of a floating or blanket lien to secure a loan against pledged inventory involves drawing a security agreement giving the lender a security interest in the inventory owned by the borrower. Such a lien does not specify the items of inventory pledged or provide any control by the borrower over such inventories. Such an arrangement is convenient to the borrower in that it is free to move the inventory, process it, display it, or sell it at will. But lenders tend to have a low regard for such an arrangement for essentially the same reasons. At any given time the lender does not know how much of what inventory is securing its loan, the value of the inventory, where it is, or, in fact, whether or not it exists at all. Lenders usually regard such a lien as a "hunting license" that will give them the right upon default of the loan to seize and liquidate any pledged inventory they can find, *if* they can find it. They simply have seen or learned of too many cases in which such inventories (and often the borrowers) have disappeared.

Yet, in many cases, the blanket or floating lien is the only practical means of securing a loan by inventory. The work in process inventory of almost any manufacturing company simply must be available to the borrower to be processed; there is no way that it can be put under lock and key or that a guard representing the lender can hover over it. Most retail firms must have merchandise inventory displayed on their sales floors, and it continually fluctuates as merchandise is sold and replaced by the purchase of new inventories. Thus, inventories that are not subject from a practical standpoint to perfection of liens stronger than a blanket or floating lien generally are not considered as highly desirable collateral.

When a floating lien is considered by a lender as the sole collateral supporting a loan, the amount of the loan generally will be only a small percentage of the estimated value of the inventories, say 25 to 50 percent. Even this will require that the lender have a high regard for the character of the principal(s) of the borrowing firm in order to minimize the risk of inventory disappearance. Often, however, when a lender is relying primarily upon other collateral, such as assigned accounts receivable and/or a chattel mortgage on equipment, a blanket lien will also be placed upon inventories (1) to provide a little additional protection to the lender and (2) so that the borrower cannot pledge the inventories to someone else, jeopardizing the lender's position relative to those inventories in event of bankruptcy. It must be admitted that there also may be another motive. Some lenders believe that, "When you've got 'em over a barrel, take anything they've got."[5]

Trust receipts

A somewhat stronger lien may be obtained through the use of trust receipts. Under this arrangement, the lender holds title to the inventory and the borrower is entrusted with physical possession of it. Each item of pledged inventory is specifically identified by serial number, and the lender periodically audits the inventory; any missing inventory that has not been accounted for through sale and repayment of the loan against it indicates that the borrower has breached the trust. Legal implications of a breach of trust are much stronger than simple default on a loan.

This device usually is used on an ongoing basis, each new item of inventory being added to the collateral and each sale releasing collateral, with the amount loaned on that item remitted to the lender as a payment on the loan. Trust receipt financing is used extensively to carry the inventories of dealers in automobiles, major appliances, furniture, and heavy equipment; the arrangement is called "floor-planning." The largest lenders on this basis are captive finance company subsidiaries of the manufacturers of such products. This type of financing is also done by commercial banks and independent finance companies.

Although this arrangement provides tighter control of the inventory by the lender than a blanket or floating lien, it still is not by any means foolproof. Almost any lender can cite cases in which such security has been sold without remitting the proceeds or, at the extreme, in which both the inventory and the dealer have disappeared, occasionally never to be found. Such lenders realize that a piece of paper called a trust receipt does not create a trustworthy borrower, so they place considerable emphasis upon integrity of the borrower in analyzing such loans.

Borrowing against warehoused inventories

The strongest lien exists when pledged inventories are required to be stored under the control of a third party, a warehousing company, that is responsible to the lender for physical security of the property. This can be accomplished either through storing inventories in a public warehouse or through setting up a field warehouse located on the borrower's premises.

[5]An alleged example of this occurred in 1980 when the Hunt brothers, who reputedly had been one of the wealthiest families in the world, got into financial difficulty with their huge speculation in the silver markets. A group of banks that bailed them out was reported to have required the pledge of not only their silver and silver futures contracts, the securities reflecting ownership in their oil companies, their cattle ranches, and racing stables, but even the pledge of Bunker Hunt's Rolex wristwatch.

Public warehousing If public (sometimes called terminal) warehouse receipts are used, the borrower stores the pledged inventory in a public warehouse and the warehouse company issues a negotiable *warehouse receipt*. The warehouse receipt must be presented to the warehousing company to obtain release of the stored inventory. The borrower transfers the warehouse receipt to the lender to provide the required security on the loan.

Commercial banks or finance companies usually will lend against such receipts a relatively high proportion of the value if the pledged inventory is a standard marketable commodity. The security agreement provides that in the event the quoted market value falls close to the amount of the loan, the holder of the warehouse receipt, upon specified notice to the borrower, may sell the commodity to pay off the loan. This arrangement is often used to finance the carrying of commodities inventories such as grains (stored in public grain elevators), oil, cotton, sugar, or metals. The arrangement is almost foolproof when the warehousing company is reliable; even if not, it normally is bonded to cover the full value of the stored inventories. There is the possible risk that forged or stolen warehouse receipts may be used as collateral. Such arrangements are not necessarily limited to financing standard commodities, but often cost and inconvenience of transportation and storage limit feasibility of borrowing against other inventories under this arrangement. If so, a field warehousing arrangement may be more practical.

Field warehousing Under a field warehousing arrangement, the pledged inventory is stored in a segregated warehouse located on the borrower's premises but under the control of a warehousing company that is obligated to act in the interest of the lender. A firm specializing in setting up and controlling field warehouses is brought in to manage this arrangement. Often the field warehouse will simply be the raw materials or finished goods warehouse at the borrower's plant. Sometimes it is necessary to physically secure such a warehouse by constructing a chain-link fence segregating a portion of the borrower's plant or perhaps enclosing an outdoor area adjacent to the plant. One or more persons employed by the field warehousing company are placed in charge of physical security and accounting for all inventories moving in or out of this restricted area, which is now a field warehouse. These employees are bonded for the maximum contemplated amount of the loan and are responsible to the lender.

Borrowing under such an arrangement usually is ongoing, the lender agreeing to advance a given percentage of cost of warehoused inventories to the borrower. As new inventories are moved into the warehouse, the amount that may be borrowed is increased, and as inventories are released from the warehouse, appropriate payments must be made to the lender. By utilizing such an arrangement the flexibility of the borrower is greatly increased as compared to public warehousing. However, the costs may be quite high because the borrower must pay all costs of the field warehousing arrangement in addition to interest required on the loan.

From the lender's standpoint, while the lien is more secure than either a blanket lien or trust receipts, there still are ways by which a dishonest borrower could defraud the lender. The most famous case of such fraud occurred in the 1960s, when Allied Crude Vegetable Oil Refining Corporation defrauded over 50 major banks and other lenders of about $175 million under a field warehousing arrangement covering pledged inventories of vegetable oil. As this debacle was sorted out, the principal owner of the company, Anthony DeAngelis, went to prison, the field warehousing company went bankrupt, and the lenders who held the warehouse receipts absorbed horrendous losses.[6]

Cost of borrowing The cost of securing borrowing by pledging inventories generally is quite high and varies greatly depending upon the legal and physical means by which the lien is perfected as well as the nature and quality of the inventory collateral. Borrowing against trust receipts (floor-planning) or against public warehouse receipts covering standard commodities usually provides the least costly inventory loans. Interest rates tend to run around 2 or 3 percent over prime, depending upon the nature, amount, and marketability of the collateral. In the latter case, an important cost element is whether or not the commodities would have to be stored in a public warehouse anyway. If so, warehousing fees should be ignored in calculating the borrower's cost. If not, such fees, tending to run from 1 to 3 percent of the value of the inventory stored, must be added, making such loans quite expensive.

The percentage of cost of the pledged inventory that may be borrowed also runs highest for these two types of loans, 80 to 100 percent (the latter where a captive financing subsidiary of the manufacturer is, in effect, subsidizing the floor-planning of its dealer's inventories) on trust receipt loans and, depending on the commodity, some 75 to 80 percent of market value on public warehouse receipts.

Inasmuch as blanket or floating liens on inventories provide relatively weak security and are often used in conjunction with other, stronger collateral, the cost of such loans is rather hard to isolate. Probably some 3 to 6 percent above the prime interest rate is a reasonable estimate. On the basis of such a lien, most lenders would advance only 25 to 50 percent of cost of the inventories. There may be exceptions to both the interest and the percentage advanced if integrity of the borrower is judged to be high and the nature of the inventory is such that use of a stronger lien would not be feasible.

[6]See N. C. Miller, *The Great Salad Oil Swindle* (Baltimore: Penguin Books, 1965), for a very interesting story of the fraudulent use of a field warehousing arrangement. Another, much shorter, description of various frauds against secured lenders commended to your reading is Monroe R. Lazere, "Swinging Swindles and Creepy Frauds," *Journal of Commercial Bank Lending,* September 1977, pp. 44–52.

Total costs of borrowing under field warehousing arrangements also are difficult to identify categorically. Interest rates, depending upon the quality of the inventory collateral, usually run about 3 to 5 percent over prime. But incremental field warehousing costs vary widely. If the existing plant warehouse can be utilized without modification except changing the lock on the door and the present warehouseman becomes an employee of the warehousing company, little additional cost would be incurred except for bonding this warehouseman and paying the warehousing company for its services in reporting to the lender. On the other hand, if a special facility must be built and additional warehouse employees are required, unless such costs can be spread over a very large loan, the incremental field warehousing costs may be prohibitive. The net of this is that total costs range up to the point at which such an arrangement must be ruled out as too expensive.

Other secured financing

Theoretically, any asset of the borrowing firm might be pledged to secure a short-term loan if the lender asks for such a pledge and the borrower is willing to make it. Assets other than accounts receivable or inventories that might be pledged are stocks or bonds of other corporations, equipment, or the cash value of life insurance policies. Real estate is rarely mortgaged to secure short-term loans because of the relatively high cost of perfecting such a lien. Real estate mortgages, of course, are frequently used in connection with longer-term loans.

When *stocks or bonds,* particularly those listed on major securities exchanges, are available, they are excellent collateral. The securities are turned over to the bank along with a hypothecation certificate, which gives the lender the right to sell the securities in event of default or, with adequate notice to the borrower, if their market value falls to a level only sufficient to cover the loan. In addition, a form stating that the proceeds of the loan are not to be used for the purpose of purchasing or carrying securities must be furnished to the bank in compliance with Federal Reserve regulations governing margin requirements.

Depending upon the quality of the pledged securities, banks may lend up to 90 percent of market value and charge interest rates ranging from perhaps one half of 1 percent over prime on large loans secured by the pledge of high-quality securities to some 3 or 4 percent over prime on smaller loans secured by lower-quality collateral. Many loans to individuals are collateralized in this way, but few business loans are so secured because usually firms either do not own such securities or, if they do, they would sell them to obtain financing rather than borrow.

Equipment may be pledged under a security agreement (formerly called a *chattel mortgage,* which is simply a mortgage on any tangible property except real estate). Desirability, and the consequent percentage that will be loaned, depends not only on current appraised value but also on the marketability of the equipment. Standard machinery, such as lathes or milling machines, and transportation equipment, such as freight cars, trucks, tractors, or airplanes, will have relatively high loan value, whereas specialized machinery that has been custom designed for use in the firm's manufacturing processes probably will have no loan value at all. The lender also considers the ease and cost of liquidation in event of default. Security agreements pledging equipment are used most frequently in connection with longer-term loans, but they may be used to secure short-term loans in some cases.

Often firms own *life insurance policies* on their key people. The *cash values* of these may be utilized either by borrowing against them from the issuing insurance company or by assigning them to secure a loan from the bank. The appropriate alternative depends upon the interest rate. The interest applicable to policy loans from an insurance company usually is fixed at the date of issue of the policy. On policies that have been outstanding for some years, it may be substantially lower than current bank rates. However, the opposite may be true in a period when the money markets are soft. Then the use of such policies as collateral for bank loans may be appropriate.

Another way a lender may facilitate a loan that would not otherwise be justified is to require that some other individual or corporation sign the note in addition to the required signature of the borrower. Many loans to small, closely-held corporations require the personal signatures of the principal owners in addition to the corporate signature to cut through the corporate limitation of liability and put the personal assets of the principals behind the loan. Such a *comaker loan* may also be used to enhance the credit worthiness of an individual borrower. For example, you may wish to borrow in connection with starting a new business before your credit standing is sufficient to support such a loan. A bank may agree to make the loan if your parents will also sign the note. (If your parents just happen to be millionaires, you may suddenly find that the note is worthy of the prime rate!) Here the bank is looking to the comakers to support the loan in event of default by the principal borrower. The requirement of comakers can also have a coercive effect upon the borrower in inducing payment of the loan.[7]

On some occasions loans have been guaranteed by the U.S. government.

[7]The author learned this by taking the note of a rather irresponsible individual. On the advice of a close banker friend, the signatures of his wife, his parents, and his in-laws (who were wealthy) were also required. When this individual defaulted on the note, the mere mention that the note might be presented to be his father-in-law for payment if the principal and accrued interest were not received within a few days brought forth a check by return mail paying the obligation in full!

In wartime, this has been done on a large scale. But the peacetime bail-out of the Chrysler Corporation in 1980 through a U.S. government guarantee of its obligations wrote a new and perhaps lamentable chapter in financial history. For the lenders, the security is great, but the use of the national credit for this purpose may be questionable.

Summary

When a short-term loan cannot be justified on an unsecured basis, evidenced by a simple promissory note, then the lender looks to specific assets that the borrower might pledge or assign to secure the loan. Any asset acceptable to both parties might be used as collateral, but in practice such security usually will be the assignment of accounts receivable or the pledge of inventories. The feasibility of a secured loan arrangement will depend upon three factors: (1) legal and physical perfection of the lien, (2) value of the collateral, and (3) cost of administration. Short-term secured loans are made by commercial banks and finance companies.

Financing of accounts receivable may be obtained either by assigning the accounts to secure a loan or by factoring the receivables. If the accounts are assigned, the lender will appraise the credit worthiness of the borrower's credit customers, using such analyses as aging the receivables, credit-rating classification analysis, and review of the borrower's collection experience on the accounts over a past period. Then the lender will decide either to take a specific assignment of the accounts considered to be sound collateral and agree to lend a given percentage of these, or to take a general (blanket) assignment of all the accounts and lend a given (smaller) percentage of the total amount. These percentages range from about 50 to 90 percent, depending upon the quality of the assigned receivables. Usually such lending arrangements are ongoing and may be made on either a notification or nonnotification basis. The cost of such loans may include fees related to auditing the accounts as well as interest.

Factoring is the sale of accounts receivable to a financial institution. The factor charges a fee based upon the amount of receivables purchased and provides advances at a stated interest rate to the firm up to the amount of the uncollected receivables less a specified reserve. These arrangements usually are ongoing, without recourse, and on a notification basis.

Inventory may be used to secure a loan by using a floating (blanket) lien, trust receipts, or warehousing the inventory either in a public warehouse or a field warehouse and using the warehouse receipts as collateral. Feasibility of such lending arrangements depends upon (1) the degree of control over the inventory that can be provided the lender, (2) the nature of the inventory in terms of certainty and stability of value and marketability in the event that liquidation should be required, and (3) the cost of maintaining the security arrangement. The cost to the borrower of such loans varies widely up to the point at which it is prohibitive.

Other assets that might be used to secure loans are marketable stocks or bonds, equipment, or cash value of life insurance policies. Another way a loan might be secured is by obtaining the signature(s) of one or more financially responsible parties on the note in addition to that of the borrower. If the note is not honored by the borrower, the comaker(s) can be held liable for payment.

Questions

1. If the simplest and most desirable form of short-term borrowing is an unsecured loan evidenced by a straight promissory note, why are many short-term loans secured by the pledge or assignment of collateral?
2. Why are assignment of accounts receivable and the pledge of inventories the most widely used collateral arrangements in securing short-term commercial loans?
3. What might be the reaction of trade creditors to a firm's assignment of its accounts receivable to secure a loan? Why?
4. What is a security agreement? How is it used?
5. State and discuss briefly the three general considerations of a lender in assessing the acceptability of a secured loan arrangement.
6. How might a banker appraise the quality of a firm's accounts receivable? On the basis of this appraisal, how can the banker establish the amount or percentage that the bank will lend against them?
7. Why will a lender rarely, if ever, lend over 90 percent of an assigned receivable, even if that receivable is from a customer of unquestioned credit standing?
8. Why would a borrower prefer that accounts receivable be assigned on a nonnotification basis? What risk does the lender assume under such an arrangement?
9. How does factoring receivables differ from borrowing secured by assignment of receivables?
10. List the various legal means by which a lien on inventories pledged to secure a loan might be perfected. Describe each and indicate its relative strength as collateral.

11. From the viewpoint of a lender, select—in order of their desirability as security—among the following forms of collateral (assuming cost of the pledged inventories to be the same). Briefly indicate your reasons.

a. Trust receipts covering an inventory of new automobiles.
b. Warehouse receipts covering an inventory of grain stored in a public grain elevator.
c. A floating lien on the inventory of a small department store.
d. A field warehousing arrangement covering the finished goods inventory of a high-fashion women's clothing manufacturer.
e. A field warehousing arrangement on the finished goods inventory of a fruit and vegetable canning company.

12. If your firm wished to borrow against the cash value of life insurance policies on its key employees, how would you proceed?

13. Why might a bank require the personal signature(s) of the principal owner(s) of a closely-held corporation in addition to the corporate signature by an authorized officer on a note evidencing a loan to the corporation?

Problems

(Note: Problems 1 and 2 are a series.)

1. Moorhead Furniture Manufacturing Corporation has applied to the First National Bank for a loan of $480,000 to be secured by a general assignment of accounts receivable. As a starting point for analysis, the banker is willing to lend 85 percent on Moorhead's receivables under 30 days old, 70 percent on those from 31 to 60 days old, 35 percent on those from 61 to 90 days old, and nothing on those over 90 days old. An aging of Moorhead's receivables indicates:

Age	Amount
0–30 days	$342,000
31–60 days	205,000
61–90 days	97,000
>90 days	43,000

a. What is the maximum amount and percentage of total receivables that the bank might lend on the basis of this aging analysis?
b. If the bank's policy is to grant accounts receivable loans on a basis of 70 percent or better, what should the banker do?

2. See Problem 1. Further analysis of Moorhead's receivables by credit-rating classification indicates:

D&B credit appraisal class	Amount
High	$373,000
Good	212,000
Fair	62,000
Limited	40,000

The banker generally lends to firms in the furniture industry 85 percent against receivables in D&B's "high" classification, 70 percent on accounts classified "good," 40 percent on "fair," and nothing on "limited."

a. What is the maximum amount and percentage that the bank might lend on the basis of this credit-rating classification?

b. What should the banker do?

3. Roxbury Distributing Company, a wholesaler of office supplies, has been turned down on a loan requested from its bank and referred to the Acme Commerical Finance Company. Acme offers an ongoing loan arrangement to be secured by a general assignment of accounts receivable on a 60 percent basis. The interest charge would be 16 percent per annum on the outstanding loan balance. In addition, a service fee of $150 per month would be charged to cover accounting and auditing costs incurred in administering the loan. Roxbury estimates that it would be borrowing the maximum amount available against its receivables, which average about $140,000. What would be Roxbury's average annual cost of this financing *(a)* in dollars and *(b)* as a percentage of funds available?

(Note: Problems 4 through 6 are a series.)

4. The Heydon Corporation is factoring all of its receivables on a nonrecourse basis. The factor's fees are 2 percent of all receivables discounted. Heydon draws the maximum advance available, which is the uncollected balance less a 10 percent reserve, at 1½ percent interest per month. Heydon's average credit sales are $200,000 per month, and the average collection period on the receivables is 30 days. Heydon estimates that its credit department costs, including bad debt losses, would be 1 percent of credit sales if it did not factor.

a. What is Heydon's net annual incremental cost attributable to factor's fees?

b. What is the average amount advanced to Heydon?

c. What is the total annual interest paid on these advances?

d. What is the incremental annual cost of Heydon's using the factoring arrangement in dollars and as a percentage of the funds available through advances?

5. Heydon Corporation (Problem 4) has just been offered a continuing accounts receivable loan on an 80 percent basis by the Central National

Bank at 14 percent annual interest rate plus a $1,500 per month service fee. Should Heydon accept this offer when the factoring agreement expires next month and establish its own credit department?

6. Would your answer to Problem 5 differ if Heydon's credit costs, including bad debt losses, were 2 percent of sales (equal to the factor's fees)?

7. Tastee Cereal Company could borrow 90 percent of cost of its $4 million inventories of wheat and oats by storing these inventories in public grain elevators and securing the loan by furnishing warehouse receipts to the Metropolitan Bank. The bank would charge 11 percent interest. In addition, Tastee Cereal would pay warehouse fees of $20,000 per month and would incur additional handling costs of $5,000 per month. The warehouse fees are $3,000 per month greater than the costs Tastee Cereal would incur by storing the grain elsewhere. What would be the effective cost of funds borrowed, stated as an annual rate?

8. Central Valley Canning Company borrows from the Farmers National Bank to finance its finished goods inventories of canned fruits and vegetables. Under a field warehousing arrangement, the products are stored in the warehouse at Central Valley's canning plant under the control of the United Warehousing Company, which has been designated by Farmers Bank. The additional cost of warehousing if $500 per month. The bank lends 80 percent of cost of inventories stored in the field warehouse. In September, when the loan was initiated, inventories costing $1 million were in the warehouse and Central Valley borrowed $800,000. By November 30, $2.8 million of additional inventories had been placed in the warehouse and $1.2 million of inventories had been withdrawn for delivery to customers. Farmers Bank charges 12 percent per annum interest on the loan balance.

a. What is the amount of the loan on November 30?

b. What is the effective cost of the funds borrowed, stated as an annual rate?

Part Four
Capital Investment Decisions

Chapter 11
The Time Value of Money

The focus of our discussion will soon shift back to the asset side of the balance sheet, particularly to management of the fixed assets. Chapters 12 through 15 will deal with capital investment, the very important analytical and decision-making processes by which managers determine the long-term investments to be made in fixed assets. Such decisions, because they determine the directions the firm is going and the business(es) it will be in, are vital to its success.

If you are to understand the analytical techniques required to deal with capital investments (and a number of other subjects treated later in this book, such as capital structure determination, lease-versus-buy-and-borrow decisions, and bond refunding decisions), you must first understand the time value of money. This subject requires the use of some relatively simple mathematics. Any capital investment involves the outlay of money now (and sometimes more in the future) in the expectation that this outlay will result in net cash benefits at a future date or at various times in the future. Mathematical techniques are the only means by which the value of cash flows at different times may be compared. You must be able to use them to make intelligent capital investment decisions.

In his classic treatise, *The Theory of Investment Value,* J. B. Williams in 1938 developed the thesis that the value of any asset is the present value of the future benefits that will flow to its owner.[1] This is the essence of modern theory of value and capital investment decision making. In order to transform future benefits to present value, the future benefits (cash flows) must be *discounted* to reflect the time value of money. The *discount rate* reflects the rate of return on a riskless investment plus a premium based upon the perceived risk that expected benefits will not materialize. But this is getting ahead of our story. First we must explore the nature of the time value of money, compound interest, and discount.

Simple interest

You are all familiar with interest. Some of you have earned it, some have paid it, and all have been concerned with it in earlier parts of this book. Now we shall try to be more precise about its nature. *Interest* is essentially a *rate of exchange* between the expectation of a sum of money at a future date and that sum of money at the present time. If you invest $1,000 in a savings account at a bank or savings and loan association for one year at 7 percent interest, you will receive $1,070 at the end of a one-year period. This is *simple interest* of 7 percent, or $70, reflecting an exchange rate of 7

[1]J. B. Williams, *The Theory of Investment Value,* (Cambridge, Mass.: Harvard University Press, 1938).

percent between the sum of $1,000 now and the expectation that $1,070 will be returned to you in one year. This exchange rate reflects the time value of money—to you and the institution you invest it in—in a contract called a savings account. You are willing to forego the use of the money for one year for 7 percent interest ($70), and the institution you invest it in is willing to pay that much to be able to use your money.

To put this into a formula, let P_0 represent your original investment, the *principal* of $1,000 at time 0 (now), P_1 will be the principal balance at the end of 1 year, and i will be the interest rate of 7 percent (expressed in decimal form as .07), Then

$$\begin{aligned} P_1 &= P_0 (1 + i) \\ &= \$1,000\ (1.07) \\ &= \$1,070 \end{aligned}$$

Compound interest

In the illustration above your account balance will be $1,070 at the end of one year. Now let us assume that you do not withdraw the account, but rather leave this money with the institution to earn more interest. During the next year you will be earning interest on $1,070, which consists of the original investment of $1,000 *plus* the $70 interest earned the first year. This is what compound interest is all about. At the end of the second year, your account balance will be $1,144.90, determined as follows:

Balance at end of first year	$1,070.00
Interest on $1,070 for second year at 7%	74.90
Balance at end of second year	$1,144.90

or

$$\begin{aligned} P_2 &= P_1 (1 + i) \\ &= P_0 (1 + i)(1 + i) \\ &= P_0 (1 + i)^2 \end{aligned}$$

$$\begin{aligned} P_2 &= \$1,000\ (1 + .07)^2 \\ &= \$1,000\ (1.1449) \\ &= \$1,144,90 \end{aligned}$$

If you left this money in the account for another year, the $1,144.90 again would earn interest at 7 percent. At the end of the third year, your balance would be $1,225.04, determined by

$$\begin{aligned} P_3 &= P_0 (1 + i)^3 \\ &= \$1,000\ (1.22504) \\ &= \$1,225.04 \end{aligned}$$

Generalizing this formula,

$$P_n = P_0 (1 + i)^n \qquad (11\text{–}1)$$

where

P_0 = The principal, or initial amount, at time 0
i = The interest rate
n = The number years interest is compounded
P_n = The principal value at the end of n years

As you see from the above illustration, *compound interest* is interest earned not only upon the original principal investment but also upon the retained (or reinvested) interest accumulated from previous periods. For example, if you invested $1,000 at 7 percent interest, compounded annually (as above) for 5 years, at the end of that period your investment would amount to

$$\begin{aligned} P_5 &= \$1{,}000\ (1 + .07)^5 \\ &= \$1{,}000\ (1.40255) \\ &= \$1{,}402.55 \end{aligned}$$

Simple interest, which assumes that you withdraw the interest at the end of each year and leave only the original principal invested, would have been 5 × $70, or $350. The net effect of compounding (earning interest on interest) was:

Interest earned with annual compounding	$402.55
Less simple interest earned	350.00
Net effect of annual compounding	$ 52.55

The power of compound interest can be tremendous when many years are considered. For example, if your $1,000 were invested at 7 percent annually compounded for 50 years, the balance at the end of that period would be $29,456. In another 10 years (totaling 60 years), it would be $57,946. As the interest rate increases, these figures increase remarkably. For example, $1,000 invested at 14 percent for 50 years would amount to $700,197, and for 60 years, $2,596,000.

Future value

In demonstrating compound interest, we have calculated future values of a sum invested at interest compounded annually. Now let us change our terminology and mathematical notation to reflect this. Simply substitute FV_n

(future value at the end of n years) for P_n and PV (present value) for P_0 in Equation 11–1:

$$FV_n = PV\,(1 + i)^n \quad (11\text{–}2)$$

This is the general equation for calculating *future value* of a sum compounded annually, where

PV = Present value
i = Interest rate
n = Number of years of compounding
FV = Future value

Future value tables

The term $(1 + i)^n$ is rather laborious to calculate if n is a large number. Two labor-saving aids are available to simplify this. One is the *FV* button on some hand-held calculators. The other is a future value interest factor *(FVIF)* table (sometimes called a compound interest or compound value table). A future value interest factor *(FVIF)* is the future value of $1 at the end of n years. The *FVIF* is substituted for the term $(1 + i)^n$ in Equation 11–2 when using such a table. Then

$$FV_n = PV \times FVIF_{i,n}$$

An *FVIF* table is constructed by starting with the term $(1 + i)$ for one year hence, raising it to the second power for two years hence, to the third power for three years hence, and so on. Table 11–1 demonstrates the construction of an abbreviated *FVIF* table at 7 percent interest.

Table 11–1 Future value interest factors *(FVIF)* at 7 percent

Years hence	Computation	*FVIF*
1	$1 + .07$	1,070
2	$(1 + .07)^2$	1.145
3	$(1 + .07)^3$	1.225
4	$(1 + .07)^4$	1.311
5	$(1 + .07)^5$	1.403
6	$(1 + .07)^6$	1.501
7	$(1 + .07)^7$	1.606
8	$(1 + .07)^8$	1.718
9	$(1 + .07)^9$	1.838
10	$(1 + .07)^{10}$	1.967

Note: In this table all *FVIFs* have been rounded to the nearest thousandth; therefore they do not exactly agree with the computations made earlier, compounding $1,000 to the nearest cent.

Table 11–2 is an *FVIF* table for interest rates of 1 through 10 percent and for periods *(n)* 1 through 50. The portion of it that was constructed in Table 11–1 appears under the 7 percent column. Let us now use the *FVIF* table to find the value of \$14, 382 compounded at 8 percent for 14 years:

$$FV_{14} = \$14{,}382 \times 2.937$$
$$= \$42{,}240$$

(The 2.937 was found by reading across the 14 year line to the 8 percent column.)

The increase in future value through the years in exponential curves is shown in Figure 11–1. This figure also illustrates how future values rise much more rapidly as the compound interest rate is increased.

Table 11–2 Future value interest factors *(FVIF)*
Future value of \$1 at the end of *n* periods at interest rate *i*.

	Interest rate, *i*									
n	1%	2%	3%	4%	5%	6%	7%	8%	9%	10%
1	1.010	1.020	1.030	1.040	1.050	1.060	1.070	1.080	1.090	1.100
2	1.020	1.040	1.061	1.082	1.102	1.124	1.145	1.166	1.188	1.210
3	1.030	1.061	1.093	1.125	1.158	1.191	1.225	1.260	1.295	1.331
4	1.041	1.082	1.126	1.170	1.216	1.262	1.311	1.360	1.412	1.464
5	1.051	1.104	1.159	1.217	1.276	1.338	1.403	1.469	1.539	1.611
6	1.062	1.126	1.194	1.265	1.340	1.419	1.501	1.587	1.677	1.772
7	1.072	1.149	1.230	1.316	1.407	1.504	1.606	1.714	1.828	1.949
8	1.083	1.172	1.267	1.369	1.477	1.594	1.718	1.851	1.993	2.144
9	1.094	1.195	1.305	1.423	1.551	1.689	1.838	1.999	2.172	2.358
10	1.105	1.219	1.344	1.480	1.629	1.791	1.967	2.159	2.367	2.594
11	1.116	1.243	1.384	1.539	1.710	1.898	2.105	2.332	2.580	2.853
12	1.127	1.268	1.426	1.601	1.796	2.012	2.252	2.518	2.813	3.138
13	1.138	1.294	1.469	1.665	1.886	2.133	2.410	2.720	3.066	3.452
14	1.149	1.319	1.513	1.732	1.980	2.261	2.579	2.937	3.342	3.797
15	1.161	1.346	1.558	1.801	2.079	2.397	2.759	3.172	3.642	4.177
16	1.173	1.373	1.605	1.873	2.183	2.540	2.952	3.426	3.970	4.595
17	1.184	1.400	1.653	1.948	2.292	2.693	3.159	3.700	4.328	5.054
18	1.196	1.428	1.702	2.026	2.407	2.854	3.380	3.996	4.717	5.560
19	1.208	1.457	1.753	2.107	2.527	3.026	3.616	4.316	5.142	6.116
20	1.220	1.486	1.806	2.191	2.653	3.207	3.870	4.661	5.604	6.727
21	1.232	1.516	1.860	2.279	2.786	3.399	4.140	5.034	6.109	7.400
22	1.245	1.546	1.916	2.370	2.925	3.603	4.430	5.436	6.658	8.140
23	1.257	1.577	1.974	2.465	3.071	3.820	4.740	5.871	7.258	8.954
24	1.270	1.608	2.033	2.563	3.225	4.049	5.072	6.341	7.911	9.850
25	1.282	1.641	2.094	2.666	3.386	4.292	5.427	6.848	8.623	10.834
30	1.348	1.811	2.427	3.243	4.322	5.743	7.612	10.062	13.267	17.449
40	1.489	2.208	3.262	4.801	7.040	10.285	14.974	21.724	31.408	45.258
50	1.645	2.691	4.384	7.106	11.467	18.419	29.456	46.900	74.354	117.386

Figure 11–1 Future value of $1 @ 5, 10, and 15 percent interest compounded annually

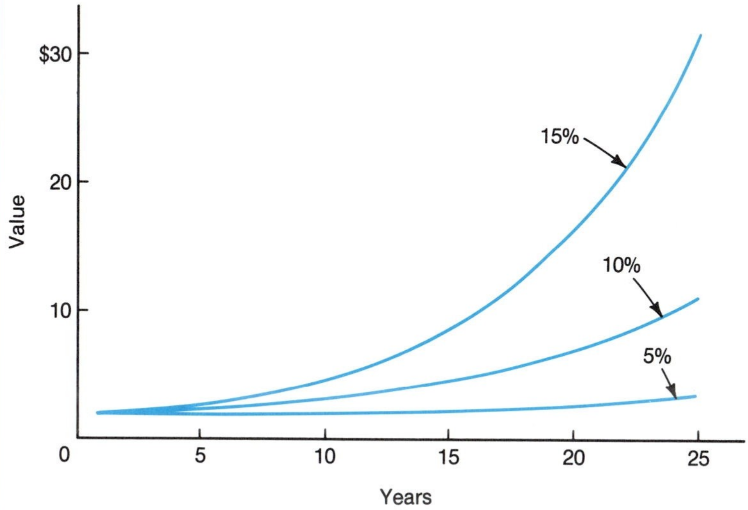

More frequent compounding

To this point our discussion of compound interest has assumed annual compounding. The interest was added to the principal at the end of each one-year period. However, this is not always the case. Bonds usually pay interest semiannually. Savings institutions may compound interest semiannually, quarterly, monthly, daily, or continuously. If such is the case, Equation 11–2 may be modified to determine the exact future value.

For example, let us assume that $1,000 is invested at an annual rate of 7 percent interest compounded semiannually. Then interest of 3½ percent will be compounded at the end of six months and the amount earning interest will be $1,035 for the next six months. Interest on this amount will be $36.23 ($1,035 × .035), making the total value at the end of the year $1,071.23. Modifying Equation 11–2, this can be expressed as

$$\begin{aligned} FV_1 &= \$1,000\left(1 + \frac{.07}{2}\right)^2 \\ &= \$1,000\,(1.035)^2 \\ &= \$1,071.23 \end{aligned}$$

If the investment were compounded quarterly, the value at the end of the year would be

$$FV_1 = \$1{,}000\left(1 + \frac{.07}{4}\right)^4$$
$$= \$1{,}000\ (1.0175)^4$$
$$= \$1{,}071.86$$

This modification of the future value formula (Equation 11–2) can be generalized to

$$FV_n = PV\left(1 + \frac{i}{m}\right)^{mn} \qquad (11\text{–}3)$$

where

n = Number of years the interest is compounded
m = Number of times per year interest is compounded

Applying this formula, if interest were compounded monthly, then

$$FV_n = PV\left(1 + \frac{i}{12}\right)^{12n}$$

or, if compounded daily, then

$$FV_n = PV\left(1 + \frac{i}{365}\right)^{365n}$$

More frequent compounding increases the effective interest rate. At a 7 percent annual rate, semiannual compounding yields an effective interest rate of 7.123 percent, quarterly compounding yields 7.186 percent, and daily compounding yields 7.245 percent.

If *FVIF* tables based upon annual compounding, such as Table 11–2, are used, the period n may be multiplied by m and the interest rate i divided by m. For example, with semiannual compounding at an 8 percent annual rate for 10 years, look up in Table 11–2 the *FVIF* at 4 percent for 20 periods. You should find it to be 2.191 (compared to 2.159 for 10 years at 8 percent compounded annually).[2]

[2]Tables have been developed to show the year-end accumulation of $1 received in various periodic installments during the year at various interest rates. These can be used to adjust from standard future value and present value tables based on annual compounding to any periodic payments from semiannual to continuous. Such a table may be found in Appendix C-3 of J. Keith Butters, William E. Fruhan, Jr., David W. Mullins, and Thomas R. Piper, *Case Problems in Finance,* 8th ed. (Homewood, Ill.: Richard Irwin, 1981), pp. 616–17.

Present value

Up to now we have addressed the question, "What is the future value of a given present investment compounded at an interest rate for so long a time?" Now we reverse this question to, "What is the *present value* of a given sum to be received at some future time if this sum is *discounted* at a given interest rate?" To put the latter question a different way, "How much money would you be willing to pay now for the right to receive a given sum of money at a specified time in the future if you required a given compound interest return on your investment?"

You will remember that if you require a 7 percent annual interest return on your money, then the future value of $1,000 compounded annually for five years is $1,402.55 (from the earlier example illustrating compound interest). Therefore, for the future sum of $1,402.55 to be received in five years, you should be willing to pay $1,000 now. How much would you pay now for $1,000 to be received five years hence? The amount would be $712.99, which is $1,000 divided by 1.40255 (the *FVIF* for five years at 7 percent).

Now we are getting somewhere. Instead of dividing $1,000 (the *PV* in the initial example) by 1.40255, you could have multiplied it by 0.71299, which is the *reciprocal* value. The reciprocal is simply the inverse relationship, the result of turning a fractional relationship upside down. The *present value (PV)* of $1 is the *reciprocal* of the *future value (FV)* of $1. To prove this, let us go back to the general formula for future value (Equation 11–2):

$$FV_n = PV\,(1 + i)^n$$

Solving this for *PV,* we get

$$PV = \frac{FV_n}{(1 + i)^n}$$

or

$$PV = FV_n \left[\frac{1}{(1 + i)^n}\right] \qquad (11\text{–}4)$$

Equation 11–4 is the general formula for *present value.* This rearrangement is useful because our chief concern with compound interest in capital investment analysis is to establish the present value *(PV)* of estimated future cash flows (*FVs*) expected to take place at various times. These present values are obtained by *discounting* the estimated future cash flows at some interest rate, usually called a *discount rate* when used in this connection. (We shall use these terms interchangeably.) Thus, in a sense, discounting is the application of compound interest in reverse, allowing us to transform future values back to the present, rather than present sums to future values.

To illustrate the use of present values, assume that you are offered a contract under which you will receive $1,000 at the end of three years if you will pay $775 now. You require an 8 percent return on the investment. To decide whether to accept or reject this offer, you wish to discount $1,000 for three years at an annual compound discount rate of 8 percent.

$$PV = \$1,000 \left[\frac{1}{(1 + .08)^3}\right]$$
$$= \$1,000 \left[\frac{1}{1.2597}\right]$$
$$= \$1,000 \times .79384$$
$$= \$793.84$$

You would accept the offer because getting something worth $793.84 for $775 is a bargain. In other words, the implicit interest rate in this contract is greater than the 8 percent you require.

Present value tables

You will not have to do calculations such as the one shown above by hand. The *PV* button on some hand-held calculators will do this for you. Present value interest factor *(PVIF)* tables also are available. They show the present value of $1 discounted annually for various numbers of years at various interest rates. You simply substitute the *PVIF* from the table for $1/(1 + i)^n$ in Equation 11–4 as follows:

$$PV = FV_n \times PVIF_{i,n} \qquad (11\text{–}5)$$

A *PVIF* table for $1 discounted at 7 percent for years 1 through 10 is constructed in Table 11–3. To demonstrate the relationship between *FVIF*s and *PVIF*s, the *FVIF*s from Table 11–1 are also shown in this table. Note that each factor is the reciprocal of the other.

The decline in present values as the years of compound discounting increase is shown in Figure 11–2. As discount (interest) rates increase, the decline in present value increases remarkably. Thus, at high discount rates, cash flows expected many years in the future are almost valueless.

Full-blown *PVIF* tables are reproduced in the Appendix at the end of this book. Here we will use Table A, showing the present value of $1 at the end of *n* years discounted at an interest rate of *i*. Let us assume that, as part of a capital investment consideration, we expect the sale of a machine at the end of 10 years to yield $4,000 cash. We wish to know the present value of

Table 11–3 **Future value interest factors *(FVIF)* and present value interest factors *(PVIF)* @ 7 percent**

Years *(n)*	*FVIF* $(1 + .07)^n$	*PVIF* $\frac{1}{(1 + .07)^n}$
1	\$1.070	.935
2	1.145	.873
3	1.225	.816
4	1.311	.763
5	1.403	.713
6	1.501	.666
7	1.606	.623
8	1.718	.582
9	1.838	.544
10	1.967	.508

Note: In this table all *FVIF*s and *PVIF*s have been rounded to the nearest thousandth; therefore, they do not exactly agree with the computations made earlier, compounding \$1,000 to the nearest cent.

Figure 11–2 **Present value of \$1 *(PVIF)* discounted at 5, 10, and 15 percent, compounded annually**

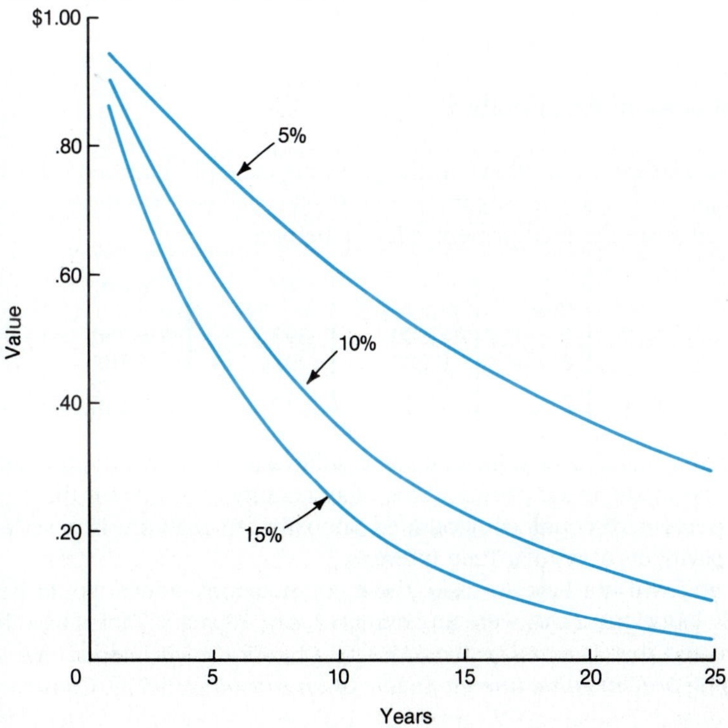

that sum discounted at 15 percent. We look down the 15 percent column in Table A to 10 years to find the *PVIF* of .247. Multiplying this by $4,000 tells us that $988 is the present value of the expected proceeds from sale of the machine.

Or perhaps we have an opportunity to make a capital investment of $14,000 that is expected to yield cash inflows of $5,000 the first year, $7,000 the second, and $4,000 the third year, at the end of which it is expected to be valueless. Our required rate of return on such an investment is 12 percent. To find the present value of these expected future cash flows we proceed as follows:

Year	Amount	*PVIF* @ 12%	Present value
1	$5,000	.893	$ 4,465
2	7,000	.797	5,579
3	4,000	.712	2,848
			$12,892

The total present value of $12,892 is less than the required outlay of $14,000. We probably should not make this investment; its return is expected to be less than the required 12 percent.

Present value of a level stream: An annuity

If the expected cash flows in the previous example had been the same each year, that is, a level stream of, say, $6,000 each year for three years, we could calculate the total present value as before:

Year	Amount	*PVIF* @ 12%	Present value
1	$6,000	.893	$ 5,358
2	6,000	.797	4.782
3	6,000	.712	4,272
			$14,412

This total, $14,412, which incidentally is sufficiently high that the investment should be made, is the present value of an annuity of $6,000 for three years at 12 percent discount compounded annually. An *annuity* is a series of equal payments at regular time intervals.

But you will not have to make these computations, which would be extremely laborious if this were an annuity of, say, 18 years. Tables have been constructed that accumulate the *PVIFs* by years for each interest rate, thus providing *present value interest factors of an annuity (PVIFA)*. Construction of an abbreviated *PVIFA* table for years 1 through 10 at 7 percent is illustrated in Table 11–4.[3]

Table 11–4 Present value interest factors (@ 7 percent) for an annuity (*PVIFA*)

Years (*n*)	*PVIF*	*PVIFA*
1	.935	.935
2	.873	1.808
3	.816	2.624
4	.763	3.387
5	.713	4.100
6	.666	4.767
7	.623	5.389
8	.582	5.971
9	.544	6.515
10	.508	7.024

Note: Because all figures in this table are rounded to the nearest thousandth, they do not exactly accumulate or agree with computations retaining a larger number of significant digits.

A *PVIFA* table is reproduced in Table B in the Appendix at the end of this book. Referring to it, let us find the *PVIFA* at 12 percent interest rate for three years to get our answer to the previous example in an easier way. The *PVIFA* is 2.402. Designating the present value and the future installments of an annuity by the subscript a and defining *PVIFA* as the present value interest factor of an annuity, we may write

$$\begin{aligned} PV_a &= FV_{a,n} \times PVIFA_{i,n} \\ &= \$6{,}000 \times 2.402 \\ &= \$14{,}412 \end{aligned} \tag{11–6}$$

To combine a future sum and an annuity into an illustration, assume that Brooks Processing Company is considering an investment in capital equip-

[3]For simplicity, we have omitted from the text the equation for the present value of an annuity. It is

$$\begin{aligned} PV_{a,n} &= \sum_{t=1}^{n} \left[\frac{a}{(1+i)^t} \right] \\ &= a \sum_{t=1}^{n} \left[\frac{1}{(1+i)^t} \right] \end{aligned}$$

where

a = Amount of each periodic payment
n = Number of periods
t = Each integer from 1 through n

ment. This investment is expected to result in net cash inflows of \$8,000 each year for nine years and an additional inflow of \$5,000, the net proceeds from sale of that equipment at the end of the nine-year period. Assume further that 11 percent is the required rate of return on this investment. What is the present value of such an investment? First, we can use Table B to get the *PVIFA* for nine years at 11 percent. This is 5.537.

$$\$8,000 \times 5.537 = \$44,298$$

Next, we must get from Table A the *PVIF* for nine years at 11 percent. This is .391.

$$\$5,000 \times .391 = \$1,995$$

Combining these:

PV of the nine-year operating stream	\$44,298
PV of the liquidation at end of nine years	1,995
Total *PV* of the investment	\$46,293.

Perpetuities

A *perpetuity* is a series of equal periodic payments that goes on forever. An example of a perpetual security is a British consul, which is an obligation of the British government to pay interest at a stated rate forever (or as long as the British government exists and is willing and able to pay). As a practical abstraction, we sometimes conceive of a corporation's stock as participating in a perpetual income stream. More will be said about this later. Now we are concerned with the present value of a perpetuity.

You may have noticed in studying Table B in the Appendix at the end of this book that as the number of years increases, the *PVIFAs* approach the reciprocal of the discount rate. Thus at 10 percent discount rate, \$1 to be received annually for 50 years is worth \$9.915 (compared to \$1/10 = \$10), at 20 percent \$1 for 50 years is worth \$4.999 (compared to \$1/20 = \$5), and so on. Some higher mathematics (the calculus) would tell us that as an infinite number of years is approached (forever), the *PVIFA* will become the reciprocal of the discount rate. Therefore, the formula for obtaining the *present value of a perpetuity* (a perpetual annuity) is

$$PV = FV_a\left(\frac{1}{i}\right)$$

or

$$PV = \frac{FV_a}{i} \qquad (11\text{–}7)$$

where

FV_a = Amount of each annual payment

To illustrate determination of the present value of a perpetuity, assume you can buy a perpetuity of $10,000 annually and you require 8 percent compound interest on your investment. What would you be willing to pay for it?

$$PV = \frac{\$10{,}000}{.08} = \$125{,}000$$

Use of present value tables

Now that you understand the nature of present value and how to use present value tables (*PVIF* and *PVIFA*) to determine the present value of a sum or an annuity to be received in the future, we shall introduce another use of the present value tables and some of the finer points and complications connected with their use.

Finding the discount rate

To this point we have used present value tables only to find the present value when the discount rate and the future value(s) are known (or at least assumed). Now we wish to use them to find the discount rate when the present and future value(s) are given. In many applications of the time value of money to capital investment analysis, it will be necessary to find the discount rate that equates the future value(s) (cash flows) to the present value (investment in a capital project).

Assume that Echo Speaker Company plans to build a new general office building three years from now. It has the opportunity to buy suitable land for this project now for $118,000. The cost of such land three years from now is estimated to be $150,000. Taxes will be ignored for simplicity. What is the discount rate that equates the present value of $118,000 to the future value of $150,000? From Equation 11–5,

$$PV = FV_3 \times PVIF_{i,3}$$

$$PVIF_{i,3} = \frac{PV}{FV_3} = \frac{\$118{,}000}{\$150{,}000} = .787$$

Searching the 3-year line on Table A, we find that the *PVIF* at 8 percent is .794 and at 9 percent is .772. Thus the discount rate is between 8 and 9 percent, visually estimated at about 8⅓ percent. (We could interpolate and find that it is 8.32 percent, but that comes later in our discussion and it is seldom necessary considering the uncertainty in the estimate of future value.)

This technique has general application whenever you seek the discount rate that equates present and future *sums*. Simply divide the *PV* by the *FV* to get the *PVIF*. Then scan the year line *(n)* to find that *PVIF* or the two *PVIF*s that this one falls between. The percent column of that *PVIF* is the applicable discount rate. Interpolate if necessary.

Now let us find the discount rate for the case of a level stream of periodic future receipts, an annuity. Echo is considering purchasing an electronic testing instrument for $9,800. This instrument is expected to reduce cash outlays for production by $2,600 for each of the next five years and to have no value at the end of five years. What discount rate will equate the $9,800 present value with the $2,600 annuity for the next five years? From Equation 11–6,

$$PV_a = FV_{a,5} \times PVIFA_{i,5}$$

$$PVIFA_{i,5} = \frac{PV_a}{FV_{a,5}} = \frac{\$9{,}800}{\$2{,}600} = 3.769$$

Searching the 5-year line on Table B, we find that the *PVIFA* at 10 percent is 3.791 and at 11 percent is 3.696. Thus the discount rate is between 10 and 11 percent. Offhand, this would be about 10¼ percent. (We could interpolate but this would seldom be necessary for the reason indicated above.)

This technique, which is similar to the one used when dealing with sums, has general application to find the discount rate when *annuities* are involved. Divide the PV_a by the $FV_{a,n}$ to get the *PVIFA* or the two that this one falls between. The percent column of that *PVIFA* is the discount rate applicable. Interpolate if necessary.

Interpolation We have referred to interpolation in the above illustrations and pointed out that it is seldom necessary in connection with capital investment analysis because the uncertainty of the estimates of future cash flows makes precision in determining discount rates rather superfluous. Nonetheless, you may encounter applications in which it is useful. *Interpolation* is simply the location of a term that is intermediate between two terms of a series. Here we can use it to approximate the discount rate if our *PVIF* is between two values shown on the present value table.

For example, in determining the discount rate equating a present and future sum, we found the *PVIF* to be .787. Table A indicated that the *PVIF* at 8 percent is .794 and at 9 percent is .772. To interpolate the discount rate reflected by .787,

PVIF @ 8% =	.794		.794
@ 9% =	.772	Exact *PVIF*	.787
Difference =	.022		.007

$$\frac{\text{Difference @ 8\% from exact } PVIF}{\text{Difference @ 8\% from @ 9\%}} = \frac{.007}{.022} = .32$$

$$8.00\% + .32\% = 8.32\%$$

By interpolation, we have determined that the discount rate that equates the two sums is 8.32 percent.

The same can be done regarding the example dealing with an annuity. Do this yourself to be sure you can interpolate. The discount rate is 10.23 percent.

Uneven cash flow streams

Perhaps we have oversimplified our illustrations of present value calculations by assuming the estimated future values to be either a sum or an annuity. In many real-life applications, expected future cash flows resulting from a capital investment are an uneven stream with the amounts differing each year. In some cases, even though the pretax cash benefits may be a steady stream, accelerated depreciation results in uneven tax payments, making the net cash flows irregular. In other cases, the anticipated cash flows may increase each year, for example, if the project is to produce a new product that is expected to increase in sales each of the first few years as market penetration improves. For the purchase and use of new machinery, anticipated net cash flows may decrease through the years as cash outlays for maintenance increase. Anticipated inflation also tends to create uneven expected cash flow streams.

Present value calculation Where the expected future cash flows (*FVs*) are uneven, the calculation of present value (*PV*) must be done the long way by multiplying the future value of the sum each year by the appropriate *PVIF* from Table A and accumulating the present values of each to get the total present value of the stream.[4] Assume that Devon Products Company is considering tooling up for the manufacture of a new line of cooking utensils. This line is expected to produce net cash benefits as indicated in Table 11–5. The required rate of return on the project is 12 percent. The present

Table 11–5 Calculation of present value (*PV*) of an uneven cash flow stream

Year	(1) Expected cash flow	(2) *PVIF* @ 12%	*PV* of cash flow (Col. 1 × Col. 2)
1	$100,000	.893	$ 89,300
2	130,000	.797	103,610
3	150,000	.712	106,800
4	160,000	.636	101,760
5	160,000	.567	90,720
6	120,000	.507	60,840
7	80,000	.452	36,160
Total			$589,190

[4]Some hand-held calculators with memories will handle the accumulation of the *PVs* of uneven *FVs*.

value, $589,190, of these cash flows is calculated as shown in Table 11–5. There is no chortcut to this calculation. It is rather laborious if the time span of the project is long, say 20 years or so.

In cases in which the uneven stream includes an annuity, a shortcut may be taken by separating the annuity from the additional sums included in the stream. For example, if the expected cash flows from a project were $150,000 the first year, $125,000 the second, and $100,000 each of the third through seventh years, then a $100,000 annuity for seven years may be separated, leaving additional sums of $50,000 in year 1 and $25,000 in year 2. The *PV*s of the annuity and the additional sums are then determined and accumulated. The calculation of the present value of these expected cash flows is shown in Table 11–6.

Table 11–6 Calculation of present value (*PV*) of an uneven cash flow stream

A.

Year	Expected cash flow	Annuity	Additional sums
1	$150,000		$50,000
2	125,000		25,000
3	100,000		—
4	100,000	$100,000	—
5	100,000		—
6	100,000		—
7	100,000	↓	—

B. Calculation:

PV of $100,000 annuity for 7 years discounted @ 12%:	
$100,000 × 4.564 (the *PVIFA*)	$456,400
PV of $50,000 sum in 1 year discounted @ 12%:	
$50,000 × .893 (the *PVIF*)	44,650
PV of $25,000 sum in 2 years discounted @ 12%:	
$25,000 × .797	19,925
PV of the expected cash flows:	
$456,400 + $44,650 + $19,925	$520,975

Discount rate calculation We found the discount rate that equated the present value of either a future sum or an annuity by calculating the *PVIF* or the *PVIFA* and then scanning the year *(n)* line of the appropriate present value table to locate the discount rate. Where future cash flow (*FV*) streams are uneven, determining the discount rate is much more complicated and laborious. The only way it can be done by hand with the tables is by trial and error. Choose a trial discount rate. Then calculate the present value as we did in Table 11–5 (or, if appropriate, as in Table 11–6). If this calculated *PV* is lower than the known *PV*, then choose a *lower* discount rate (*PV*s increase as discount rates decrease) and repeat the *PV* calculation. If the resulting calculated *PV* is now higher than the known *PV*, the discount rate must be between those used in the first and second calculations. Repeating this process as often as necessary will bracket the discount rates that are immediately above and below the one that equates the *PV* and *FV*s of the uneven stream. Interpolate if necessary. Computer programs have been developed to do this electronically and some hand-held calculators have an IRR (internal rate of return) button that will do it for a limited number of uneven flows.

More frequent payments

The present value tables we have used, those in the Appendix at the end of this book and most others that may be available, are based upon annual compound discounting. This assumes that future cash flows (*FV*s) will occur at the end of each year. However, in real-life applications cash flows often will occur at more frequent semiannual, quarterly, monthly, weekly, or daily intervals, or even continuously. Where payments are expected to occur more frequently, to be technically correct present values should be calculated by more frequent compounding of the discount.

Because estimated future cash flows often are highly uncertain, this relatively small discrepancy usually is not significant. Illustrations and problems in this book and most of those encountered in practice will ignore it. But on some occasions you may wish to discount future cash flows on a more frequent compounding basis. There are three ways to accomplish this. First, there are tables available based upon more frequent compounding. For example, one that applies monthly compounding to the present value of annuities shows the *PVIFA*s as "Present value of 1⁄12 of $1 received monthly for *n* years." The second way of handling this is to use a conversion table, such as the one cited in footnote 2 earlier in this chapter, to adjust from the regular (annually compounded) tables to any periodic payment from semiannual to continuous that appears appropriate to the nature of the cash flows under consideration. The third way is to adjust the formulas or use of the tables in the fashion indicated earlier in this chapter under "Compound interest—More frequent compounding."

Summary

To do the analysis required to make capital investment decisions (and several other types of financial decisions) one must understand the time value of money and the mathematical techniques used to account for it.

Money has a time value because the use of it through time will produce income. Therefore a dollar available now is worth more than one that will become available at a future date. Interest is the exchange rate between a present and an expected future value. Simple interest is computed on the original principal for one period. Compound interest is interest earned not only on the original principal but also on the reinvested interest accumulated from previous periods. The basic formula for future value at annually compounded interest is

$$FV_n = PV\,(1 + i)^n$$

This calculation may be simplified by substituting for $(1 + i)^n$ an *FVIF* (future value interest factor) obtained from an *FVIF* (compound interest) table. If interest is compounded more frequently than once a year, the basic formula may be modified to

$$FV_n = PV\left(1 + \frac{i}{m}\right)^{mn}$$

where m is the number of times per year interest is compounded.

We are, however, more interested in determining present value (*PV*) of expected future cash flows (*FV*s) in the analysis required for capital investment decisions. Present value of $1 is the reciprocal of future value of $1. Therefore the general formula for present value is

$$PV = FV_n\left[\frac{1}{(1 + i)^n}\right]$$

Here the interest rate *(i)* usually is referred to as the discount rate, and compound discount is employed to transform future value to present value. This calculation may be simplified by substituting a *PVIF* (present value interest factor), obtained from a *PVIF* table (also called a present value table or a compound discount table), for $1/(1 + i)^n$ in the above equation. Then the formula becomes

$$PV = FV_n \times PVIF_{i,n}$$

Sometimes we will wish to find the present value of a level stream of periodic payments in the future. Such a stream is an annuity. Tables are available showing the present value interest factors for an annuity (*PVIFA*). To find the present value of an annuity for n years discounted at i compound interest rate, use the formula

$$PV_a = FV_{a,n} \times PVIFA_{i,n}$$

Some types of financial analysis require finding the present value of an annuity that goes on forever. This is a perpetuity. The *PV* of a perpetuity is the reciprocal of the discount rate times the amount of each annual payment, or

$$PV = \frac{FV_a}{i}$$

Present value tables also may be used to find the discount rate that equates given present values and future values. To do this, divide the *PV* by the *FV* to get the *PVIF*. Then search the appropriate *n* line on the *PVIF* table to locate the matching *PVIF*. The rate at the head of that column is the discount rate. Interpolate if necessary. If you are doing this for an annuity, the process is the same but uses the *PVIFA* determined by dividing the PV_a by $FV_{a,n}$.

Where uneven streams of future cash flow are anticipated, calculation of present values and discount rates becomes more complex and laborious. The present value of the sum to be received each year must be calculated and these *PV*s accumulated to get the total present value. If one is seeking the discount rate that equates a present value with an uneven stream of expected cash flows, it must be found by trial and error. Present values are calculated as above for various discount rates until one has bracketed the rate that equates the values. Interpolate if necessary. Computer programs can identify the discount rate, and some hand-held calculators will do it for a limited number of uneven flows.

Technically, future values that are expected to flow at more frequent intervals than each year should be discounted as they would occur. But the use of tables based upon annual discounting creates only a small discrepancy that usually is unimportant. If necessary, more frequent discounting may be handled in several ways.

Questions

1. How does compound interest relate to simple interest? (Include in your answer the formulas for simple and compound interest.)

2. How does the present value (*PV*) of a future sum relate to the future value (*FV*) of a present sum?

3. How does more frequent compounding of interest affect the future value of a present sum invested at a positive interest rate? Why?

4. *a.* What is a *PVIF*?

   b. How does a *PVIF* table facilitate the computation of the present value (*PV*) of a sum to be received at a future date (FV_n) at a given compound discount rate (*i*)?

5. *a.* What is a *PVIFA*?
   b. How is a *PVIFA* table constructed from a *PVIF* table?
   c. How does a *PVIFA* table facilitate computation of the present value (*PV*) of a sum to be received at the end of each period for a given number of periods ($FV_{a,n}$) discounted at a specified interest rate (*i*)?

6. What is a perpetuity? How can one determine the present value of a perpetuity at a given interest rate?

7. If the present value (*PV*) and the future value of a sum (FV_n) are known, how can the discount rate (*i*) that equates them be identified?

8. If the present value (PV_a) and the amount of an annuity for a given number of periods ($FV_{a,n}$) are known, how can the discount rate (*i*) that equates the two values be identified?

9. What is the effect of an increase in the discount rate (*i*) upon the present value (*PV*) of a future sum (FV_n)? Is the effect the same if the future sum is to be received annually for a given number of years (an annuity)?

10. Explain why present value (*PV*) decreases at an increasing rate with the length of time after which the payment is to be received.

11. How can present value tables be used to calculate the *PV* of a mixed (uneven) stream of expected future cash flows when the discount rate (*i*) is specified?

12. If the present value (*PV*) is known and the future cash flows (*FVs*) are a mixed (uneven) stream, how can present value tables be used to identify the discount rate (*i*) that equates the *PV* and the *FVs*?

Problems

1. You have been offered the choice of two prizes, $10,000 now or $16,000 to be received five years from now. If you can invest at 10 percent interest compounded annually at the same perceived risk as that of receiving the prize in five years, which prize would you accept? Why? (Ignore income tax considerations.)

2. Sales of the Sundial Company are expected to increase 8 percent annually for the next five years. If sales for 1982 were $5 million, what are sales for 1987 expected to be?

3. Sally Crafton has just inherited $20,000 and wishes to purchase an annuity to pay her equal amounts each year for the next four years. If an insurance company offers annuities based upon a 9 percent interest rate, how much will Sally receive at the end of each year?

4. You need $30,000 at the end of six years. If you have excess funds available now, how much will you have to invest at 9 percent compounded annually to provide the $30,000 in six years?

5. How much would you pay for a $1,000 non-interest-bearing note to mature in three years if you require a 10 percent return compounded annually?

6. Greenbriar Manufacturing Company has an opportunity to make a capital investment of $250,000 that is expected to produce net cash inflows of $100,000 the first year, $140,000 the second, $90,000 the third, and $20,000 the fourth year, at the end of which it will be valueless. If Greenbriar requires a rate of return of 14 percent on this investment, should the investment be made?

7. Colby Corporation could make an investment of $250,000 that is expected to produce net cash inflows of $60,000 annually for each of the next five years. If Colby requires a 12 percent rate of return, should this investment be made?

8. Linden Corporation is considering two investments with the following expected cash flow streams:

	Cash flow from investment	
Year	A	B
1	$10,000	$50,000
2	20,000	40,000
3	30,000	30,000
4	40,000	20,000
5	50,000	10,000

a. Compute the present value of the cash flow stream from each investment discounted at 15 percent.

b. If the investment required for each were $100,000 and Linden required a rate of return of 15 percent on each, which investment would it make? Why?

c. What general observation, if any, do you draw from solving this problem?

9. What is the present value of a perpetuity of $30,000 annually discounted at 9 percent? How does this value compare with that of an annuity of the same amount for 50 years discounted at 9 percent? Why is there so little difference? What general observation do you draw from solving this problem?

10. If you have the choice of $10,000 now or $20,000 ten years hence, what discount rate will equate the present values of the two opportunities?

11. Eagle Corporation is considering purchasing for $10,000 a machine that will reduce cash outlays by $2,100 each year for the next seven years

and be worthless at the end of that period. What is the discount rate that will equate the purchase price and the $2,100 cash savings each of the next seven years? If Eagle required a return of 12 percent on this investment, should it buy the machine?

12. What is the present value of the following cash flow stream discounted at 14 percent?

Year	Cash flow	Year	Cash flow
1	$10,000	6	$11,000
2	10,000	7	10,000
3	10,000	8	10,000
4	14,000	9	10,000
5	15,000	10	20,000

(Hint: Save time; minimize the number of calculations.)

13. Determine to the nearest percent the discount rate that will equate the values of the present outlay of $180,00 and the following future cash flows.

Year	Cash flow
1	$40,000
2	50,000
3	30,000
4	35,000
5	65,000

Chapter 12
Capital Investment Decisions: Analytical Methods

Capital investments are those outlays (expenditures) that are expected to yield benefits to the firm over a period greater than one year. Most capital investments are made to acquire fixed assets, such as a new plant, warehouse, or office building, to buy one or more new machines, to modernize a production line or, in a marketing firm, to open a new store or expand an existing one. Such investments, however, are not limited to the acquisition of fixed assets. They also include research projects to develop new products, improve existing products, or increase the efficiency of production. Advertising and promotion campaigns designed to produce long-term marketing benefits should also be considered as capital investments. Additional working capital required in connection with fixed-asset or product-line expansion projects should be included in the capital investment. Not all of these outlays will be capitalized in the accounting process or for income tax purposes. The distinguishing characteristics are the *long-term nature of expected benefits* and *the analytical techniques* appropriate to the decision-making process.

The importance of the capital investment decision-making process (often called *capital budgeting*) cannot be overemphasized. The success of nearly all of our great corporations ultimately may be attributed to their developing capital investment opportunities, identifying those that enhanced the value of the firm, and investing in these projects in a timely fashion. Conversely, the economic graveyards are littered with the corpses of firms that failed to identify such opportunities or to invest in them when they were available.

The importance attached to capital investment decisons reflects (1) the relative size of the outlays involved, (2) the long time-span of the investments, and (3) their great influence upon the future directions of the firm. In most firms, the amounts of money committed in major capital investment decisions are many times larger than those that might be involved in decisions relating to working capital, such as extending credit to a customer or purchasing inventories. In some large firms, individual capital investment decisions may involve hundreds of millions or even billions of dollars.

The time period over which benefits may be expected from capital investments varies from 2 or 3 years to as much as 30 or 40 years. Therefore, a major capital investment decision, by committing resources for such a long time, limits the firm's flexibility. If the decision is right, the firm benefits for a long time. But if it is wrong, either resources are tied up for a long time or severe losses must be sustained to salvage the remaining value of the investment. In addition to increasing the importance of such decisions, the long time-span greatly increases the difficulty of analyzing capital investment proposals and making appropriate decisons. This results from the increased uncertainty of the benefits to be received and the difficulty of making meaningful estimates of such benefits at all.

The major capital investment decisions of a firm are directly interrelated with the firm's long-term operating strategy. This strategy, involving such broad considerations as the ways in which the firm is going to compete, the markets it intends to penetrate, and ultimately the nature and scope of the firm's operations, will be implemented by the capital investment decisions that are made.

Responsibility for capital investment decisions

Capital investment decisions rarely, if ever, will be made *solely* by the financial manager. Rather, the financial manager and his or her staff usually will have a substantial influence upon the guidelines governing such decisions and the analytical format to be used in the decision-making process. The finance department will serve as a funnel through which the relevant data will be collected and processed. The financial officer will have a direct influence upon major capital investment decisions through membership on the responsible committees and an indirect influence upon minor decisions through informal liaison with the responsible operating officers.

The formal organization of capital investment authority and responsibility will vary among firms. A rather common pattern for a medium-sized manufacturing firm will authorize department managers to approve minor outlays, up to perhaps $5,000, while plant managers may authorize expenditures up to, say, $50,000. Major capital investments—say, up to $500,000—would be authorized by a capital investment committee including perhaps the chief executive officer, the chief operating officer, and the vice presidents for finance, production, and marketing. Larger capital investments, after approval by this committee, may then be submitted to a capital investment committee of the board of directors and perhaps to the entire board for final approval. The chief financial officer, usually a member of the board and of this committee, will have considerable influence upon the discussions and the final decisions. Formal guidelines governing the minor decisons (those that may be authorized by the department or plant manager) might be developed jointly by the financial and production vice presidents.

In smaller firms, the chief executive officer often must approve all capital expenditures over a few hundred dollars. At the other extreme, in a large firm organized into operating divisions (profit centers), guidelines and sometimes maximum annual capital expenditures for each division may be determined at the corporate level, with responsibility for all except very large capital outlays delegated to the division managers. In such cases, the pattern of authority within each division will then be broken down in the fashion previously described for the medium-sized firm.

Two points are important here. First, although the analytical processes essential to sound capital investment decision-making are financial in nature, the decisions will be made by individuals many of whom are not primarily finance-oriented. All executives involved in such decisions must have at least a working understanding of the pertinent analytical processes. Second, the financial manager and staff must be able to work with other executives of the firm to familiarize them with the analytical techniques and informally, as well as formally, influence the capital investment decisions.

Generation of capital investment proposals

The genesis of a successful capital investment program is the generation of proposals for promising investment projects. This should be as obvious as the fact that a profit cannot be made without sales. Yet many firms die on the vine simply because either the people in the organization do not generate good proposals for capital investments or their proposals are stifled at the lower level before they are forwarded to a level of authority where such decisions can be made.

Research and development efforts are importantly related to this process. Contrast the growth and profitability of our electronic computer industry over the past two or three decades to that of our steel industry. Innovation, capital investment, and economic prosperity of a firm, an industry, or, perhaps, a nation appear to go hand in hand. Innovation relates not only to organized research and development but also, and perhaps more importantly, to the generation and forwarding of ideas from throughout the organization to the decision-making level.[1] We have much to learn about creating appropriate attitudes, mechanisms, and incentives for the generation of more and better capital investment proposals.

The cost-benefit analytical framework—Introduction

The basic concept underlying capital investment decision-making is cost-benefit analysis. As shown in Figure 12–1, the cost of making each proposed

[1] Perhaps this is one of the most important reasons that Japanese industry has outcompeted American and some other western-based industries in many markets during recent years. The organization of people in the major Japanese industrial firms provides both attitudes and incentives favorable to the generation of constructive ideas, their development into formal proposals, and action by management to consider these proposals. For example, in such firms the worker who proposes the use of a machine to do his or her job is not only immune to layoff but is guaranteed a promotion and pay increase if the proposal is accepted. This is a far cry from the suggestion box the contents of which are periodically dumped into the wastebasket.

Figure 12–1 Capital investment analysis
Cost-benefit concept

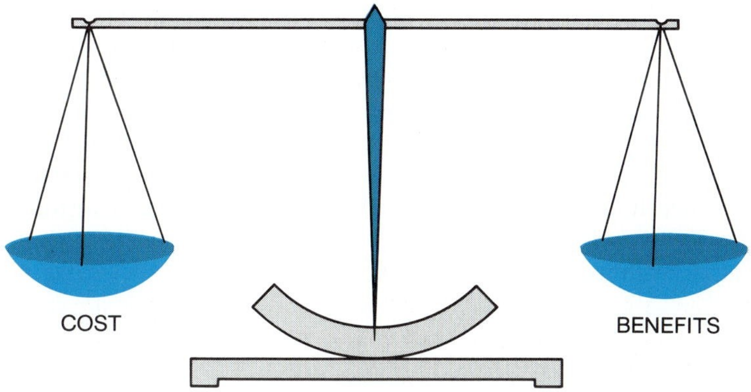

capital investment is compared to the benefits expected to result from that investment project, as if each were placed on a balance scale. Note that cash benefits may be either net cash inflows or cash savings. If the present value of the benefits exceeds the cost, the capital investment should be approved. If the present value of the benefits is less than the cost, the proposal should be rejected. This cost-benefit concept strives to accomplish the general goal of maximizing the value of the firm.

One method of applying the concept is the *net present value method.* If the capital investment to be made presently, the amount of that investment will be its present value. If the present value of expected future benefits, discounted at an appropriate rate, is greater than the initial investment outlay, the value of the firm is increased by investment in the project.

Another way of applying the cost-benefit concept is the *internal rate of return method.* It considers the benefits in terms of the expected rate of return on the investment and the cost in terms of the required rate of return on such an investment. If the benefits exceed the cost, then the value of the firm is increased by investment in the project.

Independent and mutually exclusive proposals

The above discussion assumes that the various capital investment proposals are *independent,* that is, that the acceptance of one will not preclude acceptance of another. Examples of independent proposals are those to buy a given new machine, build a warehouse, or introduce a new product.

Two or more proposals are *mutually exclusive* if acceptance of one would preclude the acceptance of another. Examples of mutually exclusive proposals are those to purchase a new machine, to purchase a different machine to perform the same function, or to renovate the old machine that either of these two machines would replace. In considering mutually exclusive proposals, the alternative with the greatest excess of present value of the expected future benefits over the present value of the investment normally would be chosen. This would tend to maximize value and thus be compatible with the general goal of the firm.

Initial simplifying assumptions

Two of the major difficulties of implementing the cost-benefit concept arise from (1) the uncertainty (risk) of future benefits to be achieved and, to a lesser degree, the initial investment required and (2) establishing the required rate of return. These problems are interrelated. To order our discussion of the capital investment decision, we shall at this point make some simplifying assumptions:

1. That the perceived risk related to each proposed project is equal to the average risk of the firm.
2. The required rate of return of the firm, therefore that of each project, will be assumed.
3. That all proposed projects are equally compatible with the strategic policies of the firm.

These simplifying assumptions allow us to develop the basic analytical methods in this chapter and to identify the relevant cash flows in Chapter 13. Project risk differentials and strategic policy considerations will be treated in Chapter 14, and the required rate of return of the firm will be estimated in Chapter 15.

DCF methods of analysis

The only theoretically valid methods of analyzing capital investment proposals are those that fully recognize the time value of money. These are called *discounted cash flow* (DCF) methods because they involve discounting estimated future cash flows to their values at the contemplated inception of the proposed project, time zero. They take into account both the magnitude and timing of expected cash flows throughout the life of the proposed project. There are two basic DCF analytical methods, *internal rate of return* (IRR) and *net present value* (NPV). A correlary of the NPV method is the profitability index (sometimes called the benefit/cost ratio). Although the methodology differs, both basic methods apply the fundamental cost-benefit approach and will yield the same decisions in cases where that approach can be fully applied.

Net present value method

To calculate the net present value (NPV) of a proposed project, we simply *subtract the initial outlay,* or present value of net cash outflows, *from the present value of the expected future net cash benefits.* Present value of expected future net cash benefits is determined by discounting those cash benefits at the required rate of return (RRR):

$$\text{NPV} = \text{Present value of future cash benefits} - \text{Initial investment} \quad (12\text{–}1)$$

This process is illustrated in Figure 12–2.

Figure 12–2 Net present value

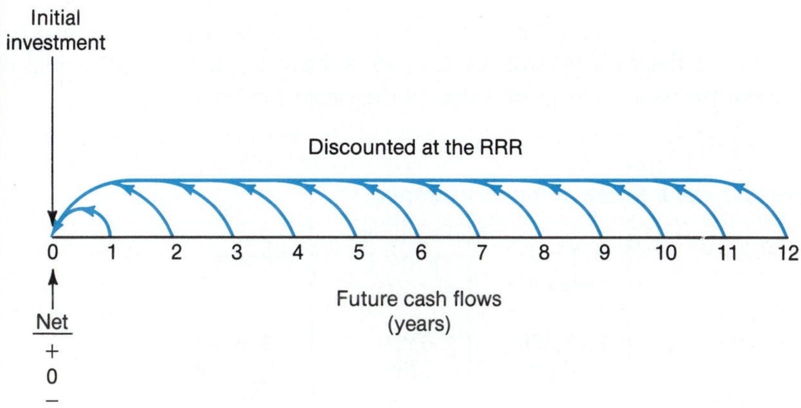

To illustrate computation of the net present value (NPV) of a simple project where the estimated future cash benefits are a steady stream (an annuity), assume a project requiring an initial investment of $17,600 in year zero. Expected net cash benefits are $3,200 for each of the next 10 years, and there is no terminal value. Also assume that the required rate of return is 12 percent. The discount factor at 12 percent for an annuity of 10 years (*PVIFA* from Table B in the Appendix) is 5.650. As shown in Table 12–1, multiplying this *PVIFA* factor by the estimated net cash benefits of $3,200 per year indicates a present value of $18,080. The initial investment in the

Table 12–1 **Net present value (simple example)**

	Amount	Discount factor @ 12%	Present value
Net cash benefits (years 1–10)	$ 3,200	5.650*	$18,080
Net cash investment (initial outlay, year 0)	−17,600	1.000	−17,600
Net present value			$ 480

*$PVIFA_{.12,10}$ from Table B in the Appendix.

project at year zero is $17,600, and its present value factor is 1. Subtracting the $17,600 present value of this outlay from the present value of the estimated net cash benefits of $18,080 results in a net present value of the project of $480.

To develop the NPV of a slightly more complex project, use the same data but also include an estimated terminal value of $3,000 at the end of 10 years. In this case, as shown in Table 12–2, the present value of the estimated annual net cash benefits from operations is the same, $18,080. The present value of the $3,000 estimated terminal value at the end of ten years is discounted at 12 percent by multiplying it by the *PVIF* of .322 obtained from Table A in the Appendix. This present value is $966, making a total present value of the cash benefits of $19,046. Subtracting the $17,600 initial investment yields a net present value of the project of $1,446.

Table 12–2 **Net present value (more complex example)**

	Amount	Discount factor @ 12%	Present value
Net cash benefits			
(years 1–10)	$ 3,200	5.650*	$18,080
(year 10)	3,000	.322†	966
Present value of inflows			19,046
Net cash investment (initial outlay, year 0)	−17,600	1.000	−17,600
Net present value			$ 1,446

*$PVIFA_{.12,10}$ from Table B.
†$PVIF_{.12,10}$ from Table A.

If the project under consideration involved different estimated net cash benefits for each successive year, the calculation of the NPV would be a bit more complicated. The estimated cash benefit each year would be multiplied by the appropriate *PVIF* from Table A in the Appendix. The resulting net present values would then be accumulated. The initial investment would be subtracted from this positive value of the benefits to obtain the net present value of the project. Similarly, if the net cash investment contemplated for the project were spread into future years, these outlays would also be discounted to the year zero by using appropriate *PVIFs* from Table A in the Appendix.

Acceptance criterion If the net present value (NPV) of the project is *positive,* the project will be *approved.* Conversely, if it is negative, the project will be rejected. The logic is that acceptance of any project showing a positive net present value, when expected cash flows are discounted at the required rate of return, will increase the present value of the firm and thereby enhance the value of its common stock. By the same logic, rejection of a proposed project having a negative present value will prevent making an investment that would reduce the value of the firm.

Profitability index The *profitability index* (PI) (sometimes called the *benefit/cost ratio)* is a correlary of the net present value method. To find the profitability index of a proposed project, the present value of estimated future net cash benefits is *divided by* the present value of the initial net cash investment:

$$\text{Profitability index} = \frac{\text{Present value of net cash benefits}}{\text{Initial investment}} \qquad (12\text{–}2)$$

To illustrate, the profitability index of the project in our more complex example is 1.08, calculated as follows:

$$\text{Profitability index} = \frac{\$19{,}046}{\$17{,}600} = 1.08$$

As the alternative term, benefit/cost ratio, implies, the profitability index indicates the relative advantage (or disadvantage) of the project in relation to a value of 1.0 representing a neutral effect on the value of the firm.

The decision criterion using a profitability index is that if the index is *greater than 1,* the project should be *accepted,* whereas if it is less than 1, the project should be rejected. This, of course, will accept or reject exactly the same projects as the NPV criterion (or the IRR criterion). However, if proposed projects are mutually exclusive or if capital is being rationed (subjects that will be treated later), the profitability index may be useful in ranking the desirability of projects. For example, assume that only one of two projects, A or B, is to be accepted and project A has a profitability index of 1.23 while that of project B is 1.14. The superiority of project A over project B is shown by its higher profitability index.[2]

[2]Note that the term *profitability index* is, in a sense, a misnomer in that it does not refer to profitability in the usual sense of accounting income determined by an accrual system. Perhaps it would be better titled "cash-flow benefit index."

Internal rate of return (IRR) method

The internal rate of return method answers the question: "What is the expected rate of return on the investment in the project under consideration?" It seeks to establish the *compound rate of return that equates the present values of (1) the initial cash outlay(s) and (2) the future cash benefits* that are expected to result from acceptance of the project. Figure 12–3 illustrates the concept underlying the IRR method. To put this into a formula, let I_0 be the initial investment in the project at year zero, *FV* equal the expected net cash benefits each year in the future, noted by subscript 1, 2, 3, etc., and *i* equal the internal rate of return. Then,

Figure 12–3 The internal rate of return

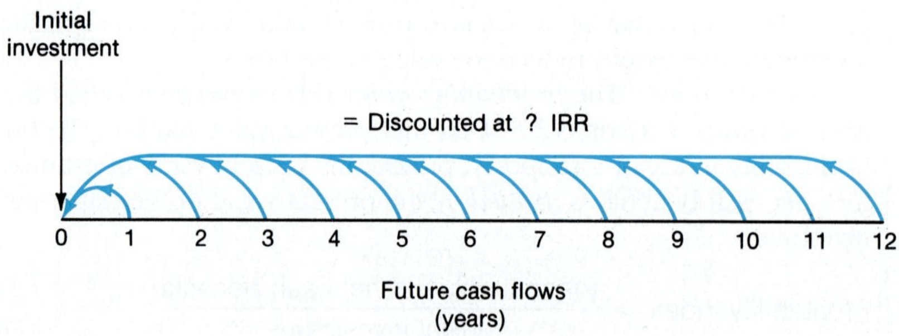

$$I_o = \frac{FV_1}{1+i} + \frac{FV_2}{(1+i)^2} + \frac{FV_3}{(1+i)^3} + \ldots \frac{FV_n}{(1+i)^n}$$

Substituting $PVIF_{i,n}$ for $1/(1+i)^n$, this equation may be written

$$I_0 = FV, (PVIF_{i,1}) + FV_2 (PVIF_{i,2}) + FV_3 (PVIF_{i,3}) + \ldots FV_n (PVIF_{i,n}) \quad (12\text{–}3)$$

To solve for *i*, the *internal rate of return* (IRR), use the procedures developed in Chapter 11. If the expected annual net cash benefits (*FV*s) are a steady stream (an annuity), finding the IRR by using the *PVIFA* table (Table B in the Appendix) is relatively simple. However, if the expected annual net cash benefits are not equal, laborious trial and error computations must be used to find the IRR from Tables A and B in the Appendix. This may be done as described in Chapter 11 or by using either a suitably programmed computer or a calculator with an IRR button.

To illustrate finding the IRR if the cash benefit pattern is an annuity, assume a project with a net cash investment in year zero of $17,600 and estimated net cash benefits of $3,200 in each of the years 1 through 10, as shown in Table 12–3. The present value interest factor of the annuity (*PVIFA*) is 5.500, determined by dividing $17,600 (the initial outlay, I_0) by $3,200 (the annuity for 10 years, FV_{10}). Searching the *PVIFA* table (Appendix Table B), we find that the *PVIFA* for 10 years at 12 percent is 5.650 and, at 13 percent, 5.426. Multiplying each by $3,200 reveals that, discounted at 12 percent, the annuity of $3,200 for ten years has a present value of $18,080, whereas, discounted at 13 percent, it has a percent value of $17,363. Thus, we know that the internal rate of return of this project is between 12 percent and 13 percent. Interpolating these data indicates that the more precise IRR is 12.7 percent.

Table 12–3 Internal rate of return (simple example)

	(1) Amount	(2) Discount factor	(1) × (2) Present value
Net cash investment (year 0)	−$17,600	1.000	−$17,600
Net cash benefits (years 1–10)			
IRR = 12%	3,200	5.650*	18,080
IRR = 13%	3,200	5.426†	17,363

Interpolation:

@ 12%	$18,080	@ 12%	$18,080
@ 13%	17,363	@ (12 + x)%	17,600
1%	$ 717	x%	$ 480

$$\frac{x}{1} = \frac{\$480}{\$717} = .7;\ \text{IRR} = 12\% + .7\% = 12.7\%$$

*$PVIFA_{.12,10}$ from Table B.
†$PVIFA_{.13,10}$ from Table B.

Now, to find the IRR under a more complex proposal, we include a $3,000 estimated terminal value at the end of year 10 and approach the problem by trial and error. As shown in Table 12–4, we utilize Appendix Table B to determine the present value of the $3,200 annuity for 10 years and Table A to find the present value of the additional $3,000 estimated net cash inflow at the end of year 10. These values discounted at 13 percent yield a present value of $18,248, a sum larger than the $17,600 initial investment. Therefore we know that the discount rate that will equate the present value of the net cash investment and benefits is greater than 13 percent. We then try 14 percent and find that the present value of the net cash inflows is $17,501. This is so close to the initial investment of $17,600 that we probably would not bother to interpolate. We see that the internal rate of return (IRR) of this proposed project is slightly less than 14 percent.

In actual practice, proposals frequently are still more complex, with dif-

Table 12–4 Internal rate of return (more complex example)

	(1) Amount	(2) Discount factor	(1) × (2) Present value
Net cash investment (year 0)	−$17,600	1.000	−$17,600
Net cash benefits			
IRR = 13%			
Years 1–10	3,200	5.426*	$17,363
Year 10	3,000	.295†	885
			$18,248
IRR = 14%			
Years 1–10	3,200	5.216‡	$16,691
Year 10	3,000	.270§	810
			$17,501

No interpolation necessary; IRR is slightly less than 14 percent.

*$PVIFA_{.13,10}$ from Table B.
†$PVIF_{.13,10}$ from Table A.
‡$PVIFA_{.14,10}$ from Table B.
§$PVIF_{.14,10}$ from Table A.

fering cash benefits expected each year. Determination of the IRR by using tables requires calculating the present value of each year's cash benefits using *PVIFs* from Appendix Table A for a given discount rate. The sum of these present values is compared to the initial investment. Then, by repeating the process using *PVIFs* for different discount rates, by trial and error we will locate the closest IRRs, and interpolation will determine the IRR more precisely.

Acceptance criterion The internal rate of return (IRR) must be compared with the *required rate of return* (also variously known as the *target rate, hurdle rate,* or *cutoff rate*). At this point we shall assume that the required rate of return (RRR) is 12 percent. (Establishing the required rate of return will be treated in Chapters 14 and 15.) *If the IRR is greater than the RRR,* the proposal will be *accepted.* If the IRR is less than the RRR, the proposal will be rejected. Therefore either of the above proposals would be accepted. The logic underlying the acceptance criterion is that if the IRR exceeds the RRR, acceptance of the proposal will increase the value of the firm. This, in turn, assumes that the RRR fully reflects the risk of the project under consideration.

Comparison of NPV and IRR methods

If all capital investment proposals that have either a positive net present value or an internal rate of return greater than the required rate of return are to be accepted, then it really doesn't make any difference which basic analytical method, NPV or IRR, is used. The accept-versus-reject signals will be the same. This is also true with respect to the profitability index corollary method as compared to either of the basic methods.

However, when a number of proposed projects having positive NPVs and IRRs exceeding the RRR must be ranked because they will *not* all be accepted, then it does make a difference which analytical method is used. The reason for this is that the *rankings* of two or more proposed projects may differ when established according to their internal rates of return as compared to rankings according to their net present values. One is faced with the question, "If project D has a higher internal rate of return than project E, but E has a higher net present value than D, which project should be accepted if only one can be accepted?" This question arises only under two conditions, (1) if the projects are mutually exclusive, such as proposals to buy machine D *or* machine E to perform the same function but only one machine is needed, or (2) it capital is rationed, *i.e.,* funds available for investment are limited and capable of financing only a smaller number of proposed projects than those that would be acceptable under general criteria.

Why can the IRR method and the NPV method result in different rankings? Two factors may be responsible. The first, and simplest, is that the IRR method reflects *rate* of return per dollar of investment in the projects, but does not reflect the magnitude (in dollars) of the cash flows related to the projects. On the other hand, the NPV directly reflects the *magnitude* (in dollars) of the present value advantage of the projects, but does not directly reflect the rates of return. Rates of return, however, can be related indirectly by the corollary method based upon NPV, the profitability index, which isolates rate of return from the side effects of cash flow magnitudes.

The second, more serious and complex, reason conflicting rankings may appear relates to implicit assumptions regarding the *reinvestment* of positive cash flows developed by the projects. The IRR method implicitly assumes that such positive cash flows are reinvested at the *project rates,* that is, the internal rates of return (IRR) of the projects. Thus, if a project has an IRR of say 18 percent, then the positive cash flows developed the first year, second year, third year, and so on are assumed to be reinvested to yield an 18 percent compound rate of return for the remainder of the project life.

In contrast, the NPV method implicitly assumes that such positive cash flows developed by the projects are reinvested at the *required rate* of return (RRR). Thus, if the RRR is 12 percent, positive cash flows developed each year are assumed to be reinvested to yield a compound rate of return of 12 percent for the remaining life of the project. This difference in implicitly assumed reinvestment rates may create significant differences in the rankings of projects under the IRR method versus the NPV method.

Which method is best? From both theoretical and practical standpoints, the net present value method (NPV), accompanied where appropriate by its corollary, profitability index, is superior. The rate of return versus magnitude of present value problem can be resolved by using profitability index information to accompany the net present value data.

Which assumption regarding the reinvestment of positive cash flows is sound? The answer requires reasoning through the probable reinvestment of such funds. Logically, there is no reason to believe that funds developed by a project with, say, a 24 percent IRR would be reinvested at any higher or lower rate than those developed by a project with a 13 percent IRR. Future reinvestment will be made from a pool comprised of all available funds and not identified by a particular source. If the firm will invest in future projects yielding down to the required rate of return (which constitutes the cutoff or hurdle rate), then one would expect that the marginal reinvestment would bring an expected rate of return only marginally higher than the required rate. Although some reinvestment may take place at a rate higher than the RRR, there would be no relationship between particular reinvestments at higher rates and the origin of the funds to finance them from higher IRR projects. Thus the use of the NPV method where there is a conflict between the two would be theoretically and practically superior.[3]

Nonetheless, the IRR method is widely used in practice. Even though NPV is both theoretically superior and, in practice, much easier to calculate when uneven streams of future cash benefits are involved, some managements find that executives involved in the capital investment decision-making process understand rates of return on investments better than net present values. This is a matter of ways of thinking and effectiveness of communication. Also, in some firms the top management does not wish to disclose to lower levels of management the required rates of return that are being used in the capital investment decision-making process. Reasons for this could range from strategic security to discouraging lower-level managers from massaging the figures so they would just clear the criterion for acceptance.

The net result of these considerations is that many firms use both the IRR and NPV methods, each as a check on the signals of the other. Also, as will be discussed in Chapter 14, considerations of risk differentials and strategic policy materially affect final capital investment decisions. Such decisions are not by any means simply matters of arithmetic.

Capital rationing

Capital rationing occurs whenever a constraint is placed upon total capital investments that results in rejection of any proposed projects that would otherwise be acceptable under conventional NPV or IRR criteria. To illustrate, assume that a firm is considering the capital investment proposals

[3]Another highly technical reason the NPV method is superior to IRR is that some unusual cash-flow patterns may yield more than one IRR. Such multiple IRRs are theoretically possible if future cash benefits change in sign from positive to negative, back to positive, and so on.

shown in Table 12–5 for a given year. Under the NPV criterion (accept all projects with positive NPVs) or the IRR criterion (accept all projects with IRRs greater than the RRR, not shown in the table) projects A through F would be accepted and only projects G and H would be rejected. Such a decision would maximize the net present value of the firm. However, if the firm were rationing capital, a limit of, say, $4 million total capital expenditures for that year may have been established. Under this constraint, all of the projects A through F could not be accepted because the total initial outlay required would be $5.4 million. Then the decisional problem would be, "Which of projects A through F should be accepted?"

Table 12–5 Capital investment proposals

Proposal	Initial outlay ($000)	Net present value	Profitability index
A	$1,000	$430	1.43
B	800	216	1.27
C	1,100	209	1.19
D	800	88	1.11
E	1,100	99	1.09
F	600	11	1.02
G	900	−36	.96
H	400	−44	.89

Note that in theory the rationing of capital to a limit of $4 million cannot result in selection of proposed capital investment projects that will maximize the net present value of the firm. Some projects with positive net present values will have to be rejected. In other words, capital rationing theoretically is a suboptimal policy. Does its use then mean that the management of a firm that rations capital is ignorant (ought to go back to college and take a good financial management course), or perhaps unintelligent? Possibly it does, but probably not. Many apparently well-managed firms ration capital. It is hard to believe that their managements are all ignorant or irrational, so there must be some other explanations.

Reasons for capital rationing There are many logical explanations for deviating from the strict theory of capital investment decision making by rationing capital. Among these is the recognition that capital is not the only resource required for the success of capital investment projects. A very important other resource is the people who will manage them. Often firms with numerous excellent opportunities for capital investments find it prudent to limit their expansion short of the theoretical financial optimum because acceptance of projects to that optimum would spread their managerial talent too thin. In other words, management reasons that placing unseasoned executives in charge of expansion projects would cause the cumulative actual returns from the accepted projects to be lower than the sum of the individually forecasted returns from each of the projects. Inferior management would be responsible for such a shortfall. This is a nonquantifiable factor that conventional analysis does not take into account.

Another reason for capital rationing is understood when one observes a family-controlled firm limiting its capital expenditures to those that can be financed without requiring the sale of additional common stock outside the family. Here the utility of the increase in value of the firm that would result from acceptance of additional projects is judged by members of the controlling family to be less than the disutility of having to share ownership with others or, in some cases, possibly losing control to others. Perhaps this is not strictly an economic consideration, but it is nonetheless an important logical explanation of management behavior.

Still another explanation of capital rationing is provided by the following illustration. A banker friend of the author, while playing golf with an officer and member of the controlling family of a medium-sized regional corporation, suggested that with the excellent acceptance of their product they should expand and penetrate the national market. That officer explained why they were not even considering it by saying, "Look, Phil, if we did that I wouldn't be out here playing golf with you. I'd be far too busy." He followed by pointing out that members of the family had all the wealth they reasonably needed.

Project selection Understanding that capital rationing is prevalent in many firms and that it is not fully irrational, then how does one select the proposed projects that will optimize the value of the firm within the constraint of limited capital investment? The objective is to maximize the present value of the combination of investments made. If the number of otherwise acceptable projects is large and the relative initial outlays are small, then ranking them by their profitability indexes and adding, from the top down, their initial outlays to the total amount available for capital investments usually will accomplish this objective.

If the available projects are relatively large and require greatly differing initial outlays, this method might not result in the proper selection. Adding the outlays in order of the profitability indexes of the projects may leave a significant amount of available capital unused. Referring to Table 12–5, we see that if capital were rationed at $4 million, this method would accept projects A through D, requiring a total of $3.7 million, and leave $300,000 not invested in capital projects.

The question then is, "What would be done with that $300,000?" Presumably it would be invested in the next most attractive opportunity, which probably would be marketable securities. The net present value of such an investment would be zero because the yield obtainable on marketable securities would reflect the required rate of return on such an investment, the pure interest rate plus a minimal premium for risk.

We seek to maximize the net present value of investment of the $4 million available capital. Noting that the net present value of project D is $88,000, whereas that of project E is $99,000, we would now substitute project E for D and add the initial outlays for projects A, B, C, and E. This accounts for the entire $4 million. The net present value of these projects would be $954,000, compared to $943,000 for projects A through D plus investment of the remaining funds in marketable securities, an advantage of $11,000. Therefore projects A, B, C, and E should be selected. The important thing is to select the combination of investments—capital investment projects and any noncapital investments required—that will maximize the net present value of investment of the available rationed capital.[4]

Other capital investment analytical methods

There are two methods of capital investment analysis in common use that do not apply a discounted cash flow approach. These are the *payback period* and the *accounting rate of return* methods. They are both less sophisticated than the methods discussed above and are subject to theoretical shortcomings. Nonetheless, under certain conditions they may be useful, particularly when used in conjunction with the NPV or IRR approaches.

Payback period

The payback period is the *number of years required to recover the initial investment.* Under the payback method, management decides the *maximum* payback period that will be acceptable for capital investment projects. To illustrate, assume that projects A and B each require an initial investment of $1,400. The estimated cash inflows from each of these projects are shown in Table 12–6. Management has established a minimum payback period of three years as the criterion for acceptance. Project A is expected to result in estimated cash flows of $800 the first year and $600 the second, totaling $1,400, the initial investment, in two years. Therefore, under this method it would be approved. Project B is expected to result in cash flows of $200 the first year, $400 the second, and $600 the third, totaling $1,200 in three years. As project B is expected to produce a cash flow of $800 in year four,

[4]Integer programming, a rather complex mathematical technique for optimizing an objective subject to constraints, can be used to determine the optimal group of acceptable projects under capital rationing. Such a sophisticated technique, however, is beyond the scope of this text.

its payback period is three years plus $200/$800, or 3.25 years (three years and three months). Inasmuch as this payback period is greater than the established maximum of three years, project B would be rejected if the criterion were strictly applied.

Table 12–6 Estimated cash benefits
Payback method

	Estimated cash inflows	
Year	Project A	Project B
1	$800	$ 200
2	600	400
3*	100	600
4	50	800
5	0	1,000

*Maximum payback period.

The obvious advantage of the payback method is its simplicity. But that is also its weakness. It considers the time value of money only in a very crude way. Within the payback period, it does not account for differences in cash-flow patterns. Early cash flows clearly have a greater present value than later ones. For example, if two projects, C and D, each had an initial investment of $1,000 and project C had expected cash flows of $500 the first year, $300 the second, and $200 the third (payback period three years), whereas project D had cash flows in the reverse order, $200 the first year, $300 in the second, and $500 in the third (payback period three years), C would clearly be superior to D. But the payback method would not reveal this difference and would consider the two projects to be equally acceptable.

The second shortcoming is that the payback method ignores expected cash flows beyond the payback period. Thus the expected large cash flows of $800 in the fourth year and $1,000 in the fifth of project B in Table 12–6 are ignored, and that project would have been rejected even though its net present value at any reasonable discount rate would have been greater than that of the accepted project A. A third shortcoming of the payback method is that the acceptance criterion must be rather arbitrary: there is no explicit link to the value-maximization objective of the firm.

Despite its shortcomings, the payback method has some appropriate applications. First, it can be used as a rough screening device for capital investment proposals with a view to applying more sophisticated discounted cash flow analysis to those projects which appear to be in the ball park. Second, it may be used in conjunction with other methods by firms that foresee serious liquidity problems requiring relatively high cash inflows in the near future, thus a short payback period may be required. Third, some projects entail such a high degree of uncertainty that estimated cash inflows beyond a few years can be little more than guesses. The use of a relatively short payback period, say three or four years, may be preferable to just guessing cash flow expectations over a longer period and utilizing a more sophisticated method of analysis, falsely implying validity of the results.

Accounting rate of return

The *accounting rate of return* (sometimes called average rate of return) is determined by dividing the average accounting profit after taxes expected from the project by the investment in the project:

$$\text{Accounting rate of return} = \frac{\text{Average profit after taxes}}{\text{Investment}} \qquad (12\text{–}4)$$

The profit after taxes is estimated under the accrual accounting process, which includes the deduction of annual depreciation and other noncash charges. The investment depends upon which version of this method is being used. Under one version, this is the *initial* investment in the project; in this case, the method is sometimes called accounting return on investment. If, for example, the initial investment in a project were $10,000 and the average accounting profits after taxes were expected to be $2,000 over the five-year estimated life of the project, the accounting rate of return on initial investment would be 20 percent, calculated as follows:

$$\text{Accounting rate of return on initial investment} = \frac{\$\ 2{,}000}{\$10{,}000} = 20\%$$

Under the other version of this method, the investment is considered to be the *average book value* of the asset, that is, the original investment less accumulated depreciation. Using the same data as in the above example, if the asset were estimated to have no terminal value and straight-line depreciation were used, the book value of the asset would decline $2,000 each year, reflecting depreciation. The average investment would be $5,000, and the accounting rate of return on investment calculation would be:

$$\text{Accounting rate of return on average investment} = \frac{\$2{,}000}{\$5{,}000} = 40\%$$

If the accounting rate of return method is used to compare capital investment proposals, comparability must be maintained by consistently using either one or the other of these two versions.

The decision criterion under this method is to accept only those projects with accounting rates of return greater than a given percentage established by management. This rate of return usually would, in turn, be related to the firm's present or past average accounting rate of return on assets (gross assets, if initial investment is used in the calculation, or net assets, if average book value is used).

The purported advantages of the accounting rate of return method are (1) simplicity, (2) familiarity of management personnel with the concept of accounting profits, and (3) the ease of monitoring subsequent performance of projects because the appropriate data are readily available from accounting records.

In most cases, the shortcomings outweigh the advantages. The major shortcomings of this method are (1) the time value of money is totally ignored, (2) differing time patterns of both expected accounting profits and cash flows are ignored, and (3) establishment of the acceptance criterion is not as soundly based as that of the discounted cash flow methods. Nonetheless, this method is rather widely used, particularly in conjunction with more sophisticated discounted cash flow analysis. From a practical viewpoint, its use can be justified if project lives are relatively short and maintenance or improvement of reported accounting profits is deemed to be of great importance to maintain or improve the market value of the firm's securities.

Summary

Capital investments are those outlays that are expected to yield benefits to the firm over a long period of time. The long time-span between such cash outlays and expected cash benefits requires that sound analysis of capital investment proposals recognize the time value of money. Therefore, the cost-benefit analysis should incorporate discounted cash flow (DCF) techniques. The two basic DCF analytical methods are net present value (NPV) and internal rate of return (IRR).

The NPV method determines the net present value of the project by subtracting the initial outlay, or present value of cash outlays, from the present value of the expected cash flow benefits. The discount rate used to determine the present values is the required rate of return (RRR). The decision criterion is that to be acceptable the NPV must be positive. A corollary of the NPV method is the profitability index (or benefit/cost ratio). It is determined by dividing the present value of the net cash benefits by the initial outlay, or present value of cash outlays. The profitability index indicates the relative advantage of the project.

The IRR method determines the discount rate that equates the present values of the capital outlay(s) and the future cash flow benefits expected from the project. This discount rate (IRR) is compared to the required rate of return (RRR). The decision criterion is that to be acceptable the IRR must be greater than the RRR.

The IRR, NPV, and profitability index methods will give the same accept-reject signals if all capital investment proposals that would enhance the value of the firm can be accepted. They will not, however, provide the same ranking. If projects must be ranked because they are mutually exclusive or capital is being rationed, the NPV method is superior. This is true because the NPV method implicity assumes reinvestment of cash benefits at the RRR, while the IRR method assumes reinvestment at the project rate of return.

There are two other methods of capital investment analysis in common use, payback period and accounting rate of return. Neither fully considers the time value of money and each suffers from other shortcomings. Nonetheless each may have appropriate uses in conjunction with the more sophisticated discounted cash flow methods.

Questions

1. What are the basic characteristics that identify a capital investment? Under what circumstances might an advertising campaign, a research and development project, or an additional working capital requirement be considered to be a capital investment?

2. Why are capital investment decisions probably the most important decisions made by management?

3. "Discounted cash flow (DCF) methods of analyzing capital investment proposals are essentially special types of cost-benefit analyses." Explain how the net present value (NPV) method and the internal rate of return (IRR) method apply the cost-benefit concept.

4. If all estimates used are correct, how do the acceptance criteria of the net present value (NPV) and internal rate of return (IRR) methods tend to accomplish the goal of maximizing value of the firm?

5. Why must a theoretically valid method of capital investment analysis fully recognize the time value of money? How do the NPV and IRR methods take into account the time value of money?

6. List four considerations other than the decision criteria of formal discounted cash flow (DCF) methods of analysis that might influence capital investment decisions.

7. Why are DCF methods of analysis usually not applicable to decisions regarding the management of current assets?

8. What is a profitability index (benefit/cost ratio)? How is it calculated? How does it relate to the NPV method? What will be the profitability index of a project when its NPV is zero?

9. How do the reinvestment assumptions implicit in the NPV and the IRR methods differ? Can these assumptions influence the *ranking* of theoretically acceptable projects under the two methods?

10. What is capital rationing? When capital is rationed, which method, NPV or IRR, is superior in establishing the ranking of projects? Why? Under what conditions can profitability indexes be useful in selecting acceptable projects under capital rationing?

11. The accounting rate of return method of capital investment analysis is theoretically inferior to DCF methods but is widely used. Why is it theoretically inferior? Why is it widely used?

12. What is the payback period? What are the shortcomings of the payback method of capital investment analysis? Under what conditions might its use be justified in conjunction with DCF methods? What is the built-in bias of the payback method?

Problems

1. Which of the following cash outlays normally would be considered to be a capital investment? Why?.

a. Building a new warehouse for $1 million.
b. Spending $200,000 on a research project to develop a new product.
c. Purchase of a new desk-top computer for $10,000.
d. Purchase of $1,000 worth of office supplies.
e. Spending $300,000 on an advertising campaign designed to promote sales of our present product line.
f. Spending $200,000 on an advertising campaign to introduce a new product.
g. Purchasing for $250,000 the patent rights to a process for manufacturing a new product.
h. A semiannual royalty payment of $180,000 for the use of a patent.
i. Purchase of $100,000 worth of inventories.

2. Bear Mountain Ski Resort is considering investing in a new restaurant-lounge at the top of its gondola lift. The initial investment of $350,000 is

expected to generate aftertax cash flows of $75,000 each year for a 10-year period, at the end of which the property would be valueless. For each of the required rates of return listed below, (1) calculate the net present value (NPV) of the project, (2) calculate the profitability index (PI), and (3) indicate your decision whether or not to accept the project.

a. 14 percent.
b. 18 percent.
c. 20 percent.

3. Abbey Manufacturing Company can acquire a new machine at an initial cost of $58,000 to replace a manual process. The annual net cash flow saving would be $14,000 for eight years, at the end of which there would be no salvage value. The required rate of return (RRR) is 16 percent.

a. What is the net present value (NPV)?
b. What is the profitability index (PI)?
c. What is the internal rate of return (IRR)?
d. Should Abbey accept or reject this proposal? Why?

4. Calculate the net present value (NPV) and internal rate of return (IRR) for each of the following projects. Each project has a 10-year life and no salvage value. Assume a required rate of return (RRR) of 15 percent.

a. Initial outlay of $25,000; annual net cash inflows of $3,500.
b. Initial outlay of $40,000; annual net cash inflows of $7,000.
c. Initial outlay of $11,000; annual net cash inflows of $2,500.

5. Wildwood Corporation is considering a proposal to tool up for production of a new product. The initial outlay will be $850,000. Expected cash inflows are $240,000 each year 1 through 6. A net salvage value of $100,000 is expected at the end of year 6. The required rate of return (RRR) is 18 percent.

a. Compute the NPV.
b. Compute the profitability index (PI).
c. Compute the IRR.
d. Decide whether or not to proceed with the project.

6. Nottingham Manufacturing Company is considering two alternative capital investments: (1) renovating an old machine at an initial cash outlay of $15,000 or (2) replacing the machine with a new, more efficient machine at an initial cash outlay of $60,000. The renovation will result in annual cash savings of $5,000 in each of the next five years. The new machine will save $19,000 annually for the same five-year period. The required rate of return is 15 percent.

a. What is the net present value (NPV) of each project?
b. What is the profitability index (PI) of each?
c. Which alternative should Nottingham choose? Explain why.

7. Bellevue Corporation is considering a capital investment of $700,000 in a project that is expected to yield the following cash inflows:

Years	Cash inflows
1	$150,000
2	180,000
3–7	140,000
8	200,000

The required rate of return (RRR) is 14 percent.

a. Calculate the net present value (NPV) of the project.

b. Calculate the internal rate of return (IRR) of the project.

c. Should Bellevue accept or reject the project? Explain why or why not.

8. The Tanglewood Corporation uses a payback period of four years as its capital investment decision criterion. It is considering a project requiring an initial outlay of $10,000 with expected cash inflows of $3,000 the first year and $2,000 annually in years 2 through 10. What would be its decision regarding this proposed project? What does this tell you about the payback method of capital investment analysis?

9. Flagstaff Corporation uses the accounting rate of return method of capital investment analysis. It is considering two proposals. Each requires an initial investment of $20,000 and is depreciated (for accounting purposes) on a straight-line basis over its five-year life with no salvage value. The accounting profits after taxes expected to be generated by each project are as follows:

Year	Project A	Project B
1	$5,000	$2,000
2	4,000	3,000
3	3,000	4,000
4	2,000	5,000
5	2,000	5,000

a. What is the accounting rate of return on each project if initial investment is used?

b. What is the accounting rate of return on each project if the average investment (book value) is used?

c. If Flagstaff required an accounting rate of return on initial investment of 18 percent, which project would be accepted?

d. What shortcoming of this method of capital investment analysis is illustrated?

10. The Latin American subsidiary of Amalgamated Mining Company uses a three-year payback period as its criterion for choosing among capital investment proposals. The major reason is the political risk, particularly that of nationalization of its properties. It is currently considering two proposals,

one to invest $600,000 to improve a tin mine in Bolivia, and the other a $1 million investment to modernize port facilities in Peru. Estimated net cash savings from the two projects are as follows:

Year	Cash savings: Mine improvements	Cash savings: Port facilities
1	$300,000	$300,000
2	200,000	300,000
3	150,000	300,000
4	100,000	200,000
5	50,000	200,000
6	?	200,000

a. What are the payback periods of these investments?
b. Which project(s) would be accepted under the payback criterion?
c. Is this criterion generally appropriate under the circumstances?
d. What other considerations might be pertinent to the decisions?

Chapter 13
Estimating Relevant Cash Flows

The previous chapter established the superiority of discounted cash flow (DCF) methods of analyzing capital investment opportunities. The relevant net cash outlays and benefits were simply assumed in order to illustrate the methodology. Once the DCF methodology has been mastered, the more difficult tasks of estimating the relevant cash flows must be undertaken. In practice, most poor capital investment decisions result from errors in estimates of cash outlays and/or benefits, particularly the latter.

The information required to analyze proposed capital investments is both quantitative and nonquantitative. It should indicate the amounts and timing of the expected cash flows that would result from the acceptance of each proposal and reveal as much as possible about the degree of risk (uncertainty) inherent in the project. Risk relates to the probability that expected cash flows will materialize as estimated. In this chapter we shall be concerned only with estimating the relevant cash flows. We have assumed that the perceived risk of each proposed project is equal to the average risk of the firm. Risk differentials among projects will be treated in Chapter 14.

Note that we are utilizing *cash flows* rather than accounting income and expense data. The reason for this is that the *financial* results of accepting a project are expressed in terms of cash. The investment requires the outlay of cash. The tangible benefits of making the investment are the receipt of cash or the avoidance of cash outlays that otherwise would have to be made. Accounting income and expense data are less direct in that they are influenced by noncash items such as depreciation expense. Although these items are legitimate accounting charges against income, the firm neither receives anything nor gives up anything when they are recorded.

We are interested in *aftertax* cash flows. Tax payments and tax shields, the avoidance of paying taxes that otherwise would have to be paid, affect cash flows just as any other payment or saving. Different projects have different tax implications, therefore comparability among projects cannot be maintained unless taxes are fully considered in the analysis.

The initial review of a capital investment proposal requires careful scrutiny. Are all cash flows that would result from acceptance of the proposal included? Are the estimates reasonable? Do the estimates make adequate provision for such things as work stoppages, downtime for maintenance and repair, and the fact that production will not always be at 100 percent of capacity? One must always remember that the project proposal was originated by someone who has a stake in its acceptance. Often the reviewer has the unpleasant task of whittling overly optimistic estimates down to size.

The test of a *relevant* cash flow is the answer to the question, "Would this cash flow (or cash saving) occur if the decision were 'go' but not occur if it were 'no go'?" We are concerned only with differential (incremental) cash flows identified by *the "go" versus "no-go" criterion* because this is basically a *marginal* cost-benefit analysis.

Cash-flow patterns

A cash-flow pattern shows the *net* cash flow expected through time from a project. Figure 13–1 illustrates the simplest type of cash-flow pattern. The proposed investment is the purchase and installation of a machine for $5,000. Use of the machine is expected to reduce cash expenditures by $1,000 each year for each of the next 10 years. At the end of 10 years the machine is expected to be worn out and have no scrap value. You will recognize this pattern as an *annuity,* which was discussed in Chapter 11. Such a pattern is easy to analyze but unfortunately is not often found in practice.

Figure 13–1 Annuity cash-flow pattern

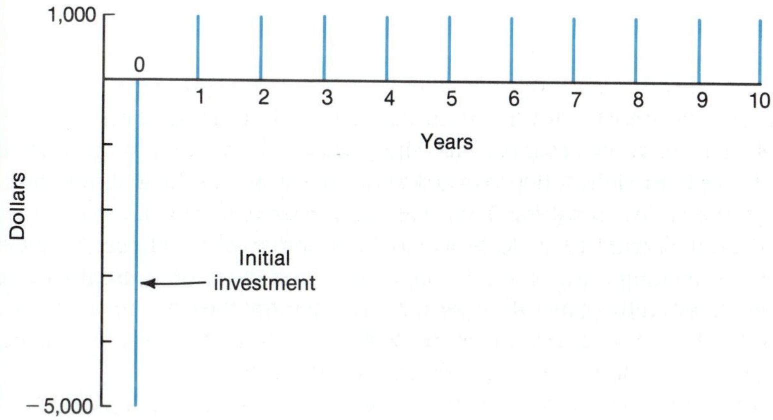

A more complex cash-flow pattern, called a *mixed* pattern, is illustrated in Figure 13–2. This capital investment proposal is to build a new plant to produce a new product. It will require an outlay of $5 million at year zero. Start-up costs, advertising, and promotion during the first year are expected to require large cash outlays that are not completely offset by cash inflows from operations. Therefore, a net cash outflow of $500,000 is expected that year. During the second and third years, net cash inflows of $1 million and $1.6 million, respectively, are expected from operations. Then plant capacity will be reached, and in year four a $3.6 million plant addition (phase 2) will be required. This cash outflow will be partially offset by a $1.6 million

Figure 13–2 Mixed cash-flow pattern

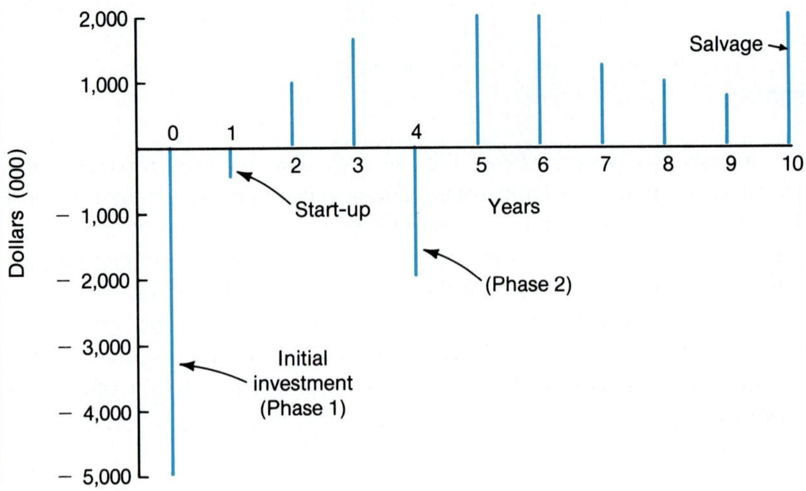

cash inflow from operations, resulting in a $2 million net cash outflow that year. During the fifth and sixth years, $2 million net cash inflows are expected. By the seventh year, competitors are expected to be producing products superior to ours, resulting in a decline in net cash inflows until the tenth year. We estimate that the plant could be sold at the end of the tenth year to yield a net cash inflow of about $1.7 million in addition to a $300,000 inflow resulting from operations that year. This illustration is fictitious but is used to provide a notion of some of the elements that enter into estimating cash flows through time and how they usually result in mixed cash-flow patterns rather than simple annuities.

Estimating the net cash investment

The net cash investment usually is the net cash outflow that will occur initially (year zero) as the result of a "go" decision on the capital investment proposal. This cash flow may consist of three elements: (1) the cash cost of the capital asset, (2) proceeds from the sale of the asset(s) that may be eliminated with a "go" decision, and (3) tax effects.

These cash flow elements can best be illustrated by the example summarized in Table 13–1. The plant manager of Jefferson Manufacturing Company has proposed the purchase of a new milling machine to replace an old one. The manufacturer's price is $32,000. Delivery would cost $400 and installation $600. The old machine that would be replaced has an unrecovered cost

Table 13–1 Jefferson Manufacturing Company capital investment proposal
Estimate of net cash investment

Cost of new machine:		
Purchase price	$32,000	
Delivery cost	400	
Installation cost	600	$33,000
Less proceeds from sale of present machine		−14,000
		$19,000
Tax effects:		
Investment tax credit	−$3,300	
Tax on sale of present machine	+ 1,600	− 1,700
Net investment (cash outflow)		$17,300

(depreciated value) of $10,000, and a used machinery dealer has offered $14,000 for it.

Cash cost

Cash outlays directly related to the cost of the new machine are $32,000, which would be paid to the manufacturer, plus the cash outlays required to put the machine in place and ready for use. These additional outlays are $400 for delivery and $600 for installation, making a total of $33,000. This illustration is relatively straightforward. Now let us complicate it a bit by proposing an addition to the cost of the machine of $500 spent last month by the plant manager to attend a machinery trade show to select this machine and discuss custom specifications with the manufacturer. The answer is no. This is a "sunk cost". It already has been incurred at the time the capital investment decision is to be made; therefore, it could not *result* from a "go" versus a "no-go" decision. Change the illustration to indicate that, *if* the proposal were approved, then the plant manager will have to go to the manufacturer's plant next month to discuss custom specifications with the manufacturer's engineers. The additional $500 outlay for this trip *would* be included in the cash cost. It would not be incurred if the decision were "no go" but would be incurred if it were "go." This little bit of nitpicking illustrates the basic criterion in determining relevant cash flows.

Proceeds from sales of assets

If Jefferson invests in the new machine, the firm will sell the old machine for $14,000 cash. This cash receipt is a proper deduction from the cash outlay as it results directly from a "go" decision. Note that the $10,000 unrecovered cost (depreciated value) is *not* pertinent to our analysis *at this point.* It reflects a sunk cost related only to the decision to purchase that old machine years ago and to depreciate it to arrive at this value. The unrecovered cost of the old machine, however, will later be pertinent because it will influence the tax effects of the capital investment decision.

Applying the same logic in reverse, some capital investment analyses require charging to the proposed investment cash receipts that would be foregone if the decision were "go." For example, if a proposed project would occupy a building owned by the firm that would be sold if the project were not accepted, then the cash proceeds that would be foregone should be considered part of the cash investment. The tax effects of such a potential transaction should also be considered in estimating the net cash investment in the project. This again illustrates the way in which the "go" versus "no go" criterion provides the test of a relevant cash flow.

Tax effects

Almost any capital investment decision will affect the firm's income tax liability. Such tax implications may take three forms: (1) the investment tax credit, (2) the effects on reported ordinary income subject to tax at the firm's incremental income tax rate, and (3) capital gains or losses subject to special tax treatment.

The investment tax credit, discussed in Chapter 2, provides a direct dollar-for-dollar credit against the federal income tax liability for the year in which the asset is placed in service. In our illustration, if the investment tax credit were 10 percent, Jefferson would have a tax credit of $3,300 (.10 times $33,000) on its income taxes for this year if the proposal were accepted. This assumes that the machine is classed as five-year or greater property under the accelerated cost recovery system (ACRS). If it were three-year property under ACRS, the applicable investment tax credit would be 6 percent. This tax credit is a direct deduction from required cash outlays in estimating the net cash investment.

Jefferson will have to pay income tax on the difference between the $14,000 cash it receives from sale of the old machine and its unrecovered cost (depreciated value) of $10,000 because the IRS will consider this gain of $4,000 to be a recapture of depreciation. The reasoning is that if the asset is now worth $14,000 while its depreciated value is only $10,000, Jefferson must have charged $4,000 too much depreciation during the years that it has owned the machine. Assuming that Jefferson's incremental tax rate is 40 percent, this transaction will increase its income taxes for this year by $1,600 (.40 × $4,000). The additional tax expenditure should be included in estimating the net cash investment.

In some cases, sale of an asset to be replaced will result in a tax shield rather than additional tax liability. For example, if Jefferson could sell the old machine for only $8,000, this would result in a loss for tax purposes of

$2,000 and reduce its tax liability for the year by 40 percent of $2,000, or $800. The reduction in tax liability would reduce the net cash investment.

In some other cases, sale of an asset resulting from a "go" decision may result in a capital gain or loss. If the asset sold is a capital asset as defined by the IRS and has been held for over one year, then such a long-term capital gain would be taxable to a corporation at 20 percent. A long-term capital gain would be incurred only for the amount received from sale of the asset that was greater than its original cost. The difference between the depreciated value and original cost would be considered a recapture of depreciation and taxed at regular incremental income tax rates.

To illustrate this, assume that the original cost of the old machine was $15,000, that the depreciated value is $10,000, and that the machine could be sold for $19,000. Then $5,000 of the gain ($15,000 − $10,000) would be taxed at the assumed 40 percent incremental tax rate on ordinary income, resulting in additional tax liability of $2,000 (.40 × $5,000). Only the long-term capital gain of $4,000 ($19,000 − $15,000) would be taxable at the 20 percent rate, resulting in additional tax liability of $800. Total additional taxes of $2,800 ($2,000 on ordinary income plus $800 on the long-term capital gain) would be included in the net cash investment related to the proposed project.[1]

Summary: Net cash investment

In its simplest form, ignoring the various complications we have introduced, the estimated net cash investment of Jefferson Manufacturing Company in the proposed acquisition of a new milling machine to replace an old one is $17,300, as shown in Table 13–1. This consists of $33,000, the cost of the new machine delivered and installed, less $14,000, the proceeds from the sale of the old machine and net tax savings of $1,700.

Although the immediate cash cost of the asset, the proceeds from sale of the old asset, and the tax effects are all of the elements included in the net cash investment in this example, there are two other elements that may be

[1]Technically, the tax effects of acceptance of a capital investment project do not occur exactly at time zero, the date the investment is made. Additional taxes will be paid (or the benefits of the investment tax credit and tax shields will reduce the amount of taxes paid) on the date the firm files its income tax return for the year in which the transactions took place. This date might, of course, be several months later. Usually this fact will not make a material difference in the outcome of the capital investment analysis and should therefore be ignored. The purist may wish to discount such cash flows for the intervening months to their present value at time zero. The appropriate discount rate would be the yield on short-term government securities maturing at the income tax return filing date because the degree of risk of a payment to or a claim against the federal government would be essentially the same as the risk of the federal government paying its debt obligations.

included in some more complex capital investment proposals. These are additional net working capital that may be required if the capital investment proposal is accepted and additional investments required at a later date.

Additional net working capital

If the capital investment project were, for example, the introduction of a new product, an additional investment in net working capital probably would have to be considered in estimating the net cash investment. Additional inventories of the new product would be carried as well as the accounts receivable resulting from the additional sales and, perhaps, larger cash balances to cover the lack of coincidence between cash inflows and outflows related to production and sale of the new product. This investment in additional current assets would be partially offset by spontaneous current liabilities, such as accounts payable, accrued wages, and accrued income tax liabilities. The net increase in working capital should be included as a component of the estimated net cash investment. Investment in additional net working capital would be recovered when the projects's life is terminated.

Subsequent capital outlays

Up to now, we have dealt only with capital outlays that would be made at time zero or sufficiently close to it that usually no consideration of the time value of money would be required. This is not always the case. For example, the additional net working capital requirements discussed above may be made over a period of years as the volume of operations related to the project increases. Another example of subsequent cash outlays is the expected expansion of a plant several years after its construction (illustrated by phase 2 in our example of a mixed cash flow pattern in Figure 13–2). Still another is the present purchase of a machine that is expected to require a major overhaul after, say, five years to maintain its productivity for another five years. In such cases, analysis requires recognition that the present value of an investment to be made sometime in the future is less than that of one to be made at time zero.

Expected subsequent cash investments may be handled in one of two ways. The simplest is to subtract subsequent cash investments from the expected cash inflows in the year (or years) that the additional investments are to be made. The net figure is the estimated future cash flow for that year (or years). (Estimating the future cash inflows will be considered in the next section of this chapter.) The other way subsequent investments may be handled is to discount them from the year that they are expected to be incurred back to time zero at an appropriate rate. This discounting will yield the present value at time zero of the future cash outlay(s), which should then be added to the initial investment elements to estimate the net present value of the total investment.

Estimating future cash benefits

The next step in assembling relevant cash flow information is to estimate the *incremental aftertax cash benefits* expected to result from investment in the proposed project. The words italicized above indicate the three key points that identify the relevant cash flows. Each constitutes a test. Does each figure represent a *cash* benefit? Have the *taxes* that will have to be paid been deducted? Is the cash flow *incremental*, that is, does it reflect the difference between the cash flow if the decision were "go" and that which would occur if the decision were "no go"?

To illustrate this portion of the capital investment analysis, let us assemble additional information regarding the Jefferson Manufacturing Company's proposal to replace the present machine with a new one. Estimated annual operating expenses of the present machine and the proposed new one for each of the next ten years are shown in Table 13–2. Reductions of $3,000 in labor costs, $600 in materials costs, and $400 in energy costs are contemplated in each of the next 10 years. The estimated total annual cash saving from reduced operating expenses is $4,000.

Table 13–2 Jefferson Manufacturing Company capital investment proposal
Comparison of annual operating expenses

	Present machine	New machine	Difference
Operating expenses, years 1–10			
Labor costs	$31,000	$28,000	−$3,000
Materials costs	60,000	59,400	− 600
Energy costs	4,000	3,600	− 400
Total	$95,000	$91,000	−$4,000

The new machine, to be placed in service in 1983, can be depreciated for tax purposes under the accelerated cost recovery system (ACRS). It qualifies as a five-year asset under ACRS; therefore, its capitalized cost of $33,000 less one half of the investment tax credit, $1,650, or $31,350 can be depreciated according to the schedule shown in the top portion of Table 13–3. Note that although the useful life of the new machine is 10 years, the ACRS provides for cost recovery (depreciation) for tax purposes over a much shorter period, 5 years. This cost recovery in the early years is the principal feature of the ACRS incorporated in the Economic Recovery Act of 1981.

Table 13–3 Jefferson Manufacturing Company capital investment proposal
Depreciation schedule

	Depreciation allowed	
	Percent*	Amount
New machine		
Year 1	15%	$4,703
Year 2	22	6,897
Years 3–5	21	6,583
Years 6–10	0	0
Present machine		
Years 1–5	—	2,000
Years 6–10	—	0

*From Table 2–1, Chapter 2.

Depreciation for tax purposes on the present machine, which was placed in service in 1978, was calculated on a declining balance basis during the early years of its life and changed to straight-line depreciation of $2,000 for each of the later years, as provided by the tax regulations applying to assets acquired prior to 1981. This machine will be fully depreciated at the end of five years hence (1988).

Now we shall identify the relevant cash flows through the 10-year expected life of the project.

Cash flows over the life of the project

As shown in Table 13–4, direct reductions in operating cash outflows during each of the next ten years are expected to be $4,000. These cash benefits are incremental, that is, they reflect the differences estimated to result from a "go" decision as compared to a "no go" decision.

If these operating costs are reduced by $4,000, then Jefferson will be subject to additional income tax each year of $1,600 (.40 assumed tax rate times $4,000). However, another important change in Jefferson's tax bill each year will result from the change in allowable depreciation. During the first five years, the tax shields provided by depreciation of the new machine under the ACRS (40 percent of the ACR amounts calculated in Table 13–3) are much larger than those provided by allowable depreciation of the present machine (see Table 13–4). These tax shields reduce Jefferson's income tax liabilities, thereby reducing cash outflows.

Net cash inflows each year that would result from acceptance of the pro-

Table 13–4 Jefferson Manufacturing Company capital investment proposal
Estimated net cash benefits

	Years			
	1	2	3–5	6–10
Cash savings from operations	$4,000	$4,000	$4,000	$4,000
Tax effects				
Taxes on operating savings .40 × $4,000	–$1,600	–$1,600	–$1,600	–$1,600
Tax shields from depreciation				
New machine:				
.40 × ACR amount*	$1,881	$2,759	$2,633	0
Less present machine:				
(Years 1–5) .40 × $2,000	– 800	– 800	– 800	0
Years net tax shield	$1,081	$1,959	$1,833	0
Net tax effects	–$ 519	$ 359	$ 233	–1,600
Net cash inflow	$3,481	$4,359	$4,233	$2,400

*Accelerated cost recovery from Table 13–3.

ject are summarized at the bottom of Table 13–4. The only remaining relevant cash flows to be considered are are those related to the terminal value of the machine at the end of its 10-year useful life.

Terminal cash benefits

Jefferson's management estimates that the milling machine could be sold at the end of 10 years for $3,000. As the unrecovered cost of the machine at that time would be zero (it was fully depreciated under ACRS), Jefferson would be subject to tax on the $3,000 net proceeds at its incremental rate on ordinary income. The IRS would consider the gain to be a recapture of depreciation. Therefore, if the firm's incremental tax rate is 40 percent, tax of $1,200 would be paid. The net aftertax cash inflow upon termination would be $1,800.

In other cases, there may be additional considerations in estimating net cash flow at the termination of a project. If the cost of the asset has not been fully recovered through depreciation, the unrecovered cost is subtracted from the net proceeds of liquidation to determine the gain subject to taxation. For example, if Jefferson's unrecovered cost at termination were $2,000, then only $1,000 would be taxed at 40 percent, resulting in a tax of $400. In the unlikely event that terminal value is expected to exceed original cost of the asset, that portion of the proceeds of liquidation representing the difference between net proceeds and unrecovered cost would be taxed as a recapture of depreciation at the ordinary rate. The portion in excess of original cost would be taxed as a long-term capital gain at a 20 percent rate. If the net proceeds of liquidation were expected to be less than unrecovered cost, the loss would create a tax shield at the ordinary rate.

In analyzing any capital investment proposal that included additional net working capital as part of the investment, the recapture of this net working capital should be considered a cash inflow at the termination of life of the project or whenever the net working capital will no longer be required.

Summary: Cash flow estimates

Now we have completed assembly of the cash flow estimates relevant to Jefferson Manufacturing Company's proposed capital investment in a new machine. These data are summarized in Table 13–5. The net cash investment (outflow at time zero) is estimated to be $17,300. Net cash benefits through the life of the project are $3,481 in year 1, $4,359 in year 2, $4,233 each of years 3 through 5, and $2,400 each in years 6 through 10. At the end of year 10, an additional net aftertax cash inflow of $1,800 is expected from termination of the project.

You may recognize that the illustration has been somewhat simplified for clarity of discussion and analysis. This example deals with the proposed replacement of one machine by another. Consider the increased complexity of a proposal to build a $10 million dollar plant to produce a new product. First, nearly all cash flows would be very difficult to estimate because of the great uncertainty of both cash outflows to get the plant into production and cash benefits from sales of the new product. Second, the plant would include many different machines and processes involving selection among several alternatives of the ones economically feasible. Third, choices would have to be made ranging from production of all component parts and assembling the product to purchasing each of various components from outside suppliers and confining the firm's investment to facilities required to assemble them. Fourth, the sheer magnitude of the project increases the importance of the decision, thereby placing a greater burden on the analyst regarding accuracy of the detailed estimates and the application of relevancy criteria.

Perhaps fortunately for the finance field, the development of such data and their analysis is done largely by engineers specializing in plant design and engineering economy. At any rate, we have established the fundamentals of estimating net capital investment and future cash benefits.

Mutually exclusive projects—Time horizon

In Chapter 12 we established the superiority of the net present value (NPV) method in ranking mutually exclusive projects. Applying this method, we should accept the project with the highest NPV. But we may encounter

Table 13–5 Jefferson Manufacturing Company capital investment proposal
Summary: Cash flow estimates

	Year					
	0	1	2	3–5	6–10	10
Initial net cash investment (Table 13–1)						
Cost of new machine	−$33,000	—	—	—	—	—
Proceeds from sale of present machine	$ 14,000	—	—	—	—	—
Tax effects	+ 1,700	—	—	—	—	—
Net cash benefits						
Cash savings from operations (Table 13–3)	—	+$4,000	+$4,000	+$4,000	+$4,000	—
Net tax effects (Table 13–4)	—	− 519	+ 359	+ 233	− 1,600	—
Net terminal cash inflow	—	—	—	—	—	+$1,800
Net cash flow	−$17,300	+$3,481	+$4,359	+$4,233	+$2,400	+$1,800

Note: + indicates cash inflow; − indicates cash outflow.

a complication in estimating the relevant cash flows for this analysis if the mutually exclusive projects have *unequal* useful lives.

If the projects are strictly one-shot investments, that is, if they are expected to relate to operations only through their useful lives and not be replaced, the discrepancy in useful lives does not influence the analysis. For example, if project A is expected to have a useful life of five years and project B, one of seven years, then conventional NPV analysis implicitly assumes that the cash inflows from project A would be zero for years six and seven. This is a reasonable assumption if project A would simply expire at the end of five years.

However, in most cases mutually exclusive projects are related to ongoing operations. Thus if project A, the purchase of a machine, were accepted, it would be replaced at the end of its five-year useful life by another machine to continue performing its function. To avoid an apples-and-oranges comparison, analysis of these two mutually exclusive projects must incorporate the same time horizon. This can be handled in either of two ways. The first and simplest method is to reduce the analysis of project B to a five-year time horizon by establishing a *hypothetical terminal value* at the end of five years. That hypothetical terminal value would usually be the value at the end of the fifth year of the estimated cash benefits from operations for years six and seven plus any estimated net terminal value at the end of year seven. This approach would then equitably compare the two projects on a five-year time horizon.

Another, somewhat more complicated, method of handling this problem would be to establish a seven-year time horizon and modify project A to include its replacement by another machine at the end of the fifth year. This analysis would include the present value of the negative cash flow from investment in the replacement machine at the end of the fifth year and the present values of the cash benefits expected to result from it in the sixth and seventh years. Then a terminal value of project A at the end of seven years would be established in the same fashion as used for project B above. This method, called "chaining," is theoretically sound, but it is rather complicated and involves making two highly uncertain estimates. One is the outlay required to replace the machine at the end of five years and the other is the terminal value of that machine at the end of seven years.

Inflation considerations

We must emphasize that all capital investment analysis is based upon forecasted data. The initial investment usually is a relatively short-term forecast of cash outlays. But the expected future net cash benefits through the estimated life of the project rest upon numerous forecasts of revenue and cost elements that may be highly uncertain. A major element in these forecasts is the expected inflation factored into each.

Through most of the period from about 1952 through 1972, when annual inflation rates varied from roughly zero to 5 percent and averaged about 2½ percent, net cash flows expected to result from capital investment projects could be estimated almost entirely on the basis of existing prices. Relatively low inflation rates were presumed to affect cash inflow and outflow items about equally and therefore would be offsetting in their effects upon net cash flows.

But since 1973 annual inflation rates have been so high, in some years ranging into double digits, with increases in prices of some particular cost (or revenue) elements such as energy and petrochemicals rising at much higher rates, that the influence of future inflation could not safely be ignored. This has greatly complicated capital investment analysis.

The principal implications are that inflation must be accepted as a fact of life, and estimates of expected future inflation must be included in the forecasts of each future cash inflow and outflow item. To disregard future inflation is, in effect, forecasting that the rate of inflation will be zero for the life of each project. Such an assumption would be considered naive by most people. Even the initial outlay for a large project, in which the investment would be made over a period of several months or perhaps a few years, must be adjusted for future inflation to be realistic. Assuming that inflation will not influence cash benefits resulting from operation of a project over a large number of future years would be totally unrealistic.

To cope effectively with this problem, the analyst must estimate not simply the general inflation rate expected in the future but specific inflation rates relative to particular cash inflow and outflow items, such as sales revenues and costs of materials, labor, and energy. For example, take a simple machinery replacement project in which the major future benefit elements are reduction in use of energy and labor. The prices of energy and labor wage rates over the useful life of the machinery must be estimated. Obviously, this is not an easy task. Then multiply this many times for all the various alternatives related to the design of a major production plant, and you will see that this problem becomes horrendous.

Another implication of inflation is that it significantly increases the degree of uncertainty of the cash-flow forecasts. In other words, the risk that the benefits expected will materialize from the projects is significantly increased. This, as we shall see in Chapters 14 and 15, materially increases the required rate of return. It also increases the difficulty of estimating required rate of return. Thus, the capital investment decision-making process, always a difficult one in practice because of the uncertainty involved, has become still more difficult as the reality of inflation has been recognized.

Summary

This chapter deals with estimating the relevant cash flows to be used in employing discounted cash flow (DCF) methods of analyzing capital investment opportunities. Relevance is determined by the test, "Would the cash flow (or cash saving) take place if the decision were 'go' but not occur if it were 'no go'?" This identifies the incremental (or differential) cash flow. Only *cash* flows, not to be confused with accounting income or costs, are relevant. As tax payments (or shields) affect cash flows, all data must be reduced to an aftertax basis.

The net cash investment may consist of four elements: (1) the cash cost of the capital asset, (2) proceeds from the sale of assets that may be eliminated upon a "go" decision, (3) tax effects, and (4) additional net working capital required. Cost of the capital asset includes delivery and installation. Tax effects include the investment tax credit as well as taxes or tax shields resulting from disposition of any assets eliminated. Sunk costs (any outlays that have been incurred before the decision) are not pertinent except as they may influence tax payments or savings.

Future net cash benefits consist of the net cash inflows expected through the life of the project and any terminal cash flows. Cash benefits through the life of the project are estimated by totaling the cash inflows and then subtracting the related taxes less the tax shield from incremental depreciation (cost recovery). Terminal cash benefits include estimated aftertax proceeds of liquidation of the capital asset at the end of its useful life and recapture of net working capital associated with the project.

A special problem is encountered in comparing mutually exclusive projects with unequal useful lives whenever such projects relate to ongoing operations. In such cases, the simplest solution is to establish a hypothetical terminal value of the longer-lived project at the terminal date of the shorter-lived one. Another, more complex, method of equalizing the time horizon is chaining. This requires assuming replacement of the shorter-lived project, operation of the replacement until the end of life of the longer-lived one, and establishing a hypothetical terminal value of the replacement at that time.

Estimating relevant cash flows has always been difficult because uncertainties are great. But the necessity in recent years of factoring in future inflation has further complicated the task. It now appears necessary to forecast and allow for specific estimated inflation rates for each major component of future cash flows, including sales revenues and the cost of materials, labor, energy, and other cost elements. Additional implications of persistent inflation are greater uncertainty of the cash-flow estimates and increased required rates of return.

Questions

1. Why do the sophisticated methods of capital investment analysis utilize cash flows rather than accounting income? Why are *aftertax* cash flows relevant rather than pretax flows?

2. What is the basic criterion identifying a *relevant* cash flow?

3. Why in practice is the pattern of relevant future cash flows usually mixed (uneven) rather than a simple annuity?

4. Explain how *(a)* the investment tax credit and *(b)* the accelerated cost recovery system (ACRS) tend to induce firms to modernize their plants. How does this modernization relate to productivity of the economy?

5. What is a *sunk cost*? Are sunk costs relevant in estimating net investment outlays? Explain.

6. Depreciation expense (cost recovery) is not a cash flow but rather a noncash accounting entry. Should depreciation expense be included in calculating future net cash flows in a capital investment analysis? How does it relate to the analysis?

7. Indicate which of the following items should be added to or subtracted from the purchase price of a new machine in estimating the net investment outlay.

   a. Installation cost of $1,000.
   b. Investment tax credit of $1,500 on the new machine.
   c. Severance pay of $1,400 to an employee who will be dismissed because his services will not be required if the old machine is replaced.
   d. Sale price of $3,000 of the old machine being replaced.
   e. The book value (unrecovered cost) of the old machine of $5,000.
   f. Cost of $400 to modify electrical and plumbing outlets to accommodate the new machine.
   g. An expenditure of $500 to test and adjust the new machine.
   h. Cost of training the operator of the new machine of $1,000.

8. Why and under what conditions should additional working capital be included in the estimated cash outlay in analyzing a capital investment project?

9. Why do inflation considerations greatly complicate the analysis of capital investment projects? How can expected future inflation be incorporated in such analysis?

10. What are the pertinent elements to be considered in estimating the cash flows to be obtained upon termination of a project? In practice, what are the difficulties encountered in making such estimates?

11. A special problem is encountered when comparing net present values of two or more mutually exclusive (competing) projects having differing estimated life spans. What is this problem? How can it be handled in capital investment analysis?

Problems

(Note: Problems 1 through 4 are a series.)

1. The Flagstaff Corporation in considering investing in a new machine to perform an assembly function presently done by hand. The machine will cost $82,000. Transportation costs of $450 will be incurred, and installation will cost $900. The assembly workers replaced will be transferred to other jobs within the firm. A new employee must be recruited and trained, at a cost of $1,500, to operate the machine. The machine is expected to have a useful life of 10 years but qualifies as a five-year property for depreciation purposes under ACRS. The investment tax credit for such property is 10 percent. What is the net cash investment if the proposal is adopted?

2. Flagstaff's management estimates that the new machine (Problem 1) will save $14,000 each of the next 10 years in labor costs. This saving will be partially offset by $2,500 additional annual energy costs. The machine will be depreciated under the ACRS at 15 percent the first year, 22 percent the second, and 21 percent each of the third through fifth years. The estimated incremental tax rate is 40 percent. What will be the net aftertax cash savings each of the next 10 years if the proposal is adopted?

3. At the end of 10 years, the machine (Problem 1) is expected to be sold for $8,000. What will be the net aftertax cash proceeds at termination of the project?

4. If the required rate of return (RRR) on the Flagstaff assembly machine project (Problem 1) is 15 percent, what is the net present value (NPV) of the project? Should Flagstaff approve the project?

5. Columbine Corporation is considering the purchase of a new delivery truck priced at $10,700, including transportation, dealer preparation, and sales taxes, to replace an old truck. The new truck qualifies as three-year property under ACRS. This entitles Columbine to a 6 percent investment tax credit. The old truck, which is fully depreciated for tax purposes, can be sold for $3,400. Columbine's incremental tax rate is 40 percent. What is the net cash investment outlay if this proposal is accepted?

6. Centennial Manufacturing Corporation is considering the replacement of several old machines. The old machines cost $500,000 eight years ago, now have a depreciated book value for tax purposes of $200,000, and could be sold for $140,000. The old machines have a remaining useful life of 10 years, would be depreciated on a straight-line basis at $20,000 per year, and are expected to have no salvage value.

The proposed new machines would cost $1 million delivered and installed. They are classified under ACRS as five-year assets, entitling Centennial to a 10 percent investment tax credit and cost recovery (depreciation) of 15 percent the first year, 22 percent the second, and 21 percent each of the third through fifth years. The new machines are estimated to have a salvage value of $100,000 at the termination of their useful life in 10 years. Centennial estimates that operating expenses would be reduced by $200,000 each of the next 10 years by replacing the machines. The firm's incremental tax rate is 40 percent.

a. What is the net cash investment in year 0?

b. What is the net incremental cash inflow in each of years 1 through 10?

7. Briarwood Corporation is considering the purchase of *one* of two additional woodworking lathes. The first can be purchased for $5,000, has a useful life of eight years, and will cost $10,000 per year to operate. Its before-tax salvage value is estimated at $500. The second, a highly automated model, costs $25,000, has a useful life of eight years, and will cost only $5,000 per year to operate. Its before-tax salvage value is estimated to be $4,000. Both machines are classed as five-year property under the ACRS. Briarwood's incremental tax rate is 40 percent.

Estimate the negative net present values (NPV) of each machine, employing a discount rate of 16 percent. Which machine should Briarwood purchase? Why? (Note: Briarwood's available data do not provide information on the cash inflows expected from operation of the two machines. They are unknown but equal.)

8. At present price levels, the annual cost savings that could be achieved by replacement of a machine are:

Costs	Old machine	New machine	Cost savings
Labor	$120,000	$106,000	$14,000
Materials	212,000	205,000	7,000
Energy	84,000	64,000	20,000
Total	$416,000	$375,000	$41,000

If labor costs increase at 8 percent, materials costs at 9 percent, and energy costs at 14 percent annual rates, what will be the cost savings for each of the next five years? Why is this aspect of capital investment analysis important?

Chapter 14
Risk Differentials and Strategic Considerations

In the previous two chapters we assumed that the perceived risk of each proposed capital investment project was equal to the average risk of the firm. This assumption implied that the probability that each estimated cash flow would materialize was equal to the probability that the estimated cash flow from the total operations of the firm would occur as forecasted.[1] This simplifying assumption was convenient. It made it possible to discount all proposed projects at the same required rate of return (RRR), the estimated overall cost of capital of the firm. Thus the acceptance criterion could be standardized.

Now we must face reality. Rarely, if ever, would all of the capital investment opportunities considered by a firm entail the same degree of risk. Some projects will appear to be relatively safe, others might be about as risky as the average risk of the firm, still others may be considerably more risky, and perhaps a few will entail so much risk that they will either make the firm rich or result in loss of the entire investment. Consider an integrated oil company analyzing several proposed capital investment projects: (1) replacing storage tanks at a refinery, (2) drilling additional wells in an established oil field, (3) developing a new oil field where exploratory drilling has indicated the presence of oil, (4) starting a wildcat drilling project in an area where geological surveys have indicated the probable presence of oil, and (5) undertaking a geological survey project in Greenland to determine whether or not there might be oil in this region. Obviously, these proposals have been arranged in order of their perceived risk, with the first project perceived to entail less risk than the average risk of the firm and the fifth project bearing many times as great a risk.

The capital investment decision-making process must recognize such differences in perceived risk. Investors generally are risk averse. They are willing to accept greater risk only when it is accompanied by the expectation of a higher rate of return. The relationship between risk and the required rate of return is shown in Figure 14–1. The minimum required rate of return is the return anticipated on a risk-free investment. Such an investment guarantees specific future cash flows with certainty. The return is the pure interest rate, which is compensation only for foregoing the use of money. As perceived risk increases, so does the required rate of return. The RRR of

[1]Note that the material in the two preceding chapters does not assume *certainty* of cash flows (as is stated in some of the similar literature of capital investment analysis). If certainty were assumed, then the discount rate used would have to be the pure interest rate, the rate of return on a riskless investment. Rather the assumption that project risk equalled the average risk of the firm implied that the degree of *uncertainty* of the cash flow from each project was equal to the uncertainty of the overall cash flows from operations of the firm. This assumption validated discounting project cash flows at the required rate of return (RRR) of the firm, its estimated cost of capital.

Figure 14–1 Risk-return relationship

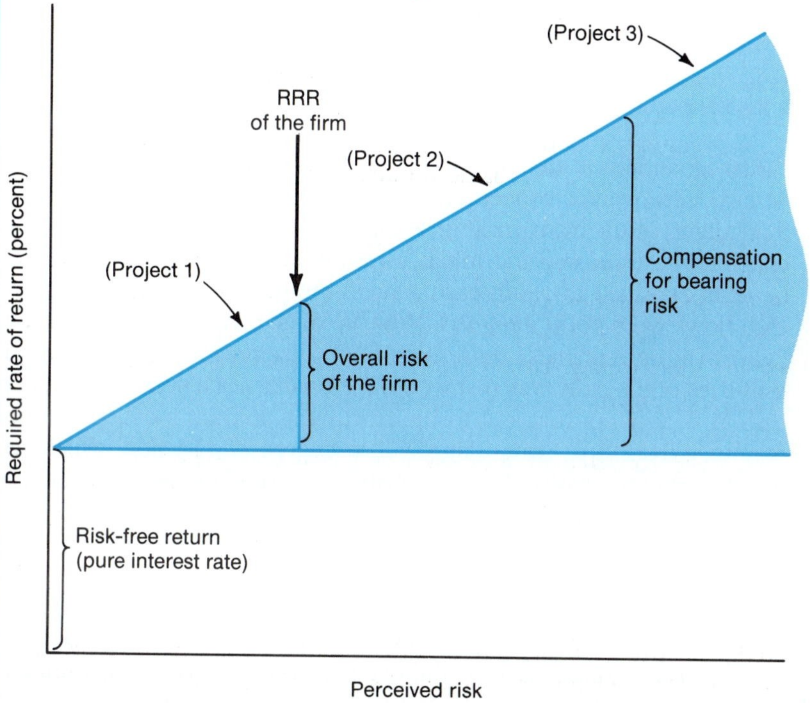

the firm is the return that provides the risk-free return plus compensation for the overall risk of the firm.

Recognizing project risk differentials from the overall risk of the firm requires locating the projects under consideration on the upward-sloping line in Figure 14–1 in relation to the point on that line indicating the RRR of the firm. As you may suspect, this is easy to illustrate but hard to do. The projects undertaken may affect the required rate of return of the firm. The value of the firm will be increased only if the rate of return on each project exceeds the rate of return required to compensate for bearing its risk. Thus, recognition of project risk differentials provides the heretofore missing link tying capital investment decisions to our general goal of maximizing value of the firm.

Now we shall proceed to develop the concepts of risk and some means of measuring risk. Then we shall develop techniques by which project risk differentials may be incorporated into capital investment decisions. Finally, the relationship between the capital investment decision-making process and strategic policy of the firm will be considered.

Risk concepts and measures

Risk generally is defined as the degree of potential variability of outcomes. Here we are concerned with the degree of variability of cash flows that might result from making a capital investment. In the previous two chapters we estimated the initial investment in a project and the net cash benefits expected to result each year in the future from the project. These cash flows were *point estimates*. Now we must recognize that each of those figures (point estimates) represented only a *central tendency* of a group of estimates of the cash flow that would materialize each year. Each anticipated cash flow may not turn out to be exactly the amount indicated, but rather may vary from it to some degree. The degree of variation, which reflects the risk, may be depicted by a probability curve elaborating the estimate to show the various outcomes that might occur.

This is illustrated by the probabilistic cash-flow pattern shown in Figure 14–2. Here the analyst indicates not only the most probable cash flow (the vertical line from the high point of each curve) but also the probability of occurrence of higher or lower cash flows (shown by the probability curves). This more realistically depicts the expected outcome of the investment. The greater the variability of expected cash flows, as expressed by the greater flatness of the probability curves, the greater the risk of the investment.

Figure 14–2 **Probabilistic cash-flow pattern**

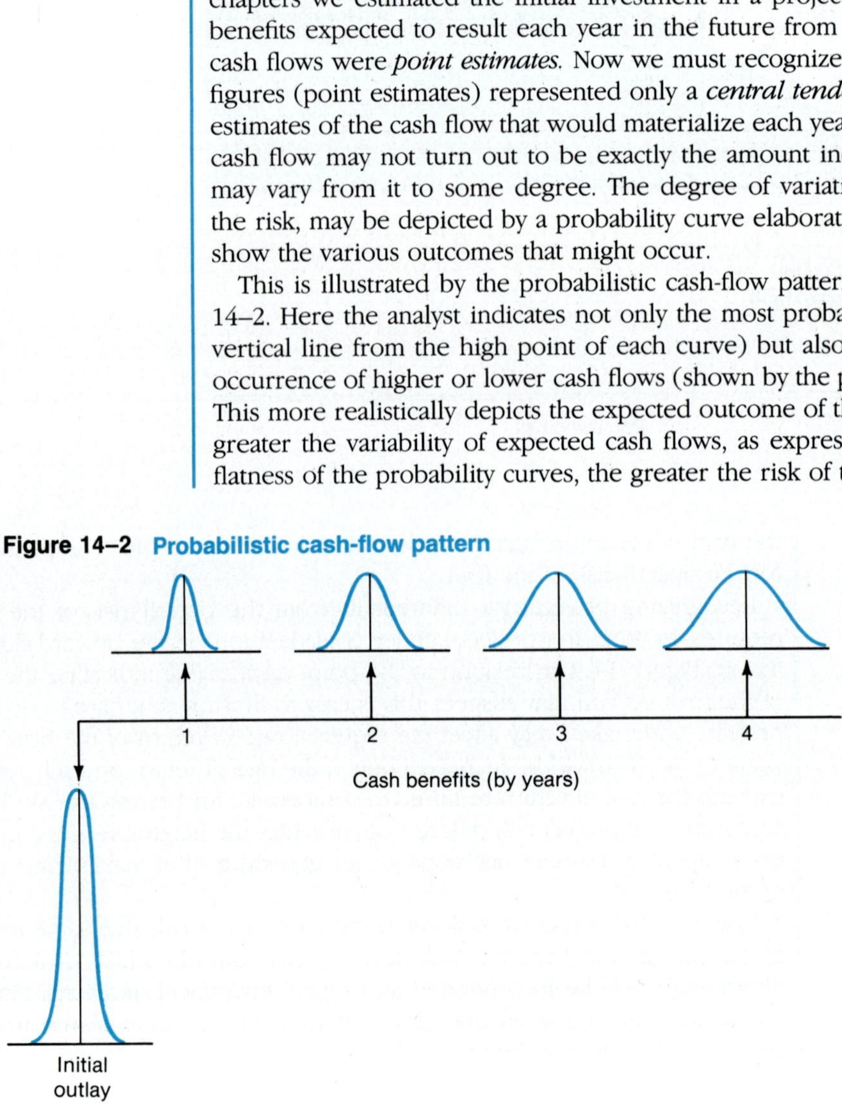

Table A Present value interest factors (PVIF)

Present value of $1 to be received at the end of *n* periods discounted at *i* interest rate

$$PVIF\,(i, n) = \left[\frac{1}{(1+i)^n}\right]$$

Period (n)	Discount rate (i) 1%	2%	3%	4%	5%	6%	7%	8%	9%	10%	11%	12%	13%
1	0.990	0.980	0.971	0.962	0.952	0.943	0.935	0.926	0.917	0.909	0.901	0.893	0.885
2	0.980	0.961	0.943	0.925	0.907	0.890	0.873	0.857	0.842	0.826	0.812	0.797	0.783
3	0.971	0.942	0.915	0.889	0.864	0.840	0.816	0.794	0.772	0.751	0.731	0.712	0.693
4	0.961	0.924	0.888	0.855	0.823	0.792	0.763	0.735	0.708	0.683	0.659	0.636	0.613
5	0.951	0.906	0.863	0.822	0.784	0.747	0.713	0.681	0.650	0.621	0.593	0.567	0.543
6	0.942	0.888	0.837	0.790	0.746	0.705	0.666	0.630	0.596	0.564	0.535	0.507	0.480
7	0.933	0.871	0.813	0.760	0.711	0.665	0.623	0.583	0.547	0.513	0.482	0.452	0.425
8	0.923	0.853	0.789	0.731	0.677	0.627	0.582	0.540	0.502	0.467	0.434	0.404	0.376
9	0.914	0.837	0.766	0.703	0.645	0.592	0.544	0.500	0.460	0.424	0.391	0.361	0.333
10	0.905	0.820	0.744	0.676	0.614	0.558	0.508	0.463	0.422	0.386	0.352	0.322	0.295
11	0.896	0.804	0.722	0.650	0.585	0.527	0.475	0.429	0.388	0.350	0.317	0.287	0.261
12	0.887	0.788	0.701	0.625	0.557	0.497	0.444	0.397	0.356	0.319	0.286	0.257	0.231
13	0.879	0.773	0.681	0.601	0.530	0.469	0.415	0.368	0.326	0.290	0.258	0.229	0.204
14	0.870	0.758	0.661	0.577	0.505	0.442	0.388	0.340	0.299	0.263	0.232	0.205	0.181
15	0.861	0.743	0.642	0.555	0.481	0.417	0.362	0.315	0.275	0.239	0.209	0.183	0.160
16	0.853	0.728	0.623	0.534	0.458	0.394	0.339	0.292	0.252	0.218	0.188	0.163	0.141
17	0.844	0.714	0.605	0.513	0.436	0.371	0.317	0.270	0.231	0.198	0.170	0.146	0.125
18	0.836	0.700	0.587	0.494	0.416	0.350	0.296	0.250	0.212	0.180	0.153	0.130	0.111
19	0.828	0.686	0.570	0.475	0.396	0.331	0.277	0.232	0.194	0.164	0.138	0.116	0.098
20	0.820	0.673	0.554	0.456	0.377	0.312	0.258	0.215	0.178	0.149	0.124	0.104	0.087
25	0.780	0.610	0.478	0.375	0.295	0.233	0.184	0.146	0.116	0.092	0.074	0.059	0.047
30	0.742	0.552	0.412	0.308	0.231	0.174	0.131	0.099	0.075	0.057	0.044	0.033	0.026
40	0.672	0.453	0.307	0.208	0.142	0.097	0.067	0.046	0.032	0.022	0.015	0.011	0.008
50	0.608	0.372	0.228	0.141	0.087	0.054	0.034	0.021	0.013	0.009	0.005	0.003	0.002

Period (n)	Discount rate (i) 14%	15%	16%	17%	18%	19%	20%	25%	30%	35%	40%	50%
1	0.877	0.870	0.862	0.855	0.847	0.840	0.833	0.800	0.769	0.741	0.714	0.667
2	0.769	0.756	0.743	0.731	0.718	0.706	0.694	0.640	0.592	0.549	0.510	0.444
3	0.675	0.658	0.641	0.624	0.609	0.593	0.579	0.512	0.455	0.406	0.364	0.296
4	0.592	0.572	0.552	0.534	0.516	0.499	0.482	0.410	0.350	0.301	0.260	0.198
5	0.519	0.497	0.476	0.456	0.437	0.419	0.402	0.328	0.269	0.223	0.186	0.132
6	0.456	0.432	0.410	0.390	0.370	0.352	0.335	0.262	0.207	0.165	0.133	0.088
7	0.400	0.376	0.354	0.333	0.314	0.296	0.279	0.210	0.159	0.122	0.095	0.059
8	0.351	0.327	0.305	0.285	0.266	0.249	0.233	0.168	0.123	0.091	0.068	0.039
9	0.308	0.284	0.263	0.243	0.225	0.209	0.194	0.134	0.094	0.067	0.048	0.026
10	0.270	0.247	0.227	0.208	0.191	0.176	0.162	0.107	0.073	0.050	0.035	0.017
11	0.237	0.215	0.195	0.178	0.162	0.148	0.135	0.086	0.056	0.037	0.025	0.012
12	0.208	0.187	0.168	0.152	0.137	0.124	0.112	0.069	0.043	0.027	0.018	0.008
13	0.182	0.163	0.145	0.130	0.116	0.104	0.093	0.055	0.033	0.020	0.013	0.005
14	0.160	0.141	0.125	0.111	0.099	0.088	0.078	0.044	0.025	0.015	0.009	0.003
15	0.140	0.123	0.108	0.095	0.084	0.074	0.065	0.035	0.020	0.011	0.006	0.002
16	0.123	0.107	0.093	0.081	0.071	0.062	0.054	0.028	0.015	0.008	0.005	0.002
17	0.108	0.093	0.080	0.069	0.060	0.052	0.045	0.023	0.012	0.006	0.003	0.001
18	0.095	0.081	0.069	0.059	0.051	0.044	0.038	0.018	0.009	0.005	0.002	0.001
19	0.083	0.070	0.060	0.051	0.043	0.037	0.031	0.014	0.007	0.003	0.002	0
20	0.073	0.061	0.051	0.043	0.037	0.031	0.026	0.012	0.005	0.002	0.001	0
25	0.038	0.030	0.024	0.020	0.016	0.013	0.010	0.004	0.001	0.001	0	0
30	0.020	0.015	0.012	0.009	0.007	0.005	0.004	0.001	0	0	0	0
40	0.005	0.004	0.003	0.002	0.001	0.001	0.001	0	0	0	0	0
50	0.001	0.001	0.001	0	0	0	0	0	0	0	0	0

Source: Adapted from O. Maurice Joy, *Introduction to Financial Management*, rev. ed. (Homewood, Ill.: Richard D. Irwin, 1980), Appendix Table C, pp. 589–92.

Table B Present value interest factors for an annuity (PVIFA)

Present value of \$1 to be received at the end of each of *n* periods discounted at *i* interest rate

$$PVIFA\ (i, n) = \sum_{t=1}^{n} \frac{1}{(1+i)^t}$$

Period (n)	1%	2%	3%	4%	5%	6%	7%	8%	9%	10%	11%	12%	13%
	Discount rate (i)												
1	0.990	0.980	0.971	0.962	0.952	0.943	0.935	0.926	0.917	0.909	0.901	0.893	0.885
2	1.970	1.942	1.913	1.886	1.859	1.833	1.808	1.783	1.759	1.736	1.713	1.690	1.668
3	2.941	2.884	2.829	2.775	2.723	2.673	2.624	2.577	2.531	2.487	2.444	2.402	2.361
4	3.902	3.808	3.717	3.630	3.546	3.465	3.387	3.312	3.240	3.170	3.102	3.037	2.974
5	4.853	4.713	4.580	4.452	4.329	4.212	4.100	3.993	3.890	3.791	3.696	3.605	3.517
6	5.796	5.601	5.417	5.242	5.076	4.917	4.767	4.623	4.486	4.355	4.231	4.111	3.998
7	6.728	6.472	6.230	6.002	5.786	5.582	5.389	5.206	5.033	4.868	4.712	4.564	4.423
8	7.652	7.325	7.020	6.733	6.463	6.210	5.971	5.747	5.535	5.335	5.146	4.968	4.799
9	8.566	8.162	7.786	7.435	7.108	6.802	6.515	6.247	5.995	5.759	5.537	5.328	5.132
10	9.471	8.983	8.530	8.111	7.722	7.360	7.024	6.710	6.418	6.145	5.889	5.650	5.426
11	10.368	9.787	9.253	8.760	8.306	7.887	7.499	7.139	6.805	6.495	6.207	5.938	5.687
12	11.255	10.575	9.954	9.385	8.863	8.384	7.943	7.536	7.161	6.814	6.492	6.194	5.918
13	12.134	11.348	10.635	9.986	9.394	8.853	8.358	7.904	7.487	7.103	6.750	6.424	6.122
14	13.004	12.106	11.296	10.563	9.899	9.295	8.745	8.244	7.786	7.367	6.982	6.628	6.302
15	13.865	12.849	11.938	11.118	10.380	9.712	9.108	8.559	8.061	7.606	7.191	6.811	6.462
16	14.718	13.578	12.561	11.652	10.838	10.106	9.447	8.851	8.313	7.824	7.379	6.974	6.604
17	15.562	14.292	13.166	12.166	11.274	10.477	9.763	9.122	8.544	8.022	7.549	7.120	6.729
18	16.398	14.992	13.754	12.659	11.690	10.828	10.059	9.372	8.756	8.201	7.702	7.250	6.840
19	17.226	15.678	14.324	13.134	12.085	11.158	10.336	9.604	8.950	8.365	7.839	7.366	6.938
20	18.046	16.351	14.877	13.590	12.462	11.470	10.594	9.818	9.129	8.514	7.963	7.469	7.025
25	22.023	19.523	17.413	15.622	14.094	12.783	11.654	10.675	9.823	9.077	8.422	7.843	7.330
30	25.808	22.396	19.600	17.292	15.372	13.765	12.409	11.258	10.274	9.427	8.694	8.055	7.496
40	35.835	27.355	23.115	19.793	17.159	15.046	13.332	11.925	10.757	9.779	8.951	8.244	7.634
50	39.196	31.424	25.730	21.482	18.256	15.762	13.801	12.233	10.962	9.915	9.042	8.304	7.675

Period (n)	14%	15%	16%	17%	18%	19%	20%	25%	30%	35%	40%	50%
	Discount rate (i)											
1	0.877	0.870	0.862	0.855	0.847	0.840	0.833	0.800	0.769	0.741	0.714	0.667
2	1.647	1.626	1.605	1.585	1.566	1.547	1.528	1.440	1.361	1.289	1.224	1.111
3	2.322	2.283	2.246	2.210	2.174	2.140	2.106	1.952	1.816	1.696	1.589	1.407
4	2.914	2.855	2.798	2.743	2.690	2.639	2.589	2.362	2.166	1.997	1.849	1.605
5	3.433	3.352	3.274	3.199	3.127	3.058	2.991	2.689	2.436	2.220	2.035	1.737
6	3.889	3.784	3.685	3.589	3.498	3.410	3.326	2.951	2.643	2.385	2.168	1.824
7	4.288	4.160	4.039	3.922	3.812	3.706	3.605	3.161	2.802	2.508	2.263	1.883
8	4.639	4.487	4.344	4.207	4.078	3.954	3.837	3.329	2.925	2.598	2.331	1.922
9	4.946	4.772	4.607	4.451	4.303	4.163	4.031	3.463	3.019	2.665	2.379	1.948
10	5.216	5.019	4.833	4.659	4.494	4.339	4.192	3.571	3.092	2.715	2.414	1.965
11	5.453	5.234	5.029	4.836	4.656	4.486	4.327	3.656	3.147	2.752	2.438	1.977
12	5.660	5.421	5.197	4.988	4.793	4.611	4.439	3.725	3.190	2.779	2.456	1.985
13	5.842	5.583	5.342	5.118	4.910	4.715	4.533	3.780	3.223	2.799	2.469	1.990
14	6.002	5.724	5.468	5.229	5.008	4.802	4.611	3.824	3.249	2.814	2.478	1.993
15	6.142	5.847	5.575	5.324	5.092	4.876	4.675	3.859	3.268	2.825	2.484	1.995
16	6.265	5.954	5.668	5.405	5.162	4.938	4.730	3.887	3.283	2.834	2.489	1.997
17	6.373	6.047	5.749	5.475	5.222	4.988	4.775	3.910	3.295	2.840	2.492	1.998
18	6.467	6.128	5.818	5.534	5.273	5.033	4.812	3.928	3.304	2.844	2.494	1.999
19	6.550	6.198	5.877	5.584	5.316	5.070	4.843	3.942	3.311	2.848	2.496	1.999
20	6.623	6.259	5.929	5.628	5.353	5.101	4.870	3.954	3.316	2.850	2.497	1.999
25	6.873	6.464	6.097	5.766	5.467	5.195	4.948	3.985	3.329	2.856	2.499	2.000
30	7.003	6.566	6.177	5.829	5.517	5.235	4.979	3.995	3.332	2.857	2.500	2.000
40	7.105	6.642	6.233	5.871	5.548	5.258	4.997	3.999	3.333	2.857	2.500	2.000
50	7.133	6.661	6.246	5.880	5.554	5.262	4.999	4.000	3.333	2.857	2.500	2.000

Source: Adapted from O. Maurice Joy, *Introduction to Financial Management*, rev. ed. (Homewood, Ill.: Richard D. Irwin, 1980), Appendix Table D, pp. 593–96.

We have been using the terms *probability* and *probability distributions* rather loosely. Now we must more precisely develop these concepts.

Probability distributions

A *probability* is the percentage chance of occurrence of a given outcome. A *probability distribution* depicts a set of possible outcomes and the percentage chance of occurrence of each outcome. The probability distributions we are interested in are the various cash flows that might materialize related to the percentage chance that each might occur.

We must recognize at the outset that such probability distributions may be estimated with varying degrees of precision. One probability distribution may rest upon highly reliable information while another may simply reflect the analyst's guesses. An *objective probability distribution* is one that is statistically determined from historical information. Of course, history may not repeat itself, but nonetheless, such a probability distribution may be quite reliable. A *subjective probability distribution* is one that reflects the opinions of the person who developed it. Whenever a project involves doing something new and different, this is the only kind of probability distribution that can be developed. The subjectivity of such a probability distribution may vary all the way from sophisticated estimates based upon engineering studies, extensive market research, and pilot plant experience to outright guesses. Unfortunately, subjective probability distributions are the only ones available for use in many capital investment project analyses.

Probability distributions may be either discrete or continuous. A *discrete probability distribution* is one in which only a limited number of outcomes is possible and a probability is assigned to each. These are displayed in a bar chart. A *continuous probability distribution* is one in which an unlimited (infinite) number of outcomes is possible. These outcomes and their related probabilities are shown in a line graph. These two types of probability distributions will now be developed.

Discrete probability distributions Discrete probability distributions are based on the assumption that the probability of each of a limited number of possible outcomes can be established. To illustrate the use of such probability distributions, let us compare two proposed projects, A and B. Project A is an investment in machinery to manufacture a product having a stable market. Project B is an investment in machinery to manufacture a luxury product sold in a market that is highly sensitive to economic conditions. We have estimated the net cash flows expected from each project under each of five possible states of the economy: deep recession, moderate recession, normal, moderate prosperity, and great prosperity. The estimates are shown in column 2 of Table 14–1. Although each project is expected to develop cash flows of $10,000 annually under normal economic conditions, the cash flows of project A would drop to $6,000 in a deep recession but those of project B would drop to 0. At the other extreme, the cash flows from project A would be $14,000 under great prosperity; those of project B would be $20,000. These estimates may have been developed through statistical analysis of historical data or computer simulation of operations under the various assumed states, or they may be completely subjective estimates.

Table 14–1 Expected values of cash flows of projects A and B

(1)	(2) Estimated annual cash flow		(3)	(4) Weighted value (2) × (3)	
	Project A	Project B	Probability of state occurring	Project A	Project B
State of the economy					
Deep recession	$ 6,000	$ 0	.05	$ 300	$ 0
Moderate recession	8,000	5,000	.20	1,600	1,000
Normal	10,000	10,000	.50	5,000	5,000
Moderate prosperity	12,000	15,000	.20	2,400	3,000
Great prosperity	14,000	20,000	.05	700	1,000
Expected value				$10,000	$10,000

The next step is to estimate the probability of occurrence of each of the five states of the economy. These estimates must be relatively subjective because they refer to the unknown future over the lives of the projects. Each of the estimated project cash flows is multiplied by the probability of its occurrence to obtain weighted values. The sums of these weighted values are the *expected values.* These expected values will then be discounted at appropriate required rates of return to obtain the present values of each project.

The discrete probability distributions of annual cash inflows of projects A and B are shown in Figure 14–3. The tightness of the project A distribution as compared to that of project B in the bar charts indicates that project A is substantially less risky than project B. The essence of risk is variability of return, and these probability distributions show the variability to be less for project A than for B. Because project A is less risky than project B, the expected value of its annual net cash flows should be discounted at a lower required rate of return (RRR) than those of project B.

In this illustration the expected values are identical to the central values (means, medians, and modes) of the probability distributions. The example was designed this way for simplicity. In practice, this might not be the case. The distributions could be skewed or even bimodal; therefore, the means, medians, modes, and expected values might differ from each other.

Continuous probability distributions In developing discrete probability distributions, we assumed only a limited number of possible states (five in

Figure 14–3 **Discrete probability distributions of cash inflows of projects A and B**

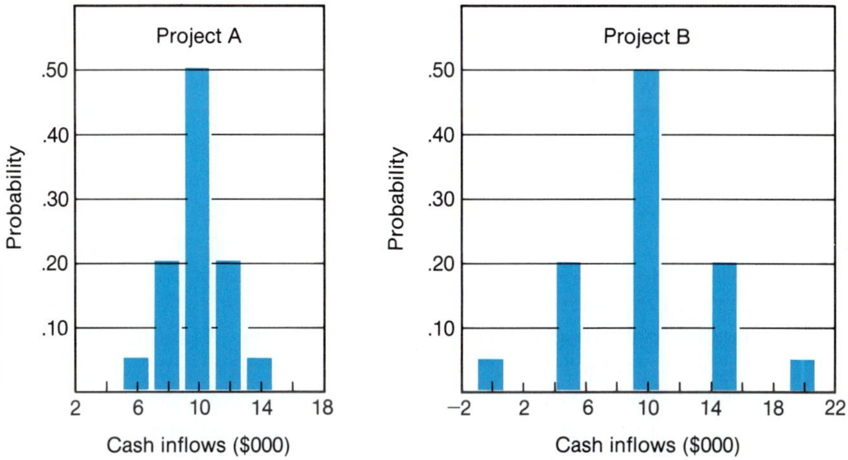

our illustration). In reality, there are an unlimited number of possible outcomes and an unlimited number of probabilities associated with each of these outcomes. If data regarding such possibilities were available, continuous probability distributions could be developed to depict all possible outcomes and their respective probabilities. The resulting continuous probability distributions would be depicted by line graphs as shown in Figure 14–4. The tighter the probability distribution, that is, the more peaked the distribution, the less the riskiness of the outcome. Conversely, the flatter the distribution, the more risky the outcome. From such a distribution we can statistically measure the dispersion, that is, the relative flatness or spread of the distribution, to establish numerical measures of relative risk.

Figure 14–4 **Continuous probability distributions of cash inflows of projects A and B**

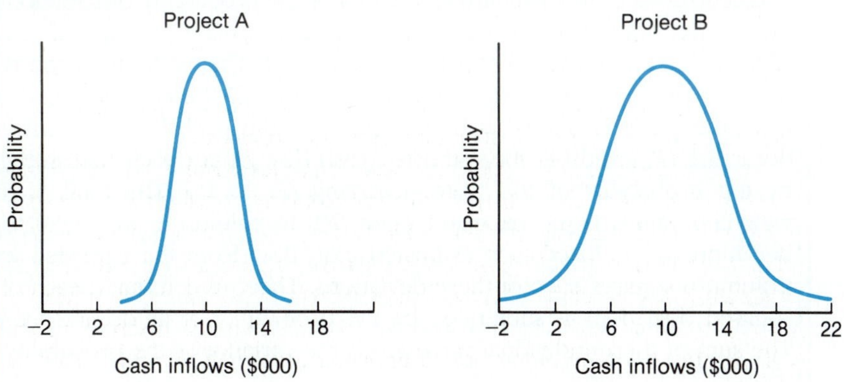

Measures of dispersion

There are three useful measures of dispersion of a probability distribution: the range, the standard deviation, and the coefficient of variation.

Range The *range,* a simple and crude measure of dispersion, is simply the *difference between the lowest and the highest estimates of outcome.* If we had only a most pessimistic estimate and a most optimistic one, the range would be the difference between one and the other. This measure is very crude because it identifies only the two extremes and tells us nothing about the shape of the distribution between them. As a theoretical point, the tails of a continuous normal probability curve approach, but never reach, the horizontal axis of the graph. Therefore, the range is infinite. But, as a practical matter, estimates by knowledgeable business executives that one project might have a range of annual cash flows from 0 to $1 million while another project might have a range of only $400,000 to $600,000 provide a great deal of information regarding the riskiness of the two projects.

Standard deviation The *standard deviation* of a distribution is *the square root of the weighted average squared deviations of the individual outcomes from the expected value.* The formula for calculating the standard deviation is

$$\sigma = \sqrt{\sum_{i=1}^{n} (E_i - \overline{E})^2 \times P_i} \qquad (14\text{–}1)$$

where

σ (sigma) = the standard deviation
n = the number of possible outcomes
E_i = the outcome for the ith case
$\overline{E}$ = the expected value
P_i = the probability that the ith outcome will occur

Calculations of the standard deviations of the probability distributions for our project A and project B are shown in Table 14–2. Columns 1 through 4 of this table are drawn directly from Table 14–1. They indicate, respectively, for each project, (1) the state of the economy, (2) the estimated cash flow from the projects under each state *(E_i)*, (3) the probability of each state occurring *(P_i)*, and (4) the estimated cash flow under each state weighted by the probability of that state occurring *($E_i \times P_i$)*. The total of these weighted values is the expected value *($\overline{E}$)*. In column 5, we calculate the deviation *($E_i - \overline{E}$)* of each estimated cash flow from the expected value. Column 6 squares each of these deviations. Then, in column 7, each of the squared deviations is multiplied by the probability of its occurrence *(P_i)*. The sum of these individual variances is the variance of the probability dis-

Table 14–2 **Calculation of standard deviations of cash flows from projects A and B**

(1) State of the economy*	(2) Estimated cash flow E_i	(3) Probability of state occurring P_i	(4) Weighted value $E_i \times P_i$	(5) Deviation $E_i - \overline{E}$	(6) Squared deviation $(E_i - \overline{E})^2$	(7) Individual variance $(E_i - \overline{E})^2 \times P_i$
Project A						
1	$ 6,000	.05	$ 300	$ −4,000	$ 16,000,000	$ 800,000
2	8,000	.20	1,600	−2,000	4,000,000	800,000
3	10,000	.50	5,000	0	0	0
4	12,000	.20	2,400	2,000	4,000,000	800,000
5	14,000	.05	700	4,000	16,000,000	800,000
			$10,000†			$ 3,200,000‡
		Standard deviation (σ) = $\sqrt{\text{Variance}}$ = $1,789				
Project B						
1	$ 0	.05	$ 0	$ −10,000	$100,000,000	$ 5,000,000
2	5,000	.20	1,000	− 5,000	25,000,000	5,000,000
3	10,000	.50	5,000	0	0	0
4	15,000	.20	3,000	5,000	25,000,000	5,000,000
5	20,000	.05	1,000	10,000	100,000,000	5,000,000
			$10,000†			$20,000,000‡
		Standard deviation (σ) = $\sqrt{\text{Variance}}$ = $4,472				

*1 = Deep recession; 2 = Moderate recession; 3 = Normal; 4 = Moderate prosperity; 5 = Great prosperity.

†This figure, the total of the weighted values, is the *expected value*, $\overline{E}$.

‡This figure, the sum of the individual variances, is the *variance* of the distribution.

tribution. The standard deviation is calculated by taking the square root of the variance.

From Table 14–2 we see that the standard deviation of project A is $1,789, and that of project B is $4,472. Since both projects have the same expected value, $10,000, and the standard deviation of project B is about 2½ times that of project A, we conclude that project B is about 2½ times riskier than project A.

If, as in this example, we are considering a *normal* probability distribution (one that is symmetrical and bell-shaped), then 68 percent of the outcomes will fall within one standard deviation ($\pm 1\sigma$) of the expected value, 95 percent will fall within two standard deviations ($\pm 2\sigma$), and 99 percent will fall within three standard deviations ($\pm 3\sigma$) of the expected value. This is illustrated in Figure 14–5. The percentages indicate the portion of the area under the probability curve included within one, two, and three standard deviations from the expected value.[2]

The standard deviation is a valid measure of relative risk only for projects having the same expected value. In comparing projects of differing expected values, one must convert the standard deviation to the coefficient of variation.

Coefficient of variation The *coefficient of variation* measures the risk *per dollar* of expected returns. It is *calculated by dividing the standard deviation by the expected value.* Let *CV* represent the coefficient of variation, σ the standard deviation, and $\overline{E}$ the expected value; then

$$CV = \frac{\sigma}{\overline{E}} \tag{14–2}$$

Figure 14–5 Area under a normal probability curve

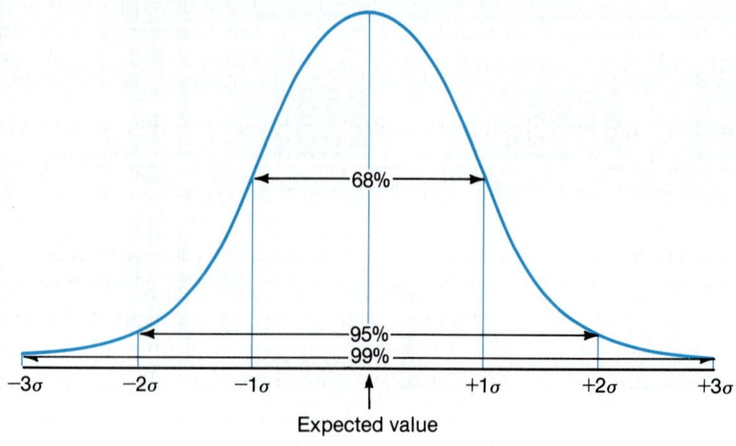

[2]Tables indicating the area under the normal curve within a range from .01 through at least 3.0 standard deviations from the expected value may be found in most standard statistics texts.

The coefficients of variation for our projects A and B are

$$CV_A = \frac{\$1,789}{\$10,000} = 0.179$$

$$CV_B = \frac{\$4,472}{\$10,000} = 0.447$$

The coefficient of variation of project B is about 2½ times that of project A. In this case, as pointed out earlier, it would not be necessary to calculate the coefficients of variation because the expected values of the two projects are equal. But if we were comparing these two projects to another, project C, having a different expected value, calculation of the coefficients of variation would be necessary. If the probability distribution of the expected annual cash flows from project C indicated a standard deviation of $6,700, and its expected value were $24,000, then its coefficient of variation would be 0.279 ($6,700/$24,000). This would indicate that its riskiness fell between that of projects A and B.

Inasmuch as the coefficient of variation may be used to compare project risk regardless of the relative size or expected value of different projects, as a general rule this is the measure of dispersion to be used.

Risk-time relationship

One of the factors relating to risk is time. Changes in the economic, technological, political, and social environment that affect cash benefits from projects take place through time. We usually can estimate cash flows that will take place next year more accurately than those 5 years hence, and the latter more accurately than those 10 years hence. To this point we have ignored this fact as we developed probability distributions of expected annual cash flows. In reality, the dispersion of the probability distributions usually will increase through time. In other words, the curves will become flatter.

The risk-time relationship is depicted by Figure 14–6. Envision this figure as a three-dimensional model with the probability distributions standing up vertically from the page. The distribution for the 1st year is the tightest, that for the 5th year is somewhat flatter, and those for the 10th and the 15th years become progressively flatter. This increase in dispersion through time is shown more precisely by the lines indicating the range spanned by plus and minus one standard deviation ($\pm 1\sigma$). Note the increase in the distance within one standard deviation of the expected value as the time increases.

The importance or magnitude of this time-risk relationship will, of course, vary among projects. Other things being equal, longer-lived projects are more risky than shorter-lived ones. The time factor would be less important in an almost riskless project than in a highly risky one. For example, the time-risk relationship would be of negligible importance in building a

Figure 14–6 Risk-time relationship

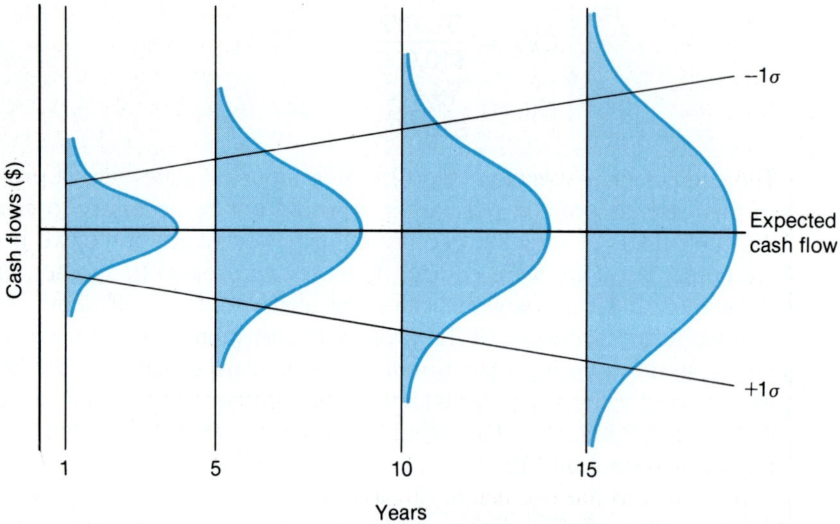

post office to be leased under a fixed rental to the Postal Service for its useful life. It would be very important in a project involving the introduction of a new product that might become popular and be sold for many years or be forgotten after a year or two.

Incorporating project risk differentials into capital investment decisions

There are two conventional methods of incorporating project risk differentials into the capital investment decision-making process. The first, the *certainty equivalent method,* involves adjusting the estimated future cash flows. The second method involves the use of *risk-adjusted discount rates.*

The certainty equivalent method

The first step in the certainty equivalent method is to adjust each estimated future cash flow to a certainty equivalent. In essence, such a *certainty equivalent* is the minimum amount receivable with certainty at the given future date that the investors would exchange for the uncertain (risky) expectation of receiving whatever amount might be generated by the project at that future date. The concept of the certainty equivalent is compared to that of the uncertain (risky) expectation in Figure 14–7. The uncertain expectation of cash flow from a given project in year four is shown in distribution B. The expected value of that distribution of possible outcomes is \$2,000, but the probability distribution of those outcomes is relatively flat. The probability of achieving the \$2,000 cash flow is about 40 percent, with a 20 percent probability of generating \$1,000 or \$3,000, and a 10 percent probability of generating \$600 or \$3,400.

Figure 14–7 Certainty equivalent versus uncertain (risky) expectation for year 4

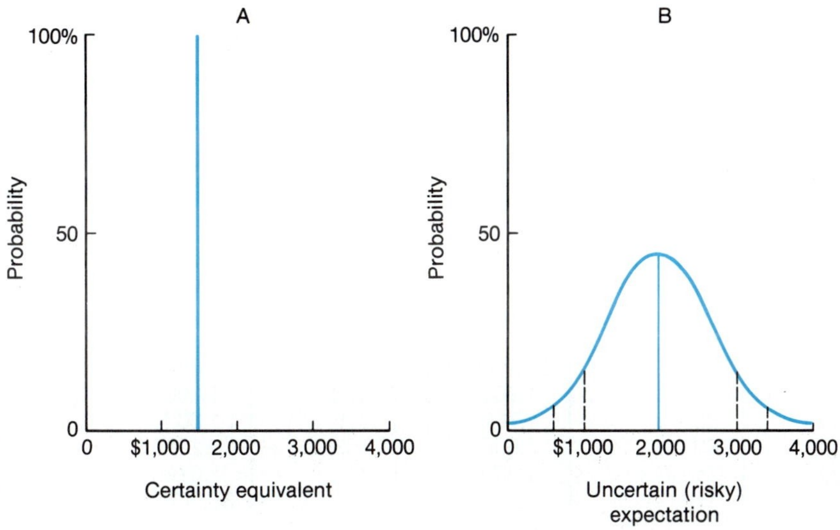

The certainty equivalent of this uncertain expectation reflects two factors. The first is the risk as revealed by the probability distribution. The second is the perceived aversion to risk of the firm's investors. In this case the certainty equivalent is \$1,500, as illustrated by the vertical line on distribution A, indicating 100 percent probability that this amount will be generated four years hence. Put another way, the investors would be indifferent in their valuation of \$1,500 certain or the uncertain cash flows from the project.

Risk is removed from each estimated future cash flow by establishing a certainty equivalent for that cash flow. The *certainty equivalent coefficient* (CE_t) represents the ratio of the acceptable certain outcome to the expected value of the uncertain (risky) expectation, as shown by the following equation:

$$CE_t = \frac{\text{Certain cash flow}_t}{\text{Expected value of uncertain cash flow}_t} \tag{14–3}$$

where t refers to the tth year. The *CE* may vary from 1, indicating certainty, to a value approaching 0 as uncertainty of the outcome becomes extremely great.

Now let us illustrate the calculation of the present value of a series of cash inflows using the certainty equivalent method. A project requires an initial investment of $5,000 and, as shown in Table 14–3, is expected to generate net cash flows of $1,000 the first year, $1,400 the second, and $2,000 each of years three through five, with no salvage value at the end of the fifth year. Certainty equivalent coefficients (CE_t) are estimated at .95 for the first year and to decrease by .05 each year thereafter, as shown in column 3. The certainty equivalent cash flow each year (column 4) is then calculated by multiplying the expected cash flow (column 2) by the appropriate certainty equivalent coefficient (column 3).

Table 14–3 Calculation of present value
Certainty equivalent method

(1) Year	(2) Expected cash flow	(3) Certainty equivalent coefficient (CE_t)	(4) Certainty equivalent cash flow (2) × (3)	(5) Present value factor @ 7%	(6) Present value (4) × (5)
1	$1,000	.95	$ 950	.935	$ 888
2	1,400	.90	1,260	.873	1,100
3	2,000	.85	1,700	.816	1,387
4	2,000	.80	1,600	.763	1,221
5	2,000	.75	1,500	.713	1,070
Total					$5,666

The present value of the certainty equivalent cash flow for each year is calculated by discounting at the *risk-free rate* (or certainty rate). Note that the required rate of return (RRR) here is the rate of return on a risk-free investment rather than the RRR of the firm. This is so because risk has been removed from the expected cash flow by converting it to a certainty equivalent. To do otherwise would be to account for risk twice. Usually the yield on U.S. Treasury securities of equivalent maturity is used as the risk-free rate. In this case we have assumed that rate to be 7 percent and implicitly assumed that the yield curve is flat. The appropriate present value interest factors (*PVIF*s) in column 5 have been obtained from Table A in the Appendix at the end of this book.

The present value of the certainty equivalent cash flow for each year is calculated in column 6 by multiplying the certainty equivalent cash flow (column 4) by the appropriate present value factor (column 5). These present values are then summed to obtain $5,666, the present value of the certainty equivalent inflows. Subtracting the initial investment of $5,000 from this yields a net present value of the project of $666. Applying the decision criterion of the net present value method, the project would be accepted because its risk-adjusted NPV is positive.

Risk-adjusted discount rates

Another, probably most widely used, method of incorporating project risk differentials into the capital investment decision-making process uses risk-adjusted required rates of return (RRRs) to discount expected future cash flows. This method takes several forms, ranging from adjustment of the RRR for each individual project to classifying projects by type or profit center and establishing benchmark RRRs for each classification. Adjustment of the RRRs may be based on either the firm's overall RRR or the risk-free RRR.

Individual project RRRs In many small to middle-sized firms, where only a few capital investments are being evaluated, the executives making the decisions will simply adjust the RRR for each individual project upward or downward from the estimated RRR of the firm (cost of capital) on the basis of subjective judgment. Thus, if the RRR of the firm is estimated to be 12 percent, the executive(s) might judge that project A entails sufficient risk that the RRR for this project should be 15 percent, whereas project B appears to bear about the same risk as the average for the firm, so 12 percent will be its RRR. Project C, because of a stable market for the asset at or above its purchase price even if the project should not be successful, might be approved even if its expected rate of return were only 10 percent. The aggregate projects approved, of course, will be subject to the firm's RRR, assuming that the firm's overall risk would not be changed. Each of these judgments implicitly reflects the executives' perception of the dispersion of possible outcomes of each project relative to the dispersion of possible outcomes of the firm's overall operations.

In other cases, individual project RRRs might be established on the basis of more sophisticated analysis. Probability distributions of each project may be developed, incorporating as much objectivity as possible, and the project RRRs based upon their coefficients of variation.

Classification by type of project In large firms, many capital investment projects must be evaluated, and a formal classification system may be developed. Each class of projects will be identified by a brief description of the characteristics of the projects, and an RRR for each class will be established. That RRR will reflect the responsible executives' judgment of the relative risk of each type of project. Their judgment, in turn, will be based upon experience with each type of project and sometimes formal analysis of that experience.

Such a project classification for Kohlman Manufacturing Company is shown in Table 14–4. The increasing dispersion of possible outcomes and the degree of subjectivity in estimating the probability distributions are reflected by the increasing RRRs as one moves down this table. The RRR for each type of project usually does not constitute a hard and fast rule, but rather is used as a benchmark to guide the final decision-making process. For example, a project in classification 6, "New facilities using existing technology to produce new products," might involve a new product very closely related to a present product line. In such a case it might be accepted even if its expected rate of return were only 16 percent rather than the benchmark 17 percent. On the other hand, another project in the same classification might involve a new product rather far afield from present product lines, and selling that product would require marketing efforts somewhat foreign to Kohlman's marketing organization. A return of perhaps 18 or 19 percent might be required for its approval. The value of the classification system lies more in its providing benchmarks to narrow the appraisal of risk differentials of individual projects than in providing inflexible decision rules.

Table 14–4 Project classifications and RRRs
Kohlman Manufacturing Company

Type of Project	Risk	RRR
1. Repair of existing equipment	Very low	9%
2. Replacement of existing equipment	Low	10
3. Additions to existing facilities to produce present product lines	Slightly below normal	12
4. New facilities using proven technology to produce present product lines	Normal	13
5. New facilities using new technology to produce present product lines	Above normal	15
6. New facilities using existing technology to produce new products	Higher	17
7. New facilities using new technology to produce new products	High	20
8. Development of new technology and new products	Very high	25
9. Development of new technology, products, and markets	Highest	30

Classification by profit centers Many large firms operate in several different industry sectors. Such firms usually are organized into semiautonomous profit centers or divisions, each responsible for operations in an individual industry sector. Because risk characteristics differ greatly among different industries, the central management usually will establish an RRR for each of the profit centers or operating divisions. An example of such profit center classifications is shown in Table 14–5. Multi-industry Corporation is engaged in five different industries, each with differing risk characteristics. Its corporate management has established various RRRs for its respective profit centers to reflect the differing risk characteristics of these industries. These RRRs range from 10 percent for the Natural Gas Transmission Division, which operates an interstate pipeline system, to 28 percent for its Oil and Gas Exploration Division, which is engaged in the high-risk business of wildcatting in search of oil and gas deposits.

Table 14–5 Profit center classification and RRRs
Multi-industry Corporation

Profit center (Division)	Risk	RRR
1. Natural Gas Transmission	Low	10%
2. Natural Gas Distribution	Moderate	12
3. Petrochemicals	Higher	16
4. Oil and Gas Production	High	19
5. Oil and Gas Exploration	Very high	28

How can appropriate RRRs for such diverse profit centers be established? Multi-industry Corporation's securities (stock and bonds) are actively traded in the markets. As we shall see in Chapter 15, we can estimate Multi-industry's overall required rate of return (its cost of capital) from these markets. But those securities reflect interests in the whole corporation, not any one of its individual parts. Thus, it is necessary to establish a rate of return that would be required by each of Multi-industry's divisions if it were standing alone.

The usual approach to this problem is to estimate the RRR (cost of capital) of each profit center by estimating the cost of capital of several similar firms that operate only in that individual industry sector. Thus, to establish the RRR for Multi-industry's Petrochemicals Division, one would estimate the weighted average cost of capital (which you will learn how to do in Chapter 15) for several similar firms that are engaged only in the production and marketing of petrochemicals. By noting the cost of capital of each of these firms and considering any differences that may exist in their operations from those of the Petrochemicals Division of Multi-industry Corporation, one should be able to establish an appropriate required rate of return for the Petrochemicals Division standing alone.

However, this RRR may later require adjustment to take into account that the Petrochemicals Division does not stand alone, but rather is part of Multi-industry Corporation. It is quite possible that after going through this same process for the other four divisions, one will find that the individual RRRs of the divisions, when weighted by the asset investments in each, yield a weighted average RRR higher than that estimated for Multi-industry Corporation as a whole.

In such a case there must be some economic advantage of Multi-industry's diversification and/or the integration of these divisions. For example, the Petrochemicals Division may benefit from its captive source of supply of feedstock from the Oil and Gas Production Division or the Natural Gas Transmission Division. At any rate, if we assume that the overall RRR for Multi-industry Corporation is estimated to be 14 percent and the weighted average of the separately estimated RRRs of the divisions is 15 percent, then those separately estimated divisional RRRs might be scaled down by 1 percent to reflect the economic advantage of their being parts of the Multi-industry Corporation.

The RRRs established for different profit centers or divisions refer only to the *aggregate* of the capital investment proposals of those divisions, not to individual projects. In using them, the management of each division then will adjust from the divisional RRR for the perceived risk differentials of individual projects proposed within the division. This may be done either by estimating individual RRRs for various projects or by utilizing project classifications within the division along the lines illustrated in Table 14–4. Thus, within the Petrochemicals Division, there may be a number of different project classifications with benchmark RRRs ranging from, say, 12 percent for the repair of existing equipment to 30 percent for the development of new technology, products, and markets. The aggregate of the capital investment projects of the Petrochemicals Division, however, must have a positive net present value (NPV) based upon discounting at 16 percent.

Portfolio risk and the capital asset pricing model

To this point in our discussion of project risk, with the exception of mentioning the possible adjustment of profit center RRRs, we have treated the risk of each project as if that project stood alone. But each capital investment does not stand alone; rather, it is a part of a portfolio of assets owned and operated by the firm. We shall first consider this portfolio effect and then discuss the way in which the capital asset pricing model (CAPM), or at least the concept that lies behind it, may be used to account for risk in a portfolio context.

The portfolio effect

The *portfolio effect* recognizes the influence of a particular investment or set of investments upon the overall risk exposure of the firm. Ideally, a capital investment proposal should be considered in terms of its net effect upon the risk and cash generation of the firm. In other words, the *incremental* effect of the project's acceptance is the focus of the analysis. Otherwise the decision may not be fully consistent with the firm's value-maximization goal.

To illustrate the portfolio effect, assume that a supermarket chain expects its net cash flows to expand in periods of prosperity and contract in recessions. It may be considering investing in discount food stores to handle limited lines of generic groceries and household products. Net cash flows from these stores are expected to be countercyclical, that is, to contract in prosperous periods but expand in periods of recession. Thus, the addition of the discount food stores should reduce the overall risk of the firm. In other words, the dispersion of the probability distribution of the firm's overall net cash flows will be decreased. This decrease should be considered in the supermarket chain's capital investment decision-making process. Presumably it would give an advantage to the discount food store projects compared to proposals to open additional regular supermarkets with the same expected rates of return.

Portfolio risk The effect of a particular investment (an added asset) upon the overall risk of the firm's aggregate investments (a portfolio of assets) depends upon the *correlation* of returns from the project with returns from other assets in the portfolio. *Positively correlated* investments, such as the addition of additional regular supermarkets in our illustration, will have little or no effect upon the risk of the portfolio. The cash flows from such investments will move in the same direction as economic conditions change. Such positively correlated investments will not diversify away risk.

On the other hand, *negatively correlated* investments, such as the discount food stores in our illustration, will reduce the overall risk of the portfolio because their returns will move in the opposite direction from those of other assets in the portfolio as economic conditions change.

Other projects might be totally *uncorrelated* with the aggregate of other assets in the portfolio. There simply is no relationship between the fluctuations in rates of return on these assets and those of the remainder of the portfolio. Investment in uncorrelated assets will reduce variation in the overall rate of return of the portfolio, but to a lesser degree than negatively correlated investments. Some risk is diversified away because of the law of large numbers. The larger the number of independently fluctuating cash flow streams, the less will be the dispersion of the aggregate cash flows from the portfolio.

The degree of correlation between projects, or between a project and the remainder of the portfolio, may be quantified by developing the *coefficient of correlation.* This statistical measure takes on values ranging from +1 through 0 to −1. If the cash flows from two projects always moved in the same direction and in the same magnitude, their coefficient of correlation would be +1. If the direction of movement were totally uncorrelated, that is, random, then their coefficient of correlation would be 0. If the direction of movement were always of the same magnitude and consistantly in the opposite direction, that is, negatively correlated, then their coefficient of correlation would be −1. Perfect positive or negative correlations (+1 or −1) of combinations of investments are rarely found in the real world. This is particularly true of negatively correlated investments. Therefore, the analyst usually would be concerned with the relative degree of correlation, say +.2 versus −.4 rather than the extremes of +1 or −1.

The effect of investment in a project that is negatively correlated with the portfolio of investments of the firm is illustrated in Figure 14–8. The portfolio effect upon risk is demonstrated by the reduced fluctuation of aggregate net cash flows from prosperity to recession after adding the negatively correlated project to the firm's portfolio.

Figure 14–8 Effect of negative correlation upon risk

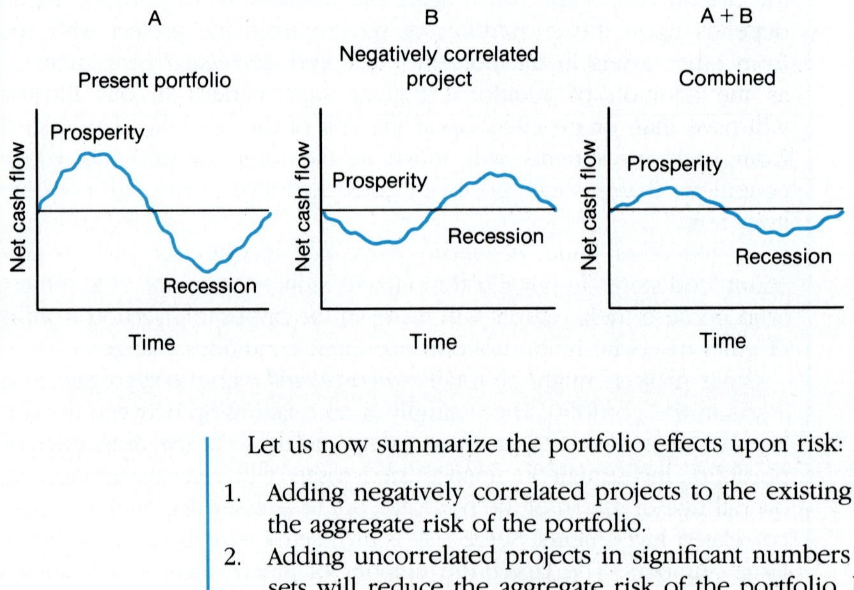

Let us now summarize the portfolio effects upon risk:

1. Adding negatively correlated projects to the existing assets will reduce the aggregate risk of the portfolio.
2. Adding uncorrelated projects in significant numbers to the existing assets will reduce the aggregate risk of the portfolio, but to a lesser degree than adding negatively correlated projects.
3. Adding perfectly positively correlated projects to the existing portfolio will not reduce the aggregate risk of the portfolio.

Evaluation of portfolio opportunities Modern portfolio theory was developed primarily as it relates to investment in financial assets (securities), especially common stocks.[3] It seeks to identify combinations of assets (portfolios) that will satisfy two objectives:

1. Provide the highest possible rate of return for any given level of risk.
2. Provide the lowest possible risk for any given rate of return.

An *efficient portfolio* is one that satisfies these two objectives. To identify such portfolios, the risk-return combinations for all possible portfolios of assets are plotted on a graph as shown in Figure 14–9. Each of the points represents the risk-return relationship of the present portfolio of assets and a different possible combination of additional assets under consideration. The umbrella-shaped area enclosing these points is called the *attainable set*. The efficient portfolios are those that lie on the upper left boundary of the attainable set.

In Figure 14–9, the efficient portfolios are A, B, C, and D. Among the possible combinations, these are the ones that reflect the best attainable risk-return relationships. Portfolio A would yield the highest return for the

Figure 14–9 The attainable set and the efficient frontier

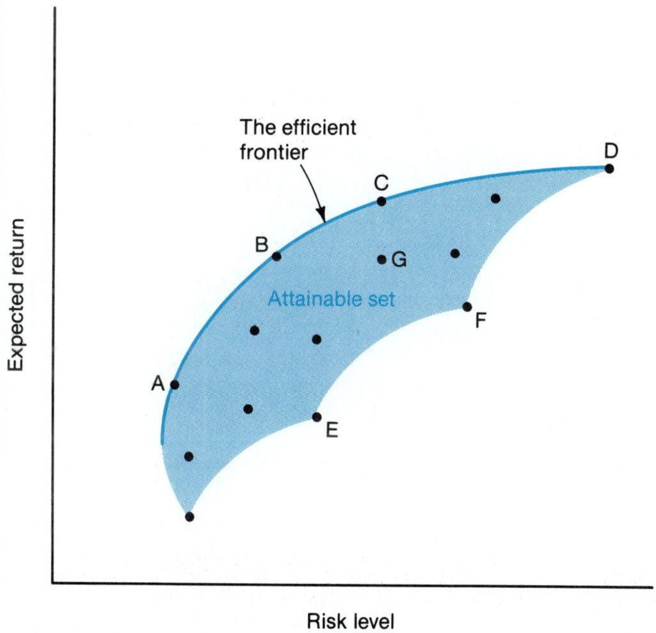

[3]Portfolio theory was originally developed with reference to investment in common stocks by Harry M. Markowitz in his classic article, "Portfolio Selection," *Journal of Finance*, March 1952, pp. 77–91.

lowest risk, B a higher return for a somewhat higher risk, C a still higher return for a higher risk, and D the highest return for bearing the highest risk. All of the other possible combinations within the attainable set are not efficient because their risk-return relationships are inferior to the four efficient portfolios. For example, portfolio G has the same expected return as B but entails greater risk, and it has about the same risk level as C but is expected to yield a lower return. The curve connecting the efficient portfolios (the top of the umbrella) is the *efficient frontier*. Any point on the efficient frontier reflects the highest possible risk-return relationship attainable.

Where along the efficient frontier should an investor be? The answer to this question will determine whether that investor selects portfolio A, B, C, or D, each of which is equally efficient. That answer depends upon the investor's degree of risk aversion. This risk aversion, in turn, is portrayed by a parallel series of indifference curves, as shown in Figure 14–10. An *indifference curve* indicates that the investor would be equally satisfied with a risk-return combination at any point on that curve. In other words, the investor's utility function (or scale of values) is reflected by his or her indifference to the low risk-return combination indicated by the left end of the curve or any point moving to the right along the curve, indicating increasing expected returns for increasing risk. Actually, a given investor will have an

Figure 14–10 Indifference curves

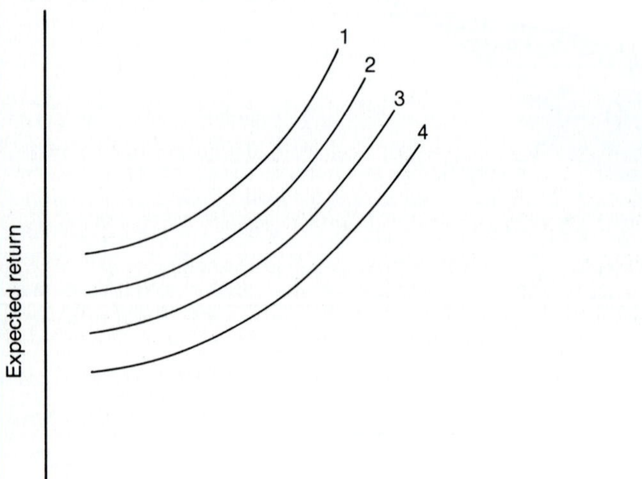

infinite series of parallel, upward-sloping indifference curves. We have simplified by showing only four of these in Figure 14–10. The indifference curves of a highly risk-averse investor would slope steeply upward. Those of a moderately risk-averse investor would be similar to those shown in Figure 14–10. Those of an investor totally indifferent to risk would be horizontal lines.

Selecting the optimal portfolio The series of indifference curves of the investor can now be combined with the efficient set of portfolios to identify the optimal portfolio for that investor. The *optimal portfolio* will be the one closest to the point of tangency of the investor's indifference curves and the efficient frontier. As shown in Figure 14–11, the optimal portfolio for the investor whose indifference curves are shown in Figure 14–10 is portfolio B. This investor, of course, would like to obtain a portfolio having a risk-return combination along curve 1 or 2. But such a portfolio is not attainable; this is wishful thinking. A risk-return combination offered by a portfolio lying along curve 4, although attainable, either would not provide the most favorable risk-return combination (it would be inefficient) or would not satisfy this investor's scale of values (risk-aversion characteristics).

Thus portfolio B, which is efficient, lying on the efficient frontier at its point of tangency with indifference curve 3, is the optimal risk-return combination attainable by this investor. If the investor were highly risk-averse,

Figure 14–11 Selection of the optimal portfolio

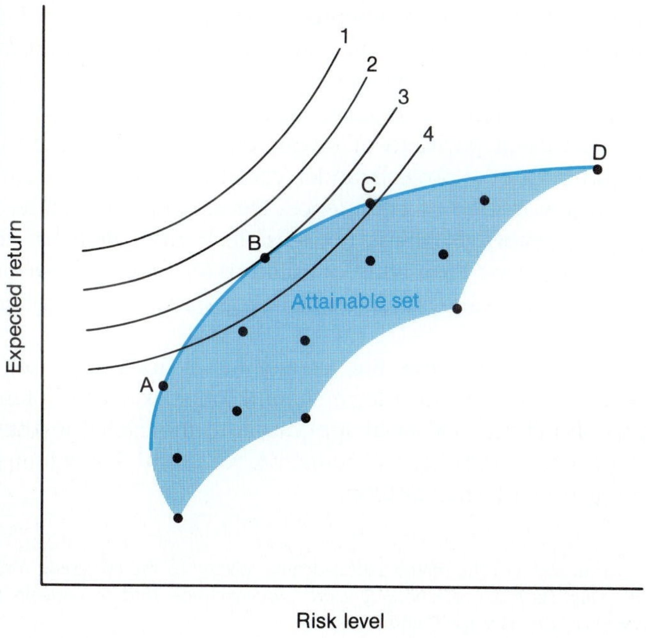

with steeper-sloping indifference curves, the point of tangency might be closer to portfolio A on the efficient frontier; therefore, portfolio A would be optimal for that investor. At the opposite extreme, an investor who was indifferent to risk would choose portfolio D, which would lie at the point of tangency with a series of horizontal indifference curves.[4]

Practical application of portfolio theory Although the logic underlying modern portfolio theory is sound, its application to real-world capital investment decisions of a firm is, at best, very limited. Proposed projects that are positively correlated with the existing portfolio of investments of the firm frequently are those with low degrees of uncertainty. Many of these projects are closely related to the present business activities of the firm, such as repair or replacement of existing equipment, adding facilities to produce present product lines, or expanding present product lines. Conversely, uncorrelated or negatively correlated projects are more likely to be ones that involve venturing out of "the woods that we know" into "the woods that we do not know." Such projects might involve efforts to develop and market new products that are unrelated to the firm's present lines, to invade new territories with which the firm's marketing personnel are unfamiliar, or the acquisition of totally unrelated businesses. The increased uncertainties of venturing into the woods that we do not know tend to offset the portfolio risk advantages of uncorrelated or negatively correlated projects. Many firms learned this the hard way in the 1970s as they diversified into lines of business they did not understand. The subsequent withdrawal can be very painful.

Also, the technical problems encountered in attempting to apply portfolio theory to investment in real assets often are difficult or insurmountable. Establishing the points representing the risk-return combinations of each possible portfolio of investments requires measurement of the correlation coefficients of the present portfolio of investments of the firm with each possible combination of new projects under consideration. This often cannot be done with any degree of confidence. Developing the indifference curves of a firm's investors usually is not feasible. A firm often has many different investors, perhaps thousands or millions of them, whose utility functions as reflected by series of indifference curves are individually different and not obtainable.

Even though in most cases this line of analysis is not practicable, the concepts embodied in it are valuable in shaping one's way of thinking to incorporate portfolio effects. Informal application to the capital investment decision-making process probably will remain more useful than attempts to utilize this approach in a formal fashion.

[4]For a complete explanation and the mathematical details relating to the foregoing material, see Harry M. Markowitz, *Portfolio Selection: Efficient Diversification and Investments* (New York: John Wiley & Sons, 1959), chaps. 7 and 8.

The capital asset pricing model

In recent years the capital asset pricing model (CAPM) has received a great deal of attention, particularly in academic circles, as a means of measuring the risk of assets in a portfolio context.[5] This model, which is based upon the portfolio theory previously discussed, was developed with reference to investment in financial assets, particularly common stocks. Such financial assets are divisible (the stock of a company is divided into a large number of shares) and available in large numbers (the stocks of thousands of different companies being available to an investor). They generally are traded in broad markets, which allows the assumption of an "efficient market."

An efficient market is one with a large number of fully informed buyers and sellers. It is assumed that complete information regarding the available assets and the market in which they are traded is available to all investors. Other assumptions include that investors are not restricted as to the assets they may hold and that they are subject to neither taxes nor transaction costs. Thus, the market price of each available asset may be assumed to be efficiently determined.

Although these assumptions are quite utopian in relation to investment in financial assets (securities), the body of theory is useful in such applications. In relation to investment in real assets by a firm, the assumptions are somewhat unrealistic. Most capital investment projects are not divisible; one cannot invest in part of a machine, a plant, a store, or a warehouse. Markets for real assets usually are neither broad nor efficient. Information is limited and often of a subjective nature. Transactions costs sometimes are high, and the firm is subject to substantial taxes.

For these reasons, the theory as applied to internal capital investment decision-making rarely is *operational* in the sense that one can push the numbers on it and come out with answers. Nonetheless, the *concepts* are transferrable and relevant to the appraisal of project risk in the capital investment decision-making process. In some limited cases, particularly in connection with establishing benchmark rates of return for divisions or profit centers of a diversified firm, much of the CAPM theory may be operational in a formal sense.

Components of risk Under the CAPM, risk is broken down into two components, diversifiable risk and nondiversifiable risk. *Diversifiable risk* (some-

[5]The CAPM was first developed by William F. Sharpe in his classic article, "Capital Asset Prices: A Theory of Market Equilibrium under Conditions of Risk," *Journal of Finance,* September 1964, pp. 425–42. Many authors have further developed, tested, defined, and sometimes maligned the theory based upon this model. Our treatment of the CAPM here must of necessity be only introductory and confined to its relevance to the capital investment decision-making process in a firm.

times called *unsystematic* risk or avoidable risk) is risk that relates to a specific asset but that can be diversified away by combining a number of assets into a portfolio. Such specific risks as strikes, unfavorable regulatory action, or competitive developments fall into this category. *Nondiversifiable risk* (sometimes called *systematic* risk or unavoidable risk) is defined as the risk that effects all assets, such as political events, changes in general economic conditions, or international crises. This risk, although it affects all assets, will do so in varying degrees. It cannot be diversified away by combining individual assets into a portfolio.

Assuming that assets are combined by investors into portfolios, only the nondiversifiable risk is pertinent to risk adjustment of expected cash flows from individual investments. The appropriate adjustment can be established by comparing this risk to that of a fully diversified portfolio of assets (securities), referred to as the *market portfolio.* When the CAPM is used in connection with investment in common stocks, a broadly-based index, such as the Standard & Poor's 500 Stock Composite Index or the New York Stock Exchange Composite Index, is used as a proxy for the market portfolio. The nondiversifiable risk of an individual asset (stock) is a function of its behavior as compared to that of the market as a whole.

The model The capital asset pricing model (CAPM) is stated in the following equation:

$$K_j = R_F + (K_M - R_F)\,\beta_j \tag{14–4}$$

where

K_j = the required rate of return on the individual investment j
R_F = the risk-free rate of return
K_M = the required rate of return on the market portfolio
β_j *(beta)* = the beta coefficient, the index of comovement of the rate of return on the individual investment j relative to the rate of return on the market portfolio

To spell this out, the required rate of return on an individual asset equals (1) the risk-free rate of return plus (2) the product of the premium for risk of the market as a whole $(K_M - R_F)$ times the beta coefficient. The yield on a short-term U.S. government security would usually be used as a proxy for the risk-free rate of return (R_F). The net yield, combining the change in market price as well as dividends paid during an arbitrary holding period, of a broadly based stock index, such as the S&P 500, would be used to represent the required rate of return on the market (K_M). The beta coefficient (β_j), the index of comovement of the individual asset's return (price movement as well as dividends) relative to the market return, is evaluated by regression analysis.[6] *Beta* (β_j) measures the nondiversifiable (systematic) risk.

The beta coefficient of the market is 1. The beta of an individual asset reflects the relative responsiveness of returns on that asset to changes in returns of the market portfolio. An asset whose returns are more volatile than the market returns might have a beta of 2, indicating that it is twice as risky as the market as a whole. A relatively stable asset might have a beta of 0.5, indicating that it is only half as risky as the market. Most widely traded common stocks have betas roughly in the range from 0.3 to 2.0. A negative beta, such as −0.4, indicates that returns on the asset tend to be negatively correlated with those of the market; these are quite rare.

The CAPM is depicted graphically by the *security market line (SML),* as shown in Figure 14–12. In this illustration, the risk-free rate of return *(R_F)* is assumed to be 7 percent. The required rate of return on the market *(K_M)* is 12 percent, reflecting a 5 percent premium over the risk-free rate. The

Figure 14–12 The security market line (SML)

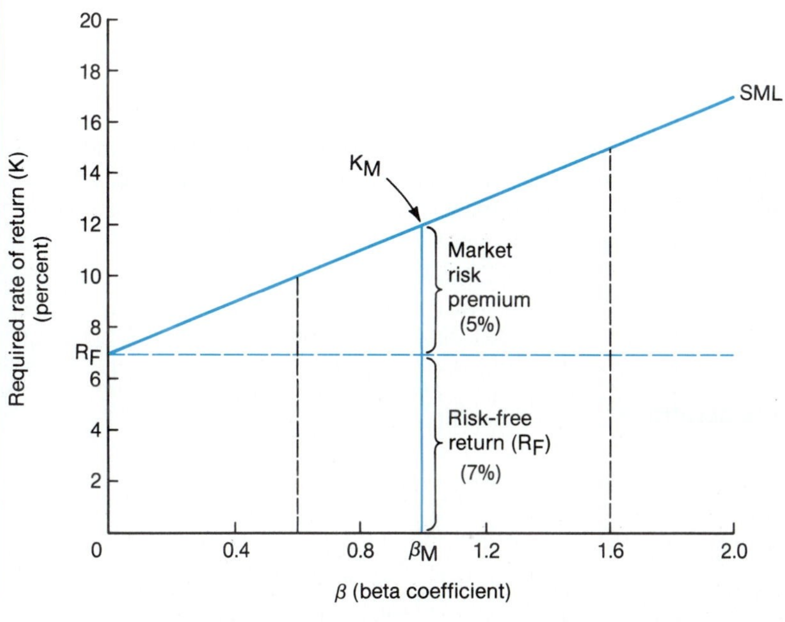

[6]The measurement of beta using historical data requires the use of some rather complex mathematics. The reader is referred to William J. Sharpe, *Investments,* 2d ed. (Englewood Cliffs, N.J.: Prentice-Hall, 1981), for full treatment of this subject. Beta coefficients for large numbers of common stocks are published by *Value Line* and several of the major stock brokerage firms, such as Merrill Lynch, and Paine, Webber.

required rate of return on any asset (K_j) will fall on the security market line (SML) according to the beta coefficient of that asset. Thus, an individual asset with a beta coefficient of 1.6 will have a required rate of return of 15 percent, reflecting a risk premium of 8 percent over the risk-free rate. An asset with a beta of less than 1, say 0.6 percent, indicating that it is only 60 percent as risky as the risk of the market portfolio, will require a rate of return of only 10 percent, reflecting a 3 percent premium over the risk-free rate. If the beta coefficient of an individual asset can be determined, then its required rate of return can be read off the SML.

Note that the security market line (SML), as shown in Figure 14–12, appears to be essentially the same as the risk-return relationship depicted earlier in this chapter in Figure 14–1. At that stage of our discussion, however, we were referring to the risk of the individual asset in isolation, as that risk might be perceived through the use of a probability curve. A significant difference between Figures 14–1 and Figure 14–12 is that the concept of risk embodied in the SML considers risk in a portfolio context. Risk here is measured by a beta coefficient, which reflects only the nondiversifiable risk (systematic risk) of the asset. It is assumed that the diversifiable risk (unsystematic risk) has been eliminated by including the asset in a portfolio.

Portfolio theory, including the CAPM, rarely is operational in connection with capital investment decision making in a sense that we can find the numbers and calculate them to provide the specific required rate of return on a real asset such as a machine, a plant, or the development of a new product. This theory does, however, provide an insight, an additional dimension, to the decision maker's perception of risk. This may be of value in a subjective sense.[7]

Strategic policy considerations

Throughout our discussions of capital investment decision making to this point, it may have appeared that any proposed project that showed a rate of return exceeding its required rate of return would be approved by management. This often is not the case. Capital investment decision making takes

[7]A counterargument questions the value of this theory because the very basis of portfolio theory as it is applied to investment in financial assets (securities) is that investors in a firm can and do diversify away their diversifiable risks by investing in portfolios of stocks. If the firm's stockholders achieve efficient external diversification, then no additional value of the firm could be achieved by internal diversification of its assets. This is an argument to which no satisfactory empirical answer has been found.

place in the context of the strategic policy of the firm. That *strategic policy* sets forth the means by which the firm will pursue its long-range goals. Although the general goal of the firm may be to maximize the value of its common equity, the means by which this may be accomplished requires translation into operational policies. These policies define and constrain the type or types of businesses in which the firm will engage, the markets it will enter, and the advantages it will attempt to exploit.

Such strategic policies will be determined by top management largely through assessment of the firm's unique competence(s) and recognition of its weaknesses. These strengths and weaknesses, in turn, may be in part financial but also depend upon abilities of personnel, possession of physical assets, reputation, market positions, and the like. The resulting strategic policies must be meshed with capital investment decisions made by the firm. Otherwise investments might be made that are inconsistent with the fundamental directions of the firm. If a firm spreads its efforts in different directions in a haphazard manner, it may find itself in numerous different lines of business in which it does not have the competitive strength to survive.

This intermesh of strategic policy and capital investment decision making is necessary because the policy is *implemented* through the capital investments made by the firm. Viewed from the opposite direction, capital investments made by the firm will *determine* its policy. The businesses the firm will be engaged in, the products it will offer, the markets it will attempt to penetrate, and the production processes it will utilize will be determined by the capital investment proposals that are accepted.

There are two ways in which this required coordination may be achieved. One is the outright limitation of projects that will be considered and the other is the modification of project required rates of return (RRR) on the basis of strategic considerations.

Limitation of types of projects considered

If the top management of a firm recognizes unique competence or abilities of the organization, projects eligible for consideration may be limited to those in which that competence can be utilized. For example, Philip Morris possesses a great deal of competence in the mass marketing of consumer goods, particularly those promoted through media advertising and marketed primarily through supermarkets. As that firm diversified from its base of tobacco products, it expanded into beer (Miller Brewing Company) and soft drinks (7-Up). The management of that firm probably would restrict major product-line expansion proposals to those that would utilize its recognized competence. For an extreme example, it probably would not be at all interested in a proposal to invest in a plant to manufacture heavy industrial equipment. Such a limitation of projects to be considered would not really be arbitrary. Rather it simply would recognize that, even though formal analysis of the risk-return combination might look favorable, the uncertainty resulting from the firm's total lack of knowledge of the industry should dominate the consideration.

An example of a smaller firm's limiting its consideration of projects would be a merchant operating a men's clothing shop. A jewelry store down the street might be for sale at a price that appeared to be a good value. But the clothing merchant might not be interested in considering purchasing it because he simply does not know anything about the jewelry business and considers it unwise to walk in the woods that he does not know. He might, however, seriously consider investing in the women's clothing store next door because its business is more closely related to his competence. Almost all firms, with the exception of the outright conglomerates, place some limitations on the types of projects in which they will consider investment.

Strategic adjustments of required rates of return

The other method of relating capital investment decision making to strategic policy is to adjust required rates of return to express that policy. For example, a manufacturer of road-paving machinery might see that the direction of technological development in this field is to employ microcomputer automated systems to control many of the operations of such machinery. Sensing the firm's lack of technological capability in this area, management might lower the required rate of return on a project involving the development of such controls below that determined strictly on the basis of expected future cash flows from the project. Here the consideration would be the possibly immeasurable technological advantages that might accrue to the other operations of the firm.

On the other hand, management might have made a strategic policy decision to withdraw gradually from a particular industrial sector or market. Such a policy might be implemented by increasing the required rates of return on projects in that sector to discourage new investment and to allow the capital assets employed to be reduced through depreciation.

In summary, one often sees in practice either the outright limitation of projects to be considered or adjustments of required rates of return upward or downward on specific types of projects. These limitations or adjustments are based upon strategic policy considerations. Such actions might appear to be arbitrary, or even capricious, to a person not familiar with the overall policy of the firm. However, they often make a good deal of sense when the policy is understood. Recognition of uncertainty and estimates of future benefits generally lie behind such actions, but they may not be reduced to quantitative analysis.

Summary

The capital investment decision-making process must incorporate recognition of differences in perceived risk among proposed projects. If investors are risk-averse, they are willing to bear greater risks only when accompanied by expectation of higher rates of return. Risk generally is defined as the degree of potential variability of outcomes. This variability can be expressed by probability distributions of various possible outcomes, which may be objectively or subjectively determined. The dispersion of a probability distribution may be expressed by the range, the standard deviation, or the coefficient of variation, the latter being the most useful as a comparative measure of risk. Usually risk will increase through time, thus longer-lived projects tend to be more risky than those with shorter lives.

There are two conventional methods of incorporating project risk differentials into the capital investment decision-making process. The certainty equivalent method requires adjusting each estimated annual cash flow to a certainty equivalent, which reflects risk related to the cash flow and the risk aversion of the firm's investors. These certainty equivalents are then discounted at the risk-free rate to calculate the present values of future cash flows. The other method involves discounting the point estimates of future cash flows by risk-adjusted required rates of return. These risk-adjusted rates may be established for each individual project or for classes of projects by type or profit center.

When it is recognized that each capital investment does not stand alone but rather is a part of a portfolio of assets, then the effect of the added asset upon the risk of the portfolio may be considered. This effect depends upon the correlation of the returns from the project with the returns from the other assets comprising the portfolio. Returns may be positively or negatively correlated or uncorrelated. The degree of correlation is measured by the coefficient of correlation. Adding negatively correlated or uncorrelated projects will tend to reduce the aggregate risk of the portfolio, whereas adding positively correlated projects will not.

Efficient portfolios are those that achieve the best attainable risk-return relationships among the possible combinations of assets. The optimal portfolio for an investor depends upon that investor's degree of risk aversion as expressed by indifference curves. The optimal portfolio is the efficient portfolio that lies closest to the point of tangency of the investor's indifference curves and the efficient frontier. Although the logic underlying portfolio theory is sound, practical considerations and technical problems often render it inoperable as a formal model in capital investment decision-making of the firm. The concepts embodied in it, however, are valuable and may be informally incorporated in the decision-making process.

The capital asset pricing model (CAPM), which is based upon portfolio theory and the assumption of an efficient market, is limited in its practical application to capital investment decision-making of the firm. Nonetheless, the concepts are relevant to the appraisal of project risk in a portfolio context.

This model segregates nondiversifiable (systematic or unavoidable) risk and uses the measure of it, beta (β), to relate the risk of an individual asset to that of the market as a whole.

The CAPM is

$$K_j = R_F + (K_M - R_F)\beta_j$$

where K_j is the required rate of return on investment j; R_F is the risk-free rate of return; K_M is the required rate of return on the market; and β_j (beta) is nondiversifiable risk as indicated by the index of comovement of the rate of return on the investment j relative to the rate of return on the market portfolio. In essence, the required rate of return on asset j is the risk-free rate of interest plus the premium for risk, $(K_M - R_F)\beta_j$. This risk premium reflects the risk of the market as a whole $(K_M - R_F)$ and the beta coefficient. Under the CAPM, comovement of the asset's rate of return relative to that of the market portfolio (calculated from historical data) is the key factor in appraising the risk of the individual asset and determining its required rate of return. The CAPM is depicted graphically by the security market line (SML). For each beta, the required rate of return of the asset can be read off the SML.

A final consideration in the capital investment decision-making process is the interrelationship of capital investment decisions and the strategic policies of the firm. There are two ways the required coordination can be achieved. The first is simply to limit the types of projects that will be considered to those that will implement the policies. The second is to adjust required rates of return for specific projects or types of projects to express strategic policies.

Questions

1. Why is it important to consider perceived risk differentials among projects in the analysis of capital investment proposals? Why might a proposal with a 20 percent internal rate of return (IRR) be rejected while another with an IRR of 15 percent be accepted by an intelligent decision maker?

2. What is risk? What is a probability distribution? How is the degree of risk of a project expressed in terms of a probability distribution?

3. What is the shape of the graph of the probability distribution of an absolutely certain cash flow? Of a completely uncertain cash flow? Most future cash flows fall between these two extremes. Discuss briefly the three statistical measures of dispersion of a probability distribution. Which is the most meaningful in comparing the risk associated with different projects of varying size?

4. What is the difference between an objective and a subjective probability distribution? If objective probability distributions have greater validity as measures of risk than subjective ones, why are objective probability distributions only infrequently used in appraising risk of major capital investment projects?

5. What is the typical relationship between risk and the time at which cash flows are expected (other things being equal)? Why?

6. What is a *certainty equivalent?* What two factors influence the certainty equivalent of a given expected cash flow? How can certainty equivalents be used to incorporate project risk into capital investment decision making?

7. How can risk-adjusted discount rates be used to incorporate project risk into capital investment decision making?

8. Where risk-adjusted discount rates are used as benchmarks for capital investment analysis in various divisions or profit centers of a multi-industry firm, how can the risk-adjusted required rate of return (RRR) for each division be established?

9. Define the following terms used in portfolio theory: *(a)* portfolio, *(b)* efficient portfolio, *(c)* efficient frontier, *(d)* indifference curves, and *(e)* optimal portfolio.

10. What is the effect of an added asset upon the overall risk of a portfolio if the returns from the added asset are *(a)* positively correlated, *(b)* negatively correlated, or *(c)* uncorrelated with the returns of the initial portfolio? Define and explain the coefficient of correlation.

11. Define and explain the difference between *diversifiable* (unsystematic) risk and *nondiversifiable* (systematic) risk. Why does the capital asset pricing model (CAPM) consider only nondiversifiable risk to be pertinent in recognizing and adjusting for risk of an individual asset (security or investment project)?

12. What is the *beta* coefficient (β) for a given asset, as used in the CAPM? How does beta provide a means of recognizing and adjusting for risk differentials among different assets in a portfolio?

13. State the capital asset pricing model (CAPM). (Define your terms.) Why is it operational in connection with management of some portfolios of fi-

nancial assets (securities) but of limited use in capital investment management (investment in real assets)?

14. What is the *security market line* (SML)? Construct a graph of the SML where the market return (K_M) is 14 percent and the risk-free return (R_F) is 10 percent.

Problems

1. Maxwell's Mens Store is considering adding a new line of men's clothing. Joe Maxwell, the proprietor, estimates annual net cash flow from the new line as follows:

Possible market acceptance	Probability	Annual cash flow
Low	.20	$ 5,000
Moderate	.40	10,000
High	.30	15,000
Very High	.10	20,000

a. What is the *expected value* of the annual cash flow from the new line?
b. What is the *range*?
c. What is the *standard deviation* (σ)?
d. What is the *coefficient of variation* (*CV*)?

2. Sandra McDonald is analyzing two mutually exclusive projects for her company. She has made the following estimates:

	Project A	Project B
Initial investment	$25,000	$80,000
Useful life	10 years	10 years
Expected annual cash flow	$ 7,000	$20,000
Standard deviation	$ 3,000	$ 7,000

a. Which is the riskier project? (Use coefficient of variation as the comparative risk measure.)
b. If Ms. McDonald requires a risk-adjusted rate of return of 17 percent on the riskier project and 15 percent on the less-risky project, what is the NPV of each?
c. Which project should she recommend be accepted? (Use profitability index.)

3. Mixmatch Clothing Manufacturing Company is considering three capital investment projects. Possible annual cash flows and their respective probabilities of occurrence are:

	Project A		Project B		Project C	
	Cash flow	Probability	Cash flow	Probability	Cash flow	Probability
Low	$1,000	.20	$1,000	.25	$1,500	.25
Medium	2,000	.60	3,000	.40	2,500	.50
High	3,000	.20	6,000	.35	3,500	.25

Rank the riskiness of each project by computing its coefficient of variation.

4. The Roget Corporation is evaluating two capital investment projects to produce and market new products, A and B. Frank Sanchez, its analyst, has estimated the following cash flows and their probabilities:

		Annual cash inflow	
Market acceptance	Probability	Product A	Product B
Very Poor	.10	$ 100	$ 300
Poor	.20	400	700
Average	.40	800	1,500
Good	.20	1,200	2,300
Excellent	.10	1,500	2,700

a. Construct a chart depicting the discrete probabilities of the annual cash flows from each project.

b. Using the chart developed in *(a)*, evaluate the relative riskiness of the projects.

c. Calculate the expected value of the annual cash flow from each project.

d. Calculate the standard deviation (σ) of each.

e. Calculate the coefficient of variation (*CV*) of each.

f. Using the information developed in *(e)*, evaluate the relative riskiness of the projects.

g. If your answer to *(f)* differs from your answer to *(b)*, explain why. Which provides the best measure of relative risk?

5. Catalin Corporation uses the *certainty equivalent* method of adjusting for project risk. It is considering investing $2 million in a high-risk project. Management subjectively estimates annual cash flows for years 1 through 8 from the project and the probability of each as follows:

Annual cash flow	Probability
0	.10
$ 200,000	.20
500,000	.40
800,000	.20
1,200,000	.10

At the end of eight years, the project is expected to be worthless.

After much debate, the capital investment committee of Catalin has agreed that a certainty equivalent of 60 percent of the expected value of the annual cash flows would be appropriate. The risk-free rate of return is estimated to be 9 percent, and Catalin considers its overall required rate of return to be 13 percent. Compute the risk-adjusted net present value (NPV) of this project and decide how you, as a member of the capital investment committee, will vote on its acceptance or rejection.

6. Delbert Corporation must choose between two mutually exclusive projects. Both projects involve the same capital outlay and have the same useful lives with no salvage value. Project A has an expected annual cash flow of $308,000, and the riskier project B has an expected annual cash flow of $376,000. Delbert's capital investment committee has reviewed the relative risks and decided that the certainty equivalents of the expected cash flows of these projects are 85 percent for project A and 70 percent for project B. Which project should be accepted?

7. The Egbert Corporation uses the certainty equivalent method to adjust for project risk. It is considering a project requiring an initial outlay of $45,000 with a useful life of five years and no salvage value. Expected cash flows and their certainty equivalent coefficients are:

Year	Expected cash flow	Certainty equivalent coefficient
1	$12,000	.95
2	14,000	.90
3	17,000	.85
4	17,000	.85
5	10,000	.80

The estimated risk-free rate of return is 10 percent, and Egbert estimates its overall required rate of return to be 14 percent.

a. Compute the risk-adjusted net present value (NPV) of the project.

b. Decide whether to accept or reject the project.

8. Filmore Soap Corporation uses risk-adjusted discount rates to account for risk differentials among projects. Although its overall RRR is 15 percent, Filmore requires a 20 percent rate of return on projects using new technology to produce new products. One such project being considered is production of a new cleanser developed by Filmore's research laboratories. The initial outlay is estimated to be $600,000, and the following cash flows are expected:

Year	Cash flow
1	$ 50,000
2	200,000
3	300,000
4	250,000
5	200,000
6	100,000

At the end of year 6, the project is expected to have a net aftertax terminal value of $75,000. Estimate the risk-adjusted net present value (NPV) of the project and decide whether to accept it.

9. Conglomerate Enterprises, Inc., is evaluating three capital investment opportunities in the form of companies that it might attempt to acquire. It employs the capital asset pricing model (CAPM) to estimate the risk-adjusted required rate of return (RRR) on these projects. The risk-free rate (R_F) is estimated at 9 percent, the current yield on short-term U.S. government securities. The required rate of return on the market portfolio (K_M) is estimated to be 14 percent, the return on the S&P 500 Stock Composite Index. The beta coefficients (β) of the companies under consideration are as follows:

Company	Beta
A	.6
B	1.2
C	1.9

a. Graph the security market line (SML).
b. Locate each of the three companies on the SML.
c. Calculate, using the CAPM, the required return (K) of each of the companies.
d. Why might this be a viable approach for analysis of external investments (acquisition of companies) by Conglomerate Enterprises but not for analysis of internal investments (acquisition of real assets, such as machinery, plants, and warehouses) by the Acme Hardware Manufacturing Company?

Chapter 15
Cost of Capital

As we developed the analytical methods for capital investment decision making in Chapter 12, we frequently referred to the required rate of return (RRR) of the firm. Then in Chapter 14, as risk differentials among proposed projects were considered, we used the RRR of the firm as a benchmark from which to establish risk-adjusted RRRs for different types of projects or individual projects. *The required rate of return of the firm is its overall cost of capital.* To this point in our dicussions of capital investment analysis we have assumed the cost of capital of the firm. Now we must direct our attention to the nature of the firm's cost of capital, the methods by which we can estimate this cost, the problems encountered in the estimating process, and the uses of cost of capital analysis in various areas of financial decision making.

This chapter will discuss the cost of capital of the firm in the following order:

1. Uses of cost of capital analysis.
2. The rationale of overall cost of capital.
3. Estimating the cost of the various components of capital: debt, preferred stock and common stock equity.
4. Estimating the weighted average cost of capital of the firm.
5. Effects of inflation upon the firm's cost of capital.

Uses of cost of capital analysis

A realistic estimate of the overall cost of capital of the firm is vital to sound capital investment decision making. Cost of capital analysis also has many applications in other areas of financial management treated in the remainder of this book.

Capital investment analysis applications

If the perceived risk of a proposed project is equal to the general risk of the firm, capital investment decision criteria are directly related to the firm's overall cost of capital. Chapter 12 pointed out that under the internal rate of return (IRR) method, projects would be accepted if the IRR is greater than the RRR, the overall cost of capital of the firm. If the net present value method is used, the estimated future cash flows from the project are discounted at the RRR of the firm, the overall cost of capital. If the NPV (based upon discounting at the cost of capital) is positive, the project would be accepted.

If the perceived risk of a proposed project (or class of projects) differs from that of the firm, risk-adjusted project RRRs may be used. Adjustments are made from the benchmark of the firm's overall cost of capital. Even if risk-adjustment methods are not related directly to a required rate of return under the certainty equivalent method or analysis employing the CAPM, the aggregate of accepted projects must have a rate of return greater than the estimated overall cost of capital of the firm.[1] Whenever risk differentials must be considered, overall cost of capital still plays a part in the capital investment decision-making process. Otherwise, the fundamental value-maximization objective of the firm would not be accomplished.

Capital structure policy applications

Capital structure policy relates to the use of financial leverage by employing debt and/or preferred stock in the capital structure as well as common stock equity. In selecting the appropriate proportions of such securities to be employed in the capital structure, management seeks to minimize the firm's overall cost of capital while maintaining solvency and financial flexibility. The role of cost-of-capital analysis in accomplishing this objective will be discussed in Chapter 17.

Other financial decision-making applications

Evaluating the feasibility of bond refunding, new borrowing to pay off existing long-term debt, employs the concepts and techniques related to measuring the cost of debt capital. This subject will be discussed in Chapter 18.

When a firm considers leasing assets rather than buying them and borrowing the money to pay for them, cost-of-capital concepts are employed to measure the cost of rental compared to the cost of owning and borrowing. This analysis will be treated in Chapter 19.

In Chapter 6 we discussed in a general way the feasibility of financing various proportions of temporary and permanent working capital requirements through short- and long-term debt. Detailed analysis relative to such decisions requires estimating the cost of debt capital.

In addition, some of the concepts and techniques of cost of capital analysis may be employed in connection with preferred and common stock management (Chapter 20), the use of convertible securities (Chapter 21), retained earnings and dividend policy (Chapter 22), mergers and acquisitions (Chapter 23), and reorganization in bankruptcy (Chapter 24).

[1]This statement is subject to the qualification that the aggregate of the accepted projects does not materially alter the operating risk of the firm. This qualification reflects one of the general assumptions underlying the use of cost of capital as a standard or benchmark in capital investment decision making.

Overall cost of capital—Rationale

This chapter will focus primarily upon the use of cost of capital in connection with capital investment decision making. *The cost of capital of the firm is the rate of return required by the investors who furnish the capital.* This constitutes the required rate of return (RRR) of the firm because if that rate of return were not achieved, investors would not be willing to furnish the capital required. In essence, management acts as an agent of the investors in selecting capital investment projects that investors in the firm are willing to finance. This willingness, in turn, is a function of expected returns to be received by the investors as compensation for foregoing the use of the invested funds (the pure, or riskless, rate of return) and for bearing the risk that those returns will not materialize. This relationship is illustrated in Figure 15–1.

Figure 15–1

To put this concept another way, the cost of capital is *the rate of return the firm must achieve on its aggregate investments for the market value of its securities to remain the same.* Since the firm must obtain its funds directly or indirectly from the securities markets, the rate of return required by investors in its securities is the firm's cost of capital. This probably is obvious if one considers external sources of funds, such as new issues of debt securities (bonds), preferred stock, or common stock. The firm goes to market and must offer potential investors an expected return that will induce them to invest their money.

This market influence may not be so obvious in the case of funds obtained by retaining earnings for capital investment within the firm. Here the influence of the market is indirect. If common stockholders are not satisfied with investments being made by the firm's management, they may sell their stock, thus depressing its market price. Or they may replace the management by exercising their rights to elect the board of directors who are charged with management of the firm. In either event, management will not fulfill its responsibility of maximizing the value of the common stock if it invests in capital projects that do not satisfy the investors required rate of return. Thus, the fundamental concept of cost of capital of the firm involves looking to the securities markets to establish that cost and thereby establish its required rate of return.

Opportunity cost concept

The cost of capital is an *opportunity cost.* In this sense, the cost of capital invested in a given internal capital project is the value of the cash flows foregone by not accepting a competing opportunity to invest at similar risk. The cost of each component of capital of the firm, debt, preferred stock, or common stock equity, likewise is the return that the investor must forego if he or she is to invest in the firm's securities. If an investor is going to buy the bonds of X company, those bonds must offer an interest yield equal to or greater than that offered by other bonds of equal perceived risk available in the market. The same principle applies to preferred stock or common stock. For any particular security at any given time, suppliers and demanders of funds make a market with the price reflecting the required rate of return on the security.

Funds obtained internally through the retention of earnings also have an opportunity cost. If these funds are to be invested in proposed capital projects, the alternative disposition of the funds would be either external investment in the securities of other firms or the payment of dividends to the common stockholders. The opportunity cost of the internal investment is the return that the firm could obtain from external investments at similar risk or that which the stockholder could earn by reinvesting dividends in other securities of similar risk.

This opportunity cost concept will be readily understood if you consider yourself to be the sole owner-manager of a firm. As you consider the opportunities for additional capital investments by your firm, you will weigh the return obtainable on such investments against your opportunity to invest the required funds elsewhere. The cost of the capital required for the internal investment will be the opportunity foregone by not investing the funds elsewhere at similar risk. This will be true whether the funds were generated internally by your firm (retained earnings) or by additional investment of your money in the firm. Since the management of a firm with many investors is in the middleman position illustrated in Figure 15–1, the same opportunity cost concept applies to capital investment decision making of any firm.

The overall cost concept

A firm may obtain capital from several different sources. The most common sources are long-term debt (bonds or term loans), preferred stock, the sale of new common stock, and retained earnings. The cost of capital from each of these sources differs, largely because of the differences in the contractual relationships between the firm and its investors.

The *overall cost of capital* used in capital investment decision making *is a weighted average of the costs of the various components of the capital structure.* The weight applied to each component reflects the proportion of total capital to be raised from each source in the long run.

Computation of the overall cost of capital is illustrated in Table 15–1. This table also indicates the symbols that will be used to designate the cost of the various types of capital. The costs of individual sources of capital are estimated, weights are assigned to each, and the weighted cost is computed by multiplying the estimated cost of each type of capital by its appropriate weight. The weighted average cost is the sum of the individual weighted costs. Inasmuch as both the costs and the weights are estimates, stating that the overall cost of capital of Electrophonics Corporation is 12.7 percent might imply a degree of accuracy that simply does not exist. Perhaps it would be reasonable to say that this cost is probably between 12 and 13 percent.

Table 15–1 Cost of Capital
Electrophonics Corporation

Source of capital	Symbol	(1) Estimated cost (after tax)	(2) Proportion (weight)	(3) Weighted cost (1) × (2)
Debt	K_d	7.2%	40%	2.88%
Preferred stock	K_p	13.5	5	0.68
New common stock	K_c	17.0	20	3.40
Retained earnings	K_r	16.4	35	5.74
Totals			100%	12.70%

Weighted average cost of capital (K) = about 12.7%.

The estimated cost of each component of capital is stated on an *aftertax* basis. It is important that aftertax costs be used because taxes are included in the cash flow estimates developed in appraising proposed capital investment projects.

The relevant cost is the *cost that would be incurred* if the firm raised capital from each source *at the present time* or in the near future. Current costs must be used to evaluate capital investments that will be made now or in the near future. Past costs, such as the cost of bonds issued several years ago that are now on the firm's books, are not pertinent. These *embedded costs* were incurred to finance projects in the past and reflect capital markets of the past. New projects will be financed in the immediate future with funds obtained in the market at costs that may differ substantially from costs prevalent in the past.

Why not specific costs? At first glance one might think that if a given project (or set of projects) could be financed by a particular type of capital, say a bond issue with estimated aftertax cost of 7.2 percent, this cost should be the standard or benchmark for evaluation of the project(s). This appears to be plausible until one realizes that any given firm requires a reasonable balance of different types of capital comprising its capital structure. Otherwise it will either deplete its financing capability or finance at suboptimal costs. (We shall deal with capital structure policy in Chapter 17.)

If the firm utilizes relatively low-cost debt to finance this project (or set of projects), then future projects will require financing from more expensive equity sources—say, retained earnings or a new common stock issue costing about 16 or 17 percent—to bring its capital structure back into balance. If projects with expected returns of 8 or 9 percent (exceeding the 7.2 percent estimated cost of debt capital) were accepted this year, then projects with expected rates of return of 15 percent would be rejected next year because they would have to be financed with capital costing more than that expected return. This would be patently unreasonable. One would be measuring the required rate of return with a rubber yardstick. For this reason, the overall cost of capital (weighted average cost) must be used as the required rate of return of the firm in the capital investment decision-making process. This is the only way that one can be consistent in choosing among projects considered at various times.

Assumptions

Market-determined costs are based upon the required rate of return on riskless capital (the pure interest rate) plus a premium reflecting the perceived risk of the particular security. At any given time the portion of this cost reflecting the riskless rate of return will be the same for all securities of all issuers. (Note that this riskless rate will change through time, reflecting changes in the supply and demand for funds, expectations of inflation, and other factors.) The required premium for risk includes two components, that related to the operating risk of the firm and that related to the financial risk of the security. Two assumptions are necessary if market-determined cost of capital is to be a valid measure of the required rate of return of the firm.

The first assumption is that *the accepted capital investment projects will not materially change the perceived operating risk of the firm.* In other words, the set of projects accepted will have about the same risk as the general risk of the firm. As we have seen in Chapter 14, perceived differences in project risk from the general risk of the firm must be considered in the decision-making process.

The second assumption is *that the financing* of any given project or set of projects *will not materially change the financial risk relating to any particular security* of the firm. As financial risk relates to the financial leverage employed in the capital structure, this assumption generally will be met as long as management consistently maintains the proportionality of various types of capital in the long run. The proportions should be those used in the weighting process employed in estimating the overall cost of capital.

The first step in developing the overall cost of capital of the firm is to estimate the aftertax cost of capital that might be obtained now or in the immediate future from each of the specific sources.

Cost of debt

In the simplest case, in which debt may be issued at par and no flotation costs will be incurred, the before-tax cost of debt is the stated (or coupon) interest rate. For example, assume that a life insurance company has indicated its willingness to lend $5 million to Electrophonics Corporation for 10 years at 12 percent interest. Under this proposed loan Electrophonics will receive the full $5 million and will incur no significant flotation costs (underwriting fees or out-of-pocket costs, such as accounting, legal, clerical or other expenses) to obtain this capital. Electrophonics' only obligation will be to pay 12 percent interest annually on the loan and to pay off the $5 million principal at maturity.

Each 12 percent annual interest payment ($600,000) will be an expense for tax purposes. If Electrophonics is expected to operate at a profit during the next 10 years, and its average marginal income tax rate is expected to be 40 percent, the aftertax cost of this debt capital will be 12 percent times (1 − .40), or 7.2 percent. To put this into a formula, let K_d be the cost of debt capital; i, the interest rate, and t, the estimated marginal income tax rate. Then

$$K_d = i\,(1 - t) \tag{15–1}$$

The same would be true if Electrophonics were to learn from its investment bankers that they could sell a $5 million issue of 12 percent bonds at 102.[2] The investment bankers would charge 1.5 percent, or $75,000, for their services in underwriting and marketing these bonds, and Electrophonics would incur an estimated $25,000 out-of-pocket cost in preparing the

[2]Bonds are quoted in cents on the dollar of principal. Thus a bond quoted at 102 is selling at 102 percent of its principal or face value. As bonds usually are sold in $1,000 denominations, each bond in this example would be sold to the public at $1,020.

issue for sale. The net proceeds to Electrophonics would be $5 million, or 100 percent of the principal amount of bonds. The point is that if the net proceeds to the issuer are equal to the principal amount of the borrowing, no adjustment of the interest cost would be required. The only adjustment necessary to obtain the aftertax cost of capital would be to account for the tax shield created by the interest payments.

In most instances of raising long-term debt capital, however, the computation of cost is not as simple as illustrated above. This is because the net proceeds to the issuer are not the same as the principal amount of the debt. When bonds are issued, the stated interest rate usually is set at the nearest of one eighth of 1 percent of the going market rate for the issue, and the bond is then sold at a discount or premium to "meet the market." If the going market rate were estimated to be 12.41 percent, the bonds would carry an interest rate of 12⅜ percent and be sold at a discount to provide a *yield to maturity* of 12.41 percent to the investors who buy them. Conversely, bonds might be sold at a premium if the going interest rate is estimated to be less than the nearest one eighth of 1 percent. The investment bankers' fees and out-of-pocket costs directly incurred in preparing the issue for sale must then be deducted. The result is that net proceeds to the issuer usually will be different from the principal amount of the bond issue.

When this is the case, the nominal interest rate must be adjusted to a true *cost to maturity* to take into account two factors. First, the interest payment will be the nominal interest rate times the principal amount of the bonds outstanding, 12⅜ percent times $5 million in the above example. Second, although an amount greater or less than the principal will be received upon issue, the principal amount must be paid at maturity. Therefore, the difference must be amortized over the life of the issue.

The simplest way to determine the true cost to maturity is to look it up in a *bond yield table*. Such tables are available in almost any securities broker's office, investment banking house, bank, or library.[3] If, for example a 20-year, 12 percent bond issue of $5 million were to be sold in $1,000 denominations at 99.1 ($991 per bond), investment bankers' fees (called gross underwriting spread) were 1.7 percent ($17 per bond), and out-of-pocket costs were $50,000 (1 percent or $10 per bond), the net proceeds from each bond would be $964 ($991 − $17 − $10), or $4,820,000 from the issue. This would be 96.4 cents on each dollar of principal. Then, one would examine the bond table covering 12 percent bonds to find the yield to maturity of a 20-year bond priced at 96.4.[4] This table would tell us that

[3]Bond yield tables are rather voluminous; some of them are large books. For that reason such tables are not reproduced in this text for your reference.

[4]Bond yield tables are used primarily by investors. Therefore, they refer to *yield* to maturity and to *price* of the bond. We would be using such a table from the standpoint of the issuing firm, thus we seek *cost* to maturity in relation to *net proceeds* from the issue of the bond. The applicable figures are the same, and we will find the true cost to maturity if we simply translate the terminology.

the true cost to maturity is 12.494 percent. This cost can also be obtained by using some hand-held calculators, following the instructions for calculating "yield of bond on coupon payment date."

A simplified formula may be used to approximate the before-tax cost to maturity. Let

K_{dbt} = before-tax cost to maturity;
I = annual interest payment in dollars per bond;
P_n = net proceeds from sale of one bond;
n = time to maturity in years.

Then apply the following equation:

$$K_{dbt} = \frac{I + \left(\frac{\$1{,}000 - P_n}{n}\right)}{\left(\frac{P_n + \$1{,}000}{2}\right)} \tag{15–2}$$

Using the data in our example, we find

$$K_{dbt} = \frac{\$120 + \left(\frac{\$1{,}000 - \$964}{20}\right)}{\left(\frac{\$964 + \$1{,}000}{2}\right)}$$

$$= \frac{\$120 + \left(\frac{\$36}{20}\right)}{\left(\frac{\$1{,}964}{2}\right)}$$

$$= \frac{\$120 + \$1.80}{\$982}$$

$$= 12.4\%$$

Note that this approximation of 12.4 percent compares to the more precise 12.494 percent before-tax cost of debt capital indicated by the bond table. This degree of error may be accepted, as we are dealing with approximations throughout the overall cost of capital analysis.

It would now be necessary to adjust the 12.4 percent approximate before-tax cost of debt capital to an aftertax basis:

$$K_d = .124\ (1 - .40) = .0744 \text{ or } 7.4 \text{ percent}$$

Cost of preferred stock

Although preferred stock does not entail a firm legal contract to pay the stated dividend or face legal action, it does imply that the required preferred stock dividends will be paid if possible. If these dividends were not paid, dividends on the common stock would be restricted and the firm's ability to raise capital from any sources probably would be impaired. Therefore management usually regards the required dividend on preferred stock as a definite obligation. Preferred stock, however, normally does not have a maturity date. Capital raised from this source usually will stay with the firm for an indefinitely long period of time. The dividend requirement of a preferred stock may be stated either as a dollar amount, say a $13 preferred, or as a percentage of its par value, say a 13 percent preferred stock with a par value of $100.

The cost of preferred stock capital is simply the required annual preferred stock dividend per share in dollars divided by the net proceeds per share which could be obtained by issuing new preferred stock.[5] To put this into a formula, let K_p be the cost of preferred stock capital; d_p, the annual preferred stock dividend per share in dollars; and P_n, the net proceeds that could be obtained from the sale of one share of new preferred stock. The net proceeds would be the price to the public less flotation costs. Then

$$K_p = \frac{d_p}{P_n} \tag{15–3}$$

Thus, if new preferred stock with an annual dividend of $13 per share could be sold to the public at $100 per share, with flotation costs of $4 per share and yielding net proceeds to the issuer of $96 per share, the cost of this preferred stock capital would be

$$K_p = \frac{\$13}{\$96} = 13.5 \text{ percent}$$

Preferred stock dividends are not an expense for tax purposes; these dividends must be paid out of aftertax dollars. Therefore no tax adjustment is

[5]There are some preferred stocks, particularly those issued by public utility companies, that are intended to be redeemed through time by the issuer (sinking-fund payments are used to repurchase the outstanding preferred stock). Also some preferred stocks are convertible into common stock. At this time we shall deal only with "straight" preferred stocks, which are not intended to be redeemed. The cost of convertible preferred stocks will be treated in Chapter 21.

appropriate, and the aftertax cost of this preferred stock capital is 13.5 percent.

The estimates of cost of both debt and preferred stock capital are relatively "hard," or definite. The nature of these contracts is such that the payments to be made to investors are definite (in the case of debt) or at least limited (in the case of preferred stock). Up to now there are only two possible sources of error in our estimates. The first is that we had to estimate the future effective marginal income tax rate of the firm during the life of the debt in order to estimate its aftertax cost. Here, in effect, we were forced to estimate the actions of Congress over a considerable number of years into the future. Also, in the case of both debt and preferred stock, we were relying upon the estimated effective interest rate or preferred stock dividend cost obtained from our investment bankers or others involved in providing the capital. Since market conditions are continually in a state of flux, our estimates might err somewhat as compared to the actual rates obtainable when financing could be arranged. These possible errors are slight compared to those associated with estimating the cost of common stock equity.

Cost of common stock equity

The common stock contract involves a residual claim upon the *future* earnings, cash flows, and assets of the firm. The length of the contract is indefinitely long, presumably until the unknown date of liquidation of the firm. Thus a great deal more uncertainty, often bordering upon guesswork, is involved in estimating the ultimate cost of common stock equity. There is no way to avoid this; we simply must "bite the bullet" and get on with establishing estimates that we are willing to rely on in guiding our capital investment decisions. Such uncertainty is something that the financial executive must learn to live with. But it is vitally important that the framework of our thinking, the way that we assemble our guesstimates, is conceptually sound. Two methods by which we may proceed with this task involve the use of the dividend-growth model or the capital asset pricing model.

Dividend-growth model

To develop the logic of the dividend-growth model as a means of estimating the cost of common stock equity capital, we must answer the question, "Why is a stockholder willing to pay a given price for a share of stock?" In other words, what is the basis of valuation of common stock equity? What benefits will a stockholder receive and how does he or she value these benefits?

Valuation of common stock equity The common stockholder is simply a part owner of the firm. If we cut through the corporate shell, we find that the holder of a share of common stock participates on a ratable basis (each share equal to every other share) in the residual earnings and, ultimately, assets of the firm. But the corporate shell does exist; therefore, the holder of a share of common stock will receive from the corporation only the dividends paid on that share. Thus the shareholder benefits *directly* only from the periodic dividends paid on that share during the life of the firm and the final liquidating dividend (if any) at the eventual termination of the firm.

The value of the future dividends paid on a share of stock will be a function of the amount of those dividends and the discount rate required by the market as a rate of return on the investment. Thus, if P is the present price (value) of a share of stock, d_1 is the dividend per share expected to be paid next year, d_2 is the dividend expected to be paid the second year, and so on, and K_e is the discount rate (the required rate of return); the value of that share of stock is determined by the following model:

$$P = \frac{d_1}{(1 + K_e)^1} + \frac{d_2}{(1 + K_e)^2} + \ldots + \frac{d_\infty}{(1 + K_e)_\infty} \qquad (15\text{–}4)$$

If dividends are expected to grow, then the future dividends *(d)* to be included in Equation 15–4 will increase through time. If dividends are expected to grow at a constant compound rate, then the common stock valuation model can be stated as

$$P = \frac{d_0\,(1+g)^1}{(1 + K_e)^1} + \frac{d_0\,(1+g)^2}{(1 + K_e)^2} + \ldots + \frac{d_0\,(1+g)^\infty}{(1 + K_e)^\infty} \qquad (15\text{–}5)$$

where d_0 is the past year's dividend, $d_0\,(1+g)^1$ is the dividend expected next year, etc., and g is the expected constant compound growth rate of the dividends. This model may then be simplified to

$$P = \frac{d_1}{K_e - g} \qquad (15\text{–}6)$$

which is the simplest form of the common stock valuation model based upon dividends and growth.

The general dividend-growth model By rewriting the common stock valuation model to focus upon the cost of common stock equity (K_e) we derive the general *dividend-growth model.*[6]

$$K_e = \frac{d_1}{P} + g \qquad (15\text{–}7)$$

[6]The dividend-growth model was first published by Myron J. Gordon and Eli Shapiro in "Capital Equipment Analysis: The Required Rate of Profit", *Management Science,* October 1956, pp. 102–16. It often is called "the Gordon model".

To illustrate its use, assume that the common stock of Electrophonics Corporation is selling at \$54 per share *(P)*. It expects to pay a dividend of \$4 (d_1) during the ensuing year, and that dividend will increase at a compound rate of 9 percent per year *(g)*. Then

$$K_e = \frac{\$4}{\$54} + .09 = .164$$

and the cost of common stock equity is 16.4 percent. A rate of return of approximately 16½ percent must be earned on the common stock equity if the market price is to be maintained. If Electrophonics invests in projects perceived to have about the same degree of risk as the general risk of the firm, and these projects produce annual benefits to the common stock of less than 16½ percent, the market price of Electrophonics stock will fall. Conversely, if capital investments (assuming equality of risk) produce annual benefits to the common stock greater than 16½ percent, the market price should increase.

Put another way, if *g* should turn out to be, say, 5 percent rather than the estimated 9 percent, the valuation model (Equation 15–6) tells us that the price of the stock should fall from \$54 to about \$35.

$$P = \frac{\$4}{.164 - .05} = \frac{\$4}{.114} = \$35.09$$

Conversely, if favorable capital investment experience should increase the growth rate to 11 percent and the perceived risk of the firm remains unchanged, the market price of the stock should rise to about \$74 per share.

$$P = \frac{\$4}{.164 - .11} = \frac{\$4}{.054} = \$74.07$$

The major practical difficulty in applying the dividend-growth model is estimating the growth rate *(g)*. Estimating the dividend for the coming year involves little uncertainty, and the market price now is definite. But the growth rate of most firms is highly uncertain. If you wish to impress yourself with this fact, try to estimate the compound growth rate in the dividend of some major corporation, say General Motors, Exxon, U.S. Steel, or General Electric. Realize that this estimate is to cover the period from next year until the indefinite date of dissolution of the firm. Then realize that you are going to stake hundreds of millions or perhaps billions of dollars of capital investments on the soundness of your estimate. You will then realize that the task is not only difficult, it is horrendous. Perhaps the responsibilities of making such judgments and staking such large sums of money on their wisdom provides some explanation of the high salaries earned by major corporate executives.

Estimating the growth rate *(g)* Upon what information would the estimate of *g* be based? Past trends might be of some value. If dividends have steadily increased at a given compound rate, say 9 percent, over a considerable number of years, and management sees nothing on the horizon to change that trend, then this growth rate might be projected into the future. But such a projection might also be wide of the mark because economic, political, and social conditions continually change. One might get some help from security analysts, who from the standpoint of investors frequently estimate growth rates. But these people are only human, too, and a good deal of subjectivity enters into their estimating processes.

Sometimes g is estimated by using a formula based upon the assumption that retained earnings will be reinvested to earn a rate equal to the firm's past rate of return on common stock equity. This formula is

$$g = r_e (1 - dpo) \tag{15–8}$$

where

r_e = past rate of return on common stock equity
dpo = the dividend payout ratio (dividends/earnings to common stock)

For example, if Electrophonics' past rate of return on common equity *(r_e)* were 20 percent and its dividend payout ratio *(dpo)* 55 percent, then its growth rate *(g)* would be

$$\begin{aligned} g &= .20 (1 - .55) \\ &= .09 \text{ or } 9 \text{ percent} \end{aligned}$$

This formula assumes that the firm would retain part of its earnings rather than paying them out in dividends only if these retained earnings could be reinvested to earn a rate of return equal to that which has been earned on the common stock equity in the past. If such a rate were achieved, then the rate of growth in earnings per share would be a function of the percentage of the earnings that was retained. Thus, to find the g, the past rate of return on common stock equity is multiplied by one minus the payout ratio, or in other words, the earnings retention ratio. This formula reflects good logic *if* history repeats itself, which it often does not.[7]

Ultimately, management must assemble all relevant information available, such as past growth trends, security analysts' growth estimates, perhaps the g indicated by the above formula, information regarding competitive developments, and overall economic forecasts, and then make a hard judgment. On the theory that several heads are better than one, such judgments usually are made by trying to obtain a consensus, or at least a reasonable compromise, among members of a committee of top-level executives of the firm.

[7]In connection with a research study, the author mechanically applied this formula to estimate the cost of common stock equity capital of a large number of firms. Frankly, some of the results seemed reasonable, but some others simply did not yield cost of capital estimates that made sense. His conclusion is that this formula may be used only very selectively, and that it is not a satisfactory substitute for executives' judgment.

What does the g in the dividend-growth model mean? Does it refer to growth in *earnings* per share, *dividends* per share, or *market price* of the common stock? Theoretically, it refers to the estimated growth in *dividends* per share. But the payment of dividends, in turn, depends upon the availability of earnings. If the dividend payout ratio is expected to remain stable, then the rate of growth of dividends and earnings will be the same. To go one step further, if the price-earnings ratio and the dividend yield remain stable, the stock price should grow at the same rate as earnings and dividends. If all of these conditions indeed apply, it really doesn't make any difference which growth rate one focuses upon because they will all be the same.

Cost of new common stock The general dividend-growth model is based upon the current market price of the common stock. But if a firm is to issue new common stock, it will not receive the market price. First, a new offering of common stock must be *underpriced* in order to be absorbed by the market. When new stock is offered, an additional supply suddenly is thrown upon the market. Normally, with little or no immediate increase in demand, this additional supply will be absorbed only at a lower price than the going market price before the offering. In addition, as the number of shares is increased with no immediate increase in the firm's earnings, earnings per share will be diluted, at least until the new funds can be employed in the firm's operations. Investors' perception of this dilution tends to lower their valuation of the stock. Second, investment bankers' fees and various out-of-pocket costs in floating the issue must be absorbed.

If the percentage reduction in net proceeds from the current market price attributable to both underpricing and other flotation costs is symbolized by f, then the *cost of new common stock capital* (K_c) is

$$K_c = \frac{d_1}{P(1 - f)} + g \qquad (15\text{–}9)$$

In our example, if \$4 is the expected dividend per share next year (d_1), \$54 is the present market price of the stock (P), 9 percent is the estimated growth rate (g), and \$4 per share is the total effect of underpricing, investment bankers' fees, and out-of-pocket costs, then the total flotation costs (f) would be 7.4 percent (\$4/\$54). The cost of new common stock (K_c) would be estimated as shown below:

$$\begin{aligned} K_c &= \frac{\$4}{\$54\,(1 - .074)} + .09 \\ &= \frac{\$4}{\$50} + .09 \\ &= .08 + .09 \\ &= .17 \text{ or } 17\% \end{aligned}$$

This model may be stated another way. If the net proceeds that the firm would receive from the sale of a new share of common stock is symbolized by P_n, then

$$K_c = \frac{d_1}{P_n} + g \tag{15–10}$$

Using the above data to illustrate this version of the model,

$$K_c = \frac{\$4}{\$50} + .09 = .08 + .09 = .17 \text{ (or 17\%)}$$

Cost of retained earnings When a firm retains current earnings rather than paying them out in dividends to its stockholders, this amounts to reinvestment on the stockholders' behalf in additional assets of the firm. This reinvestment would not be justified unless the stockholders' required rate of return were satisfied. Therefore, the *cost of retained earnings* (K_r) should be considered to be identical to K_e, the cost of common stock equity as estimated by using the general dividend-growth model. That model, restated to seek the cost of retained earnings (K_r) is

$$K_r = \frac{d_1}{P} + g \tag{15–11}$$

No underpricing or other flotation costs should be considered because the firm does not have to go to market to obtain these funds—they are already in the firm.

This is the simplest way to estimate the cost of retained earnings. But is it totally valid when we consider that cost of capital is fundamentally an *opportunity cost?* The answer depends upon what the viable alternatives really are. If the viable alternative to *internal* investment is to invest the retained earnings *externally* by directly purchasing securities of similar risk, then this model is valid. The opportunity cost of retained earnings should be considered equal to the required rate of return of the firm's common stockholders because the alternative use of the funds would be external investment at the same risk and required rate of return.

If, however, the only viable alternative to retaining earnings and reinvesting them internally is paying out these earnings in dividends to the stockholders, then estimating the cost of retained earnings may be considerably more complicated. The stockholders' "opportunity" would be to pay personal income taxes on the dividends received, then reinvest the remaining funds in other securities of similar risk. The net value of such dividends to the stockholder would be their gross amount less personal income taxes. A further complication is that inasmuch as the justification for retention of earnings is that value of the stock will be enhanced, then the present value of future capital gains tax resulting from the increased value of the stock when it eventually would be sold should be considered.

As you can see, this application of the opportunity cost concept leads to severe complications. Obviously there are practical problems in employing a model to incorporate the stockholders' tax considerations. How can the average marginal personal income tax rate of the stockholders be obtained? What will be the future holding period before each stockholder will sell his or her stock? This will influence the conversion of the estimated future capital gains tax to its present value.[8]

Nonetheless, understanding that the cost of retained earnings *(K_r)* of some firms may be significantly lower than the general cost of common stock equity *(K_e)* can be of considerable importance. For example, a firm such as Mars (the candy bar maker), the common stock of which is held entirely by the Mars family, might consider its K_r to be substantially lower than K_e because the stockholders presumably are in high tax brackets. Conversely, Hershey Foods (Mars' largest competitor) probably would consider its K_r to be identical to K_e because some 56 percent of its common stock is held by the Hershey School and the Hershey Trust, non-profit charitable organizations that are not subject to any income tax.

Although adjustment to the general model is a viable concept and in some cases should be made in at least an approximate way, we shall assume in future illustrations and problems in this text that the cost of retained earnings *(K_r)* is equal to the unadjusted general cost of common stock equity capital *(K_e)*.

Capital asset pricing model

The capital asset pricing model (CAPM) was introduced in Chapter 14 in connection with recognition of risk differentials among proposed capital investment projects. There it was found to be a valuable concept in that it drew the analyst's attention to the portfolio effects of proposed projects, or sets of projects, in combination with the existing investments of the firm. But as a mathematical tool for appraising capital investment projects, it was found to be of limited use because the efficient markets assumed by the CAPM rarely exist in the markets for real assets.

The market for the common stock of large, publicly held firms traded in large volume daily on a major stock exchange may be considered to be highly efficient. Therefore, when one is looking to the market to establish

[8] If dividends are considered to be the only "opportunity," stockholders' incremental tax rates are known, and their expected holding periods can be estimated, the necessary adjustment to K_e can be made by using the following model. Let t_p equal the marginal personal income tax rate applicable to dividend income of the stockholder, and t_{ga} represent the capital gains tax adjustment. This t_{ga} reflects the tax rate that would have to be paid on a future capital gain adjusted to its present value. Then

$$K_r = K_e\,[1 - (t_p - t_{ga})]$$

the cost of equity capital of a major, publicly held firm, that market may be assumed to reflect a reliable estimate of the required rate of return of its stockholders. In such cases the CAPM is operational as a mathematical tool for estimating the cost of common stock equity *(K_e)*.

Using the CAPM, K_e is estimated as follows:

$$K_e = R_F + (K_M - R_F)\,\beta_j \tag{15–12}$$

where

R_F = the risk-free rate of return (estimated by the yield on short-term U.S. government securities)

K_M = the market rate of return on the common stock market portfolio (estimated by the return on a broadly-based index, such as the Standard & Poors 500)

β_j (beta) = the index of relative responsiveness or co-movement of the rate of return on the firm's common stock relative to the market return

Beta (β) reflects the nondiversifiable (systematic) risk of the firm's common stock relative to that of the market as a whole.[9] A beta of one indicates that the stock's risk is equal to the average risk of the market. A beta of less than one indicates that the stock is less risky than the general market to the degree measured by the difference from one. A beta greater than one indicates that the stock is more risky than the general market. The beta of the common stock of almost any publicly held firm whose stock is traded sufficiently actively for the assumption of an efficient market may be obtained from the *Value Line* service or from the "beta books" published by major brokerage houses.

For example, assume that Electrophonics Corporation is using the CAPM to estimate its general cost of common stock equity *(K_e)*. Short-term U.S. government securities are yielding about 8 percent *(R_F)*. The rate of return on the S&P 500 is 13 percent *(K_M)* and the beta (β) of Electrophonics common stock is 1.7. Then

$$\begin{aligned} K_e &= .08 + (.13 - .08)\ 1.7 \\ &= .08 + (.05 \times 1.7) \\ &= .08 + .085 \\ &= .165 \text{ or } 16\tfrac{1}{2}\% \end{aligned}$$

If Electrophonics' general cost of common stock equity *(K_e)* is estimated to be about 16½ percent, then to obtain its cost of new common stock capital, this figure would have to be adjusted upward to account for flotation

[9]The computation of beta is quite complex and considered beyond the scope of this text. For details as to its computation, the reader is referred to William F. Sharpe, *Investments,* 2d ed. (Englewood Cliffs, N.J.: Prentice-Hall, 1981).

costs. This poses a theoretical problem in that there is no price term *(P)* in the model to adjust to get a net proceeds term (P_n). However, an operational approximation of the cost of new common stock capital (K_c) can be made by multiplying K_e by P/P_n (the current market price of the stock, *P*, divided by the net proceeds that could be obtained from the sale of a new share, P_n). *P* and P_n will be obtained independently of the CAPM.

For example, Electrophonics' K_e is estimated to be 16.5 percent. The market price of its common stock is \$54, and the net proceeds that could be obtained from sale of a new common share is \$50. Its cost of new common stock capital (K_c) may be estimated by multiplying 16.5 percent by \$54/\$50 to obtain 17.8 percent as its K_c. The cost of retained earnings (K_r) would be estimated at 16.5 percent, the same as K_e.[10]

Evaluation of the dividend-growth model versus the CAPM

One might initially think that the capital asset pricing model (CAPM) solves all our problems by establishing a definite, mathematically computed cost of common stock equity capital (K_e). It appears to eliminate the uncertainty associated with estimating the growth rate *(g)* required by the dividend-growth model. But this may be deceptive; the CAPM merely substitutes another set of equally difficult problems and uncertainties associated with its practical use. These difficulties and uncertainties arise largely from the application of a strict mathematical calculation based upon historical data to a changing, uncertain world.

The market rate of return (K_M) is the weighted composite of both dividend yields and changes in market prices of stocks in the chosen index (say, the S&P 500) over some period of time, the assumed "holding period." One obtains rather widely differing figures for K_M depending upon the length of time that holding period extends into the past. How long should the holding period be; one year, three years, five years, or what? The calculation of the beta (β) is fraught with the same problem. It reflects the past comovement of the rate of return (combined changes in market price and dividend yield) of the firm's common stock relative to that of the market index. Over what period of time should that relative responsiveness or comovement be calculated to produce the beta? These two factors, K_M and β, reflect the degree of risk of the firm's stock in the CAPM. Various values of K_M and β may be obtained, depending upon the holding period chosen. Thus, different magnitudes of risk may be indicated, resulting in different estimated costs of equity capital (K_e).

[10]If one wishes to estimate the cost of retained earnings considering the payment of dividends as the only alternative, therefore the opportunity cost, this may be handled in exactly the same manner as discussed earlier in footnote 8 in connection with use of the dividend-growth model.

In addition to this problem, K_e, computed using the CAPM, assumes that the future will duplicate the past, that the responsiveness or comovement of the firm's common stock relative to the market (β) will be the same in the future as it was in the chosen holding period. This is indeed a heroic assumption in a changing socio-political-economic environment.

Blind mechanical application of the model, in effect, entails the judgments that the holding period utilized is correct and that future experience will repeat the past. Of course, the analyst may subjectively modify the data to reflect his or her judgment as to the future. For example, many security analysts modify betas from their computed figures. The point is that both the CAPM and the dividend-growth models require the exercise of similarly difficult subjective judgments. Use of either model requires facing the necessity of making these judgments rather than allowing one to escape them.

The dividend-growth model and the CAPM should yield about the same estimated cost of common stock equity capital (K_e). They both derive K_e from observation of the market but do so in a different format. The dividend-growth model encompasses the concept of risk in a portfolio context indirectly because investors collectively establish the price of the stock in consideration of its nondiversifiable (systematic) risk in the context of its inclusion in their investment portfolios.

Which method should the analyst use in estimating the K_e? The answer depends largely upon availability of information, the nature of the firm, and the market for its stock. Both models are theoretically sound and difficult to apply. If equally sound judgment is applied, they should both yield about the same answer. Perhaps it is worthwhile to have two or more people independently estimate K_e using different models and their own judgment to see whether a consensus is reached.

Finally, one must always recognize that the cost of common stock equity capital is at best a relatively imprecise *estimate* rather than a hard fact. Thus, if K_e is found to be, say, 16.458 percent, forget the final digits and conclude that it is probably about 16½ percent or, perhaps better yet, that it probably lies between 16 and 17 percent. After all, what it actually is will be determined by the fate of the firm from now until its final liquidation at an unknown date. One really would be very lucky to estimate anything so uncertain within one percentage point!

Weighted average cost of capital (WACC)

Early in this chapter we presented the rationale for the use of the estimated *weighted average* cost of capital (WACC) in connection with capital investment decision making. Then we developed the methods of estimating the cost of each component of capital. In our illustration, we estimated that these costs for Electrophonics Corporation were:

Cost of debt	7.2 percent
Cost of preferred stock	13.5 percent
Cost of new common stock	17.0 percent
Cost of retained earnings	16.4 percent

Now we must consider the various alternatives in establishing the appropriate weights to be used in developing the estimated weighted average cost. Should these weights be based upon the book values of each component in the firm's present capital structure, their market values, or the expected proportional use of each of these sources in the future (called target weights)?

Book value weights

Book value weights are derived from the stated values on the firm's current balance sheet. The amounts of long-term debt and preferred stock outstanding are used directly as stated. Common stock includes its stated value (par value times the number of shares outstanding) plus any paid-in or capital surplus reflecting amounts in excess of par value that have been received from the sale of common stock in the past. Retained earnings (or earned surplus) is used as stated. The dollar amounts of each of these types of capital are divided by the total long-term capital of the firm to determine the weights (proportions). The weighted cost of each type of capital is then determined by multiplying its estimated cost by its weight. The sum of the weighted costs of each type of capital is the estimated overall weighted average cost of capital of the firm.

Computation of Electrophonics Corporation's estimated weighted average cost of capital on the basis of book value weights is shown in Table 15–2. The computed cost is rounded to state the estimated weighted average cost

Table 15–2 Weighted cost of capital using book value weights
Electrophonics Corporation

Source of capital	(1) Estimated cost	(2) Book value ($000)	(3) Proportion (weight)	(4) Weighted cost (1) × (3)
Long-term debt	7.2%	$35,000	43.8%	3.15%
Preferred stock	13.5	6,000	7.5	1.01
Common stock	17.0	13,000	16.2	2.75
Retained earnings	16.4	26,000	32.5	5.33
Totals		$80,000	100.0%	12.24%

Weighted average cost of capital (K) = about 12.2%.

of capital at about 12.2 percent to avoid the deceptive appearance of precise accuracy.

There are two advantages of book value weights. The first is the simplicity of their use. The second is their stability. As proportions of the book values of the various types of capital usually change very slowly, the rubber yardstick problem is minimized.

But the use of book value weights has serious theoretical and practical shortcomings. Retained earnings stated on the balance sheet are subject to all of the deficiencies of the accounting process relative to the valuation of assets. Some valuation methods, such as LIFO inventory valuation and historical cost less depreciation valuation of fixed assets, do not purport to reflect current economic values. Thus, as retained earnings is the residual item on the liability and equity side of the balance sheet, it does not purport to reflect the present economic value of this portion of the common stock equity.

A further consideration is that our whole concept of considering the weighted average cost of capital to be the overall required rate of return of the firm rests upon *market* determination of these costs. If we are looking to market-determined costs, then we cannot validly ignore market-determined weights if they differ significantly from those based upon book values.

The final shortcoming of book value weights is the implicit assumption that future capital will be raised in the same proportions from each source as reflected in the present capital structure. In any given case, this may or may not be true. For example, although 7½ percent of Electrophonics' present capital structure is preferred stock, the unfavorable tax position of preferred dividends may have led Electrophonics' management to decide not to use this security in raising future capital. Then why should its cost be considered at all in relation to decisions regarding present and future capital investments to be made by the firm?

Market value weights

The use of current market values of the various securities eliminates some of the shortcomings mentioned above. The market presumably determines more realistic current values than the accounting process. Market value weights also are consistent with market-determined estimated costs of the various types of capital. Therefore, market value weights are theoretically superior to book value weights.

To illustrate the use of market value weights, assume that Electrophonics has 1 million shares of common stock outstanding. The current market price per share is $54. Its long-term debt (bonds) and preferred stock are traded in the market at par. Then its weighted average cost of capital would be estimated as shown in Table 15–3.

Table 15–3 Weighted cost of capital using market value weights
Electrophonics Corporation

Source of capital	(1) Estimated cost	(2) Market value ($000)	(3) Market value (allocated) ($000)	(4) Proportion (weight)	(5) Weighted cost (1) × (4)
Long-term debt	7.2%	$35,000	$35,000	36.8%	2.65%
Preferred stock	13.5	6,000	6,000	6.3	0.85
Common stock	17.0	54,000*	18,000*	19.0	3.23
Retained earnings	16.4		36,000*	37.9	6.22
Totals		$95,000	$95,000	100.0%	12.95%

Weighted average cost of capital *(K)* = about 13.0%.

*Market value of common stock of $54 million allocated one third to common stock and two thirds to retained earnings on basis of book value proportions.

As the market value of common stock does not differentiate between the common stock and retained earnings components, these values must be allocated in a rather arbitrary manner. In this illustration, that allocation was made on the basis of proportions of common stock and retained earnings in the current balance sheet (their book values). These were $13 million common stock and $26 million retained earnings (from Table 15–2). The proportions are one third common stock and two thirds retained earnings. The $54 million market value of the common stock equity ($54 per share × 1 million shares) was then allocated one third to common stock ($18 million) and two thirds to retained earnings ($36 million). The required arbitrary allocation of common stock equity is one of the shortcomings of using market value weights. In practice, this is relatively unimportant because the difference in estimated costs of these two types of capital usually is small; therefore, the net effect of the allocation on estimated weighted average cost of capital is minor.

A more important practical difficulty encountered in using market value weights is the rubber yardstick problem. Market values, particularly of common stocks, change almost continuously. Electrophonics' estimated cost of capital based on market weights is now 13.0 percent. But if the market price of its common stock at the end of next year were only $40 per share, then, because K_e is considerably higher than K_d or K_p, the lower weight applied to it would result in a considerably lower estimate of the overall cost of capital at that time. Conversely, if the market price of the common stock were to rise to, say, $75 per share, then the weighted average cost of capital would be estimated at a considerably higher figure next year. Perhaps these differences would be justified by changed conditions, but frequent changes in the required rate of return does result in undesirable inconsistency in capital investment decision making. Projects with exactly the same estimated rates of return and risk characteristics could be accepted one year and rejected the next.

Still another weakness of market value weights is that their use assumes that future capital will be raised from each source in the same proportions as represented by the present market values. This may or may not be true.

Target weights

Target weights are those representing *the proportions of future long-term financing expected* to be obtained from the various sources of capital. These target proportions refer to averages over the long run. It is recognized that capital is raised in "lumps," that is, capital investment projects undertaken in one year may be financed entirely by retained earnings, those of another year by a combination of, say, a bond issue and retained earnings, and those of still another year financed by an issue of preferred stock. But management usually has decided upon a policy of seeking long-term financing in given proportions over the long run. These target proportions reflect efforts to minimize the overall cost of capital to the firm. (This subject will be treated in detail in Chapter 17.)

To illustrate the use of target weights, assume that the management of Electrophonics Corporation has decided to raise future long-term capital from each source in approximately the following proportions: 40 percent from long-term debt, 5 percent from preferred stock, 20 percent by the sale of new common stock, and 35 percent through retained earnings. Then its weighted average cost of capital would be estimated as shown in Table 15–4. The resulting estimated overall cost of capital *(K)* of about 12.7 percent is the best representation of the required rate of return (RRR) of the firm.

Table 15–4 Weighted cost of capital using target weights
Electrophonics Corporation

Source of capital	(1) Estimated cost (after tax)	(2) Proportion (weight)	(3) Weighted cost (1) × (2)
Debt	7.2%	40%	2.88%
Preferred stock	13.5	5	0.68
New common stock	17.0	20	3.40
Retained earnings	16.4	35	5.74
Totals		100%	12.70%

Weighted average cost of capital *(K)* = about 12.7%.

The great advantage of using target weights is that they reflect the *expected* future financing, which is what we are seeking. In addition, they minimize the rubber yardstick problem, as they will change only infrequently as the firm's capital structure policy might be modified.

Although this is probably the best we can do, there still is a possible shortcoming if the target weights are substantially different from the market value weights. The deficiency stems from the fact that market-determined costs of the individual components of capital presumably reflect investors' appraisal of financial risk based upon observation of the current market proportions. Thus the linkage of costs and weights is imperfect. However, when target weights have been based upon minimizing overall cost of capital in the long run and their difference from market weights is not great, then the only possible deficiency is that their use might result in a slight overestimate of the overall cost of capital *(K)*. Perhaps this slight conservative bias is desirable considering the possible error in the cost estimates, particularly that of common stock equity.

Weighted marginal cost of capital (WMCC)

The weighted average *marginal* cost of capital of a firm is not necessarily independent of the *amount* of capital required during a given period of time. The cost of long-term debt and preferred stock should remain the same regardless of amounts required *as long as the basic capital structure proportions are stable.*[11]

But common stock equity capital consists of two components, new common stock and retained earnings. New common stock has a higher cost than retained earnings, because raising capital from this source entails underpricing and other flotation costs, whereas retaining earnings does not. The amount of retained earnings available during any given period is limited, being a function of the earnings of the period and the dividends to be paid. As long as the total amount of capital required is such that the common stock equity portion of it can be supplied from retained earnings, only the cost of retained earnings will be pertinent as the equity cost.

But when the total capital requirement exceeds this level, then to raise the required funds and still maintain stable proportions of long-term debt, preferred stock, and common stock equity, new common stock will have to be sold to augment the equity. This new common stock capital can be secured only at a higher cost than that of retained earnings.

Therefore, as total capital requirements increase beyond the level where common equity requirements may be financed internally, an increasing proportion of the required common stock equity must be raised through the

[11]Some authors maintain that the requirement of larger issues of long-term debt and/or preferred stock would result in higher costs, therefore increasing the WMCC. We do not believe this is generally true *as long as* the capital structure *proportions* remain unchanged. Financial risks are unchanged and flotation costs as a percentage of funds obtained are, if anything, reduced as issues become larger due to economies of scale in preparing and marketing these securities.

sale of new common stock at the higher cost. The result is that the overall cost of capital begins to curve upward, as illustrated in Figure 15–2. Thus, the *weighted marginal cost of capital* (WMCC) is stable up to the point at which new common stock must be sold and then increases at an increasing rate as the proportion of new common stock capital to retain earnings increases.

Figure 15–2 Weighted marginal cost of capital

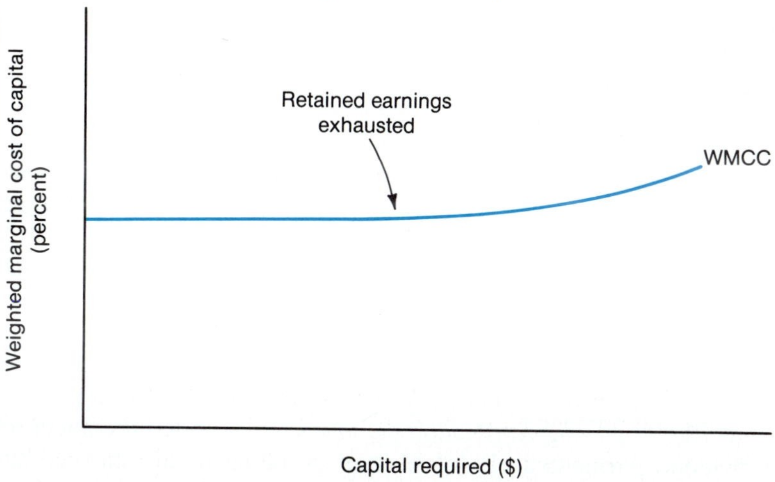

If the amount of capital required to finance investment projects will exceed the level at which required equity capital can be supplied through retained earnings (the point at which WMCC begins to rise), the increased weighted marginal cost of capital (WMCC) must be considered in deciding whether or not the marginal proposed project will be accepted. As the difference between the cost of new common stock capital and retained earnings is relatively small, and the portion of total equity capital expected to be raised through the sale of new common stock usually is relatively small, this consideration appears to be of greater theoretical than practical importance.

Effect of inflation

Inflation has greatly increased the cost of capital. During the period from 1951 to 1973, when the annual rate of inflation varied from negligible to about 5 percent and averaged only 2 or 3 percent, investors apparently either ignored or gave very little emphasis to expected inflation in determining their required rates of return. During the decade since 1973, it has become readily apparent to all investors that the expectation of inflation requires significantly higher rates of return to preserve the purchasing power of their investments as well as provide "real" rates of return sufficient to justify foregoing the use of their funds (the riskless or pure interest rate) and to provide a sufficient premium for bearing risk. In addition to this influence, the expectation of *uncertain* rates of future inflation has increased the magnitude of risk perceived by investors in both debt and equity securities.

With no expectation of inflation, investors were willing to accept, say, 3 percent on a riskless investment (such as a Treasury bill) and required, say an additional 1½ percent in the light of the then-perceived risk of a particular corporate bond. Then 4½ percent was the approximate before-tax cost of debt capital to the corporation issuing the bond. With corporate income tax rates of about 50 percent, this converted to approximately 2¼ percent aftertax cost of debt capital to the firm.

But when the investor, who may still be willing to accept 3 percent as a real rate of return on a riskless investment, adds, say, 2 percent to cover the perceived risk of the corporate bond and 9 percent to compensate for expected inflation (the reduced purchasing power of interest and principal payments), that investor then requires 14 percent rate of return on such a bond. The borrowing corporation perceives the expected tax shield related to dividend payments to be 46 percent, resulting in an estimated aftertax cost of that capital of about 7.6 percent. The cost of preferred stock capital has been increased by inflation expectations in essentially the same way except for the tax adjustment.

The cost of common stock equity capital has been influenced by the same inclusion of an inflation adjustment factor in investors' required rate of return. In addition, the required return on common stock equity has been influenced by the increased perceived risk of operating under conditions of uncertain future inflation rates and the inequality of these rates relative to prices of the firm's inputs and outputs. The net effect of these factors is seen in the fact that although the earnings, dividends, and net assets per share of many corporations had at least doubled during the past decade, their stocks were selling in the market at lower prices in 1981 than those of 10 years previously. Thus, their estimated costs of common stock equity capital were at least twice as great as those of ten years ago.

The great increase in estimated overall cost of capital of most firms has, of course, greatly increased the expected rates of return required for proposed capital investment projects to be acceptable. This, in turn, has tended to result in the gradual erosion of our industrial plants and has adversely affected the ability of many major industries to compete effectively in world markets. The serious economic problems of which we are all aware probably cannot be satisfactorily overcome unless inflation can be controlled at a level much lower than that prevailing during the past decade. How that can be done, of course, is probably the greatest unanswered economic question of our time!

Summary

The required rate of return of the firm is its overall cost of capital. The decision criteria for proposed capital investment projects are directly related to the firm's estimated overall cost of capital. In addition to capital investment decision making, cost-of-capital concepts and methods are used in connection with several other kinds of financial decisions.

The overall cost of capital of the firm is the rate of return required by its investors if the market value of its securities is to remain the same. The cost of each component of long-term capital is estimated by looking to the market to learn what rate of return it would require to furnish each type of capital to the firm now or in the immediate future. Then these costs must be weighted to reflect the proportional expected use of each source in the long run. The weighted average of these costs is the overall cost of capital.

The cost of debt capital (K_d) is a function of the effective interest rate (i) and the expected average income tax rate (t) of the firm over the life of the debt. The formula for calculating it is

$$K_d = i\,(1 - t)$$

If the net proceeds from issuing the debt differ from the principal, the nominal interest rate must be adjusted to the cost to maturity by using a bond yield table, a calculator, or an approximate yield formula.

As preferred stock has no maturity date and dividends paid on it are not an expense for tax purposes, its cost (K_p) is

$$K_p = \frac{d_p}{P_n}$$

where d_p is the preferred stock dividend in dollars and P_n is the net proceeds that could be received from the sale of a share of preferred stock.

Either the dividend-growth model or the capital asset pricing model (CAPM) may be used to estimate the general cost of common stock equity (K_e). The dividend-growth model is

$$K_e = \frac{d_1}{P} + g$$

where d_1 is the dividend expected to be paid during the next year, P is the market price of a share, and g is the estimated annual growth rate of the dividend. If the CAPM is used, K_e may be estimated as follows:

$$K_e = R_F + (K_M - R_F)\,\beta$$

where R_F is the risk-free rate of return, K_M is the market rate of return, and β (beta) is the index of relative responsiveness or comovement of the rate of return on the firm's stock relative to the market return. Either method requires the exercise of considerable judgment.

From K_e the cost of new common stock equity (K_c) may be estimated by adjusting for the required underpricing and other flotation costs. The cost of retained earnings (K_r) may either be considered equal to K_e or it may be estimated by adjusting K_e downward to reflect the personal income tax implications to the stockholders of payment of dividends as an alternative to reinvesting earnings.

Appropriate weights must then be established for each of these types of capital. The alternatives are book weights, market weights, or target weights. As target weights are the best estimates of the proportions of each source of capital that will be used in the future in the long run, their use is preferred.

The weighted marginal cost of capital (WMCC) is not always the same regardless of the amount of capital required during a given period of time. It will remain the same up to the point at which new common stock will have to be sold to maintain a stable proportion of common stock equity to the other types of capital. At that point the WMCC will begin to rise, because the cost of new common stock is greater than that of retained earnings. If acceptable capital investment projects require that this point be exceeded, the rising WMCC must be considered in the decision to accept or reject the marginal project.

Inflation, or more correctly the expectation of inflation, has greatly increased the overall cost of capital of all firms. This increase is the result of investors' requiring rates of return not only to compensate for their foregoing the use of funds and bearing risk but also for absorbing the loss of purchasing power of the dollars to be received in the future. The great increase in the cost of capital during the past decade has had dire repercussions upon the viability of many firms and the economy as a whole.

Questions

1. Explain why the overall cost of capital *is* the firm's required rate of return in capital investment analysis.

2. If the capital investment projects undertaken this year are to be financed entirely by issuing long-term debt, should the cost of this debt be used as the benchmark in deciding which projects to accept? Explain why or why not.

3. The cost of capital is an *opportunity cost.* Explain from the viewpoints of the firm and the investors in its securities.

4. What is meant by the *overall* cost of capital of a firm? In general, why is this cost, at best, a useful estimate rather than a hard fact?

5. What is meant by the statement, "The cost of each component of capital is a *market-determined* rate"? How does this market determination of costs link the actions of the firm to the general economy of a society?

6. Why is the cost of debt generally lower than the cost of other types of capital?

7. Why are the net proceeds from sale of a bond issue usually different from the principal amount of the bonds? What are the implications of this difference? How can one compute the cost of debt capital to account for this difference?

8. If bonds are priced to yield 11 percent and preferred stock to yield 10.5 percent in the market, which has the higher cost to the issuer? Why?

9. State the general *dividend-growth model* used in estimating the cost of common stock equity (K_e). What is the most difficult term in that model to estimate? Explain why.

10. Indicate three methods that might be used to estimate the growth rate, g, in the dividend-growth model. Discuss the problems in using each.

11. What would be the probable effect of each of the following on the cost of capital of most firms? (Trace the logic of your answers.) (Consider each independently.)

- *a.* The Congress lowers corporate income tax rates.
- *b.* The Federal Reserve takes action to tighten the money supply.
- *c.* Prices in the stock market move sharply lower.
- *d.* Congress approves a budget that will result in large deficit spending (larger expenditures than revenues).

12. Under what conditions is growth (g) in dividends, in earnings, and in common stock price the same?

13. Do the costs of new common stock capital and retained earnings differ? Why or why not?

14. How is the cost of common stock equity capital estimated under the capital asset pricing model (CAPM)?

15. What characteristics must exist in the market for a firm's common stock for the CAPM to yield a valid estimate of the firm's cost of common stock equity? What is the major judgment required in using the CAPM to estimate the cost of common stock equity?

16. Discuss the difference between *book value* and *market value* weights. What are the advantages and disadvantages of each?

17. What are *target* weights? What are the advantages and possible disadvantages of their use?

18. How may the weighted *marginal* cost of capital (WMCC) differ from the weighted *average* cost of capital (WACC)? Under what conditions is the difference pertinent in capital investment analysis?

19. How does inflation affect the cost of capital?

Problems

1. *a.* Valtech Corporation has been offered a 10-year loan of $4 million by the American Life Insurance Company at an interest rate of 12½ percent. Valtech estimates its average marginal tax rate for the next 10 years to be 45 percent. What is Valtech's cost of long-term debt capital (K_d)?

   b. If the insurance company informed Valtech that it could make the loan only at a 3 percent discount from the principal value (lending $3.88 million with $4 million payable in 10 years), what would be Valtech's approximate cost of long-term debt capital (K_d)? (Use the simplified approximate cost-to-maturity formula.)

2. Ravenwood Corporation currently has outstanding $5 million of 6¾ percent bonds due in 1988. Its investment bankers, Bottemly Brothers, indicate that they could sell a new issue of 12¼ percent 20-year bonds to the public at 99. Bottemly estimates that the investment bankers' fees would be 2 percent of the principal amount and Ravenwood would incur out-of-pocket costs equal to about one half of 1 percent of the principal amount. Estimate Ravenwood's cost of debt capital, using the simplified approximate cost-to-maturity formula.

3. Oxbridge Corporation could issue 12 percent preferred stock to the public at its par value of $100 per share. Investment bankers' fees and out-of-pocket costs would equal $2.50 per share. What is Oxbridge's cost of preferred stock capital (K_p)?

4. Estimate the cost (K_p) of each of the following preferred stocks:

	Per share		
Issuer	Par value	Annual dividend	Flotation costs
Company A	$100	$10.50	$4.00
Company B	$ 50	$ 6.25	5%
Company C	$ 70	12%	7%

5. The Jordan Company is estimating its cost of common stock equity capital. Jordan expects to pay dividends of $1.20 per share next year. Its stock is traded in the market at $15 per share. Management estimates that both earnings and dividends per share will increase about 7 percent annually in the future.

a. Estimate Jordan's cost of retained earnings (K_r).

b. Jordan could sell additional stock to the public at $13.50 per share. It would incur investment bankers' fees and out-of-pocket costs equal to $1 per share in connection with this offering. Estimate Jordan's cost of new common stock capital (K_c).

6. The Barnsley Food Company has paid the following dividends on its common stock during the past six years while maintaining a payout ratio of approximately 55 percent:

Year	Dividends
1982	$1.47
1981	1.34
1980	1.21
1979	1.12
1978	1.02
1977	.94

Barnsley's management expects the past trend in earnings and dividends to continue and is planning to pay $1.61 in dividends during 1983. Its common stock is selling for $30 per share in January 1983. Barnsley's investment bankers indicate that new common stock could be sold to net about $27 per share after flotation costs.

a. Estimate the growth rate in dividends (g).

b. Estimate the cost of retained earnings (K_r).

c. Estimate the cost of new common stock capital (K_c).

7. Westmor Corporation uses a formula based on the past return on common stock equity and its dividend payout ratio to estimate its dividend growth rate (g). Its rate of return on common stock equity over the past five years has averaged 15 percent, and its target payout ratio is 60 percent of earnings.

a. Estimate Westmor's dividend growth rate (g).

b. Using the dividend-growth model, estimate the cost of retained earnings (K_r) if Westmor's common stock is selling at $25 per share and dividends of $2 per share are planned for next year.

c. If Westmor would incur flotation costs equal to 7 percent of the current market price in selling additional stock, what is its estimated cost of new common stock capital (K_c)?

8. The Morrison Company, a large international manufacturing and marketing firm, uses the capital asset pricing model (CAPM) to estimate its cost of common stock equity (K_e). The current interest yield on Treasury bills is

9.2 percent and the return on the S&P 500 over a holding period considered to be valid has been 14 percent. Morrison's beta (β) for the same holding period is 1.3.

a. Estimate Morrison's cost of retained earnings capital (assuming $K_r = K_e$).

b. If Morrison's common stock is currently selling for $58 per share, and net proceeds from a new issue would be $54 per share, what is Morrison's estimated cost of new common stock capital (K_c)?

9. Edinboro Corporation's current balance sheet indicates the following capital structure:

8% Bonds due 1986	$40 million
9% Preferred stock	6 million
Common stock (6 million shares)	60 million
Retained earnings	32 million
Total capital structure	$138 million

Edinboro's outstanding securities are currently quoted in the market at:

	Market price
8% Bonds	89½
9% Preferred stock	78
Common stock	24

Edinboro's management has established a capital structure policy of financing approximately 25 percent of future long-term capital requirements by issuing long-term debt and 75 percent from equity sources. It believes that two thirds of its equity requirement can be obtained through retained earnings and that the remainder will be financed by selling new common stock. Edinboro does not plan to issue preferred stock in the future because of the unfavorable tax status of preferred dividends compared to interest on bonds.

a. Determine Edinboro's book value weights.

b. Determine its market value weights.

c. Determine its target weights.

10. Maxim Corporation currently could issue 11½ percent bonds to mature in 20 years at $1,000 per bond. Flotation costs would be 3 percent of the principal amount. It could also issue 12 percent preferred stock at par of $100 per share, with net proceeds after flotation costs of $96 per share.

Maxim's common stock is currently selling at $50 per share. It plans to pay dividends of $3.50 per share on this stock during the next year. Management believes that the firm's earnings and dividends per share will increase in the future at a compound rate of 8 percent. Flotation costs equal to 5 percent of market price will be incurred when Maxim sells additional common stock.

Management has established a policy of financing 35 percent of future capital requirements by issuing additional long-term debt, 5 percent by issuing preferred stock, and the remainder by common stock equity. Two thirds of the additional common stock equity will be provided by retained earnings. The remaining one third of common equity requirements will be supplied by selling additional common stock.

Maxim expects its future marginal income tax rate to average 40 percent.

a. Estimate Maxim's cost of long-term debt capital (K_d). (Use the simplified approximate cost-to-maturity formula.)

b. Estimate its cost of preferred stock capital (K_p).

c. Estimate its cost of retained earnings (K_r).

d. Estimate its cost of new common stock capital (K_c).

e. Establish appropriate weights for each component of the capital structure.

f. Estimate Maxim's overall cost of capital (K). (Assume that target weights are similar to current market value weights.)

Part Five
Long-Term Financing

Chapter 16
Raising Funds in the Capital Markets

The next seven chapters will deal with the long-term financing of the firm. We shall study capital structure planning and policy in Chapter 17, the various debt, quasi-debt, and equity instruments used in raising long-term funds in Chapters 18 through 21, and finally internal equity financing through retained earnings in Chapter 22. But first we must familiarize ourselves with the institutional structure of the financial markets from which long-term financing may be obtained. Where do we go to get long-term funds? How do we get there? Where does the supply of funds come from and what factors influence the terms on which we may obtain them?

This chapter will first establish the role of financial markets in a capitalistic economic system. Then the primary capital markets will be examined, considering in some detail the investment banking function in raising capital for business firms. The alternative of direct placement of securities will be considered. Secondary markets will be discussed. Finally, government regulation of the capital markets will be treated.

Role of financial markets

In the most primitive society, each caveman who is to survive must obtain on a day-to-day basis sufficient necessities of life. The first step in evolution toward a capitalistic society occurs when some persons are able to accumulate a surplus over daily needs, making time available to fashion crude implements, such as spears or fishhooks, to increase their productivity. These implements are *capital assets* in their purest form. The next step is the development of *exchange* through barter, whereby the surplus production made possible by the use of capital assets may be traded among individuals of the society. Then some crude form of *money* will evolve as a generally accepted medium of exchange and a store of value.

The next step in economic development will be the emergence of a *financial market.* Some individuals (let us now call them economic units), the savers, will constitute the supply side of this market. They will be willing to lend or invest their surplus money, savings, to other economic units who need these funds and are willing to pay a price, interest, for the use of them. The borrowers comprise the demand side of this market. When a trade takes place, a financial transaction, a *financial asset* comes into existence in the hands of the saver and a *financial liability* of the borrower is created. Holders of financial assets may then trade these assets for consumer goods, capital assets, or other financial assets.

Eventually, a modern capitalistic economic society emerges with millions of economic units comprised of households, governmental bodies, and business firms that hold real assets (including capital assets) and financial assets and owe financial liabilities. The net balance of assets owned in excess of financial liabilities constitutes their equity capital or net worth.

Note the vital importance of financial markets in creating a modern industrial society. These markets provide *fluidity of capital* by making possible the transfer or allocation of savings in the economy to the demanders. Without financial markets, the ability of each economic unit to acquire real assets (such as inventories, plant, and equipment for businesses; roads, bridges, dams, and schools for government; or housing, automobiles, and so on for households) would be limited to the savings of that unit. Economic development by the society would be stifled, resulting in much lower productivity and wealth accumulation.

A *financial market* is anywhere that suppliers and demanders of funds meet, create or exchange financial assets and liabilities, and establish a price of the financial instruments exchanged. The price mechanism of the financial markets allocates the savings of society to the demanders of funds in a highly efficient fashion.

Financial intermediaries

As financial markets develop in a society, various financial intermediaries are created to facilitate the flow of savings to the ultimate demanders of funds. A *financial intermediary* is an institution that pools the savings of many economic units and reinvests these accumulated funds in debt or equity securities. The principal financial intermediaries in the United States are commercial banks, savings and loan associations, life insurance companies, pension funds, mutual savings banks, credit unions, and various types of investment companies or mutual funds.

The process of intermediation, the type of savers whose funds are pooled, and the kind of investments made varies among these institutions. For example, savings and loan associations, mutual savings banks, and credit unions solicit funds in relatively small amounts from individual savers and invest most of these pooled funds in real estate mortgages and consumer installment loans. The primary function of life insurance companies is writing insurance policies providing death benefits to the beneficiaries and/or retirement annuities to the policyholders. But by collecting premiums over many years to provide these benefits, life insurance companies accumulate large policyholders' reserves, which are invested mainly in real estate mortgage loans, government and corporate bonds, and some preferred and common stocks. Pension funds pool the contributions of employers and employees and invest those funds largely in debt securities of both government and corporate issuers and in preferred and common stocks. Investment companies, such as mutual funds, sell their securities to individual savers and invest the pooled funds in portfolios of securities ranging from common stocks of various investment characteristics to highest-quality money-market instruments.

Some financial intermediaries directly lend funds to individuals, governmental bodies, and business firms. Others purchase financial instruments (securities) in the financial markets. In either case, intermediaries tend to increase the efficiency of financial markets by pooling funds, and by providing portfolio diversification and professional management in the investment of those funds. They are able to concentrate greater information and analytical capability in the investment process than would be the case if each individual saver were to make his or her separate small investments directly.

The capital markets

Financial markets are classified rather arbitrarily as money markets or capital markets according to the time to maturity of the financial instruments exchanged. *Money markets* are those dealing with instruments maturing within one year. In the broad sense, the money markets include the short-term lending activities of such institutions as commercial banks and finance companies. These were discussed in Chapters 9 and 10. In the narrow sense, the term money markets designates the markets for highest-quality short-term securities, such as Treasury bills, federal agency securities, commercial paper, and negotiable certificates of deposit. We have discussed these markets in Chapter 7 in connection with management of the firm's marketable securities portfolio.

Our present interest is in the capital markets (often called securities markets).[1] The term *capital markets* refers to the markets for *long-term* securities, such as bonds, preferred stock, convertible securities, and common stock. With the exception of retained earnings, funds comprising the capital structure of the firm are raised in the capital markets.

A capital market exists wherever such securities are issued or traded. Thus AT&T enters the capital markets when it issues $300 million worth of bonds or 10 million shares of additional common stock. Likewise Jane and Joe's Restaurant, Inc., enters the capital markets when it borrows $50,000

[1]The term *capital* is used in a variety of ways. Economists consider capital to be wealth used in the production of additional wealth. In that sense they refer to the factors of production as land, labor, and capital. In a broader sense they sometimes also include consumer durable goods such as housing, automobiles, and major appliances. Accountants and lawyers sometimes use the word *capital* to mean the owners' equity in the firm. We have in preceding chapters used the term *capital* to mean either long-term investment in real assets of the firm (as in capital investments decision making) or the long-term financing of the firm (as in the cost of capital). Here the term *capital* refers to long-term financial instruments, such as bonds, preferred stock, and common stock, which are issued by business firms, governmental bodies, or (rarely) individuals to providers of long-term funds. Thus capital in this sense provides the funds to be used to acquire real assets, such as plant and equipment, inventories, and so on.

from its bank by placing a 20-year mortgage on the restaurant or when it sells additional common stock for $15,000 to Dr. Smith, whose office is down the street. Also Mary Johnson enters the capital markets when she asks her broker to sell 50 shares of AT&T common stock she owns and to buy 100 shares of Coca-Cola stock for her account. Prudential Life Insurance Company also enters the capital markets when it invests $10 million in the bonds being issued by AT&T or $5 million in U.S. Treasury bonds.

Capital markets are classified as primary and secondary markets. *Primary capital markets* are those related to *the issue of new securities* by business firms, governmental bodies, or other organizations to raise new funds. The sale of additional bonds or stock by AT&T referred to above involves the primary capital markets. *Secondary capital markets* relate to the *trading of already outstanding securities* among investors. For example, Mary Johnson's sale of her AT&T stock and purchase of Coca-Cola stock were secondary market transactions. Secondary markets provide liquidity to investors by allowing them to manage their portfolios by buying or selling outstanding securities before their maturity.

Primary capital markets

The primary capital markets are relatively unstructured in that there is no central organized marketplace where new issues of securities are sold to investors. Small business firms, such as Jane and Joe's Restaurant, must seek out individual or institutional investors in their communities. Jane and Joe found their local bank willing to make the mortgage loan and Dr. Smith down the street willing to buy some stock in their restaurant. Larger firms usually enter the primary capital markets through investment bankers who operate essentially as merchant middlemen by marketing new securities issues to individual and institutional investors. Thus, AT&T's $300 million bond issue would go to market via the investment banking mechanism. Its 10 million share common stock offering might be handled either through investment bankers or by a direct offering of the additional stock to its present stockholders. Another middle-sized to large firm might directly place its $10 million bond issue with one or a group of life insurance companies.

The institutional mechanisms through which firms gain access to the primary capital markets are of great interest to business financial executives. They must know where to go for long-term funds, how to select an appropriate investment banker, and how that investment banker operates to place the firm's securities with investors.

Competition for funds in the primary capital markets

The financial manager is interested in the competition among demanders of funds for the savings available in capital markets. Who else will be demanding funds in these markets and how will their demands influence the availability and cost of long-term funds to business firms?

In recent years the total amount of new long-term securities issued, excluding household borrowings such as home mortgage and consumer installment debt, has been on the order of $160 to $180 billion per year. New securities issued by corporations accounted for only about one third of this financing. The other two thirds represented long-term borrowings by the U.S. government, various federally sponsored credit agencies, and state and local governmental bodies. Although it is hoped that the proportion of demand in the capital markets by governments will decline in the future, the financial manager must recognize that demand by governmental bodies probably will continue to exceed that of business corporations. As long as that is true, governmental transactions will tend to have a greater influence upon the availability and cost of funds in the capital markets than the competition among corporations for these funds.

Within the corporate sector, over three fourths of the dollar amount of new financing in recent years has been obtained through the sale of bonds. Some 5 or 6 percent reflects the sale of preferred stock, nearly all of this by public utility companies. Less than 20 percent of new corporate financing in the capital markets has been obtained through the sale of common stock. Thus, *less than 7 percent* of the total dollar amount of new securities sold in the primary capital markets in recent years reflects the sale of new common stock by business firms. This is indeed a sobering statistic for a highly industrialized nation operating under a capitalistic economic system.

The investment banking process

An *investment banker* (also called an investment banking firm or investment banking house) is a financial middleman engaged in raising long-term funds for business firms and governmental bodies by arranging the sale of their securities to investors.[2] The basic function of the investment banker in business finance is to bridge the gap between the firm requiring long-term funds to invest in real assets (such as inventories, plants, and equipment)

[2]The term *investment banker* is a misnomer in that such firms neither *invest* by holding securities for a long term nor engage in a *banking* business in the sense of accepting deposits from the public and making loans. There is no such thing as an investment *bank*. The term probably originated in the period prior to 1933 when many banks operated as both commercial and investment bankers. The Banking Act of 1933 prohibits commercial banks from doing any investment banking business except in municipal bonds. In most European countries, banks have much wider latitude in their financial activities and continue to engage in the investment banking business.

and the savers or financial intermediaries who invest in long-term financial assets.

Investment banking functions

The usual functions of investment bankers are to (1) originate securities issues, (2) underwrite the issues by guaranteeing their sale in the primary capital markets, (3) manage the distribution of these securities to the ultimate investors, and (4) advise their corporate clients regarding long-term financial matters.

Origination Nearly all securities offerings by industrial corporations are originated by negotiation between officers of the issuing firm and an investment banking house. Once the firm's management has determined that long-term funds are needed and contact with an investment banker has been established, negotiations begin.[3]

Initial discussions Initial discussions (sometimes called preunderwriting conferences) are concerned with determining the proper amount of capital to be raised, the security to be issued, and the particular terms of that issue. The value of these discussions to the issuer derives largely from the investment banker's intimate knowledge of the capital markets. He or she is in daily contact with these markets and recognizes the ability of the markets to absorb a new issue. Thus, if it were determined that a $10 million bond issue were to be floated, the investment banker would advise as to the specific provisions that would be required for the issue to be absorbed by the market. Although the exact interest rate, price to the public, and required compensation for performing the investment banking functions probably would not be crystallized at this point, the investment banker would provide fairly close approximations of these. If it were determined that common stock would be issued, then the approximate number of shares, underpricing required, and whether or not the stock would be offered under privileged subscription to the present stockholders would be determined.

Investigation As the preliminary discussions proceed to the point where it appears that a security offering will be made, the investment banking firm will begin its investigation of the issuing corporation and an appraisal of the security to be offered. This investigation serves two purposes. The first is to assure the investment banking firm that its reputation with other investment bankers and investors will not be tarnished by selling a security that does not satisfy investors' expectations. The second is that the information gathered will be required in registering the issue with the Securities and Exchange Commission (SEC).

Various professional specialists will be brought into this investigation as required. Certified public accountants audit the books of the issuing cor-

[3]Selection of an appropriate investment banker will be treated in a later section of this chapter.

poration and develop the required financial statements. Lawyers investigate the legal aspects of the issue and develop the required documents and opinions. If the issue involves financing of an engineering project, consulting engineers may be retained to render opinions regarding the technical feasibility of the project. If mineral resources are involved, independent geologists estimate the mineral reserves, and perhaps mining engineers appraise the technical feasibility of extracting those minerals. The investment bankers will analyze the financial condition, operating results, and future prospects of the company.

Negotiation When the preliminary discussions and the investigation have proceeded to the point that it is quite definite that a security flotation will take place, officers of the issuing corporation and the investment banking firm will negotiate the terms of the offering. This involves determining the precise amount and terms of the security to be offered, including in the case of a bond issue the maturity, specific security, if any, sinking-fund or other repayment provisions, call provisions, and the various protective clauses to be included in the bond indenture.[4] *The gross underwriters' spread,* which is the difference between the price at which the security will be offered to the public and the amount to be remitted to the issuing corporation, will be determined by negotiation. This spread, plus various out-of-pocket costs to be paid by the issuing corporation, constitutes the flotation cost of the issue.

The financial manager of the issuing corporation must understand that the investment banker, as a merchant middleman, may be somewhat biased in favor of terms of the security that will tend to minimize the risk of selling the issue to investors and in favor of maximizing the underwriters' spread. For this reason the financial manager must negotiate regarding these terms and provisions for the benefit of his or her firm. Although this negotiation takes place on a friendly basis, there frequently are differences of opinion or possible trade-offs. Bargaining may result in terms of the security and underwriting arrangements more favorable to the issuing corporation than those initially proposed by the investment banker. The exact price at which the security is to be offered will not be crystallized at this point. Its determination will be delayed until the latest possible time before the offering is to take place.

When negotiations are completed, a tentative *underwriting agreement* will be signed. This agreement will contain "out clauses," which allow either party to withdraw in the event of specified future developments that might jeopardize the offering.

Registration Under the Securities Act of 1933 nearly all new securities publicly offered in interstate commerce must be registered with the Securities

[4]These arrangements and provisions will be discussed in detail in Chapter 18 dealing with long-term debt.

and Exchange Commission (SEC). The issuing corporation must file a *registration statement* with the SEC, disclosing *all material facts regarding the security, the issuing corporation, and the underwriting arrangements* under which the security is offered.[5] Although the registration statement technically is filed by the issuing corporation, it is developed largely by the investment banker.

The registration statement may be a rather voluminous document; it must be meticulously prepared, because the potential liability is great to the issuing corporation, its officers, and the investment banker if it contains a misstatement or fails to state a material fact. Twenty days ordinarily must elapse after the filing before the securities may be offered for sale. During this period the staff of the SEC examine the statement for errors, omissions, or evidence of fraud. Often the SEC requests the filing of supplementary information, which further delays the effective date of the registration statement.

A part of the registration statement is the *prospectus,* which is a document that must be furnished to each prospective buyer of the securities. The prospectus contains the necessary information to inform the buyer of all material facts regarding the issue. During the waiting period between filing and the effective date of the registration statement, a *preliminary prospectus* may be distributed to securities dealers and prospective investors. This preliminary prospectus does not contain pricing information or the issue date. It is called a "red herring" because printed in the left margin in red ink is a statement indicating that the information is tentative only and that it does not constitute an official offer to sell the securities. Only after the registration statement has become effective can the official prospectus containing all information be offered to the investing public.[6]

In addition to registration with the SEC, the investment banker must qualify the offering under the securities laws of the various states in which it is to be offered for sale. These laws vary greatly among the states, ranging all the way from requiring notice of the offering to empowering their securities commissions to prohibit the sale of securities that are deemed to be highly risky.

Underwriting The term *underwriting* means assuming the risk. When a new issue of securities is underwritten, investment bankers agree to pay the issuing corporation the net proceeds (price to the public less the gross underwriting spread) on a given closing date, usually a few days after the

[5]Other aspects of SEC regulation will be discussed near the end of this chapter.

[6]At this writing, the SEC is allowing on a trial basis simplification of registration requirements for new issues of securities by large corporations whose securities are listed on major securities exchanges and which have regularly filed required reports for at least three years with the SEC. This allows such corporations to file a *shelf registration* in advance, which may become effective at a subsequent date upon filing a brief amendment.

registration statement is effective and the offering begins. Thus, the underwriters assume the risk that the offering will be successful.

During the origination period described above, the originating investment banker will form an *underwriting syndicate* by inviting other investment banking firms to participate in bearing the risk of the issue. At this point the "originating house" becomes the "manager of the underwriting syndicate." Depending largely upon the size of the issue, the underwriting syndicate may include only a few investment banking firms or perhaps one or two hundred of them. Each agrees to underwrite a given portion of the issue and to pay for that portion at the closing date. Each underwriter assumes the risk of the successful sale of its portion of the offering. For example, if the offering is a $10 million bond issue, the manager of the syndicate may underwrite $1.5 million of the bonds (15 percent of the issue), 10 other houses may underwrite $500,000 each, and 15 other houses underwrite amounts varying from $400,000 to $50,000 each. If the bonds are to be sold at par and the gross underwriting spread is 4 percent, then each of the houses underwriting $500,000 of bonds must pay $480,000 on the closing date whether or not the bonds have been sold.

There are three reasons that the originating house forms an underwriting syndicate rather than bearing all of the risk of an issue itself. First, it may not have $9.6 million available to risk on the securities offering. Second, even if it does have the financial capability, the originating house does not wish to have all its eggs in one basket. By laying off all but $1.5 million of the bonds to other members of the syndicate, it limits its risk on this particular issue and frees part of its funds to participate in other underwritings. Thus, it diversifies its risks by participating in say 8 or 10 other offerings at the same time. Third, it wishes to be invited to join the syndicates formed by other investment banking houses and recognizes that it will be invited largely in accordance with its inviting other houses to participate in the deals which it originates. In other words, there is an element of reciprocity. Notice, however, that the originating house normally underwrites a somewhat larger portion of the issue than it asks other syndicate members to take. This shows its good faith that the offering is expected to be successful.

The members of the underwriting syndicate sign the *purchase agreement* with the issuing corporation and the *agreement among the underwriters,* binding each other and authorizing the manager of the syndicate to act for them in forming a selling group, conducting market stabilization efforts, and otherwise to act on behalf of the syndicate in managing orderly distribution of the securities.

At a time just before the registration statement is to be effective, ordinarily after the close of the securities exchange on the day before the offering is to be made, members of the underwriting syndicate and the major officers of the issuing corporation hold a meeting at which the syndicate members may ask any last-minute questions of the corporate officers, the current condition of the market is appraised, and the offering price of the security is agreed upon. Then the final documents are signed, information is dispatched for overnight printing into the prospectus, advertising of the issue is placed, and the offering is announced to the press.

If the offering is highly successful, all of the securities may be sold within hours, or sometimes minutes, of the "opening of the book" by the managing underwriter on offering day. But, lest one get the impression that securities underwritings yield quick profits for doing almost nothing, one must understand that sometimes securities offerings turn sour and the underwriters are stuck with substantial losses. For example, a $1 billion IBM bond offering went to market on Friday, October 4, 1979. The bond market weakened that Friday and only about $600 million of the bonds were sold. Over the weekend the Federal Reserve Board announced policies designed to tighten credit. The bond market fell the following week. An underwriting syndicate of 227 houses, managed by Salomon Brothers and Merrill Lynch, lost almost $10 million when it became necessary to "break the syndicate" and allow each underwriter to sell its unsold bonds in the market.[7] This illustrates what underwriting is all about. IBM received the net proceeds of this issue, $987 million, on the closing date. Many underwritings are successful and the underwriters make money on them. But occasionally some are not. The underwriters must take their losses in stride.

A related aspect of underwriting is the market stabilization effort of the managing underwriter. Often the manager places bid orders in the secondary market at the offering price. If there is a slight downward pressure on the market during an offering, the market will be stabilized at the offering price through the execution of these buy orders. But such efforts are successful only if the selling pressure is slight and temporary. If the pressure is great and protracted, the underwriters find themselves buying such large quantities of the securities that the effort cannot be sustained. As a result, they may take still greater losses by being stuck with a larger portion of the securities than if there had been no stabilizing effort. Such measures are far from foolproof in assuring successful underwriting.

Distribution Members of the underwriting syndicate that have extensive retail facilities, such as the major brokerage houses, usually will sell the full amount of securities they underwrite through their own sales organizations. Other underwriters, who may have greater financial resources than retail selling facilities, wish to have all or part of the securities they have underwritten sold by other securities dealers. Therefore, the managing underwriter usually will form a *selling group* in order to broaden the market coverage of the retail selling effort. In a large national security offering, the selling group may include several hundred securities dealers scattered about the country. For example, 80 firms may be members of the under-

[7] *The Wall Street Journal,* October 12, 1979.

writing syndicate bearing the risk and distributing part of the issue, while another 300 firms may be members of the selling group distributing the remainder of the securities.

Under the selling agreement, each member of the selling group is granted a *selling concession,* which is less than the gross underwriting spread and provides compensation only for its selling efforts, not for bearing any risk. While the gross underwriting spread may be 4 percent, or $40 per bond, the selling concession may be only 2 percent, or $20 per bond. In addition, a small concession, of perhaps .5 percent or $5 per bond, may be offered to any member of the National Association of Securities Dealers (NASD) that takes an accepted order for the security. By allowing this concession, the distribution facilities are broadened from the retail efforts of the members of the underwriting syndicate to include nearly all of the securities dealers in the country.

Investment bankers' compensation To illustrate the compensation of the various parties involved in the distribution of a new securities issue, assume that the Marlowe Corporation negotiates a $10 million bond issue with Dean Witter as the managing underwriter. The gross underwriting spread is 4 percent, or $400,000; therefore, the net proceeds to Marlowe are $9.6 million. Under the agreement among the underwriters, Dean Witter is to receive $50,000 as a management fee to compensate it for performing the origination function and its services as manager of the underwriting syndicate, leaving $350,000, or 3½ percent of the issue, to compensate for underwriting and selling. Dean Witter underwrites $1.5 million of these bonds, and 25 other members of the underwriting syndicate underwrite various amounts ranging from $500,000 down to $50,000. If Dean Witter sells all of the bonds it underwrites, it will receive an additional $52,500 (3½ percent of $1.5 million) as compensation for its underwriting and distribution services. A selling group of 50 securities dealers is formed, with a selling concession of 2 percent or $20 per bond.

Each member of the underwriting syndicate will net 3½ percent, or $35 per bond, for the bonds it sells, but only 1½ percent, or $15 per bond, for the securities it underwrites but does not sell. Those bonds it does not sell will be allocated to members of the selling group. Thus, E. F. Hutton, which underwrites $300,000 and sells all of these bonds will receive $10,500 (3½ percent of $300,000). F. Eberstadt and Co., which also underwrites $300,000 of the bonds but sells only $100,000 of them, allocating $200,000 to the selling group, will receive $6,500 (3½ percent of the $100,000 it sold plus 1½ percent of the $200,000 it underwrote but did not sell). First of Michigan Corporation, which participated in the selling group only and sold $20,000 of bonds, receives $400 (2 percent of $20,000) for its selling services only.

Marlowe Corporation's total flotation costs were the $400,000 gross underwriters' spread plus $55,000 direct out-of-pocket costs to cover lawyers' and accountants' fees, travel expenses, SEC filing fees, and other costs incurred in connection with the issue.

Advising The relationship between a corporation and its investment banker (managing underwriter) often continues far beyond that of a particular securities offering. Much as a firm's commercial banker is its advisor regarding short-term financial matters, the investment banker becomes its advisor regarding long-term financial matters. Such advisory services relate not only to raising additional long-term capital but also to acquisitions, mergers, refinancing, long-term financial planning, arranging foreign financial connections, and so on. In many cases, a firm's investment banker will sit on its board of directors. Financial advisory services have been the most rapidly growing sector of the investment banking field in recent years.

Variations in the process

Our discussion of the investment banking process to this point has been confined to the context of a negotiated, fully underwritten public offering of securities. Although this is the most common form of flotation of new securities, there are several possible variations in the process, the most important of which are competitive bidding, "standby" underwriting, and "best-efforts" distribution.

Competitive bidding Bond issues may be initiated by competitive bidding rather than by negotiation between the issuing corporation and an originating house. This method of origination is usually used in connection with the bond offerings of governmental bodies. In the private sector, it is the method of origination of many public utility bonds but is rarely used by industrial corporations. Its use in public utility financing generally has been brought about by requirements of various public utility commissions that regulate the industries in this sector.

Under this method, the underwriting syndicate is determined by competitive bids submitted to the issuer. Where it is used, the issuer often retains an investment banking firm on a consulting basis to aid in determining the terms and timing of the issue. The issuing firm distributes the terms to many investment banking houses and advertises a call for sealed bids to be submitted to its offices at a stated time. Then investment banking houses interested in managing the underwriting form bidding syndicates and submit bids of the prices their syndicates offer to pay for the issue (net proceeds to the issuer). At the appointed time, bids are opened, and the issuing corporation usually accepts the highest bid. The winning syndicate then becomes the underwriting syndicate and proceeds to market the bonds in the manner indicated above.

The principal advantage claimed for competitive bidding is that, by eliminating an ongoing relationship between the issuing firm and its investment banker, the highest possible price will be obtained for the security because the investment banker cannot use its influence in determining the price. Evidence supporting this contention is mixed. The argument against competitive bidding is that, by destroying the ongoing advisory function of the investment banker, the underwriting risk relative to any given issue is increased, and that this increased risk in the long run results in higher rather than lower flotation costs to the issuer.

Standby underwriting When a corporation issues additional shares of common stock (or, in some cases, of securities convertible into common stock), often these securities will be offered under *privileged subscription* to the present stockholders on a ratable basis. For example, if a company with 10 million shares of common stock presently outstanding issues an additional 1 million shares, it will distribute *rights* to each present stockholder to subscribe to one new share for each 10 shares held.[8] These rights may be exercised any time within a given period—say, three weeks—to purchase new shares at a stated price, somewhat under the market price of the stock at the time the rights are issued.

To illustrate, if the market price of the stock at the time the rights are issued is $22¼, the exercise price of the rights might be $20 per share. The firm's investment banker might handle this offering by originating it in the normal fashion and doing the paperwork connected with soliciting the present stockholders and taking their orders for the new issue. For this service the investment banker might receive a fee of, say, 20 cents per share subscribed through the exercise of the rights. Under this arrangement, however, the issuing corporation would run the risk that the price of the stock during the rights offering period might drop below $20 with the result that few or none of the new shares would be sold.

If the issuer wishes to protect against that risk, the investment banker may arrange a *standby underwriting*. He will form a standby underwriting syndicate, which agrees to pay the issuer $19 per share for all shares not subscribed through exercise of the rights. In essence, this underwriting syndicate agrees to stand by during the rights offering to pick up any shares that are not sold. If the rights offering is successful, which it will be if the market price of the stock stays above the exercise price of the rights ($20 per share) during the offering period, the underwriters will do nothing and receive an underwriters' spread of perhaps 50 cents per share for bearing the risk. However, if the market price of the stock should fall below the exercise price during the offering period, the underwriters will be obligated to purchase a considerable portion or perhaps all of the new issue of stock at $19 per share. If that should occur, the underwriters probably will be buying the unsubscribed stock from the issuing corporation at a price considerably above its market value at the time.

This again illustrates the underwriting function of risk bearing; the members of the standby underwriting syndicate will have to take their beating by either selling the stock in the market at whatever price can be obtained

[8]The use and valuation of rights will be discussed in detail in Chapter 20, dealing with common stock.

or by having their money tied up in an inventory of it while they wait and hope for the price to recover. The issuing corporation will get at least $19 per share for the stock, regardless of what happens.

Best-efforts distribution Some securities offerings, particularly those of common stock in new or unseasoned corporations, are so risky that investment bankers are not willing to underwrite them at any reasonable spread. In such a case, the investment banker may enter into a *best-efforts agreement,* obligating itself to use its best efforts to sell the securities at a stated price to the public and to remit a specified lower price to the issuer for each share sold. Usually the price to the issuer is some 10 to 20 percent lower than that to the public because such issues are hard to sell. The investment banker's salespeople must "pound the pavements" to solicit orders. Most issuers would prefer a full underwriting to a best-efforts distribution because under the latter there is no guarantee of a successful sale of the securities. Thus, best-efforts distributions usually are used when they are the only method available to reach the capital markets. However, in some cases, a strong corporation will choose a best-efforts distribution to avoid the cost of the underwriting function.

Selection of the managing underwriter

Investment bankers vary greatly in integrity and reputation. Just as there are reputable lawyers and shysters, excellent medical doctors and quacks, there are investment bankers of highest standing in the financial community and some fly-by-night securities peddlers who, at the limit, stoop to selling fraudulent securities and departing for parts unknown with the proceeds. Obviously it behooves the financial manager to seek an association with an investment banker of the highest repute possible.

A small or middle-sized corporation going to market for the first time faces a major problem in that the leading investment banking houses, such as Morgan Stanley; Salomon Brothers; First Boston Corporation; Goldman Sachs; Merrill Lynch; or Lehman Brothers, Kuhn, Loeb usually are not interested in managing underwritings for such corporations. They do the bulk of their business with corporations of the Fortune 500 class.

There are, however, somewhat smaller national and regional houses that have long-standing good reputations and are accessible to small and middle-sized issuers. By all means, the financial officer should seek an investment banker who has been in business for a considerable period of time and has a reputation for honest dealing in his local community. Never do business, either as an issuer or a buyer of securities, with a securities firm that is not well and favorably known. Often a company's commercial banker can be of help in introducing the officers of its corporate client to an appropriate investment banker. Once a sound relationship is established through an initial successful securities issue, the relationship with a good investment banker, like that with a commercial bank, may prove to be of great value through the years.

Direct placement

As the markets for securities have become increasingly institutionalized, it has become possible to place even large issues of bonds and/or preferred stocks directly with one or a few institutions, such as life insurance companies, directly administered pension funds, trust departments of banks (often investing pension funds), charitable foundations, university endowment funds, and—sometimes—wealthy individuals. In addition, corporations sometimes directly place additional issues of common stock with their present stockholders by using rights offerings, which are made directly without utilizing the investment banking process.

Direct placement with institutions

Direct placements (sometimes called private placements) with institutional investors have accounted for over one third of the total dollar amount of corporate bonds issued during recent years. The process involves direct negotiations between the firm and investment officers of one or more institutional investors to arrange a sale of an entire debt issue. Often an investment banker is employed as an agent to place the issue on behalf of its corporate client. The advantage of this is that the investment banker knows which particular institutions would be interested in a given bond issue and the people to contact. He or she may utilize an intimate knowledge of the capital markets in negotiating with officers of the institutions regarding the interest rate, price, maturity, specific security, if any, and the various provisions of the issue, such as sinking-fund requirements, call features, and protective covenants. This improvement in bargaining power to get the best deal available usually is worth the placement fee.

Possible *advantages* of direct placement are:

1. Reduction of flotation costs. Even if an investment banker is employed to place the issue, placement fees generally are considerably lower than the underwriters' spread in a public issue. In addition, if an issue is directly placed with 25 or fewer investors (as is always the case), registration with the SEC is not required.
2. Speed. Direct placement, by avoiding SEC registration with its minimum 20-day waiting period, reduces the time-lapse between a decision to issue the security and the receipt of funds by the issuer. Inasmuch as

this time-lapse involves the risk of change in capital market conditions, risk also may be reduced.

3. Privacy. In some cases, issuers do not wish to make public certain information that would have to be contained in the SEC registration statement. In a private placement, such information can be treated in confidence in dealing with one or a few investment officers of institutions.
4. Flexibility. By dealing directly with the ultimate investor, particular provisions of the security may be tailored to fit the circumstances of the issuer. These terms might have to be more standardized to be acceptable to a large number of investors in a public issue. In addition, the process of negotiating any change in the provisions of an issue while it is outstanding may be very cumbersome in the case of a public issue held by many investors. Renegotiation may be greatly simplified by direct discussions with one or a few investors holding a directly placed issue.

These advantages must be weighed against the possible *disadvantages* of private placement:

1. Interest cost may be higher. Investment officers of major financial institutions are quite shrewd and may be able to drive a harder bargain than a broader public market would require. This is a debatable point in any given issue, as investment bankers also are shrewd negotiators. Interest cost also may be higher because the security is less liquid. There will not be an established secondary market for it.
2. Other terms of the security may be disadvantageous to the issuer. The institutional investment officer may drive a harder bargain in terms of restrictions and protective covenants than the broader public market would require. This, too, is a debatable point in a particular issue.
3. The advantages to the issuer of having its securities known to the investment public and seasoned in the market are foregone. It is always most difficult to go to the public market the first time. The ground simply is not cultivated. The issuing corporation, with a view to future public offerings of its securities, may find it disadvantageous to directly place an issue now and thus delay the cultivation of the public market.
4. The possibility of buying back the firm's debt at a discount in the open market is foregone. Assuming no change in the credit worthiness of the issuer, if interest rates increase above those existing at the time of issue, the price of a bond in the open market will fall to a value that will reflect the yield to maturity at that later time on newly issued securities. Thus, if bonds were issued at a 10 percent interest rate and the going market rate later increased to 13 percent, the issuer of publicly held bonds could buy its own bonds back in the secondary market at a substantial discount. If its bonds had been directly placed with one or a few institutional investors, however, no such opportunity would exist.

Those investors would be unwilling to sell the bonds to the issuer at a discount. Depending upon fluctuation in future interest rates and the financial requirements of the issuer, this may be a highly significant disadvantage of direct placement.[9]

Rights offerings (without underwriting) Some corporations, when offering additional common stock under privileged subscription, make the rights offering directly to their stockholders without participation by investment bankers or standby underwriting. This can safely be done if the exercise price of the right is substantially below the going market, so that the probability that the market value will fall below the exercise price is extremely small. AT&T has on several occasions utilized this method of raising common stock equity capital. It might also be feasible if the issuing corporation does not urgently need the additional funds on a timely basis. The advantage, of course, of handling a rights offering in this fashion is elimination of underwriting costs. That advantage must be weighed against the probability and the possible consequences of an unsuccessful issue.

Secondary capital markets

In any given time period, the volume of secondary market trading in securities already outstanding is many times greater than the volume of new issues coming onto the market. The relatively large and continuous flow of transactions has led to a more elaborate and formal institutional development of the secondary capital markets. These markets are divided into two categories, the organized securities exchanges and the over-the-counter markets.

Organized securities exchanges

The organized securities exchanges are tangible markets, that is, trading on them is organized on a formal basis and takes place at a central location where representatives of buyers and sellers meet. They are called *stock exchanges,* but this term is a misnomer because bonds are also traded on some of them. Most of the trading is done by *brokers* who represent their clients, although there are some *floor traders* and *specialists* who trade on their own accounts.

Trading on an organized securities exchange is conducted by double auction, in which buyers bid against each other and sellers ask against each

[9]Redemption of bonds and refunding to take advantage of reduced interest rates will be treated in Chapter 18.

other until a price of the transaction is reached. The exchanges are equipped with elaborate telecommunications systems by which quotations of all transactions are transmitted almost instantaneously to the offices of their member-brokers. Accounting and settlement procedures are handled through the exchanges.

Organized securities exchanges may be either national or regional in scope. The New York Stock Exchange (NYSE), sometimes called the "big board," and the American Stock Exchange (AMEX) are national exchanges; there are five registered regional exchanges including the Midwest Stock Exchange and the Pacific Coast Stock Exchange.

The New York Stock Exchange is by far the largest organized securities exchange in the United States (and the world). It accounts for between 80 and 85 percent of the dollar volume of trading on organized securities exchanges of this country. Over 2,000 common and preferred stocks, representing over 1,500 companies, are listed for trading. In addition, over 2,000 bond issues are listed. Trading in bonds, however, on this and other organized exchanges is relatively light. Membership in the NYSE, which carries with it the right to trade on the floor, is limited to 1,366 "seats." All of the major national securities brokerage firms and most of the prominent regional firms are members of NYSE. Many smaller regional and local brokerage houses handle their transactions through correspondents who are members.

When Mary Johnson asked her broker at a Kansas City office of Merrill Lynch to buy for her account 100 shares of Coca-Cola common stock, that broker wired the order to the firm's New York office, where it was relayed to one of the seven officers of Merrill Lynch on the floor of the NYSE. That officer then went to the "stall" where Coca-Cola and several other stocks are traded. There he or she indicated a bid and bought the stock at the lowest available price resulting from the ensuing auction. Confirmation of the transaction was then transmitted back to the Kansas City office. The broker who sold the shares of Coca-Cola perhaps was representing a customer of E. F. Hutton who had placed a sell order in one of their offices in Detroit. In this fashion various buyers and sellers of stock throughout the country are brought together via the securities brokerage mechanism to effect their transactions on the floor of the exchange.

Because trading on the NYSE is limited to round (100-share) lots, Mary Johnson's order to sell 50 shares of AT&T was handled differently by her broker at Merrill Lynch. The New York office had to go through an odd-lot dealer, who buys and sells less than 100-share lots at one eighth of a dollar per share over or under, as the case may be, the price of the last regular transaction on the exchange. Of course, Ms. Johnson is charged brokerage fees by Merrill Lynch for performing these services.

Economic benefits Although securities exchanges, as secondary capital markets, do not directly participate in the process of capital formation, they do have an important bearing upon the efficiency of that process. By maintaining continuous markets for the outstanding securities listed on them, they greatly increase the marketability of new issues of these securities. Liquidity, the ability to turn a security into cash on short notice, is highly valued by investors, particularly those investing in common stocks. When a listed corporation offers additional shares of stock in the primary market to obtain new funds, investors in that stock are willing to pay a higher price for it because they know that when and if they wish to sell the stock, this can be done easily and quickly.

In addition to providing sheer marketability (the ability to sell at some price), securities exchanges tend to create more stable and just prices. These attributes result from two factors. First, the market for any given security tends to become both broader and deeper when the security is traded on an organized exchange. The mechanism of accessing the market through many securities brokerage houses tends to bring the investment characteristics of the security to the attention of a larger number of investors. This, in turn, tends to broaden participation in the market for that security, increasing total demand for it, thereby increasing the depth of the market.

The second factor relates to the effect that securities exchanges have upon the information base available to investors. There is a continuous flow of information regarding prices and volume of trading of listed securities. Furthermore, firms whose securities are listed on registered exchanges must comply with the accounting and reporting requirements of the SEC, including the filing of extensive financial information (Form 10K reports, which are available to the investing public).

The net result of the above factors is that the organized securities exchanges tend to enhance the *efficiency* of the markets for securities traded on them. "Just" or "fair" prices are directly related to market efficiency. Efficient markets allocate the available funds of a society to their most productive uses. Although the organized securities markets may not be perfectly efficient, they do contribute substantially to increasing the efficiency with which capital is allocated in our economy.

Listing considerations The requirements for listing a security on the NYSE are as follows:

1. The firm must have demonstrated earnings of at least $2.5 million before federal income taxes during the previous year and $2 million before taxes during each of the two preceding years.
2. The firm must have at least 2,000 stockholders owning 100 or more shares each.
3. At least one million shares must be publicly held.
4. The publicly held shares must have a total market value of at least $16 million.
5. The net tangible assets of the firm must total at least $16 million.

These requirements are designed to assure that the firm is sufficiently well established, the stock is "seasoned," and that there will be adequate trading activity in the stock. Listing requirements of the AMEX and regional exchanges are less stringent.

Advantages of listing are prestige, publicity, and the direct and indirect benefits related above. Disadvantages include the required listing fees and the possible reluctance of management to disclose the detailed financial and operating information required of listed corporations. In general, listing is feasible only for middle-sized to large corporations whose stock is relatively widely held and actively traded. Choice of the securities exchange depends upon the geographical distribution of the stock and the formal listing requirements.

Over-the-counter markets

The term *over-the-counter* (OTC) markets refers to all securities trading that does not take place on organized exchanges. The OTC markets are intangible in the sense that trading is not centralized at a particular location as it is on an organized exchange. Rather, trading is conducted by individual securities dealers throughout the country. A *dealer* buys or sells securities for its own account, as contrasted to a broker who transacts business on an organized exchange as an agent for the client. Nearly all of the major securities brokerage houses also act as dealers in the OTC market. Many smaller local securities firms are dealers only, but some of these also conduct a brokerage business through correspondents that are exchange members. Most securities dealers operating in the OTC markets are linked by telecommunications networks, which include telephone, telex, and an electronic quotation system, the National Association of Securities Dealers Automated Quotation System (NASDAQ).

Various securities dealers "make a market" for particular OTC securities. The "market maker" for a stock maintains an inventory and stands ready at any time to buy that stock at a quoted bid price and to sell it at a higher quoted asked price. Thus, the market maker is the wholesaler that buys or sells the stock to other dealers, who act as retailers in transactions with their customers.

To illustrate, assume that Mary Johnson wished to buy 200 shares of Affiliated Bankshares of Colorado (a bank holding company whose stock is traded over the counter). If she buys this from her broker-dealer, Merrill Lynch in Kansas City, Merrill Lynch will obtain the asked wholesale quotation from its NASDAQ terminal. Then it will contact Boettcher & Company in Denver (a market maker for this stock) by telephone and negotiate a firm price to buy at wholesale the 200 shares of ABC stock. Merrill Lynch will then sell the 200 shares to Mary Johnson at a slightly higher price, sufficient to cover its retail margin.

A much larger number of issues of common stock is traded in the OTC markets than on the organized stock exchanges. However, the dollar volume of stock trading is much lower. Since most OTC stocks are those of smaller companies, trading is less frequent and in smaller dollar amounts.

Nearly all of the trading in corporate, municipal, and U.S. government bonds is done in the over-the-counter markets. Although many corporate bonds are listed on the New York Stock Exchange, the floor trading in these bonds is only a small fraction of the volume traded OTC. Since most bond trading is among financial institutions and in large blocks, it is more feasible to negotiate such transactions than to establish a price through the double-auction mechanism of the organized exchange.

For example, if an institutional holder, say a life insurance company, wished to sell $5 million of a particular issue of Pacific Gas and Electric bonds, simply offering these bonds on the New York Stock Exchange would jolt the market, because buying orders for that large a block would not be readily available. A bond dealer being offered these bonds can look around among other institutional investors to locate enough buyers to absorb the bonds. Thus the dealer probably can negotiate a higher price than would result from throwing the bonds onto the organized exchange.

Two special types of additional markets developed during the 70s within the OTC market system. These are known as the third and fourth markets. The *third market* is OTC trading by nonmember securities dealers in stocks listed on organized securities exchanges. This trading usually involves large blocks for which such dealers can arrange trades at lower spreads (profit to the dealers) than the commissions that would be charged by brokers for handling such transactions on an exchange. This development has subsequently been countered by elimination of fixed commission rates charged by broker-members of the exchanges so that they can better compete with the third market dealers.

The *fourth market* is trading directly among institutional investors of large blocks of securities. This fourth market trading eliminates the middleman entirely. Its development reflects the increased prominence of institutional investors in the capital markets. Fourth market trading is facilitated by a computerized quotation system called *Instinet,* with terminals located in the offices of major institutional investors.

Regulation

Both interstate distribution of new securities issues and securities trading on the organized exchanges are regulated by the Securities and Exchange Commission. The major purpose of this regulation is to protect the investing public from fraud and manipulation and to increase the efficiency of the markets in allocating the capital of the economy. The two major laws administered by the SEC are the Securities Act of 1933, which governs the sale of new securities, and the Securities Exchange Act of 1934, which governs trading in the secondary markets.

Securities Act of 1933

The sale of *new issues* of securities in interstate commerce is governed by the Securities Act of 1933. The main thrust of this law is the requirement of *full and fair disclosure of all material facts* regarding the security, the issuer, and the investment banking arrangements under which it is sold. This requirement explains why it is called the "truth-in-securities act." Disclosure is accomplished through *registration* of the issue with the SEC. The registration statement has been discussed earlier in this chapter in connection with origination of a securities issue. It contains full detail regarding the security, the issuer, and the underwriting arrangements.[10] The SEC has a minimum of 20 days to examine the registration statement before the security can be offered for sale. If its examiners question any of this information or require additional data to be included, the waiting period is extended. Even after public offering has begun, the SEC may issue a stop order, which bars further sale of the issue until such an order is lifted.

When a registered security is offered for sale, the prospective buyers must be furnished a copy of the final *prospectus* containing the required information. The buyer must make a personal judgment as to the quality and risk of the security. Prior to issue, a preliminary red-herring prospectus may be circulated among potential buyers. Note that the SEC does *not* issue any opinion regarding the soundness or risk of the security. Its function is solely to provide a high degree of assurance that the true facts are disclosed.

The "teeth" in this law are that the issuing corporation, its officers and anyone who participated in the registration, such as the accountants, lawyers, engineers, and the investment bankers, may be sued for damages by securities holders if they have suffered losses due to either misstatements or failure to disclose material facts in the prospectus. In addition, if fraud is evident the SEC may file criminal charges against the responsible parties.

There are numerous exemptions to the registration requirement. These include:

1. Issues that are offered only to residents of a single state.
2. Offerings totaling less than $500,000.
3. Offerings of short-term debt instruments maturing in 270 days or less.
4. Issues controlled under the jurisdiction of other federal regulatory

[10]See footnote 6 regarding simplification of registration requirements.

agencies, such as the Federal Communications Commission, the Federal Energy Regulatory Commission, or the Interstate Commerce Commission.
5. Securities which are offered to fewer than 25 investors.

Securities Exchange Act of 1934

The Securities Exchange Act of 1934 extends the concept of full and fair disclosure to a large segment of the secondary securities markets and seeks to improve the efficiency of these markets by regulating or prohibiting specific practices considered detrimental to the public interest. In addition to creating the Securities and Exchange Commission (the Securities Act of 1933 had previously been administered by the Federal Trade Commission), the major provisions of this act are:

1. The Act requires major organized securities exchanges and their member-brokers to register with the SEC and to submit to its regulation.
2. All companies whose securities are listed on a registered exchange must register with the SEC and provide similar information to that required of new issuers under the Securities Act of 1933. In addition, these companies must file annual reports (Form 10K) and quarterly reports (Form 10Q) with the SEC. Accounting practices underlying these reports are subject to SEC rules. These reports are quite detailed and are available to the public. This requirement has significantly enhanced the availability of operating and financial information to the investing public.
3. Various practices that had previously been used to manipulate market prices of securities, such as price-rigging pools and wash sales, are prohibited.
4. "Insider" trading (by officers, directors, major stockholders, and their relatives) is regulated. Such insiders must file statements with the SEC indicating their holdings and all transactions in the stock of their corporations. Profits made by insiders from short-term trading (holding period of less than six months) or short sales must be restored to the corporation. The SEC releases for publication the record of stock transactions reported by insiders, thus improving the information available to the investing public.
5. The SEC is empowered to regulate the solicitation of proxies by listed corporations.[11] This regulation requires the submission of a Proxy Statement to each stockholder, supplying information regarding the background and affiliation of proposed directors, management and opposition statements regarding proposals to be brought before the meeting,

[11]A proxy is an authorization by an absent stockholder for someone else to vote his or her shares at a stockholders meeting. The proxy mechanism will be further discussed in Chapter 20.

and the use of proxies enabling the stockholder to designate a vote for or against each proposal.

6. The Board of Governors of the Federal Reserve System is empowered to set margin requirements for stock trading. This enables the Board to control the credit available for stock transactions.
7. Under the amendments of 1975, the SEC has been empowered to supervise the establishment of a national exchange (which has not yet materialized at this writing), and the exchanges are prohibited from setting fixed brokerage commissions to be charged by their members on securities transactions.

Summary

This chapter dealt with the financial market environment in which long-term corporate funds are raised and the institutional mechanisms through which these markets are accessed.

The role of financial markets is to provide fluidity of capital by making possible the transfer of savings to economic units that require funds to invest in real assets. A financial market exists anywhere that suppliers and demanders of funds meet to create or exchange financial assets and liabilities. The price mechanism of these markets quite efficiently determines the allocation of capital in our society. Financial markets are vitally important to the development of a modern industrial economy. Various financial intermediaries facilitate the flow of capital by pooling savings of many investors and, in turn, investing these savings in the money and capital markets.

Capital markets are those in which long-term securities, such as bonds, preferred stock, convertible securities, and common stock, are created or traded. Primary capital markets are those related to the issue of new securities, whereas secondary capital markets relate to the trading in already outstanding securities among investors.

Most new securities of business firms are marketed through the investment banking process. An investment banker is a merchant middleman who arranges the sale of securities issues. The functions performed are (1) origination, (2) underwriting, (3) distribution, and (4) advising. Origination usually is arranged by negotiation but may be handled by competitive bidding. Underwriting is bearing the risk that the issue will not be sold. Usually an underwriting syndicate will perform this function. When securities are offered under privileged subscription, a standby underwriting may be used. When investment bankers consider the risk of sale of an issue to be too great to be underwritten, such securities may be offered for sale on a best-efforts basis. Distribution may be accomplished by forming a selling group to participate with the underwriters in selling the securities. The advising function of the investment banker involves ongoing counsel to the firm regarding its long-term financing, mergers, acquisitions, and the like.

An alternative to offering securities through the investment banking process is directly placing a bond or preferred stock issue with one or a small number of institutional investors. Here the terms of the issue are directly negotiated with the institution either by the company's financial officer or by an investment banker acting as an agent and being compensated by a placement fee. Another possible alternative relating to an additional issue of common stock is a direct privileged subscription offering to present stockholders without underwriting.

Secondary markets are divided into two categories, the organized securities exchanges and the over-the-counter markets. The existence of relatively efficient secondary markets indirectly affects the raising of new long-term capital by business firms by increasing marketability and, therefore, the value of new securities issues.

Interstate distribution of new securities issues is regulated by the SEC under the Securities Act of 1933. The principal requirements are the filing of a registration statement and the offering of a prospectus to prospective purchasers of the issue. Trading on registered organized securities exchanges is regulated by the SEC under the Securities Exchange Act of 1934.

Questions

1. What are financial markets? How do financial markets relate to the development of a capitalistic industrial society?

2. Distinguish between the money market and the capital market. What types of financial instruments are created or transferred in each of these markets? Indicate some of the financial institutions that participate in each of these markets.

3. Distinguish between the primary and secondary capital markets. What are the major financial institutions engaged in each of these markets?

4. Who are the major competitors of business firms for funds in the primary capital markets? How does the magnitude of the federal deficit influence demand for funds in the capital market?

5. What is a financial intermediary? What functions do financial intermediaries perform to facilitate the flow of savings to the ultimate demanders of funds in an economy?

6. What is an investment banker? What functions are performed by investment bankers?

7. Why do investment bankers extensively investigate firms whose securities they are going to underwrite even though they intend to sell the securities as soon as possible rather than maintain investments in these firms?

8. What is underwriting? Why is an underwriting syndicate usually formed in connection with a large securities offering?

9. What is the gross underwriters' spread in connection with a new issue of securities? How is it divided among the originating house (manager of the underwriting syndicate), members of the underwriting syndicate, and members of the selling group?

10. How is a standby underwriting used in connection with an additional issue of a firm's common stock? Explain why a firm might use a standby underwriting arrangement. Under what circumstances might a firm *not* wish to have an additional issue of common stock underwritten?

11. What is a direct placement of securities? Why might a firm choose a direct placement rather than a public offering of a bond or preferred stock issue?

12. Secondary capital markets consist of the organized securities exchanges and the over-the-counter (OTC) market. Explain the differences between these two types of markets.

13. What economic function is performed by the New York Stock Exchange and its member-brokers?

14. Why do most transactions in outstanding bonds take place in the over-the-counter market?

15. The Securities Act of 1933, governing the sale of new securities in interstate commerce, is called the "truth-in-securities act." Why? What provisions exist for dealing with violations of this law?

16. How does the Securities Exchange Act of 1934 tend to increase efficiency of the secondary market for securities traded on registered organized securities exchanges?

Problems

1. Sheridan Corporation is offering for sale a $10 million bond issue to mature in 15 years. Its investment bankers, Blackwell and Company, indicate that bonds bearing an interest rate of 11 percent can be sold to the public at par. The gross underwriters' spread will be 1½ percent, and Sheridan will incur out-of-pocket costs of $45,000 preparing the issue for sale.

   a. What is the gross underwriters' spread in dollars?

   b. What are the total flotation costs in dollars?

c. What are the net proceeds to Sheridan after all costs?

d. What are the total flotation costs and the net proceeds per $1,000 bond?

e. What is the approximate cost to maturity (before taxes) of the net proceeds from this bond issue? (Use the approximate cost-to-maturity formula discussed in Chapter 15.)

2. Sparks Electronics Company is considering raising $20 million of 20-year debt by either a direct placement with Midwestern Life Insurance Company or a public offering through its investment banker, Sidley and Company.

Midwestern Insurance offers to buy the bonds at par at an interest rate of 10¾ percent. Sparks' cost of arranging this placement will be $25,000.

Sidley indicates that the gross spread will be 1 percent of par on 10½ percent bonds sold to the public at 99. Sparks' out-of-pocket costs of preparing a public issue are estimated at $110,000.

a. What would be the net proceeds to Sparks after all costs of each alternative?

b. What would be the approximate cost to maturity (before tax) of the net funds available to Sparks under each alternative? (Use the approximate cost-to-maturity formula from Chapter 15.)

c. On what basis would you decide which alternative to pursue?

3. Jeffco Electric Company is offering 100,000 shares of $100 par 12 percent preferred stock. Wadleigh Brothers, its investment banker, can sell the preferred stock to the public at $102 per share. The gross underwriters' spread is $1.65 per share, and Jeffco incurs out-of-pocket costs of $70,000 preparing the issue.

a. What are the net proceeds of this financing to Jeffco after all costs?

b. What is the aftertax cost (assuming infinite maturity) of this preferred stock capital? (See Chapter 15, if necessary, for the formula used to calculate the cost of preferred stock.)

4. The Whittemore Corporation is going public. All its 500,000 common shares presently are owned by the Whittemore family. Aftertax annual earnings currently are $2,000,000. John Whittemore, the chief executive officer, has arranged with the First of Iowa Corporation, investment bankers, to offer 200,000 additional shares of common stock to the public at $17 per share under a best-efforts distribution. First of Iowa will charge a gross spread of $2 per share, and Whittmore will incur out-of-pocket costs of $25,000 preparing the issue. If all the shares are sold:

a. What will be the net proceeds to Whittemore?

b. What are the earnings per share (EPS) before the issue? What are the EPS immediately after the issue?

c. What aftertax rate of return will Whittemore have to make on investment of the net proceeds from this stock issue to restore the earnings per share to the pre-issue level (to avoid dilution of EPS)?

d. If Whittemore intends to pay a dividend of $3 per share next year and future dividends grow at a compound rate of 7 percent, what is Whittemore's estimated cost of this new common stock capital (K_c)? (Refer to the dividend-growth model in Chapter 15, if necessary.)

5. Kerry Corporation, which currently has 3 million common shares outstanding, is offering 500,000 additional shares to its present stockholders under privileged subscription. Each stockholder is issued rights to purchase one new share for each six shares presently owned. Wellbody and Company, investment bankers, have formed a standby underwriting syndicate to insure the success of this offering. Kerry's stock is selling in the market at $27 at the time of the offering, and the subscription price of the new shares is $24. The underwriters will receive 50 cents per share subscribed through the exercise of rights and agree to purchase all shares not subscribed at $23 per share.

a. If the market price of the stock remains above $24 per share through the offering period and all shares are subscribed through exercise of rights, how much compensation will the investment bankers receive? What will be the net proceeds to Kerry (ignoring out-of-pocket costs)?

b. If the market price of Kerry stock falls during the offering period to $21 per share and no stock is subscribed through exercise of rights, what will happen? What will be the net proceeds to Kerry? What can the members of the standby underwriting syndicate do?

6. Obtain a prospectus issued in connection with a new securities offering. Indicate:

a. The type and major provisions of the securities offered.

b. The price of the security and the total dollar amount of the offering to the public.

c. The gross underwriters' spread per unit and on the total issue.

d. What investment banker(s) was the manager and what was the management fee?

e. How many members participated in the underwriting syndicate? What were the maximum and minimum participations?

f. What were the net proceeds to the issuer in dollars? In percent of the price to the public?

g. Was there provision for a selling group? If so, what was the selling concession?

Chapter 17
Capital Structure Planning and Policy

This chapter deals with planning the firm's long-term funds requirements and determining its capital structure policy. The latter involves establishing the proportions of debt and equity to be used in financing long-term capital requirements. This, in turn, seeks to maximize the value of the common stock by striking an optimal balance between risk exposure and profitability sought by the common stockholders.

We shall first briefly review the process of long-range financial forecasting. Then the relationship between capital structure and operating characteristics of the firm will be shown. Operating and financial leverage analysis, which was introduced in Chapter 3, will be further developed. Then the theory underlying capital structure policy will be reviewed. Finally, establishment of target capital structure proportions will be discussed.

Long-range financial planning

Just as the short-term cash forecast provides the backdrop for cash and marketable securities management, the long-range financial forecast underlies long-term financial management. But long-range financial planning is more difficult and subject to greater uncertainty (therefore error) than short-term planning for three reasons.

First, long-range planning usually is done by annual periods covering a time span of some four or five years. Uncertainty is, to a large degree, a function of time. Much more change may take place in the economic, political, and social environment of the firm over the next five years than during the coming year. Therefore, the degree of uncertainty in long-range forecasting is far greater. It is more difficult to get dependable figures to incorporate in the forecast, and the reliability of the indicated financial requirements is much lower. Nonetheless, long-range forecasts are highly useful in forewarning management of the financial consequences of their operating plans. Long-range forecasts usually are revised annually to incorporate perceived changes and pushed a year further into the future.

Second, long-range financial forecasts are based upon the overall policies and strategies of the firm. Since these are more nebulous than specific short-range operating plans, it is more difficult to quantify their financial effects.

Third, the influence of inflation is both more difficult to estimate and more profound in its effect upon financial requirements over a long period of time. Although the task is both difficult and fraught with uncertainty, management must acknowledge the challenge and proceed to forecast long-range capital requirements. Failure to do so entails the risk of proceeding with operating plans that either cannot be financed or that require financing from a position of weakness, resulting in "paying the price" by existing stockholders. The sale, merger on unfavorable terms, or failure of many firms has been the result of either lack of long-range financial forecasting or gross errors in such forecasts.

The long-range sales forecast

The forecast of capital requirements must be based upon the long-range sales forecast. Future sales, in turn, will relate to the general state of the economy, the demand for the products of the industry, and the market share that can be attained by the particular firm. Therefore, the long-range sales forecasting process usually is initiated by the firm's economist. The starting point is estimating the general state of the economy in which the firm is to market its products. Usually this will be expressed in terms of broad measures of economic activity such as gross national product (GNP), personal consumption expenditures (if the firm produces consumer goods), or plant and equipment expenditures (if it produces capital goods). Then the economist will try to find a statistical relationship between demand for the industry's products and one or more of these broad economic measures, using this to estimate industry demand.

Next, the economist and the marketing manager, recognizing the firm's strategic plans to penetrate the market, develop a long-range sales forecast. If this forecast initially is made on a unit volume basis, it must be converted to sales in dollars, factoring in forecasted inflation. We must emphasize that the financial forecast is only as strong as the sales forecast upon which it is based and is subject to its inherent uncertainty.

Projecting financial requirements

Once the sales forecast is accepted, the financial people develop pro forma income statements and balance sheets based upon the sales estimates. This involves the use of various statistical techniques to project costs and expenses in developing the pro forma income statements and to estimate the various components of the pro forma balance sheets.

Forecasting the income statements Some of the costs and expenses associated with forecasted sales may be estimated by the *percent-of-sales method.* The percentages may be estimated on the basis of past experience. Thus, if the cost of goods sold has varied from 50 to 52 percent of sales during the past five years and has averaged 51 percent, this item might reasonably be projected into the pro forma income statements at 51 percent of sales.

One must be very careful, however, to recognize that only *variable costs* may be projected validly as percentages of sales. Any costs that would remain *fixed* through the volume of forecasted sales must be projected as fixed costs, rather than variable costs. Some other types of costs, such as depreciation and interest, are not directly related to sales. These must be estimated independently. Depreciation charges relate to the estimated depreciable assets, and interest charges to the amounts expected to be borrowed and the interest rates thereon. Income taxes, of course, will be a function of estimated pretax income and the estimated tax rates.

The principal reason for developing the pro forma income statements is to forecast the net profit after taxes expected in each of the future years. This amount, less anticipated dividend payments, will be added to retained earnings to forecast that account in the pro forma balance sheets.

Forecasting the balance sheets Several statistical methods, of varying degree of sophistication, may be used in forecasting items of the balance sheet.

Percent-of-sales method The simplest, but often the least satisfactory, method of developing pro forma balance sheets is to forecast each of the asset requirements (and some of the liabilities) as a percentage of the estimated sales. The implicit assumption is that each asset will vary directly with sales volume. This approach will be valid only if experience and logic indicate that the relationship between sales and the investment in a particular asset will be linear and that the regression line will pass through the origin, as shown in Figure 17–1. If past experience verifies this relationship, as shown by the points plotted in Figure 17–1, and the firm's strategic policy does not contemplate any change that would influence this relationship, this method should be used.

Figure 17–1 Percent-of-sales method

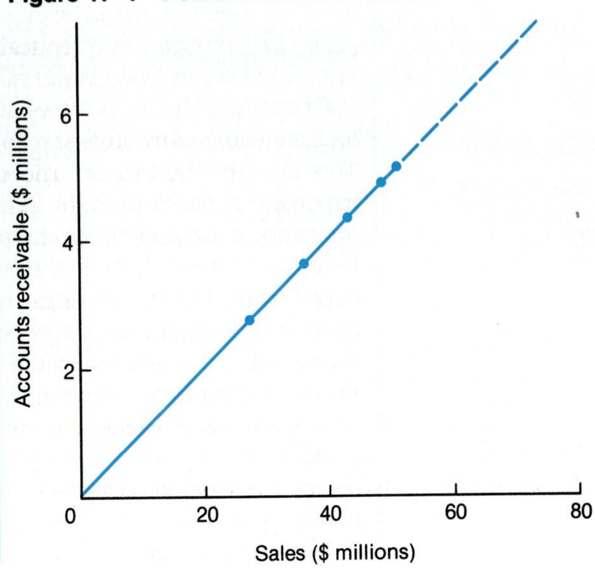

In many cases, the method would be applicable to forecasting required working cash balances, accounts receivable, and inventories. For example, if no changes in terms of sale, credit standards, or collection policies were contemplated and the collection period were expected to remain stable, accounts receivable would vary directly in relation to sales. However, if the firm's strategic policy were to achieve increased sales volume by relaxing credit standards, lengthening the terms of sale, and relaxing collection efforts, then the collection period would be expected to increase and the line in Figure 17–1 would curve upward as sales increased. Thus, if such a strategy were to be used, forecasting the investment in accounts receivable by this percent-of-sales method would be misleading. The effect of the strategy upon accounts receivable balances would have to be estimated directly. On the liability side, such spontaneous current liabilities as accounts payable or accrued wages often may be validly estimated as a percentage of sales.

Use of a percentage of sales as an estimate of all assets and all current liabilities, however, very rarely would be valid. Fixed asset investments usually take place in "lumps." For example, the firm may plan to replace machinery only in amounts approximately equal to depreciation charges over the next two years, utilizing presently excess capacity to accommodate increasing sales until the end of that period. Then, in the third year, it plans to invest several million dollars in a major plant expansion. About five years hence, it may plan to build a new warehouse or office building to replace the present structure.

On the liability side, accrued income taxes will not relate directly to sales volume, but rather will be a function of pretax income and tax regulations. Retained earnings, of course, will change as the result of net income after taxes and dividends paid, rather than as a direct function of sales volume.

So one must be very skeptical of forecasted financial requirements based entirely upon the percent-of-sales forecasting method. Such forecasts are too simplistic. In many cases, the oversimplification results in erroneous and misleading forecasts.

Simple linear regression The use of simple linear regression analysis to forecast balance sheet items differs from the percent-of-sales method in that it does *not* assume that the regression line relating sales to the balance sheet item passes through the origin. Its use involves first plotting a scatter diagram showing the historical relationship between sales and the particular item, say inventories. A regression line can then be fitted to the plotted points, either visually or mathematically by using the least squares regression method, as shown in Figure 17–2.

This is an improvement upon the percent-of-sales method in that it avoids the possibly erroneous assumption that the line of relationship (regression) passes through the origin. For example, the regression line between inventories and sales may not pass through the origin because certain base inventories of various raw materials and finished goods must be maintained even at low sales volumes. At increasing sales volumes, the inventories may increase at a lower rate than sales. These factors are illustrated in Figure 17–2: the regression line does not pass through the origin, and its slope is less than would result from using a percentage of sales.

Figure 17–2 Simple linear regression

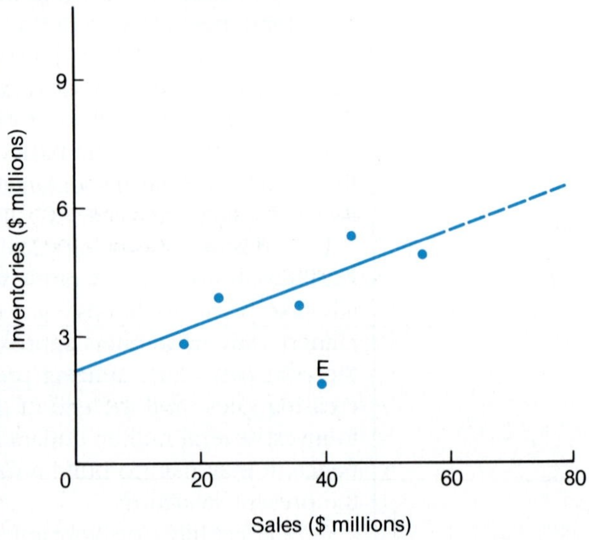

A simple linear regression method is appropriate if (1) the scatter diagram indicates that the regression line would not pass through the origin, (2) the relationship is linear, that is, a straight line is the best fit to the plotted points, (3) the deviations are small, and (4) no policy change is contemplated that would modify the historical relationship. In using any regression method, care must be taken to eliminate any points from the scatter diagram that resulted from circumstances not expected in the future. In Figure 17–2, a very low plot for inventories at the end of one year (labeled E) was eliminated because it was the result of an unusually protracted strike by a major supplier, which nearly caused the firm to run out of inventories.

Curvilinear regression A curve might fit a given scatter diagram of historical relationships better than a straight line. In other words, the relationship may be curvilinear rather than linear. For example, if technological change in inventory control methods is causing an inventory-sales curve to bend into a curvilinear relationship, this may be taken into account in forecasting by fitting a curve rather than a straight line to the plotted points. The curve may be fitted visually or mathematically, by utilizing suitable techniques.

Multiple regression It also may be evident in some cases that one or more factors other than sales may influence the level of investment in a given asset. In such cases, multiple regression analysis, which introduces additional variables, may be employed to increase precision of financial forecasting. However, considering the degree of uncertainty inherent in long-range forecasting, such technical refinement usually would not be required and is considered beyond the scope of this text.

Assembling the financial forecast After the asset items and spontaneous current liabilities have been forecasted, there remains the task of forecasting external capital requirements. We would, at this point, have developed the forecasted assets and all current liabilities except bank loans on the pro forma balance sheets. These estimates and the assumptions underlying them for Lashley Industries, Inc., are shown in Table 17–1. Short-term bank loans are estimated on the basis of the presently available line of credit and expected increases through the years. Now we can subtract the forecasted total current liabilities from total assets to obtain the long-term debt and equity required to finance the firm in each of the forecasted years.

The present capital structure (at the end of 1982) of Lashley Industries consists of $14 million long-term debt, $10 million common stock, $2 million capital surplus, and $7 million retained earnings. We can project the retained earnings account by adding the estimated net profit after taxes each year and subtracting contemplated dividends equal to 60 percent of these net profits.[1] By adding the forecasted retained earnings to the present combined long-term debt, common stock, and capital surplus of $26 million, we determine the total amount of long-term financing available each year without going to the capital markets for additional funds. Finally, the external capital required is determined by subtracting the total available capital each year from the forecasted required long-term debt and equity.

According to this forecast, Lashley will have to go to the capital markets for about $750,000 each of the next two years and for nearly $5 million in each of the years 1985 through 1987. Over the five-year period, external financing of about $16 million will be required. This long-range financial forecast provides the basis for planning the acquisition of funds in the capital markets. If, for example, Lashley's management has established a capital structure policy of maintaining a long-term debt ratio of approximately 40 percent, then $6.5 million of the five-year requirement can be financed through the sale of bonds, requiring the firm to raise an additional $9.5 million from the sale of common stock during the period.[2]

[1]Dividend policy will be treated in Chapter 22. For illustrative purposes, we are assuming that the firm has an established dividend policy of paying out about 60 percent of its net aftertax profits each year in dividends and retaining the remaining 40 percent.

[2]Determination of capital structure policy will be treated later in this chapter.

Table 17–1

Lashley Industries, Inc.
Long-Range Financial Forecast
1983–1987
($ millions)

	1983	1984	1985	1986	1987	Assumptions
Pro forma income data						
Sales (constant dollars)	$100.0	$106.0	$112.4	$119.1	$126.2	+ 6% per year
Sales (adjusted for inflation)	108.0	123.6	141.5	162.0	185.4	8% annual rate
Net profit after taxes	5.0	5.8	6.7	7.9	9.5	(From pro forma income statement)
Pro forma balance sheet						
Current assets						
Cash and marketable securities	$ 3.2	$ 3.7	$ 4.2	$ 4.9	$ 5.6	3% of sales
Accounts receivable	10.8	12.4	14.2	16.2	18.5	10% of sales
Inventories	11.6	12.9	14.3	16.0	17.8	(From simple regression)
Other	1.1	1.2	1.4	1.6	1.9	1% of sales
Total current assets	26.7	30.2	34.1	38.7	43.8	
Fixed assets*	20.0	20.0	25.0	25.0	27.0	
Total assets	$ 46.7	$ 50.2	$ 59.1	$ 63.7	$ 70.8	
Current liabilities						
Accounts payable	$ 4.3	$ 4.9	$ 5.7	$ 6.5	$ 7.4	4% of sales
Accrued expenses	3.2	3.7	4.2	4.9	5.6	3% of sales
Income taxes payable	1.4	1.6	1.9	2.2	2.7	28% of net profit (after taxes)
Notes payable—Bank	2.0	2.0	2.5	2.5	2.7	
Total current liabilities	10.9	12.2	14.3	16.1	18.4	
Required long-term debt & equity	35.8	38.0	44.8	47.6	52.4	(Total assets – Current liabilities)
Less:						
Long-term debt—end of 1982	14.0					
Common stock—end of 1982	10.0	26.0	26.0	26.0	26.0	
Capital surplus—end of 1982	2.0					
Retained earnings†	9.0	11.3	14.0	17.2	21.0	
Total available capital	35.0	37.3	40.0	43.2	47.0	
External capital required	.8	.7	4.8	4.4	5.4	

*Replacements equal depreciation. Plant expansion in 1985 and new warehouse in 1987.
†Retained earnings equal end of 1982 of $7 million plus net profits after taxes less dividends of 60 percent of net profits after taxes.

Relating to corporate strategy

Corporate strategy involves the long-range practices by which the firm is to compete in its present markets and its plans to shift into other markets. This strategy is flexible through time and, in essence, expresses the intentions of management to change the nature of the firm's operations. Because there is a corporate strategy, the long-range plan cannot be merely a projection of past trends and relationships. Rather, the plan must incorporate the firm's strategy. Top-level management must be involved in the planning process and modify the documents to express its intentions.

We previously mentioned one example of this in connection with modification of forecasted accounts receivable to incorporate a strategy of competing for additional sales by liberalizing credit and collection policies. In another case, a firm's strategy might call for modifying projected inventory levels to reflect intentions to broaden the variety of products offered or provide better service to customers by warehousing inventories at additional regional locations. Often the forecast of fixed asset investments will reflect corporate strategy, such as to lower costs by automating production facilities, to invest in plant facilities to produce new products, or perhaps to invade new markets. The point is that, rather than being the result of a mechanical forecasting process, the long-range plan incorporates the strategic policy of the firm, where it intends to go, and how it intends to get there.

Of equal or perhaps greater importance, long-range planning allows management to examine various strategic alternatives and to appraise the feasibility of each. Potential changes in operating results and financial requirements may be forecasted to reveal their effects upon the firm's viability. This aids in determining the strategy to be adopted. Thus, long-range planning is a valuable policy-making tool.

Effect of inflation

Inflation has a profound effect upon capital requirements. Recall that to accomplish rather modest real growth in sales of 6 percent annually, Lashley Industries required about $16 million additional external capital financing over a five-year period, as shown in Table 17–1. This large amount of required financing resulted entirely from factoring in anticipated inflation of 8 percent per year. The long-range financial forecast for Lashley Industries, assuming exactly the same *real growth* in sales but *no inflation,* is shown in Table 17–2. This forecast indicates that the firm would not have to raise a single dollar in the capital markets over the next five years in the absence of inflation. Its sales growth of 6 percent per year could be financed entirely through retained earnings.

Table 17–2

Lashley Industries, Inc.
Long-Range Financial Forecast
Assuming No Inflation
1983–1987
($ millions)

	1983	1984	1985	1986	1987	Assumptions
Pro forma income data						
Sales	$100.0	$106.0	$112.4	$119.1	$126.2	+ 6% per year
Net profit after taxes	4.6	5.0	5.3	5.8	6.5	Same % of sales as Table 17–1
Pro forma balance sheet						
Current assets						
Cash and marketable securities	3.0	$ 3.2	$ 3.4	$ 3.6	$ 3.8	3% of sales
Accounts receivable	10.0	10.6	11.2	11.9	12.6	10% of sales
Inventories	11.0	11.5	12.0	12.5	13.1	Same regression as Table 17–1
Other	1.0	1.1	1.1	1.2	1.3	1% of sales
Total current assets	25.0	26.4	27.7	29.2	30.8	
Fixed assets*	20.0	20.0	24.0	24.0	25.4	
Total assets	$ 45.0	$ 46.4	$ 51.7	$ 53.2	$ 56.2	
Current liabilities						
Accounts payable	$ 4.0	$ 4.2	$ 4.5	$ 4.8	$ 5.0	4% of sales
Accrued expenses	3.0	3.2	3.4	3.6	3.8	3% of sales
Income taxes payable	1.3	1.4	1.5	1.6	1.8	28% of net profit (after taxes)
Notes payable—Bank	2.0	2.0	2.4	2.4	2.5	
Total current liabilities	10.3	10.8	11.8	12.4	13.1	
Required long-term debt and equity	34.7	35.6	39.9	40.8	43.1	(Total assets – Current liabilities)
Less:						
Long-term debt—end of 1982	14.0					
Common stock—end of 1982	10.0	26.0	26.0	26.0	26.0	
Capital surplus—end of 1982	2.0					
Retained earnings†	8.8	10.8	12.9	15.2	17.8	
Total available capital	34.8	36.8	38.9	41.2	43.8	
External capital required	(.1)	(1.2)	1.0	(.4)	.7	

*Replacements equal depreciation. Plant expansion in 1985 and new warehouse in 1987 in constant dollars.
†Retained earnings equal end of 1982 of $7 million plus net profits after taxes less dividends of 60 percent of net profits after taxes.

Why does inflation have such a great effect on capital requirements? This is explained by noting that current asset requirements are almost entirely dependent upon *dollar* sales volume. For example, when dollar sales increase by 14.5 percent annually (1.06, reflecting real growth, times 1.08, reflecting inflation, equals 1.145), the required investment in cash and marketable securities, accounts receivable, and other current assets increase by 14.5 percent. The required investment in inventories increases at a somewhat slower rate (11.3 percent) because it is forecasted by a simple regression intersecting the vertical axis at $3 million, reflecting required base inventories. Investment in fixed assets, however, is not so directly related to dollar sales volume, because the existing investment in these assets reflects past costs and only the incremental investment (cost of the plant expansion in 1985 and the new warehouse in 1987) reflect costs in current dollars. Profits increase with inflation but are reflected on the balance sheet only as incremental additions to retained earnings less the dividend payout.

The net result is that inflation increases the required investment in assets, particularly current assets, *much more than* it increases the internal generation of equity capital through retained earnings. The shortfall in long-term capital must be raised externally in the capital markets.

The seriousness of this effect of inflation upon external capital requirements is reflected by the fact that, in the period of very high inflation since 1974, many otherwise sound small and middle-sized firms have found it necessary to merge with large, cash-rich corporations in order to finance continuation of their operations. This has been especially onerous because, at the same time that large amounts of external financing have been required due to inflation, interest rates have been extremely high, long-term debt funds limited in availability, and stock prices low relative to earnings (all functions of the same inflation).

Elements of capital structure policy

Capital structure policy involves determination of the proportions of long-term debt, preferred stock, and common stock equity that may soundly be included in the capital structure of a firm. The basic trade-off is between potential increased profitability on the common stock equity, which can be obtained by utilizing long-term debt and/or preferred stock, and the increased risk borne by the common stockholders, resulting from fixed commitments to service long-term debt and/or prior commitments to service preferred stock.

Basic characteristics of securities

The obligations under long-term debt are to pay fixed interest periodically, to pay the principal at maturity or according to various forms of installment arrangements, and to abide by the restrictions of the debt contract. Thus, long-term borrowing via a term loan or bond issue involves a *rigid* capital contract. The risk to the common stockholders takes two forms. The first relates to the magnification of changes in net operating income on earning available to the common stockholders. This results from the fixed interest obligation. The second risk is that sometime during the period that such a contract is outstanding, the firm will suffer from restriction of its ability to finance operations, find it difficult to keep its promises under the debt contract, or, at worst, face bankruptcy because of its inability to keep one or more of those promises.[3]

Preferred stock involves the commitment to pay dividends at a stipulated rate before any dividends may be paid to the common stockholders. In liquidation, the preferred stockholders usually must be paid a par or stated value in full before the common stockholders may receive anything. In addition, preferred stocks may include various restrictions. Thus, while the preferred stock contract is not as rigid as that of long-term debt, there still are significant risks to the common stockholders. Financial flexibility as well as ability to pay dividends on the common stock is limited if preferred dividends have accumulated in arrears.

The common stock contract is almost completely *flexible.* The corporation is obligated to pay dividends only as, if, and when declared by the board of directors. The common stockholders' claim in liquidation is residual. All creditors' and preferred stockholders' claims must be fully satisfied before the common stockholders receive anything.[4] Thus, common stock equity financing is highly flexible, involves no fixed commitments, and thus imposes no additional financial risks.

Objective of capital structure policy

Financial management, acting in the interest of the common stockholders, is obligated to seek the profitability-risk combination of the various types of long-term financing that will maximize the value of the common stockholders' investment. Therefore, capital structure policy should be designed to assume prudently some financial risks in seeking higher profitability on the

[3]This is merely an introduction to the basic nature of the long-term debt contract. Specific obligations, various restrictive covenants, and so on will be treated in detail in Chapter 18.

[4]This description of preferred and common stockholders' rights is only introductory. These rights will be treated in detail in Chapter 20.

common stock equity, but only those risks that are outweighed by the profitability potential. Thus, the value of the common stock may be maximized.

The *total risk* borne by the common stockholders is the product of the *operating risk* (also called "business risk"), that is, the risk of the business as a whole, which relates to the nature of its operations, and the *financial risk* imposed by the existence of fixed or limited financial contracts in its capital structure. Capital structure policy can be determined only after appraising the operating risk of the firm. In general, if the operating risk is high, the capital structure should contain little or no debt or preferred stock. Conversely, if the operating risk is low, then the use of a large proportion of fixed or limited capital contracts in the capital structure may be prudent.

The operating risk of the firm is a function of its *operating characteristics.* You will recall from Chapter 3 that these characteristics reflect the nature of the firm's operations as they influence the rate of return on the assets and the variation in that rate that may result from changes in the operating environment. Capital structure policy must be based upon an understanding of the operating characteristics, because the cash flows required to service financial contracts usually must come from operations.

The first step in analyzing operating risk is to estimate the volatility of future sales volume. Then one must estimate the effect of fluctuation in sales volume upon net operating income.

Operating leverage analysis, utilizing an operating break-even chart, with its associated break-even point and degree of operating leverage at various sales levels, provides an appraisal of the cost-related aspects of operating risk. Such analysis, which was introduced in Chapter 3, will be fully developed in the next section of this chapter.

Just as operating risk is a function of fluctuation in sales volume and the operating leverage created by fixed operating costs, financial risk is a function of the financial leverage created by fixed or limited financial costs resulting from the use of long-term debt and/or preferred stock in the capital structure. Financial risk may be appraised by using financial leverage analysis. This involves developing the financial leverage chart and calculating the financial point of indifference and the degree of financial leverage at various levels of earnings before interest and taxes (or net operating income). Finally, total risk borne by the common stockholders may be perceived as a function of (1) fluctuation in sales volume, (2) the degree of operating leverage, and (3) the degree of financial leverage.

Operating leverage analysis

Operating leverage is the responsiveness of net operating income (before taxes) to fluctuation in sales volume. If a firm's costs were entirely variable, its net operating income would vary in direct proportion to a change in sales volume. In such a case, the operating leverage would be unity, or 1. If only a portion of costs were variable and the rest were fixed, then the responsiveness of net operating income to a change in sales volume would be in a ratio of greater than 1. If, for example, a decline in sales volume of 10 percent would result in a 20 percent reduction in net operating income, then the operating leverage would be 2 (.20/.10).

Operating leverage is a direct result of the existence of fixed costs. By definition, *fixed costs* (sometimes called indirect or overhead costs) remain the same as volume of output changes through a relevant range. Some costs that usually are fixed are officers' salaries, depreciation, property taxes, maintenance, and insurance. *Variable costs* (sometimes called direct costs) fluctuate in direct proportion to changes in volume. The principal costs that are entirely variable are direct labor and materials in a manufacturing operation or cost of goods sold in a marketing firm. Some types of costs are partly variable and partly fixed; for example, energy costs related to heating the plant and offices usually are fixed but those associated with operating machinery and equipment are variable. Likewise, the base salaries of salespeople are fixed but commissions paid to them are variable.

Data regarding the classification of various costs as fixed or variable are obtained from the cost accountants and utilized in operating leverage analysis. Initially, we shall assume that all operating costs may be identified as either fixed or variable over the entire range of possible output. Later we recognize that life is not this simple and that some costs, called *semifixed costs,* change in a stairstep pattern within the range of possible output.

Operating break-even chart An operating break-even chart is used to show the fixed costs, variable costs, total costs, and total revenues through the range of possible output of a firm. To illustrate, let us assume that Rangley Corporation, a manufacturing company, has an operating capacity of 120 million units per year. Its fixed costs are $30 million, and its variable costs are $1 per unit. The selling price of its product is $1.50 per unit. As shown in Figure 17–3, the total revenue line is plotted by multiplying the selling price ($1.50) by the number of units produced and sold. Fixed costs remain at $30 million regardless of volume, and total costs are determined by adding to that $30 million the variable costs per unit ($1) times volume.

The *break-even point* (BEP) is 60 million units, the intersection of the total revenue and total cost lines. Net operating income (NOI) at any output level over 60 million units is indicated by the vertical distance between the total revenue and the total cost lines. For example, at a volume of 100 million units, total revenues are $150 million and total costs $130 million. Therefore, the net operating profit is $20 million. At volume levels below the break-even point (60 million units), net operating losses are shown by the vertical distance between the total revenue and cost lines. At a volume of 40 million units, total revenues are $60 million and total costs $70 million; therefore, a net operating loss of $10 million results.

Figure 17–3 **Operating break-even chart—Rangley Corporation**

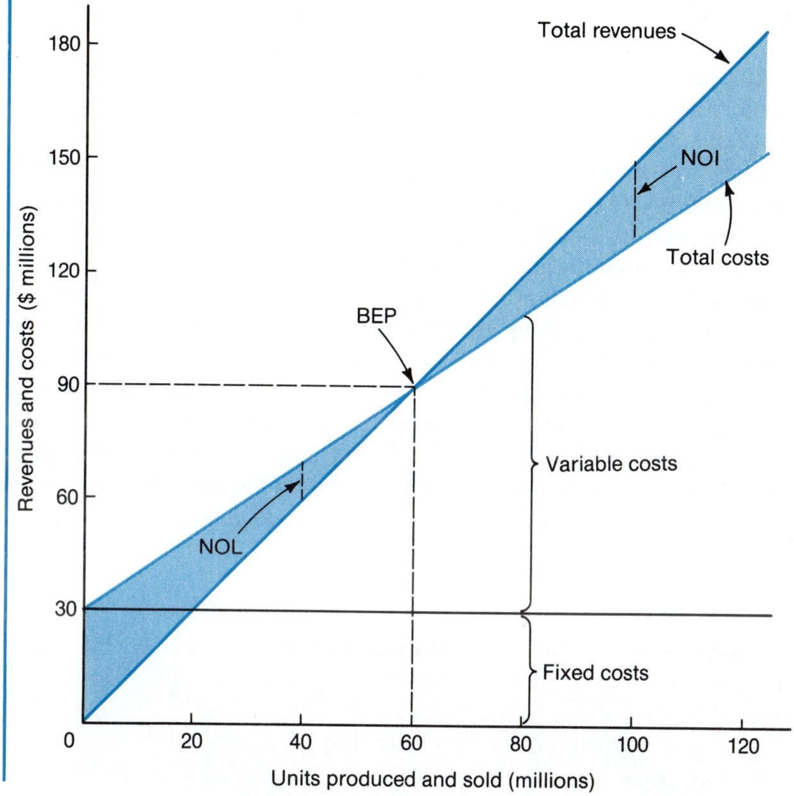

Having developed the operating break-even chart, management can then apply the range, or perhaps a subjective probability distribution, of expected sales volumes to estimate the levels of net operating income (or losses) at various volumes. For example, if Rangley Corporation expected future sales volumes to range between 80 million and 120 million units, net operating income may range between $10 million and $30 million (read off the chart from the vertical distances between the total revenue and total cost lines). If management has developed a probability distribution of various sales volumes, the probability that each volume will occur may be applied to the net operating income at each volume level. Such data may aid management in its decision to assume fixed financial obligations in the firm's capital structure.

On the other hand, if Rangley's management expected the volume of operations to vary widely—say, between 30 million and 100 million units—net operating losses that would occur at lower sales volumes could be predicted. Unless adequate sources of funds were to cover fixed financial obligations when such operating losses occurred, the firm's management probably would forgo use of any long-term debt financing in the capital structure.[5]

Through the use of break-even charts, we can illustrate the effects of different cost structures upon the break-even point and net operating income at various volumes of operations. In Figure 17–4, the chart labeled "Low Leverage" represents a firm with very low fixed costs (FC) and relatively high variable costs (VC) per unit. This cost structure usually would be found in a firm with low capital intensity, such as a labor-intensive manufacturing operation or a marketing operation in which cost of goods sold is a high percentage of total costs. The result is a relatively low break-even point (BEP) and low operating leverage (except at volume levels close to the break-even point).

The opposite cost structure is reflected in the chart labeled "High Leverage." This highly capital-intensive firm, which might be an automated manufacturing operation, has high fixed costs and low variable costs per unit. The result is a higher break-even point and higher operating leverage. Other things being equal, management of the firm with low operating lev-

Figure 17–4 **Operating break-even charts**

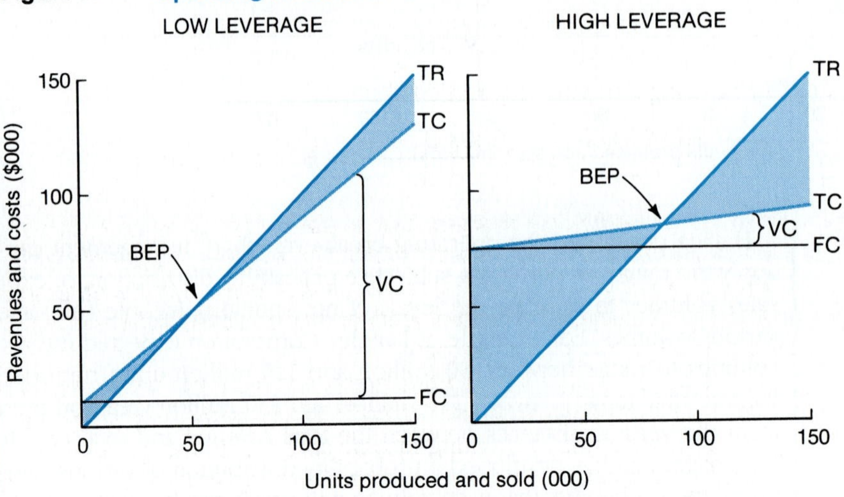

[5]The operating break-even chart also is useful in planning and control of operations. For example, if a firm is considering modernizing its plant, which would increase fixed costs but lower variable costs, the chart can be used to estimate the effects of such a change on the break-even point and levels of net operating income at various volume levels. A retail store considering terminating a lease on which payments are based on a percentage of sales (a variable cost) and buying the building (creating fixed costs) may evaluate such a decision by developing operating break-even charts for the two alternatives. Effects on its break-even point and on net operating income at various forecasted sales levels may be observed.

erage might assume more financial risk by financing a larger proportion of the capital structure through debt securities than would the management of the high operating leverage firm.

Break-even point formula The break-even point may also be determined by formula, Let

x = the break-even point
F = fixed costs
v = variable costs per unit
p = selling price per unit

Then solve the following equation for x:

$$F + vx = px \tag{17–1}$$

Using the price and cost data for Rangley Corporation (Figure 17–3),

$$\begin{aligned} \$30{,}000{,}000 + \$1.00\,x &= \$1.50\,x \\ -\$.50\,x &= -\$30{,}000{,}000 \\ x &= 60{,}000{,}000 \text{ units} \end{aligned}$$

This formula may be restated in a form called the "contribution margin" approach:

$$x = \frac{F}{p\text{-}v} \tag{17–2}$$

Again using Rangley Corporation data:

$$x = \frac{\$30{,}000{,}000}{\$1.50 - \$1.00} = \frac{\$30{,}000{,}000}{\$.50} = 60{,}000{,}000 \text{ units}$$

Here the *contribution margin,* that is, the contribution of each unit sold toward covering the fixed costs, is \$.50. Dividing the contribution margin of \$.50 into the fixed costs of \$30 million indicates the break-even point of 60 million units. Beyond this point, each additional unit of sales will contribute \$.50 toward net operating income.

Cash break-even analysis To this point, our break-even analysis has dealt with accounting income. Some of the costs properly charged against revenues in determining accounting income are noncash charges such as depreciation or depletion. Financial management may wish to do a *cash break-even analysis,* considering only those costs that require immediate cash outflows. This analysis might be useful because financial obligations are serviced by the payment of cash. During a period of depressed sales volume, a firm may incur net operating losses but still be able to generate sufficient cash from operations to pay bond interest, installment payments on the principal, and the like. Positive cash flows might be accomplished by stringently limiting or eliminating replacements and additions to fixed assets during a period when operating losses were incurred. This, of course, can be done only over a limited period of time, because, if fixed assets are not replaced, the firm is gradually liquidating through wearing out these assets. But such action may tide the firm over a recessionary period.

Cash break-even analysis eliminates noncash charges from the operating costs. For example, if Rangley's fixed costs of $30 million include $10 million depreciation charges, the operating break-even chart may be recast on the basis of $20 million fixed *cash* outlays ($30 million fixed costs less $10 million depreciation charges). The *cash break-even point* would be

$$\frac{\$20{,}000{,}000}{\$1.50 - \$1.00} = \frac{\$20{,}000{,}000}{\$.50} = 40{,}000{,}000 \text{ units}$$

Degree of operating leverage The degree of operating leverage (DOL) is the relationship between the rate of change in volume of operations and the resulting rate of change in net operating income (NOI). In other words, it indicates the magnification of a change in volume upon net operating income.

$$\text{DOL} = \frac{\text{Percentage change in net operating income}}{\text{Percentage change in unit volume}} \quad (17\text{–}3)$$

The simplest way to understand the degree of operating leverage is to develop an abbreviated income statement at a particular unit volume of sales. Then develop a similar income statement at a given incremental increase (or decrease) in sales volume, say 10 percent. By comparing the change in net operating income to the given change in sales volume (10 percent) you will determine the degree of operating leverage at that volume of operations.

The first column in Table 17–3 shows that at the volume of 70 million units, Rangley Corporation would have a net operating income of $5 million. A 10 percent increase in volume to 77 million units (second column) would result in a net operating income of $8.5 million. The increase in NOI of $3.5 million ($8.5 million less $5 million) is 70 percent. By dividing the 70 percent increase in NOI by the 10 percent increase in volume we determine that the degree of operating leverage (DOL) at the 70 million unit volume level is 7.0. In other words, the incremental rate of change in net operating income (NOI) is 7 times as great as the rate of change in unit volume. Of course, this also works the other way around. A 10 percent decrease in unit volume would result in a 70 percent decrease in NOI.

The last two columns of Table 17–3 show that, at the 100 million unit volume level, a volume increase of 10 percent would result in a 25 percent increase in NOI. Therefore, at this higher volume of operations, the degree of operating leverage (DOL) is 2.5. If we were to develop the same analysis at the break-even point (BEP) of 60,000 units, we would find that the degree of operating leverage is indeterminate. Any positive change in volume would result in NOI changing from zero to a positive figure and any de-

Table 17–3 Degree of operating leverage—Rangley Corporation
(000 except percent)

	70,000 units	77,000 units	100,000 units	110,000 units
Total revenues (@ \$1.50)	\$105,000	\$115,500	\$150,000	\$165,000
Fixed costs (\$30,000)	30,000	30,000	30,000	30,000
Variable costs (@ \$1.00)	70,000	77,000	100,000	110,000
Total costs	\$100,000	\$107,000	\$130,000	\$140,000
Net operating income	\$ 5,000	\$ 8,500	\$ 20,000	\$ 25,000
Increase in NOI	$\frac{3,500}{5,000} = 70\%$		$\frac{5,000}{20,000} = 25\%$	
Increase in volume	$\frac{7,000}{70,000} = 10\%$		$\frac{10,000}{100,000} = 10\%$	
Degree of operating leverage	$\frac{70\%}{10\%} = 7.0$		$\frac{25\%}{10\%} = 2.5$	

crease in volume would result in NOI changing from zero to a negative figure, a net operating loss.

From this we can observe that, as unit volume moves away from the break-even point (BEP), the degree of operating leverage (DOL) changes from indeterminable to a high figure that gradually decreases, approaching 1 but never reaching it. The degree of operating leverage is a function of two factors: (1) the relationship between fixed and variable costs and (2) the difference in unit volume from the break-even point.

DOL formula Computation of the degree of operating leverage (DOL) from any volume level may be simplified by the use of a formula. Let Q = the unit volume level from which DOL is calculated. Then

$$\text{DOL} = \frac{Q\,(p-v)}{Q\,(p-v) - F} \tag{17–4}$$

The degree of operating leverage equals the operating income before fixed charges divided by the operating income after fixed charges.

To illustrate this, let us calculate the degree of operating leverage of Rangley Corporation at the 100 million unit volume level.

$$\begin{aligned}\text{DOL} &= \frac{100{,}000{,}000\ (\$1.50 - \$1)}{100{,}000{,}000\ (\$1.50 - \$1) - \$30{,}000{,}000}\\ &= \frac{\$50{,}000{,}000}{\$20{,}000{,}000}\\ &= \frac{5}{2} = 2.5\end{aligned}$$

This, of course, agrees with our computation of the DOL the long way in Table 17–3.

Risk implications of operating leverage Operating risk results from volatility of net operating income. This, in turn, relates to changes in sales volume that might result from change in the economic environment of the firm, competitive developments, technological change, sociological factors, and the like. So the analysis of operating risk starts with estimates of future levels of sales volume under varying possible conditions. These estimates may be expressed only in terms of a crude measure of dispersion, such as a range, or they may be developed into a subjective probability distribution of various sales volumes.

These possible changes in sales volume will be magnified by operating leverage in their effects upon net operating income. The use of break-even charts and computation of the degree of operating leverage at various probable sales volume levels will clarify management's understanding of operating risk. Estimates of expected levels of net operating income, fluctuation in that income, and the probability of suffering net operating losses should emerge. At the extreme, management will be concerned with the risk of bankruptcy, that is, the possibility of failure due to inability to meet obligations. Only after management fully understands these operating risks should it consider assuming additional financial risks through the use of fixed or limited cost securities in the capital structure.

Complications and limitations To this point, we have assumed that fixed costs remain the same throughout the range of levels of operations from zero units to plant capacity. We also have assumed that variable costs per unit and selling prices per unit remain the same throughout the range. Thus, total costs and total revenues are linear. This assumption was made to clarify explanation and illustration of the basic principles. In many cases, this represents an oversimplification.

Most firms will have some *semifixed* costs, which will be fixed through a given range of operating volume and then increase in a stair-step fashion. For example, an office may require three people up to a certain volume of activity and then a fourth must be added. Beyond another level, a fifth person must be added, and so on. In constructing a detailed, realistic break-even chart, these semifixed costs must be incorporated.

Variable costs per unit may also change. In a large manufacturing operation, only the most efficient machinery and equipment, with the lowest variable cost per unit required for its operation, may be utilized at low volume levels. As volume increases, older, less efficient equipment may be put into operation. Eventually, as capacity production during the regular eight-hour day is reached, overtime wage premiums must be paid and/or less efficient second or third shifts must be added. These will increase variable costs per unit.

Selling prices per unit might not be stable throughout the entire volume range. In order to achieve higher volume, a firm may reduce its prices, grant rebates, or produce products to be sold under private labels at reduced prices.

These factors all tend to modify the nice neat straight lines we have shown on the break-even chart to perhaps something like those on the chart shown in Figure 17–5. The result is that the net operating income (vertical distance between the total revenue and total cost lines) may be considerably more stable through a fairly wide range of volume levels than implied by the simplified break-even chart (Figure 17–3).

Figure 17–5 Complex operating break-even chart

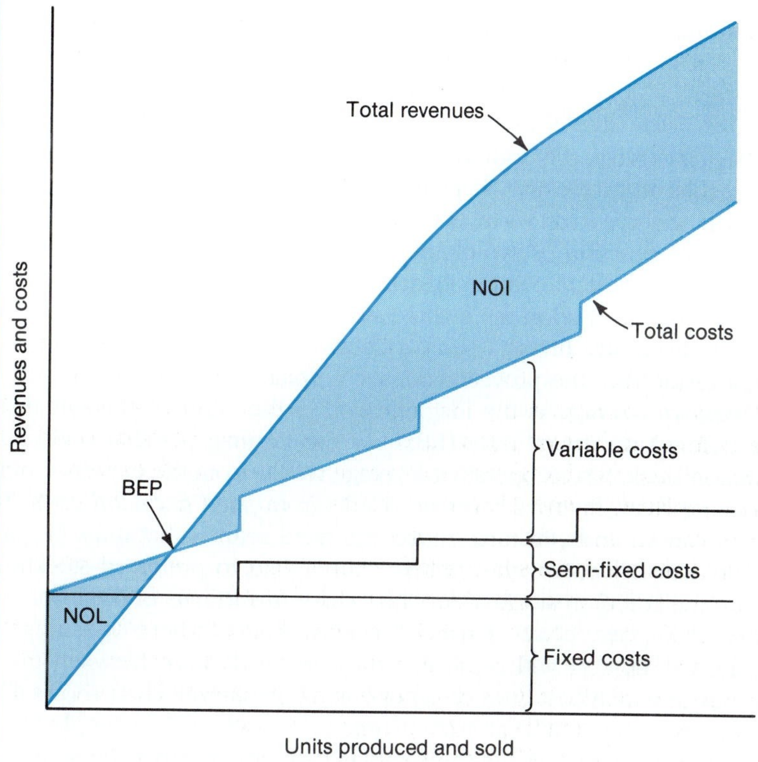

A limitation of operating leverage analysis relates to the timeliness of the cost and revenue data. Especially in a period of inflation, operating break-even charts become obsolete in a very short time. Costs, particularly variable unit costs, change every time a supplier changes the price of a raw material, employees are granted raises, or utility companies change their rates. Thus, it may be difficult or impossible to keep operating break-even charts up to date. This tends to limit their usefulness.

In multiproduct firms, operating leverage analysis is complicated by changes in the product mix. Also, in multiplant firms, different plants have different sets of fixed and variable costs associated with their operation. Shifts in production from one plant to another change the cost structure.

So, if you wish to become thoroughly confused, think of the problems connected with this type of analysis in a conglomerate firm, producing many different types of products, with hundreds of different models and sizes in each line, and operating perhaps 20 or 30 different plants at varying volume levels from nearly shut down to overtime operations. While it is virtually impossible to develop an operating break-even chart for the whole firm, these problems are reduced to more manageable proportions by divisional organization, delegating responsibility to smaller units in which such information may be more meaningful.

Financial leverage analysis

Financial risk is the additional risk borne by the common stockholders that results from the use of fixed- or limited-return securities (long-term debt or preferred stock) in the capital structure. This risk, as mentioned earlier, is a function of two elements. The first is the greater fluctuation in earnings per share of common stock that results from fixed or limited prior claim of securities upon the income stream. The second is the possibility of limited flexibility, financial embarrassment, or, at worst, default, which might result from the provisions of such capital contracts.[6]

Financial leverage is the magnification of the effect of changes in earnings before interest and taxes (EBIT) on the earnings per share (EPS) of the common stock. Just as operating leverage results from the existence of fixed operating costs, financial leverage results from *fixed financial costs.* These fixed financial costs, in turn, reflect the fixed returns that must be paid to the holders of debt or the limited returns paid to preferred stockholders before the common stockholders may share in earnings of the firm.

Financial leverage chart

Financial leverage begins where operating leverage leaves off. You will recall that the vertical distance between the total revenue and total cost lines on an operating break-even chart shows the net operating income (NOI) at each volume of operations. In a simple firm, net operating income (NOI) is the same as earnings before interest and taxes (EBIT). Although some firms may have nonoperating income and/or expenses, these often are insignificant or balance each other out. If so, NOI and EBIT are essentially the same. Then the NOI from the operating leverage chart *is* the EBIT indicated on the horizontal axis of the financial leverage chart, as shown in Figure 17–6.

A *financial leverage chart,* as shown in Figure 17–7 (also variously called an *EBIT chart,* a *range of earnings chart,* or an *EPS-EBIT chart*), shows the earnings per share on the common stock that wold result from the use of

[6]Various provisions of debt and preferred stock contracts and their risk implications will be discussed in Chapters 18 and 20.

Figure 17–6 **Schematic relationship of operating break-even chart to financial leverage chart**

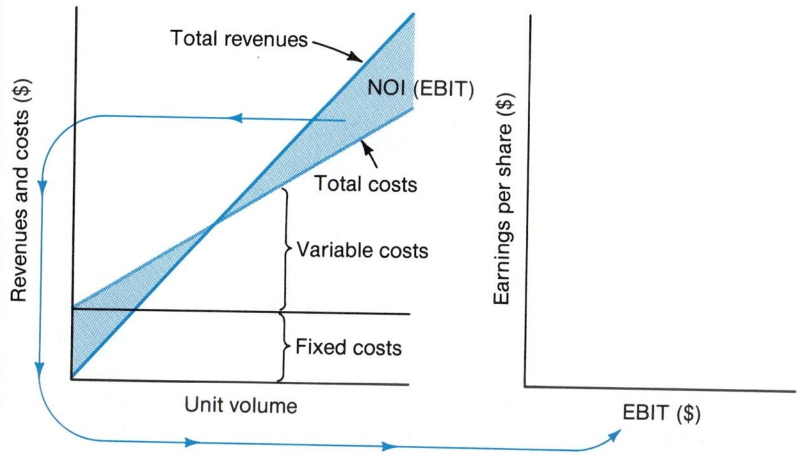

two or more capital structures under consideration. Let us consider two possible capital structures for Rangley Corporation:

A. All common stock:	
2 million shares common stock @ $10	$20 million
Retained earnings	30 million
Total capital	$50 million
B. 40 percent debt and 60 percent equity:	
10% bonds	$20 million
1.2 million shares common stock @ $10	12 million
Retained earnings	18 million
Total capital	$50 million

At $20 million EBIT (assuming an income tax rate of 40 percent), earnings per share (EPS) on the common stock under capital structure A will be $6, as calculated below:

EBIT	$20.0 million
Taxes @ 40%	8.0 million
Earnings after taxes	$12.0 million
Number of shares common stock	2.0 million
Earnings per share (EPS)	$6

At zero EBIT, earnings per share (EPS) will be $0. Now the line showing earnings per share under capital structure A at all levels of EBIT can be drawn through the origin of the chart and the plot of $6 EPS at $20 million EBIT (see Figure 17–7).

The line showing earnings per share with the complex capital structure B, consisting of 40 percent bonds at a 10 percent interest rate and 1.2 million shares of common stock, can be located by plotting any two points in a similar fashion. At $20 million EBIT, earnings per share on the common stock would be $9, as calculated below:

EBIT	$20.0 million
Interest ($20 million @ 10%)	2.0 million
Earnings before taxes	$18.0 million
Taxes @ 40%	7.2 million
Earnings after taxes	$10.8 million
Number of shares common stock	1.2 million
Earnings per share (EPS)	$9

Earnings per share will be $0 at $2 million EBIT, because the $2 million bond interest will absorb all EBIT. Thus, the second point can be plotted on the horizontal axis at $2 million. Now the line showing EPS under capital structure B at all EBIT levels can be drawn through the two points (see Figure 17–7).

The financial *point of indifference* is indicated by the intersection of the lines reflecting the two capital structures. This point indicates the EBIT level

Figure 17–7 **Financial leverage chart—Rangley Corporation**

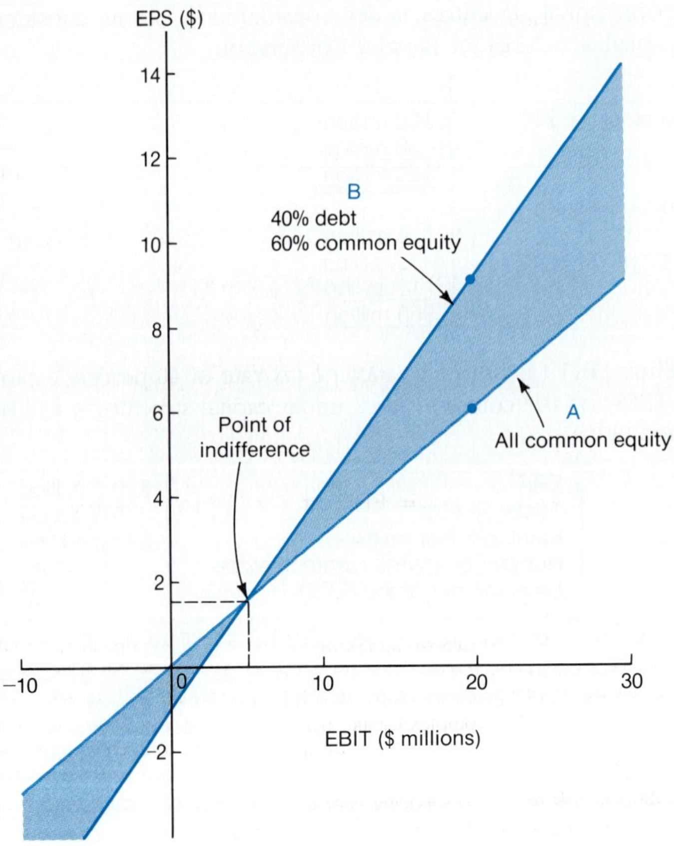

at which earnings per share (EPS) would be identical under each of the capital structures being compared.[7] At all levels of EBIT above the point of indifference, EPS will be higher under B, the complex capital structure (including debt), than under A, the simple all-common-stock structure. The vertical distance between the two lines indicates the advantage. Conversely, below the point of indifference, B, the complex capital structure, results in lower EPS. The disadvantage is measured by the vertical distance between the lines. Below $2 million EBIT, earnings per share (EPS) under B, the complex capital structure, become negative while EPS is still positive under A, the all-common-equity structure. As EBIT becomes negative, losses are magnified by the financial leverage under B, the complex capital structure.

Point of indifference formula The financial point of indifference can also be determined by formula. Let

x = EBIT at the point of indifference;
N_1 = shares of common stock in the all-common-equity capital structure;
N_2 = shares of common stock in the complex capital structure;
I = interest requirement on debt (in dollars);
t = corporate income tax rate.

Then

$$\frac{x\,(1 - t)}{N_1} = \frac{(x - I)\,(1 - t)}{N_2} \tag{17–5}$$

Solving this equation, using the data for Rangley Corporation, we find

$$\frac{x\,(1 - .40)}{2.0\text{ million}} = \frac{(x - \$2.0\text{ million})\,(1 - .40)}{1.2\text{ million}}$$

$$\frac{.60\,x}{2.0\text{ million}} = \frac{(x - \$2.0\text{ million})\,.60}{1.2\text{ million}}$$

$$x = \$5\text{ million}$$

$$= \text{EBIT at point of indifference.}$$

[7]The term *point of indifference* is a misnomer and perhaps an unfortunate one. It should be understood as the point at which EPS would not be different under the two capital structures being compared. But management would *not* be indifferent in choosing between these two capital structures if the central tendency of the probability distribution of expected EBIT were at the point of indifference. The complex capital structure (utilizing debt) entails the assumption of additional risk as compared to the simple all-common-stock structure. Management would not be indifferent to the choice under these circumstances. Rather it would be foolhardy to assume additional risk related to servicing debt in the absence of an expectation of additional benefits to the common stockholders in the form of higher EPS.

Degree of financial leverage The *degree* of financial leverage (DFL) at any given level of EBIT indicates the relationship between the rate of change in EBIT and the resultant rate of change in EPS.

$$\text{DFL} = \frac{\text{Percentage change in EPS}}{\text{Percentage change in EBIT}} \tag{17–6}$$

In other words, it shows the degree of magnification of a change in operating earnings as it affects earnings to the common stockholders. The degree of financial leverage resulting from a simple all-common-equity capital structure is unity, or 1. The capital structure is unleveraged since it entails no fixed costs. The easiest way to understand the degree of financial leverage resulting from a leveraged capital structure (one including fixed or limited return securities) is to calculate it the long way, as shown in Table 17–4. Columns 1 and 2 demonstrate that a 10 percent increase in EBIT from a level of $10 million would result in a 12.5 percent increase in EPS under capital structure B. Therefore, the degree of financial leverage at that EBIT level is 1.25. Columns 3 and 4 show that a 10 percent increase from the $20 million EBIT level would result in an 11.1 percent increase in EPS, the degree of operating leverage being 1.11.

Table 17–4 Degree of financial leverage—Rangley Corporation
(000 except EPS)

	(1)	(2)	(3)	(4)
EBIT	$10,000	$11,000	$20,000	$22,000
Interest	2,000	2,000	2,000	2,000
EBT	8,000	9,000	18,000	20,000
Tax @ 40%	3,200	3,600	7,200	8,000
EAT	$ 4,800	$ 5,400	$10,800	$12,000
Number of shares	1,200	1,200	1,200	1,200
EPS	$ 4.00	$ 4.50	$ 9.00	$ 10.00
Increase in EPS(%)	$\frac{.50}{4.00}$ = 12.5%		$\frac{1.00}{9.00}$ = 11.1%	
Increase in EBIT(%)	$\frac{1,000}{10,000}$ = 10.0%		$\frac{2,000}{22,000}$ = 10.0%	
Degree of financial leverage	1.25		1.11	

As the level of EBIT decreases, the degree of operating leverage increases until it become indeterminate at the point where EBIT equals the interest charges and EPS reaches zero. Thus, on the financial leverage chart (Figure 17–7), the degree of financial leverage is indeterminate at the point where the complex capital structure line, B, intersects the horizontal axis. Financial leverage is highest immediately above (or below) that point and declines as EBIT increases, approaching 1 but never getting there.[8]

DFL formula The degree of financial leverage may be determined by a simple formula. Let

Y = EBIT level from which DFL is calculated
I = interest requirement on debt (in dollars)

Then

$$\text{DFL} = \frac{Y}{Y - I} \qquad (17\text{–}7)$$

Using this formula, the degree of financial leverage at \$20 million EBIT for Rangley Corporation under the complex capital structure, B is calculated as follows:

$$\text{DFL} = \frac{\$20 \text{ million}}{\$20 \text{ million} - \$2 \text{ million}} = \frac{\$20 \text{ million}}{\$18 \text{ million}} = 1.1$$

At \$5 million EBIT,

$$\text{DFL} = \frac{\$5 \text{ million}}{\$5 \text{ million} - \$2 \text{ million}} = \frac{\$5 \text{ million}}{\$3 \text{ million}} = 1.67$$

At \$2 million EBIT,

$$\text{DFL} = \frac{\$2 \text{ million}}{\$2 \text{ million} - \$2 \text{ million}} = \frac{\$2 \text{ million}}{\$0} = \infty$$

Use of financial leverage analysis Just as operating leverage analysis is useful when applied within the range of forecasted volumes of sales, financial leverage analysis is useful within the range of forecasted EBIT levels. For this reason, the financial leverage chart is sometimes called a *range-of-earnings chart*. Management must first have in mind the range of expected future EBIT levels, or perhaps more sophisticated subjective probability estimates of EBIT, before it can meaningfully employ financial leverage analysis as an aid in determining capital structure policy. These expected EBIT levels are derived from the preceding sales fluctuation and operating leverage analyses.

The financial leverage chart and the degree of financial leverage at various EBIT levels within the appropriate range may be used to choose among various contemplated capital structure policies. If a new firm is being started

[8]Note that the indeterminate degree of financial leverage is not in any way related to the point of indifference on the financial leverage chart. In this example, the degree of financial leverage of capital structure B at the point of indifference is 1.67, but this cannot be generalized.

and management has a choice as to the proportion of debt to be employed in the initial financing, financial leverage analysis may be used to indicate the relative EPS advantage of various long-term debt ratios within the range of probable EBIT levels. Similarly, when a going concern requires additional long-term capital, management can assess alternative sources in terms of their effects upon EPS to aid in making the decision.

One must exercise caution by recognizing that *value* and anticipated *earnings* are not the same. Value of the common stock is a function of *both* anticipated earnings and risk. In almost all cases, a financial leverage chart will indicate higher expected EPS to result from additional use of debt as compared to equity. This will be true as long as the expected pretax rate of return from operations exceeds the rate of interest to be paid on the debt. But remember that the economic graveyard is full of the corpses of firms whose managers were both overly optimistic and too greedy. If a little is good, a lot is *not* necessarily better. Financial leverage is beneficial only when the EPS advantage is not outweighed by the disadvantage of increased risk. (The next section of this chapter will deal with estimating a prudent proportion of debt to be incorporated in the capital structure in an effort to maximize the *value* of the common stock, recognizing both income and risk elements.)

Total leverage analysis

Total leverage (TL) is the magnification of a change in sales volume as it affects earnings per share:

$$\text{TL} = \frac{\text{Percentage change in EPS}}{\text{Percentage change in unit volume}} \qquad (17\text{–}8)$$

In other words, the degree of total leverage (DTL) at any given sales volume is the degree of operating leverage multiplied by the degree of financial leverage:

$$\text{DTL} = \text{DOL} \times \text{DFL} \qquad (17\text{–}9)$$

Let us apply this total leverage concept to Rangley Corporation. At a unit sales volume of 100 million units, this firm has a degree of operating leverage (DOL) of 2.5 (from Table 17–3). At that volume level, its net operating income (NOI) is $20 million. Assuming that its NOI and EBIT are equal, Table 17–4 indicates that at the EBIT level of $20 million, Rangley has a degree of financial leverage (DFL) of 1.11 if its capital structure is 40 percent debt and 60 percent common equity. Therefore, its degree of total leverage (DTL) at the 100 million unit volume level is calculated as follows:

$$\text{DTL} = 2.5 \times 1.11 = 2.78$$

This is the simplest and most explanatory formula for calculating the degree of total leverage.

Degree of total leverage also may be determined by using a formula that combines the DOL and DFL formulas as follows:

$$\text{DTL} = \frac{Q\,(p - v)}{Q\,(p - v) - F - I} \qquad (17\text{–}10)$$

where Q equals unit sales volume, p equals price per unit, v equals variable cost per unit, F equals fixed costs, and I equals interest in dollars.

Applying Rangley Corporation data to this formula,

$$\text{DTL} = \frac{100 \text{ million } (\$1.50 - \$1)}{100 \text{ million } (\$1.50 - \$1) - \$30 \text{ million} - \$2 \text{ million}}$$

$$= \frac{\$\,50 \text{ million}}{\$\,50 \text{ million} - \$30 \text{ million} - \$2 \text{ million}}$$

$$= \frac{\$\,50 \text{ million}}{\$\,18 \text{ million}}$$

$$= 2.78$$

One of the general objectives of financial management is to manage total risk, through control of both operating and financial leverage, so that leverage is used to magnify benefits to the common stockholders within prudent risk limits. The other objective is to minimize the overall cost of capital to the firm. These two objectives are fully compatible.

Minimizing overall cost of capital

Just as we have sought to maximize the value of the assets in the management of current assets in Part III and of fixed assets in Part IV of this book, now we seek to minimize the overall cost of capital on the right side of the balance sheet. By so doing we pursue the goal of the firm of maximizing the value of the common stock. You will recall from Chapter 15 that we estimated the overall cost of capital of the firm by weighting the lower aftertax cost of debt (K_d) and the higher cost of equity capital (K_e).[9] But there we either accepted the existing capital structure or assumed optimal proportions. Now we must seek the proportions of debt and equity that will

[9]In our discussions here, we shall assume that the capital structure is comprised of long-term debt and equity only. Elimination of preferred stock increases clarity of the discussion. We also shall not quibble about the minor difference between the cost of new common stock (K_c) and retained earnings (K_r), but rather will designate the cost of all common stock equity as K_e. This is done for the same reason. The terms *overall* and *weighted* cost of capital (K) will be used interchangeably.

minimize the overall cost of capital *(K)*. When the overall cost of capital is minimized, the optimal capital structure will be achieved.

An overview of capital structure theory

Considerable controversy has surrounded capital structure theory. The crux of the controversy has been whether or not the use of debt to create financial leverage can affect the overall cost of capital. If so, how? In other words, "What is the shape of the cost-of-capital curve?"

The *cost-of-capital curve* depicts the aftertax cost of capital (on the vertical axis) in relation to the long-term debt ratio, that is, the percentage debt in the capital structure (on the horizontal axis).

The naive theory The naive theory (sometimes called the *dependence theory* or the *net income theory*) holds that the overall cost of capital *(K)* declines throughout the range of increasing debt ratios, as illustrated in Figure 17–8. As its title indicates, this is merely a "straw man" set up to illustrate the nature of debt and equity costs. It assumes that the aftertax cost of debt (K_d) remains stable as the percentage of debt in the capital structure increases. It also assumes that the cost of equity (K_e) remains stable throughout the range. Inasmuch as K_d is lower than K_e, K declines as larger proportions of K_d are weighted with smaller proportions of K_e.

Figure 17–8 The naive cost-of-capital curve

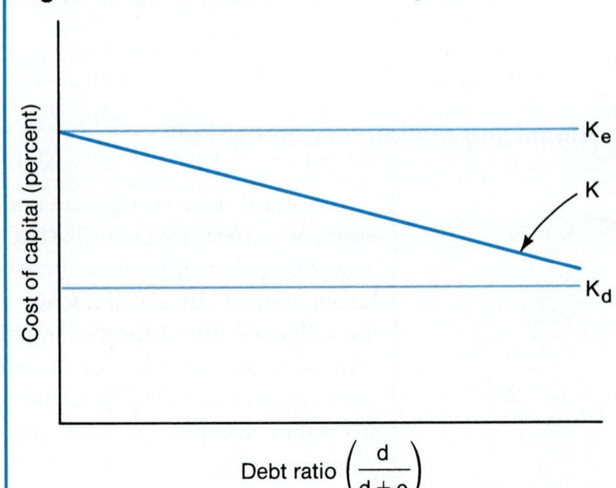

But capital costs do not behave in this way. As the debt ratio increases to the point at which risk of default is recognized, lenders will require higher interest rates to compensate for that risk. Thus the K_d line will curve upward. The risk of default will increase at an increasing rate until, at some point, the default becomes imminent and no one will lend to the firm at any rate. Figuratively, the firm will wear out its welcome on Wall Street and successively move to Main Street, side streets, alleys, and perhaps the Mafia to obtain debt capital on increasingly onerous terms.

The cost of equity capital (K_e) will not remain stable, either. As the debt ratio increases, common stock investors will recognize the increased risk to their investments. This increased risk takes two forms: (1) the increased fluctuation in EPS resulting from financial leverage and (2) the risk that default on the debt will jeopardize or eliminate the value of the common stock. Recognition of these risks will affect the market price of the common stock by inducing investors to capitalize anticipated earnings and dividends at higher rates. In other words, the stock will trade in the market at lower price-earnings ratios. Thus, the K_e line will curve upward at an increasing rate. These criticisms of the naive theory lead us to the traditional theory.

The traditional theory The traditional theory recognizes the behavior of capital costs indicated above. This results in a shallow, U-shaped overall cost-of-capital (K) curve, as shown in Figure 17–9. When the capital structure is entirely common stock equity, K and K_e, of course, are identical. As increments of lower-cost debt are combined with higher-cost equity, K will decline. But this will be true only through the range in which the risk of default on the debt is slight. Through this range the increase in both K_d and K_e will be minor. A significant factor in the decline of K is the advantage provided by income tax laws, which allow interest on debt as an expense but not dividends on the common stock.

Figure 17–9 The traditional cost-of-capital curve

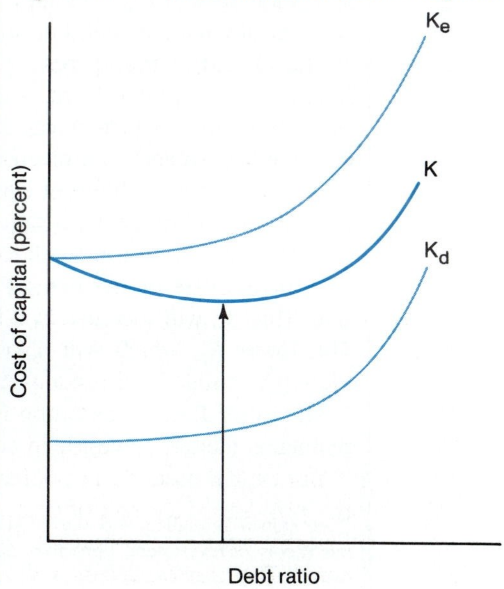

Then, as the debt ratio is further increased, the risk of default (also called the risk of bankruptcy or bankruptcy cost) will be recognized in the capital markets and cause both K_d and K_e to curve upward at an increasing rate. As these increasing component capital costs outweigh the effect of combining lower-cost debt with higher-cost equity, the downward slope of K will be reversed and it will begin to slope upward. As the debt ratio is increased still further, the increased risk of default causes both K_d and K_e to rise at increasing rates, resulting in an increasing upward slope of the K curve. Eventually, as default becomes imminent, debt capital will not be obtainable in the market on any reasonable terms and the common stock will have fallen into complete disrepute because of the extreme leverage upon EPS and the great risk of default.

Under the traditional theory, the optimal capital structure will be comprised of debt and common stock equity proportions indicated by the arrow on Figure 17–9. This is the bottom of the U-shaped K curve, the point at which the curve is tangential to the horizontal axis. This theory appears to be substantially correct in relation to recognized real-world behavior of capital costs. But there remains a question as to whether or not there is an exact point at the bottom of the U that identifies a unique optimal capital structure for a particular firm.

The M and M theory The original M and M theory (also known as the *independence theory* or the *net operating income theory*), so called because its leading proponents are Professors Modigliani and Miller, holds that the overall cost of capital *(K)* is flat throughout the range of possible debt ratios, as shown in Figure 17–10.[10] This theory caused great excitement in the financial world because it, in effect, maintained that there was no such thing as capital structure *policy* and that any proportions of debt and common stock equity were as good as any others.

The M and M theory rests primarily upon two lines of reasoning. The first, in oversimplified form, is that "no matter how you slice it, it is still the same bologna." A firm is capable of generating a given net operating income and is subject to a given degree of operating risk. When that income is divided between different classes of securities holders (bondholders and common stockholders), no value can be created or destroyed. The increase in EPS to the common stockholders resulting from financial leverage will be exactly offset by the market's capitalizing the increased EPS at a higher rate. Thus K_e will increase in a linear fashion as the debt ratio is increased. The lower K_d, which will also rise linearly, will be exactly offset by the higher K_e, thus K will remain stable.

The other line of reasoning is the "homemade leverage" argument. This maintains that any investor in common stock of a firm can make his or her

[10]See Franco Modigliani and Merton H. Miller, "The Cost of Capital, Corporation Finance and the Theory of Investment," *American Economic Review,* June 1958, pp. 261–97.

Figure 17–10 The M and M cost-of-capital curve

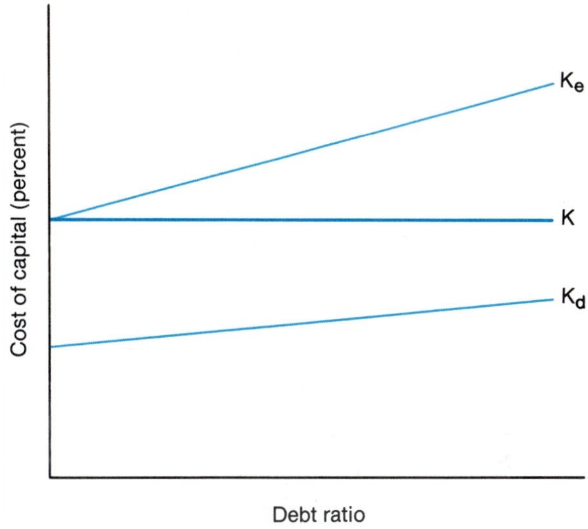

own financial leverage just as economically as the firm can. For example, if the investor buys stock in an unleveraged firm and wishes to assume additional risk in the quest of higher return, that investor can borrow any proportion of the amount invested in the stock to create his or her own financial leverage just as economically as the corporation can. Thus, the effect of any given debt ratio that might be created by the corporation can just as economically be created by the individual common stockholder.

The internal mathematical consistency of the M and M model has not been refuted. But this model is based upon a number of assumptions, several of which do not apply to the world we live in. The critical assumptions are that (1) there are no corporate or individual income taxes, (2) there are no institutional deterrents to holding either bonds or stock or to the creation of "homemade leverage," (3) there are no transactions costs, and (4) all investors can borrow in the same amounts and at the same interest rates as the corporation. These assumptions are patently unreal. We *do* have corporate and individual income taxes; many financial institutions *are* limited by law, their charters, and/or their investment policies with regard to the types of securities they hold and their borrowing practices; we *do* have transactions costs (brokers and lenders do not work for free); and many investors *do not* have the credit worthiness of many corporations.

Modigliani and Miller later corrected their theory to account for the existence of corporate income taxes.[11] This modification (called "M and M

[11]Franco Modigliani and Merton H. Miller, "Corporate Income Taxes and the Cost of Capital: A Correction," *American Economic Review,* June 1963, pp. 433–43.

modified") resulted in a downward sloping linear overall cost-of-capital *(K)* curve throughout the range of possible debt ratios. Under this theory, the optimal capital structure would be almost all debt and almost no equity. The *K* curve is substantially the same as that of the naive theory (but for different reasons). It is not applicable as a guide to capital structure policy, because the latter three critical assumptions are still unreal and because it fails to recognize fully the effect upon the market of the risk of default.

This is not to say that the M and M theory has not made a contribution to the study of capital structure. It has contributed in two ways. First, it inspired a great intellectual ferment among both academicians and practitioners to seek a valid theory of capital structure. Second, that ferment led to questioning of the traditional theory, the reasoning and evidence supporting it, and particularly its contention that a unique optimal capital structure exists for each firm. This questioning led to the development of the saucer-shaped cost-of-capital theory.

The saucer-shaped cost-of-capital theory Most, but not all, academicians and practitioners now agree that the saucer-shaped cost-of-capital theory, as illustrated in Figure 17–11, is a valid guide for determining capital structure policy. This theory is similar to the traditional theory, differing in only one respect. The traditional theory holds that there is a unique point at the bottom of the U-shaped overall cost-of-capital *(K)* curve at which *K* is mini-

Figure 17–11 The saucer-shaped cost-of-capital curve

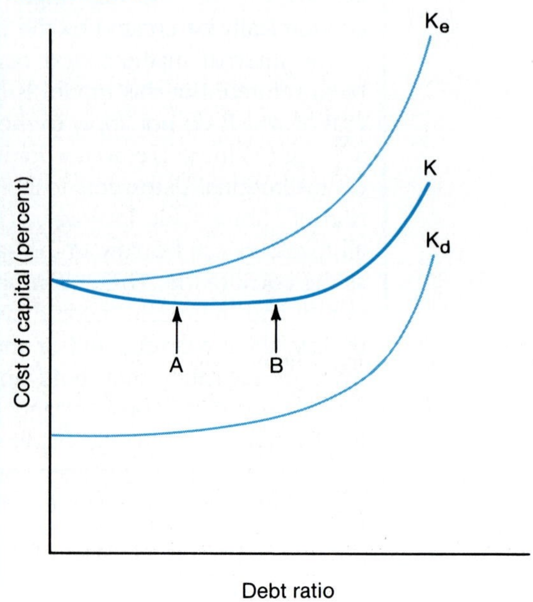

mal, and that the capital structure at that point is optimal. The saucer-shaped cost of capital theory holds that there is a *range* along the bottom of a saucer-shaped K curve before K begins to rise in an increasingly ascending pattern. Thus, this theory holds that there is *not* a unique *point,* but rather an *area* across the bottom of the saucer through which K remains stable. Capital structure proportions are optimal at any point along that flat area.

The overall cost of capital (K) falls as lower-cost debt is combined with higher-cost equity through the range in which K_d and K_e increase only slightly, because the risk associated with the debt is considered relatively insignificant. Then, through the flat range of the saucer (from point A to point B in Figure 17–11), the increasing K_d and K_e will be exactly offset by the increasing proportion of lower-cost debt to higher-cost equity in the capital structure. Beyond point B, the greater increase in K_d and K_e—resulting from recognition of risk reflecting higher financial leverage and probability of default on the debt—will cause K to rise in an increasingly ascending curve. Eventually, K will rise very rapidly until neither debt nor common stock equity may be obtained in the capital markets on feasible terms.

This modification of the traditional theory is important to financial managers, because it indicates that they have some room for discretion in the flat area between A and B on the K curve through which the overall cost of capital will remain stable. Thus, if this area is between, say, a 30 percent and a 40 percent debt ratio for a given firm, management may establish a policy that will keep within that range and still be optimizing the firm's capital structure.

Target capital structure proportions

In line with its overall goal of maximizing the value of the common stock, financial management should seek to minimize the overall cost of capital (K) of the firm. This requires a capital structure policy that will utilize such proportions of debt and common stock equity that K will remain within the flat area of the saucer-shaped overall cost-of-capital curve.

This objective, in turn, dictates that in periods when environmental conditions and the operating results of the firm are favorable, management should seek a capital structure near the left end (point A) of that flat area. The reason for this is that such a conservative capital structure may be utilized at no cost in terms of lowering the value of the common stock. To utilize a lower debt ratio would be ultraconservative in the sense that it would lower the value of the stock by increasing K.

The choice of seeking the lower end of the flat range, rather than the middle or the upper end (near point B), is based upon the financial *flexibility* available under adverse conditions. If either general economic conditions or the economic state of the particular firm should become adverse at a time that additional external capital were required, the firm would then have the choice of obtaining capital from either the debt or equity markets. At such a time, the price of the common stock probably would be depressed. Additional stock could be sold only at a high cost in terms of the large number of shares required to obtain a given amount of funds. At this time the firm's borrowing power would be adequate to obtain the required funds on a reasonable basis through the sale of additional debt securities, because such borrowing would not increase its debt ratio beyond point B. In other words, management could exercise its freedom to move from A to B at no cost in terms of lowering the value of its stock. Later, if external and/or internal conditions improve, then management could move in the direction of point A to restore its reserve of borrowing power.

The important point is to maintain, when feasible, a *reserve of borrowing power* to be utilized under adverse conditions. If, in good times, management's policy were to borrow up to point B, then under adverse conditions it would have to pay a price to obtain additional debt financing by moving beyond point B and thereby increasing its overall cost of capital *(K)*. The alternatives would be to sell common stock at a price detrimental to the present stockholders or not obtain needed funds at all.

How can a financial manager establish points A and B for a particular firm? This is indeed a difficult question. Ultimately its answer will be based upon the analysis of probable fluctuations in sales volume and the effects of these upon net operating income as developed through operating leverage analysis. Some further light upon this question can be shed by such historical information as past long-term debt ratios (long-term debt/equity or long-term debt/total capital structure), interest coverage ratios, fixed charge coverage ratios, and total burden coverage ratios (all discussed in Chapter 4) of both the firm and the industry in which it operates. Such ratio analysis, comparing the firm to its industry, will give the manager some idea of the standards applied by the capital market in appraising debt capacity.

Another useful pursuit is to relate capital structure policy to bond ratings. (These will be discussed in detail in Chapter 18.) For example, the management may estimate that the optimal range for its capital structure exists when its bonds are rated AA or A. (These are the second and third highest classifications, respectively.) Based upon this estimate, it would seek to maintain a AA bond rating under favorable conditions and to exercise extreme effort to hold its bond rating at A under adverse conditions.

Ultimately, management and stockholder attitudes also will affect capital structure policy. These range all the way from those of some ultraconservative managements that will not borrow a dime under any circumstances to some that will borrow every dollar they can get on the thinnest of equity. Stockholders' propensity to bear or avert risk has an important influence upon a firm's capital structure policy.

Summary

This chapter dealt with forecasting long-term funds requirements; operating, financial, and total leverage analysis; the theory of capital structure; and establishing target capital structure proportions. The long-range financial forecast provides the backdrop for capital structure planning, policy, and decision making. It begins with a sales forecast covering a four- or five-year period. Then pro forma financial statements are developed. Asset requirements and current liabilities are projected by various methods, including percentage of sales, simple regression, and, in some cases, curvilinear or multiple regression. These projections are modified to reflect the corporate strategy. Then the forecasted data are assembled to estimate future long-term capital requirements.

Capital structure policy involves determining the proportions of debt, preferred stock, and common stock equity that may be used to finance the firm's capital requirements. The objective is the risk-profitability combination that will minimize the overall cost of capital in the long run and thereby maximize the value of the common stock.

In most cases, the firm's operations must provide the funds to service the securities comprising its capital structure. Therefore, one must first thoroughly understand the operating characteristics. This begins with estimating the future volatility of sales volume. Then the effect of fluctuation of sales volume upon net operating income must be analyzed, using an operating break-even chart and determining the degree of operating leverage at the various probable volume levels. This analysis provides an understanding of the firm's operating risk, which results from the volatility of net operating income inherent in the business.

Financial risk is the additional risk borne by the common stockholders that results from the use of fixed- or limited-return securities in the capital structure. This risk, in turn, is a function of two elements: (1) magnification of fluctuation in earnings per share resulting from financial leverage and (2) the risk of default. Financial leverage may be analyzed by using financial leverage charts and by calculating the degree of financial leverage at various probable levels of EBIT.

Total leverage is the magnification of change in sales volume as it affects earnings per share of the common stock. Operating leverage multiplied by financial leverage equals total leverage. A management policy objective is to control the total risk exposure of the common stockholders relative to the opportunity to increase their return in such a way as to maximize the value of their stock. This objective implies seeking an optimal combination of operating and financial leverage that will at the same time avoid significant default risk.

A compatible management objective is to minimize the overall cost of capital *(K)*. By so doing, the value of the common stock will be maximized. Development of capital structure theory has been controversial. The naive theory holds that *K* declines throughout the range of increasing debt ratios. It has been discarded, because it fails to recognize the increasing cost of both debt and equity capital as the debt ratio increases. The traditional theory recognizes the pattern of capital cost behavior. It holds that the *K* curve is U-shaped and that each firm has a unique optimal capital structure, the debt-equity proportions represented by the bottom of the U. The original M and M theory holds that the *K* curve is flat throughout the range of possible debt ratios; therefore, no particular capital structure is superior to any other. The M and M modified theory recognizes the existence of corporate income taxes and concludes that *K* declines throughout the range of increasing debt ratios. Both M and M theories are rejected because they are based upon assumptions as to institutional factors, transactions costs, and borrowing capacities that do not reflect real-world conditions.

Most academicians and practitioners now agree that the overall cost-of-capital *(K)* curve is saucer-shaped, declining through low debt ratios, flat through some range, and then sloping upward at an increasing rate as default risks (bankruptcy costs) are recognized by the capital markets. This provides some flexibility in capital structure management. The overall cost of capital *(K)* is minimal at any debt ratio within the flat of the saucer.

Target capital structure proportions should be established as a range within the flat of the saucer. Under favorable economic and operating conditions, management should seek the lowest debt ratio within that range. This provides flexibility to borrow when conditions may be unfavorable without increasing the overall cost of capital. By moving back and forth within the optimal range, financial management may maintain a minimum cost of capital and thus maximize the value of the common stock.

Questions

1. Why is long-range financial planning more difficult and subject to greater uncertainty than short-term financial planning?

2. A long-term financial forecast takes the form of a series of pro forma balance sheets. Why must pro forma income statements be developed in connection with the long-term financial forecast? What are the basic shortcomings of pro forma income statements based entirely on the percent-of-sales method? How can these deficiencies be overcome?

3. Explain the difference between the percent-of-sales method and the simple linear regression method of forecasting balance sheet items. Why is the linear regression method superior? If the regression line of best fit is curvilinear, what should the forecaster do?

4. How do corporate strategic considerations explain the fact that long-term forecasts usually are reviewed (and often modified) at the highest managerial levels?

5. Explain the rigidity of long-term debt and the relative flexibility of common stock. How does the difference between these two types of capital contracts relate to capital structure policy?

6. Define: *(a)* operating leverage, *(b)* financial leverage, and *(c)* total leverage. Other things being equal, how does operating leverage limit the prudent use of financial leverage?

7. Indicate and explain the effect (to raise, lower, or leave unchanged) on the operating breakeven point (BEP) of each of the following: (Consider each item independently.)

- *a.* A reduction in the variable costs per unit.
- *b.* An increase in wage rates (not accompanied by an increase in productivity).
- *c.* An increase in property tax rates.
- *d.* An increase in the price of the product (not accompanied by a change in costs).

8. What does an operating break-even chart tell you? How can a firm's estimates of potential fluctuation in sales volume be applied to its operating break-even chart to appraise the effects of sales fluctuations upon net operating income? What bearing does such analysis have upon capital structure policy?

9. Why might management wish to make a *cash* operating break-even analysis to supplement the analysis based upon accounting revenues and costs?

10. What does a financial leverage chart tell you? How can a firm's estimates of potential fluctuation in EBIT be applied to a financial leverage chart to appraise two or more different capital structure policies under consideration?

11. What does the financial point of indifference mean? Would you be indifferent as to which capital structure to use if EBIT were expected to hover about the point of indifference?

12. Why is the naive theory—of the relationship between the overall cost of capital *(K)* and the capital structure—naive? How does the traditional theory differ from the naive theory?

13. The original M and M theory holds that the overall cost of capital *(K)* is flat, and the modified M and M theory holds that it declines throughout

the range of possible debt ratios because of the effect of corporate income taxes. Why are these theories not practicable as bases for capital structure policy determination?

14. What is the saucer-shaped cost-of-capital theory? What are its significant implications regarding capital structure policy?

Problems

1. Frontier Manufacturing Company's balance sheet as of December 31, 1982 is shown below:

Assets		*Liabilities and Capital*	
Cash	$ 10,000	Accounts payable	$ 28,000
Accounts receivable	41,000	Accruals	18,000
Inventories	88,000	Notes payable—bank	30,000
Fixed assets (net)	75,000	Long-term debt	42,000
		Common stock	25,000
		Retained earnings	71,000
Total assets	$214,000	Total liabilities and capital	$214,000

Sales, which were $300,000 in 1982, are expected to increase 20 percent annually during the next two years. Current assets and spontaneous current liabilities are forecasted to increase directly in proportion to sales. Replacements of fixed assets are expected to equal depreciation charges in 1983 and 1984, but an additional investment of $25,000 is planned for 1984 to expand the plant. Frontier's line of credit at its bank of $30,000 is expected to be increased $5,000 each of the next two years. Net profits after taxes are forecasted to equal 10 percent of sales, and a dividend payout ratio of 75 percent is planned. No long-term debt will be retired.

a. Forecast the external long-term financial requirements for 1983 and 1984.

b. How much would these requirements for the two-year period be changed if Frontier reduced dividends to 40 percent of earnings?

2. In connection with its long-range financial forecast, O'Neil Corporation is analyzing the historical relationship between its sales and inventory levels. The following data are available ($ millions):

Year	Sales	Inventories
1977	$10.1	$3.2
1978	9.0	2.5
1979	16.2	3.4
1980	18.3	3.2
1981	23.4	4.1
1982	29.0	4.0

a. Plot a scatter diagram showing the relationship between sales and inventories.

b. Visually fit an appropriate regression line on the scatter diagram.

c. Is the regression linear or curvilinear?

d. If sales are forecasted at $31.0 million for 1983 and $33.4 million for 1984, what inventory levels would you forecast for those years (assuming no change in inventory policy or control technology)?

3. The Brooklawn Corporation has fixed operating costs of $400,000 per year and variable costs of $30 per unit. The selling price of its product is $48 per unit.

a. Draw its operating break-even chart.

b. Compute its breakeven point in units by formula.

c. What is Brooklawn's net operating income before tax (NOI) at 30,000 units?

d. What is the degree of operating leverage at 30,000 units? At 40,000 units? At what unit volume would Brooklawn's degree of operating leverage be indeterminate?

4. Merlin Corporation has fixed costs of $1 million and variable costs of $2.20 per unit. The selling price of its product is $2.60 per unit.

a. At what unit volume is Merlin's operating break-even point?

b. How much will Merlin's net operating income before taxes (NOI) be increased if it can increase sales from 3 million units to 3.6 million units? What is the degree of operating leverage (DOL) at 3 million units?

c. What would Merlin's degree of operating leverage (DOL) be at 4 million units? Why is the DOL lower?

5. How and why would the following actions affect a firm's operating break-even point (BEP)? (Consider each action independently.)

a. Raising the selling price of the product.

b. Lowering the variable costs per unit through increased productivity.

c. Increasing fixed costs because of increase in property taxes on the plant.

6. Short Temper Garden Tool Company is considering two proposals to finance a plant expansion. Short Temper presently has an all-common-stock equity capital structure consisting of 500,000 shares of common stock at a par value of $10 per share and $3.2 million retained earnings. Plan A is to issue 100,000 additional common shares at $20 per share. Plan B is to place $2 million of 12 percent bonds with Acme Life Insurance Company. Assume a 40 percent income tax rate.

The firm's management expects annual EBIT to range between 0 and $3 million in the future.

a. Prepare a financial leverage chart comparing the two financing plans.

b. Calculate the EBIT at the financial point of indifference under the two resulting capital structures.

c. What is the degree of financial leverage (DFL) under Plan B at an EBIT level of $1.4 million? At EBIT of $500 thousand?

d. At what EBIT level will financial leverage be indeterminate?

7. Supersafe Corporation has a capital structure comprised of 10 million shares of $10 par common stock and $80 million retained earnings. Shoestring Corporation has a capital structure comprised of $150 million of 14 percent bonds, 1 million shares of $10 par common stock, and $20 million retained earnings. (Assume 40 percent tax rate.)

a. Compare the earnings per share (EPS) of Supersafe and Shoestring when each has EBIT of $15 million, $25 million, and $50 million.

b. What is the degree of financial leverage (DFL) for each corporation at each EBIT level indicated in (*a*)?

c. What are your general observations regarding financial leverage of these two corporations?

d. Under what conditions relative to sales volume and operating leverage might Supersafe's or Shoestring's capital structure be appropriate?

8. McCann Corporation has fixed operating costs of $2 million per year and variable operating costs of $18 per unit. The selling price of its product is $32 per unit. McCann's capital structure is comprised of $2 million 12 percent bonds, 500 thousand shares of $10 par value common stock, and $1.5 million retained earnings. The firm's income is taxed at 40 percent.

a. Draw McCann's operating break-even chart covering operating volumes from 0 to its capacity of 500,000 units annually.

b. Compute its operating break-even point in units.

c. Compute its degree of operating leverage (DOL) at volumes of 200,000 units and 400,000 units.

d. Compute McCann's degree of financial leverage (DFL) when operating at volumes of 200,000 units and 400,000 units. (Assume that the firm has no nonoperating income or expense except interest and taxes, so that NOI equals EBIT.)

e. Compute McCann's degree of total leverage (DTL) at operating levels of 200,000 and 400,000 units.

Chapter 18
Long-Term Debt

In Chapter 17 we learned that the judicious use of debt financing will lower the overall cost of capital and thereby increase the value of a firm's common stock. The lower cost of debt capital results from both the tax deductibility of interest and its limited prior claim upon the income stream and assets in liquidation. But risk to the common stockholders is increased by financial leverage and greater probability of default. Therefore the use of long-term debt must be controlled within a reasonable range.

What are the legal arrangements under which long-term debt financing is obtained? What financial instruments may be used? What trade-offs must be considered among explicit costs and the various possible privileges and constraints of long-term debt contracts? This chapter will attempt to answer these questions and consider various aspects of debt management.

Long-term borrowing is considerably more complex than short-term because risk is, to a large degree, a function of time. In the case of, say, a 90-day note, there is little probability that changes in the operations and financial condition of a firm would materially affect its credit worthiness. If the note were to be renewed, the lender would have the opportunity to reappraise the credit before accepting a new note. But when debt financing involves a commitment over many years, numerous possible contingencies must be provided for in the contract. Therefore, the agreement is much more formal, spelling out in detail just where the lender and the borrower stand if and when any such contingencies materialize.

The two ways that long-term debt financing may be obtained are through the sale of *bonds* and by directly borrowing under a *term loan* from one or a group of financial institutions. We shall first discuss the use of bonds and then treat term loans and the various sources from which they may be obtained.

Bond financing

Most long-term corporate debt is financed through the issuance of bonds. A bond is a long-term *promise to pay interest* periodically (usually semiannually) at a stated rate and the *principal* at maturity. In addition, the issuer promises *to abide by* the various *provisions,* called covenants, *of the bond indenture.* Bonds are referred to by the name of the issuer, the stated interest rate (the *coupon* rate), and the maturity date. Bond prices are quoted as a percentage of face value. For example, the AT&T 13¼s of '91 were quoted on April 15, 1981, at 96. Since these, and most bonds, are issued in $1,000 denominations, one bond was worth $960 on that date. The bonds of U.S. corporations normally are denominated in a fixed number of dollars.[1] Bonds usually mature in 10 to 30 years and are issued in lots of five to several hundred million dollars.

As indicated in Chapter 16, bond issues may be either privately placed with institutional investors or publicly offered through the investment banking mechanism. When privately placed, details of the agreement normally can be handled by a contract between the issuing corporation and the institutional investors. When publicly offered, a more complex arrangement involving a trustee and an indenture must be used.

The indenture

When a bond issue is sold by public offering, there will be many bondholders, perhaps tens of thousands of them, widely scattered throughout the country or perhaps the world. The bond *indenture,* executed and enforced by the trustee, *provides a mechanism for centralizing and protecting the interests of the scattered and unrelated bondholders.* The bond itself is a relatively simple single-page instrument stating only the highlights of the issuer's obligation. But it contains a statement and a trustee's certificate indicating that this is one of the bonds fully described by the indenture executed between the issuing corporation and the trustee and subject to all of the rights, privileges, and obligations contained in the indenture.

The indenture is a lengthy document, ranging from perhaps 50 to several hundred pages, in which all of the details of the terms, protective covenants, redemption provisions, reporting requirements, action required in event of default, and other contractual agreements are stated. If the bonds are secured by the pledge of specific property, the legal descriptions of such property also are included. Thus, in effect, the contractual relationship between the issuer and the bondholders is set forth in the indenture.[2]

The trustee

The trustee usually is the trust department of a major commercial bank. It is selected and paid for its services by the issuing corporation. *The trustee*

[1]This is not always the case. A few bonds have variable interest rates tied to the price of a commodity or a general price index. Many bonds issued by corporations in countries that have undergone severe inflation are indexed to various indicators of general price levels, such as their countries' consumer price indexes. These arrangements, of course, are in response to investors' fears that the value of their bonds will be eroded by inflation.

[2]The reader should not infer that a bondholder must read the indenture in order to understand the important provisions of a bond contract. The prospectus (discussed in Chapter 16) must contain the essence of all material provisions. In addition, manuals published by the major investors services, Moody's and Standard & Poor's, contain summary descriptions of all bonds that are widely held by the public.

is obligated to act as the "watchdog" of the bondholders to protect their interests in assuring that all of the provisions of the indenture are carried out. In event of default, the trustee usually must take legal action to force the corporation to comply and/or to protect the interests of the bondholders.[3] The trustee also administers the sinking fund arrangement, if any.

Types of bonds

Bonds may be specifically *secured* by the pledge of collateral, such as a mortgage on real property in the case of a mortgage bond, or securities, such as stocks or other bonds, in the case of collateral trust bonds. Or they may be *unsecured* in the sense that no specific security is pledged, as in the case of debentures. Some bonds may hold an inferior claim in liquidation, as in the case of subordinated debentures. They may be classified as to *priority of claim,* in which case one issue of bonds may be the *senior* issue while another, with an inferior claim, will be the *junior* issue. Sometimes these classifications are referred to as *first-line, second-line,* and so on in order of their priorities of claim. Bonds also may be classified as to their retirement provisions, such as sinking fund bonds or convertible bonds.

Mortgage bonds

A *mortgage bond* is *secured by a lien on real property* in the form of land and the improvements such as buildings that are permanently attached to the land. But mortgages may differ as to their priorities in liquidation and the flexibility of future financing.

Closed-end mortgage bonds If a closed-end mortgage is used, specific real property is pledged to secure the debt, and *only the bonds of that issue may have the first claim against the value of the pledged property.* These will be called *first mortgage* bonds. Additional borrowing against the same property will have an inferior claim against the value of that property and be called *second mortgage* bonds. Still further borrowing will have a third mortgage claim, then a fourth mortgage claim, and so on.

This is essentially the type of mortgage you would use if you were to buy a house or condominium. Let us say you buy a house valued at $100,000 and borrow $60,000 from a savings and loan association, executing a first mortgage to the lender. If you wish to borrow additional funds to be secured by that house, you might execute a second mortgage to secure a loan of, say, $15,000 from a finance company. Perhaps your father-in-law will lend you another $10,000, secured by a third mortgage. If you should be

[3]The indenture and the trustee must comply with the requirements of the Trust Indenture Act of 1939, which is administered by the SEC. In essence, this act requires that (1) the indenture fully disclose the terms of the issue, (2) the trustee be independent of the issuer and have sufficient power to act on behalf of the bondholders, and (3) the trustee take prompt protective action if default occurs.

unfortunate enough to fail to make the payments and the mortgage were foreclosed, the first mortgage holder, the S&L, would receive from the sale of the house the total amount owed to it before the second mortgage holder, the finance company, would get anything. Then the finance company would be entitled to the full amount owed to it before your father-in-law would get anything. He would get the full amount owed to him before anything would be left for you.

In business finance, the use of closed-end mortgages can be cumbersome as a firm expands, acquires additional real properties, and issues bonds secured by various priority liens against its properties. Each bond issue will entail different credit risks related to differing priorities of claim in relation to assets of differing values.

Open-end mortgage bonds An *open-end mortgage allows additional borrowing having the same priority of claim against real property. Unlimited* open-end mortgage bonds simply would not be salable, because the security provided by the mortgage to the original bondholders might be diluted by excessive issue of additional bonds having the same priority of claim against the property. But the *limited open-end mortgage,* with proper safeguards against overissue, has proven to be a viable and convenient means of securing bond financing.

Under this arrangement, a *blanket first mortgage* is executed to the trustee when the first bond issue (called series A) is sold. This mortgage contains an *after-acquired clause,* which says that these bonds and any additional bonds issued under the mortgage will be secured by real property specified in the indenture *and all other real property hereafter acquired.* The issue of additional first mortgage bonds will be limited to (1) a stated maximum ratio of bonds outstanding in relation to value of the pledged property (in effect, a *property coverage* ratio) and (2) a minimum ratio of earnings before interest and taxes (EBIT) of the firm in relation to interest required to service the bonds (an *interest coverage* ratio).

As the firm acquires additional real property (covered by the after-acquired clause) and earnings increase, it can issue additional first mortgage bonds (called series B, series C, series D, and so on) that have the same first claim against the pledged assets. The corporation may issue additional first mortgage bonds, however, only as long as it can qualify these bonds under the property value and earnings coverage limitations.

To illustrate the use of the open-end mortgage, assume that the American Public Utility Corporation (APUC) began operations with an electric generating plant and distribution facilities valued at $100 million. At that time, it issued $50 million of open-end 5 percent first mortgage bonds (series A). Its initial EBIT was $7.5 million in relation to the interest requirement of $2.5 million. The bond indenture contains an after-acquired clause. Additional issuance of bonds is limited to 50 percent of real property value and

EBIT for the 12 preceding months must be equal to or greater than three times the interest requirement on the then outstanding bonds plus the new issue.

Subsequently, APUC acquired additional property that increased its real property value (net of depreciation) to $200 million, and its annual EBIT increased to $18 million. It could then sell an additional issue of first mortgage bonds (series B) of $50 million at a 6 percent interest rate (the rate required by the market at that time). In subsequent years if further increased its assets and earning power to qualify the issue of series C, series D, and so on.

APUC now has outstanding $2 billion of first mortgage bonds secured by net real property valued at $4.3 billion. These bonds require interest payments of $180 million per year, as compared to the firm's EBIT of $600 million. Last year it issued series R. Series A through L have already been paid off at their maturities. APUC presently is qualified to issue $150 million additonal first mortgage bonds (series S) at a 13¼ percent interest rate. Property coverage would be reduced to 2 times ($4.3 billion/($2 billion + $.150 billion) and interest coverage would be 3 times ($600 million/$180 million + $19.88 million).[4]

Largely because of their capital intensity, the public utility industries (electric utilities, natural gas distribution and pipeline companies, and the like) account for the largest portion of corporate long-term borrowing. Most of the firms in these industries use a limited open-end first mortgage to secure their first-line debt.

Collateral trust bonds Collateral trust bonds are secured by the pledge of securities, usually stocks or bonds owned by the issuing corporation. They are issued primarily by *holding companies,* firms that own controlling interest in the stock of subsidiary operating companies.[5] The holding company deposits securities of its operating subsidiaries with the trustee and issues collateral trust bonds secured by these securities. In event of default on the bonds, the trustee may seize the collateral to protect the bondholders.

Equipment trust certificates Equipment trust certificates are used primarily by transportation companies, such as railroads, airlines, trucking companies, barge lines, and ocean shipping companies, to finance their equipment. The equipment, say a number of transport aircraft, is purchased and title held by the trustee, usually a major commercial bank. The money to pay the manufacturer for the aircraft is provided by a down payment, of, say, 20 percent by the airline, and the remaining funds are provided by selling equipment trust certificates to investors. These certificates bear interest and

[4]This qualification refers only to the indenture restrictions. The *market* might impose more rigid limitations.

[5]Holding companies will be discussed in Chapter 23.

mature serially, that is, some of them mature each year for, say, the next 10 years.

The airline then leases the aircraft from the trustee, with the rental payments arranged to cover the interest payments, serial maturities, and the trustee's fees. When the final rental payment is made at the end of 10 years, the trustee transfers title to the aircraft to the airline. In the event the airline fails to make the rental payments or otherwise breaches the terms of the lease, the trustee, after due notice, may order that the aircraft be assembled at a designated airport and turned over to the trustee to be held or liquidated for the benefit of the equipment trust certificate holders.[6]

Debentures A debenture is often called an unsecured bond. It is not secured by the pledge of any specific asset, such as real property or securities collateral. But, in another sense, a debenture is secured by *the general credit of the issuer,* which, in turn, rests upon the firm's ability to maintain sufficient earnings to cover its financial obligations and asset values greater than its liabilities.

The dominant trend in long-term debt financing of industrial corporations has been toward the use of debentures rather than mortgage bonds. This reflects the relative simplicity of debentures and recognition that the ultimate value of a long-term debt security rests upon the earning power of the issuer rather than the lien against specific physical assets.

The claim of a debenture holder in liquidation is that of a general creditor. Thus, the debenture holders stand in the same position as unsecured bank creditors or trade creditors. Debentures may be first-line debt or second-line debt, depending upon whether or not specific assets have been pledged to secure claims. Many public utilities and some industrial firms use debentures as second-line debt, ranking under the first mortgage bonds, which comprise a large portion of their capital structures. In such cases, the credit standing of the debentures clearly is inferior, so the cost of this second-line debt is relatively high. On the other hand, some public utilities and most industrial corporations do not have any secured long-term debt; therefore, debentures constitute their first-line or senior debt and may be of very high credit standing.

If debentures are used as first-line debt, the indenture usually contains one of two provisions to protect the debenture holders from dilution of their claims. Subsequent pledge of specific assets to secure senior debt would force the debentures into a junior position. If the debentures are privately placed, the contract will include a *negative pledge clause,* under which the issuer is prohibited from pledging specific assets to secure other

[6]Technically, from the standpoint of the airline, this arrangement is a form of leveraged lease. (Leasing will be discussed in Chapter 19.) However, the equipment trust certificate is discussed here as a type of secured bond because the financial and investment characteristics of the instrument are essentially the same as those of a bond.

debt unless the debenture holder agrees to amend the bond contract. If the debentures are publicly offered, the indenture usually will include an *equal and ratable security clause.* This provides that if the issuer were to pledge specific assets to secure other debt, the debentures would automatically share equally in the claim against those assets with the secured creditors. In other words, if the issuer were to place a first mortgage on its real property, the debentures would automatically become first mortgage bonds.

Either of these arrangements adequately protects the debenture holders against being forced into a junior position by an action of the issuer. When debentures are the first-line debt and are protected by such a clause, most investors consider their quality to be about the same as if they were first mortgage bonds of an issuer of equal credit worthiness.

Subordinated debentures The term *subordinate* means inferior to or standing in order or rank below another. The claim of a *subordinated debenture* is subordinate to that of any other creditor(s) named in the indenture. Usually the claim is inferior to straight (senior) debentures and/or bank loans.

The cost of subordinated debenture financing usually is higher than that of other debt because of the greater risk resulting from subordination. They often are used when the borrowing power of the issuer under straight debentures is limited either by contractual provisions or by the threat that its bond rating would be downgraded if additional senior debt were issued. Subordinated debt serves as if it were equity in supporting senior debt, because its claim is inferior. The stockholders, however, view subordinated debt as a contractual obligation that must be met. Thus, the use of subordinated debentures tends to reduce the risk of senior creditors but increase that of the stockholders.

Income bonds An *income bond* (or income debenture) requires the payment of interest only when that interest has been earned. If the issuer sustains losses or does not have sufficient earnings to pay the interest, a default does not occur. Usually the interest is *cumulative,* that is, any interest that has not been paid in previous years must be paid when earnings are sufficient to do so. The principal must be paid at maturity. The indenture clearly specifies the accounting methods that must be applied in determining earnings.

Historically, income bonds often have been issued in the reorganization of failed corporations. In such cases, the income provision may apply only to a limited period, say three years. This allows the reorganized firm to establish its earning power during the initial years of operation without the fear that default will cause it to fail again. Another appropriate use is where the seller(s) of a firm accepts income bonds as partial or full payment of the purchase price. Here, in effect, the purchase of the firm is financed on a long-term or installment basis while avoiding the possibility of default resulting from a short period of insufficient earnings.

Income bonds often are subordinated to bank loans and/or senior long-term debt. Since the subordination and the income feature entail high risk, the interest rate is considerably higher than that of straight debt. Subordinated income debentures are very similar to preferred stock, materially differing only in the firm obligation to pay the principal. Because interest payments on subordinated income debentures are an allowable expense for income tax purposes, whereas preferred stock dividends are not, subordinated income debentures may advantageously be used when preferred stock otherwise would be appropriate. Some corporations have refinanced preferred stock by offering subordinated income debentures in exchange for the outstanding shares of preferred stock. Such refinancing improves the corporation's tax position and also slightly improves the claim of the investors without materially increasing the risk borne by the common stockholders.

Convertible bonds A *convertible bond* is a long-term debt security that is *convertible at the option of the holder into a given number of shares of common stock.* Some debentures, and many subordinated debentures and income debentures are convertible. This hybrid security has investment characteristics of both a bond and the common stock into which it is convertible. Convertible bonds will be treated in detail in Chapter 21.

Protective provisions

In addition to promising to pay interest periodically and the principal at maturity or in some form of installment arrangement, the firm issuing bonds promises to abide by other covenants of the indenture. These other covenants are the various provisions established for the protection of the bondholders. Some are routine safeguards; others may seriously constrain the financial and operating activities of the borrower.

Standard protective provisions Nearly all bond indentures contain several standard provisions requiring that management act in a prudent and responsible fashion. The borrower is required to maintain adequate records according to generally accepted accounting principles and to render timely audited financial statements to the trustee. These reporting provisions are necessary to assure that specific operating and financial requirements of the indenture are met. The borrower is required to maintain its properties in sound condition and to carry adequate insurance against property and casualty losses. Taxes and other liabilities must be paid when due. Bondholders, of course, are aware that default on such obligations could jeopardize their position by creating liens against property or, at worst, forcing the issuer into bankruptcy.

The final, but most important, standard provision is the *acceleration clause,* stating that if any provision of the indenture is breached, the trustee may declare a default and the entire amount of principal and accrued interest of the bonds will become due and payable in, say, 30 days. This allows a grace period for the issuer to correct the breach but also, at the expiration of that period, gives the trustee the power to take legal action to protect the bondholders.

Constraints on additional borrowing As discussed earlier, the indenture usually limits additional issue of bonds of the same class to a stated percentage of net property value and/or a stated minimum earnings coverage of interest requirements. These restrictions protect against overissue of bonds that would dilute the investment quality of the outstanding bonds. In some cases, short-term borrowing and/or total borrowing is limited.

Constraints on asset management Debenture issues of industrial corporations usually require the maintenance of a minimum net working capital (current assets less current liabilities) and/or a minimum current ratio. This covenant recognizes that continued operation of the firm depends upon its maintaining a sound current position. Insufficient liquidity would increase the bondholders' risk by increasing the probability of default in payment of maturing current liabilities. In addition, some indentures prohibit the sale or assignment of accounts receivable or the pledging of inventories. Such actions might dilute the firm's liquidity and place the bondholders in a junior position relative to the value of these assets in liquidation.

Liquidation or pledging of fixed assets may be limited or prohibited. Here again, the bondholders are protected against dilution of their asset coverage or giving another creditor a prior claim on assets. In issues that are publicly offered, this contingency usually is covered by the *equal and ratable security clause,* discussed earlier. Lease obligations sometimes also are prohibited or limited.

Constraints on dividends Payment of dividends withdraws the most liquid asset, cash, from the firm and transfers it to the stockholders. If not limited, it might be possible for stockholders to "bleed" the corporation through the payment of excessive dividends, which would reduce liquidity and the equity cushion protecting the bondholders. Therefore, the indenture usually will include a limitation upon dividends.

The indenture commonly limits dividend payments to earnings accruing after the bonds have been issued. In other words, retained earnings may not be reduced below those existing at the time of issue. Or a restriction of this type may allow payment of dividends equal to subsequent earnings plus a stated amount, say $200,000. The dividend clause may be more restrictive by limiting dividends to a given percentage, say 50 percent, of subsequent earnings.

Cash and the equity cushion might also be reduced by the corporation's repurchasing its stock. This has the same effect as the payment of dividends. Therefore, the same restrictions usually apply to stock repurchase.

Other restrictions Various other restrictive covenants might be included in the indenture. Perhaps the vote of a stated majority of the bondholders will be required if the firm is to be merged into another corporation. Officers' salaries, bonuses, or stock options might be limited. Certain investments in assets also might be restricted.

It should be recognized that *all* of the above discussed restrictive provisions are not necessarily included and how tight or loose they may be depends upon the financial condition and risks of the issuing firm and the trade-offs required by the marketplace. In a privately placed bond issue, the protective provisions, as well as the interest rate, maturity date, payment provisions, and so on are the result of bargaining between the issuer and the investing institution(s). In a publicly offered bond issue, the investment banker bargains with the issuer for such provisions as are believed necessary to facilitate sale of the issue.

Bond ratings

Publicly offered bonds are rated on quality scales by the two major investment services, Standard & Poor's Corporation and Moody's Investors Service, Inc. These ratings depict the estimated probability of default (that the issuer will fail to fulfill the obligations of the bond). When bond issues are scheduled for offering, the rating agencies will thoroughly investigate the issuing corporation both quantitatively and qualitatively.[7] The ratings determined will have a considerable effect upon marketability of the issue and the interest rate required.

The rating scale and an abbreviated interpretation are shown in Table 18–1. As a general rule, a straight bond issue requires a rating in one of the

Table 18–1 Bond ratings

Standard & Poor's	Moody's	Interpretation
AAA	Aaa	Highest quality—minimal risk
AA	Aa	High quality—low risk
A	A	Medium-high quality—some risk
BBB	Baa	Medium quality—moderate risk
BB	Ba	Low-medium quality—speculative elements recognized
B	B	Low quality—speculative
CCC	Caa	Poor quality—speculative
CC	Ca	Highly speculative—some in default
C	—	Income bonds not paying interest
—	C	Extremely poor quality
DDD, DD, D		In default

Note: Standard and Poor's uses plus (+) and minus (−) in ratings AA through BB. Moody's adds numbers to its letter system in ratings Aa through B. Number 1 indicates the high end of the rating category, number 2 denotes the midrange, and number 3 designates the low end of the category.
Source: Standard & Poor's *Bond Guide* and Moody's Investors Service *Bond Guide*.

[7]A comprehensive discussion of factors influencing bond ratings is contained in Standard & Poor's *Rating Guide* (New York: McGraw-Hill, 1980).

top four classifications to be readily marketable. Many institutional investors are limited by law or their policies to bond investments in these four categories. The interest rate required will be inversely related to the rating. Interest rate differentials among ratings tend to be relatively narrow in strong bond markets when funds are plentiful. They widen considerably when bond markets become tight and funds are scarce.

The capital structure policies of many firms will dictate that bond ratings be kept within a range of two classifications if possible. Thus if a firm's first-line debt is rated AA in good times, management will be extremely reluctant to issue bonds under adverse conditions that would lower its rating below A. For example, it might issue second-line (junior) debt if confronted with a high probability that an additional senior issue would lower the rating to BBB. A less conservative management might strive to maintain A or BBB on its first-line debt. Falling below BBB would be particularly onerous because such issues usually must contain "sweeteners" in the form of convertibility or attached warrants to purchase common stock in order to be marketable. An alternative, of course, is the issue of additional common stock to reinforce the equity cushion and thus maintain the bond rating.

Downgrading the rating of a firm's bonds has a two-pronged effect. First, the interest rate on the new issue will be increased, thus increasing the cost of new capital. Second, the market prices of all of the firm's outstanding bonds will tend to fall to bring their yields into line with that on the new issue. This impairs the reputation of the firm in the bond market. Although bond ratings usually are changed only when new issues are offered, the rating agencies may change a rating at any time. Such changes typically are made in response to material adverse developments affecting the firm's credit worthiness.

Bond retirement

Contractual arrangements for the retirement of bonds may seriously affect the firm's risk, cost, cash flows, and flexibility. Therefore the financial manager must consider these arrangements when evaluating the trade-offs involved in designing and placing a bond issue.

Payment at maturity The repayment terms may simply require that the issuer will pay the principal at maturity. Thus if a $20 million, 12 percent, 20-year bond were issued on July 1, 1983, the entire $20 million principal would be payable on June 30, 2003.

There are three possible problems in connection with such a repayment arrangement. First, the issuer might not need the funds for the full 20-year period. In such a case, it still would be obligated to continue to pay interest until 2003. Second, if interest rates decline to, say, 7 percent during the interim period, the issuer could not pay off these bonds and borrow the money at the lower rate. Third, the issuer might not have $20 million available on June 30, 2003, to make the principal payment. If so, it would have to *refund* the bonds by selling another bond issue to obtain the funds to make the principal payment. Who knows the condition of the bond market and the interest rate that would be required to borrow this amount on or a little before June 30, 2003? The issuer would be taking the risk that the bond market might be weak at that time and that it would be forced to borrow on onerous terms to obtain the required funds.

Some corporations, particularly the larger public utility firms such as AT&T, issue bonds on such repayment terms. They can do this because they expect to need the funds throughout the period to maturity. They are marketing one or more bond issues each year and can distribute the maturities in approximately equal annual amounts to spread the refunding risk. Some years they may have to refund at high interest rates, but this will be balanced off by other years in which they can refund at low rates. But most firms are not in such a position. They issue bonds only infrequently and prefer to provide for the gradual payoff of the principal each year. They also wish to reserve the right to pay the outstanding bonds if they do not need the funds or if they could refund on advantageous terms. Therefore, most industrial bonds and some public utility issues include one or more of the following repayment provisions.

Sinking funds The term *sinking fund* is a misnomer. Nothing is sunk and no fund is created. A *sinking fund* simply *is a means of gradually repaying all or a portion of the principal of a bond issue prior to its final maturity.* If a *full* sinking fund is used, an equal face amount of bonds will be redeemed each year so that the outstanding principal of the issue will decline as shown in Figure 18–1. At the maturity date, June 30, 2003, only $1 million will remain outstanding and have to be paid.

In the case of publicly issued bonds, the issuer usually may meet the sinking fund requirements by *presenting to the trustee* on each anniversary date *either* (or any combination of) *cash or face amount of bonds* ($1 million in our example). This option may be advantageous to the issuing corporation.

If the bonds are selling in the market at a *discount,* the issuer will quietly purchase in the open market sufficient bonds to meet the sinking-fund requirement by presenting these bonds to the trustee on the anniversary date. In that way, it may be able to pay off debt at a discount. This opportunity would reflect a rise in interest rates between the date of issue and the particular period preceding the anniversary date. Thus, if in 1988 the going rate on newly issued 15-year bonds of the same credit standing and maturity were 15 percent, outstanding bonds of this 12 percent issue could be purchased in the market at a substantial discount and used to make the sinking-fund payment. This option, of course, would not be available if the bonds had been privately placed. The sinking-fund requirement could be met only by paying the bondholder(s) $1 million cash to redeem that face amount of bonds.

On the other hand, if the going rate on newly issued bonds in 1988 were

Figure 18–1 Sinking fund (Full)

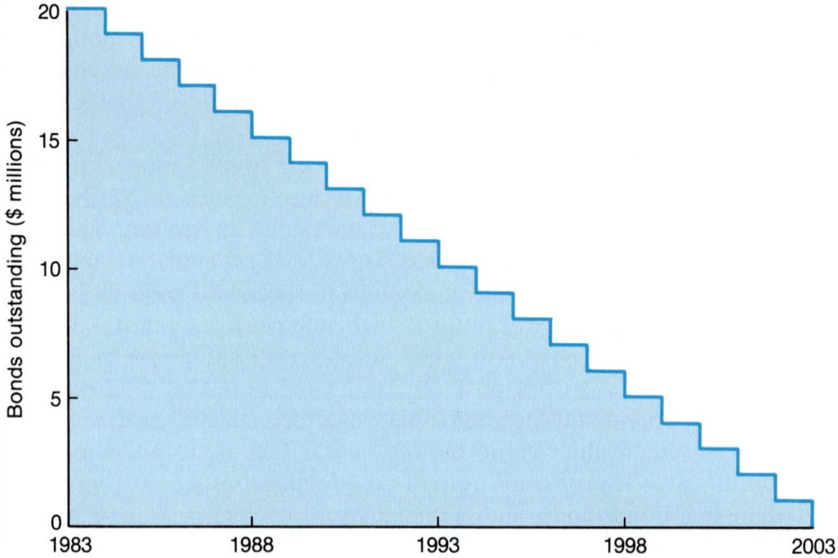

10 percent, this 12 percent issue would trade in the market at a premium. The issuing corporation would meet its 1988 sinking-fund requirement by presenting a check for $1 million to the trustee. The trustee would then be obligated to call $1 million face amount of the bonds. The particular bonds to be called would be selected by lot (usually using a random number generator) and the unlucky bondholders notified that they must relinquish their bonds and accept from the trustee payment at the call price. This call price (for sinking fund purposes only) usually is the par value or the original issue price of the bonds. In either case the amount of bonds outstanding will have been reduced by $1 million.

Nearly all sinking-fund arrangements operate as discussed above. There are occasional exceptions. For example, a corporation with a small first mortgage bond issue outstanding might float a large debenture issue with the intention that the debentures will, as soon as possible, become its first-line debt. In such a case, the sinking-fund provision of the debenture issue might stipulate that the payments of the first few years be used to redeem the senior first mortgage bonds until they are extinguished. Subsequent sinking-fund payments would redeem the debentures. In this way the elimination of the senior issue would strengthen the credit worthiness of the debentures.

Almost *never* is a *fund* (in the sense of an earmarked asset) accumulated and invested to provide cash for the redemption of the bonds at maturity. This is a common misconception. It simply is not feasible, because the most economical investment is the periodic redemption of the security that the sinking fund is provided to protect.

Some sinking-fund arrangements, however, do not provide for redemption of an equal amount of the bonds each year or for redemption of the entire issue during the period to maturity. In some cases, sinking-fund payments begin at the end of, say, the third or fifth year after issue. This delayed payment may be provided to allow the issuing corporation to establish the earning power of the assets acquired with the proceeds of the bond issue before the cash drain of gradually paying off the debt begins. In other cases, a *partial* sinking fund may provide for repayment of only part of the issue, leaving a *balloon payment* to be made at maturity. The amount of bonds outstanding under a delayed partial sinking fund with a balloon maturity is illustrated in Figure 18–2. Another arrangement sometimes used to provide for flexible sinking-fund payments is a percentage of annual income of the issuer, perhaps with a fixed minimum requirement.

Figure 18–2 Sinking fund (Delayed, partial)

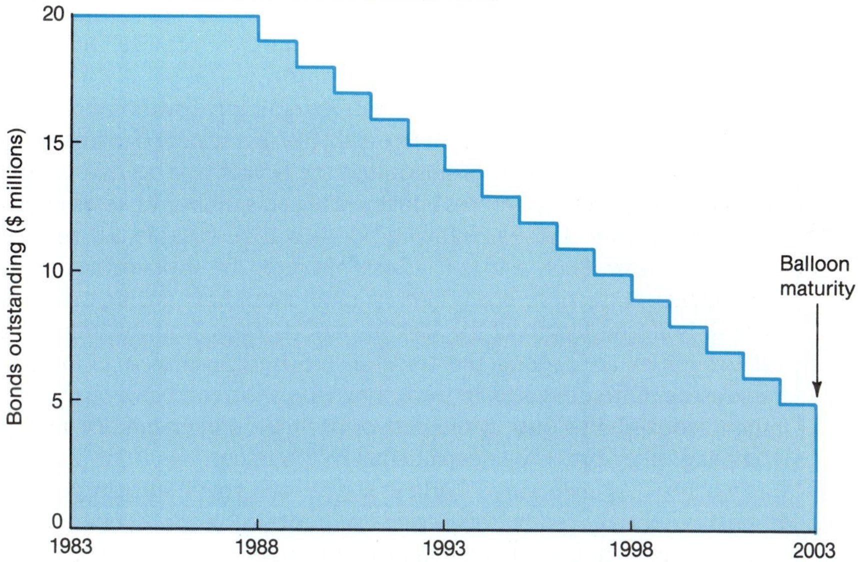

Serial maturities A serial bond issue is one in which *a portion of the individual bonds mature each year.* For example, $1 million of individual bonds may mature in each of 20 years after issue. The individual bonds (shorter maturities usually being labeled notes) may bear different coupon interest rates recognizing the shape of the yield curve at the time of issue. This arrangement allows individual investors to pick the maturities to satisfy their requirements. For example, commercial banks usually want short maturities, whereas life insurance companies and pension funds prefer the longer maturities.

Serial maturities are rarely used in corporate mortgage or debenture issues. Equipment trust certificates usually are issued in serial maturities. Serial maturities are most common in municipal bond issues.

Optional call It is to the advantage of the issuer to have the option of paying off its bond issue(s) before maturity. At some unknown time it might simply not need the funds any more and wish to pay off the debt. But more important, if interest rates should fall, it might save substantial amounts by *refunding,* that is, by issuing new bonds at the prevalent lower interest rate and using the proceeds to pay off the outstanding bonds. Investors, of course, take a dim view of this because they would have to give up the high-interest bonds at a time that they were valued at a premium.

To achieve this advantage the issuer would like to have an *optional call* privilege. The optional *call price* normally will be at a premium required by the investors to compensate them for the risk of call. This *call premium* will relate to the condition of the bond market at the time of issue, being higher in a tight bond market and lower in a loose one. Usually the premium will start at approximately one year's interest requirement and gradually descend as the bond approaches maturity.

In tight bond markets, when investors' bargaining power is strong, a *lock-in* clause may be required by investors or the investment bankers who must sell the issue. This lock-in requires that the bonds will be noncallable (except for sinking-fund purposes) during a stated number of years after issue, say, 5 or 10 years. Subsequently the bonds will be callable at a premium as indicated above. Such a lock-in clause protects the investor against call of the high-coupon-rate bonds if interest rates should fall during the stipulated period. Both the length of the lock-in period, if any, and the amount of the call premium are among the trade-offs to be considered in designing a bond issue. Often the lock-in period may be shortened and/or the call premium reduced, but only at the cost of paying a higher interest rate and/or accepting other provisions detrimental to the issuer.

Conversion As mentioned earlier, a type of hybrid security, convertible bonds, may be retired by their conversion into common stock. This conversion may be voluntary on the part of the bondholder or forced through action taken by the issuer. Convertible bonds and possible action by the issuer to induce voluntary conversion or force conversion into common stock will be fully discussed in Chapter 21.

Bond refunding decisions

If interest rates have declined and outstanding bonds can be called at the issuer's option, the firm should consider refunding the issue. When should a bond issue be refunded? What amounts can be saved and what increase in value of the firm can be achieved? These questions can be answered by utilizing a type of cost-benefit analysis similar to that used in capital investment decision making.

Income tax considerations Before making such an analysis, we must clarify the relevant income tax considerations. The *call premium* required to pay off the outstanding bonds can be treated as a tax-deductible expense in the year of the call.

When the outstanding bonds were issued, they might have been sold to the public at a premium or discount. In addition, flotation costs such as the investment banker's spread and various accounting, legal, clerical costs were incurred. On the issue of $20 million face amount of bonds, the issuer might have received net proceeds of $19.5 million. The $500,000 difference (discount) between the face amount of bonds issued and the net proceeds must be amortized over the life of the bonds, say 25 years. Each year this amortization of $20,000 ($500,000/25) is considered an expense for tax purposes.

If and when those bonds are called, the *unamortized discount* is treated as an expense for tax purposes in the year of call. (Conversely, if there were a net premium, the unamortized premium would be treated as income in the year of call.) Discount and flotation costs of the new issue must also be amortized annually over the life of that issue.

Analysis required The analysis required to decide whether or not to refund an outstanding bond issue can best be explained by an illustration. The Brice Corporation has outstanding $20 million of 13 percent bonds maturing in 20 years. These bonds were initially issued five years ago and sold to the public at 99. The discount of $200,000 plus flotation costs of $300,000 resulted in net proceeds to Brice of $19.5 million. One fifth of the $500,000 difference has been amortized and $400,000 unamortized discount and flotation costs remains. These bonds are presently callable at 112 ($1,120 per bond).

A new issue of 20-year 10 percent bonds could be sold to the public at par. Flotation costs on the new issue are estimated to be $400,000. Brice's current and expected future income tax rate is 40 percent. If a refunding takes place, a one-month overlap period is expected during which interest will have to be paid on both the old and the new bonds.

Initial cash flows First we calculate the initial cash flows, as shown in Table 18–2. The *initial cash outflows* consist of (1) the outlay to call the old bonds, $22.4 million and (2) the overlapping interest payments for one month on the old bonds, $216,667. These cash outflows total $22,616,667.

The *initial cash inflows* consist of (1) the net proceeds to Brice from the sale of the new bonds, $19.6 million, (2) the tax shields arising from *(a)* the deductibility of the call premium, $960,000, *(b)* writing off the unamortized discount and flotation costs of the old bonds, $160,000, and from *(c)* the tax

Table 18–2 Bond refunding analysis—Brice Corporation
Initial cash flows

		Cash flow
Initial cash outflow		
Call of old bonds (1.12 × $20,000,000)		$22,400,000
Interest on old bonds for one month overlap (1/12 × .13 × $20,000,000)		216,667
Total cash outflow		$22,616,667
Initial cash inflow		
Proceeds from sale of new bonds		
Face amount	$20,000,000	
Less flotation costs	400,000	
Net proceeds		$19,600,000
Tax shields		
From call premium (.40 × $2,400,000)		960,000
From unamortized discount and flotation costs of old bonds (.40 × $400,000)		160,000
From overlapping interest on old bonds (.40 × $216,667)		86,667
Total cash inflow		$20,806,667
Net initial cash outflow		$ 1,810,000

deductibility of the overlapping interest on the old bonds, $86,667. The total cash inflows will be $20,806,667. Thus, the *net initial cash outflow* will be $1,810,000.

Annual cash savings Next we must calculate the annual cash savings that will result from the refunding. Inasmuch as the old bonds and the new ones would mature at the same date, the cash savings each year will be the same and we avoid the apples-and-oranges comparison problem that would exist if the maturity dates differed.[8] Table 18–3 shows the calculation of annual cash savings for each of years 1 through 20. First we calculate the annual net cash outflow if the *old bonds* were to remain outstanding. This would be the annual interest payment at 13 percent, or $2,600,000, less the tax shields resulting from these interest payments, $1,040,000, and from amortization of discount and flotation costs of the old issue, $8,000. The annual *net* cash outflow from the old bond would be $1,552,000.

[8]The maturity date of the new bonds in this example was set equal to that of the outstanding bonds to avoid the unequal life problem. This problem is essentially the same as that which we encountered in dealing with the time horizon problem in comparing capital investment proposals in Chapter 13. If the proposed new bonds have a maturity date differing from that of the old bonds, the problem may be handled by establishing a terminal value at the maturity of the shorter of the two. The reader may wish to refer to an advanced financial management text for a detailed analysis of refunding with issues of unequal maturity.

Table 18–3 Bond refunding analysis—Brice Corporation
Annual cash savings, years 1 through 20

	Annual cash outflow
Old bond	
Annual interest payment (.13 × \$20,000,000)	\$2,600,000
Less tax shields	
From interest (.40 × \$2,600,000)	(1,040,000)
From amortization of discount and flotation cost $\left(.40 \times \frac{\$500{,}000}{25}\right)$	(8,000)
Annual net cash outflow—old bond	\$1,552,000
New bond	
Annual interest payment (.10 × \$20,000,000)	\$2,000,000
Less tax shields	
From interest (.40 × \$2,000,000)	(800,000)
From amortization of discount and flotation cost $\left(.40 \times \frac{\$400{,}000}{20}\right)$	(8,000)
Annual net cash outflow—new bond	\$1,192,000
Annual cash flow savings	\$ 360,000

If the *new bonds* were sold to refund the old issue, annual interest payments of 10 percent would be \$2,000,000. From this would be subtracted the tax shields resulting from these interest payments, \$800,000, and from amortization of the flotation cost of the new issue, \$8,000. The annual *net* cash outflow under the new bond would be \$1,192,000. Subtracting these annual cash outflows from those associated with the old bond, \$1,552,000, indicates that the refunding would result in *annual cash flow savings* of \$360,000 during each of the next 20 years.

Net present value Finally, we must determine the net present value of the decision to refund. This requires comparing the net initial cash outflow (the investment at time 0) of \$1,810,000 (from Table 18–2) to the present value of the annual cash flow savings of \$360,000 (from Table 18–3). This requires discounting the annual cash flow savings at an appropriate rate. But how do we determine that discount rate?

As we learned in Chapter 14, future cash flows should be discounted at a rate *reflecting the degree of uncertainty of those flows.* Here the cash flows under the old bond or the new one are almost certain. They are comprised entirely of contractual interest payments and tax shields; therefore, they have the same degree of certainty as the firm's payment of the interest obligations. The effective aftertax interest cost at which the firm could currently *borrow* funds over the time period of the cash flows under consideration embodies the market's estimate of the discount rate that should be applied to these annual cash flow savings.

For Brice Corporation, the interest rate on the new issue of bonds would be 10 percent.[9] Then this pretax cost must be adjusted to an effective after-tax cost:

$$.10\ (1 - .40) = .06 = 6 \text{ percent}$$

Table B in the Appendix at the end of this book indicates that the present value interest factor of an annuity *(PVIFA)* of $1 for each of the 20 years discounted at 6 percent is 11.470. Multiplying the annual cash flow savings of $360,000 by this factor indicates a present value of the annual cash flow savings of $4,129,200 as shown in Table 18–4. As the net initial cash outflow would be only $1,810,000, the positive net present value of a decision to refund is $2,319,200. Thus, the quantitative analysis indicates that the proposed refunding should be carried out.

Table 18–4 Bond refunding analysis—Brice Corporation
Present value

	Cash flow	*PVIFA* of $1 @ 6%	Present value
Cash savings, years 1–20	$ 360,000	11.470	$4,129,200
Net initial outflow, year 0	(1,810,000)	—	(1,810,000)
Net present value			$2,319,200

Other considerations Although a bond refunding decision usually can be made on the basis of quantitative analysis, there may be nonquantifiable factors to consider. One must do some "guesstimating" of future trends in interest rates. The refunding as soon as possible of Brice Corporation's bonds appears to be highly advantageous. But if the financial manager expects interest rates to decline further, he or she might delay the refunding in the hopes that new bonds could be sold, say six months from now, at an interest rate of around 9½ percent. Also, inasmuch as the call premium usually declines through time, waiting another six months might allow a call of the old bonds at say 111½ rather than 112.

[9]In this illustration we have dispensed with the calculation of the *exact* cost to maturity for convenience in using the available present value table. If greater precision were necessary, the flotation costs of $400,000 should be taken into account. The firm will have the use of $19.6 million, which is 98 percent of the face amount of the new bond issue. The yield to maturity of a 10 percent bond maturing in 20 years priced at 98 is 10.24 percent. The tax-adjusted cost to maturity is 6.14 percent [.1024 (1 − .40)].

On some rare occasions, bond refunding might be advantageous even though the quantitative analysis indicates a negative present value. This might arise through the possibility of eliminating or modifying onerous provisions of the old bond indenture. For example, perhaps a tight minimum working capital requirement might be modified to provide more financial flexibility or a limitation on future borrowing relative to asset or interest coverage might be modified to allow larger amounts to be borrowed.

Often the quantitative analysis relative to a refunding decision is more complicated than that illustrated because of two factors. The amount of new bonds to be issued may be significantly greater than the amount of the old bonds to be called. Thus, the new issue would be a combination of refunding and additional long-term financing. Also, particularly if the outstanding bonds are within a few years of maturity, the new bonds to be issued might mature many years later, thus providing debt financing for a substantially longer period of time.

Term loans

Intermediate and long-term corporate borrowing, particularly by small firms, often entails term loans rather than the issuance of bonds. Term loans generally range in maturity from 2 or 3 years to 20 years and usually are repaid in installments. They are used primarily to finance the purchase of fixed assets such as land, buildings, machinery, and equipment. The lender usually is relying on cash flows generated through earnings and depreciation to repay a term loan, rather than on the liquidation of current assets during a seasonal cycle. Thus, the lender's analysis of the borrower's credit worthiness is similar to that of a bond investor. Term loans may be unsecured or secured; they are made by various financial institutions, and may range in size from a few thousand to many millions of dollars.

Sources

The largest dollar amount of term lending is done by the commercial banks and life insurance companies. Term loans also are made by pension funds, the Small Business Administration, small business investment companies (SBICs), and finance companies.

Commercial banks generally make term loans in the maturity range from about three to eight years. Sometimes, particularly when the loan is relatively small, the bank will carry the entire loan. Large loans may be syndicated among a number of banks. If the borrower needs a longer term loan than the bank wishes to carry, the banker often will arrange syndication with one or more life insurance companies to carry the longer maturities, say 8 through 15 years, while the originating bank and perhaps other banks will carry the shorter maturities, say up through 7 years. The originating bank will be responsible for administration of the loan. Syndication is used both to spread the risk and to comply with legal limitations upon the maximum amount that a commercial bank may lend to a single borrower. Term loans by banks may be unsecured (similar to debentures) or secured by a mortgage or other collateral, such as the pledge of machinery or equipment. In rare cases, they may be secured by the pledge of inventories or a continuing general assignment of accounts receivable.

Life insurance companies also do a large amount of term lending. Their loans usually are secured, often by real estate mortgages, and tend to be of longer maturity, up to about 20 years. Some life insurance company term loans to business are arranged and serviced through local mortgage bankers or brokers as well as commercial banks.

Term loans made by pension funds administered by trust departments of commercial banks, life insurance companies, state and local governmental bodies, or individual trustees are similar in their characteristics to those made by life insurance companies.

The Small Business Administration (SBA), an agency of the federal government, engages in term lending to qualifying small business firms in several different ways. It may guarantee the payment of a term loan made and serviced by a commercial bank. It may also participate in such a loan by furnishing a portion of the required funds, the servicing bank furnishing the remainder. Or, in some cases, it directly makes term loans when the borrower shows evidence that it has been refused such accommodation by its local bank. Interest rates on SBA loans generally are below or at most equal to those charged by commercial banks.

Small business investment corporations (SBICs) are institutions chartered by the federal government that obtain their equity financing from private sources and debt financing from the SBA. They make term loans to small businesses, usually receiving some potential equity interest, called a "kicker," such as convertibility to common stock or warrants to purchase common stock. Their term loans often are made to small businesses with significant growth potential, the SBIC looking to both the interest on the loan and the potential value of their equity interest as compensation. Some SBICs are affiliated with commercial banks or other financial institution holding companies. If the commercial bank cannot make a term loan to its customer, sometimes it may arrange the loan through its affiliated SBIC.

Term loans are an important and rapidly growing area of finance company activity. These loans often are used to finance machinery or equipment purchases, the finance company holding title until the term loan is paid off. Such loans usually are of relatively short maturity, in the range of two to eight years, and are repaid in equal installments including the interest and amortizing the principal.

Maturities and repayment schedules

As mentioned above, term loans generally range in maturity from 2 or 3 years to 20 years. Those made by different financial institutions vary in their maturity and repayment characteristics. Term loans usually are repayable in quarterly or semiannual installments. In some cases these installments repay equal amounts on the principal and interest on the outstanding balance. In other cases the installments are equal through the life of the loan, each payment covering both interest and amortization of the principal. The latter repayment arrangement is similar to that used in connection with home mortgages and personal installment loans.

The loan agreement

Because a term loan will be held by one or a few financial institutions, it is not necessary to employ a trustee and use an indenture to specify the detailed terms, restrictions, procedures, and so on as in a publicly offered bond issue. There is, however, a term loan agreement, which often is a rather lengthy document specifying about the same things as a bond indenture. The usual standard provisions and constraints regarding additional borrowing, asset management, dividends, repurchase of stock, and the like are contained in this agreement. Failure to make timely principal and interest payments or breach of any of these provisions usually make the entire principal balance and unpaid interest due and payable within, say, 30 days.

Sometimes the financial officer arranging a term loan may be rather shocked by these protective provisions in the proposed loan agreement. A frequent reaction of a bank customer is, "Why are you getting so tough? We have been borrowing here for years by signing simple unsecured notes. These many pages of restrictive provisions seem to indicate that you are apprehensive and don't trust us any more. Maybe you also want to put my grandmother in the dungeon and want me to leave a pint of blood!"

Although this reaction is understandable, the financial officer must realize that the proposed term loan will be outstanding over a long period of time and therefore must provide for the many contingencies which might occur. Each time he or she signed an unsecured short-term note, the banker had the opportunity to examine the firm's financial condition and probably was applying the same standards, such as minimum working capital and current ratio, asset coverage of debt, and earnings coverage of interest, as are now reflected in the term loan agreement. Those tests of credit worthiness that had been administered on an informal basis now are being cast in the formal terms of a complex legal document.

Cost

The cost of a term loan probably will be about the same as that of a bond issue of comparable quality, size, maturity, and other terms. Avoidance of flotation costs may make the term loan slightly less expensive, but on the other hand dealing with one or a few financial institutions limits the market and may lead to slightly higher costs.

But many term loans are of considerably smaller size than bond issues. To some degree, costs are related to size. The investigation connected with credit appraisal, arranging the loan, and administering it are largely fixed costs. Therefore, the cost of smaller term loans tends to be higher than that of larger bond issues for borrowers of the same credit worthiness.

General considerations in long-term debt financing

Now we shall briefly review and integrate some of the major factors to be considered in long-term debt financing. These may be discussed under the headings of cost, effect upon overall cost of capital, limitation of flexibility, and trade-offs to be considered in long-term borrowing.

Cost

The *explicit cost* of debt nearly always will be lower than that of equity financing. This lower cost reflects the prior claim of debt upon the income stream and assets in liquidation. Tax deductibility of interest payments further contributes to this explicit cost advantage.

The explicit before-tax cost is determined by the stated (coupon) interest rate adjusted to account for amortization of premium or discount and flotation costs. This effective interest cost is then further adjusted—by taking account of the estimated incremental tax rate of the firm during the life of the debt—to obtain the aftertax cost. But in a broader sense this explicit cost does not fully reflect what the firm gives up when it incurs long-term debt. There are other nonquantifiable *implicit* or indirect costs incurred.

Effect on overall costs of capital

You will recall from Chapter 17 the saucer-shaped overall cost-of-capital curve. This cost declines as moderate portions of debt are added to the capital structure. Then it is flat through an area in which increasing perceived risk of both debt and equity increase their cost, but the rising proportion of lower-cost debt offsets these higher component costs. When debt is utilized beyond the flat of the saucer, the overall cost of capital rises. This results from the capital market's increasing recognition of the risk of default (bankruptcy risk).

The risk of default, in turn, reflects the probability of failure to comply with any of the firm's obligations. These obligations include principal and interest payments and compliance with all of the other provisions of the debt contract(s). Consequently, to fulfill its goal of value maximization, management must refrain from issuing debt that would carry it into the rising portion of the overall cost-of-capital curve. If excessive long-term debt is issued, the firm will go through successive stages of first having its overall cost of capital increase, then losing its ability to raise additional capital, and finally defaulting on its obligations and facing bankruptcy.

Limitation of flexibility

Financial flexibility is an extremely valuable intangible corporate asset. To maintain it, management must always "keep the debt door open." By so doing it has the choice of which security to use in raising required funds, as contrasted to being forced to accept onerous terms dictated by the furnishers of capital.

This flexibility relates not only to limitations imposed by restrictive debt provisions, such as minimum asset and earnings coverage ratios, but also informal restrictions imposed by the marketplace. The latter are reflected in such actions as downgrading of the firm's bond rating(s) or requiring extremely high interest rates and/or kickers as compensation for supplying funds. Extreme lack of financial flexibility may force a firm to sell large amounts of common stock at inopportune times (and prices) or to merge under unfavorable terms.

An additional, but less severe, flexibility consideration relates to such matters as lock-in clauses and/or optional call premiums as they influence ability to refund long-term debt at opportune times.

Analysis of trade-offs

In the bargaining process under which the terms of a bond issue or term loan are developed, trade-offs among the provisions usually are possible. For example, by paying a higher interest rate, a lock-in clause may be eliminated or a lower call premium obtained. Or, by agreeing to a full sinking-fund requirement, perhaps the interest cost may be reduced or less stringent minimum working capital requirements imposed. The financial manager must be very careful to obtain terms that the firm can tolerate. Such trade-off considerations relate not only to future flexibility but also to the risk of default. The acceptance of any provision that might eventually result in loss of control of the firm or even bankruptcy in order to get a little lower interest rate would be foolhardy. These trade-offs require a great deal of balanced judgment.

Summary

This chapter discussed long-term debt financing through the use of bonds and term loans. A bond is a long-term promise to pay interest periodically and the principal at maturity. The issuer also promises to abide by the various provisions of the bond indenture. The indenture is the detailed agreement covering the obligations of the issuer and the rights of the bondholders. It is executed and enforced by the trustee, who acts as the "watchdog" of the bondholders.

Bonds may be secured or unsecured. The most widely used security is a mortgage on real property. The mortgage may be closed-end or open-end, the latter allowing additional borrowing having the same priority of claim, limited by specific restrictions. Other types of secured bonds are collateral trust bonds and equipment trust certificates. Debentures are unsecured bonds relying upon the general credit of the issuer. Some debentures are subordinated to specified other debt. Income bonds (often subordinated) require the payment of interest only when earned. Convertible bonds may be converted at the holder's option into common stock.

Various protective provisions are included in bond indentures. Some of these merely require prudent and responsible management. Others may constrain additional borrowing, asset management, dividend payments, repurchase of stock, merger, or other actions that might impair the credit of the issuer. Finally, the indenture will state that if any of the protective provisions are breached, the unpaid principal and interest will become due a specified number of days after notice by the trustee. This provides the "teeth" in the bond agreement.

Some bond issues may be retired simply by payment at maturity. But other retirement provisions may be desired by either the issuer or the bondholders. The most common provision allows periodic redemption through sinking-fund payments. Such payments may retire all of the bonds through the period to maturity or only part of the issue, leaving a "balloon" payment at maturity. A few corporate bonds issues mature serially. Many bonds are callable at a premium at the issuer's option. Convertible bonds, of course, may be extinguished by conversion into common stock.

Bond refunding may be considered if interest rates have declined and outstanding bonds are callable. A refunding decision may be based upon cost-benefit analysis. First, the initial net cash outflow from calling the outstanding bonds and selling new ones is determined. Then, the present value of future annual net cash savings is determined by discounting at the after-tax cost of debt. The value of refunding is determined by subtracting the initial net cash outflow from the present value of the net cash savings. If this value is positive and nonquantifiable considerations do not outweigh this advantage, the bonds should be refunded.

Another means of long-term debt financing is the term loan. Such loans are made primarily by commercial banks and life insurance companies but also may be obtained from pension funds, the SBA, SBICs, or finance companies. They usually range in maturity from 3 to 20 years and are payable in installments. Some term loans are accompanied by "kickers" in the form of convertibility or warrants to purchase common stock. The loan agreement is similar to, but somewhat less complex than, a bond indenture.

The long-term borrower must consider, in addition to explicit costs, the effects of such borrowing upon overall cost of capital, financial flexibility, and ability to live with the provisions of the contract.

Questions

1. Define a bond. What is a bond indenture? What is the function of the trustee under a bond indenture?

2. What is the difference between a closed-end and an open-end mortgage as each may be used to secure bond issues? Why has the open-end mortgage achieved greater acceptance in business finance? How does an "after-acquired" clause relate to an open-end mortgage? What are the two types of limitations on additional issues usually contained in an open-end mortgage bond indenture?

3. What are the principal types of *secured* bonds? Of *unsecured* bonds?

4. If you were a bond investor, why would you insist upon an equal and ratable security clause or a negative pledge clause in first-line debentures that you would purchase?

5. Why might bond investors require the following protective provisions?
   a. Maintenance of a minimum net working capital and/or a minimum current ratio.
   b. Prohibition of sale or assignment of accounts receivable.
   c. Limitation of dividend payments to earnings accruing after the bonds have been issued.

6. What are bond ratings? Who establishes the ratings? Why are they important to an issuer?

7. Why would a firm issuing bonds wish to have an optional call provision if it expects interest rates to decline in the future? Why would bond

investors prefer that there be no such provision, or at least that call be delayed for several years?

8. What is a sinking fund? Distinguish among a *full* sinking fund, a *delayed* sinking fund, and a *partial* sinking fund.

9. What option does a firm usually have in meeting annual sinking-fund requirements? How might this option benefit the firm?

10. Why might an issuing firm prefer that a sinking-fund arrangement be used in its bond issues? What might be the disadvantge to the issuer of a sinking-fund requirement?

11. Why do investors usually prefer that bonds either have a sinking-fund requirement or serial maturities? Is there any possible disadvantage to the investor relating to the operation of a sinking-fund arrangement?

12. Why is a bond refunding decision based primarily upon cost-benefit analysis? In discounting future cash benefits from a bond refunding, why is the appropriate discount rate the firm's aftertax cost of debt rather than its overall (weighted average) cost of capital?

13. What is the relationship between bond prices and interest rates? Explain. If interest rates were to increase, which market price would be affected most, that of a 6 percent bond maturing in 3 years or a 6 percent bond maturing in 20 years? Why?

14. Why might a bank require many protective provisions in a short term loan to the same customer to which it lends on short-term unsecured notes with no protective provisions at all?

15. What is the *basic* difference between a bank's appraisal of a term loan and that of a short-term loan to provide temporary working capital?

16. Why do banks often syndicate term loans among a number of banks and/or life insurance companies or other financial institutions?

17. During the 1970s and early 80s, with a generally weak stock market, corporations have borrowed heavily and interest rates have soared. Explain how these factors have affected interest coverage ratios, cost of debt, and overall cost of capital of those capital-intensive firms, such as public utilities, that require large amounts of external long-term financing.

Problems

1. The Beasley Corporation has three bond issues outstanding:

First mortgage bonds	$5 million
Debentures	2 million
Subordinated debentures	1 million

Beasley is liquidated in bankruptcy. Net proceeds (after court costs and other priority claims) are $2 million from current assets and $4 million from real property pledged to secure the first mortgage bond issue. Short-term common creditors claims total $1 million. How much would be received by each class of bondholders?

2. Sparks Electric Utility Company has $224 million in first mortgage bonds outstanding. These bonds require annual interest payments of $23.5 million. The indenture of the open-end mortgage limits additional issues by the following two clauses: (1) bonds outstanding must not exceed 60 percent of net property value, and (2) EBIT for the 12 months prior to issue must be at least 2.5 times the interest requirement on then outstanding bonds plus the new issue.

Sparks eligible property is valued at $470 million. Its EBIT for the past 12 months was $65 million. If additional bonds would require an interest rate of 12 percent, what is the maximum amount of additional bonds that Sparks can issue?

3. Acme Steel Company has $100 million of 13 percent debentures outstanding. The indenture limits additional borrowing to $50 million or total interest coverage (EBIT/interest requirement) of 3 times (whichever allows the least borrowing). Acme's EBIT last year was $52 million. How much could Acme borrow under a term loan at 15 percent interest without breaching the indenture restriction?

4. Sherill Manufacturing Company has an issue of 9 percent sinking-fund debentures outstanding, which requires an annual sinking-fund payment of $4 million. This requirement may be met by presenting cash or face amount of the bonds to the trustee on or before June 30 this year. In March, the bonds are trading in the market to yield to maturity 12.31 percent. As treasurer of Sherill, what would you do? Would your action be different if the bonds were trading to yield 8.51 percent? If, rather than having been publicly issued, the bonds had been privately placed with a pension fund, what could you do?

5. The Petrol Corporation five years ago sold $40 million of 14 percent bonds to mature 20 years from the date of issue. The discount and flotation costs on this issue totaled $400,000. One fourth of this amount has been amortized to date. These bonds currently are callable at 110. A new $40 million issue of similar bonds to mature in 15 years could now be sold at par with a 12 percent coupon rate. Flotation costs would be $300,000. Petrol expects future income to be taxed at a 40 percent rate. Petrol management does not expect interest rates to decline further in the forseeable future. Appraise this proposed refunding, assuming there would be no overlapping interest costs. (*Note:* You may round the discount rate to the nearest percent.) What would you, Petrol's financial manager, propose to do (assuming that nonquantifiable considerations do not influence this decision)?

6. Barker Industries has a $25 million 11 percent debenture issue outstanding, which matures in 12 years. These bonds were issued 8 years ago at a premium equal to the flotation costs. They are currently callable at a 7½ percent premium. A new $25 million debenture issue to mature in 12 years could now be sold at 99 with a 10¼ percent coupon interest rate. Flotation costs would be $250,000. Barker management does not expect interest rates to decline further and estimates the firm's future income tax rate to be 40 percent. If the refunding were carried out, there would be an overlap of interest payments of one month. Appraise this refunding proposal. (You may round the discount rate to the nearest percent.) Do you recommend proceeding with the refunding (assuming that nonquantifiable considerations do not influence the decision)?

Chapter 19
Lease Financing

A firm may obtain the *use* of fixed assets by leasing them as an alternative to buying them and directly financing their purchase. The basic difference is that under a lease, title to the asset is held by the *lessor.* The *lessee* has the right to use the asset in accordance with the lease contract. This compares to owning, where the firm takes title to the asset and arranges for its financing through capital contracts.

Although leasing has existed for many centuries, until recently its use has been largely confined to land and buildings. During the past two or three decades, leasing has become much more prevalent and its use broadened to include almost any type of capital equipment as well as real estate. About 20 percent of the capital equipment recently put into use has been leased. Today a firm can lease anything from light machinery to supertankers or industrial plants to potted plants. Therefore, leasing must be considered as a practical alternative to buying and financing almost any fixed asset.

This chapter will first discuss the nature of the lease contract and the types of leasing arrangements available. Then, the tax and accounting considerations peculiar to leasing will be set forth. Next the analysis required to compare leasing to buying and borrowing will be treated. Finally, the advantages and disadvantages of leasing will be evaluated.

The lease contract

A lease provides for the simultaneous *acquisition* and *financing* of a fixed asset. The *lease contract* provides that the owner of the asset, the lessor, will allow the lessee to use that asset for a stipulated period of time provided that the lessee fulfills the obligations set forth.

Basic obligations

The first and most important obligation of the lessee is to make *rental payments* (alternatively called lease payments) periodically during the term of the lease. These payments may be required annually, semi-annually, quarterly, or monthly and usually must be made in advance. Sometimes an additional deposit must accompany the first payment. The amount of the required rental payment is designed to provide (1) amortization of the lessor's investment in the asset, (2) interest on the funds invested, and (3) compensation for any services that are to be paid for by the lessor, such as maintenance, property taxes, or insurance.

Many leases require that maintenance, taxes, and/or insurance be paid by the lessee. The lease contract may require documentation of these payments and provide for inspection by the lessor to verify required maintenance. Usually improvement, modification, or alteration of the property must be approved by the lessor.

A lease may be *cancellable* or *noncancellable.* If cancellable, penalty provisions usually apply. Possession of the property, of course, must be returned to the lessor upon cancellation or expiration of the lease. Failure by the lessee to comply with any of the terms of the lease will constitute a default and, after stipulated notice, give the lessor the right to seize the property and sue the lessee for damages. In the event of bankruptcy, the lessor may seize the property and claim damages, which normally are limited to one to three years' rental payments.[1]

A lease usually will be *renewable* at the option of the lessee. If so, the terms of renewal will be specified. In addition, some leases provide that the asset may be purchased by the lessee during the term of the lease or upon expiration. If so, these terms of purchase will be included. Often the lease provides that at expiration the lessee will have the *right of first refusal.* This gives the lessee the opportunity to match the best offer available from another party to purchase the asset or lease it for an additional period.

Types of leases

Leases may be classified as operating leases and financial leases.

Operating leases An *operating lease* (sometimes called a service lease or maintenance lease) is identified by its (1) relatively *short term,* (2) *cancellation* feature, and (3) *maintenance* of the asset being provided by the lessor. The term of an operating lease is considerably shorter than the expected life of the asset, typically one to five years. Thus, the lessor does not expect to recover fully its investment during a single lease period. Rather, the asset is expected to have a positive market value at the expiration of the lease, and the lessor expects to recover the remainder of its investment by either re-leasing the asset or selling it. The lessee usually has an option to renew or purchase the asset upon expiration of the lease. Some operating leases provide an option to purchase during the term of the lease.

An operating lease generally is cancellable before expiration at the option of the lessee. This feature is important to the user-firm because it increases its flexibility; the asset may be returned and future rental payments eliminated if its services are no longer required. The cancellation clause, however, often requires a penalty payment.

[1] In a reorganization, this limit is three years' interest, whereas the limit is one year in a bankruptcy involving liquidation. The limit applies only to leased real property. No limit is applied regarding other leased property, such as machinery and equipment.

Maintenance, property taxes, and insurance usually are provided by the lessor. Under an operating lease, the lessee obtains not only the use of the asset but also this package of services. The rental payments include compensation for the costs and risks associated with the service obligations as well as compensation for providing financing. In addition, the lessor bears the risk that technological obsolescence might result in either cancellation of the lease or a lower than expected market value of the asset at expiration. Rental payments must also include compensation for bearing this risk.

Operating leases most commonly cover such equipment as computer hardware, photocopy machines, typewriters, word processors, automobiles, trucks, light standard machinery, or cash registers.

Financial leases A *financial lease* (often called a capital lease) (1) is for a *long period of time,* roughly equivalent to the expected useful life of the asset, (2) is *noncancellable,* and (3) usually requires *maintenance, property taxes, and insurance* to be provided *by the lessee.* This type of lease generally is used in connection with the leasing of land and buildings, such as industrial plants, warehouses, retail stores, and office buildings, or large pieces of equipment, such as ships, heavy industrial machinery, aircraft, or oil-drilling rigs.

The term of a financial lease usually approximates the estimated useful life of the asset. By accounting definition, it must be at least 75 percent of the useful life. There may be some expected salvage value at the expiration; this is particularly true if all or part of the leased asset is land. Rental payments are designed to fully amortize the lessor's investment (less expected salvage value) and to provide a rate of return on the unamortized investment approximately equal to that which would be charged on a similar long-term loan. Thus, the basic economics of a financial lease are similar to those of a term loan for the full amount of the investment in the asset.

A capital lease is noncancellable; therefore, the lessee is obligated to make the rental payments until expiration of the lease agreement, whether or not use of the asset is required. In many cases, however, the lessee may sublease the asset with permission of the lessor. The importance of this noncancellable provision is that the lessee is committed to a fixed financial obligation over the entire period of the lease. This obligation also is essentially the same as that under a term loan. Inasmuch as maintenance, taxes, and insurance usually are obligations of the lessee, the lessee bears the costs or risks associated with these required services.

The title, *financial* lease, is appropriate. Such a lease is essentially a medium by which long-term financing of an asset is obtained by the lessee in return for the fixed financial obligation to make periodic rental payments throughout the term of the lease.

Acquisition of leased assets

There are some differences in leases related to the arrangements under which the lessor may acquire the asset to be leased. Some are direct leases; others are sale-leaseback transactions.

Direct leases A *direct lease* is created when the lessor either already owns the asset to be leased or acquires it for the purpose of leasing. The lessor may be the manufacturer or distributor of the asset, or a subsidiary organized for the purpose of acquiring and leasing assets manufactured by its parent company. In other cases, the lessor may be a financial institution, such as a specialized leasing company, a leasing subsidiary of a commercial bank holding company, a life insurance company, pension fund, or one or a group of wealthy individuals. If the lessor is a financial institution or individual, the user-firm selects the asset and arranges with the potential lessor to purchase it and simultaneously enter into a lease agreement with the lessee. This arrangement usually involves a financial lease.

A particular type of direct leasing agreement, which has become quite popular in recent years, is the *leveraged lease*. Here, the lessor purchases the asset specified by the user-firm, financing that purchase by borrowing a large portion of the required funds from institutional investors, such as life insurance companies. The loans are secured by the asset. Then the lessor enters into a lease agreement with the lessee. By borrowing 70 to 90 percent of the required funds, the lessor may utilize leverage to increase its rate of return. The lessor also increases its risk, because it must repay the loans even if the lessee fails to meet its obligations. Leveraged leases generally are feasible only in relative large (about $5 million or over) financial leases.

Sale-leasebacks In some cases a firm wishes to sell an asset it owns and lease that asset back for a period approximating its remaining useful life. For example, a department store that owns its store building may wish to sell the land and building to a financial institution and simultaneously lease the store back. In this way the department store may improve its liquidity position by turning fixed assets, land and building, into cash. Similarly, supermarket chains often acquire locations and build store buildings, either directly or through a real estate subsidiary. Immediately upon completion, the property is sold to a financial institution or individual investor, and the supermarket chain simultaneously enters into a financial lease for the estimated useful life of the property.

Such an arrangement, called a *sale-leaseback,* may have income tax advantages if a large portion of the value of the property relates to the land. Land cannot be depreciated for income tax purposes. But a similar effect may be attained through a sale-leaseback under which tax-deductible rental payments include amortization of the land value as well as that of the building (less any estimated residual value). Other tax considerations will be discussed in the next section.

Tax and accounting considerations

In the past, proponents of leasing sometimes have claimed income tax and/or accounting advantages of this type of financing. Some of the alleged advantages have been eliminated by the scrutiny of the Internal Revenue Service and by relatively recent changes in tax laws and accounting standards.

Tax status of leases

Rental payments under a lease are allowable expenses for income tax purposes in the year in which the services of the asset are received. Because lease payments usually are made in advance, the year in which the payments are made and that in which the expense is deductible may not coincide.

Deductibility of rental payments is contingent upon the Internal Revenue Service's recognizing that the contract is a bona fide lease rather than an installment purchase camouflaged as a lease.[2] Therefore it is important that the contract will be considered to be a bona fide lease and that the parties to a major lease obtain a favorable opinion from the IRS before proceeding with the transaction.

In general terms, the IRS requires that *all* of the following qualifications be met:

1. The term of the lease must be less than the estimated useful life of the asset and, in any case, less than 30 years.
2. The rental payments must be reasonable, that is, they must include a rate of return to the lessor within a reasonable range of returns obtainable on similar leases or loans at the time.

[2]This scrutiny arises from the fact that under a lease the entire rental payment is tax deductible, whereas under an installment purchase only the interest on the unpaid balance is deductible and the purchased asset may be depreciated according to the Accelerated Cost Recovery System (ACRS). If the term of a contract purporting to be a lease were substantially shorter than the cost recovery period of the asset and the so-called lessee in effect became the owner of the asset, then the tax deduction would be greater than under an installment purchase. The IRS naturally takes a dim view of this and may hold that such a lease is an installment purchase for tax purposes.

3. In a leveraged lease, the lessor must provide equity capital equal to at least 10 percent of the purchase price of the asset.[3]

The investment tax credit may be taken by either the lessor or the lessee. The disposition of the investment tax credit should be covered in the lease contract.

Accounting for leases

Prior to 1977, the only disclosure requirement regarding leases was that a footnote to the financial statements indicate the existence of any leases, outline their terms, indicate the total rental payment obligation, and list rental payments required for the next five years. Liabilities related to leases did not have to be disclosed on the balance sheet proper. At that time leasing was considered to be "off-balance sheet financing." This was purported to be advantageous, because the debt ratios derived from the balance sheet were lower than if the firm had purchased assets and financed them by borrowing. But sophisticated financial analysts made due allowance for this omission when comparing a firm that leased large amounts of assets to another that did not. In many cases, analysts recast the balance sheet of the firm that leased assets to show the approximate value of those assets and the related liabilities on the reconstituted balance sheet. This action is called "capitalizing leases."

In November 1976, the Financial Accounting Standards Board (FASB) issued Statement No. 13, which *requires the lessee to capitalize a financial (capital) lease.*[4] This statement requires capitalization of any lease containing *one or more* of the following features:

1. The lease transfers title to the property to the lessee upon its expiration or contains a purchase clause giving the lessee the option to buy the property at a bargain price.
2. The term of the lease is equal to 75 percent or more of the estimated useful life of the property.

[3]Qualification of a bona fide lease is a delicate area of income tax law. Anyone entering into a substantial lease contract should obtain competent tax counsel. The 1981 tax act greatly liberalized this qualification and some of these liberal provisions were modified or replaced by the 1982 act.

[4]Financial Accounting Standards Board, *Statement of Financial Accounting Standards No. 13,* "Accounting for Leases" (Stamford, Conn., November 1976). The FASB is the standard-setting board of the public accounting profession. Its standards must be followed by firms if their financial statements are to receive unqualified certification by CPAs. FASB No. 13 sets forth in detail the conditions under which a lease must be capitalized and prescribes the methods for capitalizing it.

3. The present value of the lease payments equals or exceeds 90 percent of the fair value of the property at the inception of the lease less any investment tax credit retained by the lessor. The discount rate used to calculate this present value is the lower of *(a)* the lessee's borrowing rate or *(b)* the implicit rate of return used by the lessor in determining the rental payments.

Under FASB No. 13, a financial lease is capitalized as shown in Table 19–1. At the time the lease contract is initiated, the value of *Leased Property under Capital Leases* is established by *discounting all required lease payments* at a rate equal to the lower of *(a)* the lessee's incremental borrowing rate for a secured loan over the same term as the lease or *(b)* the rate of return used by the lessor in determining the rental payments. A corresponding liability, *Obligations under Capital Leases,* is booked. Rental payments due in the first year are shown as current liabilities and the remainder as long-term. The net effect is that debt ratios calculated from the balance sheet will be substantially the same as if the firm owned the leased assets and borrowed the money to finance them.

Table 19–1 Capitalizing a lease ($000)

Assets		*Liabilities*	
Leased property under capital leases less accumulated amortization	$5,000	Current: Obligations under capital leases	$ 500
		Long-term: Obligations under capital leases	4,500
	$5,000		$5,000

Each year's rental payments are split into their interest components, which are charged as *Interest Expense* on the income statement, and their amortization components, which are booked as *Accumulated Amortization of Leased Property* and a reduction of the liability, *Obligations under Capital Leases.* Note that if a lease qualifies under IRS regulations, the entire rental payment is an expense for tax purposes. The split referred to above applies only for accounting purposes.

In addition to capitalization on the balance sheet, the lessee under a capital lease must disclose in footnotes to the financial statements such information as (1) the gross amount of assets under financial leases by classes according to their nature or uses, (2) the accumulated lease amortization, (3) rental payment obligations for each of the next five years, and (4) total rental obligations.

An operating lease, according to FASB No. 13, is any lease not identified as a capital lease. Operating leases do not have to be capitalized on the balance sheet but must be disclosed in a footnote. That footnote must show the rental expenses for the year along with any contingent rentals and list the total minimum rental obligations as well as detail these obligations for the next five fiscal years.

FASB No. 13 probably had little effect upon the knowledge and judgments of sophisticated financial analysts, such as commercial bank and life insurance company loan officers. They were capitalizing financial leases informally in their analyses before the FASB statement was issued. But it has been beneficial to trade creditors, some bondholders, and many stockholders by providing clearer disclosure of the nature of lease obligations and their effect upon the financial status of the firm.

Evaluating lease versus buy-borrow alternatives

As mentioned early in this chapter, leasing involves the simultaneous acquisition of the use of an asset and providing for its financing. In the decision-making process, these two aspects of the lease transaction must be separated. The analytical processes and decision criteria appropriate to the *acquisition* of an asset (capital investment) differ in both concept and application from those that apply to the *financing* of that asset. A great deal of controversy among both academicians and practitioners has arisen regarding the analysis and decision-making process relative to leasing. Much of this controversy is rooted in confusion of these two aspects of the lease. We shall now try to clarify this matter and develop an appropriate method of evaluating the two separate facets of the leasing decision. Our consideration will focus upon the financial (capital) lease, although some of the points developed are equally applicable to operating leases.

Lessee's perspective

The lessee's view of a leasing decision is depicted in Table 19–2. As shown on the left side of that table, the first decision is whether or not to *acquire* the use of the asset.

The acquisition decision The decision to acquire the asset is a *capital investment decision* that should be based upon the analytical methods and decision criteria discussed in Chapters 12 through 14. You will recall that the usually superior analytical method involves estimating the net present value of the net cash inflows expected to result from use of that asset in the operations of the business.

The discount rate(s) applied to estimated future cash flows should reflect the degree of uncertainty (risk) that they will materialize. If the uncertainty

Table 19–2 Leasing decisions—lessee's perspective

Acquisition	Financing
Decision	Decision
To acquire or not to acquire the asset (a capital investment decision)	To lease or to finance in an alternative way (a financing decision)
Analysis	Analysis
NPV of estimated net cash inflows	NPV of estimated net cash outflows
(Discount rate(s) reflecting uncertainty of net cash inflows from *operating* the asset)	(Discount rate(s) reflecting uncertainty of net cash outflows from *financing*)

of cash flows from operation of a particular asset (or class of assets) were believed to be equal to the average uncertainty of cash flows of the firm, then the weighted average cost of capital would establish the appropriate discount rate to be used in estimating the net present value of the asset. This discount rate would be adjusted to reflect perceived differences in risk of such cash flows from the average risk of the firm. Almost certain cash flows might be discounted at a relatively low rate, approximating the firm's aftertax cost of debt capital, whereas highly uncertain cash flows would be discounted at a much higher rate.

The general decision criterion would be to acquire the asset if its net present value were positive. Note that the particular *means of financing* the investment in an individual asset is not directly related to the decision to acquire that asset.[5] For this reason the necessity of separating the acquisition decision from the financial decision in lease analysis is emphasized.

The financing decision Once the decision to acquire an asset is made, then the question of how to finance it may be considered. Here we seek the financing that is *least costly* in the long run. Leasing is one means of financing the asset. The cost of leasing should be compared to the cost of the alternative means of financing that is most comparable in the characteristics of its contractual obligations to those incurred under the lease. The most directly comparable financial obligation clearly is long-term debt such as a term loan. Both a term loan and a lease involve fixed obligations to make periodic payments that return the initial investment to the furnisher of capital and provide a fixed or calculated rate of return to that investor. That these obligations are approximately equivalent is recognized by FASB State-

[5]The possible exception to this is that *if* the cost of financing under a lease were *so much lower* than the cost of borrowing that it would materially reduce the overall cost of capital to the user-firm, then it might be necessary to revise the estimated cost of capital in analyzing the acquisition decision. This would rarely, if ever, be true in competitive financial markets.

ment No. 13 in its requirement that financial leases be capitalized on the balance sheet as if the asset had been purchased and its financing had been obtained through long-term debt.[6]

If we are to evaluate a lease as a means of financing, we must estimate its costs versus those that would be incurred if the required financing were obtained via a term loan for a period of time equal to the term of the lease. This analysis requires (1) *calculating the net cash outflows* under the lease versus the owning and borrowing option, (2) *determining the net present value of each* alternative by discounting the cash flows at appropriate rates, and (3) selecting the alternative with *the lowest NPV* (subject, of course, to nonquantifiable considerations).

To illustrate this analysis, let us assume that in December 1983, the Macron Tool Company decided to acquire an electronically controlled milling machine. The manufacturer's price of this machine is $100,000. Universal Leasing Company has offered to purchase the machine and lease it to Macron for a period of seven years with annual rental payments of $13,200, payable in advance. The lease would be noncancellable. Macron (the lessee) would be responsible for all maintenance, property taxes, and insurance. The investment tax credit would be taken by the lessor, Universal Leasing.

Alternatively, Macron could buy the machine from the manufacturer for $100,000. If it did so, Macron would be eligible for an investment tax credit of 10 percent ($10,000) in the year of purchase. It could obtain the remaining required funds by borrowing $90,000 under a seven-year term loan from the First National Bank. The principal of this loan would be paid in equal annual installments of $12,857 at the end of each year. Interest at the rate of 15 percent on the unpaid balance would also be payable at the end of each year. The machine would be classed as five-year property and depreciated for tax purposes under the Accelerated Cost Recovery System (ACRS) at 15 percent of the eligible amount (cost less one half the investment tax credit, or $95,000) the first year, 22 percent the second year, and 21 percent each of the third through fifth years. Macron management guesstimates that the machine could be sold at the end of the seventh year for about $20,000. It is possible that technological obsolescence might result in the machine's being worth considerably less than that or that inflation during the seven-year period would result in its value's being considerably greater. Macron expects to be subject to a 40 percent tax rate on incremental income.

[6]FASB Statement No. 13, p. 49, states, "a lease that transfers substantially all the benefits and risks incident to the ownership of property should be accounted for as the acquisition of an asset and the incurrence of an obligation by the lessee." Such an obligation, required to be booked as a *liability,* the amount due within one year classified as current and the remainder as long-term, is, in effect, a long-term debt obligation.

Cash flows

First let us calculate the expected cash flows under the lease versus the buy-borrow alternative.

Lease The annual rental payments under the lease and the related tax savings are shown in the upper portion of Table 19–3. These payments must be made in advance, that is, at the beginning of each year of the lease. As the beginning of the year is the same as the end of the previous year, then rental payments of $13,200 will be made at the end of each of years 0 through 6. Rental payments may be expensed for tax purposes only in the year in which the services of the asset are received. Therefore the tax shields of $5,280 ($13,200 × .40) will be available in each of years 1 through 7. Thus, there will be no tax shield in year 0 and a tax shield but no rental payment in year 7. The cash outflows each year, shown in column 3, will be the rental payments shown in column 1 less the tax shields in column 2.

Buy-borrow If Macron were to buy the machine and borrow the funds required to finance it, the required cash flows would be calculated as shown in the lower portion of Table 19–3. Principal payments of $12,857 each

Table 19–3 Cash outflows, lease versus buy-borrow—Macron Tool Company

Lease

Year	(1) Rental payments	(2) Tax shields	(3) Cash outflows (1) − (2)
0	$13,200	-0-	$13,200
1–6	13,200	$5,280	7,920
7	-0-	5,280	(5,280)

Buy-borrow

Year	(1) Principal payments	(2) Interest	(3) ACRS depreciation	(4) Tax deductible expenses (2) + (3)	(5) Tax shields (4) × .40	(6) Cash outflows (1) + (2) − (5)
0	-0-	-0-	-0-	-0-	$10,000*	($10,000)
1	$12,857	$13,500	$14,250	$27,750	11,100	15,257
2	12,857	11,567	20,900	32,467	12,987	11,437
3	12,857	9,643	19,950	29,593	11,837	10,663
4	12,857	7,714	19,950	27,664	11,066	9,505
5	12,857	5,786	19,950	25,736	10,294	8,349
6	12,857	3,857	-0-	3,857	1,543	15,171
7	12,857	1,929	-0-	1,929	772	14,014
7	(20,000)†				(8,000)†	(12,000)

*Investment tax credit of 10 percent of purchase price.

†Terminal sale value of $20,000 less tax base (book value) of zero yields taxable gain of $20,000. This is taxable at regular income tax rate as a recapture of depreciation. Tax is $20,000 times 40 percent, or $8,000.

would be made at the end of years 1 through 7 (column 1). Interest payments would decline from $13,500 at the end of year 1 to $1,929 at the end of year 7, because interest at 15 percent would be paid on a declining outstanding balance.[7]

Although depreciation charges do not directly result in cash flows, they are deductible expenses for tax purposes. They thereby create tax shields, which, in turn, are negative cash outflows in the sense that they reduce the amount of taxes to be paid in the year. Column 3 shows the depreciation charges, which would be allowable for tax purposes using the Accelerated Cost Recovery System (ACRS). Note that only $95,000 ($100,000 cost less one half the investment tax credit, or $5,000) can be depreciated under ACRS. This system would be used for tax purposes, because it increases the present value of the tax shields as compared to straight-line depreciation or other accelerated methods based upon useful life of the asset.

Interest (column 2) and depreciation (column 3) are tax deductible expenses. These are accumulated in column 4. Tax shields, equal to 40 percent (the assumed income tax rate) of these expenses, are shown in column 5. Cash outflows relating directly to principal and interest payments on the loan minus the tax shields for years 1 through 7 are shown in column 6. Note that the investment tax credit available to Macron in the year of purchase of the machine is shown as a tax shield in column 5 and as a negative cash outflow in column 6.[8]

Estimated terminal value at the end of seven years is shown by assuming a sale of the machine for $20,000 at that time. Such a sale would result in a taxable gain of $20,000, because the asset was fully depreciated at the end of year 5. This gain would be taxed at 40 percent, or $8,000, as a recapture of depreciation. Thus, the net terminal value is shown as a cash inflow of $12,000 in column 6.

Appropriate discount rates

Much of the controversy mentioned earlier is centered on the discount rates appropriate for determining the net present value (NPV) of the cash flows we have just calculated. Positions vary from using the firm's aftertax cost of long-term debt to discount all expected cash flows to using the firm's estimated weighted average cost of capital as the discount rate for all cash

[7]An alternative term loan might have required *equal annual payments* to include interest on the unpaid balance and an increasing schedule of principal payments (similar to the payment schedules used in connection with home mortgages and personal installment loans). If that were the case, the illustration would be slightly altered to break down each equal annual payment into its principal and interest components.

[8]Actually, the investment tax credit would not be received at the exact time of purchase but several months later, when the firm filed its income tax return. If we had known these dates and required precise accuracy, we should have included interest on a short-term loan of $10,000 for the intervening period.

flows. The position we believe to be most logical is to discount each risk (uncertainty) class of cash flow by a rate commensurate with its risk.[9] This is in accordance with the fundamental principle that the discount rate embody the pure (or risk-free) interest rate plus a premium for risk.

Fixed cash flows Rental payments required under the lease and all payments, principal and interest, on the loan are *fixed* by the respective contracts. They must be paid or the user-firm would default and face bankruptcy. Tax shields arising from rental payments under the lease and from interest and depreciation charges under the buy-borrow alternative are almost certain. The only reason to question their certainty is the possibility of error in estimating the firm's incremental tax rate. The investment tax credit that the firm would receive under the buy-borrow alternative is certain. Therefore, it is reasonable to consider all of these cash flows to be as certain as any that the firm will experience. This degree of certainty is embodied in the firm's after-tax borrowing rate for a period equal to the term of the lease or loan. In our illustration, that rate for Macron is 9 percent, calculated by multiplying the pretax interest rate on the term loan, 15 percent, by 1 minus the tax rate of 40 percent.[10]

Uncertain interim cash flows If the lease agreement provides that the lessor will be responsible for maintenance, property taxes, insurance, or any other payments that the user-owner would have to pay under the buy-borrow alternative, then such payments should be discounted at a rate reflecting their perceived uncertainty. (Our example, illustrating a financial lease, does not involve any such payments, but that of an operating lease often would.) Such payments probably would be subject to about the same degree of uncertainty as the average of all cash flows of the firm. Therefore, the estimated amounts of these payments (after tax) should be discounted at the firm's overall cost of capital. This rate, of course, would be higher than its debt cost.

Uncertain terminal values If the buy-borrow alternative were chosen, the owner-firm would benefit from the terminal value of the asset at the end of

[9]For positions to the contrary see R. W. Johnson and W. G. Lewellen, "Analysis of the Lease-or-Buy Decision", *Journal of Finance,* September 1972, pp. 815–23, and L. D. Schall, "The Lease or Buy and Asset Acquisition Decisions", *Journal of Finance,* September 1974, pp. 1203–14.

[10]Some analysts argue that a slightly higher rate, perhaps 0.5 or 1 percent higher, should be applied to the tax shields because of the possibility of error in estimating the firm's incremental tax rate. This is a legitimate argument. We feel, however, that from a practical standpoint this refinement would make such a small difference in the resulting NPVs that its use is not justified.

Also an argument is made that inasmuch as the lessor's claim in bankruptcy is limited whereas the lender's claim covers the entire unpaid principal and delinquent interest, the rental payments under the lease should be discounted at a higher rate than payments required under the loan. From the lessee's standpoint, this argument is without merit. If the firm is bankrupt, its owners probably will lose their entire investment and have no further interest in the firm. How the creditors might pick the bones of the bankrupt estate has no bearing upon the certainty of the obligations of the firm to make payments while it is solvent.

the lease period, whereas the lessee may give up this value under the terms of the lease. In most cases the value of the asset at the termination of the lease is highly uncertain. This was implied by the term "guesstimate" of the terminal sale price of the milling machine owned by Macron. The aftertax terminal value under the buy-borrow alternative should be discounted at a rate reflecting the degree of uncertainty that it would materialize. In our illustration, we consider a discount rate of 20 percent to reflect this uncertainty. In any case, the appropriate rate for discounting such a terminal value would be much higher than the firm's aftertax borrowing rate and usually somewhat higher than its overall cost of capital.[11]

Net present values

Finally, the net present values (NPVs) of the cash flows under the two alternatives are determined as shown in Table 19–4. Under the lease the

Table 19–4 Present value of cash flows, lease versus buy-borrow—Macron Tool Company

	(1) Net cash outflows	(2) Present value factors @ 9%	(3) Present value of net cash outflows (1) × (2)
Leasing			
Year 0	$13,200	1.000	$13,200
Years 1–6	7,920	4.486	35,529
Year 7	(5,280)	.547	(2,888)
Total			$45,841
Buy-borrow			
Year 0	($10,000)	1.000	($10,000)
1	15,257	.917	13,991
2	11,437	.842	9,630
3	10,663	.772	8,232
4	9,505	.708	6,730
5	8,349	.650	5,427
6	15,171	.596	9,042
7	14,014	.547	7,666
7	(12,000)	.279†	(3,348)*
Total			$47,370
NPV advantage of *lease* ($47,370 − $45,841)			$ 1,529

*After tax terminal value of asset discounted at 20 percent.
†*PVIF* at 20 percent.

[11]Alternatively, the NPV of the terminal value could be estimated by using the *certainty equivalent method* described in Chapter 14. Using this approach, one would estimate the certainty equivalent of the estimated (but uncertain) net terminal value. Then the firm's aftertax cost of debt capital (its certainty rate) would be applied to this certainty equivalent. The product would be the NPV of the terminal value.

NPV of the initial payment at time 0 is the full amount of the rental payment, \$13,200 (from Table 19–3). The net aftertax cash outflows of \$7,920 for years 1 through 6 are multiplied by the present value interest factor of an annuity (*PVIFA*) at 9 percent obtained from Table B in the Appendix of this book. Then the negative cash outflow (cash inflow) of the tax shield available in year 7 is multiplied by the present value interest factor (*PVIF*) at 9 percent, found in Table A in the appendix. The NPV of the net cash outflows under the lease is \$45,841.

Under the buy-borrow option, the present value of the available income tax credit is \$10,000, a negative cash outflow (cash inflow). Then, each of the cash outflows from column 6, Table 19–3, is multiplied by the appropriate *PVIF* at a 9 percent rate (from Table A). The cash inflow of \$12,000, reflecting the aftertax terminal value at the end of seven years, is multiplied by the *PVIF* at the higher discount rate of 20 percent due to the much higher uncertainty of that flow. The NPV of the net cash outflows under the buy-borrow alternative is \$47,370.

Therefore the NPV advantage of the lease as compared to the buy-borrow alternative is \$1,529. On the basis of this quantitative analysis only, the decision to lease the machine would be preferred to buying it because the present value of the net cash outflows is lower. However, the advantage is so small that nonquantitative considerations might determine the decision.

Factors affecting the lease versus buy-borrow comparison

There are two types of factors that may affect the lease versus buy-borrow comparison and the ultimate decision of which financing method to use. First, there are some factors that might favorably influence the cost and availability of leasing. Second, there are a number of alleged nonquantifiable advantages of leasing that must be critically evaluated.

Cost and availability advantages of leasing

Three possible cost and availability advantages of leasing will now be discussed.

Differing tax status of lessor and lessee In some cases, advantageous lease terms may be offered by a lessor because its tax status will provide greater tax advantages than those available to the lessee under the buy-borrow alternative. This might be true if the user-firm is operating at a loss or has accumulated tax-loss carry-forwards that nullify its tax liabilities. Such a user-firm would be unable to take advantage of the investment tax credit if it purchased the asset or of subsequent tax shields from accelerated depreciation. A lessor that can utilize the tax credit and subsequent tax shields should be able to purchase and lease the asset on terms providing a lower net present value of cash outflows of the lessee than would result from its buy-borrow alternative. A similar situation exists if the user is a tax-exempt organization, such as a university, governmental body, church, or museum.

Sometimes a significant difference in tax status of the lessor and lessee may occur if the lessor is a high-income individual or a partnership of such individuals. The lessor's personal incremental tax bracket may be higher than the corporate income tax rate, thus it obtains greater advantage from the tax shields than the user-firm could under the buy-borrow alternative. This factor may be particularly important if a leveraged lease is used and the wealthy individual lessor may obtain tax advantages from both ACRS depreciation and interest on the borrowing that provides a large portion of the funds required to purchase the asset.

Greater residual value to the lessor Especially in operating leases, the manufacturer, its leasing subsidiary, or a specialized leasing company may be able to realize greater residual value from the asset at the expiration of the lease than the user-firm could. This results from its greater access to the market to re-lease or sell the asset. For example, a computer manufacturer could more readily locate another lessee or buyer of a used computer than could a lumber company that used the computer. Therefore, competition among such lessors might force rental charges down to a level at which the NPV of the lessee's net cash outflows would be lower than under the buy-borrow alternative.

Availability of financing There are two factors that might favorably influence the availability of lease financing compared to a loan to finance purchase of an asset. The first is that, particularly in connection with operating leases, the manufacturer or distributor of the asset looks to *both* its profit on the sale of the asset to its leasing subsidiary and the rate of return that the subsidiary can earn on the lease. In a sense, such a manufacturer or distributor views leasing as a selling device. This may lead to its willingness to lease the asset to a firm that might not be able to obtain debt financing on a reasonable basis. Even if the user-firm were able to obtain such financing, the lease arrangement may be less costly than borrowing.

The other factor influencing availability of leases is that it generally is less difficult and time-consuming for a lessor to seize a leased asset if the lessee defaults than for a long-term lender to foreclose on pledged property and obtain possession of it. This factor is particularly important if the asset is real estate. Evicting a tenant from leased property is considerably less cumbersome than foreclosing a mortgage and subsequently evicting the mortgagor.

Note that most of the factors discussed above are not general influences upon cost or availability of lease financing but rather refer to specific individual circumstances under which some economic advantages may exist.

Alleged subjective advantages of leasing

Several nonquantifiable advantages of leasing may be claimed, particularly by leasing institutions. These must be carefully scrutinized by the user-firm, because in many cases they either lack merit or must be weighed against counterbalancing disadvantages.

Cleaner balance sheet Prior to 1977, it was widely claimed that leasing resulted in a more favorable balance sheet of the user-firm. Because the liability related to lease obligations did not appear on the balance sheet, debt ratios were lower. On the face of this, the debt-plus-lease financing capacity of the lessee would be greater than under the buy-borrow alternative. It is doubtful, however, that potential lenders would ignore the effect of lease obligations upon the firm's debt capacity. Astute financial analysts simply capitalized the leases.

At any rate, FASB Statement No. 13 eliminates this possible advantage of a financial (capital) lease by requiring that it be formally capitalized on the balance sheet. Operating leases, however, do not have to be capitalized. It is possible that minor operating leases may be ignored by some lenders. In such cases the cleaner balance sheet argument may have some validity. It is doubtful that this would be true if the firm acquired the use of a significant portion of its assets through operating leases.

One hundred percent financing A similar claim is that leasing provides 100 percent financing of the acquired asset and thus enhances the financial capability of the firm. This argument has little merit. If the asset is purchased, the firm becomes eligible for an investment tax credit up to 10 percent of the purchase price. As compared with a lease agreement in which the lessor retains the investment tax credit, this provides 10 percent of the required financing. In addition, rental payments under a lease usually must be made in advance. If annual rental payments are required under a 10-year lease, the initial rental payment would be the equivalent of a 10-percent down payment under the buy-borrow alternative. Considering both the investment tax credit forgone and the advance rental payment, the financing provided under such a lease would be comparable to a purchase with 80 percent of the financing provided by a term loan.

Even if leasing provided 100 percent financing, this should not favorably affect the user-firm's debt capacity. Logically, a firm with a given earning power and equity cushion is capable of supporting a limited amount of fixed financial obligations. If obligations to service a lease are just as definite (fixed) as those to service a loan, then leasing uses up some of that borrowing power, just as a loan would. If the firm has the capacity to support financing 100 percent of the required investment in a leased asset, it then must have the same financial capacity to support borrowing 100 percent of the required funds if it purchased the asset. Therefore, the remaining borrowing power would be the same under either alternative.

Equivalent of depreciating land As mentioned earlier, if land is owned it cannot be depreciated for tax purposes. But if it is leased, the lessee may deduct for tax purposes the entire rental payment. Thus, leasing indirectly allows the lessee to obtain a tax advantage equivalent to depreciating land. This tax effect results from inclusion of amortization of the entire value of the real estate, land as well as buildings, in the lease payments. This is a valid consideration in many sale-leasebacks of urban real estate where the land represents a large proportion of the total value.

But the seller-lessee must carefully weigh this tax advantage against the disadvantage resulting from its forgoing the opportunity to benefit from possible increase in value of the land during the period of the lease. Many a seller-lessee who was enticed by the tax advantage 20 years ago regrets having ever heard of a sale-leaseback, because the property is now worth several times more than it was at the time of the transaction. But the firm does not own it; the lessor just smiles as he drives by in his Mercedes!

Increased liquidity A sale-leaseback increases liquidity by converting an existing fixed asset into cash. This conversion to cash commits the seller-lessee to fixed rental payments over the term of the lease. As sale-leasebacks almost always involve financial leases, their effects upon both liquidity and solvency of the firm are similar to borrowing the amount of the sale price on the security of a mortgage on the property. The liquidity advantage would be only the amount by which the sale price (after capital gains taxes) might exceed the principal of the loan. This liquidity advantage would be offset by the higher rental payments required to amortize the buyer-lessor's larger investment.

Reduced risk of obsolescence Under a cancellable operating lease, the lessee avoids the risk of premature obsolescence of the asset, because it can cancel if the asset is no longer useful to it. Of course, the lessor has figured into the required rental payments and the cancellation premium compensation for bearing the risk of premature obsolescence. This should be a nearly even trade-off.

The lessee bears the risk of obsolescence under a financial lease. Here the lease is noncancellable. The lessee is obligated to make rental payments throughout the term of the lease even if the asset has become obsolete and is no longer useful to it. This fact, incidentally, may induce the lessee to continue to use an obsolete asset to the detriment of its operational efficiency. An additional disadvantage of a financial lease is that if the economic longevity of the asset should prove greater than anticipated, the lessee may not have the opportunity to continue use of it.

Flexibility The financial flexibility of a lease may be greater than that under the buy-borrow alternative. A lease usually does not include as many restrictive provisions, or as stringent ones, as a term loan or a bond issue. Another consideration is that financing may be obtained at the time and in the amount required as it becomes necessary to acquire the use of assets, compared to long-term borrowing in relatively large round-lot amounts. This piecemeal financing may be both convenient and more efficient in that the timing of the financing coincides more closely with the productive use of the property acquired.

Operational flexibility, however, may be limited under leasing. Modification or improvement of the asset usually requires approval of the lessor. In some cases, the lessor might disapprove modifications or improvements that would be of value to the lessee but might limit marketability of the asset at the expiration date.

Summary

A lease is a means of obtaining the use of a fixed asset as an alternative to buying the asset and directly financing it. The lessor holds title to the asset and the lessee has the right to use it in accordance with the lease contract. The use of leasing has been broadened in recent years from its original application to real estate; now, almost any fixed asset may be leased.

An operating lease is identified by its relatively short term (considerably less than the useful life of the asset); its cancellation feature; and the provision of services, such as maintenance, taxes, and insurance by the lessor. A financial lease covers a long period of time (approximately equal to the useful life of the asset), is noncancellable, and usually requires that maintenance, taxes, and insurance are responsibilities of the lessee. The financial lease is essentially a medium by which long-term financing of the asset is obtained by the lessee in return for a fixed rental obligation for its entire period.

A direct lease is created when the lessor either already owns the asset or acquires it for the purpose of leasing. A lease is leveraged if the lessor finances a large portion of the purchase price through borrowing from third parties, thereby augmenting the rate of return from leasing the asset. Under a sale-leaseback, the owner sells the asset to the lessor, simultaneously leasing it back for approximately its remaining useful life.

Certain tax and accounting considerations are important in leasing. Rental payments are tax deductible in the year in which the services of the asset are received, which may not coincide with the year in which the payments are paid. Stringent IRS regulations define a lease on which such payments may be fully deductible. The investment tax credit may be allocated to either the lessor or the lessee by the lease contract. For accounting purposes, Financial Accounting Standards Board Statement No. 13 establishes tests for a capital (financial) lease and requires that such a lease be capitalized, thus disclosing the value of the asset and the corresponding liability on the balance sheet. Certain information regarding both financial and operating leases also must be disclosed in footnotes.

Leasing involves two distinct decisions: (1) whether to acquire the use of the asset and (2) if so, how to finance the acquisition. The acquisition decision is made independently and based upon capital investment analysis and criteria. The financing decision requires a discounted cash flow comparison of the lease versus the most directly comparable alternative financing, long-term debt such as a term loan. First, the net aftertax cash outflows each year under the two alternatives are calculated. The lease entails almost certain rental payments, partly offset by tax shields; the buy-borrow alternative entails principal and interest payments, also partly offset by tax shields from depreciation and interest. To determine their present values, these cash outflows are discounted at the firm's aftertax borrowing rate, reflecting their relative certainty. Differences in service obligations, if any, are discounted at a rate reflecting their uncertainty, usually the estimated overall cost of capital. The aftertax residual value of the asset usually is highly uncertain. It should be discounted at a rate reflecting that uncertainty, probably higher than the overall cost of capital. The decision criterion is to accept the alternative with the lowest NPV of the cash outflows, unless modified by subjective considerations.

In some cases, particular factors may favorably influence the cost and availability of leasing. These may be (1) tax advantages available to the lessor but not to the lessee, (2) greater residual value of the asset to the lessor, (3) the lessor's considering profit on sale of the asset to its leasing subsidiary as well as the rate of return on the lease, and (4) less complex and time-consuming seizure of the asset if default occurs than foreclosure under the terms of a secured loan.

Several subjective advantages of leasing have been claimed. These include claims of a cleaner balance sheet, 100 percent financing, ability to depreciate land, increased liquidity, reduced risk of obsolescence, and increased flexibility. All of these alleged advantages are tenuous at best, and several are subject to counterbalancing disadvantages.

Questions

1. What is a lease? How does an operating lease differ from a financial (capital) lease?

2. Some people hold that leasing allows a firm to obtain the use of more fixed assets with a given amount of equity capital than owning the assets. Evaluate this contention.

3. What is the difference between a direct lease and a sale-leaseback? Which arrangement allows the lessee to increase its liquidity?

4. What is meant by capitalizing a lease? Under FASB No. 13, how is a financial (capital) lease capitalized?

5. In evaluating a financial (capital) lease, why are the cash flows under the lease compared to those resulting if the asset were purchased and financed by borrowing the required funds under a term loan?

6. What cash flows are considered in the financial lease versus buy-borrow analysis?

7. In a financial lease versus buy-borrow analysis, why are the net cash outflows during the term of the lease discounted at the firm's aftertax borrowing rate rather than its estimated overall cost of capital? Why might the estimated terminal net cash inflow be discounted at a much higher rate?

8. Advantageous lease terms might be offered by a lessor in a high tax bracket to a lessee that is subject to little or no tax. Explain.

9. Under what conditions might the lessor be willing to lease an asset under an operating lease at a lower cost to the lessee than the alternative cost of borrowing by the user-firm?

10. "A sale-leaseback is advantageous compared to a long-term loan secured by a mortgage on the property because it increases the liquidity of the user-firm." Evaluate this statement.

Problems

1. Unitas Corporation is entering into a financial (capital) lease requiring rental payments of $100,000 at the *end* of each year for 20 years. Under FASB No. 13, Unitas is required to capitalize this lease. Unitas' borrowing rate for a 20-year loan secured by the asset to be leased is 8 percent, which is the same as the rate of return used by the lessor in determining the rental payments. Capitalize this lease, indicating amounts to be entered under the headings "Leased property under capital lease," "Current obligation under capital lease," and "Long-term obligations under capital lease" on Unitas' balance sheet.

2. Glenwood Corporation's lease on a plastic moulding machine requires annual rental payments of $9,000 to be made at the *beginning* of each year for 10 years. Glenwood's income tax rate is 40 percent.

a. What are the aftertax outflows each year?

b. What is the present value of these cash outflows discounted at 9 percent, the aftertax borrowing rate Glenwood would pay on a 10-year term loan secured by the machine?

3. Chatham Corporation wishes to acquire the use of a stamping press costing $240,000. Foremost Leasing Corporation has offered to purchase the press and lease it to Chatham for eight years (its estimated useful life) with annual rental payments of $35,000 payable *in advance.* The lease would be noncancellable, and Chatham would be responsible for maintenance, insurance, and taxes. The investment tax credit of 10 percent would be taken by Foremost. At the expiration of the lease, Chatham would have the right of first refusal to purchase or re-lease the press.

Chatham's alternative would be to purchase the press for $240,000, take the investment tax credit, and finance the balance by obtaining an eight-year term loan from the Security Bank. The principal of this loan would be paid in equal annual installments at the *end* of each year. Interest of 15 percent of the outstanding balance would be payable at the time each principal payment is made. The press would be classed as five-year property under ACRS and be depreciated for tax purposes at 15 percent of the amount eligible for ACRS depreciation the first year, 22 percent the second, and 21 percent each of the third through fifth years. No net salvage value is anticipated at the end of eight years. Chatham expects to be subject to a 40 percent tax rate.

Evaluate Chatham's alternatives and recommend the most economical means of acquiring the stamping press.

4. Ectron Electronics, Incorporated, wishes to acquire $150,000 worth of testing equipment for its research laboratory. Nucleonics Leasing Corporation, a subsidiary of Nucleonics, Incorporated, the manufacturer, offers to lease this equipment for three years, with rental payments of $36,000 per year payable *in advance.* Nucleonics Leasing will take the investment tax credit and agree to pay for maintenance, insurance, and taxes. At the expiration of the lease, Ectron will have the right of first refusal to re-lease or purchase the equipment.

Ectron's alternative is to buy the equipment, take the 6 percent investment tax credit for which it would be eligible, and finance the purchase by borrowing the balance of the required funds under a three-year term loan from Fidelity National Bank. The principal would be paid in three equal annual installments at the *end* of each year, and interest of 15 percent would be paid annually on the outstanding balance. This equipment would qualify as three-year property under ACRS and be depreciated for tax purposes at 25 percent of the amount eligible for ACRS depreciation the first year, 38 percent the second, and 37 percent the third year. Ectron estimates its pretax cost of maintenance, insurance, and taxes to be $4,000 per year and the net aftertax value of the equipment at the end of three years to be $40,000.

Ectron estimates its overall aftertax cost of capital to be about 17 percent. The value of the equipment at the end of three years is highly uncertain because of rapid technological change. Ectron's management feels that a 25 percent discount rate would reflect this uncertainty. Ectron is subject to a 40 percent tax rate.

Evaluate Ectron's alternatives and recommend whether it should lease or purchase the testing equipment.

5. Superyield Management, Incorporated, a consulting firm, is remodeling its offices. It is acquiring $40,000 worth of office furniture and equipment. United Leasing Company offers to lease this equipment for six years at an annual rental of $8,500 to be paid at the *end* of each year. United will take the investment tax credit. Superyield will be responsible for maintenance, taxes, and insurance. At the termination of the lease, Superyield will have the right of first refusal to re-lease or purchase the assets.

Superyield could buy the furniture and equipment for $40,000, take a $4,000 investment tax credit, and finance the remaining $36,000 by borrowing on a six-year term loan from the Merchants National Bank with principal payments due at the *end* of each year and 14 percent interest on the outstanding balance payable with each principal payment.

The furniture and equipment would qualify as five-year property under ACRS and be depreciated for tax purposes at 15 percent of the amount eligible for ACRS depreciation the first year, 22 percent the second, and 21 percent each of the third through fifth years. The furniture and equipment is expected to have aftertax terminal value of $7,000 at the end of the sixth year. Superyield is in the 40 percent tax bracket.

Appraise these alternatives for acquiring the furniture and equipment and recommend which should be chosen. (Round to the nearest percent in determining the discount rate for cash flows during the term of the lease. Consider 20 percent to be an appropriate discount rate reflecting the uncertainty of the terminal value.)

Chapter 20
Common and Preferred Stock

This chapter deals with the relationship between a corporation and its owners, the stockholders. The stockholders' position differs from that of creditors in several fundamental ways. Creditors are *owed* certain *fixed obligations,* for example, periodic interest payments and the principal at maturity. If these payments are not made, or other promises are not kept, default occurs. The creditors may resort to the courts and obtain judgments. If judgments are not paid, the creditors may then levy on the firm's property. The eventual outcome probably will be that the corporate assets will be seized by the courts and either liquidated or reorganized in bankruptcy. Stockholders have no such legal rights. Their position as part *owners* of the corporation is *residual,* their claims coming after those of all creditors. The stockholders have rights to share in distribution of residual earnings and assets, and they have control rights that relate to their ownership of the corporation. These relationships are shown in Figure 20–1.

Figure 20–1 **Stockholders' and creditors' relationship to the corporation**

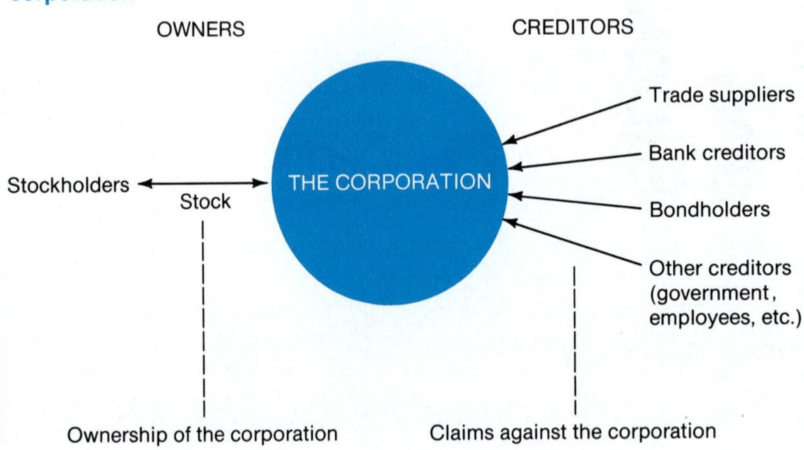

The stockholders are the true entrepreneurs of the firm. They provide the equity capital that finances part of the assets and that forms the basis upon which rests the borrowing power to finance the remainder of the assets. All of the equity capital of the firm, paid-in surplus and retained earnings as well as that booked as stock, reflects the investment of the stockholders. While most corporations have just one type of stock outstanding, common stock (sometimes called capital stock), some may have two or more types or classes of stock.

This chapter first will relate the fundamental rights of stockholders assuming that the corporation has only one type of stock. Then it will recognize that the issue of more than one type of stock results in the unequal distribution of these rights among different classes of stockholders. As the most common differentiation is between preferred and common stock, the nature of preferred stock will be treated in detail. Finally, the characteristics and managerial considerations relative to common stock will be discussed.

Fundamental rights of stockholders

The fundamental rights of stockholders are established by the corporate charter. In the narrow sense this is the *articles of incorporation.* But in the broader sense the charter includes the state's corporation laws and the body of judicial decisions interpreting them.[1] These rights may be classified as those relating to (1) earnings and dividends, (2) assets in liquidation, and (3) control and information.

Earnings and dividends

After all creditors' claims have been satisfied, the remaining earnings accrue to the benefit of the stockholders. Residual earnings may be paid in dividends to the stockholders at the discretion of the board of directors. The payment of dividends must be on a *ratable* basis, that is, each share being treated alike. Earnings that are retained should benefit the stockholder by increasing the net assets of the firm, which, in turn, provide the basis for increased future earnings. For example, the ABC Corporation earned $2.83 per share of stock in 1982, and dividends of $1.50 per share were paid to the stockholders. The remaining $1.33 per share was reinvested in net assets that, if ABC's capital investment decisions are sound, will increase the firm's future earnings per share and the value of its stock.

As the stockholders' participation in earnings and dividends is residual, it therefore is variable. Earnings will fluctuate according to the relative prosperity of the firm's operations. Direct benefits in the form of dividends will reflect both that prosperity and the dividend policy of the board of directors.[2] The corporation has no legal obligation to provide either earnings or dividends; the stockholders could not go to court if they did not materialize. If losses are sustained, these losses reduce the net equity of the firm. Such

[1]State corporation laws are quite similar but not identical. The material in this chapter is, of necessity, generalized. There are differences among state corporation laws, leading decisions of state courts, and the articles of incorporation of different firms incorporated within the same state.

[2]Dividend policy will be discussed in Chapter 22.

losses are absorbed by the stockholders as their investment in the corporation is thereby reduced.

Assets

The net assets (total assets less liabilities) are, in a sense, owned by the stockholders. But this ownership is indeed indirect. The stockholders hold *stock certificates,* which provide only such rights as exist in the corporate charter. These rights in relation to the corporate assets are limited to distribution of assets, usually cash, through dividends and the residual right to assets if and when the corporation is dissolved. That usually will take place when the firm becomes bankrupt. In bankruptcy, the assets will be liquidated or the firm will be reorganized. In either case, all creditors' claims must be satisfied before the stockholders may receive anything. Unfortunately, there usually is nothing left for the stockholders.[3] Occasionally a solvent corporation is dissolved. In such cases, significant distributions of assets may be made to the stockholders on a ratable basis.

Control and information

In general, the stockholders collectively control the corporation through their rights to elect the board of directors and to approve changes in the corporation that materially affect its nature and activity. The board of directors, as representatives of the stockholders, then appoint the officers and establish the basic operating and financial policies of the firm. The officers, in turn, are responsible for execution of these policies and day-to-day operation of the firm.

This mechanism appears to be quite straightforward. In many small, closely held firms, it is. However, in considering the large, publicly held firm, one must recognize that the real mechanisms of control may be vastly more complex. Who controls AT&T, General Motors, Exxon, General Electric, or many other major corporations with stock so widely dispersed that no individual or group of stockholders holds a majority interest? Who selects the individuals to be nominated for election to the board? Is the board, in effect, self-perpetuating? Do the directors control the officers or vice versa? These are indeed important and often unanswerable questions. Discussion of the power structure of the modern national or multinational corporation is beyond the scope of this text. However, it would be naive to imply that control of such corporations is as simple as implied by the legal mechanism.

Voting rights Voting for the board of directors and on other matters of vital importance to the corporation takes place at the annual stockholders' meeting. Because many stockholders cannot be physically present, absen-

[3]Bankruptcy will be treated in Chapter 24.

tees may vote by proxy. A *proxy* is a temporary power of attorney giving another person the right to vote a stockholder's shares. Management solicits proxies from the stockholders before the meeting. If nonmangement individuals or groups are vying for control of the corporation, they also may solicit proxies. In such a case, a *proxy fight* ensues. Proxy fights usually are heated, with repeated communication by letter and in the press. Each side will accuse the other of acting against the best interests of the stockholders collectively and attempt to justify its own position in pursuing the stockholders' proxy votes. Proxy fights are somewhat akin to political campaigns.

Large, publicly held corporations subject to the jurisdiction of the SEC are required to follow specific procedures in soliciting proxies. These include the submission of a *proxy statement* indicating the background and stockholdings of nominees to the board of directors and the details of other matters that are to be voted upon at the annual meeting. Management may include statements supporting its positions on these matters, and any stockholder may require inclusion of statements opposing the management view. The proxy itself allows the stockholder to vote his or her preference on matters to be voted upon.

The election of the board of directors usually is the most important control right of the stockholders. Voting rights also extend to (1) amendment of the articles of incorporation, (2) adoption or amendment of bylaws, (3) approval of mergers or consolidation, (4) sale or mortgaging of a major portion of the corporate assets, and (5) authorization of additional shares of stock or different classes or types of stock. State corporation laws define the specific majority, simple or two-thirds, required to approve these matters. Direct stockholder approval is required because these actions may materially change the nature of the corporation or even result in termination of its existence.

Information rights Related to their control rights are certain rights of the stockholders to information. A stockholder, in theory, has the right *to inspect the books.* As a practical matter, corporations cannot have stockholders wandering into the accounting office physically inspecting the books or competitors buying one share of stock and sending someone over each day to gain confidential information. It is important, however, that stockholders be adequately informed regarding the operating results and financial condition of a corporation of which they are part owners. Normally this right is satisfied by the published annual reports to stockholders and, where required, the filing of 10K reports with the SEC.

The stockholder also has the right *to know the names and addresses of* his or her fellow *stockholders.* This is required by law, because the list is necessary for a stockholder to engage in a proxy fight. The stockholder must be able to support the legitimacy of the need; the corporation obviously does not have to comply with requests of direct-mail marketers for choice mailing lists.

A final general right of a stockholder is *to sue the directors* in a court of equity. Such a suit, based upon evidence that those in control of the corporation have acted beyond their legal authority for personal gain to the detriment of the stockholders in general, is called a stockholders derivative suit. Such a suit asks that damages be determined and the amount restored to the corporate treasury. Such civil suits sometimes accompany criminal prosecution on such charges as embezzlement or misappropriation of funds.

Risk, income, and control

The position of the stockholders relative to creditors can be compared in terms of risk, income, and control. The stockholders bear the *residual risk.* They stand to lose their entire investment before any creditors may lose anything. This is the reason their investment in the corporation is referred to by creditors as the *equity cushion.* The equity absorbs operating losses and/or direct losses of asset value, while the creditors' position remains intact until the owners' equity is eliminated.

But risk is a two-edged sword. In return for bearing the residual risks, the stockholders stand to benefit from the good fortunes of the firm. The earnings, and ultimately dividends, benefiting the stockholders also are residual. Whereas the creditors are entitled to fixed interest payments, earnings to the stockholders are unlimited. Fluctuation in the rate of return on the firm's operations will not directly affect the income of the creditors unless default occurs. The income benefiting the stockholders changes more or less continuously and may range from negative to perhaps a very high rate of return.

As a general principle, investors who bear the risk should control the firm. As long as debt obligations are properly serviced and their value remains intact, the risk is borne by the stockholders. It is their money that will be lost if the firm is poorly managed, and they are the ones who will benefit from good management. Therefore, the stockholders control the firm.

However, this is true only as long as debt obligations are properly serviced. If the firm gets into trouble, the stockholders' equity may be seriously impaired. Then the ability to service debt becomes questionable and the creditors may be jeopardized. At this point, default on obligations to creditors, such as failure to make interest and sinking-fund payments or breach of protective provisions, becomes imminent. From a practical viewpoint, even though the balance sheet might not show it, the equity cushion is exhausted. Creditors may then be expected to move in and seize control. The stockholders have risked and lost. The creditors are now in the risk-bearing position.

When default is imminent, in spite of the legal mechanism that stockholders elect the directors, who in turn appoint the officers to run the company, the stockholders must relinquish control. The creditors are in a position to press their claims through the courts if default occurs and management, representing the stockholders, is in no position to do anything about it. The defaulted creditors may take control informally by demanding that the stockholders elect their representatives to the board, who will in turn invite their Mr. Smith to come over and run the company. Their alternative is to go to court and force the firm into bankruptcy. Then the court will seize the corporate assets and appoint a trustee to manage or liquidate them for the benefit of creditors.

In summary, the stockholders control the corporation, and the creditors do not have or want control rights as long as the debt is properly serviced and supported by the equity cushion. If and when debt cannot be properly serviced, control may shift to the creditors. Control properly lies with those investors who are at risk.

Unequal distribution of rights among stockholders

Most firms have only one class or type of stock. This is common stock, sometimes called capital stock. Each share has the rights previously indicated. Alternatively, it is possible to have two or more types or classes of stock. In such cases, the rights attaching to one type differ from those of another. Such differences are not standardized, but rather are designed to accomplish the needs of incorporators or controlling stockholders to raise equity funds and/or to maintain control.

An example of such unequal distribution of rights among stockholders is *classified stock*. The corporation may have class A and class B stock. The class B stock (held by the management) may have full voting rights, whereas the class A stock (sold to the public) is identical in its rights to dividends and assets in liquidation, but is nonvoting. Classification is used in this case to assure control of the corporation by the management group. For example, in the Adolph Coors Company (Coors beer), the regular common stock is held by the Coors family and the class B nonvoting stock by the public. The Ford Motor Company uses a variation in this type of stock classification. The relatively small issue of class B stock held by the Ford family is entitled to 40 percent of the voting power, while the much larger issue of common stock held by the public has 60 percent of the voting power. While not absolutely assuring control of the corporation by the family, this arrangement provides a greatly exaggerated voting power for their class B shares.

In some cases classified stock may involve unequal rights to dividend distributions. For example, the class A stock may be entitled to dividends, whereas dividends on the class B stock are restricted.[4] Such an arrangement is sometimes used in financing a new corporation if the buyers of the class A stock require dividends as an incentive to purchase but the management-held class B stock is not entitled to dividends until retained earnings are built up to a stated level.

A far more prevalent use of different types of stock involves unequal distribution of rights between preferred and common stockholders.

Preferred stock

Preferred stock is a hybrid security and in a sense a misnomer. Perhaps it would be better understood if it were called *preferred but limited* stock. From the viewpoint of the common stockholders, its characteristics are similar to those of a junior bond in that its claims upon income and assets in liquidation are superior to those of the common stock. But from the viewpoint of the creditor, preferred stock is equity. Its claims are inferior to those of debt; therefore, it constitutes part of the equity cushion supporting the debt.

Priorities and limitations

Preferred stock has a priority on dividend distributions and assets in liquidation.

Dividends The first and most important priority and limitation of preferred stock relates to dividends. This may be stated either as a percentage of par value or a specified dollar amount per year. A 12 percent preferred stock with a par value of $100 entitles its holder to dividends of $12 per year ($3 per quarter) before any dividend distribution may be made to the common stockholders. A $12 preferred stock provides the same priority upon dividends.

This priority does *not* imply that the corporation *must* pay the preferred stockholder $12 per year in the sense that failure to do so would constitute a default and provide legal remedies to the holder. It only requires that the preferred dividend be paid *before* any dividend distribution is made to the common stockholders. Preferred dividends are limited to the stated per-

[4]In cases where such class B stock is convertible into class A at an increasing conversion ratio based upon dividends paid to the class B, the IRS may take a dim view of the arrangement. Its position is that the escalating conversion ratio, if linked to dividend payments on the class A stock, provides constructive benefits of dividends to the class B stockholders. Any firm contemplating the use of such classified stock should obtain competent tax counsel.

centage of par or dollar amount, regardless of the firm's earnings or cash available for distribution. The only exception to this limitation is the case of participating preferred stock, which will be discussed later.

Preferred stock nearly always is *cumulative.* If the board of directors fails to declare and pay preferred dividends, these dividends will *accumulate in arrears.* All dividend arrearages plus the current periodic dividend must be paid to the preferred stockholders before any future dividends may be paid to the common stockholders. From a practical standpoint, newly issued preferred stock must have a cumulative feature to be salable. Otherwise the corporation, controlled by the common stockholders, could omit preferred dividends for years, then pay one quarterly dividend on the preferred and a large dividend on the common stock. In effect, this would destroy the basic concept of preferred stockholders' priority. A few noncumulative preferred stocks have been issued as a result of reorganization in bankruptcy. These may be noncumulative only for a period of perhaps two or three years or until the earning power of the reorganized corporation has been established.

The cumulative feature does not, however, always result in the preferred stockholders' receiving the full amount of arrearages if the ailing firm should recover its earning power. The common stockholders may have bargaining power to settle preferred arrearages for something less than their full amount. The preferred stockholders are not in a position to go to court to collect arrearages. They can only bargain for a satisfactory settlement if the common stockholders control the corporation.

Assets in liquidation Another priority and limitation of preferred stock relates to assets in liquidation. Preferred stockholders typically have the right to receive the par value (usually $100 per share) or a stated value—say, $100 per share—plus any dividend arrearages in liquidation before the common stockholders may receive anything. This claim is inferior to the claims of all creditors. If a solvent corporation were liquidated, the preferred stockholders might recover their investment in full. Since corporations usually are liquidated in bankruptcy, however, the proceeds of liquidation frequently are not sufficient to cover all creditors' claims and neither the preferred nor common stockholders will receive anything.

Protective provisions

Some preferred stock contracts contain protective provisions similar to those in bond indentures. These covenants may limit the issue of debt securities and/or additional preferred stock according to such tests as asset coverage of combined long-term debt and preferred stock or earnings coverage of interest and preferred dividends. Such tests usually are less restrictive than those contained in bond indentures or term loan agreements. In addition, payment of common stock dividends or repurchase of common stock may be limited to amounts that will not reduce retained earnings below a stated figure. Other protective provisions may include maintenance of minimum working capital and/or a minimum current ratio.

If protective provisions are breached, the corporation usually is prohibited from paying dividends on the common stock, and the contingent voting rights discussed below become effective. Note, however, that the enforcement provisions are not as strong as those relating to debt contracts. Preferred stockholders usually cannot declare a default and go to court to enforce their contract as under a bond indenture or a term loan agreement.

Voting rights

Control rights relating to preferred stocks usually are nonexistent or weak as compared to those of common stock as long as the preferred dividends are paid and protective provisions are not breached. Some preferred stocks have no voting rights at all. While others may have full share-for-share voting rights along with the common, the number of common shares outstanding usually is so much greater than preferred that the preferred stockholders cannot elect any directors. Some other preferred stocks have classified voting rights, under which the preferred stockholders voting as a class may elect a stated number of directors. Usually that number is only a small minority of the board. In such cases, the preferred stockholders may have a representative on the board but certainly do not have control of the firm. This absence or weakness of control rights is quite appropriate as long as the investment expectations of the preferred stockholders are satisfied by the regular payment of dividends and compliance with all protective provisions. They do not bear the risk; the common stockholders do.

But control rights are important to preferred stockholders *if* and *when* preferred dividends are not paid or protective provisions are breached. For that reason many preferred stocks provide *classified and contingent voting rights.* This arrangement provides that, after the omission of, say, four consecutive quarterly dividends or lapse of a stated period of time after notice of breach of a protective provision, the preferred stockholders as a class shall have the right to elect a stated number of directors. If that number of directors is only a minority, the preferred stockholders are not well protected. But if they may elect a *majority* of the board, this will enable the preferred stockholders to take control and attempt to protect their investment. This is consistent with the concept that the investors at risk should have control. Under such conditions, the common equity cushion has failed to absorb the risk and the preferred stockholders' investment is in jeopardy.

If contingent and classified voting rights are provided, the preferred stockholders' right to elect directors will cease after dividend arrearages have been paid and the firm is again on schedule in paying preferred dividends and/or after the breach of protective provisions has been corrected.

Retirement provisions

Preferred stock, unlike debt, has no maturity. But some provision usually is made for its retirement. This may be by optional call, operation of a sinking fund, or conversion into common stock.

Call provisions Nearly all preferred stocks are callable at the option of the issuer. The call provision is essentially the same as that contained in bond indentures. The initial call premium usually is about equal to one year's dividend requirement, say 12 percent, and gradually declines through time. Often there is a lock-in clause providing that the issue will be noncallable for a period of several years after issue.

The call feature provides financial flexibility to the issuing corporation by allowing it to refinance its outstanding preferred stock if this can be done at a significantly lower dividend rate. Preferred dividend rates fluctuate in direct relation to changes in market interest rates. Analysis of the feasibility of refinancing preferred stock is similar to that applied to bond refunding but more nebulous because the period of time the existing preferred stock would be outstanding is indefinite.[5]

If there were no call provision, the only way the firm could retire outstanding preferred stock would be to purchase it in the open market or to make a *tender offer* to redeem it. Such a tender offer would have to be either for cash or another security of value exceeding the existing market price. Otherwise, the preferred stockholders would refuse to tender their shares. (Tender offers will be discussed in greater detail later in this chapter.)

Sinking fund Some preferred stocks provide for the gradual redemption of shares through the operation of a sinking fund. The sinking fund operates essentially the same as under a bond issue. The firm is required to present periodically to the trustee either face amount of preferred stock that has been acquired in the open market or cash to be used by the trustee to call by lot a given number of preferred shares. In some cases the sinking-fund requirement, rather than being a fixed amount, is a stated percentage of earnings during the preceding period.

Convertibility Many preferred stocks are convertible into a stated number of common shares. For example, each share of convertible preferred might be convertible at the option of the holder into three shares of common stock. In some issues, the conversion ratio changes periodically through time. The convertible feature may be provided either as a "sweetener" to attract investors or with a view to eventually forcing conversion to eliminate

[5]This type of analysis, of course, is further complicated and more nebulous if it is contemplated that the preferred stock will be refinanced by issuing a differing type of security. Sometimes preferred stock will be refinanced by selling junior bonds.

the superior claim of the preferred and augment the common stock equity. Convertible preferreds are often used as the currency of exchange in connection with mergers and acquisitions. (Convertibility will be treated in detail in Chapter 21 and mergers and acquisitions in Chapter 23.)

Participating preferred stock

A *participating preferred stock* is a hybrid security that is entitled to its regular preferred dividend and also may participate under some conditions in additional distributions of income. For example, a $12 participating preferred stock might require regular dividend payments of $12 per share before any dividends could be paid on the common stock. Then the common stockholders might be entitled to say up to $12 per share in dividends. The preferred stockholders would then participate in any additional distribution of earnings in that period on a prespecified basis, say share for share. In this example, if the corporation were to pay $15 per share dividends to the common stockholders, then the preferred stock would be paid the required initial $12 and an additional $3 dividend. In another period in which only $8 dividends were paid on the common, the participating preferred stockholders would receive only their regular $12 dividend with no extra. Nearly all preferred stocks are nonparticipating; the use of the participation feature is quite rare.

Appropriate uses of preferred stock

Even though preferred stock has several advantages to the issuer, it is not extensively used in financing industrial firms. This requires explanation.

Advantages of preferred stock The advantages of preferred stock relate largely to its *flexibility.* It provides the benefits of leverage to the common stockholders without their incurring some of the risks resulting from the rigidity of debt. Although most issuers of preferred stock consider the dividend requirement as an obligation that will be met if possible, still if the firm should incur adversity the preferred dividend payments may be omitted. Such omission, although it may impair the firm's ability to obtain additional financing, will not jeopardize its continued existence. Further, since preferred stock does not have a maturity, the issuer does not run the risk related to payment of the principal. Many preferred stock issues do not require sinking-fund payments, and those that do often have less stringent requirements. Protective covenants also are less restrictive and their enforcement provisions less onerous in most cases.

Another factor favoring the use of preferred stock relates to the *tax status of dividends received by corporations* holding preferred stock. A corporation is subject to federal income tax on only 15 percent of dividends received from another corporation. If the corporate recipient is subject to a tax rate of 46 percent, then such dividends are taxed at only 6.9 percent (.15 × .46). As income tax regulations do not differentiate between preferred and common stock dividends, this provides a substantial tax advantage to corporate investors holding preferred stocks as compared to bonds on which the interest is taxed at the full 46 percent rate.

Because of this tax break, high-grade preferred stock issues often can be sold at dividend yields slightly lower than the interest yields on bonds of the same issuers. Thus, even though the investment quality of a preferred stock is clearly inferior to a bond of the same issuer in light of its junior claim, the *before-tax* cost to the issuer may be lower.

The overwhelming disadvantage For most firms, however, all these advantages are outweighed by the *tax status of preferred dividends paid by the issuer.* Such dividends are *not* a deductible expense, whereas interest on debt is deductible. Therefore, even though the before-tax cost may be slightly lower than that of long-term debt, the *aftertax cost* is almost double. This tax consideration makes the use of preferred stocks by most industrial corporations prohibitively costly.

Use by public utilities Most of the straight (nonconvertible) preferred stock issued in recent years has been sold by public utility firms. Regulatory bodies consider income taxes to be part of the cost of furnishing public utility services. Therefore the tax burden is included in the rates charged to their customers. This enables the public utility firm to pass the tax differential incurred by using preferred stock on to its rate-payers.

As public utility firms are highly capital-intensive, they require huge amounts of external financing. They usually use bonds to finance as much as possible of their capital requirements. This borrowing is limited by the market, restrictive covenants in their indentures, and their regulatory bodies. Inasmuch as preferred stock constitutes a part of the equity cushion sustaining debt capacity, they usually sell preferred stock when feasible to restore borrowing power. This, of course, is limited by the adequacy of the residual equity cushion provided by the common stock equity. The net result of these considerations is that public utility corporations tend to finance about 10 percent of their long-term capital requirements with preferred stock.

Industrial corporations rarely issue straight preferred stock. Many of those that formerly had preferred stock outstanding have refinanced those issues with junior debt such as subordinated debentures.

Use of convertible preferred stock in mergers Convertible preferred stock has been used extensively as the currency of exchange in connection with mergers. Here a convertible preferred stock of the acquiring firm may provide a priority on dividends sufficiently attractive to induce the common stockholders of the acquired corporation to exchange their shares. Their exchange of common stock for a convertible preferred is considered as a tax-free exchange by the IRS, whereas an exchange for a debt security is not. Further, it provides some period of time for the acquiring corporation to reflect increased earnings per share on the common stock resulting from the acquisition before those earnings per share are diluted by the conversion. (This use will be further developed in Chapters 21 and 23.)

Common stock

The common stockholders provide the residual equity of the firm. In most corporations, where only one type of stock is outstanding, the common stockholders have all the fundamental rights discussed earlier. If preferred stock is outstanding, then because the preferred has a priority and limitation on distribution of income and assets, only the common stock represents the true residual equity. In such cases, the rights of common stockholders are subject to the prior rights established by the preferred stock contract.

As the residual owners, the common stockholders bear the residual risk. They stand to lose their entire investment before the preferred stockholders or any creditors will suffer loss. Due to the limited liability of the corporation, common stockholders are protected against loss beyond their investment in the stock. But they also share directly or indirectly in all residual earnings of the corporation. Relating to this residual risk and participation in earnings, the common stockholders normally control the corporation through their voting rights.

Legal, accounting, and valuation concepts

Certain legal, accounting, and valuation terminology and concepts regarding common stock must be understood by both investors and issuers.

Authorized, issued, and outstanding shares The corporate charter (articles of incorporation) specifies the number of *authorized shares* of common stock. The corporation does not have to issue all of these shares; often, some of them are reserved for future use. For example, Juniper Corporation has 8 million shares authorized but has issued only 6 million of them, as shown in Table 20–1. The charter must be amended, requiring a stated majority vote of the stockholders, to increase the authorized shares. *Issued shares* are those that have been sold to the public. A corporation may have fewer *outstanding shares* than issued shares because it has repurchased some of its shares. Juniper Corporation has repurchased 28,420 of its shares and is holding them as *treasury stock*. Thus, it has 5,971,580 shares outstanding.

Table 20–1

Juniper Corporation
Common Stockholders' Equity Accounts
December 31, 1982
(000)

Common stock—$10 par—authorized 8 million shares; issued 6 million shares	$ 60,000
Additional paid-in capital	88,000
Retained earnings	112,000
Total common stockholders' equity	260,000
Less 28,420 shares treasury stock (at cost)	1,387
Net common stockholders' equity	$258,613

Treasury stock and/or unissued shares may be sold in the future or used in connection with exercise of stock options, conversion of other securities, mergers, stock splits, or stock dividends.

Accounting for common stock equity If the stock has a *par value,* the common stock account is carried at par times the number of issued shares. Juniper Corporation's common stock has a par value of $10 per share; therefore, the common stock account is $60 million ($10 × 6 million issued shares). Some stocks have only nominal par value, say 5 or 10 cents per share. Other stocks have no par value, in which case they may be booked either at a nominal stated value or the value at which they are sold.

Usually common stock is sold to the public at a price exceeding its par value. The amount received in excess of par (or stated) value is booked as *additional paid-in capital* (sometimes called capital surplus, paid-in surplus or premium on common stock). Juniper Corporation has sold its common stock through the years at various prices, the total premium over par value being $88 million.

The *retained earnings* account (formerly called earned surplus) reflects the accumulated past earnings of the corporation less the dividends that have been paid through the years of its life. In essence, this account reflects *reinvestment* of earnings that accrued to the common stockholders but were retained in the firm. Retained earnings of Juniper Corporation are $112 million. The total common stockholders' equity is $260 million. From this, the cost of 28,420 shares of treasury stock, $1,387,000, is deducted to arrive at the net equity of $258,613,000 represented by the 5,971,580 shares of common stock outstanding.

Valuation of common stock A share of common stock may be valued in several different ways, some meaningful and some not. *Par value,* or stated value, is almost meaningless. Its legal importance is that in many states, if stock has been sold by the corporation at less than par value, stockholders may be held liable by creditors for differences between the prices paid and the par value. Stock is very rarely sold below its par value.

The *book value* per share is determined by dividing the net common stockholders' equity by the number of shares outstanding. For example, the book value per share of Juniper Corporation's outstanding common stock is \$43.31 (\$258,613,000 ÷ 5,971,580 shares outstanding). Inasmuch as book value is based upon the balance sheet, which is subject to all of the aberrations of accounting processes that have been applied in the past, the figure may differ substantially from a meaningful current value.

There are exceptions. The book value of common stock of some financial institutions, such as commercial banks, may closely approximate current liquidation value. This results from the facts that nearly all of their assets are financial instruments representing the debt obligations of others and their assets are subject to evaluation by regulatory authorities. The book value of common stock of utility companies also may be meaningful, because their regulatory bodies base their rates (thus their earning power) upon an allowable rate of return on the book value of their assets (subject to some modification).

Liquidation value differs from book value in that it is based upon the current market values of the firm's assets less the amount of total liabilities, preferred stock, and liquidating expenses. It is, of course, meaningful if the firm is to be liquidated. Liquidation value also is meaningful if it is greater than the value of the firm as a going concern. It establishes the *floor value* of a firm's common stock in the sense that, if the firm is worth more dead than alive, the value of the corpse predominates. This is subject to the qualification that control of the firm could be obtained by the party valuing its stock.

Market value per share, of course, is the price at which a share of stock is currently trading in the market. Validity of market value relates to the depth and breadth of the market. It may be a valid measure of economic value of a small holding of a stock traded in large volume on a major exchange. On the other hand, it may not be a good indication of value of a large block of a stock traded infrequently in small lots in the over-the-counter market.

Going-concern value per share is the theoretical value of the common stock of a firm that is expected to continue in operation indefinitely. It is the present value of expected future dividends per share discounted at a rate reflecting the riskless rate of return plus a premium for risk. This going-concern value is based upon the theory that was employed in Chapter 15 under *Value of common stock equity* in explaining the cost of common stock equity.

It may be estimated by using the dividend-growth model

$$V = \frac{d_1}{K_e - g} \tag{20–1}$$

where

V = going-concern value per share of common stock
d_1 = dividend per share expected to be paid next year
K_e = the required rate of return on common stock (the riskless rate + premium for risk)
g = the expected compound growth rate of dividends

This is the common stock valuation model based upon dividends and growth discussed in Chapter 15 with V substituted for P, the price of a share of stock.

For most common stock valuation purposes, this is the most meaningful value. It is also the most difficult to estimate, because both g and the risk premium included in K_e are subjective.

Voting rights

Each share of common stock is entitled to vote on a ratable basis in the election of the board of directors. The way in which the votes are cast, however, depends upon the system of voting incorporated in the corporate charter. Under a *majority* voting system, holders of a simple majority of the shares may elect the entire board of directors. A *cumulative* voting system allows holders of a sufficiently large minority of shares to elect one or more directors roughly proportionate to the stock held. These voting systems are discussed and illustrated in the Appendix to this chapter.

Preemptive right

The *preemptive right* gives each common stockholder the opportunity to purchase on a proportionate basis any new issue of common stock or securities convertible into common stock. This right allows the stockholder to maintain his or her proportionate voting rights and participation in earnings and assets in liquidation. If the common stock did not have this right, majority stockholders controlling the corporation could cause it to issue additional shares to themselves at low prices, thereby diluting the voting power and the value of minority shareholdings.

For example, assume that the MNO Corporation has outstanding 1 million shares of common stock, 600,000 of which are owned by the Owens family, Thus, the family now owns 60 percent of the stock, and minority stockholders hold 40 percent. The current market value is $50 per share. If MNO were to issue 500,000 additional shares at $25 per share to the Owens family and none to the minority stockholders, the family would then own 1.1 million of the 1.5 million total shares outstanding. This would increase their holdings from 60 percent to 73.3 percent. The market value of each share of common stock would be diluted because new shares were added at a price only half that of the old shares in the market. The price immediately should fall to about $41⅝ per share, assuming the expectation that the added equity would be employed as efficiently as the old equity had been. The Owens family, of course, would gain from this because they paid only $25 each for their additional 500,000 shares. But the minority stockholders would, in effect, be cheated out of about $8⅜ per share.

The preemptive right prevents this from happening by requiring that, if 500,000 new shares are offered at $25 each (or any price), they must be offered to all stockholders on the basis of one new share for each two shares held. This enables all shareholders to maintain their proportionate positions relative to voting rights, future dividends, and assets in liquidation. The market price will fall to about $41⅝ per share, but all stockholders exercising their rights will have acquired sufficient additional shares at $25 to come out even. Any stockholders not wishing to exercise their rights could have sold them in the market to others who wish to buy the stock at a price that would compensate them for the drop in market price of shares held.

Most, but not all, common stock is entitled to the preemptive right. A few states require it, but others may allow this right to be omitted from the articles of incorporation. Also the stockholders may waive their preemptive rights. In short, this right, which originally was common law, has been somewhat watered down by some state corporation statutes. Application of the preemptive right to the issue of new common stock will be discussed in the next section of this chapter.

Management of common stock

Because common stock represents residual ownership and basically is permanent financing, there is relatively little that the managers of a corporation may do to manage it. In a sense, the common stockholders control the management of the firm rather than the firm's management relating to the stockholders as external furnishers of capital. Management's policies and decisions relating to common stock are limited to (1) selling more of it, (2) redeeming some of it, and (3) maintaining stockholder relations.

Selling additional stock

The decision to sell additional common stock usually is made reluctantly, because such an offering requires either that the present owners invest more funds in the firm or that stock be sold to outsiders, allowing these new holders to share in future control, earnings, and assets of the firm. In essence, if you and your fellow stockholders have a good thing going for you, you naturally are reluctant to allow others to join you and share your good fortune. But the realities of life are that in a growing firm, even though a large proportion or all of the earnings are retained, sale of additional common stock may be required from time to time to finance expansion and provide an adequate equity cushion to support increased debt.

Generally there are four ways by which additional common stock might be sold: (1) rights offerings, (2) nonrights offerings to the public, (3) employee stock purchase plans, and (4) the exercise of stock options.

Rights offerings Additional common stock usually is sold under a *rights offering* (also called a *privileged subscription*). New stock is offered to the old stockholders in proportion to their present shareholdings. This may be required under the preemptive right discussed above. However, even if the charter does not require the preemptive right, this method often will be used, because present stockholders constitute a receptive market for additional shares. They probably would not hold the stock if they did not consider it an appropriate investment or were not satisfied with the firm's managerial policies.

To illustrate a rights offering, let us assume that the Apex Corporation presently has outstanding 9 million shares of common stock with a market price of $40 per share. It wishes to raise $35 million by offering 1 million new shares at $35 each.

Mechanics and terminology After deciding to raise these funds through a rights offering of common stock and initiating registration with the SEC, management of Apex announces the offering and sets a *record date,* which is the date at which the stockholders listed on the firm's stock record will be mailed their rights. A *right* is a document authorizing its holder to subscribe to additional shares according to the terms of the offering. Apex announces the rights offering on January 24, 1983, with a record date of February 10. Until February 6 the stock will be traded *rights-on* (sometimes called *cum rights*). A person buying the stock when it trades rights-on will be entitled to the rights when issued. Trading in the rights on a when-issued basis will begin after the announcement.

Beginning February 6, Apex stock will be traded *ex-rights,* that is, the buyer of the stock will not receive the rights. The rights will be furnished to the former stockholder. The ex-rights date is four business days before the record date because the stock exchange requires this time to clear stock transactions. The market price of the stock automatically will fall by the value of a right when the stock goes ex-rights.

One right attaches to each share of the outstanding stock. Apex will issue 9 million rights. *Nine rights* and the *subscription price,* $35, must be presented to the designated corporate office on or before the *subscription date,* which usually is about a month after the record date, say March 10, to subscribe to each share of the new stock.

Determining the subscription price The crucial factor in determining the subscription price is that the market price of the common stock must be higher than the subscription price during the period immediately preceding the subscription date. Otherwise the rights will be valueless and will not be exercised. Because a considerable time elapses between the announcement date and the subscription date (45 days in our example), allowance must be made for possible market price fluctuation during that period.

The financial manager should analyze past downward fluctuations in market price, appraise current and estimated future price volatility, and then allow a prudent safety factor in setting the subscription price. Dilution resulting from the new issue must be recognized in this analysis. In our example, dilution will be 50 cents per share (which will be explained below). Therefore, after considering dilution, Apex has provided for \$4.50 possible decline in market price due to other factors. This is 11.4 percent [(\$39.50 − \$35)/\$39.50]. If Apex stock were more volatile, the rights offering period were longer, or a greater safety margin were desired, then the subscription price would be set lower, at say, \$30 per share.

Value of a right The theoretical value of a right when the stock is selling *rights-on* may be determined by the following formula:

$$R = \frac{M_0 - S}{N + 1} \tag{20–2}$$

where

R = theoretical value of a right
M_0 = market value of the stock, rights-on
S = the subscription price of a new share
N = number of rights required to buy one new share

Applying this formula to the Apex rights offering

$$R = \frac{\$40 - \$35}{9 + 1}$$
$$= \frac{\$5}{10} = \$.50$$

The market price of the stock will drop by the value of a right when the stock goes ex-rights, since the right no longer attaches to the stock but rather becomes a separate financial instrument. The following formula may be used to determine the theoretical value of a right when the stock is selling *ex-rights:*

$$R = \frac{M_e - S}{N} \tag{20–3}$$

where M_e = market value of the stock, ex-rights.

Assuming that Apex stock closes at $40 the day before it goes ex-rights (February 5) and no extraneous factors affect the market overnight, it will open ex-rights at $39.50 the next day (February 6). Applying the formula

$$R = \frac{\$39.50 - \$35.00}{9}$$

$$= \frac{\$4.50}{9}$$

$$= \$.50$$

Note that the theoretical value of a right is identical when calculated on either a rights-on or ex-rights basis.

During the period between announcement of the rights offering and the subscription date, the market prices, of course, may fluctuate almost continually. At any given time, the relationship between the price of the stock and the right should tend to reflect the theoretical value. Otherwise *arbitrage,* the simultaneous sale of one instrument and purchase of the other, should take place, bringing them into their theoretical relationship. However, this may not always be true in practice. Speculators may obtain a much greater "play" from the commitment of a given amount of funds by trading in the rights rather than in the stock. Therefore, if speculators are optimistic, expecting the stock price to rise in the short term, they may bid the rights up well above their theoretical value. Conversely, if they expect the price of the stock to fall, they may sell the rights short in sufficient quantities to force their price below theoretical value.

Effect on stockholder's position The stockholder neither gains nor loses economic value as the result of a rights offering. If the stockholder exercises his or her rights, the apparent bargain subscription price is exactly offset by the dilution of value of the old shares held. For example, the holder of 90 shares of Apex stock suffers dilution of 50 cents per share (the value of a right) when the stock goes ex-rights. That is a $45 drop in market value of the holding. He or she uses the 90 rights received to purchase 10 shares of new stock at a discount of $4.50 under the diluted market price of $39.50 after the stock goes ex-rights. The discount amounts to $45, exactly offsetting the $45 dilution suffered on the old shares. There has been no gain or loss.

If the stockholder chooses to sell the 90 rights at 50 cents each, the $45 received exactly offsets the $45 resulting from dilution of the 90 shares of common stock held. Again, there is no gain or loss. In effect, this stockholder has liquidated $45 worth of his or her investment in the common stock of Apex Corporation. After the rights offering, this stockholder owns a slightly smaller proportion of the common stock equity of the corporation.

Underwriting of rights offerings As discussed in Chapter 16, rights offerings may or may not be underwritten by investment bankers under a *standby underwriting*. The underwriters, for a fee, guarantee the success of a rights offering by agreeing to purchase any unsubscribed shares at the termination of the offering. The risk the underwriters assume depends upon the probability that the market price of the stock will fall below the subscription price in the period immediately preceding the subscription date or that they will have to prevent this by purchasing stock in the secondary market to support the price.

The advisability of having a rights offering underwritten relates to two factors: (1) the spread between the subscription price and the diluted market price and (2) the length of time during which the offer will be outstanding. The narrower the spread and longer the period, the greater the importance of underwriting the issue, but also the higher will be the underwriters' fees. If the subscription price is very low compared to market price, underwriting will be unnecessary.

Oversubscription privilege Many rights offerings include an *oversubscription privilege,* which allows the shareholder, in addition to exercising his or her normal rights, to elect to be allocated any shares that are left over after the termination of the offering on a pro rata basis. Usually a small proportion of the shares offered, perhaps 1 or 2 percent, will not be subscribed even though the rights are valuable. The stockholder who picks up a few shares by oversubscription receives a true bargain because he or she has suffered no dilution of market value of old shares held related to the additional shares obtained at the lower subscription price.

Nonrights offerings Where the charter permits, common stock sometimes is offered to the public through a nonrights offering. Even though the charter may include the preemptive right, this right may be waived by the stockholders. Nonrights offerings usually are used when closely held corporations "go public." As the reason for going public is to obtain equity capital from outsiders and to broaden the base of common stock ownership, the present stockholders relinquish preemptive rights if they exist.

A nonrights offering usually will be made through investment bankers, often under a best-efforts agreement rather than a full underwriting. Particularly in the case of a firm going public, the risk may be too great for the investment bankers to agree to underwrite the issue.[6]

When a nonrights offering is made, the price is set as high as it is believed the market will bear (with a little safety cushion). Naturally the present stockholders do not wish to part with more shares than necessary to obtain a given amount of money.

Specialized types of nonrights offerings are made in connection with employee stock purchase plans and the exercise of stock options.

Employee stock-purchase plans Some firms have stock-purchase plans under which employees may subscribe to common stock on a preferential

[6]A best-efforts offering may also be used if the perceived risk is so small that the issuing firm chooses to bear it.

basis. Typically, each employee may purchase stock at annual intervals in amounts up to say 10 percent of his or her salary at a bargain price of 10 or 15 percent under the market price at the time. Such a plan usually is not primarily a financing device, rather it is used to enhance employee loyalty and motivate the employee-stockholders toward the goal of maximizing the value of the stock. Considerations regarding the effectiveness of such plans as personnel motivating devices are beyond the scope of this text. They will be left to the employee relations people.

Exercise of stock options Many firms provide stock options to their key officers and employees as part of their compensation. Such options allow their holders to purchase a given number of shares at a fixed price based upon the market price at the time the options are issued. Exercise usually is limited to a stated period, say within 5 or 10 years. There are two motivations for granting stock options. The first is to provide an incentive to key personnel to act in a fashion that will tend to maximize the stock's value. Second, as partial compensation of the officer or employee, stock options may have a tax advantage. If the stock options are issued under a plan that complies with regulations of the IRS, profit made through the exercise of stock options may be considered as a capital gain at the time of sale of the stock (provided the sale occurs at least one year after exercise of the options). Only 40 percent of long-term capital gains are subject to taxation, as compared with 100 percent of earned income received in cash.

Redemption of common stock

Once issued, common stock cannot be redeemed through optional call or other prearranged device. Usually the only way a corporation may reduce its outstanding stock is by purchase in the open market or by making a tender offer to repurchase it. Repurchased common stock usually is held as treasury stock.

Open-market purchases The corporation may, from time to time, purchase its stock in the open market. It must, of course, pay the going market price. In some cases, such purchases must be disclosed to the SEC. As a practical matter, purchases are limited to relatively small amounts because attempts to repurchase large amounts of common stock would force its market price to increase unreasonably.

Tender offers Some corporations holding excess cash and marketable securities may seek to redeem large amounts of their outstanding stock through tender offers. A *tender offer* is an offer to stockholders to purchase up to a given number of shares at a certain price. The price offered must be sufficiently above the market price at the time to attract stockholders to tender their shares. If the number of shares tendered exceeds the number to be repurchased, the tendered shares must be purchased on a pro rata basis. For example, Selma Corporation might make a tender offer for 1 million shares of its common stock. If 1.25 million shares were tendered, then Selma could redeem 800 shares from a stockholder who tendered 1,000 shares (1,000,000/1,250,000 = .80). If only 900,000 shares were tendered, all offers would be accepted. Occasionally some flexibility is provided by the tender offer's indicating that the company will repurchase up to, say, 1 million tendered shares, but has the option to accept up to an additional 300,000 shares.

The motivation for such a tender offer usually is to increase the earnings per share by reducing the number of shares outstanding. It is hoped that this will increase the future market price of the stock. If the corporation is employing its working assets at a higher rate of return than the rate received on the marketable securities liquidated to repurchase its shares, earnings per share will increase. Whether this will be reflected by increase in the market price of the stock depends upon whether the increased EPS is offset by perceived increase in the risk borne by the remaining stock resulting from the decreased equity and liquidity. If the cash and marketable securities were truly redundant, the tender premium not too high, and the firm overcapitalized, then the value of the remaining stock might be increased.

Stockholder relations

Although sometimes considered in the realm of public relations rather than financial management, stockholder relations are a very important responsibility of the financial manager and his or her staff. The relative prosperity of the corporation, as translated into earnings per share, dividend payments, and stock prices, of course, is the most important element in stockholder relations. Maximizing the value of the stock in the long run is the overall responsibility of all management personnel.

But there are many other management responsibilities in maintaining stockholder relations. One is establishing a dividend policy that satisfies the needs of the stockholders. The most direct communications with the stockholders are the dividend checks mailed to them each quarter. Other communications are annual and quarterly reports to the stockholders. We refer not to the format, typography, and illustration of such reports created by the public relations staff, but rather to the information content and the signals sent to the stockholders regarding the firm's operations, financial condition, and strategic policies.

Relations with the financial press also are important. Press releases that create misunderstandings or unwarranted expectations may greatly damage stockholder relations. Of perhaps greater importance is the relationship maintained with securities analysts and other members of the financial community who influence stockholders and potential stockholders through their advice and recommendations. For example, financial managers of major publicly held corporations usually meet at least once a year with the New York Society of Securities Analysts (NYSSA) and similar local or regional groups. Such meetings, held privately, may have a profound effect upon market activity and price of the stock. We are not referring to touting the stock—that will backfire—but rather to providing frank, correct, and useful information to the analysts. Any faulty or misleading statements or forecasts can incur ill will of the analysts, whereas sound information will be valuable to them. This will be reflected in their appraisals and recommendations regarding the firm's stock.

Finally, the personal relationships with large and important stockholders are of utmost importance. Their personal reactions can have profound effects upon the firm (and the financial officer)!

Summary

This chapter discussed the relationship between the corporation and its owners, the stockholders. The stockholders' position is residual; their claims are junior to those of all creditors. The fundamental rights of stockholders are established by the corporate charter. These rights are to share on a ratable basis in (1) distribution of earnings, (2) distribution of assets in liquidation, and (3) control of the firm through voting for the board of directors and on other matters that materially affect the nature of the corporation. Because the stockholders' equity is increased by residual earnings and decreased by losses, they bear the residual risk. To manage that risk, they control the firm as long as obligations to creditors are properly serviced.

Most firms have only one class or type of stock. If two or more types of stock are outstanding, these rights are unequally divided among the stockholders. Classified stock usually provides that the voting rights of one class differ from those of the other. In some cases, rights to dividends may differ.

The most prevalent differentiation of rights is between preferred and common stockholders. Preferred stock has a priority and limitation upon dividends and assets in liquidation. It may have protective provisions. Dividends usually are cumulative. Voting rights of preferred stock usually are weak as long as the security is properly serviced. However, if dividend arrearages accumulate and/or protective provisions are breached, often the preferred stock has contingent and classified voting rights to elect a given number of directors. Preferred stock usually is callable and sometimes may be retired through a sinking fund or conversion into common stock.

Although preferred stock financing has important advantages compared to debt, the disadvantage of nondeductibility of preferred dividends for tax purposes has limited its use by industrial firms. Convertible preferred stock, however, is widely used as the currency of exchange in mergers.

Common stockholders' claims upon earnings and assets are junior to those of creditors and preferred stockholders, if any. Common stock may be valued in different ways: par value, book value, liquidation value, market value, and going-concern (or theoretical) value, listed in their general order of validity as measures of true economic value. Common stockholders elect directors under either majority or cumulative voting systems, depending on the corporate charter. Cumulative voting allows holders of a sufficient minority of shares to elect one or more directors; under the majority system holders of a simple majority of the stock elect all directors. Common stockholders usually have the preemptive rights to subscribe on a proportionate basis to additional issues.

Additional shares generally are sold through a rights offering. Each present stockholder is issued one right for each share held. A given number of rights is required to subscribe to a new share at the subscription price, which must be less than the market price if the offering is to be successful. The offering may or may not be underwritten under a standby agreement. Additional stock sometimes is sold to the public under a nonrights offering. Other means of selling additional shares are through employee stock-purchase plans and the exercise of stock options.

Redemption of common stock is limited to open-market purchase or a tender offer to repurchase a specified number of shares at a given price. Redemption of common stock reduces the firm's liquidity and its equity.

Financial management is also responsible for stockholder relations. In addition to such broad aspects as the benefits provided to stockholders in terms of earnings, dividends, and stock prices, this area includes providing informative annual reports and maintaining liaison with the financial press, securities analysts, and the larger stockholders.

Questions

1. What are the fundamental differences between debt and equity capital? Why does a firm incur less risk by employing equity capital than by using debt financing?

2. Most stockholders vote their shares by proxy. What is a *proxy?* A *proxy statement?* A *proxy fight?*

3. As a general principle, investors who bear the risk should control the firm. Explain why, in a financially healthy firm, the common stockholders collectively control the firm through their voting rights. How does control

change if the firm is not in a position to service its debt obligations? Explain the logic underlying this shift in control.

4. What is *classified stock*? How might class A and class B stock differ? Why would a firm use classified stock?

5. What is *preferred stock?* How does a creditor view preferred stock? How does a common stockholder's view differ?

6. Why do investors usually require that a preferred stock be *cumulative?* Why do they also prefer that a preferred stock have *classified* and *contingent* voting rights?

7. Why does the issuer of preferred stock prefer that it be *callable?*

8. In recent years, public utility firms have been the dominant issuers of straight preferred stock. Explain why. What change in income tax laws might greatly increase the use of preferred stock by industrial firms?

9. What is *participating* preferred stock? Can you think of circumstances under which participating preferred stock might be issued?

10. Explain how the common stockholders benefit from the residual earnings of the firm whether or not the earnings are paid out in dividends. If losses are incurred, how is the common stock equity affected?

11. Why is *going-concern value* usually the most meaningful value of a firm's common stock? Under what circumstances might liquidation value predominate?

12. What is a *rights offering* of common stock? How does it relate to the *preemptive right*? How does an issuer determine the subscription price in a rights offering?

13. When is a stock traded *rights-on?* When does trading become *ex-rights?* If there are no extraneous market influences, why does the market price drop when the stock goes ex-rights?

14. What is a *tender offer?* How may it be used by a corporation to redeem a portion of its outstanding stock? Why would a firm want to redeem some of its common stock?

Problems

1. Ameron Electric Utility Company is issuing 1 million shares of 11 percent $100 par preferred stock to the public at $107 per share. Flotation costs are $3 per share.

   a. What will be the total annual dividends on this preferred stock issue?

b. What will be the net proceeds to Ameron from this issue?

c. What is the aftertax cost of this preferred stock capital? (Assume that the issue will not be called or redeemed through a sinking fund.)

2. The Last Ditch Mining Company has 100,000 shares of 12 percent $100 cumulative preferred stock outstanding. Quarterly dividends have not been paid for the past five years. During the past year, Last Ditch developed a rich deposit of nickel ore, and its operations became highly profitable. Management wishes to resume dividend payments on both its preferred and common stock. If dividends on the common stock are to be paid on March 31 this year, how much will have to be paid to the preferred stockholders? If the preferred stock was noncumulative, how much would have to be paid?

3. Coron Corporation has two classes of common stock outstanding. The 2 million shares of class A stock held by the public are entitled to one vote per share. Each of the 100,000 shares of the class B stock held by the Coron family is entitled to 10 votes. Under the majority voting system incorporated in Coron's charter, how many shares of the class A stock must be voted with the class B stock from the Coron family to elect all nine directors of Coron Corporation?

4. The Denim Corporation is being liquidated. Creditors' claims (combined long- and short-term) total $4 million. Denim's 25,000 shares of $100 preferred stock are entitled to par value in liquidation. How many dollars per share will the preferred stockholders receive if the net proceeds from liquidation of Denim's assets are $5 million? What is they are only $3.8 million? What if they are $7 million?

5. You are an investment officer of a corporation subject to a 40 percent tax rate on incremental ordinary income. You would be willing to purchase the preferred stock of the Maxon Corporation at a 2 percent greater *aftertax* yield than Maxon's bonds, on which the before-tax yield is 12 percent. What before-tax yield would be acceptable to you on the Maxon preferred stock?

6. Maxon Corporation could sell preferred stock at a net dividend cost of 10 percent or bonds at a before-tax cost of 12 percent. What would be its aftertax cost of each of these two types of capital if Maxon is subject to a 40 percent income tax rate? Which has the lower cost?

7. Fairview Corporation has 1.4 million shares of *authorized* common stock and 1 million shares *outstanding*. It holds 48,000 shares of *treasury stock*. If its common stock could be sold to net $28 per share, how much money could be raised by selling all of the stock Fairview could legally offer without amending its articles of incorporation?

8. Gourand Corporation expects to pay dividends next year of $1.80 per share on its common stock. Dividends are expected to increase in the future at a compound rate of 8 percent. The estimated required rate of return on

Gourand common stock is 15 percent (encompassing the riskless rate of 9 percent and a 6 percent premium for risk). What is the going-concern value per share of Gourand common stock?

9. Carlos Corporation which has 1 million shares of common stock outstanding, is issuing 100,000 additional shares of its common stock under a rights offering. Each holder of record of 10 shares on May 20 may subscribe to 1 new at $24 per share on or before June 20.

a. The market price of Carlos common stock on May 5, when this offering is announced, is $29 per share. Why is the subscription price so low? What factors would have been considered by Carlos' management in setting the subscription price?

b. On May 16, the price of Carlos stock is expected to drop. Why? If the stock closes at $27 per share on May 15, what is the theoretical value of a right on that date? At what price will Carlos stock open on May 16 if no extraneous factors affect the market overnight?

c. Mary Smith owns 500 shares of Carlos stock. If she exercises her rights, how many shares will she buy and how much will they cost her? If she sells her rights on June 10, when the price of Carlos stock is $26½ per share, about how much will she receive for them (before considering brokerage fees)? Should Ms. Smith consider this to be a windfall gain?

Appendix 20–A—Majority and Cumulative Voting Systems

The way in which votes may be cast by stockholders in the election of the board of directors depends upon the system incorporated in the corporate charter.

Majority voting Under a *majority voting system* (sometimes called noncumulative or statutory voting), each stockholder may cast one vote for each share held in the election of *each* director. Thus if nine directors are to be elected, the holder(s), directly or by proxy, of the votes a simple majority of the shares voted may elect all nine directors. No directors may be elected by the holder(s) of a minority of the shares.

Cumulative voting A few states require and most states permit the corporate charter to allow *cumulative voting*. This system provides that each shareholder is entitled to votes equal to the number of shares held times the number of directors to be elected. Thus, if nine directors are to be elected, the holder of 100 shares is entitled to 900 votes. Those 900 votes may be distributed among any of the candidates in any way that stockholder chooses. For example, all 900 votes could be cast for a single candidate, or they could be distributed 300 each to three candidates.

A cumulative voting system allows the holder(s) of a sufficiently large minority of the shares to elect one or more directors. A formula may be used to determine how many shares of stock must be voted to elect any given number of directors under cumulative voting. Let

N_r = the number of shares required to elect a desired number of directors

N_v = the total number of shares voted

D_e = the number of directors desired

D_t = the total number of directors to be elected

Then calculate N_r from the following formula:

$$N_r = \frac{N_v \times D_e}{D_t + 1} + 1 \qquad (20A\text{–}1)$$

For example, assume that XYZ Corporation will elect nine directors at its annual stockholders' meeting. Ninety thousand shares are expected to be voted. A group of stockholders opposed to management hope to elect three directors by concentrating their votes on three candidates. How many shares will they have to control to elect these three directors? Solve for N_r as follows:

$$\begin{aligned} N_r &= \frac{90{,}000 \times 3}{9 + 1} + 1 \\ &= \frac{270{,}000}{10} + 1 \\ &= 27{,}001 \text{ shares} \end{aligned}$$

This assumes that management controls all of the remaining 62,999 shares and would spread their votes in an optimal fashion. If there were additional candidates and other minorities seeking to elect directors, this group possibly could elect three directors by voting fewer shares than indicated. There is a certain amount of gamesmanship involved in proxy fights.

Note that less than one third of the shares voted (slightly over 30 percent) were required to elect one-third (33.3 percent) of the directors. Although cumulative voting results in roughly proportional representation of opposing stockholder groups, it is not exactly proportional. Also note that 9,001 shares are required to obtain one seat on the XYZ board. Any minority position smaller than that is ineffective.[1]

[1]If this formula is used to determine the number of directors that can be elected by voting a given number of shares, any *fractional* number of directors must be dropped. Clearly, one cannot elect a part of a person.

The relative merits of cumulative voting versus majority voting are debatable. The cumulative system appeals to our democratic instincts and implies greater equity in the representation of the stockholders on the board. In some cases, minority representation may be beneficial by providing consideration of divergent views. There is, however, another side to this coin. In some cases, minority representation has resulted in constant bickering among the directors, impairing managerial efficiency.

On net balance, the superior voting system appears to relate to the nature of the firm's operations. If operations are relatively routine and strategic policies may be deliberated at length without endangering the firm's viability, cumulative voting appears advantageous. These conditions seem to apply to most public utilities and some relatively stable industrial firms. On the other hand, many firms operate in dynamic, highly competitive markets in which technological and market changes occur frequently and rapidly. In such firms, timing of strategic policies and actions, such as development of new products and/or efforts to capitalize on emerging marketing opportunities, is of the essence. In such a firm, divergent factions on the board may engage in bickering about strategic actions while their majority-controlled competitors are acting to seize opportunities. At the extreme, minority representation may result in loss of operational viability of the firm.

Question

1. Stockholders of Devlin Corporation elect its nine directors annually. If you owned a controlling interest of 53 percent of the voting stock of Devlin Corporation, which voting system would you prefer, cumulative or majority voting? Why? Which voting system would you prefer if you held 28 percent of Devlin's stock and were skeptical regarding the integrity and/or wisdom of Devlin's management? Why?

Problem

1. If the Marlow Corporation, with 800,000 shares of common stock outstanding, elects its seven directors annually, how many shares must you vote to elect one director under cumulative voting if all of the stock were voted? If only 80 percent of the stock held by others were voted, how many directors could you elect by voting 180,000 shares? How many directors could you elect if all of the shares were voted?

Chapter 21
Convertible Securities and Warrants

In Chapters 18 and 20, we mentioned convertibility as a means by which bonds and preferred stock issues might be retired. But that was just "the tip of the iceberg." We must understand the nature of convertible bonds (debentures) and preferred stocks, the managerial considerations related to their issue, and their appropriate uses. In addition, the use of warrants, another possible component of a securities package giving the holder the right to acquire common stock, should be considered. This chapter will deal with the nature and valuation of convertible securities and warrants, managerial considerations related to these securities, and their appropriate use in a firm's capital structure.

Convertible securities

A convertible security is a bond (debenture) or preferred stock that may be exchanged for a specified number of shares of common stock at the option of its holder. Such a hybrid security appeals to two divergent motivations of investors. As a fixed- or limited-return security, it provides the stability of income associated with its senior claim. But it also holds forth the opportunity of capital gain if the market price of the common stock should rise. For clarity, our discussion will focus on convertible bonds unless otherwise indicated. However, it generally can be applied to convertible preferred stocks as well.

The privilege to convert into common stock may be stated in terms of either the conversion ratio or the conversion price. The *conversion ratio* is the number of shares into which one bond (or one share of preferred stock) may be converted at the holder's option. For example, in 1980 Folsom Corporation issued $20 million of 8 percent convertible debentures in $1,000 denominations due in 1995. Each debenture is convertible into 25 shares of common stock. Thus the conversion ratio is 25.

The *conversion price* is the effective price paid per common share if the stock is obtained through conversion. It may be stated in the contract or determined by dividing the face or par value of the convertible security by the conversion ratio. The conversion price of the Folsom convertible debentures is $40 per share ($1,000/25). The conversion price usually is in the range of 10 to 20 percent above the market price of the common stock at the time the convertible securities are issued. Folsom stock was selling in the market for $35 per share at the time of issue, thus the conversion price was set at 14.3 percent above market [($40 − $35)/$35]. Since the holder of one Folsom convertible debenture may exchange it at any time for 25 shares of Folsom common stock, in effect the investor paid $40 per share for that stock if the convertible debenture was purchased at par.

In some cases, the conversion ratio (and the conversion price) may change during the period the convertible security is outstanding. For example, a conversion ratio might initially be 25 and drop to 22.5 after 5 years and to 20 after 10 years. In this case, the respective conversion prices would be $40, $44.44, and $50.

The conversion privilege usually is effective throughout the life of the security. However, convertibility may be delayed until perhaps the end of the third year. In other cases, the conversion period may be limited—to say, 10 years, where the period to maturity of the bond may be 20 years. As preferred stocks have no maturity, their conversion privileges often are limited. The conversion ratio and price are protected by an antidilution provision. Equitable adjustments will be made if the firm issues additional stock at less than the market price, issues stock dividends, or has stock splits.

Convertible securities generally are callable at the option of the issuer at a call premium approximately equal to the annual interest requirement. The Folsom convertible debentures are callable at 108 ($1,080 per bond). In some cases the security may become callable only after a delay—say, three years after issue.

Value of convertible securities

A convertible bond is a hybrid security consisting of two elements, the *bond* itself and the *option to convert* that instrument into common stock. Therefore it has two fundamental values, (1) that of the bond and (2) that of the common stock into which it is convertible. Since the convertible bond is traded in the market as a "package" containing these two elements, its market value reflects both features.

Straight bond value

The *straight bond value* (sometimes called "investment value") is what the bond would sell for in the market in the absence of the conversion feature. The value of a straight bond is based upon the future interest payments and the principal payment at maturity, both discounted at a rate reflecting the pure interest rate plus the premium for risk. Therefore, the straight bond value of the convertible security may be determined by discounting these payments at the going yield to maturity of a straight bond of the same quality and maturity. In our example, Folsom Corporation would have paid 10 percent interest on straight debentures identical in maturity and protective provisions to the convertible debentures carrying an 8 percent interest rate. This differential is typical. Convertible bonds usually are marketable at interest rates 1 to 3 percentage points lower than similar straight bonds of the same issuer because of the value placed by investors upon the conversion privilege.

Computation of the straight bond value of the Folsom convertible debenture at the time of issue is shown in Table 21–1. The $608.48 present value of the interest payments of $80 ($1,000 × .08) for years 1 through 15 is found by multiplying the annual payment by the present value interest factor of an annuity (*PVIFA*) for 15 years at 10 percent (obtained from Table B

Table 21–1 Straight bond value of convertible debenture—Folsom Corporation

Years	(1) Payment	(2) Present value factor @ 10%	(3) Present value (1) × (2)
1–15	$ 80	7.606	$608.48
15	1,000	.239	239.00
Straight bond value			$847.48

in the appendix of this book).[1] The $239.00 present value of the $1,000 principal payment at maturity is determined by multiplying it by the *PVIF* of a sum to be received at the end of the 15th year at 10 percent (obtained from Table A in the appendix). Thus, the total present value of the bond payments discounted at 10 percent is $847.48. This is the straight bond value.[2] It establishes the *floor value* of the convertible bond even if the value of the conversion privilege were zero.[3]

The straight bond value remains stable only if going interest rates in the market and the credit worthiness of the issuing firm do not change. If, for example, interest rates and/or Folsom's credit standing should so change that its straight borrowing rate were 12 percent, then the straight bond value would fall to $727.88. If its borrowing rate should decline to 8 percent, the straight bond value would be $1,000.

Conversion value The *conversion value* (sometimes called the "stock value") is the market value of the common stock into which the security is convertible. This value is calculated by multiplying the market price of the common stock by the conversion ratio. At the time of issue, the conversion

[1]Here we have assumed that the interest payments are to be made at the end of each year. Actually, bond interest payments usually are made semiannually. The more complex method of determining the present value of semiannual payments was discussed in Chapter 11. We have made the annual payment assumption here to avoid complicating analysis of the subject at hand.

[2]This value may also be obtained from a bond table or by using some hand-held calculators. It is the value of an 8 percent coupon bond yielding 10 percent to maturity in 15 years and selling at 100 (par).

[3]Calculation of the straight preferred stock value of a convertible preferred differs because preferred stock does not have a maturity date. It may be calculated as the present value of a perpetuity (developed in Chapter 11). The straight preferred stock value is found by the formula

$$V = \frac{\text{Dividend rate on convertible preferred}}{\text{Dividend yield on straight preferred}}\left(\begin{array}{c}\text{Par value of the}\\ \text{convertible preferred}\end{array}\right)$$

For example, if a $100 par convertible preferred has a dividend rate of 9 percent and a straight preferred stock of the same quality would yield 11.5 percent, then the straight preferred stock value would be $78.26 [(.09/.115)$100)].

value of the Folsom convertible debenture was $875 ($35 market price of the common times the conversion ratio of 25). If the stock is now selling at $50 per share, the conversion value is $1,250. On the other hand, if the stock were to fall to $20 per share, the conversion value would be only $500. Various conversion values of the Folsom convertible debenture at different market prices of the firm's common stock are shown in Table 21–2. Note that the conversion value is equal to $1,000, the face or par value of the convertible debenture, when the common stock is priced at $40, the conversion price of the issue.

Table 21–2 Conversion value of convertible debenture—Folsom Corporation
(Conversion ratio = 25)

Market price of common stock	Conversion value of convertible debenture
$80	$2,000
70	1,750
60	1,500
50	1,250
40	1,000
30	750
20	500

Theoretical value The *theoretical* (or minimum) *value* of a convertible bond is the *higher* of its straight bond value or its conversion value. This theoretical value is indicated by the heavy black line in Figure 21–1. When the conversion value exceeds the straight bond value, it predominates because the convertible bond is exchangeable for common stock at the option of its holder. However, when the conversion value is less than the straight bond value, the latter predominates because the convertible debenture still has the rights and value of a straight bond. In Figure 21–1, if the conversion value were to fall below $847.48 (the straight bond value), the convertible bond would have a minimum value of $847.48 regardless of its conversion value.

Market value The *market value* of a convertible security usually will exceed its theoretical value, as shown in Table 21–3. This excess reflects the value to the investor of the fact that the two opportunities, (1) to receive the fixed interest and principal payments under the bond and (2) to gain from an increase in the market value of the common stock, are packaged into a single security, the convertible bond.

The premium This excess is the *premium* (sometimes called the "market premium"). The premium of market price over theoretical value is shown

Figure 21–1 Values of convertible debenture—Folsom Corporation

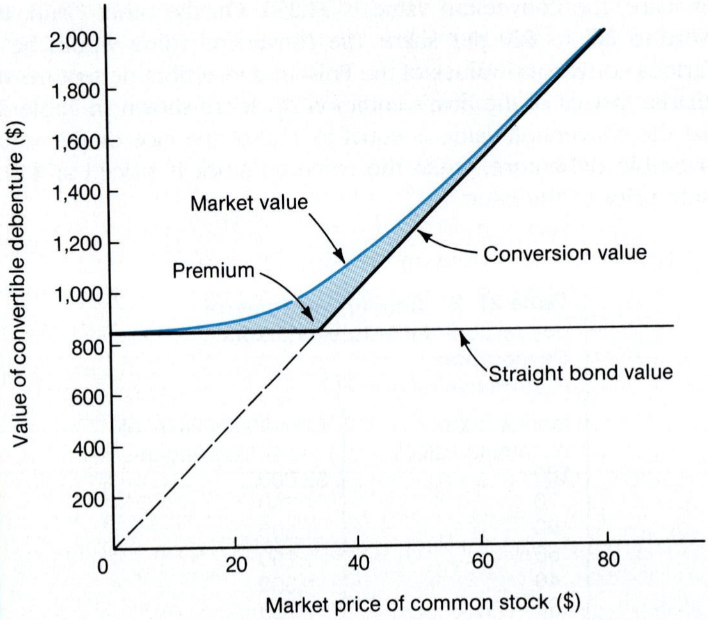

in dollars in Table 21–3. It is illustrated graphically in Figure 21–1 by the vertical distance between the theoretical value (shown by the heavy black line) and the market value. Note that the premium is greatest near the point where the straight bond value line intersects the conversion value line in Figure 21–1. At this point, where the market price of the common stock is

Table 21–3 Convertible debenture—Folsom Corporation
Market value versus theoretical values

(1)	(2)	(3)	(4)	(5)
Market value		Theoretical value		
Stock	Convertible debenture	Straight bond value	Conversion value	Premium
$80	$2,000	*	$2,000	$ 0
70	1,760	*	1,750	10
60	1,540	*	1,500	40
50	1,325	*	1,250	75
40	1,115	*	1,000	115
30	980	$848	*	132
20	900	848	*	52
10	870	848	*	22
5	848	848	*	0

*Not shown because lower than other value. The higher of the two values is the theoretical value.

about $34, the holder of the convertible debenture in a sense has the best of two worlds. If the stock price rises beyond $34, the conversion value will increase in direct proportion. If the price of the stock falls, the straight bond value functions as a floor to prevent the convertible debenture from falling below $848. To benefit from this limited downside risk and participate in the potential gain, investors are willing to pay a premium of about $145 per bond.

Another inducement for investors to pay a premium over the conversion value is that while holding a position in the common stock, the convertible bondholder will receive interest on the bond. This interest yield often is greater than the dividend yield on the common stock.

There also are institutional reasons for the premium. Brokers usually require lower margins on convertible securities than on common stock. Therefore, the investor can hold a given position in the common stock indirectly through the convertibles using less of his or her own money than by holding the stock directly. This provides greater personal leverage. Another reason is that some financial institutions, including life insurance companies and some pension funds, are limited in their investment in common stock by regulations or their investment policies. These constraints may be circumvented by holding convertible securities, which provide a position in the common stock.

If the market price of the common stock should fall below the intersection point ($34 in our example), the premium would diminish. This premium reduction reflects the declining potential for gains through conversion to common stock. For example, if the market price of Folsom common stock were $17 per share, it would have to double before the conversion value would equal the straight bond value. At this level investors are willing to pay only about $40 premium over the straight bond value of $848. At the extreme, if the market price of the stock should fall to $5 per share, the opportunity for gain through conversion would be so remote that it would be virtually valueless. The convertible debenture would trade as a straight bond, the premium having disappeared.

The premium also gradually will diminish as the market price of the common stock increases beyond $34. Downside protection of the straight bond floor becomes more remote. The advantage of receiving an interest yield on the convertible debenture greater than the dividend yield on the common stock may be reduced or eliminated. Increased common stock dividends usually accompany increased market prices.

Another factor that will tend to decrease the premium is that after a substantial increase in the price of the common stock, investors recognize that further growth is limited. They may be reluctant to pay a significant premium for limited growth potential.

Also, as the convertible bond price increases significantly above the call price, paying a premium becomes very risky. If, for example, you were to pay a premium for the convertible bond when the stock was selling at $60, you run the risk of waking the next morning to learn that the convertible debentures have been called and that you will be forced to convert to common, the premium having disappeared overnight. (The details and considerations of forced conversion through call will be treated later in this chapter.)

Finally, at some point as the market price of the common stock rises, the premium will disappear and the convertible debenture will trade as if it were identical to the shares of common stock into which it is convertible. In many cases, this point will be reached when forced conversion through call is imminent or the conversion privilege is about to expire.

Managerial considerations

There are four types of managerial considerations related to the use of convertible securities. At the outset, one must consider the trade-offs related to whether or not to issue convertible securities instead of adopting some financing alternative, and, if so, decide the terms of the convertible issue. Further considerations relate to forcing conversion into common stock, the risks of an overhanging convertible issue outstanding, and the potential dilution of earnings per share and voting rights.

Issue trade-offs When management considers raising additional long-term funds, various alternatives—including long-term debt, preferred stock, convertible debt or preferred stock, and common stock—will be compared. The use of convertible bonds or preferred stock usually will be considered in relation to an issue of straight bonds or additional common stock.

Compared to straight bonds, inclusion of a conversion feature might reduce the required interest rate some 1 to 3 percentage points. The convertibility feature might also provide the necessary trade-off to loosen or eliminate some protective provisions. In considering this decision, management must weigh against these advantages the potential dilution from conversion and the risk that the convertible securities might remain unconverted for a longer time than expected.

In many cases, issuing convertible securities is viewed as an alternative to selling additional common stock. Optimistic managers typically consider their firm's common stock to be underpriced and expect its market value to increase in the future. Therefore, they are tempted to issue convertible securities with the expectation of forcing conversion later after the common stock price has risen, thereby eliminating the debt and augmenting the equity. This may be well and good *if* the future turns out that way. The vital managerial consideration is the risk that it will not. If the common stock price does not increase sufficiently that conversion may be forced, financial flexibility may be impaired by the overhanging, unwanted debt. Management may deeply regret not having issued the required additional common stock in the first place. This highly subjective decision requires level-headed, unbiased judgment.

Once the decision to issue a convertible security has been made, trade-offs among its terms must be considered. The major bargaining areas are the interest rate and the conversion price (or conversion ratio). The lowest interest rate may be obtained if the conversion price is close to the present market price of the stock. For example, perhaps Folsom Corporation could have sold its convertible debentures at a 7½ percent interest rate rather than 8 percent if it had been willing to set the conversion price at $37 rather than $40. Conversely, if the conversion price were set at $43, it might have had to pay 8½ percent interest. The higher the conversion price as compared to the present market price, the less attractive is the opportunity for gain through conversion. Therefore, investors will not pay as high a premium over the straight bond value. In other words, investors will require a higher interest rate.

From the issuer's standpoint, the higher the conversion price, the less will be the dilution of the common stock upon conversion because fewer shares will have to be issued. On the other hand, the higher conversion price means that the market price of the common stock will have to increase by a greater amount before conversion can be forced. Therefore, the risk of an overhanging convertible is increased. The financial consequences of each of these considerations must be weighed in establishing the appropriate interest rate and conversion price.

To further complicate matters, the call price and various protective provisions also involve trade-offs related to the interest rate and/or the conversion price. For example, by paying a little higher interest rate or setting a lower conversion price, the call price might be lowered or a lock-in clause eliminated. All such trade-offs involve bargaining between the issuer and the investment bankers to design a convertible security that will be marketable and that the issuer feels it can live with.

Forcing conversion The conversion privilege gives the investor the *option* of exchanging the convertible security for a specified number of shares of common stock. Technically, the issuing corporation cannot *require* the investor to convert. But there are ways by which the issuer can make it uneconomical for the investor *not* to convert, thereby *forcing conversion.* If the market price of the common stock increases sufficiently, the issuer may *call* the convertible security. After the call announcement, the securities holders have a limited period, usually about 20 days, in which to return their convertible securities and be paid the *call price,* which in the Folsom convertible debenture is $1,080. During this *call period,* the holder may alternatively exercise the conversion privilege, returning the convertible security in exchange for common stock at the conversion ratio. This would be 25 shares per Folsom convertible debenture.

The *call equivalent* is the market price per common share at which the 25 shares will be equal in value to the call price. In Folsom's case, this is $43.20 ($1,080/25). If the common stock market price is sufficiently above the call equivalent that management believes it cannot fall during the call period to $43.20, then the convertible debentures may safely be called. Their holders will convert them before expiration of the call period. The investors have the option, but they would be foolish not to convert and accept the call price.

To illustrate this, assume that the market price behavior of Folsom common stock is as shown in Figure 21–2. The stock was at $35 on the date Folsom issued its convertible debentures, June 15, 1980. In December it reached $40, penetrating the conversion price, and went through the call equivalent early the following month, January 1981. If Folsom had attempted to force conversion at that time, it would have been foiled because the stock would have dropped through the call equivalent during the call period, investors would not have converted, and Folsom would have had to pay them cash of $21,600,000 at the call price.

Folsom management estimates, on the basis of analysis of past downward market price fluctuations and providing a reasonable safety factor, that the maximum 20-day downward fluctuation might be 15 percent of market price. Therefore a "safe" call could be made only when the market price of the common stock exceeded $51 [$43.20, the call equivalent/(1 − .15) = $50.82]. During most of 1981 the stock fluctuated from about $36 to $48. Finally, in early December 1981, it rose above $51, the safe call price. Beyond $51, Folsom management could call its convertible debentures, confidently expecting that this action would force conversion. Note that while

Figure 21–2 Common stock prices—Folsom Corporation

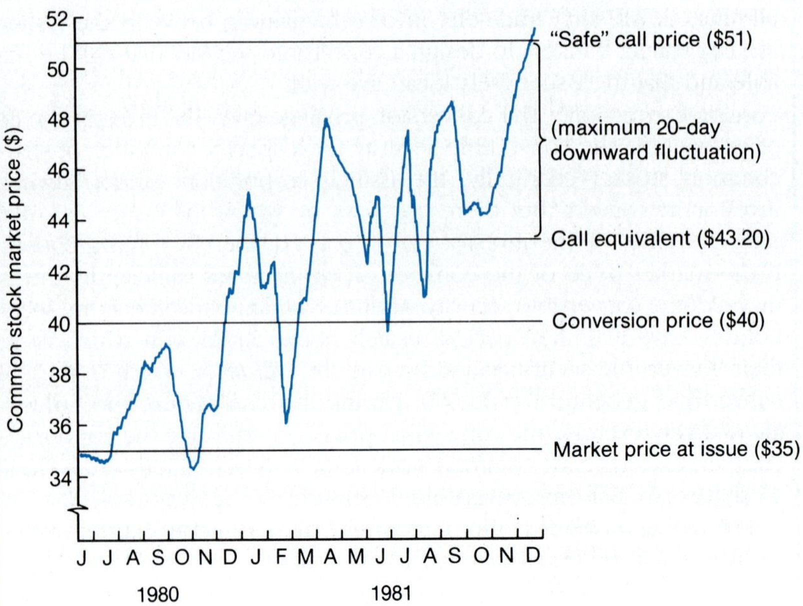

the conversion price is less than 15 percent above market at the time of issue, the common stock price must rise about 46 percent before conversion may safely be forced through a call.

A firm might or might not force conversion by call when the market price of its common stock is in the safe call range. Often call is desirable to "open the top" by extinguishing the debt and augmenting the common stock equity. Although, the firm has this option, it may not choose to exercise it if foreseen financial needs do not require strengthening of the capital structure.

There are other means by which conversion may be forced. If the conversion ratio is about to decline, say from 25 to 22.5, and the market price exceeds the conversion price, investors are motivated to convert before the step-down becomes effective. In addition, if the conversion privilege is about to expire and market price of the common stock exceeds the conversion price, investors will convert to preserve that excess value. Also, as common stock dividends are increased, the income available from holding the common may considerably exceed the interest received from the convertible bonds. This may motivate investors to convert voluntarily.

Risk of a "hung" convertible If a firm has planned to force conversion within a limited period of time, but this has not been possible because the common stock price has either declined or has not risen sufficiently to allow a safe call, the outstanding convertible security is called a *hung* or *stuck* convertible. It is overhanging the market in two senses. The firm may wish to issue additional debt but is prevented from doing so because the debt presently outstanding, including the convertible debentures, exhausts its borrowing power. The firm had hoped to extinguish the convertible debt and augment its equity cushion through conversion, but things have not worked out this way and it is stuck with the unwanted convertible debt.

At the same time, the firm's ability to raise additional funds by selling common stock may be impaired for two reasons. First, the common stock price is lower than anticipated. Second, the *potential dilution* from eventual conversion will cause the market price of the common stock to be lower than if the convertible securities were not outstanding. This potential dilution is overhanging the market for the common stock.

The net effect of a hung convertible may be that the firm's ability to finance additional capital requirements is seriously impaired. At this point, the optimistic management of a growing firm with increasing capital requirements may regret that they ever heard of convertibles. They have taken a risk and lost.

On the other hand, if additional financing is not required or the issue of convertible debentures did not exhaust the firm's debt capacity, a hung convertible may not have serious consequences. The interest cost of the debt is lower than it would have been if straight debt had been issued. If there is no pressing need to extinguish it, this low-cost debt may not be bad at all from the issuing corporation's standpoint. The convertible debenture holders, of course, would be unhappy. They paid a premium over the straight bond value and the security has turned out from a practical standpoint to be a straight bond.

Dilution When conversion takes place, common stock equity is substituted for debt. Earnings per share of common stock will be diluted by the additional number of shares outstanding. But this will be partially offset by the relief from paying interest on the convertible debt.

To illustrate this dilution, assume that Folsom Corporation's earnings per share before conversion were $4.02, as shown in the first column of Table 21–4. After conversion of its $20 million of 8 percent convertible debentures

Table 21–4 Earnings per share—Folsom Corporation
Before and after conversion

	Before conversion	After conversion
Earnings before interest and taxes	$15,000,000	$15,000,000
Less: Interest expense	1,600,000	-0-
Earnings before taxes	$13,400,000	$15,000,000
Less: Income taxes (assumed 40% rate)	5,360,000	6,000,000
Earnings after taxes	$ 8,040,000	$ 9,000,000
Common shares outstanding	2,000,000	2,500,000
Earnings per share	$4.02	$3.60

into 500,000 shares of common stock (20,000 bonds × 25, the conversion ratio), its earnings per share would be $3.60. This reflects dilution of 42 cents per share. Note that Folsom would be relieved of its obligation to pay $1.6 million annual interest on the debentures ($20 million × .08), but this would be more than offset by the additional 500,000 shares of common stock outstanding.

The effect of conversion on the market price of the common stock is unknown. The common stockholders' potential gain from financial leverage has been reduced, but this has been accompanied by a reduction in financial risk. Presumably investors would have anticipated the earnings per share dilution of the potential conversion, and this would already have been recognized in the market price of the common stock. The *quality* of earnings per share has been enhanced by the reduced debt and increased equity. This might justify a higher price-earnings ratio.

Accounting Principles Board Opinion No. 15 requires that if material dilution could occur because convertible securities, warrants, and/or stock options are outstanding, the financial statements must disclose both primary and fully diluted earnings per share.[4] *Primary earnings* per share normally are the earnings available to common divided by the number of shares outstanding. *Fully diluted earnings* per share are the *adjusted* earnings divided by the number of shares that would be outstanding if all rights to obtain them were exercised. The adjustment to earnings would eliminate the interest payments on convertible debentures (or the preferred dividend payments on convertible preferred stock), as shown in Table 21–4.[5] Therefore, under APB Opinion No. 15, Folsom's earnings per share while its convertible debentures were outstanding would be reported:

Primary earnings per share	$4.02
Fully diluted earnings per share	$3.60

Uses of convertible securities

There are several possible motivations for issuing convertible securities. We shall now discuss their uses (1) as sweeteners to enhance marketability, (2) to "sell" common stock at a higher price, (3) to raise temporarily inexpensive funds, (4) to achieve increased earnings before dilution, and (5) as currency of exchange in mergers.

As sweeteners If a firm's credit standing is weak and/or the debt markets currently are tight, it may not be able to borrow on reasonable terms. Either the interest rate would be prohibitively high or protective provisions onerous. In such cases a sweetener may have to be provided to market a debt issue. Often this sweetener is a convertible feature making the issue sufficiently attractive to investors who desire an opportunity to participate in appreciation of market value of the common stock.

For example, in many cases in which a straight bond issue would be rated BB or B and would not be marketable, a convertible bond could be sold. Often, venture capital firms, such as small business investment companies (SBICs), will lend to fledgling firms only on a convertible basis or when the debt is accompanied by warrants (which will be discussed later in this chapter). The firm's outlook may be favorable, but it is not sufficiently seasoned

[4]The Accounting Principles Board (APB) is the predecessor of the Financial Accounting Standards Board (FASB). It was the standard-setting board of the National Association of Certified Public Accountants (NACPA). Its standards must be followed by a firm if its financial statements are to receive unqualified certification by CPAs.

[5]APB Opinion No. 15 also requires that, if a convertible security paid interest or dividends equal to less than two thirds of the bank prime rate existing at the time it was issued, *primary earnings* must be determined by considering the convertible security to be a common stock equivalent. Convertible securities rarely are issued at such low rates of return. When they are, the conversion price probably is lower than the current market price of the common stock; therefore, the theoretical value at the time of issue is the conversion value.

to justify straight debt financing. The lender requires a debt position, giving it a prior claim in event of failure, and the convertibility feature, providing an opportunity for gain if the firm is successful.

To "sell" common stock at a higher price An expanding firm may wish to sell additional common stock but consider its current market price to be unfavorable compared to management's estimate of its future price. But funds to finance capital expansion are required now, and management believes that this expansion will increase earnings per share and the market price of the common stock. By issuing a convertible security, it will obtain the required funds now, and the common stock will suffer less dilution later when and if conversion takes place.

For example, the management of Folsom Corporation could have sold common stock at only about $33 per share in June of 1980. Underpricing of about $2 per share from the current market price of $35 would have been required to market the issue. To obtain the $20 million needed would have required the issue of 606,000 shares of common stock. (20 million/ $33). Convertible debentures were issued with a conversion price of $40 per share. When and if the stock should rise high enough that a safe call will force conversion, only 500,000 shares will be issued. *If* the future works out as anticipated, Folsom, in effect, will have sold 500,000 shares of common stock at $40 per share as compared to selling 606,000 shares at $33 per share now.

This appears to be very attractive, almost like getting something for nothing. But there are some catches. The first is that if Folsom's management is correct in its estimate that within a relatively short period, say one to three years, the market price of its common stock will rise to over $51 per share, where a safe call could force conversion, would it not be a better decision to borrow the $20 million temporarily and sell $20 million worth of stock later at $49 per share, giving up only about 408,000 shares?

The second consideration is that Folsom's management clearly is more optimistic than the market in general. If there is any validity to the efficient markets theory, the current market price of $35 per share fully reflects all available information relative to anticipated future earnings per share and the degree of uncertainty that such earnings will materialize. The management is, in effect, saying "We are smarter than the market." The question is, are they really merely saying "We are *more optimistic* than the market"?

The third consideration is the risk of a hung convertible. If the future does not turn out as anticipated and the market price of the common stock does not rise high enough to allow conversion, what will be the consequences? These, as earlier discussed, may range from nothing serious to disruption of the firm's ability to finance its requirements. By issuing the convertible debentures, motivated by the intention to obtain more for the common stock than would be possible at the time, management is assuming the risk of unsatisfactory market performance in return for the benefits of less common stock dilution if the future turns out as anticipated.

To raise temporarily inexpensive funds The aftertax *interest cost* of convertible debentures usually is lower than from alternative sources of capital available to the firm. The interest rate tends to be some 1 to 3 percentage points lower than the rate on straight debt of the same issuer. Thus, by using convertibles the firm may obtain temporarily inexpensive financing. This differential in interest cost, however, is not a gift. Rather it is expected to be paid for eventually by the dilution of earnings per share on the common stock after conversion.

Of course, if conversion never takes place, this saving in interest cost is effective throughout the life of the bond. But that is little consolation to the residual owners, the common stockholders, because it can occur only when they have not been able to benefit from a significant increase in market value of their common stock.

The use of convertible bonds to achieve this temporary cost saving, however, can be a wise strategy for an expanding firm. It provides the cheaper funds at a time when limited cash flows may place a premium on conserving cash. Later, when earnings have increased as a result of expansion, the firm can better afford to pay for the previous saving as conversion takes place.

In some cases, the temporary interest cost saving may be prolonged by not forcing conversion even though it is feasible because the common stock price has risen above that necessary for a safe call. The firm may simply wait until the convertible bondholders voluntarily convert immediately prior to a step-down in the conversion ratio or expiration of the conversion privilege, which usually is the maturity date of the bonds. It may logically be argued that such a strategy will not really achieve greater value of the common stock equity of the firm. The market will perceive the potential dilution and reflect it in the price of the common stock. But from the immediate standpoint of reported primary earnings per share and required cash flows to pay dividends, some at least superficial advantage may result.

To achieve increased earnings before dilution A closely related motivation for issuing convertible securities is to delay the dilution of earnings per share during a development or construction period until the expected earnings benefits have been achieved. For example, assume that a high-technology electronics firm requires financing of research and development expenditures to develop a new line of electronic measurement equipment. Already low earnings will be further depressed during the development period but are expected to increase substantially after the new line is introduced. To issue additional common stock presently would result in severe dilution because the present stock price is low and earnings per share would be further depressed.

The firm might choose a strategy of issuing convertible debentures now to finance the R&D outlays. Then, after the new line has been marketed and the higher earnings per share are achieved, it expects to force conversion by call. This will extinguish the debt and increase the equity with less dilution of the earnings per share than if common stock were issued now. Conversion, in turn, will establish the equity base for future debt financing (straight debt or convertible) of additional expansion projects. The viability of such a strategy, of course, is dependent upon the success of the new line; there lies the risk.

As currency of exchange in mergers As briefly discussed in Chapter 20, convertible preferred stock often is used as the currency of exchange in mergers. Assume that company A, a rapidly growing firm, wishes to acquire company B. Company A's stock sells at a high price-earnings ratio but a low dividend yield because most of its earnings are being retained to finance growth. Company B's earnings have been relatively stable for several years. Its stock is held largely by income-motivated investors because the dividend yield is relatively high. The company B stockholders are not willing to exchange their shares for the common stock of A at a reasonable exchange ratio because their dividend income would decrease substantially.

This roadblock may be overcome if company A offers to exchange its convertible preferred stock, which would have a dividend rate providing an attractive income to the company B stockholders. The conversion ratio would be set to achieve a market value of the company A convertible preferred stock somewhat higher than the exchanged holdings of company B common. The conversion feature offers the company B stockholders the opportunity to benefit from capital gains if the market price of the common stock of A increases in the future. This package, in the form of company A convertible preferred stock, is sufficiently attractive to induce company B common stockholders to exchange their shares. The preferred dividends satisfy their income needs, and the conversion feature provides capital gain potential.

Note that company A did not propose exchanging convertible debentures. If a substantial portion of the common shares of company B are held by stockholders who purchased that stock at lower prices than the value of company A convertible debentures that would be received, they would be subject to capital gains tax on the difference in the year of exchange. Exchange of any kind of debt for common stock is viewed by the IRS as a taxable exchange. This tax consideration would deter the company B stockholders from agreeing to the merger. But exchange of stock for stock is a tax-free exchange. The IRS does not distinguish among common, preferred, or convertible preferred stock in such an exchange. Therefore, there will be no immediate tax consequences to company B stockholders from exchanging their common shares for company A convertible preferred stock. They, of course, eventually may have to pay capital gains taxes when and if they sell the company A convertible preferred or common stock into which they have converted it.

In addition to achieving an exchange offer acceptable to company B stockholders, the use of convertible preferred stock as the currency of exchange provides another benefit to company A. This allows it to achieve the earnings anticipated from the acquisition before dilution of *primary earnings per share* occurs. The acquiring company's management expects to employ the acquired assets to earn at least the rate previously achieved and often anticipates synergistic benefits from the merger. Dilution of primary earnings per share will not occur until a future time, when the convertible preferred is exchanged for common stock.

Warrants

A *warrant* (specifically, a stock purchase warrant) is a long-term option to purchase a stated number of shares of common stock at a specified price. From the standpoint of its holder, a warrant provides a speculative position related to the market price of the stock. From the issuing firm's standpoint, the warrant is a commitment to sell common stock at a definite price if and when the holder demands.

Warrants usually are issued in conjunction with bonds, preferred stock, or common stock. For example, a firm may offer as a *unit* a $1,000, 10 percent debenture in combination with warrants to purchase 15 shares of common stock at $8 per share. Or a firm might offer units, each consisting of 20 shares of common stock and warrants to purchase an additional 10 shares at $8 per share. Usually the *exercise price* is 10 to 20 percent higher than the market price of the common stock at the time the warrants are issued. The exercise price of warrants is protected by an antidilution clause providing automatic adjustment to compensate for stock splits, stock dividends, or issue of stock below market price. In some cases warrants may have differing exercise prices, increasing periodically through time. For example, a 10-year warrant may be exercisable at $8 per share during the first three years, $10 per share from the fourth through the sixth year, and $12 per share thereafter until expiration. Stepped-up exercise prices may be designed to induce holders to exercise the warrants during the period immediately preceding the scheduled increase in the exercise price. Most warrants expire at a stated date, after five or ten years. However, there are a few perpetual warrants outstanding.[6]

Although they are similar in nature and uses, there are basic differences between a convertible debenture and a unit comprised of a straight deben-

[6]The outstanding examples of perpetual warrants are those of Transcontinental Corporation. These will be outstanding as speculative vehicles, providing a position in Transcontinental common stock, until the life of the corporation is terminated.

ture and warrants. When a convertible debenture is converted, its holder must give up the debenture to obtain common stock. The holder of a straight debenture and warrants may continue to hold the debenture but either sell the warrants or exercise them to benefit from an increase in price of the common stock. In this way, the holder of such a unit may, in a sense, have his cake and eat it, too.

A warrant differs from a *right* in the length of time during which it is exercisable. A right is exercisable only within, say, 20 or 25 days after its issue, whereas a warrant usually is exercisable over a period of several years. Another difference is that a warrant usually is exercisable at a price higher than that of the common stock at time of issue while a right is exercisable at a discount from the market price.

Value of a warrant

Similar to a convertible security, a warrant has a theoretical value which is directly related to the price of the common stock, and a market value which usually is greater. The difference between these two values is the premium.

Theoretical value

The *theoretical value* (intrinsic or minimum value) of a warrant is determined as follows:

$$\text{Warrant value} = (\text{Market price of common stock} - \text{Exercise price}) \times \text{Exercise ratio}$$

or

$$V = (P - E)\,N \qquad (21\text{–}1)$$

where

V = theoretical value of the warrant
P = market price of the common stock
E = the exercise price of the warrant
N = number of shares that can be purchased with one warrant, the exercise ratio.

For example, assume that each of Cado Corporation's warrants is exercisable to purchase one share of its common stock at $12 per share. If the current market price of Cado common stock is $16 per share, the theoretical value of a Cado warrant is

$$V = (\$16 - \$12)\,1$$
$$V = \$4$$

If Cado stock should rise to $20, then the theoretical value of its warrants would be $8 each. However, if the stock should fall below the exercise price ($12) to say $9, the theoretical value of its warrants would *not* be minus $3.

Rather, it would be zero because a piece of paper giving its holder an *option* to exercise cannot have a negative value. Under such a condition it simply has no theoretical value.

Market value The market value of a warrant will almost always be greater than its theoretical value. For example, the market values of Cado warrants when the common stock is at various prices ranging from $4 to $30 per share are compared to the corresponding theoretical values in columns 2 and 3 of Table 21–5. The corresponding premiums shown in column 4 reflect the amounts by which market prices exceed theoretical values. These data are plotted in Figure 21–3.

The premium Inasmuch as a warrant, from the holder's viewpoint, is a vehicle for speculation as to the future price of the common stock, the amount of the premium reflects two factors. The first is speculators' expectations regarding future common stock price movements, and the second is the potential gain in relation to the amount of money risked. Usually the premium is greatest when the market price of the stock is close to the exercise price, as shown in Table 21–5 and Figure 21–3. When the stock is selling at $12 per share, the exercise price, the market price of the warrants may be around $4.50, which is all premium because the theoretical value is zero.

As the market price of the common stock becomes progressively lower than the exercise price, the premium is gradually reduced because the probability that positive theoretical values may be achieved becomes more and more remote. The amount of the premium when such lower stock prices prevail will be a function of the relative optimism of speculators. In

Table 21–5 Stock prices and warrant values—Cado Corporation

(1)	(2)	(3)	(4)
	Warrant value		
Common stock price	Market	Theoretical	Premium (2) − (3)
$ 4	$ 1.25	$ 0	$1.25
6	1.75	0	1.75
8	2.50	0	2.50
10	3.50	0	3.50
12	4.50	0	4.50
14	5.50	2	3.50
16	6.75	4	2.75
18	8.00	6	2.00
20	9.50	8	1.50
22	11.10	10	1.10
24	12.80	12	.80
26	14.60	14	.60
28	16.50	16	.50
30	18.40	18	.40

Figure 21–3 Warrant values—Cado Corporation

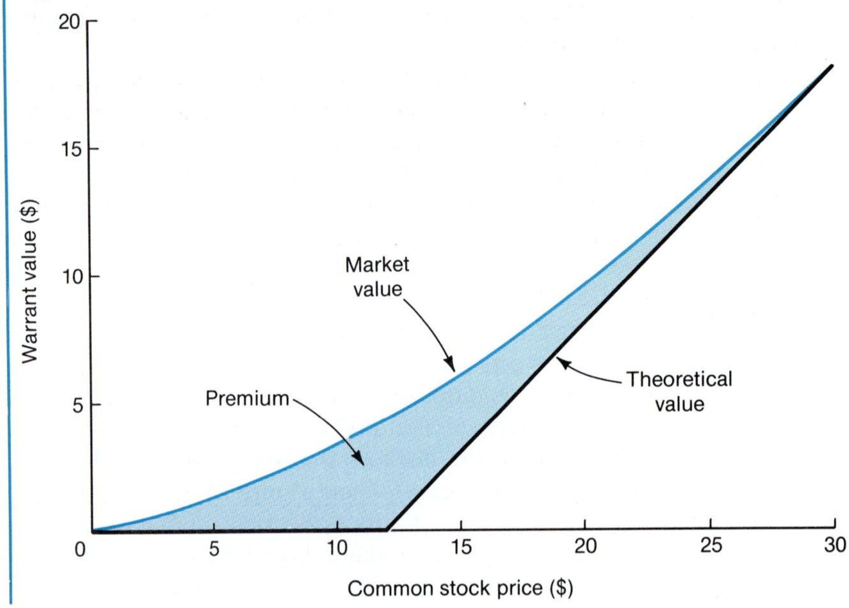

our example, they apparently are willing to pay $1.25 when the common stock is at $4, where it would have to triple in price before the exercise price were reached. Hope springs eternal!

The premium also relates to the *leverage effect* that can be obtained by holding the warrants rather than common stock. For example, when the common stock price is $14 per share, a speculator with $1,400 to risk could buy only 100 shares of stock. But if the warrants sold at their theoretical value of $2 each, 700 warrants could be purchased. If the stock rose to $18 per share, the holding of 100 common shares would be worth $1,800, reflecting a gain of $400 or 29 percent. But if the speculator owned 700 warrants, their theoretical value would have increased to $4,200 ($6 × 700), reflecting a gain of 200 percent. Thus, the warrants would have provided leverage of about 6.9 times (200%/29%).

Because this leverage is available via warrants, speculators will bid up their market price to a significant premium over their theoretical value. In this case, they are willing to pay $5.50 for a warrant, a premium of $3.50 over its theoretical value of $2. Even at this premium, the speculator still has a greater opportunity for gain if the stock price rises than from holding the stock. The $1,400 would buy about 255 warrants at $5.50. These would rise in the market to $8 if the stock went to $18, the warrants then being worth $2,040. This reflects a gain of about 46 percent, compared to the 29 percent increase in the stock price.

It must be recognized that leverage works both ways. If the market price of the common stock should decline, our speculator's losses also will be magnified by leverage.

As the market price of the common stock increases beyond the exercise price, the leverage advantage declines. This decline largely accounts for the gradual reduction of the premium as the stock price rises from $12 to $30 in Table 21–5 and Figure 21–3. Two other factors may influence the premium. The first is the dividend paid on the common stock. Warrant holders receive no dividends whereas the common stockholders do. Premiums tend to have an inverse relationship to the dividends paid. Often rising stock prices are accompanied by increased dividends; this factor may partially explain the tapering off of the premium as the stock price increases. The second factor relates to proximity of the expiration date of the warrants. If the theoretical value is positive, the warrants must be exercised before the expiration date. Therefore, the premium will approach zero as that date draws near. On the other hand, if the stock price is less than the exercise price, the market price of the warrants will tend towards zero as expiration approaches.

Managerial considerations

The principal managerial considerations are the potential effects of outstanding warrants upon the firm's capital structure and on the common stockholders' participation in earnings and control.

Retention of accompanying securities As previously mentioned, warrants usually are issued as part of a package along with other securities. These securities usually are bonds or preferred stock. In such cases, management considers such a package as an alternative to issuing convertible securities. When convertible debt is exchanged for common stock, the conversion has a two-fold effect upon the capital structure. Debt is reduced or eliminated while the common stock equity is increased. Both elements of this transaction improve the firm's borrowing power. But no additional cash is received; the additional common stock equity is paid for by surrender of the debt.

In contrast, if a package comprised of straight debt and warrants is used, exercise of the warrants will *not* affect the *debt* outstanding. It will remain a part of the capital structure until it is repaid. But exercise of the warrants does increase the common stock equity and, in contrast to conversion, brings *additional cash* into the firm equal to the exercise price times the number of common shares issued. The increase in common stock equity will augment the firm's borrowing power, but to a lesser degree than conversion would have under the alternative financing opportunity. Whether this difference is good or bad depends upon the firm's capital structure policy and its financial requirements.

Obtaining additional equity capital In some cases, issuing a package including warrants may be part of a financial strategy to arrange two financings with one offering. The firm may need $20 million now to be financed through debt and foresee an additional requirement of $10 million in equity, say, three years from now. To satisfy these requirements, it might issue a package comprised of $20 million in debentures accompanied by three-year warrants to purchase 400,000 common shares at $25 each. Such a strategy, of course, will succeed only if the market price of the common stock is above $25 immediately prior to the expiration of the warrants three years hence. If so, exercise of the warrants will bring in the required $10 million of equity money at that time.[7] Note that even if the market price of a stock exceeds the exercise price, so that the warrants have positive theoretical value, management cannot force their exercise. Warrants, unlike convertible securities, are not callable.

Dilution Some dilution of earnings per share probably will take place when warrants are exercised. But it must be recognized that additional funds will be obtained at that time. These funds presumably will be employed to enhance the firm's earnings. The additional earnings should at least partially offset the increased number of shares. Therefore, the dilution in EPS might be less than if the same number of shares had been issued through conversion of convertible securities.

APB Opinion No. 15 requires that, if the market price of the common stock *exceeds* the exercise price of the warrants, *both primary and fully diluted earnings per share* be stated *as if* the warrants had been exercised. But this adjustment includes recognition of the funds that would be received if the warrants were exercised. For example, if warrants to purchase 400,000 shares of common stock at $25 were outstanding and the current market price of the common stock were $40, the assumed net increase in the number of shares would be as shown in Table 21–6. Although 400,000 shares would be created by exercise of the warrants, an offset of 250,000 shares would be allowed. Only the remaining 150,000 shares would be added to the outstanding number of shares. This offset is calculated by dividing the cash proceeds that would be received if the warrants were exercised (item 2*a* in Table 21–6) by the current market price of the stock (item 2*b*). In effect, this adjustment adds to the existing number of shares only those shares that would be issued but would not be compensated by receipt of the current market price. Primary and fully diluted earnings per share

[7]This financial strategy was used in 1970 by AT&T, when it sold for $1.57 billion a package of debentures and five-year warrants to purchase 31.3 million shares of common stock at $52. The stock was then selling at about $47. The package sold without difficulty. However, the strategy was unsuccessful because the common stock price was slightly below $52 immediately prior to expiration of the warrants in 1975; therefore, only a small fraction of these warrants was exercised.

are then calculated by dividing the earnings available to common stock by the adjusted number of shares.

Table 21–6 Calculation of assumed net increase in common shares from exercise of warrants

1. New shares created		400,000
2. Reduction of shares from cash proceeds:		
a. Cash proceeds (400,000 shares × $25)	$10,000,000	
b. Current market price of stock	$40	
c. Assumed reduction in shares created ($10,000,000/$40)		250,000
3. Assumed net increase in shares from exercise of warrants		150,000

Dilution of voting rights might be a serious consideration in issuing either convertible securities or a package including warrants. In most cases, the added number of voting shares would not influence control. But, if a large number of potential shares are involved and management maintains control by a thin majority, this factor could indeed be serious.

Uses of warrants

Warrants usually are used as sweeteners to enhance the marketability of other securities they accompany. They also may be used to facilitate later sale of common stock or to provide part of the compensation in connection with mergers and acquisitions.

As sweeteners The most common use of warrants is to sweeten the deal in connection with the sale of senior securities, particularly bonds. Used in this way, their effect is similar to that of a conversion privilege. The attached warrants attract the type of investors who want both the security of the bond and the opportunity (provided by the warrants) to participate in increasing market value of the common stock. But the attractiveness of a package including warrants differs from convertibles. Investors may at any time decide to hold only the bonds and sell their warrants (which trade in their separate market) to speculators who wish only to hold a position relating to the common stock price. Thus, as time passes after issue, the two components of the package may gravitate to different holders.

Sometimes, particularly in the case of a new or unseasoned firm, warrants may accompany the initial public offering of common stock. Here the warrants provide an added speculative inducement to reward the holder eventually with a gain via the warrant value as well as in the price of the common stock held. In similar cases, sometimes the investment bankers marketing an initial public offering of common stock receive a batch of warrants in addition to their usual underwriting spread. This provides a sweetener to the marketers of the issue.

To facilitate later sale of stock The use of warrants to facilitate the sale of common stock at a later date was discussed briefly in the previous section. Although this strategy may have merit if the additional equity requirement is quite definite and coincides with the expiration date of the warrants, it may have some shortcomings. The first, of course, is the risk that even though the market price of the common stock might rise well above the exercise price during the period the warrants are outstanding, such a price might not exist *immediately prior* to expiration of the warrants. Only the latter is pertinent because there is no way of forcing exercise prior to expiration. In setting the exercise price, it is almost impossible for the financial manager to foresee the market price of the common stock during a short period before expiration several years hence. Unfavorable developments beyond the control of management could defeat this strategy.

The second shortcoming involves the question as to whether the strategy is *optimal,* even if it is successful in that the warrants are exercised. If exercise takes place, it must occur at a price lower than the market price of the common stock at the time. In such a case, would it not have been to the firm's advantage simply to have waited until that time to sell common stock at the higher price? One might argue that the use of warrants eliminates flotation costs of the stock issue. But such costs are very small compared to the possible difference between market and exercise prices at the date of expiration of the warrants.

The third shortcoming is the possible error in timing. The firm might need the funds perhaps a year or two before or after the expiration date of the warrants. If so, the additional funds obtained when the warrants are exercised might come in at the wrong time.

In mergers and acquisitions Sometimes the acquiring company in a merger or acquisition includes warrants as part of the package offered to the stockholders of the acquired firm. The use of warrants in this connection is largely a matter of satisfying the requirements of such stockholders. Perhaps they wish to sell their company for cash but also insist upon an opportunity to participate in future increase in the common stock value of the combined enterprise. A cash offer accompanied by warrants will satisfy those dual requirements. Or perhaps stockholders of the acquired firm want the income stability and the tax-free exchange status of preferred stock but also a chance to profit from appreciation of the common stock. The offer of a package including straight preferred stock and warrants will satisfy their needs.

Summary

This chapter discussed the nature and uses of convertible securities and warrants. Both the conversion privilege and the warrant are devices by which another security may be made more attractive to buyers by providing an option to acquire common stock at a later date. A *convertible security* is a bond or preferred stock that may be exchanged for a specified number of common shares (the conversion ratio) at the holder's option. The conversion price is the effective price paid per common share if obtained through conversion. It usually is some 10 to 20 percent above the market price at the time of issue. Most convertible securities are callable. Conversion may be forced by call when and if the common stock price is sufficiently above the conversion price. Conversion also may be induced by either a prescheduled step-down of the conversion ratio or the approaching expiration of the conversion privilege.

The theoretical value of a convertible security is the higher of its value as a straight bond (or preferred stock) or the market value of the common stock into which it is convertible (conversion value). Its market value usually is higher than theoretical value, because the holder has both the opportunity for gain if the common stock price increases and the downside protection of the straight bond value if it declines. This premium is greatest when the conversion value is close to the straight bond value.

Managerial considerations related to the use of convertible securities are (1) weighing the trade-offs regarding issue and terms of the security, (2) assessing the feasibility of forcing conversion by call, (3) recognizing the risk of a hung convertible, and (4) considering the potential dilution that will occur upon conversion. Convertible securities may be used (1) as sweeteners to enhance marketability, (2) to "sell" common stock eventually at a higher price than the present market will bear, (3) to raise temporarily inexpensive funds, (4) to achieve increased earnings before dilution, and (5) as currency of exchange in mergers.

A *warrant* is a long-term option to purchase a stated number of common shares at a specified price (the exercise price). Warrants usually are issued in package deals accompanying bonds, preferred stock, or common stock. After issue, the warrants may be separated from the accompanying securities and traded in their own market. They usually must be exercised within a limited time of, say, 5 to 10 years, and in some cases the exercise price is stepped up periodically.

The theoretical value of a warrant reflects the saving that would result from its exercise compared to purchasing common stock at the existing market price. The market value of a warrant usually is greater than its theoretical value. The premium reflects both speculators' expectations regarding future common stock price movements and the leverage obtained by holding warrants rather than the common stock. Other factors may influence the amount of the premium. The premium usually will be greatest when the common stock price is near the exercise price.

When warrants are exercised, the senior securities that originally accompanied them remain outstanding. Their exercise increases the number of common shares and brings in additional cash from payment of the exercise price. This will strengthen the firm's capital structure, but not as much as conversion of a convertible security. Some dilution of earnings per share probably will occur, but this may be tempered by increases in earnings resulting from profitable investment of the cash received. Warrants usually are used as sweeteners to enhance marketability of other securities they accompany. They may also be used to facilitate later sale of common stock or as part of the compensation offered in connection with mergers and acquisitions.

Questions

1. What is a *convertible security?* How do the motives of an investor in convertible bonds differ from those of an investor in straight bonds?

2. What is the *conversion ratio?* If you know the conversion ratio, how can you determine the *conversion price?* At the time of issue of a convertible security, what is the usual relationship between the conversion price and the market value of the common stock?

3. Convertible securities often are called *hybrid* securities. Why? What are the two elements that are combined in a convertible security?

4. How can the *straight bond value* of a convertible bond be determined? How can the *conversion value* (stock value) be determined? Under what market conditions does each of these values determine the *theoretical value* of a convertible bond?

5. The *market value* of a convertible security usually exceeds its theoretical value. Why? Demonstrate by the use of a rough graph how this excess or *premium* varies as the market value of the common stock changes.

6. A firm that contemplates issuing convertible bonds must consider the trade-off between the interest rate to be paid and the conversion price. Explain this trade-off. What will be the effect upon the interest rate of a relatively high conversion price? How will a high conversion price influence

the potential dilution of earnings per share of the common stock when and if the bonds are converted?

7. How can the issuer force conversion of a convertible security if the market price of its common stock rises to a sufficiently high level? How can the issuer determine what is a sufficiently high market price? In some cases, the issuer might *not* force conversion even though such action were feasible. Why?

8. "The use of a convertible security allows a firm to sell common stock at a higher price than could be obtained by directly issuing common stock in the current market." Critically evaluate this statement.

9. "The use of a convertible bond allows a firm to borrow at a lower interest rate than could be obtained by issuing straight bonds in the current market." Critically evaluate this statement.

10. What is a *warrant?* Why might a firm issue warrants in a package to accompany bonds or preferred stock?

11. What is the *exercise price* of a warrant? What is the usual relationship between the exercise price and the market price of the common stock at the time warrants are issued?

12. How is the *theoretical value* of a warrant determined? Why do warrants often trade in the market at substantial *premiums* over their theoretical value?

13. You are the financial manager of a rapidly growing firm that contemplates additional external funds requirements in the future. Currently you must raise $10 million by issuing either convertible debentures or a package including debentures and warrants. Indicate your preference and the reasoning underlying it.

14. How does the dilution of earnings per share on the common stock differ when warrants are exercised from that occuring when a convertible security is converted? How does the effect upon the capital structure differ?

Problems

1. What is the conversion price of each of the following convertible securities?

   a. A $1,000 convertible bond convertible into 40 shares of common stock.

   b. A $100 par convertible preferred stock convertible into five shares of common stock.

c. A $500 convertible bond convertible into 25 shares of common stock.

d. A $40 par convertible preferred stock convertible into five shares of common stock.

2. *a.* What is the *straight bond value* of a 9 percent, 15-year $1,000 par convertible bond if the straight bonds of the same issuer and maturity would be traded at an 11 percent yield?

   b. If this bond is convertible into 30 shares of common stock, what is its *conversion* (stock) *value* when the market value of the common stock is $40 per share?

   c. What is the *theoretical value* of this bond when the market value of the common stock is $35 per share? When the market value of the common stock is $25 per share?

3. *a.* What is the *straight preferred stock value* of a $100 par, 10 percent convertible preferred stock when a straight preferred stock of the same issuer would be traded at a 13 percent dividend yield?

   b. If this convertible preferred stock is convertible into four shares of common stock, what is its *conversion value* when the market price of the common stock is $22 per share?

   c. What is the *theoretical value* of this convertible preferred stock when the market conditions indicated in (*a*) and (*b*) exist?

   d. If the market price of this convertible preferred stock is $91 per share, what is the *premium?*

4. The Jackson Manufacturing Company has outstanding an issue of $1,000 par, 9 percent convertible debentures. Each debenture is convertible into 25 shares of common stock. The convertible debentures are callable at 110 ($1,100 per bond). Jackson's management estimates on the basis of past market behavior that the price of its common stock could fluctuate as much as 12 percent during a 28-day period, which is the call period required by the indenture.

   a. What is the *conversion price?*

   b. What is the *call equivalent?*

   c. What is the lowest market price of the common stock at which a *safe call* could be made to force conversion of Jackson's convertible debentures?

5. Sandham Corporation has a $100 par, 10 percent covertible preferred stock outstanding, which is callable at $109. The required call period is 21 days. Each share of preferred stock is convertible into four shares of common stock. Sandham's management estimates that the market price of its common stock might fluctuate as much as 15 percent during a 21-day period. Sandham common stock is now selling at $29 per share. Can Sandham safely call the convertible preferred to force conversion?

6. The current market price of Interco Corporation's 1 million shares of outstanding common stock is $8 per share. Interco's management estimates next year's earnings before taxes to be $1.5 million. Interco must raise $1 million additional capital by offering either (1) 137,000 shares of common stock to net $7.30 per share or (2) $1 million of $1,000 par, 10 percent convertible subordinated debentures. Each debenture would be convertible into common stock at a conversion price of $9¼. Interco's marginal income tax rate is 40 percent. What would be Interco's *primary* and *fully diluted* earnings per share next year if each of these financing alternatives were adopted?

7. The Merlin Company has outstanding a $10 million, 8 percent convertible debenture issue. Each $1,000 face amount of debentures is convertible into 50 shares of common stock. Merlin presently has 4 million shares of common stock outstanding. Management expects earnings before interest and taxes (EBIT) this year to be $30 million. The firm is subject to a 40 percent tax rate. Merlin's common stock is trading in the market at $26 per share, and management is considering calling the convertible debentures at 108 (the call price) to force conversion.

a. If management estimates maximum downward fluctuation in market price of the stock during the call period to be 10 percent, would this be a *safe call*?

b. If conversion were forced by call, how would the *primary earnings* per share be affected?

8. Rivera Electric Company has outstanding warrants that provide that each warrant may be exercised to purchase *two* shares of its common stock at $25 per share. Develop a table showing the theoretical value of a Rivera warrant when the market value of the common stock is $20, $30, $40, $50, and $60 per share. At what market price per common share will the premium of market value over theoretical value of the warrant probably be greatest?

9. Sandra Weber has $4,000 with which she wishes to speculate by taking a position that the common stock of Electrotech, Incorporated, will rise during the next year. She can either (1) purchase 200 shares of Electrotech common stock at $20 per share or (2) buy 500 Electrotech warrants at $8 each. An Electrotech warrant provides that its holder may purchase two shares of common stock at $18 per share. Electrotech does not pay dividends on its common stock. (Ignore brokerage fees.)

a. What is the *theoretical value* of an Electrotech warrant? What is the *premium*?

b. If Sandra chooses to buy the common stock and its market price is $30 a year from now, how much money will she make on this speculation? What will be her rate of return?

c. If Sandra chooses to buy the warrants and the common stock rises to $30, how much money will she make if the premium declines to one half its level at time of purchase? What will be her rate of return?

d. If, during the next year, the market price of Electrotech's common stock *declines* to $15 per share, how much will Sandra lose under each alternative, assuming that the warrant premium declines to three fourths its level at time of purchase? What percentage of her principal will she lose under each alternative?

Chapter 22
Dividend Policy and Retained Earnings

Dividends are distributions of earnings to the stockholders. Therefore, dividend policy is the counterpart of retained earnings policy. The decision to pay a given dividend reflects a simultaneous decision *not* to retain that amount of earnings. Dividend policy (or earnings retention policy) is important for two basic reasons: (1) the payment of dividends may influence the value of the common stock and (2) retention of earnings usually is the largest and most important source of additional equity capital to finance growth of the firm. As management is responsible for maintaining adequate equity capital at a minimum cost and maximizing the value of the common stock in the long run, dividend policy must be compatible with these objectives.

To focus upon dividend policy more formally, we refer to the basic dividend-growth valuation model developed in Chapter 15:

$$P = \frac{d_1}{K_e - g}$$

where

P = market price per share of common stock
d_1 = dividend to be paid next year
K_e = cost of common stock equity
g = growth rate

Every term in this valuation model relates in some way to dividend policy. The dividend to be paid next year is d_1. The growth rate *(g)* is greatly influenced by the retention of earnings to be reinvested to increase future earnings. K_e is influenced by the proportion of lower-cost retained earnings to higher-cost new issues of common stock. The resultant value of the common stock *(P)* reflects all of these factors. Therefore, management must seek an optimal balance between dividend payments and retained earnings in pursuing its goal of maximizing the value of the common stock *(P)* in the long run.

All dividends referred to in this chapter are *cash dividends,* that is, they are paid in cash. The dividend *payout ratio* is the relationship between the dividends paid and the aftertax earnings available to common stock during the period (dividends/earnings, or dividends per share/earnings per share).

This chapter is comprised of four sections. The first is a brief review of the different and conflicting dividend theories. The second will discuss the real-life considerations related to dividend policy. The third section will review various practical dividend policy alternatives. The fourth will deal with dividend payment procedures. Noncash transactions, such as stock dividends, stock splits, and property dividends, will be treated in the appendix to this chapter.

Dividend theories

There are three basic theories of dividends. Each conflicts with the other, and none by itself provides a completely satisfactory guide to determining dividend policy. Nonetheless, it is necessary to understand each concept before confronting the complexities of real-world dividend policy determination.

Residual theory

The *residual theory* holds that dividends should be *residue of the capital investment process.* The capital investment decision-making concepts developed in Part IV, Chapters 11 through 15, indicated that in any decision-making period, capital investment proposals should be accepted whenever their expected rates of return exceeded their required rates of return (risk-adjusted cost of capital). The overall cost of capital *(K)*, in turn, is a weighted average of the cost of debt (K_d) and the cost of equity (K_e), where the appropriate weights reflect the target capital structure proportions, such as 40 percent debt and 60 percent equity. The cost of equity (K_e) may have two components, the cost of retained earnings (K_r) and the cost of new common stock (K_c). The cost of retained earnings (K_r) is an *opportunity cost* reflecting the rate of return available to stockholders if earnings were paid to them in dividends and invested in other securities of comparable risk. This cost, K_r, is *lower than* K_c because the latter includes flotation costs.

Because K_r is lower than K_c, the stockholders would appear to be better off if available earnings were retained to provide the required equity financing of approved capital investments than if dividends were paid and the firm then had to issue additional common stock at a higher cost. This is the line of reasoning underlying the residual theory of dividends. It holds that dividend decisions should be made as follows:

1. Determine the dollar amount of capital investments to be made.
2. Determine the equity financing required.
3. Retain earnings to provide as much of this equity financing as possible.
4. If retained earnings are insufficient, issue additional common stock.
5. If earnings exceed the required retention, pay the *excess* in dividends.

Thus, dividend policy is a passive result (or residue) of the capital investment decision-making process. Only the earnings that are left over from financing capital investment projects should be paid out in dividends.[1]

The amounts required to finance acceptable capital investment projects will *vary* considerably from year to year. If the residual theory were accepted literally, dividends would vary from zero in years in which nothing were left over to large amounts in years when earnings substantially exceeded equity requirements to finance capital investments. To illustrate, assume that during four consecutive years Elnor Corporation approved the capital investments shown in column 1 of Table 22–1. The net funds required to finance these investments are shown in column 3. If Elnor considered a 40 percent long-term debt to total capital structure ratio to be optimal, the amounts shown in column 4 would be raised through debt financing, leaving the equity financing requirements shown in column 5. If earnings available to common in each of these years were as shown in column 6, no dividends would be paid in year 1 and $1 million would be raised through the issue of additional common stock (columns 7 and 8). In year 2, when available earnings of $9 million exceed equity financing requirements of $5.4 million, dividends of $3.6 million would be paid. But in year 3 no dividend could be paid, and in year 4, when capital investments of only $10 million were approved, $7 million would be paid out in dividends.

Table 22–1 Capital investments and dividends—Elnor Corporation
($ millions)

Year	(1) Capital investments	(2) Depreciation	(3) Net funds required (1) − (2)	(4) Debt financing .40 × (3)
1	$20.0	$ 5.0	$15.0	$6.0
2	14.0	5.0	9.0	3.6
3	26.0	5.0	21.0	8.4
4	10.0	5.0	5.0	2.0

Year	(5) Equity financing (3) − (4)	(6) Earnings after taxes	(7) Dividends paid (6) − (5)>0	(8) Common stock issued (5) − (6)>0
1	$ 9.0	$ 8.0	—	$1.0
2	5.4	9.0	$3.6	—
3	12.6	11.0	—	1.6
4	3.0	10.0	7.0	—

[1]Capital investments, as employed here, include the net working capital required as well as the investments in fixed assets.

Note that under this theory dividends are not directly related to earnings. In year 3, when Elnor's earnings increase from $9 million to $11 million, dividends would be reduced from $3.6 million to zero. Then in year 4, when earnings decrease by $1 million, dividends would be resumed and $7 million paid. The obvious practical shortcoming of the residual theory is this inconsistency of dividends.

The remaining two theories deal with the *relevance* of dividend policy to the valuation of the firm's common stock by investors.

Indifference theory

The indifference theory holds that investors are (or should be) *indifferent to the payment* (or lack of payment) *of dividends*. According to this theory, dividend policy simply does not matter because it is *irrelevant* to the value of the stock. Its proponents, Miller and Modigliani (M & M), argue that only the income stream accruing to the stockholders is relevent; whether or in what proportion it is paid out in dividends or retained does not influence the wealth of the stockholders.[2]

In brief, their arguments are that if the firm paid no dividends, this would enhance the value of the stock by the amount of the retained earnings. The individual stockholder, if he or she wanted cash, could sell some of the more valuable stock held to create "homemade" dividends. The value of that stockholder's remaining shares would be the same as if the firm had paid dividends equal to the amount received from liquidating this portion of the stock held. Conversely, if the firm paid out all of its earnings in dividends, the stockholder could use the cash received to buy additional shares if he or she preferred reinvestment of income in the firm. The wealth of each stockholder would be unchanged by either the payment of the dividend or the lack of same. Thus, stockholders' wealth is neither created nor destroyed by dividend policy.

The arguments supporting the indifference theory rest upon the following assumptions:

1. There are no taxes, either on dividends received or capital gains.
2. The firm incurs no flotation costs in issuing additional common stock.
3. The investor incurs no brokerage fees (transactions costs).

Given these assumptions, the M & M indifference theory is valid. But the assumptions are patently unreal. We live in a world of taxes, and, for most stockholders, applicable tax rates on dividend income and capital gains dif-

[2]Merton H. Miller and Franco Modigliani, "Dividend Policy, Growth and Evaluation of Shares," *Journal of Business,* October 1961, pp. 411–33.

fer. Most firms cannot sell additional common stock without incurring flotation costs, and investors cannot buy or sell stock without paying brokerage fees. As we develop the real-life considerations, we shall see that dividend policy may indeed be relevant.

"Bird-in-the-hand" theory

"A bird in the hand is worth two in the bush." Well, maybe not two but more than one! The *bird-in-the-hand theory claims that* stockholders are *not indifferent* to dividend payments versus retention of earnings; therefore, *dividend policy is relevant to the value of common stock.* The leading proponents of this theory, Lintner and Gordon, hold that stockholders value a dollar received in dividends more highly than a dollar of earnings retained.[3]

Since a dollar of cash received now as a dividend is *certain,* it is valued at $1. The benefit to the stockholder of a dollar of retained earnings reinvested in corporate assets is *uncertain.* Its value is discounted by investors to reflect the uncertainty as to whether and when it will be received in cash in the fugure. Therefore the $1 of earnings retained is valued by the stockholder at less than $1. If this is true, stockholders are not indifferent but rather prefer current dividend payments to retained earnings. Other things being equal, they should express this preference by valuing the common stock higher if a firm paid out a large proportion of its earnings in dividends (a high dividend payout ratio) than if the firm retained most of its earnings (a low payout ratio). However, other things may not be equal. If the firm were to reinvest the retained earnings at a high enough rate of return to compensate for this additional risk borne by the stockholders, the theory might not be valid.

Many empirical attempts have been made to prove or disprove the bird-in-the-hand theory. None has been completely satisfactory, because it is impossible to cope successfully with the "other things being equal" problem. No sets of firms that are identical in all respects except their dividend policies can be identified and their data analyzed. But intuitively, it appears highly probable that, ignoring tax considerations, this theory has some validity in practice. It might not be valid, however, when applied to a firm having stockholders in high income tax brackets. (The influence of taxes on dividend policy will be discussed later in this chapter.)

[3]John Lintner, "Dividends, Earnings, Leverage, Stock Prices and the Supply of Capital to Corporations," *Review of Economics and Statistics,* August 1962, pp. 243–69; and Myron J. Gordon, "Optimal Investment and Financing Policy," *Journal of Finance,* May 1963, pp. 264–72.

Real-life considerations

At this point you should be a little confused. The residual theory tells you that dividends should be the passive variable, the active variable being the retention of earnings necessary to finance attractive capital investments. The indifference theory says that you really don't have to care: dividend policy doesn't matter anyway. And the bird-in-the-hand theory insists that dividend policy is important: the larger the dividends the better.

But we live in a world influenced by laws and contractual obligations as well as internal considerations relative to investment opportunities, stability of earnings and cash generation, availability of funds, and control considerations. Most importantly, stockholders are people (or organizations owned and controlled by people) who have their individual needs, pay taxes, and exhibit differing motivations for investment in common stocks. These real-life considerations have a strong bearing upon the dividend policy appropriate to each firm and its stockholders. Now we must consider these real-life factors against the backdrop of theory.

Legal and contractual constraints

The payment of dividends may be restricted by state or federal laws or contractual provisions of senior securities.

Legal constraints Laws of the state of incorporation restrict the payment of dividends to protect creditors of the firm. In many states, dividends may be paid only from accumulated earnings as reflected in the retained earnings account. Note that dividends in excess of *current* earnings, even when losses have been incurred in the current or preceding year, may be paid so long as the retained earnings account is not entirely depleted.

This restriction is similar to the rule that *legal capital* may not be impaired by the payment of dividends.[4] The definition of legal capital, however, varies among states. Some states consider only the par or stated value of common stock to be legal capital, but others also include additional paid-in capital (sometimes labeled capital surplus or premium on stock).

Another legal restriction is that a firm cannot pay dividends when it is *insolvent* in the sense that the value of its assets is less than its liabilities and overdue liabilities have accumulated. This would constitute "bleeding"

[4]The exception is that, when a corporation is liquidated, *liquidating dividends* may be paid to the stockholders after all creditors' claims have been satisfied.

of cash by the firm's owners to the detriment of its creditors. If creditors are aware that this is about to take place, they may go to court and get an injunction prohibiting dividend payment.

Dividend policy also may be influenced by the penalty tax on unjustifiable retention of earnings. This tax may induce the payment of larger dividends than otherwise. The Internal Revenue Code provides that if a corporation has excessively retained earnings for no good reason other than to allow its stockholders to avoid personal income taxes on dividends, the IRS may levy a surtax on the improperly retained earnings. The burden of proof is on the IRS.[5]

Contractual constraints A firm's bond indenture, term loan agreement, lease contract, or preferred stock agreement often will contain restrictions limiting the payment of dividends to its common stockholders. Such provisions may prohibit the payment of dividends or limit them to amounts that will not reduce retained earnings below a stated minimum. In other cases, provisions requiring the firm to maintain a minimum working capital or current ratio may, in effect, limit the payment of cash dividends. Such provisions are designed to protect the holders of senior securities from diversion of cash to the owners and reduction of the equity cushion supporting their securities.

Internal considerations

Even though legal and/or contractual constraints may not limit the payment of any reasonable dividend contemplated by management, several internal considerations may influence a firm's dividend policy. The most important of these are (1) availability of cash, (2) capital investment opportunities, (3) stability of earnings and cash generation, (4) availability and cost of funds, and (5) control considerations.

Availability of cash Although dividends are paid out of earnings, they are paid *in cash*. Often this is the dominant restriction. Although profits have been made, these profits may not be available in cash. Rather, the cash flow has been used to finance increased accounts receivable, inventories, or fixed assets, or it may have been required to pay maturing debt obligations. Throughout this book we have stressed the difference between cash flows and profit determination under an accrual accounting system. Here this difference becomes an important influence upon dividend policy.

[5]The surtax usually is levied only in cases of flagrant abuse, where one or a few individuals are using a corporation as a vehicle to accumulate a portfolio of investments not directly related to the firm's primary business. In essence, such people are avoiding payment of personal income taxes that would result from dividends reflecting profits of the primary business. This is done by accumulating within the corporation investment securities that otherwise would be purchased by the stockholders with aftertax proceeds from dividends received. The surtax on unjustifiable retention of earnings removes the incentive to do this.

Capital investment opportunities The capital investment opportunities available to the firm have a great influence upon dividend policy. This consideration relates to the residual theory of dividends. In a growing firm, particularly one that is rather capital-intensive (having a low operating asset turnover), nearly all or perhaps more than the firm's earnings will be required to finance growth in assets. Such characteristics suggest a low dividend payout or perhaps no dividends at all in order to finance as much as possible of the required increase in equity through retained earnings. This consideration explains the no-dividend or minimal-dividend policies of many high-technology electronics firms. For example, Digital Equipment and National Semiconductor pay no dividends, and Hewlett-Packard and Beckman Instruments have very low dividend payout ratios.

On the other hand, many mature or perhaps declining firms in low-technology industries simply do not have (or their managements do not perceive) many favorable capital investment opportunities. This suggests a high dividend payout ratio, because their stockholders may be able to invest the aftertax proceeds of dividends to yield greater returns than obtainable through reinvestment of retained earnings by the firm. Examples include Beneficial Corporation and National Distillers.

In this respect, the dividend policies of public utility firms present a paradox. These firms have very high capital investment requirements largely because of their capital-intensity (low operating asset turnover). At first glance, these capital investment requirements would appear to suggest a low dividend payout ratio. But this is not the case. Investment requirements are so great that, even if all earnings were retained, they still would have to sell additional common stock frequently. Most investors in public utility stocks are income-oriented, buying these stocks largely on a dividend yield basis. Therefore, in order to attract investors to buy their frequent new issues of common stock, public utility firms generally choose the other extreme of paying out nearly all earnings in dividends to attract income-motivated investors to purchase their new issues of common stock.

Stability of earnings and cash generation There usually is a reasonable correlation between dividend payments and the earnings and cash generated by the firm. If management is to attempt to pay *stable* dividends, earnings and cash generation must be relatively stable through time. This does not imply that there cannot be some variation in earnings and cash generation; there always is. But if the variation is too great, the firm will encounter difficulties in raising sufficient funds to pay dividends when earnings and cash generation are low. When they are high, the firm will build up redundant cash and marketable securities.

At the extreme, dividend policy cannot convince the stock market that a feast-or-famine business is a stable investment. The market will bid up the price of stock when *earnings* increase and force it down when they fall almost regardless of management's attempts to stabilize dividend payments.

The old and trite expression is, "You can't make a silk purse out of a sow's ear."

Availability and cost of funds If a firm has ready access to the money and capital markets at reasonable flotation costs, its dividend policy may be considerably less critical than if it does not. For example, a small, growing firm may, as a practical matter, be limited in its access to the long-term capital market. It simply cannot sell a batch of bonds or obtain a loan when it needs the money. Likewise, its access to the equity capital market may be either nil or limited to perhaps a few local friends who might be willing to buy a little stock. In such a case, dividend payments, if any, must be rigidly limited to paying out excess cash that is not required for reinvestment within the firm. In many such cases, there is no excess cash, and the firm is using its borrowing power to the limit. Therefore, no dividends are paid and all earnings are retained to finance internal growth. The firm must adhere rigidly to the residual theory of dividends.

On the other hand a large, financially strong firm may have ready access to both the money and capital markets at reasonable costs. Its flotation costs may be so low as to be almost nominal. Its dividend payments may not be highly critical to its ability to finance internal requirements. If, in order to maintain an otherwise favorable dividend policy, its cash would be drawn down below a satisfactory working level in a given year, the firm could borrow the funds necessary to replenish the cash. Then, in another year, when excess cash may be accumulating, perhaps because of lower capital expenditures, that cash may be used to pay off the loan rather than temporarily increasing the dividend rate.

In short, ready access to the money and capital markets allows a firm to establish a dividend policy that will *in the long run* comply with the residual theory but still maintain relatively stable dividend payments. Flexible borrowings and/or occasional sales of additional stock may avoid the dividend instability that would result from precise adherence to the residual theory in the short run.

Control considerations There are two ways in which control considerations may be pertinent to dividend policy. The first relates to paying low dividends, thereby retaining a large portion of earnings to finance internal needs. Such a policy may be followed by a management that fears the alternative of selling additional stock to outsiders and risking their control of the firm. This motivation might influence dividend policy in either a small, closely held firm where owner-managers do not wish to have any outside interference or a larger one in which control by the present management is tenuous.

The other control consideration relates to the possibility of antagonizing a portion of the stockholders by reducing a dividend to which they have become accustomed. For example, if a considerable portion of a firm's stock is held by income-conscious investors, reducing or eliminating the dividend might provide the provocation that will allow an outside group to conduct a successful proxy fight to remove the present management. The appeal, of course, would be that poor management has resulted in the dividend cut and that the dividend will be restored to its previous level if the new slate is elected to the board. Fear of such a proxy fight may induce continuation of an established dividend even though other factors argue strongly against it.

Stockholder satisfaction considerations

The stockholders *own* the corporation and the most direct and meaningful communication they receive from its management is a dividend check. Therefore, it is of great importance that a firm's dividend policy satisfies their economic needs.

Type of stockholders The initial consideration is whether the stockholders seek *current income* (suggesting a high dividend payout ratio) or *capital gains* (suggesting a low payout ratio). Common stock investors vary greatly in this respect. For example, most of the stockholders of Company X, a public utility, may be individuals of modest means who depend upon income from their investments to meet their living expenses. They might be retirees or widows. The institutional investors may be income-motivated charitable foundations, university endowment funds, pension funds, and trust accounts investing to furnish income to their beneficiaries. These stockholders would be satisfied only by the payment of relatively high and stable dividends.

At the other extreme, most of the stockholders of Company Y, a high-technology electronics firm, may be individuals with high current incomes, such as medical doctors, dentists, and successful business executives. The institutional investors are largely growth-type mutual funds. These stockholders do not want current dividends—they seek the capital gains that will result from reinvestment of earnings.

Income tax status The income tax status of stockholders has a great influence upon their investment objectives. Most of the individual stockholders of Company X are in relatively low tax brackets and some of the institutional investors (the charitable foundations and university endowment funds) are tax-exempt. The holders of Company Y's stock are in high tax brackets. As only 40 percent of long-term capital gains are taxable at their incremental rates, resulting in a maximum tax of 20 percent, these stockholders much prefer receiving no dividends or only nominal ones. They seek instead the capital gains resulting from reinvestment of earnings.

Propensity to bear risk The risk-aversion versus propensity to bear risk of the stockholders also must be considered in the context of Lintner and Gordon's argument supporting the bird-in-the-hand theory. Most of Company X's stockholders probably are highly risk-averse. As a dividend received now is certain while the reinvestment of earnings is risky, they will tend to prefer a high dividend payout ratio. But the stockholders of Company Y, being wealthy and having large incomes from other sources, are more likely to be risk-bearers with regard to their investments. Such investors do not discount expected future benefits from reinvestment of earnings at high rates; they may prefer to bear this risk.

Legal limitations of some stockholders Still another stockholder consideration involves legal limitations on investments by some financial institutions. Some states, including New York, in which many important institutional investors are incorporated, require that institutions such as trusts, life insurance companies, and mutual savings banks invest only in bonds or stocks of issuers qualifying for their "legal list." A typical qualification is that dividends have been paid consecutively on the common stock over a stated period of time, say 5 or 10 years. Even institutional investors in other states consider these "legal lists" in managing their securities portfolios. If investment in a firm's bonds or stock by such institutions is important, management may be very reluctant to omit payment of a dividend. Similarly, a firm seeking to qualify its securities for legal listing to attract such institutional investors may adopt a policy of paying small regular dividends rather than no dividend at all.

Information content of dividends

The payment of dividends is perhaps the most direct and important communication of information to the market regarding the economic health of most firms. Payment of stable dividends is interpreted as a sign that the firm remains well. Management frequently will not increase the dividend unless it is confident that the higher rate may be continued in the foreseeable future. Therefore, a dividend increase sends a signal to investors indicating management's belief that earnings and cash flows have permanently improved. The market usually will react by bidding up the price of the stock. Conversely, reducing or eliminating dividend payments, particularly when they have been stable over a considerable period of time, signals that something may be wrong with the company. If accompanied by reported lower earnings, a dividend reduction may be interpreted to mean that the firm's earning power has been permanently impaired. Market reaction probably will be a drop in the price of the stock.

The market's interpretation of the information content of dividends is extremely important as it relates to the overall objective of maximizing the market value per share of the common stock. Thus, if management believes that a decline in earnings is only temporary, it may signal this by maintaining dividend payments at the existing level.

Of course, it is imperative that management not send misleading signals. Their lack of candor will be doubly damaging as the future unfolds. For example, when Consolidated Edison's financial difficulties were developing in the early 70s, it continued to pay dividends at the existing rate. When it subsequently was forced to omit the dividend in the second quarter of 1974 because sufficient funds were not available, the market price of the stock dropped by more than 50 percent in a two-week period. This violent market reaction apparently reflected not only the normal information content that Con Ed's financial capability had weakened, which was previously suspected by the market, but also that management had failed to communicate this in a timely fashion and admitted the firm's financial difficulties too late and in a drastic form.

The "clientele effect"

Stockholders desiring a particular dividend policy naturally will gravitate to holding stocks in firms that adhere to that policy. Therefore, rather than seeking to establish a dividend policy that satisfies present stockholders' desires, management might consider establishing a policy dominated by internal considerations. Then a *clientele* of stockholders whose investment objectives will be satisfied by that dividend policy will gravitate to the firm. In a large, publicly held firm this will tend to happen.[6]

But one should not infer that the clientele effect allows management to change a dividend policy without repercussions. Stockholders with various investment objectives do not gravitate from the stock of one firm to another without friction that may involve considerable risk to management. For example, Company Z for many years had been engaged in a relatively stable industry requiring low capital investment. Throughout these years it paid high and stable dividends, thus attracting a clientele of income-motivated investors. Recently the firm has been evolving into a high-technology industry. Its earnings are becoming more volatile, and its capital investment requirements are increasing substantially. Management therefore is considering changing its dividend policy from the payment of high and stable dividends to the payment of relatively low and unstable ones, a policy more suitable to the firm's internal needs.

This should lead to a change in its stockholder clientele to growth-motivated investors who are willing to assume higher risks. But this change may not go smoothly. Drastic reduction of the dividend may be interpreted to mean, "Something is wrong at Company Z." Investors, believing that its

[6]Miller and Modigliani used both the information content and clientele effect to support their indifference theory of dividends. They explained market reaction to changes in dividends as being solely the reflection of information content rather than evidence that stockholders place a higher value on one dividend policy than another. Then they used the clientele effect to support their contention that stockholders in general were indifferent to dividend policy because particular segments of them would gravitate to holding stocks in firms with dividend policies satisfying their needs. (Miller and Modigliani, "Dividend Policy.")

earning power might be permanently impaired and recognizing that the new dividend payments will not satisfy their needs for current income, may sell their stock in droves. Thus, for a few months the price of Company Z stock may decline drastically.

During this period management may run the serious risk of a takeover attempt. Someone could accumulate the stock at a low price and appeal for the votes of the remaining unhappy stockholders on the promise to restore the dividend to its previous level if control is achieved and new management installed. Eventually, if no such takeover happens, growth-motivated, risk-taking investors will be attracted to Company Z stock as the brokerage houses gradually shift Company Z from a "sell" recommendation on their income stock lists to a "buy" recommendation on their growth stock lists. The market price of the stock ultimately should recover as the result of this new demand.

In summary, there will be a risky period during which the graph of the market price of Company Z stock will be forming a V. Management may be reluctant to bear the risk and suffer sleepless nights as the bottom of that V is approached. The change in dividend policy may be successful. Or management may lose a takeover battle and find themselves out in the street.

Alternative practical dividend policies

Possible alternative dividend policies are almost infinite. A firm's management must carefully select one to encompass consideration of both its internal needs and those of its stockholders. Several basic types of dividend policies have evolved and may be considered by managers seeking to establish one that meets the needs of their firm. Five basic types that will be discussed are (1) stable and occasionally increasing dividends per share, (2) stable dividends per share, (3) a stable payout ratio, allowing dividends to fluctuate with earnings, (4) "regular" and occasional "extra" dividends, and (5) fluctuating dividends and payout ratios, reflecting internal investment needs relative to available earnings.

Stable and increasing dividends

Investors, particularly those who are income-motivated, prefer the security of being almost sure that they will receive at least a given dividend each year. Naturally, they will be happy if dividends are increased. But if dividends are reduced, their dissatisfaction probably will be reflected by reduction in the market price of the stock and possibly by attempts to remove management. Many firms adopt a dividend policy that will satisfy such stockholders. This policy is to maintain stable dividends per share unless permanent increases in earning power and ability to throw off cash allow dividends per share to be increased. Management increases dividends only when it is believed that the higher level can be maintained indefinitely. In other words, management seeks *never* to be forced to reduce the dividend. If the market has faith that such a policy will be carried out, it probably will value the stock higher than otherwise, because the stockholders' risk of receiving future dividends is believed to be minimal.

For example, Filmore Corporation's earnings per share followed a general uptrend from 1967 through 1982 but was subject to occasional downward fluctuations, as shown in Table 22–2. Management believes that retention of 50 to 60 percent of annual earnings is sufficient to provide the equity financing required for capital investments. Therefore, it strives to maintain a payout ratio roughly in the range of 40 to 50 percent. But it has some financial flexibility to allow temporary debt financing in years when either capital investment requirements may be unusually great or earnings may be temporarily depressed. It paid stable annual dividends of $1 per share each year from 1967 through 1970 as earnings gradually increased from $2 to $3.10 per share.

Table 22–2 Earnings and dividends per share—Filmore Corporation
Stable and increasing dividend policy

Year	Earnings per share	Dividends per share
1967	$2.00	$1.00
1968	2.37	1.00
1969	2.80	1.00
1970	3.10	1.00
1971	3.68	1.50
1972	2.92	1.50
1973	3.25	1.50
1974	1.40	1.50
1975	2.63	1.50
1976	3.82	1.50
1977	4.12	1.50
1978	4.39	2.00
1979	3.40	2.00
1980	3.18	2.00
1981	4.27	2.00
1982	5.15	2.00

Early in 1971 management was convinced that the higher level of about $3 per share earnings would be maintained, so it increased the annual dividend to $1.50 per share. Earnings per share dipped slightly to $2.92 in 1972 and drastically in 1974 to $1.40. Continuation of the $1.50 annual dividend in 1974 required postponing some capital investment projects and borrowing to finance others. Management, believing the drop in earnings to be temporary, continued to pay the established dividend. Their faith in the future proved well founded, and earnings increased to $4.12 per share by 1977. To this point they did not increase the dividend.

In early 1978 management estimated that earnings would probably amount to around $4 per share in the future, so they increased the dividend to $2 per share. These dividend payments were continued through 1982. At their December 1982 meeting, when it was evident that the year's earnings would exceed $5 per share, the directors decided to wait another year before adjusting the dividend. Filmore's management never wants to be in the position of having to backtrack after sending a signal to the market that the firm's capability of paying dividends had permanently increased.

Many publicly held firms seek to follow this type of dividend policy. But not all can. Its successful execution depends upon maintaining both an upward trend in earnings per share and sufficient financial flexibility that fluctuating internal capital requirements can sometimes be financed from external sources.

Stable dividends per share

If the fluctuations in a firm's earnings per share are relatively moderate and there is no pronounced trend in its earnings, a policy of paying stable annual dividends may be appropriate. It is much superior to maintaining a stable payout ratio because the latter would require dividend reductions in about half of the years. Other things being equal, the market probably will value a stock higher if its dividends are expected to remain stable than if its dividends fluctuate. Stockholders' uncertainty regarding the expectation of future dividends is reduced. If a dividend is well protected by higher and relatively stable earnings and cash flows, the stock eventually will be traded almost as if it were a bond with equal earnings and cash flow coverage. The classic historical example of such a policy is that which was followed by AT&T from 1922 to 1958. The annual dividend was $9 throughout that period, and the stock was referred to in Wall Street as "the largest bond issue in America that is printed on stock certificates."

For an example of a stable dividend policy, refer to Table 22–3. Eldorado Corporation had relatively stable earnings per share from 1967 through 1982. As its internal investment requirements were modest, it could afford to pay out about 70 percent of earnings in dividends on the average. Eldor-

Table 22–3 Earnings and dividends per share—Eldorado Corporation
Stable dividend policy

Year	Earnings per share	Dividends per share
1967	$2.00	$1.50
1968	2.18	1.50
1969	2.39	1.50
1970	2.05	1.50
1971	1.68	1.50
1972	2.12	1.50
1973	2.58	1.50
1974	1.27	1.50
1975	1.30	1.50
1976	1.88	1.50
1977	2.46	1.50
1978	2.83	1.50
1979	2.47	1.50
1980	1.72	1.50
1981	2.51	1.50
1982	1.81	1.50

ado maintained annual dividend payments of $1.50 per share throughout the period. Earnings averaged about $2.14 but ranged from a high of $2.83 in 1978 to a low of $1.27 in 1974.

In both 1974 and 1975 dividend payments exceeded earnings. If the dividend had been reduced in those years, say to $1, the market price of Eldorado stock probably would have fallen drastically. The investing public had become accustomed to the $1.50 annual dividend, and its reduction would have been interpreted as indicating that management considered the reduced earnings to be permanent. The managerial risk of continuing the stable dividend rate at such a time is that, if the reduced level of earnings should turn out to be permanent, the firm would gradually deplete its liquidity by paying out cash it could not spare. Then, when and if this reality had to be faced, the dividend would have to be eliminated entirely and this would precipitate a real crash in the market for Eldorado's stock (as in the Con Ed experience mentioned earlier).

Stable payout ratio

A firm might establish a policy of paying a constant percentage of earnings in dividends. For example, if Jarco, Incorporated, adhered strictly to a stable payout ratio, its annual dividends would be those shown in

Table 22–4 Earnings and dividends per share—Jarco, Incorporated
Stable payout ratio of 60 percent

	(1)	(2) Dividends per share	(3)
Year	Earnings per share	60% payout ratio	Adjusted to stable and increasing
1967	$2.00	$1.20	$1.20
1968	2.43	1.46	1.50
1969	2.66	1.60	1.50
1970	2.42	1.45	1.50
1971	3.12	1.87	1.90
1972	3.19	1.91	1.90
1973	3.64	2.18	1.90
1974	1.90	1.14	1.90
1975	2.10	1.86	1.90
1976	3.13	1.89	1.90
1977	3.47	2.08	2.00
1978	3.61	2.17	2.00
1979	3.18	1.91	2.00
1980	2.91	1.75	2.00
1981	4.26	2.56	2.50
1982	4.65	2.79	2.50

column 2 of Table 22–4. Since this stable payout ratio would come to be expected by its stockholders, any deviation from it might lead to suspicion that the reported earnings per share were unrealistic or at least not sustainable. If in 1981, for example, when reported earnings increased from $2.91 to $4.26, the dividend were increased from $1.75 to only $2.00 (rather than $2.56, which is 60 percent of earnings), the market price could be adversely affected. Investors might suspect that the reported earnings were inflated by either unusual transactions or possibly accounting practices that did not reflect the true economic earnings perceived by management.

The principal objection to strict adherence to a stable dividend payout ratio is that, as earnings fluctuate, dividends must be reduced in some years. In Jarco's case, dividends would be reduced in 1970, 1974, 1979, and 1980. These reductions might adversely affect the market price of Jarco stock. Furthermore, stockholders would recognize the uncertainty of the amount of dividends expected to be received each year. This uncertainty probably would be reflected by the market's valuation of the stock at the lower price than if stable dividends were expected. For these reasons few corporations adhere strictly to a stable dividend payout ratio.

However, many firms set a benchmark target payout ratio (or range), deviating from this target as appropriate to achieve relatively stable dollar dividends or stable and occasionally increasing ones. This policy is illustrated by the dividends shown in column 3 of Table 22–4. Jarco's management is using a target payout ratio of 60 percent of earnings, but adjusting the actual dividends paid to achieve stable and occasionally increasing dividends. This policy probably would have a favorable influence upon the market price of the stock by reducing the uncertainty of the dollar amounts of dividend payments and avoiding reduction of dividends in years when earnings were temporarily depressed.

Regular and extra dividends

A few firms that have relatively unstable earnings and/or capital investment requirements label their dividends "regular" and "extra." This policy recognizes the information content of dividends. The regular dividend is set at a level that management believes can be maintained regardless of fluctuations in earnings and capital investment requirements. Then, in years when additional cash is available because earnings are exceptionally high or capital investment requirements are not pressing, an extra dividend is declared at year-end. For example, General Motors paid regular dividends of 85¢ per quarter from 1966 through 1976 but paid, in addition to the 85¢ quarterly dividend, extra dividends in several years, including $2.15 in the fourth quarter of 1976. Such a policy sends the clear message to investors that regular dividends are expected to be sustained but that the extra dividend should not be counted on in the future. This labeling of dividends is designed to dampen the downward market fluctuation when the extra dividend must be reduced or eliminated.

Fluctuating dividends and payout ratios

If the residual theory of dividends were strictly adhered to, both the dollar amounts of dividends and the payout ratio would fluctuate. These fluctuations would result both from changing earnings and differing internal capital investment requirements each period. An example of the dividends that would result from following this policy was developed early in this chapter and illustrated in Table 22–1.

Such a policy would not be practical for most publicly held corporations. But strict adherence to the residual theory may be appropriate for many small, closely held firms. In such a firm, the corporate form is simply a vehicle by which one or few owner-managers organize their business. If the owners are financially self-sufficient, either because they draw stable salaries as officers or because they are private capitalists with their investment in this firm being only one of several sources of income, a dividend policy of paying out widely fluctuating dividends only at times when the cash can be spared might be highly appropriate.

The basic test in the closely held firm is, "Would our utility be maximized by reinvesting the net cash inflows in our corporate 'pocket' or by withdrawing the cash and putting it in our personal pockets?" The dividend decision, in turn, rests upon analysis of the capital investment opportunities within the corporation versus personal investment opportunities and/or personal utility of spending the money, perhaps taking a vacation or buying a new home. Of course, personal income taxes incurred on the dividends received must be considered. If the present values of the reinvestment opportunities within the firm exceed the risk-adjusted cost of capital after fully considering the personal opportunities available, then dividends should not be paid. Conversely, if the value of the personal opportunities exceeds that available within the firm, then the owner-managers should withdraw the excess cash in dividends.

This dividend policy does not receive much publicity, but it is both theoretically sound and widely practiced by small, closely held corporations. The owner-managers of such corporations do not have to consider the external factors related to satisfaction of outside stockholders.

Dividend payment procedures

Dividends may be *declared* only *by the board of directors.* The chief financial officer advises the board regarding dividend policy and often recommends the specific amounts of dividends to be declared. Dividends usually are paid quarterly, but the period is flexible, varying among firms from monthly to annually.

Terminology and sequence

There are a few terms and procedures peculiar to dividend payments.

Declaration At the conclusion of the directors' meeting at which a dividend has been declared, the financial press will be notified. A typical dividend announcement will read, "On August 12 the directors of Marmor Corporation declared the quarterly dividend of 75 cents per share payable to holders of record on August 31. The dividend will be paid September 15." At the time a dividend is declared, the firm will become liable for its payment. If Marmor has 1 million shares outstanding, the accounting entry will be:

	Dr.	Cr.
Retained Earnings	750,000	
Dividends Payable		750,000

Date of record This dividend will be paid to the stockholders appearing on the stock record at the close of business on August 31.[7] Beginning four business days before the date of record the stock will be traded *ex-dividend.* This four-day period is required by the stock exchanges to provide time for completing transfers and recording ownership of shares. Marmor stock will begin trading ex-dividend when the exchange opens August 27. Thus, a stockholder who purchased shares on or after August 27 will not receive the dividend. The dividend on the stock that he or she purchased will go to the former holder who sold it. All other things being equal, the market price of the stock will drop by the amount of the dividend, 75 cents in this case, when trading opens on the ex-dividend date.

Payment On September 15, dividend checks will be mailed to the stockholders of record of August 31. The accounting entry at this time will be:

	Dr.	Cr.
Dividends Payable	750,000	
Cash		750,000

The net effect of the dividend declaration and payment is to reduce both cash and retained earnings by the amount of the dividend, $750,000.

Dividend reinvestment plans

During the past decade many large, publicly held firms have instituted dividend reinvestment plans (DRP's) by which its stockholders may elect to have their dividends withheld and used to purchase additional shares for them. At this writing more than half of the companies whose stock is listed on the New York Stock Exchange provide this service. These plans are of two basic types, (1) those in which the dividend-paying corporation turns over the withheld dividends to a trustee, who in turn purchases stock in the open market for the participants in the plan and (2) those in which the withheld dividends are used to purchase newly issued stock from the corporation.

Under the first type of DRP, the stockholder benefits from the large block purchases made by the trustee at lower brokerage fees per share than would be paid by directly purchasing a small odd lot of the stock. These lower brokerage fees are passed on to the stockholders; usually the corporation pays the trustee for its services. Note that this type of plan does not

[7]The stock record is kept by the *Registrar and Transfer Agent,* which usually is the trust department of a major bank located in the city where the principal trading in the stock occurs.

raise any new equity funds for the firm. But it probably does slightly increase demand for the stock in the secondary market, thus tending to support its market price.

The second type of DRP may provide a significant source of additional equity capital to the firm. It is estimated that in 1979 one fourth of all new equity capital raised by large corporations was obtained through dividend reinvestment. In many cases the corporation offers a discount, commonly 3 to 5 percent, on such stock purchases. This discount roughly compensates for the flotation costs that would be incurred if the firm marketed new issues of stock through the conventional investment banking process. This type of DRP has been particularly useful to the capital-intensive public utility firms by reducing both the number and size of their conventional public offerings of common stock.

The stockholder who elects to reinvest his or her dividends from an industrial corporation through either type of DRP still has to pay income taxes as if those dividends had been received in cash. Since 1981 an exception has been provided for public utility firms' DRPs. The reinvesting stockholder may exclude from taxation up to $750 ($1,500 for a joint return) annually.

Summary

This chapter discussed dividend policy and its counterpart, earnings retention policy. Management, in pursuing its basic goal of maximizing the value of the common stock in the long run, seeks an optimal balance between paying dividends that will support the market value of the stock and retaining earnings that when reinvested will contribute to growth.

To provide a backdrop for discussion of practical dividend policy considerations, the three theories of dividends were outlined. The residual theory holds that dividends should be the residue of the internal capital investment process. Cash that is left over after financing required internal investments should be paid out in dividends. The indifference theory claims that investors are (or should be) indifferent to the payment of dividends. Therefore dividend policy is irrelevant to the value of the stock. The bird-in-the-hand theory holds that dividend policy is indeed relevant: investors value a certain dividend more highly than retained earnings with uncertain future benefits.

But in the real world, no single theory provides a satisfactory guide to dividend policy. Many practical considerations influence or constrain the payment of dividends. Legal constraints prohibit the payment of dividends if the firm is insolvent or if legal capital would be impaired. The Internal Revenue Code may induce dividend payments by providing a surtax on unjustifiable retention of earnings. A firm's bond indenture, term loan agreement, lease, or preferred stock contract may limit common stock dividends. Internal influences upon dividend policy include availability of cash, capital investment opportunities, stability of earnings and cash generation, availability and cost of funds, and control considerations.

The stockholders own the corporation. To satisfy them, dividend policy must recognize their investment motivations, income tax status, propensity to bear risk, and, in some cases, legal limitations on the securities they may hold. The information content of dividend payments must be understood. Changes in dividends send signals to the market regarding the economic health of the firm. These signals may materially affect the stock price. The clientele effect is the tendency of investors to gravitate to holding stocks adhering to dividend policies that satisfy their investment motivations. A major change in dividend policy will lead to a change in a firm's stockholder clientele. Such a transition may entail high risks to management.

Five basic types of practical dividend policies may be examined in determining the policy appropriate to a particular firm. These are (1) stable and occasionally increasing dividends, (2) stable dividends, (3) stable payout ratio, allowing dividends to fluctuate with earnings, (4) regular and occasional extra dividends, and (5) fluctuating dividends and payout ratios reflecting internal investment needs relative to available earnings. The first policy, or the second if earnings are stable, usually is sought by publicly held firms if the influential considerations are compatible. A payout ratio range often is related to it. Dividend reinvestment plans may be provided to facilitate reinvestment in the stock by holders electing to do so. The fifth policy, strictly adhering to the residual theory of dividends, may be appropriate for a closely held firm if its stockholders are financially self-sufficient.

Questions

1. What is a dividend? Who has the power to declare a dividend? When does a stock begin trading *ex-dividend?* Why?

2. How does dividend policy relate to management's responsibility to maximize the wealth of the firm's stockholders in the long run?

3. Explain the logic underlying the *residual theory* of dividends. Why is it often not feasible for a publicly held firm to execute a dividend policy based literally upon the residual theory?

4. Explain the logic underlying the *indifference theory* of dividends. Upon what critical assumptions is the indifference theory based?

5. Explain the logic of the *bird-in-the-hand theory* of dividends. What assumption regarding risk (uncertainty) is inherent in the bird-in-the-hand theory?

6. What are the principal legal and contractual constraints on the payment of dividends?

7. Explain the interrelationship between a firm's growth policy and its dividend policy. Assuming the same rate of sales growth, which industrial firm would tend to have the highest dividend payout ratio: X Corporation, a capital intensive firm with a low operating asset turnover, or Y Corporation, a firm with low capital-intensity and a high operating asset turnover? Explain your choice.

8. Why would a small, closely held firm with very limited access to the money and capital markets adopt a dividend policy based upon the residual theory?

9. If you were an investor in a high income tax bracket, what dividend policy would you prefer to be followed by a firm in which you held a large block of common stock? Why? How would your preference differ if you were the investment officer responsible for managing the endowment funds of your university? Why?

10. What is the *clientele effect*? What risk does management take in modifying a firm's dividend policy with the expectation that the stockholder clientele will change to adapt to the new policy?

11. Explain how the payout ratios of U.S. corporations generally would be affected by each of the following changes: (Consider each independently.)

   a. Elimination of taxation of capital gains.
   b. A decrease in the personal income tax on ordinary income.
   c. A general decline in investment opportunities of business firms.
   d. A decline in interest rates.

12. A director of a public utility company advocating a reduction in his firm's dividend stated, "Because the cost of retained earnings is less than the cost of new common stock, it does not make sense to pay dividends when we have to sell additional common stock to the public to finance our equity requirements." Evaluate this statement.

13. Last year the Chatham Corporation, which had incurred an operating loss because of a protracted strike, borrowed money to continue paying dividends to its common stockholders. Evaluate this action. Would your answer be the same if Chatham had incurred the loss because it had lost its largest customer? Explain why or why not.

14. A dividend decision is "the other side of the coin" of a financing decision. Explain.

Problems

1. On July 8, the board of directors of the Americal Corporation declared a quarterly dividend of $1 per share payable to common stockholders of record on July 20. The dividend will be paid August 1. The firm has 500,000 shares of common stock outstanding. Prior to this dividend declaration, pertinent balance sheet accounts were:

Cash	$ 1,400,000
Dividends payable	0
Retained earnings	14,700,000

a. What accounting entries are made on July 8?
b. When will the stock begin trading ex-dividend?
c. What accounting entries will be made August 1, when the dividends are paid?
d. What will be the effect of the dividend upon (1) current assets, (2) net working capital, (3) total assets, and (4) stockholders' equity?

2. The common stockholders' equity accounts of the Borkrum Company are:

Common stock ($10 par value)	$4,000,000
Additional paid-in capital	1,300,000
Retained earnings	800,000
Total equity	$6,100,000

Borkrum has no preferred stock outstanding. Earnings after taxes during the past year were $300,000 (included in retained earnings). Legal capital in the state in which Borkrum is incorporated is defined as all paid-in capital.

a. What is the largest dividend per share that Borkrum could legally pay?
b. If Borkrum has $200,000 cash in excess of its working cash requirements, what is the largest dividend per share it can pay without borrowing?
c. If Borkrum's payout ratio is 60 percent, what dividend per share will be paid?
d. If Borkrum pays a dividend of 40¢ per share, what will be the effect on its (1) cash and (2) retained earnings accounts?

3. Catalin Corporation's earnings per share during a 10-year period were:

Year	Earnings per share
1	$1.64
2	1.92
3	2.15
4	1.90
5	2.30
6	2.67
7	2.53
8	3.12
9	3.37
10	3.05

a. If Catalin rigidly followed a policy of paying out 60 percent of annual earnings in dividends, what would its dividend per share have been in each of these years?

b. What market considerations argue against strict adherence to the above policy?

c. The shortcomings of the dividend policy in *(a)* may be overcome by adopting a policy of paying stable and occasionally increasing dividends. Show the annual dividends that would be paid under such a policy, focusing upon a 60 percent target payout ratio and keeping within a range of 50 percent to 70 percent.

4. Delmar Corporation's earnings per share over the past eight years were:

Year	Earnings per share
1	$ .82
2	1.03
3	.68
4	1.10
5	− .30
6	1.26
7	1.64
8	1.47

Determine the annual dividend per share under each of the following dividend policies:

a. A constant payout ratio of 50 percent.

b. Pay 60 cents per share and increase to 60 percent of earnings whenever such a dividend would exceed 60 cents.

c. Pay 60 percent of earnings whenever earnings are greater than $1 per share.

d. Pay a regular dividend of 50 cents and an extra dividend equal to half of any excess annual earnings over $1 per share.

Comment on each of the above dividend policies.

5. Exor Corporation requires $2 million (in excess of depreciation) to increase its plant capacity this year. Management wishes to maintain the firm's 40 percent long-term debt to total capital structure ratio and its dividend policy of paying out 30 percent of earnings in dividends. If earnings after taxes this year are $800,000, how much external equity financing must be obtained? If Exor were to retain all earnings, how much external equity financing would be required? (Assume that Exor did not hold excess cash at the beginning of the year.)

6. Francisco Corporation will require $5 million this year to finance capital investment projects. It can borrow $2 million of the required funds. The remaining $3 million must be generated internally. Depreciation charges will be $800,000 and earnings after taxes are estimated at $3.3 million. What is the maximum amount that Francisco can pay out in dividends this year?

7. The Gaylor Corporation estimates the following aftertax net income and capital investment requirements (in excess of depreciation) for the next four years:

Year	Net income	Capital investments
1	$5.0 million	$2.2 million
2	4.0	3.0
3	5.8	4.0
4	6.3	3.8

Gaylor has 2 million shares of common stock outstanding and currently pays annual dividends of $1.50 per share.

a. If Gaylor strictly follows the residual theory of dividends, what will be its dividends per share in each of the next four years?

b. If Gaylor continues to pay annual dividends of $1.50 per share, how much external financing will be required each year?

c. If the firm maintains a 60 percent dividend payout ratio, how much external financing will be required each year?

Appendix 22–A—Noncash dividends

In Chapter 22 we were concerned only with cash dividends. These, of course, are by far the most prevalent. However, dividends may be paid in the form of stock, or the stock might be split (which is similar to payment of a stock dividend), or occasionally a property dividend is paid by distributing some asset other than cash. These noncash dividends will now be discussed.

Small stock dividends

A *stock dividend* is the payment to stockholders of additional shares of common stock (rather than cash). For example, Maxwell Corporation has 1 million shares of capital stock outstanding. If it paid a 10 percent stock dividend, each stockholder would receive one new share for each 10 held. Mary Martin, the holder of 100 shares, would receive 10 additional shares. But would she really receive anything of value?

Prior to the stock dividend distribution, Mary owned 1/10,000 of the common stock equity of Maxwell (100 shares/1,000,000 shares). After the stock dividend she still owns exactly 1/10,000 of this equity (110 shares/1,100,000 shares). Nothing tangible has been taken from the Maxwell Corporation or received by Mary Martin. This was just a paper transaction from which Mary received a piece of paper, a 10-share stock certificate, to put in her safe deposit box. The common stock "pie" of Maxwell Corporation has been cut into a larger number of pieces, and her piece, as well as those of all of the other stockholders, has been ratably adjusted. If Maxwell stock closed at $55 per share on the day before it was traded ex-dividend and nothing happened overnight to influence its value, it would open the next morning ex-dividend at $50 per share. Mary's holding of 110 shares would be worth $5,500, exactly what her 100 shares were worth before. Thus, by and of itself, the stock dividend is meaningless.

But, in the longer run, the stock dividend may or may not influence the value of Mary's holding. If Maxwell had paid no cash dividends either before or after, the value of her holding should be unchanged. This would also be true if Maxwell had paid cash dividends of $5.50 per share before the stock dividend and reduced this to $5.00 at the time the stock dividend was paid. However, if the cash dividend *per share* remained the same (or were increased), the value of each stockholders' holding might increase, because the net effect would be an increase in cash dividends he or she would receive. It would increase if the bird-in-the-hand theory were applicable in this case.

Empirical studies have indicated that when stock dividends are not accompanied by effective increases in cash dividends, they usually have no lasting effect upon aggregate market values of the stock. However, when they are accompanied by effective increase in dividends, they usually do result in increased aggregate market values.[1]

[1] C. Austin Barker, "Evaluation of Stock Dividends," *Harvard Business Review*, July–August 1958, pp. 199–214; and Eugene Fama, Lawrence Fisher, Michael Jensen, and Richard Roll, "The Adjustment of Stock Prices to New Information," *International Economic Review*, February 1969, pp. 1–21.

Use In many cases stock dividends are used by growing firms whose internal capital investment requirements are such that management wishes to retain a relatively large portion of earnings. Low cash dividends per share will be paid accompanied by stock dividends of some 5 to 15 percent each year. The information content of such stock dividends is (1) that favorable investment opportunities exist within the firm, precluding the payment of large cash dividends and (2) that the firm's earnings are expected to increase at least sufficiently to allow continuation of the existing cash dividends per share on the increased number of shares and to maintain the market price per share.

If this strategy is successful, stockholders' wealth will be increased by their receiving increasing dollar amounts of dividends and holding larger numbers of shares valued by the market at either stable prices or, preferably, slightly increasing prices. The value of their shares will appreciate largely because of the increasing number of shares held rather than increasing market value per share.

Accounting treatment The accounting effect of a stock dividend is to permanently capitalize retained earnings equal to the market value of the shares issued. For example, payment of the 10 percent stock dividend by Maxwell Corporation in stock with a market value of $50 per share would have the following effects upon the stockholders' equity section of its balance sheet:

Before	
Common stock (1,000,000 shares @ $10 par)	$10,000,000
Additional paid-in capital	20,000,000
Retained earnings	40,000,000
Total common stock equity	$70,000,000
After	
Common stock (1,100,000 shares @ $10 par)	$11,000,000
Additional paid-in capital	24,000,000
Retained earnings	35,000,000
Total common stock equity	$70,000,000

Note that the retained earnings account, from which dividends may be paid, has been reduced by the number of shares times the *market value* per share of the stock paid out in dividends, $5 million. This amount has been permanently capitalized. Administrative costs of issuing stock dividends are relatively high and are not allowable expenses for tax purposes.

Stock splits or large stock dividends

Stock splits or large (over 25 percent) stock dividends normally are used for a reason different from that for the small stock dividends we have just discussed.[2] Although technically not identical, a 100 percent stock dividend has essentially the same effect as a 2-for-1 stock split. Such a large stock dividend will double the number of shares outstanding by issuing one additional share to the holder of each share outstanding. A 2-for-1 *stock split* will replace each existing share with two new shares, each having a par value half that of an old one. The ratio of a stock split, of course, may be 1½-for-1, 2-for-1, 5-for-1 or any other ratio decided upon.

Use The usual motive for a stock split or a large stock dividend is to lower the market price of the stock to a more favorable trading range. It is generally believed that a large portion of investors prefer to buy stock selling in the range from about $20 to $80.[3] Investors prefer to buy in round lots (multiples of 100 shares), and some may be priced out of the market by a stock selling above, say, $80. Therefore, a firm whose stock has risen to $90 or $100 per share might consider a 3-for-1 stock split (or a 200 percent stock dividend) to bring the market price down to around $30 to $35 per share. If this increases demand, the stock should sell after the split at a price slightly greater than one third of its previous market price, thus enhancing the aggregate value of the firm's common stock.

Stock splits also tend to result in dispersion of the stock among a larger number of holders. Management usually considers this advantageous both from the standpoint of control and greater breadth of the market, resulting in greater price stability.

Accounting treatment Accounting for a stock split differs from that for a stock dividend in that retained earnings are not permanently capitalized. For example, if Maxwell Corporation split its stock 2 for 1, only the number of shares and the par value would be changed as indicated below:

Before	
Common stock (1,000,000 shares @ $10 par)	$10,000,000
Additional paid-in capital	20,000,000
Retained earnings	40,000,000
Total common stock equity	$70,000,000
After	
Common stock (2,000,000 shares @ $5 par)	$10,000,000
Additional paid-in capital	20,000,000
Retained earnings	40,000,000
Total common stock equity	$70,000,000

[2]The New York Stock Exchange considers stock dividends exceeding 25 percent to be stock splits.

[3]Speculators, as differentiated from investors, seem to prefer lower-priced stocks, from perhaps 10 cents to a few dollars. This accounts for the popularity of the so-called "penny stocks" issued in great volume in recent years, particularly by oil and other mineral exploration firms.

Reverse stock splits Occasionally a firm whose stock has drifted down into the range of, say, $2 to $5 will make a *reverse stock split,* exchanging one new share for several old ones to increase the market price to a more respectable trading range. For example, if the market price of Jackson Corporation's stock is $4 per share, it might make a 1-for-6 reverse split. This should result in a market price of the new shares of about $24.

Often stock splits or reverse splits are made before a closely held firm "goes public." The investment bankers suggest the price at which the public offering would be most attractive. Then the stock is split (or reverse split) to achieve that price.

Property dividends

A property dividend is a dividend paid in *assets* other than cash. Although these are rarely used, there may be interesting and creative applications. In some cases a corporation may divest itself of stock held in another corporation by distributing the latter to its stockholders as a property dividend. For example, this was done by Du Pont when it was forced by an antitrust decision to divest itself of its General Motors stock.[4] Or dividends may be paid in the products of the firm. In 1981, Ranchers Exploration and Development Corporation, a gold mining firm, paid dividends in the form of gold bars. (Stockholders entitled to less than 2½ grams of gold were paid in cash based upon the current price of gold.) There have been cases in which small distilleries or wineries have distributed their products to stockholders as property dividends.

Questions

1. What is a stock dividend? By itself, does a stock dividend benefit the stockholder who receives it?

2. Why do some firms pay small stock dividends? How do the motives for paying a large stock dividend, say 200 percent, differ?

[4]The GM stock that would have been distributed to the Christiana Securities Corporation (a personal holding company of the Du Pont family) and to members of the Du Pont family had to be sold to outsiders, but the remainder of the GM stock was distributed as a property dividend to Du Pont stockholders.

3. What is a stock split? How does it differ from a large stock dividend? Why might a closely held corporation split its stock prior to going public?

4. Explain how stock dividends or stock splits might tend to maximize the market value of a firm's common stock.

Problems

1. The stockholders' equity accounts of the Penrose Corporation are as follows:

Common stock (100,000 shares @ $10 par)	$1,000,000
Additional paid-in capital	400,000
Retained earnings	2,000,000
Total equity	$3,400,000

The current market price of Penrose common stock is $42 per share.

a. Show the effects of a 5 percent stock dividend on the stockholders' equity accounts.

b. If Penrose's earnings per share are $4 before the stock dividend, what will they be after the dividend?

c. At what price will the stock sell when it goes ex-dividend, assuming that all other market factors are unchanged?

d. If you held 100 shares of Penrose common stock before the stock dividend, what will be the value of your holding after the dividend?

2. The stockholders' equity accounts of the Carlin Company are as follows:

Common stock (300,000 shares @ $10 par)	$ 3,000,000
Additional paid-in capital	2,000,000
Retained earnings	31,000,000
Total equity	$36,000,000

The current market price of the common stock is $110 per share.

a. Show the effects on the stockholders' equity accounts of a 2-for-1 stock split.

b. At what price will the stock sell after the stock split, assuming that all other market factors are unchanged?

c. Why would Carlin declare such a stock split?

3. The Reardon Trucking Company is planning to go public. The firm's capital structure consists of 100,000 shares of common stock, held entirely by the Reardon family. Current earnings are $23 per share. The investment

bankers suggest that the stock be split 20-for-1 and that the shares could be sold for about eight times earnings. At what market price per share can the stock be sold after the split? If the Reardon family wish to sell 40 percent of the stock and the flotation costs are 8 percent, how much will the family receive?

Part Six
Expansion and Contraction

Chapter 23 Mergers and Acquisitions

Although growth by itself is not the primary objective of the firm, it often is an important secondary one. Growth usually relates to achievement of the basic corporate goal, maximization of value of the common stock in the long run. Without the expectation of growth, it may be difficult or impossible to attract and hold the aggressive managerial personnel vital to success of the firm. Growth may be attained either internally or externally. Internal growth is achieved through the capital investment process which was discussed in Part IV, Chapters 11 through 15. External growth is accomplished through business combination, commonly known as merger or acquisition. Both types of growth have figured importantly in the development of nearly all major business corporations.

Historically, there have been several major waves of merger activity in the United States. The first, known as the trust movement, occurred near the end of the 19th century. This period was typified by John D. Rockefeller's formation of the Standard Oil Trust and included such other business combinations as the sugar, tobacco, and meat-packing trusts. The next wave took place during the prosperity of the 1920s. Both of these periods were characterized by combinations within particular industries, creating monopoly power. The "conglomerate" merger movement, which occurred largely in the 1960s, witnessed the rapid rise and subsequent fall of such firms as Litton Industries, LTV (then Ling-Temco-Vought), and Gulf & Western. Beginning about 1978, the present merger movement has been highlighted by large prestigious firms that make public tender offers to acquire other large firms. Among those have been Atlantic Richfield's acquisition of Anaconda, Standard Oil of Ohio's acquisition of Kennecott, U.S. Steel's of Marathon Oil, and Du Pont's acquisition of Conoco. For each of these large, highly publicized mergers, there have been hundreds of smaller ones.

In this chapter we shall first discuss synergism, the economic basis of business combination. Then, the various legal forms of combination, through merger, consolidation, and holding companies, will be treated. The rest of the chapter will deal with the financial analysis of proposed mergers, including valuation, "currency of exchange," establishing the ratio of exchange, and methods of acquisition. Appendix A will describe the "merger game" by which the illusion of growth may be created, and Appendix B will discuss accounting treatment of mergers. Unless otherwise noted, the terms *merger* and *acquisition* will be used synonymously to include all legal forms of business combination. Primary emphasis will be placed on the standpoint of the acquiring firm, but many of the concepts also will be pertinent to the acquired firm.

Synergism—The economic basis

The nature of synergism is very simple. *Synergism* exists whenever the value of a combination is greater than the sum of the values of its parts. In other words, synergism is "2 + 2 = 5." But identifying synergism and evaluating it may be difficult; in fact, sometimes its implications may be very subtle. As broadly defined to include any incremental value resulting from business combination, synergism is the basic economic justification of merger. The incremental value may derive from increases in either operational or financial efficiency.[1]

Operating synergism

Operating synergism may result from economies of scale, some degree of monopoly (or monopsony) power, or increased managerial efficiency. The incremental value may be achieved by increasing sales volume in relation to assets employed (operating asset turnover), increasing profit margins, or decreasing operating risk. Although operating synergy usually is the result of either vertical or horizontal integration, some synergistic effects also may result from conglomerate growth or the integration of technology and/or personnel into a more efficient unit.

Vertical integration Vertical integration is the combination of functions along the chain of production and distribution between the raw materials and the ultimate consumer. For example, a vertically integrated oil company would engage in exploration, production of crude oil, refining, and marketing of petroleum products. An early classic case illustrating operating synergism achieved through vertical integration was the formation of U.S. Steel by J. P. Morgan, combining firms mining iron ore, limestone, and coal with steel ingot producers, rolling mills, and some steel fabricators. Such a combination increases control of supply and market, each producer along the chain having a captive supplier and market for its products. This type of combination among large firms may achieve an unacceptable degree of monopoly (or monopsony) power. Federal antitrust laws are designed to prevent this.[2] In many cases, particularly those involving small firms holding

[1]We are using a very broad definition, including both operating and financial synergism. Some authors use a narrow definition encompassing only operating synergism. Others identify financial, marketing, technological, organizational, and productive synergy.

[2]The principal antitrust laws are the Sherman Act of 1890, the Clayton Act of 1914, and the Celler Amendment of the Clayton Act (1950). These laws make it illegal to combine firms if the result would be the substantial lessening of competition. They are enforced by the Antitrust Division of the Department of Justice and the Federal Trade Commission.

only a minor share of the market, vertical integration still may be achieved through combination without creating potential antitrust problems.

Horizontal integration Horizontal integration involves the combination of firms engaged in the same line of business. For example, merging one supermarket chain into another is a horizontal merger. Operating synergy may be achieved by eliminating duplicate facilities, increasing marketing efficiency, or simply acquiring some degree of monopoly power in the market. Combination of two local or regional supermarket chains might result in the elimination of one or more distribution warehouses, reduction in the number of buyers required, and perhaps make it possible to purchase more items in carload lots, achieving cost savings. Advertising and sales promotion may be consolidated to achieve further savings.

Perhaps, if the merged firm controlled a large share of the market in the city or region, its profits could be increased through the exercise of monopoly power. If the latter were true, legal action probably would be taken to block the merger. But if not, such a merger might achieve considerable operating synergism, benefiting both stockholders and customers.

Conglomerate growth Conglomerate growth is achieved through a merger of firms engaged in unrelated lines of business. For example, a liquor producer might acquire an oil and coal company (as Seagram unsuccessfully attempted to acquire Conoco in 1981). In the conglomerate merger period of the 1960s, some firms acquired dozens of companies, each having no discernible operating relationship to the others. At first glance it would appear that such a combination could not provide any operating synergism: admittedly, synergism would be relatively small compared to that of most vertical or horizontal combinations. But if the operating profit patterns of the various acquired firms differ as economic changes occur, a portfolio effect might be achieved. This would make the operating risk of the combination smaller than the risks of the firms standing by themselves. If risk is reduced while the combined cash flows are unchanged, the value of the combination may exceed that of its individual components. In this sense operating synergy may result from conglomerate growth.[3]

There also may be some favorable effects resulting from flexibility of personnel and transfer of technology, even though the firms appear to be engaged in different lines of business. For example, the acquisition of Miller Brewing and 7-Up by Philip Morris allowed a synergistic transfer of mass-marketing capability.[4]

[3]The portfolio effect upon risk and value of aggregations of real assets was discussed in Chapter 14. Both the concepts and the questions regarding their validity in practice as discussed there may be applied to conglomerate mergers.

[4]One might question whether these acquisitions by Philip Morris were conglomerate mergers. This is a matter of semantics. Philip Morris could be considered in the tobacco industry or, more broadly, in the industry of producing and marketing consumer products through the use of mass-marketing techniques.

Other operating synergism Sometimes a firm may acquire another to obtain patents, copyrights, technical proficiency, marketing skills, specific fixed assets, customer relationships, or managerial personnel. Operating synergism occurs when these assets, which are intangible, may be combined with the existing assets and organization of the acquiring firm to produce an incremental value. Although that value may be difficult to appraise in dollar terms, it may be the primary motive behind the acquisition. For example, Coca-Cola acquired Duncan Foods primarily to obtain the services of Charles Duncan, a promising executive intended to be the future chief executive officer of Coca-Cola. After rising to the presidency, however, Duncan resigned as a result of policy differences. This demonstrates the risk entailed in such mergers.

Countersynergism Certain factors may oppose the synergistic effect contemplated from a merger. Often another layer of overhead costs and bureaucracy is added. Do the advantages outweigh this disadvantage? Sometimes the acquiring firm agrees to long-term employment contracts with the managers of the acquired firm. Such contracts often are beneficial but they may be the opposite. Personality or policy conflicts may develop that either hamstring operations or require buying out such contracts to remove personnel from positions of authority.

Particularly in conglomerate mergers, management of the acquiring firm simply may not have sufficient knowledge of the business to control the acquired firm adequately. Attempts to maintain control may induce resentment by personnel of the acquired firm. The resulting reduction of efficiency may eliminate expected operating synergy or even reduce the postmerger profitability of the acquired firm. The list of possible countersynergistic factors could go on endlessly; the point is that mergers do not always produce the expected results. Negative factors and the risks related to them also must be considered in appraising a prospective merger.

Financial synergism

As we are broadly interpreting the term, synergism may include financial advantages as well as operating ones. Among these are incremental values resulting from complementary internal funds flows, more efficient use of financial leverage, increased external financial capability, and income tax advantages.

Complementary internal funds flows Seasonal or cyclical fluctuations in funds flows sometimes may be reduced or eliminated by merger. If so, financial synergism results in reduction of working capital requirements of the combination compared to those of the firms standing alone. For example, Tennyson Sporting Goods Company, a maker of golf clubs, baseball, and tennis equipment, has to borrow about $3 million in late winter and spring to finance a buildup of inventories through April and to carry large receivables through June. Then, as the receivables are collected in the summer, Tennyson pays off its bank loans and develops excess cash totaling $2 million by October, when production is increased to build up inventories for the spring selling season. Tennyson seeks to acquire Alpine Ski Corporation, which has seasonal borrowing requirements peaking at $2 million in October and develops excess cash of about $2 million in the spring. If Tennyson were to acquire Alpine, its peak borrowing requirement would be reduced to about $1 million in late spring and early summer, and cash balances would be relatively stable through the rest of the year. This increase in efficiency of using working capital, by reducing the cost of seasonal financing and the risk of being able to obtain it, should result in increased value of the combined firm as compared to that of the two standing alone.

More efficient use of financial leverage Financial synergy may result from more efficient use of financial leverage. The acquiring firm may have little debt and wish to use the high debt of an acquired firm to lever earnings of the combination. Or the acquiring firm may borrow to finance an acquisition for cash of a low-debt firm, thus providing additional leverage to the combination. The financial leverage advantage must be weighed against the increased financial risk.

Increased external financial capability Many mergers, particularly those of relatively small firms into large ones, occur when the acquired firm simply cannot finance its operations. Typical of this situation is a small growing firm with expanding financial requirements. The firm has exhausted its bank credit and has virtually no access to long-term debt or equity markets. Sometimes the small firm has encountered operating difficulty, and the bank has served notice that its loans will not be renewed. In this type of situation, a large firm with sufficient cash and credit to finance the requirements of the smaller one probably can obtain a good buy by making a merger proposal to the small firm. The only alternative the small firm may have is to try to interest two or more larger firms in proposing merger to introduce competition into their bidding for the acquisition.

The smaller firm's situation might not be so bleak. It may not be threatened by nonrenewal of a maturing loan. But its management may recognize that continued growth to capitalize on its markets will require financing beyond its means. Although its bargaining position will be better, the financial synergy of the acquiring firm's strong financing capability may provide the impetus for the merger.

Sometimes the financing capability is possessed by the acquired firm. The acquisition of a cash-rich firm whose operations have matured may provide additional financing to facilitate growth of the acquiring firm. In some cases, the acquiring firm may be able to recover all or part of the cost of acquiring the cash-rich firm when the merger is consummated and the cash then belongs to it.

A similar motive explains the acquisition of a financial institution, which by nature of its operations has larger amounts of funds to invest, by an industrial firm seeking the use of some of those funds. Several industrial firms and conglomerates have acquired life insurance companies or finance companies, presumably motivated by this kind of financial synergism.

A merger also may be based upon the simple fact that the combination will make two small firms with limited access to the capital markets large enough to achieve that access on a reasonable basis. The improved financing capability provides the financial synergy.

Income tax advantages In some cases, income tax considerations may provide the financial synergy motivating a merger. For example, assume that firm A has earnings before taxes of about $1 million per year and firm B, now breaking even, has a loss carryforward of $2 million accumulated from unprofitable operations of previous years. The merger of A and B will allow the surviving corporation to utilize the loss carryforward, thereby eliminating income taxes in future periods, as shown in Table 23–1. In effect, such a merger will increase the net aftertax income of firm A by $400,000 (67 percent) for each of the next two years. The financial synergism reflects the fact that the combined firm can use the tax-loss carryforward whereas firm B might never be able to use it.[5] Operating losses may be carried forward up to 15 years whereas capital loss carryforwards are limited to 5 years.

Table 23–1 Advantage of merger utilizing tax-loss carryforward
($000)

	Year		
	1	2	3
Without merger			
Earnings before taxes	$1,000	$1,000	$1,000
Income taxes @ 40%	400	400	400
Net income to stockholders	$ 600	$ 600	$ 600
With merger			
Earnings before taxes	$1,000	$1,000	$1,000
Loss carryforward	1,000	1,000	-0-
Net taxable income	-0-	-0-	$1,000
Income taxes @ 40%	-0-	-0-	400
Net income to stockholders	$1,000	$1,000	$ 600

[5]Competent legal and tax advice should be obtained if a merger influenced by such tax considerations is contemplated. The IRS may require that the merger be economically justified on the basis of factors other than the utilization of a tax-loss carryforward. Otherwise its use may be nullified. This is a sensitive area of income tax law.

Other motives for merger

Mergers may be motivated by two other factors that perhaps should not be classified under synergism. These are the opportunity for an acquiring firm to obtain assets at a bargain price and the desire of stockholders of the acquired firm to increase the liquidity of their holdings.

"Purchase" of assets at bargain prices

Many mergers in recent years have been explained by the opportunity to acquire assets, particularly land, mineral rights, plant, and equipment, at lower cost than would be incurred if they were purchased or constructed at current market prices. During the late 70s and early 80s, market prices of many stocks have been considerably below the replacement cost of the assets they represent. Expanding firms considering constructing plants, developing mines, or buying equipment often have found that the desired assets could be obtained cheaper by acquiring a firm that already owned and operated the assets. Risk could be reduced because the assets were already in place and an organization of people knew how to operate them and market their products.

Many of these mergers have been financed by cash tender offers made to the acquired firm's stockholders at prices substantially above the current market. Even so, the assets have been acquired for less than their current costs of construction. The basic factors underlying this apparently have been inflation in construction costs not fully reflected in stock prices because of high interest rates and limited optimism (or downright pessimism) by stock investors regarding future economic conditions.

Stockholder liquidity

Where the acquired firm is a relatively small, closely held one, its stockholders may view a merger as a means of cashing in on their successful development of the firm. If they receive cash, they may then invest in a diversified portfolio of publicly traded securities or other investment media rather than having all their eggs in one basket. Similarly, if they accept publicly traded stock in the acquiring firm, they may easily liquidate all or part of that stock, according to their personal financial needs. This transformation of relatively frozen financial assets into liquid ones often appeals to such stockholders.

In addition, the stockholder-managers of the acquired firm may be offered attractive management contracts and/or seek the opportunity to rise to positions of greater responsibility in the acquired firm than would be possible within their small one.

Legal forms of combination

Most recent business combinations have been accomplished through merger. Other legal forms of combination are consolidation and the holding company.

Merger

A *merger* is a combination of two firms in which the acquiring firm continues in operation and the acquired firm ceases to exist. The assets and liabilities of the acquired firm are merged into the surviving firm. We shall use interchangeably the terms *acquiring* and *surviving firm* and the terms *acquired* and *target firm* in the remainder of this chapter. A merger may take the legal form of either a statutory merger or a purchase of assets (and often assumption of liabilities) of the target firm.

Statutory merger In a statutory merger, so called because it is executed under the statutes of the state of incorporation, the stock of the target firm is *directly exchanged* for stock of the acquiring firm, and the legal existence of the target firm automatically ceases. Although the legal form implies a stock-for-stock exchange, the acquiring firm may purchase the stock of the target for cash or by exchanging other securities and then, as the sole stockholder of the target, exchange the stock in a statutory merger.

Purchase of assets The acquiring firm might purchase the assets and, usually, assume the liabilities of the target firm. The purchase may be for cash or securities of the acquiring firm. After the purchase, the sole assets of the acquired firm are the cash and/or securities received in the exchange. After any liabilities not assumed by the acquiring firm are paid, the acquired firm is liquidated by distributing its assets (cash and/or securities of the acquiring firm) to its stockholders in a liquidating dividend. Then the acquired corporation is formally dissolved.

Regardless of the legal form used, holders of a stipulated majority, usually simple or two thirds, of the common stock of the acquired firm must approve the merger. In some cases, approval of preferred stockholders and/or creditors also may be required. Depending on its charter, approval of holders of a majority of the stock of the acquiring firm may or may not be required. In some states, minority stockholders of either firm may appeal to the courts if they object to the terms of the merger.[6]

Consolidation

A *consolidation* is the combination of two or more firms into a newly created corporation. For example, firms A and B are combined into a new firm C. This usually is accomplished by the exchange of the common shares of A and B for those of firm C. The assets and liabilities of A and B are transferred to C, and the old corporations, A and B, cease to exist.

Consolidation has not been very widely used in recent years. Its principal disadvantages, as compared to a merger, are that a new corporation must be formed, consent of a stated majority (usually simple or two-thirds) of the stockholders of each combining corporation is required, and there is no possibility of using "pooling of interests" accounting or utilizing tax-loss carryforwards.

The holding company

A *holding company* is a corporation that owns controlling interest in the common stock of one or more other companies. The *pure* holding company has no business operations of its own; its sole assets are securities of other corporations. American Electric Power and Texas Utilities are examples of pure holding companies. A *holding-operating* company is one that has operations of its own but also holds controlling interests in other operating companies. An example is AT&T, which operates the interstate long distance communications facilities but owns controlling interest in many subsidiaries such as Western Electric and "Baby Bell." Most major corporations are holding-operating companies in the sense that they hold the stock of foreign subsidiaries and some domestic ones, which are separately incorporated for convenience or economies in complying with state corporation, regulatory, or tax laws.

The holding company form of business combination differs from merger or consolidation with respect to the control of assets, financial leverage that can be obtained, risk of loss, and income taxation.

Control Through the use of the holding company, control of a larger aggregation of operating assets may be obtained with a smaller investment in common stock than by using other forms of business combination. Voting control of an operating firm does not require ownership of all of its common stock. Holding one share over 50 percent of the stock assures absolute

[6]Lawsuits often are instigated to delay or prevent the consummation of mergers. Sometimes these are protracted and expensive. In extreme cases, one of the firms may simply abandon the proposed merger in order to terminate the litigation.

control and, in firms whose stock is widely dispersed among diverse holders, sometimes a single holding of only 10, 15, or 25 percent of the stock will provide effective control. Maintaining control with a minority shareholding requires the proxy votes of enough outside stockholders to obtain a majority vote. These usually can be obtained as long as the outside stockholders are not antagonized by operating policies or results.

For example, a holding company may be able to maintain control of five operating companies, each with common equity valued at $10 million, with average holdings of 30 percent of their stock. If so, operating companies with common stock worth $50 million can be controlled by a holding company having an investment in their common stock of $15 million [.30 (5 × $10 million)]. This assumes that the capital structures of the operating companies and the holding company are comprised of all common stock equity.

If the capital structure of each operating company includes 50 percent debt, their total assets of $100 million [(5 × $10 million)/.50] may be controlled by the holding company with only a $15 million investment in their common stock. If, in turn, the holding company is financed by 50 percent debt, then a $7.5 million investment by its common stockholders will control $100 million of operating assets. Finally, if a group of its stockholders hold 50 percent plus one share of the holding company's stock, their investment of $3.75 million will control the $100 million operation.

Carried to the extreme, as occurred in the heyday of the public utility holding companies in the 20s, several layers of intermediate holding companies, each capitalized in part by debt, allows the individuals owning a controlling interest in the top holding company to magnify still further their control of operating assets. One such holding company in the late 20s utilized seven layers of corporations, with five intermediate tiers of holding companies between the operating electric utility companies and the top holding company.[7]

Financial leverage Extremely high leverage may be obtained through the use of debt financing by both operating companies and holding companies, particularly where employed in a pyramid structure. Each partially debt-financed company in this structure multiplies the leverage as the earnings stream rises through the holding companies. The net effect is that a small change in earnings per share (EPS) of the operating companies results in a large change in EPS of the top holding company. For that reason, in the Great Depression of the early 30s most of the pyramided holding compa-

[7]The financial debacle of the Great Depression in the early 30s led to the passage of the Public Utility Holding Company Act of 1935, which dismantled these holding company pyramids and limited the future use of this device in the public utility industry to one intermediate holding company, the use of which must be justified on economic grounds.

This type of use of holding companies is very rare today. In many cases the present holding companies own all or nearly all of the stock of their operating subsidiaries. Intermediate holding companies and high debt ratios of holding companies are rarely employed.

nies failed because they could not service their debt, even though downward fluctuation in earnings per share of their operating companies was only slight.

Risk Technically, a holding company is not liable for the financial obligations of an operating company it controls. The operating company is a separate corporation with limited liability; therefore, the holding company owning its stock is protected if the operating company fails. Lenders to operating subsidiaries, however, often require the guarantee of their loans by the holding company to eliminate this limitation of liability. Even without such guarantees, a holding company's reputation in the financial markets probably would be ruined if it refused to support its operating subsidiaries in time of financial difficulty.

Taxation A holding company owning less than 80 percent of the common stock of an operating company is subject to federal income tax at its regular incremental rate on only 15 percent of dividends received from the operating company. Although this tax amounts to only about 7 percent of the dividends, it still constitutes an extra layer of taxation compared to other forms of business combination. If the holding company owns 80 percent or more of the stock in an operating company, a consolidated income tax return may be filed. This eliminates intercompany dividends; therefore, no tax is paid on them.

Neither consolidations nor holding companies presently are very widely used in new business combinations; the remainder of this chapter will refer only to mergers.

Financial analysis of a proposed merger

If Acme Enterprises is considering the acquisition of Merit Corporation, what is required of its financial analysts in appraising the feasibility of this merger, the terms that might be offered, and the method to be used in making this acquisition? The analysis will consist of four steps:

1. Estimate *(a)* the *value* of each firm, Acme and Merit, standing alone and *(b)* the value added by the acquisition, taking into account synergistic effects.
2. Determine the *currency of exchange* to be offered for Merit common stock.
3. Identify a feasible range of *ratios of exchange.* Various exchange ratios within this range will then be tested to estimate their effects upon post-merger dividends, earnings per share, and the market price of Acme common stock.

4. Choose the *method of acquisition* to be used, either to negotiate a friendly merger with Merit's management or to bypass them by making a hostile tender offer directly to the Merit stockholders.

As a starting point, some of the financial data regarding Acme Enterprises and Merit Corporation are shown in Table 23–2.

Table 23–2 Financial data
Acme Enterprises and Merit Corporation

	Acme	Merit
Total earnings ($000)	$60,000	$11,250
Common shares outstanding (000)	10,000	3,000
Earnings per share	$6.00	$3.75
Price/earning ratio	10×	8×
Market price per share	$60.00	$30.00
Book value per share	$45.00	$25.00
Dividends per share	$3.00	$2.00
Annual growth rate	7%	6%

Valuation—The key element

Valuation is the key element in appraising a merger because, in essence, something is being bought and the price must be right.

Value of target firm standing alone The first task will be to value the equity of Merit Corporation standing alone, probably on a per share of common stock basis. This will provide an understanding of how Merit's management and stockholders will view their alternative of *not* merging with Acme.

The *book value* of $25 per share probably will not be very meaningful for reasons previously discussed. It is the residue of an accounting process that may yield asset values and, therefore, equity values quite different from current economic values.

The current *market value* of Merit stock, $30 per share, may or may not provide a meaningful valuation depending upon the breadth, depth, and activity of the market. If Merit stock is dispersed among many thousands of holders and actively traded on a major stock exchange, then the market might be highly efficient in establishing a sound value. On the other hand, if the majority of Merit stock is firmly held by a small number of shareholders and inactively traded over-the-counter, the market value may be an unreliable indicator of the true value of the stock. Let us assume that the latter is true regarding Merit's stock. Now the task becomes rather difficult; some of the valuation theory developed earlier in this book must be utilized.

Fundamentally, the acquisition of Merit may be viewed like any capital investment Acme might consider. To estimate its value, *future cash flows* must be estimated and *discounted* at a rate reflecting the pure (riskless) interest rate plus a premium for risk. This was developed in Part IV, which dealt with capital investment decisions. First, the earnings available to the common stock of Merit Corporation in future years are estimated. Then these are adjusted to net cash flows by adding back depreciation and other noncash charges and subtracting any additional capital investments that would have to be made to maintain the estimated earnings.

The discount rate may or may not be Acme's estimated cost of equity capital. If Merit's operations are considered to be more risky than Acme's and/or Merit's capital structure is more highly leveraged, then the discount rate should be higher. Conversely, Merit's operations or capital structure might be less risky, justifying the use of a discount rate lower than Acme's estimated cost of equity capital.

Let us assume that such analysis results in a valuation of $105 million for the common equity of Merit, or $35 for each of its common shares.[8] This value provides an indication of the *minimum* price that might be considered in exchange for the Merit stock.

Value of acquiring firm standing alone If the exchange offer is expected to be made in cash or debt, Acme stock will not have to be evaluated. But if Acme common stock or any security convertible into it is to be the currency of exchange, then its stock value is pertinent. If the acquiring firm is large and its stock is actively traded, as is true of Acme, the current market price usually may be accepted as its current value. There are two reasons for this: (1) the market probably is quite efficient in determining this value, and (2) stockholders of the acquired firm may be confident that they could liquidate the stock received at approximately this value if they wish to do so. Assume that Acme's market value of $60 per share may be accepted. If these conditions did not hold, the stock of Acme standing alone would have to be valued using the same techniques as were required for Merit.

Value added to the surviving firm The synergistic effects of the merger then must be considered. Acme's marketing vice president believes that annual aftertax savings of $600,000 will result from consolidation of sales forces and advertising efforts. Another $500,000 after taxes can be saved by eliminating the financial vice president of Merit, whose duties will be assumed by Acme's finance office, and by consolidating accounting systems. The production manager believes that another $500,000 after taxes can be saved by utilizing some of Merit's excess capacity to produce parts for one of Acme's products.

[8]If earnings per share are expected to remain stable at the present level, and replacements and additions to assets are expected to equal noncash charges, then this valuation process can be greatly simplified. The earnings per share may be divided by an appropriate capitalization rate (which is identical to the discount rate) to determine the value per share of the stock. This is called *capitalized earnings value.*

Net aftertax synergistic savings, which will amount to $1,600,000 per year, increase incremental annual earnings associated with the acquisition from $11,250,000 to $12,850,000. This will add about $5 per share ($1,600,000/$11,250,000 × $35 = approx. $5) to the value of Merit stock, making it worth about $40 per share ($35 + $5) to Acme if Merit is merged. Acme's management also hopes that it may be able to increase Merit's growth rate to 7 percent, which will equal the premerger growth rate of Acme. But it has decided that this is too uncertain to consider in valuing the synergism.

Acme naturally would like to receive the benefit of the synergism. Therefore, its management probably will make an initial offer of about $35 per share, its estimate of Merit's stand-alone value and a premium of 16⅔ percent over the current market price of Merit stock. If necessary, this offer might be increased, but not beyond $40 per share, because that value would give Merit stockholders all of the benefit of the synergism and gain nothing for Acme. Thus, the *bargaining range* probably will be from $35 to $40 per share, or $105 million to $120 million for the firm. A merger based on less than $35 per share probably would not be acceptable to the Merit stockholders, and one at more than $40 per share would pay more for Merit than it is worth.

Currency of exchange

The merger offer might be for cash or for any of a variety of securities issued by the acquiring firm. These include debt securities such as bonds or notes, preferred stock, either straight or convertible, and common stock. "Sweeteners", such as warrants or payments contingent upon future performance of the acquired firm (which would become an operating division of the surviving firm), sometimes are included in the exchange package. On some occasions optional offers are made; for example, the stockholders of the target firm may be permitted to choose either cash or stock.

This portion of the analysis requires discerning the nature of the target firm's stockholders, the identity of the major stockholders, their tax positions, and their investment motivations. In essence, one seeks to identify what currency of exchange would appeal to a sufficient number of stockholders to gain their approval of the merger. The liquidity and capital structure of the acquiring firm and the effects of the merger upon its capital structure must be considered. If a cash offer is contemplated, does the acquiring firm have the cash or can it be obtained through borrowing on acceptable terms? If debt securities were to be issued, would the surviving firm be able to live with the resulting capital structure? If common stock were exchanged, what dilution or accretion would result?

Cash or debt securities The acquiring firm might offer cash or its debt securities, notes or bonds, in exchange for the target firm's common stock. Debt securities usually can be valued at their principal (face) amount. This assumes that the interest rate on the debt is comparable to the current interest rate on obligations of similar risk and maturity. If not, the current value of the debt must be used in developing the ratio of exchange.

If an offer of cash or debt securities is considered, the tax position of the stockholders of the target firm becomes important. Exchange of their common stock for cash or debt securities will be considered to be a taxable exchange by the IRS. If many of the stockholders, particularly the larger ones, acquired their stock at much lower prices than the amounts to be received in the exchange, they would be reluctant to exchange their stock because they would be subject to capital gains taxes. In such a case, a nontaxable exchange for voting preferred or common stock would have greater appeal.

Preferred stock The use of straight or convertible preferred stock usually reflects the dividend concerns of the target firm's stockholders. If the acquiring firm pays lower dividends than the target firm, a convertible preferred stock may be offered that will yield to the stockholders dividends equal to or greater than those previously received. If the preferred stock has voting rights, this will be considered as a nontaxable exchange. (The use of convertible preferred stock as a currency of exchange was discussed in Chapter 21.)

Common stock A common stock-for-stock exchange is offered in many merger proposals. This allows the target firm's stockholders to retain a residual equity position in the surviving firm. If they hold common stock of the surviving firm, they maintain a financial interest in its continued success. On the other hand, if some stockholders wish to liquidate their holdings, they may do so by selling in the market the common stock received from the acquiring corporation. Of course, if the target firm is relatively large, the acquiring firm would be reluctant to enter into a stock-for-stock exchange if it expected a large proportion of the stock to be sold immediately after the merger. This could flood the market and result in a serious decline in its price.

"Sweeteners" If the management of the target firm owns a large protion of its stock and is to be retained to manage its operations as a division of the surviving firm, the exchange offer may include some form of sweetener. This may serve two purposes: (1) to provide an incentive to these management personnel to maximize the value of the surviving firm's stock and (2) to provide additional potential compensation to induce their approval of the merger.

One form of sweetener is the issuing of stock purchase warrants, which usually are exercisable at a higher price than the current market, to accompany the cash or securities exchanges in the merger. The other is a contingency arrangement under which the stockholders of the acquired firm may receive additional cash or securities at a later date if the performance of the acquired division meets certain standards over a succeeding period of years.

For example, such an arrangement may provide for an immediate exchange of one share of the acquiring firm for each share of the target. But if the pretax earnings of the acquired division exceed a given amount in the three years subsequent to the merger, the former stockholders of the target will receive an additional share of the succeeding firm's stock for each five shares previously exchanged. Usually the pretax earnings requirement is a little higher than previously achieved by the acquired firm. This provides a strong and direct incentive (or pressure, if you look at it that way) for the key management personnel to produce profits at the level anticipated by the acquiring firm. A variation of this is a buy-out arrangement under which only part of the purchase price will be paid on consummation of the merger, the remainder to be a percentage of the division's profits achieved during several succeeding years.[9]

To continue our example, let us assume that a majority of the common stock of Merit Corporation is held by large stockholders who acquired their shares long ago at $5 to $15 per share. The major stockholders and many of the others appear to be risk-takers who would be interested in continued holding of Acme stock if they received it from the merger. Furthermore, Acme neither has nor could easily acquire some $105 to $120 million to acquire Merit for cash. Therefore, it is determined that the appropriate currency of exchange would be the common stock of Acme Enterprises. Sufficient stock is currently authorized but unissued.

The ratio of exchange

If the currency of exchange is to be securities of the acquiring corporation rather than cash, as Acme had decided, the next step is to develop the *ratio of exchange.*

Establishing the ratio of exchange

To determine the ratio of exchange for a common stock-for-stock merger, the dollar value of the target firm's stock must be converted to the number of shares or fraction of a share of the acquiring firm's common stock that will be exchanged for each share. This conversion is made by dividing the dollar value of a share of Merit by the dollar value of a share of Acme. Thus, if the initial offer is to be based upon the estimated stand-alone value of Merit, $35 per share, and the current market value of Acme stock of $60 per share is accepted, then the ratio of exchange is calculated as follows:

$$\frac{\$35}{\$60} = .583$$

[9] The "pooling of interests" method of accounting for a merger (discussed in Appendix B) may not be used if any payments to stockholders of the acquired firm are contingent upon future performance.

The initial offer probably will be .58 share of Acme for each share of Merit. This would give the holder of each Merit share Acme stock work $34.80 compared to Merit's market price of $30.00 immediately prior to the offering, or a premium of 16 percent.

The upper limit to which Acme might be willing to raise its offer is based upon a valuation of Merit stock at $40 per share, which incorporates the contemplated synergism from the merger. This exchange ratio would be:

$$\frac{\$40}{\$60} = .667$$

Thus the *bargaining range* will be a ratio of exchange from approximately .58 to .67 share of Acme for each share of Merit.

If Acme contemplated exchanging securities other than its common stock, the ratio of exchange would be developed in a similar fashion, substituting the estimated market value of the other security, a bond or preferred stock, for that of its common stock. For example, if a preferred stock that would be valued in the market at $100 per share were to be offered, the initial exchange offer would be .35 share of Acme preferred for each share of Merit common ($35/$100 = .35).

The range of possible exchange ratios then must be tested to estimate the effects upon dividends to be received by the target firm's stockholders and upon earnings per share and market price of the surviving firm's common stock.

Dividends Will the Merit stockholders be satisfied with the dividends to be received from Acme stock? The Acme dividends they would receive if their stock were exchanged at various ratios, assuming that Acme's $3 per share dividend remains unchanged, would be:

Exchange ratio	Dividends
.58 share	$1.74
.62	1.86
.67	2.01

As dividends of $2 per share are currently paid on Merit stock, the fact that its stockholders will receive less than $2 annual dividend for each share of Merit stock exchanged, if the ratio is less than .67, might be a sticky issue in this merger. If the Merit stockholders were highly income-motivated, they might be unwilling to exchange their shares unless the ratio of exchange were at least .67. On the other hand, if they are primarily growth-oriented stockholders, the slightly lower dividend at an exchange ratio of, say, .62 may not be a significant issue.

If dividends become the only issue impeding the merger, Acme would have two choices available to satisfy the Merit stockholders. One would be to raise its dividend to, say, $3.25 per share, which, at a .62 exchange ratio, would provide the Merit stockholders with dividends of $2.015, about the same as those presently received. The other course would be to offer a convertible preferred stock that would pay dividends at least equaling those previously received by the Merit stockholders and be convertible into Acme common valued at about $37 per share. The offer for each share of Merit common stock might be .37 share of $5.50 preferred stock convertible into 1.7 shares of Acme common stock. For each share of Merit stock exchanged, the holder would receive approximately $2.03 in annual dividends (.37 × $5.50 = $2.035) if the preferred were held. Acme common stock worth $37¾ (.37 × 1.7 × $60 = $37.74), equivalent to a .629 common stock-for-stock exchange) would be received if the preferred were converted to common.

We shall now assume that a sufficient majority of the Merit stockholders are growth-oriented and do not wish to quibble about dividends if a common share-for-share exchange is offered at a satisfactory ratio. The analyst must then be concerned with the effect of the ratio of exchange upon earnings per share and market value of Acme common stock.

Earnings per share Let us assume that an exchange ratio of .62 is agreed upon. The earnings per share of Acme Enterprises forecasted to result from this merger are compared to those without the merger in Table 23–3. The analysis for year 0 indicates that if the firm had been merged for the prior year with no synergistic effects, earnings per share would have been slightly higher ($6.01 versus $6.00) than those actually achieved by Acme alone. This slight increase without any synergism reflects solely the difference between the price-earnings ratio paid for Merit stock, 9.92 times ($37.20/$3.75), and the price-earnings ratio of Acme stock, 10 times ($60/$6).[10]

Table 23–3 Pro forma earnings per share—Acme Enterprises

	Without merger		With merger	
Year	Total Earnings* ($000)	Earnings per share†	Total Earnings‡ ($000)	Earnings per share§
0	$60,000	$6.00	$ 71,250‖	$6.01‖
1	64,200	6.42	77,821	6.56
2	68,694	6.87	83,077	7.00
3	73,503	7.35	88,549	7.47
4	78,648	7.86	94,597	7.98
5	84,153	8.42	101,056	8.52

*At 7 percent compound growth rate.
†Based upon 10 million shares outstanding.
‡At 7 percent compound growth rate for Acme and 6 percent for Merit, plus additional synergistic earnings of $1.6 million beginning year 1.
§Based on 10 million original shares plus 1.86 million shares issued to Merit stockholders at .62 exchange ratio.
‖Proforma for year prior to merger with no synergistic effects.

[10]Although insignificant in this case, the ratcheting up of earnings per share by merging target firms at price-earnings ratios significantly lower than that of the acquiring company can provide the illusion of growth. This is the basis of "the merger game" discussed in Appendix A of this chapter.

In year 1, the year following the merger, earnings per share are forecasted to be 14 cents higher than if the merger did not take place ($6.56 versus $6.42). The difference reflects three factors: (1) the slightly lower price-earnings ratio at which Merit was to be acquired, as discussed above; (2) the earnings increase of $1.6 million expected to result from synergy of the merger; and (3) the lower growth rate of 6 percent from operation of the Merit division compared to the 7 percent growth rate from the premerger operations of Acme. Note that the latter factor tends to counteract advantages resulting from the first two; if Merit's growth rate were equal to that of Acme, earnings per share in year 1 would have been $6.57.

The forecasted earnings per share advantage of the merger declines slightly through succeeding years until it is only 10 cents in the fifth year. If the forecast in Table 23–3 had been carried further, the advantage would gradually decline and eventually reverse because of the forecasted lower rate of growth of earnings of the Merit division.

Market value The effect of this merger on the market price of Acme's common stock is unknown. If the market continues to pay 10 times reported earnings for Acme stock and forecasted earnings materialize, the market price should rise about 10 percent to reflect the greater expected earnings per share in future years. But if the market expects that the merger will have a negative effect on growth in EPS, the market price of the stock might rise only slightly or not be affected at all.

This merger is advantageous from the standpoint of maximizing the value of Acme's common stock in the long run if it can be consummated at an exchange ratio of .62. It would be even more attractive if Acme management could achieve improvement in the growth rate of the Merit division to equal that of Acme's other operations. If this were true, the postmerger earnings per share would continually be about 14 cents higher. This should be reflected by the market's willingness to pay a higher price for Acme stock.

The final consideration related to market price is the *market's perception* of the effect of the merger upon the *risk* of the surviving firm. The above comments assume that risk will be unchanged. If risk would be reduced—say, because the acquisition of Merit would give Acme greater control of its product markets or sources of supply—then investors might be willing to pay a higher price-earnings ratio for its stock than the premerger 10 times. Conversely, if Merit's operations entail greater risks or its capital structure is more highly leveraged, the market might be willing to pay only a lower price-earnings ratio for Acme stock, which would make this merger disadvantageous.

Let us assume that neither Acme management nor the market perceives any change in risk to result from the merger. If so, the next and last consideration is the method to use in acquiring Merit.

Method of acquisition

Once the acquiring firm's managers have decided that they wish to acquire the target firm and have determined the currency of exchange to be offered and the range of feasible exchange ratios, they must decide how to accomplish the acquisition. There are two basic alternatives, a "friendly" approach to the target firm's management or a "hostile" tender offer directly to its stockholders.

Friendly merger—Negotiation Whether a friendly merger is feasible or desirable depends upon several factors. Are the managers of the target firm amenable to a merger or do they steadfastly desire to remain independent? What portion of the outstanding common stock is owned or controlled by management? What is the influence of management upon other large and important stockholders? How important is retention of the present management to achieving successful operation and synergistic effects in the postmerger period?

It may be absolutely essential to obtain approval and active cooperation of the target firm's management. At the other extreme, it may be considered necessary to remove the present management in order to achieve operational success after the merger. If the management personnel of the target firm appear to be amenable to merger, if their approval and recommendation to the other stockholders seems to be required to achieve the necessary majority vote in favor of the merger or if their continued services are vital to success in the postmerger period, the appropriate course of action is a direct approach to management to negotiate mutually acceptable terms.

These negotiations require a great deal of tact. Friendly merger negotiations entail a corporate courtship with a view to marriage. But, in determining the price in terms of the ratio of exchange, each side utilizes its bargaining skills in an attempt to obtain as much as possible of the synergistic value expected from the merger. In Acme's attempt to acquire Merit, the bargaining probably will start with Acme's offer of around .58 share of its common stock for each common share of Merit. Management of Merit might ask an exchange ratio of around .67, depending upon its estimate of possible synergistic value. Merit's management may seek merger offers from other firms; Acme could investigate alternate acquisition opportunities or developing internal capabilities similar to those of Merit.

If the merger is to be consummated, a fairly good guess is that negotiations will result in agreement upon an exchange ratio of about .62. This would be advantageous to both firms and would almost evenly split the added value expected to result from synergism. Management contracts with the key executives of Merit, except the financial vice president, whose job is to be eliminated, might be agreed upon. These executives might also agree that, when and if they leave Acme, they will not engage in similar lines of business for, say, three years thereafter. Or possibly negotiations will be terminated without a merger ever taking place. It is estimated that approximately two out of three attempted acquisitions do not materialize.

Hostile merger—Takeover Particularly if the target firm is a large, publicly held corporation whose stock is widely dispersed among many thousands of stockholders, the acquiring firm may make a hostile tender offer directly to the stockholders. Management of the target firm and the SEC, if required, merely are notified that the tender offer will be made, and no significant negotiations precede it. This represents a takeover attempt, to which management of the target firm naturally will react in a hostile fashion.

The tender offer, often of cash, usually will represent a substantial premium (perhaps some 20 to 40 percent) over the market price of the stock immediately preceding its announcement. Elimination of the top management of the target might be contemplated by the acquiring firm. Sometimes the premium offered is considered to be the cost of separating the firm from its management. Although hostile takeover attempts have occurred for many years, their use accelerated greatly in the late 70s.

Hostile takeover attempts usually are accompanied by each management's publicly accusing the other of sinister or at least selfish motives. They often trigger lawsuits and countersuits claiming the illegality of each party's actions. Other firms frequently join the fray by making competing tender offers at still higher values. Eventually, either a merger is consummated resulting in substantial gain to the target's stockholders or management is successful in fending off the takeover, the tender offers being withdrawn, barred by court action, or rejected by a sufficient number of stockholders. The market price of the stock of the target firm then may drop back to a level similar to that existing before the take over attempt.

Avoiding hostile takeover attempts There are various means by which management of a target company may attempt to avoid a takeover. If the would-be acquirer intends eventually to finance the merger by using excess cash and marketable securities held by the target firm, these liquid assets may be eliminated by paying dividends, making a tender offer to repurchase stock, purchasing assets, or acquiring another firm for cash.

In the attempt by Texas Air to take over Continental Airlines in 1981, management of Continental arranged to double the number of common shares outstanding by selling additional shares to its employees' trust fund, the purchase to be financed by term loans from a group of financial institutions. This would have reduced the proportion of shares that had been acquired by Texas Air to about half its holding of 48.5 percent of the outstanding stock. This maneuver was unsuccessful.

Another maneuver may be to bring in a "white knight." If management is threatened by a hostile merger offer, it may negotiate a friendly merger with a firm compatible to management. That firm then comes in as the white knight with a competing tender offer approved and recommended by management to the stockholders. A means by which management may protect its position is to gain approval of long-term management contracts, called "golden parachutes", from its board of directors during the period that a hostile tender offer is outstanding. The acquiring firm then has the alternatives of withdrawing its offer, retaining the management subsequent to the merger, or buying out their management contracts.

Most of these maneuvers may be illustrated by the 1981 Du Pont–Conoco merger. Seagram first approached Conoco with a friendly offer to buy 35 percent of its shares. This was rejected by Conoco management. Then Seagram made a hostile tender offer to buy 40.7 percent of Conoco's shares at $73 per share. The market price of Conoco shares was $62 the day before this tender offer. Then Conoco management arranged long-term management contracts with its board of directors and sought a white knight.

Negotiations with Du Pont resulted in its coming in as the white knight with a tender offer to buy 40 percent of Conoco's stock for $87.50 per share in cash and to exchange 1.6 shares of Du Pont's stock for each remaining Conoco share. Seagram retaliated by increasing its cash offer. Then Mobil joined the fray with another competing tender offer. Meanwhile, it was heavily rumored that Texaco was interested. The various competing offers were increased and extended as the battle heated. Both Du Pont and Mobil raised their offers on the final day. Mobil went to a federal court, pleading for an injunction, which the judge refused.

Du Pont's successful tender offer was $98 per share for 45 percent of Conoco's stock and 1.7 Du Pont common shares (then traded at about $45¼) for the remaining Conoco shares. Total value offered was about $7.4 billion, making this the largest merger in history to that date (August 5, 1981).

Summary

This chapter discussed growth through mergers and acquisitions. Synergism is the fundamental economic basis of business combination. Operating synergism may result from vertical or horizontal integration or possibly from conglomerate growth or the integration of technology or personnel. Financial synergism may result from complementary internal funds flows, more efficient use of financial leverage, increased external financial capability, or tax advantages. Other motives for merger may be the opportunity to acquire assets at bargain prices or to increase the liquidity of stockholders of the acquired firm. The legal forms of business combination are merger, consolidation, and the holding company. Merger, either through a statutory merger or purchase of assets, is the most widely used.

Financial analysis of a proposed merger requires (1) valuation, (2) determining the currency of exchange, (3) identifying a feasible range of ratios of exchange, and (4) deciding the method of acquisition to be used, negotiating a friendly merger or making a hostile tender offer. Valuation involves estimating the value per share of the target firm standing alone and in combination with the acquiring firm, including value of the synergism. These two values establish the bargaining range, the lowest dollar value the target's stockholders could advantageously accept and the highest value the acquiring firm could afford to pay. If the currency of exchange is to be other than cash, the value of the securities of the acquiring firm that are to be exchanged also must be established.

The appropriate currency of exchange depends upon such circumstances of the target firm's stockholders as their investment objectives, tax status, and income requirements. It also may be influenced by the acquiring firm's liquidity, availability of credit, and capital structure. Cash or any securities of the acquiring firm—bonds or notes, straight or convertible preferred stock or common stock—might be offered. Sometimes sweeteners in the form of stock purchase warrants or additional compensation dependent upon future earnings of the acquired unit may be included.

The ratio of exchange is determined by dividing the dollar value of the target firm's common stock by the value of the security of the acquiring firm to be exchanged for it. The contemplated ratio of exchange must be tested to estimate its effect upon the dividends to be received by the target firm's stockholders and upon the earnings per share of the surviving firm. Then the effect of the merger upon the market price of the acquiring firm may be estimated. The latter will be a function of the anticipated EPS and the perceived risk borne by its common stockholders. If the merger is advantageous, it must result in an increase in the surviving firm's common stock value in the long run.

Whether a friendly merger or a hostile takeover should be sought is largely a function of the attitudes, stockholdings, influence, and requirement of future services of the management of the target firm. If a friendly merger is pursued, management is approached and terms are negotiated. If a hostile merger is attempted, a takeover tender offer is made directly to the stockholders of the target firm. Takeover battles usually become heated, with aggressive action by the acquiring firm, defensive action by management of the target to avoid takeover, and, sometimes, competitive tender offers.

Questions

1. What is *synergism?* Explain why some form of synergistic effects must be expected to economically justify most business combinations. Why might

significant *operating* synergism be more difficult to achieve now than when John D. Rockefeller assembled the Standard Oil Trust or J. P. Morgan formed U.S. Steel?

2. Explain the differences among *horizontal, vertical,* and *conglomerate* growth. Which types of growth have the greatest potential for operating synergism?

3. What types of *financial* synergism might economically justify business combination?

4. Under what circumstances might a firm that has been operating at a loss be considered to be a desirable merger partner?

5. What is *countersynergism?* Indicate a few factors that might reduce or nullify the contemplated synergistic effects of a business combination.

6. How can one explain the acquisition of assets at bargain prices via merger (compared to the cost of buying or constructing the same assets) during the late 1970s and early 80s? If a substantial premium over the pre-merger market price of the acquired firm's common stock was paid in such mergers, can this bargain be reconciled with the assumption of capital market efficiency? Explain.

7. What is the difference between a merger and a consolidation? How does a holding company arrangement for business combination differ from either?

8. How can the stockholders of a closely held firm increase the liquidity of their equity holdings by merging their firm into a large publicly held corporation?

9. Discuss the control, potential financial leverage, risk, and taxation aspects of the holding company form of organization of a business combination.

10. Outline the steps in analyzing and planning a prospective merger from the standpoint of the acquiring firm.

11. Valuation is the key element in appraising a merger. Explain why. How would you go about establishing the stand-alone value of the closely held stock of a prospective merger candidate firm? How would you appraise the value of that stock if the target firm were merged into your acquiring firm? How would these two values relate to your bargaining with management of the target firm to establish the terms of a friendly merger?

12. What is meant by the term *currency of exchange* in a merger? What is the *ratio of exchange*? How is the ratio of exchange established in a friendly stock-for-stock merger negotiation?

13. Under what circumstances would the following currencies of exchange be appropriate in a merger: *(a)* cash, *(b)* debt securities (bonds or notes), *(c)* convertible preferred stock, and *(d)* common stock? What sweeteners might be added in a stock-for-stock exchange?

14. How do estimated postmerger *(a)* dividends, *(b)* earnings per share, and *(c)* market value of the surviving firm's common stock influence the ratio of exchange in a stock-for-stock merger?

15. Why might the management of an acquiring firm make a hostile tender offer directly to stockholders of the target firm rather than attempt to negotiate a friendly merger? Why might stockholders of the target firm require a higher price if cash or debt securities are offered than if stock of the acquiring firm is offered?

16. Suggest a few maneuvers by which management of a target firm might try to avoid a hostile takeover.

Problems

1. Success Corporation is considering the acquisition of Flop, Incorporated. Flop has a $1 million tax loss carryforward. Projected earnings of Success for the next three years are ($000):

	1983	1984	1985
Earnings before taxes	$300	$350	$400
Taxes @ 40%	120	140	160
Earnings after taxes	$180	$210	$240

Success Corporation could immediately liquidate the assets acquired from Flop with net aftertax proceeds of $400,000 in excess of the liabilities assumed. *If* the IRS will not object to Success using the tax loss carryforward, what is the maximum amount of cash that Success could pay for Flop and still profit from the merger? (Assume that Success's management considers that a discount rate of 10 percent reflects the pure interest rate and the small risk that it might not be able to utilize the tax loss carryforward.)

2. Giant Holding Company controls $100 million of assets in company A through its investment of $20 million in A's common stock, $70 million of assets in company B through its investment of $30 million in B's common stock, and $140 million of assets in company C through its investment of $45 million in C's common stock. Giant Holding's capital structure is comprised of $40 million bonds and $55 million common stockholders' equity. Mr. A. M. Gotrocks controls Giant Holding with his block of 51 percent of Giant's common stock.

a. What is the total amount of assets controlled by Mr. Gotrocks?

b. What is the total investment of Giant Holding in stock of its operating companies?

c. What is the book value of Mr. Gotrocks' investment, which controls the Giant Holding group of companies?

(Note: Problems 3 and 4 are a series.)

3. Benton Corporation is considering the acquisition of Daly Corporation. Pertinent financial information for these firms is shown below:

	Benton	Daly
Earnings available to common stock ($000)	$3,000	$1,000
Common shares outstanding (000)	2,500	500
Earnings per share	$ 1.20	$ 2.00
Market price per share	$12.00	$15.00
Price-earnings ratio	10×	7.5×
Dividends per share	$ 0.80	$ 1.00

The ratio of exchange of Benton stock for Daly stock would be based upon a 20 percent premium over the market price of Daly stock.

a. What will be the ratio of exchange?

b. What will be the immediate postmerger earnings per share of Benton, the surviving corporation?

c. What will be the dividend per Daly share exchanged?

d. If Benton stock continues to trade at a price-earnings ratio of 10 times after the merger, what will be its market price per share?

4. (See Problem 3.)

a. If Benton's earnings from present operations grow at a 7 percent annual rate, and earnings of the Daly division grow at an annual rate of 5 percent, what will be the earnings per share of Benton, the surviving firm, for each of the next five years?

b. If after the merger the market values Benton stock at 9.5 times earnings because of the slower growth rate of the Daly division, what will be the market price of Benton stock each of the five years after the merger?

c. What would be the market price of Benton stock during each of the next five years if the merger did *not* take place, Benton's earnings grew at a 7 percent annual rate, and the market continued to value these earnings at a price-earnings ratio of 10 times? What would be the difference in market prices with and without the merger?

d. Accepting the assumptions in earlier parts of this question, would you recommend that Benton proceed with this merger? Explain your position.

5. Elton Corporation, a rather stable firm, is acquiring Bioscience, Incorporated, a rapidly growing, closely held research firm, in a two-for-one ex-

change of stock (two shares of Elton for each share of Bioscience). Financial data for the two firms are:

	Elton	Bioscience
Earnings available to common stock ($000s)	$5,000	$ 800
Shares outstanding (000s)	2,500	1,000
Earnings per share	$2.00	$0.80
Expected annual earnings growth rate	4%	30%
Price-earnings ratio	6×	N.A.

N.A. Not available because Bioscience stock is closely-held and not traded.

a. What is the dollar equivalent price that Elton is paying for Bioscience?

b. How many times earnings is Elton paying for Bioscience?

c. What is the immediate postmerger effect upon Elton's earnings per share?

d. If the price-earnings ratio of Elton stock increases to 11 times, what will be the change in the market price of this stock?

e. Why might such an increase in the price-earnings ratio occur?

(Note Problems 6 through 8 are a series.)

6. Aurora Corporation is considering acquisition of the Cress Company. Pertinent financial information for these firms is as follows:

	Aurora	Cress
Earnings available to common stock ($000s)	$9,000	$1,800
Common shares outstanding (000)	1,500	600
Earnings per share	$ 6.00	$ 3.00
Market price per share	$72.00	$24.00
Price-earnings ratio	12×	8×
Dividends per share	$ 4.00	$ 1.50
Estimated annual growth rate	8%	6%

The market prices of both Aurora and Cress common stock are believed to reflect the current stand-alone values of these securities. Aurora's management believes that it can reduce aftertax operating costs of the combined firms by $600,000 because of synergistic effects and that Aurora stock will trade at a price-earnings ratio of 11 times after the acquisition.

a. What is the maximum exchange ratio of Aurora common stock that could be offered for Cress stock? (Hint: The maximum exchange ratio is the one that will leave the market price of Aurora stock unchanged.)

b. What is the minimum exchange ratio that Cress stockholders could accept?

c. If this is to be a friendly merger, how will the actual exchange ratio be determined?

d. Assuming that the merger is consumated at an exchange ratio of .37 of an Aurora share for each Cress share, what short-run value do the Cress shareholders collectively gain? What short-run value do the Aurora shareholders gain?

7. If the Aurora–Cress merger (Problem 6) is consummated at an exchange ratio of .37 share of Aurora for each Cress share, what change will take place in the dividends received by the former holder of 100 shares of Cress stock? What will be the change in earnings accruing to this stockholder? What will be the short-term effect on the market value of his or her stockholding?

8. Assuming that the synergistic effects of the Aurora-Cress merger will be immediate, that the estimated growth rates shown in Problem 6 will materialize, and that the price-earnings ratio is 11 times, forecast the *(a)* earnings per share and *(b)* market prices of Aurora common stock for each of the next five years. How do these forecasted market prices compare to those if Aurora had not merged Cress? What are your conclusions regarding the long-run benefits of this merger to Aurora stockholders?

Appendix 23–A—The "merger game"

The term *merger game* may be used to describe a technique related to the conglomerate merger movement of the 1960s. The merger game was largely responsible for the rise and fall of the conglomerates during this period. Fortunes were made by some investors who were lucky enough to get out of the game in time. Fortunes also were lost as one by one the bubbles burst. But the game is not only of historical interest. Understanding the merger game provides valuable information to both financial executives and investors about the use and misuse of mergers.

The technique is based upon the simple fact that when an acquiring firm with a high price-earnings (PE) ratio exchanges its stock for that of a target firm with a lower PE ratio, the earnings per share (EPS) of the acquiring firm will increase even though earnings from operations have not increased at all. Repeated mergers on this basis may create the *illusion of growth,* even though operating results of both the acquiring firm and the ones that have been acquired have been stable or perhaps even have slightly declined.

If investors observe only the reported increases in EPS, they will bid up the price of the acquiring firm's stock, maintaining a high and stable PE ratio. The deception of the game arises from investors' failure to recognize that the *quality* of EPS is declining as firms with lower PE ratios are merged into the acquiring firm. If the market did recognize this, the PE ratio of the acquiring firm would decline to offset the increasing EPS; thus, the market price of its stock would remain stable.

To illustrate, let us assume that acquiring company A, a rapidly growing firm with 5 million shares of common stock outstanding, has during a series of years prior to its embarking upon the merger game shown rapidly increasing earnings resulting from internal operations. As shown in Table 23A–1, its earnings increased from $7 million to $10 million in the two years preceding its merger activity (years −2 to 0) and its EPS increased from $1.40 to $2. Earnings from operations were stabilizing at $10 million.

Table 23A–1 Earnings after taxes ($000)
Acquiring and merged companies

Year	Acquiring company A	Aquired companies B	C	D	E	F	Cumulative
−2	$ 7,000	—	—	—	—	—	$ 7,000
−1	8,400	—	—	—	—	—	8,400
0	10,000	—	—	—	—		10,000
1	10,000	$5,000	—	—	—	—	15,000
2	10,000	5,000	$7,500	—	—	—	22,500
3	10,000	5,000	7,500	$11,250	—	—	33,750
4	10,000	5,000	7,500	11,250	$16,875	—	50,625
5	10,000	5,000	7,500	11,250	16,875	$25,313	75,938

Company A's management decided to embark upon the merger game in an attempt to maintain the firm's record of increasing earnings per share by about 20 percent per year and the PE ratio of 20 times at which its stock was valued by the market. Acquisition of company B in year 1 required the exchange of 1,250,000 shares of company A's common stock, based upon valuation of company B at $50 million (10 times its earnings of $5 million) and the market price of $40 per share of company A stock (reflecting its previous year's EPS of $2 times its PE ratio of 20 times). Because company B's stock was valued at only 10 times earnings compared to company A's valuation at 20 times earnings, this merger increased company A's EPS in that year to $2.40, as shown in Table 23A–2. As A's EPS continued to maintain the past record of increase, 20 percent, the market continued to value its stock at 20 times earnings, thus increasing its market price to $48 per share.

This worked so well that company A's management forgot all about increasing earnings from internal operations. During the next four years it proceeded to play the merger game in earnest, each year acquiring a no-growth firm earning half as much as company A made during the previous year, as shown in Table 23A–1. Each firm, C through F, was acquired by exchanging company A's stock, valued at its then current market price. It paid 10 times earnings for each of these firms. Each year company A's EPS increased by 20 percent and, as the market continued to pay 20 times earnings for company A's stock, its market price increased to nearly $100 per share by the end of the fifth year, as shown in Table 23A–2. During this entire five-year period, none of the operating divisions of company A showed any growth whatever in earnings. All of the growth in EPS from $2 to $4.98 resulted from its playing the merger game.

Table 23A–2 Performance of acquiring firm A

Year	Earnings ($000)	Shares outstanding (000)	Earnings per share	Price-earnings ratio	Year-end price per share
0	$10,000	5,000	$2.00	20 ×	$40.00
1	15,000	6,250	2.40	20 ×	48.00
2	22,500	7,813	2.88	20 ×	57.60
3	33,750	9,766	3.46	20 ×	69.12
4	50,625	12,207	4.15	20 ×	82.94
5	75,938	15,259	4.98	20 ×	99.53

Note: Slight discrepancies are due to rounding.

But notice that each merger had to be larger than the preceding one (or, alternatively, there could have been more of them, or the acquisitions could have been at still lower PE ratios). This game had to end sometime. It would come to an end either when some of the divisional operations got out of control and suffered declines in earnings (or possibly losses) and/or when something prevented the acquisition during any given year of additional firms at low PE ratios. That something could be government action to block a proposed merger under the antitrust laws or simply competition among the players of the merger game, who were bidding up the PE ratios required to acquire additional firms. Please note that firms selling at low PE ratios do so because investors are aware of the low quality of their earnings, in other words, they perceive higher risk.

If in any year the growth rate of EPS were not maintained, the market price of company A's stock would fall greatly both because EPS would be lower than expected and its PE ratio would decline. The decline in the PE ratio would reflect recognition of the lower quality of earnings and that the growth formerly observed could not be sustained. This is exactly what happened to the high-flying conglomerates in the late 1960s and early 70s. Even though EPS of some of them did not show absolute declines, decrease in the *rate* of growth of EPS caused their stock to come crashing down to a small fraction of former market prices. Then the game was over. When such a firm lost its high PE ratio, its currency of exchange was devalued so much that its purchasing power was not sufficient to continue playing the merger game.

Questions

1. Explain how acquisition of firms whose common stocks have lower price-earnings ratios than that of the acquiring firm through stock-for-stock mergers may create the *illusion* of growth when operating earnings of both the acquiring and the acquired firms are stagnant.

2. What circumstances might lead to the downfall of a firm that has been playing the merger game?

Appendix 23–B—Accounting treatment of mergers

Accounting treatment of a merger may be either as (1) a *purchase* or (2) a *pooling of interests.* The method used may have a significant effect upon both the balance sheet and reported earnings of the surviving firm. The "price" paid for the acquired firm, in the form of either cash or securities, may be equal to, greater than, or less than the values at which the net assets are carried on the books of the acquired firm. If the price is equal to the net asset value, there will be no difference between purchase accounting and pooling-of-interests accounting. Each asset acquired and liability assumed will be added at its book value to the premerger accounts of the surviving firm. But if the price and the net asset values differ substantially, there will be important differences in the effects of purchase accounting versus pooling-of-interests.

Purchase accounting Under purchase accounting, the acquisition is treated as if the acquiring firm purchased the assets and assumed the liabilities of the acquired firm, paying for the net assets at the current market value of the currency of exchange used.[1] The tangible assets are booked at their fair (appraised) market values at the date of acquisition and any excess of the price paid is recorded as *goodwill,* an intangible asset. Goodwill must be written off (amortized) over a period not exceeding 40 years. The write-off is not allowed as a tax deduction.

For example, assume that firm A acquired firm B by exchanging common

[1]The use of purchase accounting is not necessarily related to the *legal form* of the merger. Thus a statutory merger may be accounted for as a purchase.

stock with a current market value of $25 million. The condensed balance sheets of firm A and firm B before the merger are shown in columns 1 and 2 of Table 23B–1. The market value of B's current assets was identical to the book value of $10 million. But the fair market value of its fixed assets was $24 million, or $4 million greater than the book value of $20 million. Under purchase accounting, as shown in column 3, the write-up of fixed assets acquired from B resulted in booking the fixed assets of the combined firm at $64 million. Common equity of B was brought onto the books of A at the current market value of the stock issued by A in the exchange, $25 million, or at $9 million in excess of the book value of the acquired firm's equity. Therefore, the postmerger common equity was $70 million. To balance the books, $5 million of goodwill, an intangible asset, was created. This purchased goodwill reflects the excess of the purchase price (market value of the A stock issued) over the fair market value of the tangible assets acquired.

Table 23B–1 Accounting for a merger
Purchase versus pooling or interests
($ millions)

	(1)	(2)	(3)	(4)
	Before		Firm A—After	
	Firm A	Firm B	Purchase accounting	Pooling of interests
Current assets	$25	$10	$ 35	$35
Fixed assets	40	20	64*	60
Goodwill	-0-	-0-	5‡	-0-
Total assets	$65	$30	$104	$95
Liabilities	$20	$14	$ 34	$34
Common stock equity	45	16	70†	61
Total liabilities and equity	$65	$30	$104	$95

*Premerger fixed assets of A plus $24 million fair market value of B's fixed assets ($4 million greater than valued on B's books).
†Premerger common equity of A plus $25 million market value of A shares issued to B stockholders.
‡Goodwill of $5 million balances the books, reflecting the excess of purchase price over fair market value of tangible assets acquired.

Management does not like to create goodwill because its annual write-off is a charge against income in succeeding years. In the case illustrated, earnings will be reduced through this write-off by at least $125,000 in each succeeding year. No tax benefits result from this write-off. Furthermore, increasing the common stock equity will reduce the calculated rate of return on the book value of common equity.

Pooling-of-interests accounting The use of pooling-of-interests accounting allows simply adding the premerger book values of all accounts of the two firms to construct the postmerger balance sheet. This is shown in column 4 of Table 23B–1. No goodwill is created; therefore, there will be no write-offs against income of future years. Common equity is the sum of the pre-merger book values. The net result is that future reported earnings and the rate of return on common equity will be higher than if purchase accounting was employed.

The use of pooling-of-interests accounting is stringently limited by six qualifications established by the Accounting Principles Board.

1. The acquiring corporation may issue only common stock identical to its outstanding voting common shares in exchange for 90 percent or more of the common stock of the acquired company.
2. The acquired firm's stockholders must maintain an ownership position in the acquiring firm.
3. The surviving firm must not intend to dispose of a significant portion of its assets within two years.
4. The merger must be consummated in a single transaction. No payments may be contingent upon future performance.
5. The basis of accounting for the acquired assets must remain unchanged.
6. Each of the combining corporations must have been autonomous for at least two years prior to initiation of the plan to merge.[2]

Many mergers do not qualify to use pooling-of-interests accounting under these rigid restrictions. One of the trade-offs to be considered in bargaining the terms of a merger is whether to adhere to these qualifications or breach them and accept accounting treatment as a purchase.

Questions

1. What is the basic difference between purchase accounting and pooling-of-interests accounting for mergers?

2. Why would a firm playing the "merger game" (Appendix 23-A) usually prefer pooling-of-interests accounting for its mergers?

3. Which method of accounting for mergers usually will result in the highest reported (1) earnings per share and (2) rate of return on equity of the surviving firm? Explain why.

[2]See AICPA, *APB Opinion No. 16,* "Business Combinations," (New York, 1970).

Problem

1. O'Neil Corporation has just been merged into Sanchez Corporation. Two shares of Sanchez were exchanged for each share of O'Neil stock. Premerger abbreviated balance sheets of each firm are shown below ($ millions):

	Sanchez	O'Neil
Assets		
Current assets	$45	$12
Fixed assets—net	50	15
Goodwill	3	0
Total assets	$98	$27
Liabilities and equity		
Current liabilities	$21	$ 8
Long-term liabilities	25	5
Total liabilities	46	13
Common stock equity	52	14
Total liabilities and equity	$98	$27

At the date of the merger, Sanchez had 2 million shares of common stock outstanding with a market value of $30 per share. O'Neil had 400 thousand shares outstanding. As O'Neil stock was closely held, its market price was not identifiable. The fair market value of O'Neil's current assets was the same as their book value, but its fixed assets were appraised at $19 million.

a. Construct the postmerger balance sheet of Sanchez, the surviving corporation, using the purchase accounting method.

b. Construct the postmerger balance sheet, using the pooling-of-interests accounting method.

Chapter 24
Failure, Reorganization, and Bankruptcy

This chapter deals with the firm in serious financial difficulty. We hope that you will never have to use this material as a manager or owner of a failing firm. If you have mastered the subjects discussed in the preceding chapters, kept your feet on the ground, exercised sound judgment, and had a little bit of luck, you probably will not face the problems of failure, reorganization, and bankruptcy of your business firm. But you still may be involved in these problems as a creditor of other firms that get into financial difficulties.

Doing business with other firms as suppliers, bankers, or other lenders involves bearing risks. When these risks materialize you must know how to exercise your rights to minimize your losses. Also, as an investor, you may have the opportunity to profit by acquiring at bargain prices securities of failed firms that will recover their value through reorganization. So this isn't the "death and dying" chapter, but rather it provides practical information of value to many business executives and investors.

A brief orientation as to the causes and magnitude of business failure and the varying degrees of financial distress will be provided first. Then informal (out of court) remedies will be discussed. Finally, legal remedies through bankruptcy proceedings will be treated. These remedies may involve either liquidation of the firm or its reorganization to continue in business in modified form.

Causes and magnitude of business failure

A long list of immediate causes of business failure could be compiled. It would include declining sales, technological obsolescence, overexpansion, insufficient net working capital, excessive short- or long-term borrowing, high interest rates, excessive credit losses, inefficient production, stringent loan restrictions, fraud, poor quality control, changes in government regulations, natural disasters, excessive competition, ad infinitum. In any given case, management of a failed firm will cite some such reason(s). But such causes are only superficial and symptomatic.

In nearly all cases, management can find the real underlying cause only by looking in the mirror. "We have found the problem and it is us!" Management is responsible for perceiving and adjusting to environmental changes, producing and selling products that are competitive, controlling costs, and arranging financing that the firm can live with. Regardless of the immediate reason(s) for failure, the ultimate responsibility rests with the firm's management. Dun & Bradstreet attributes about 95 percent of business failures to incompetent management.[1]

Symptoms of failure have been identified in terms of operating and financial ratios. The most pertinent ratios are (1) net working capital/total assets, (2) retained earnings/total assets, (3) earnings before interest and taxes/total assets, (4) market value of stock/total debt, and (5) sales/total assets. These have been incorporated into models that have some predictive power in forecasting business failures. Altman has been responsible for most of the research in this area. Although the development of such models is beyond the scope of this text, the reader may wish to refer to Altman's work.[2]

How many business firms fail? Are business failures a substantial problem in the United States? During the 1970s some 7,000 to 11,000 firms failed each year with losses to creditors. This amounted to between one fourth and one half of 1 percent of the business concerns in operation. Average liabilities per failure approximately doubled during the decade, but this is largely explained by a similar increase in price levels. Both the incidence of failure and average liabilities per failure increased during 1980 and 1981 but have not reached alarming proportions except in some particularly depressed industries and geographical areas.[3]

Statistics relating to business failures, however, do not tell the whole story. Many failing firms are not listed in the business obituary columns because they are bailed out via loans or mergers. The most spectacular bailouts have been the U.S. government's loan guarantees of Chrysler and Lockheed. Both the Federal Deposit Insurance Corporation (FDIC) and the Federal Savings and Loan Insurance Corporation (FSLIC) have arranged many mergers of failing banks and savings and loan associations with sound financial institutions.

Often, without government intervention, firms that were about to fail have been rescued by timely mergers in which the acquiring firms assumed the debt and paid very little compensation to stockholders. These actions have

[1]See Dun & Bradstreet, Inc., *The Failure Record* (published annually). The figure of about 95 percent includes D&B's detailed classifications of (1) lack of experience in the line, (2) lack of managerial experience, (3) unbalanced experience in sales, finance, production and other areas, (4) neglect, and (5) management incompetence. All of these may be considered to indicate management incompetence.

[2]Edward I. Altman, *Corporate Bankruptcy in America* (Lexington, Mass.: Health Lexington Books, 1971); "Corporate Bankruptcy Potential, Stockholder Returns and Share Valuation," *Journal of Finance,* December 1969, pp. 887–900; "Financial Ratios, Discriminant Analysis, and the Prediction of Corporate Bankruptcy," *Journal of Finance,* September 1968, pp. 589–609; and Altman, Robert G. Haldeman, and P. Narayanan, "Zeta Analysis: A New Model to Identify Bankruptcy Risk of Corporations," *Journal of Banking and Finance,* June 1977, pp. 29–54.

[3]As this goes to press in October, 1982, the incidence of failure is becoming more alarming. Reported failures in 1982 through September 16 number 17,502 and the percentage of business concerns failing in 1982 probably will be about one percent. Several prominent large firms have failed in recent months.

avoided the formalities of failure, but the parties involved recognized that their business enterprises had failed. Such actions may be economical in that they avoid the substantial costs and delays incurred in formal bankruptcy proceedings. On the other hand, particularly when government credit is pledged as in the Chrysler bail-out, they may be detrimental in the long run by continuing an uneconomical employment of resources in the economy.

Degrees of financial difficulty

The degree of financial difficulty may range all the way from occasional inability to pay a bill when it is due to forced liquidation of a firm by a bankruptcy court. Nearly all business firms at some time encounter difficulties of the first type and are able to handle such problems by stalling the creditors or arranging brief extensions of the obligations. But here we are concerned with more serious financial difficulties, which usually require "surgery" rather than "Band-Aids."

Illiquidity

Illiquidity (also called *technical insolvency*) occurs when a firm is unable to meet its financial obligations as they become due. Illiquidity may result from a *temporary* slowing or stoppage of the inflow of cash caused by slow collections of accounts receivable; curtailed sales resulting from temporarily unfavorable marketing conditions; a strike affecting the firm, its suppliers or its customers; or incurring an unforeseen obligation. Such a liquidity crisis usually can be worked out informally with the creditors. But illiquidity also can be *chronic* if the firm's normal operations are not capable of generating sufficient cash to pay recurring obligations. Chronic illiquidity requires a more permanent solution.

Insolvency

A firm is *insolvent,* sometimes referred to as "absolutely insolvent," when its liabilities exceed the real (or fair) value of its assets. In reality, it owes more than it owns, the equity capital is nonexistent, and the creditors are in jeopardy. The firm's balance sheet may not show this, but it would if the assets were written down to their real value.

Insolvency usually is a much more serious state of financial distress than illiquidity because it involves permanent inability of the firm to cover its financial obligations.

Bankruptcy

Bankruptcy is a slippery word. Sometimes a firm is said to be bankrupt when it is either illiquid or insolvent. Technically, *bankruptcy* is a legal term indicating that the firm has been admitted to a legal proceeding under the Bankruptcy Reform Act of 1978, its assets are under the control of the bankruptcy court, and it will be either liquidated or reorganized under the Bankruptcy Act. While a debtor firm is in bankruptcy, creditors may not take other legal action to enforce their claims. The Bankruptcy Act recognizes either illiquidity or insolvency as bases for petitioning the firm into bankruptcy. We shall treat bankruptcy in greater detail later in this chapter.

Economic failure

Economic failure indicates the inability of a firm to generate sufficient revenues to cover its costs, including the cost of capital. In other words, a firm has economically failed if it cannot generate sufficient profits to justify the continued employment of capital in it. The term has no legal connotation. Some firms go on year after year incurring losses or making insufficient profits to cover any reasonably estimated cost of capital.

Such a condition clearly requires that management take remedial action to turn the company around to produce profits sufficient to justify its existence. But, if the firm can maintain sufficient liquidity to meet its obligations when due and is solvent in the sense that the real value of its assets exceeds its liabilities, no crisis may arise to force reorganization or liquidation. However, when such a firm reaches the end of its rope, it may come down hard with serious losses.

Informal remedies

If a firm is in financial distress, both its management and creditors usually prefer informal remedies to the formal procedures of bankruptcy. These informal remedies are arranged privately through negotiation between management and creditors without resort to legal action. They usually are simpler, faster, and much less expensive than going to court in a bankruptcy action.

If a firm is unable to meet its maturing financial obligations and normal collection efforts by its creditors have failed, a meeting of its management and creditors is arranged. Often the adjustment bureau of the local chapter of the National Association of Credit Management will arrange this meeting and function as a catalyst in developing a settlement. At the meeting, management of the firm will explain its financial difficulties, and, if the creditors agree to pursue an informal remedy, a *creditors' committee* composed of representatives of the major creditors and a few of the minor ones will be appointed. The adjustment bureau will investigate the financial condition of the debtor and report to the creditors' committee, which will proceed to develop a proposed remedy. Eventually, if the remedy is acceptable to all creditors and the debtor, an agreement will be executed between these parties and administered by the bureau.

The informal remedy may be (1) an extension of the maturity of the overdue obligations, (2) a composition which reduces the amount of these obligations, (3) a combination of extension and composition, or (4) an assignment of the assets of the debtor to the adjustment bureau with a view either to liquidating the assets or continuing operation of the business under new management.

Extension

An *extension* simply postpones the maturity of the overdue debt obligations. The full amount still is owed. Often such an arrangement provides for installment payments, say one sixth of the amount owed to be paid at the end of each of the next six months. Trade credits often are converted to interest-bearing notes. The terms of future purchases from the extending trade creditors usually are limited to a cash basis. Sometimes the overdue obligations are subordinated to debt incurred in the future. This may make it possible for the firm to obtain credit from lenders or suppliers during the rehabilitation period.

Creditors tend to prefer an extension because it provides for the eventual payment in full of the obligations. Although extension may be a sound remedy if the debtor is temporarily illiquid but not insolvent, it is practical only if the creditors have faith that (1) the debtor is honest, (2) the debtor is capable of recovering, and (3) economic conditions in the industry are favorable to recovery. If these conditions are not met, extension may only prolong the agony and result in greater losses in the future.

In some cases, particularly if there is any question regarding the integrity and ability of the debtor, the creditors will provide safeguards during the period of the extension. They may prohibit dividends, require that the stock of the debtor firm be placed in escrow, demand security agreements pledging or assigning assets, and/or require that a designated member of the creditors' committee countersign all checks.

Composition

A *composition* is a settlement under which the creditors agree to accept a uniform percentage payment in cash and absolve the debtor of the remaining debt. For example, the creditors may agree to accept 60 cents on the dollar as full settlement of the obligations owed to them. Creditors may be willing to accept such a composition if they believe that the cash received will be greater than under the alternative of filing the firm into bankruptcy. The composition remedy usually is used where the debtor firm is insolvent but not necessarily illiquid.

Terms of the composition result from bargaining between the creditors' committee and the debtor. The debtor argues that the creditors will get more than they would if bankruptcy proceedings ensued with their high legal and administrative costs and long delays. Creditors argue that the debtor, who normally will receive nothing from a bankruptcy, will avoid the stigma of bankruptcy.

Combination—Extension and composition

If the probability is high that the debtor will recover over a period of time allowed by an extension *only if* a portion of the debt is eliminated, then a combination settlement might be worked out. For example, an agreeable settlement might provide a composition of 70 percent of the debt in the form of notes payable in equal installments over the next 12 months. This combination settlement might be agreeable to creditors if they feel that (1) the alternative of bankruptcy would result in their receiving less than 70 cents on the dollar and (2) the integrity and ability of management and economic conditions indicate that the firm would survive. As in the case of extension only, appropriate safeguards may be provided.

Assignment

Unfortunately, a large proportion of firms that get into financial difficulty do so because management lacks competence and/or integrity. In such cases, extension is not feasible because the risk is too great that it will lead to larger losses later. If the only feasible informal solution is to replace the management, the creditors' committee may demand *assignment* of all the firm's assets to the assignee (or trustee), usually the adjustment bureau. Then the bureau may either take over the management or select a suitable manager to do so. Such an assignment may lead to either orderly liquidation or continuing operation of the business.

Continuing operation If the firm is believed to be worth more as a going concern than in liquidation, the assets assigned will be continued in operation under new management. Necessary operating and financial adjustments will be made in an attempt to rehabilitate the enterprise. If successful, the obligations to creditors will be paid off in time and the firm's credit restored. The assignment may or may not provide that when obligations to the creditors are paid off, the firm will be restored to the former debtor. If not, the assignee probably will arrange sale of the firm to new owners.

Liquidation If liquidation seems to be appropriate—the firm is worth more dead than alive—the assignee may proceed to liquidate it in an orderly fashion. The advantage of assignment and liquidation in this manner is that the net proceeds distributed to creditors usually are greater than under formal bankruptcy proceedings. Rather than auctioning off the assets in a crisis atmosphere, the assignee may conduct a liquidation sale of the inventories, collect the receivables as they mature, and seek appropriate buyers of the fixed assets. Administrative costs are less than under bankruptcy.

Such liquidation usually will yield less than the amount due to creditors. The debtor effectively is relieved of remaining liabilities by a statement on the final distribution checks that endorsement acknowledges full payment of the obligations.

Pros and cons of informal remedies

The principal advantages of informal remedies are their savings in legal, investigative, and administrative costs. Working out a mutually satisfactory arrangement between the creditors and the debtor in an informal atmosphere is more expedient than going through the legal hassle of a formal court proceeding. Unfortunately, the lawyers often get more out of a bankruptcy than the creditors. In addition, if the firm can be rehabilitated informally through extension, composition, or even assignment, the creditors preserve a continuing relationship with their customer. Particularly if the debtor firm simply has a liquidity crisis and an extension will provide time for orderly collection of its excessive receivables, working off of excess inventories, and/or disposal of redundant fixed assets, the informal remedy is far more efficient than going to court.

But informal remedies require complete cooperation of the creditors and the debtor. All must agree to the settlement, whether it is a simple extension or an assignment for liquidation. The problems entailed in obtaining the cooperation of every creditor may be very difficult. Some may get a little too greedy in seeking a remedy that will benefit them more than others. Some of those owed small amounts may recognize their strategic positions by threatening to petition the firm into bankruptcy if their claims are not settled in full. This nuisance value often forces the larger creditors to agree to payment of cash in full to those owed less than, say, $100.

Management of the debtor firm sometimes is unwilling to agree to the remedy, particularly if there is to be an assignment, and threatens to file a voluntary petition in bankruptcy that will throw the firm into the courts. In essence, although informal remedies clearly are more efficient, their use may be much more difficult than superficially appears. If informal remedies do not work out, bankruptcy is the alternative.

Legal remedies—Bankruptcy

There are many reasons a firm might be petitioned into bankruptcy to obtain a legal remedy for business failure through a federal bankruptcy court. The creditors seek an equitable settlement of their claims, and the debtor seeks absolution of its debts. Often involuntary remedies have been attempted and failed. Sometimes they have not even been tried. In many cases, animosity has developed between the debtor and the creditors and sometimes among different classes of creditors. In large failures where many millions of dollars are involved, the complexities of both creditors' claims and asset management require the formality of a legal proceeding. Its advantage, of course, is the equity of a just settlement under the law. Its disadvantages are the legal formality and the costly, time consuming procedures required to comply with bankruptcy law.

Federal bankruptcy law

The Constitution empowers Congress to establish "uniform laws on the subject of bankruptcies throughout the United States."[4] The current bankruptcy law is the Bankruptcy Reform Act of 1978, which was designed to simplify and speed up the cumbersome proceedings required by the 1938 Act. Oddly, the Act consists of eight chapters numbered 1, 3, 5, 7, 9, 11, 13, and 15. (The even numbered chapters were eliminated by Congress in rewriting the act.) We are interested here in Chapter 7, which governs business liquidations, and Chapter 11, dealing with business reorganizations. The various other chapters contain general provisions and those related to municipalities and wage earners.[5] Bankruptcy is a highly complex area of the law fully understood only by lawyers specializing in the field. We shall not attempt to cover bankruptcy in detail. Rather, we shall try to provide sufficient information of a financial nature to guide business people as to the general nature of bankruptcy proceedings and the rights of creditors and the debtor involved in them.

Initial procedure A firm unable to meet its obligations may be placed in the hands of a bankruptcy court by either voluntary or involuntary petition. Management of the debtor firm may file a *voluntary* petition in bank-

[4]Constitution of the United States of America, Section 8, Paragraph 4.

[5]Care should be taken not to confuse Chapter 7 and 11, which apply to businesses, with the more widely publicized Chapter 13, which is applicable to individual wage earners with regular income.

ruptcy, which, in essence, admits its failure to meet its financial obligations and asks that the court assume responsibility for its liquidation or reorganization.

An *involuntary* petition in bankruptcy is initiated by the firm's creditors. Certain conditions must be met: (1) the debtor must not be paying debts as they become due or a custodian must have been appointed or taken possession of the debtor's property within the preceding 120 days, (2) the firm's debts must total at least $1,000, and (3) if there are twelve or more creditors, at least three of them with claims totaling at least $500 must join in the filing or, if there are fewer than twelve creditors, only one holding a claim of $500 or more may file.

If the bankruptcy petition is accepted, the court issues an *order of relief,* which bars creditors from further enforcing their claims. The court may then appoint an *interim trustee* to assume control of the firm, or it may allow management to continue in charge of the firm's affairs. Then the court calls a meeting of the creditors, notifying all parties. At this meeting the debtor is examined, the creditors may file their claims, the unsecured creditors elect a *creditors' committee,* and they may, if so decided, elect a *trustee* to assume control of the firm's affairs. Normally, additional creditors' claims will be honored if properly filed within six months after this meeting. Often the different classes of creditors (banks, secured, unsecured, subordinated, and so on) also informally organize creditors' committees to represent their respective interests.

Decision: Liquidate or reorganize The petition in bankruptcy is originally filed under either Chapter 7, requesting liquidation, or Chapter 11, requesting reorganization. However, the court may, on the basis of information developed at the creditors' meeting(s) and after hearing other interested parties, including the SEC in cases involving large, publicly held corporations, change this filing to the other chapter at any time. Therefore, a major decision of the bankruptcy court is whether the firm should be liquidated or reorganized to continue in operation. Basically, the question is whether the firm is worth more dead or alive.

This question can be answered only by establishing the going-concern value of the firm and comparing it to the net liquidation value. Going-concern value is estimated either by discounting estimated future cash flows or by capitalizing estimated future earnings. Net liquidation value is a composite of the proceeds expected from piecemeal liquidation of the assets less the administrative costs. If the firm's primary problems involve temporary illiquidity (technical insolvency), going-concern value probably will predominate and a reorganization will take place under Chapter 11. On the other hand, if the firm is insolvent and appears to be an economic failure that cannot be rectified by revamping its operations, net liquidation value probably will predominate and the firm will be liquidated under Chapter 7.

Liquidation under Chapter 7

The trustee's responsibilities under Chapter 7 are temporarily to conserve the value of the assets and to liquidate them in an orderly fashion. The net proceeds from liquidation are then distributed according to the priority of proven claims. An accounting is furnished to the creditors and the court. Finally, the debtor is discharged from its remaining debts.

Conservation and liquidation of assets

The interim trustee or his or her successor, the trustee elected by the unsecured creditors, first locates, inventories, and takes proper steps to safeguard the assets of the bankrupt firm. Then the trustee plans the liquidation of these assets. The efficiency with which the assets are liquidated has a great effect upon the ultimate proceeds. Procedures may vary from auctioning them off in a routine fashion ("knocking them down on the courthouse steps") to orderly collection of the receivables and carefully searching the market to locate suitable buyers of the inventories and fixed assets.

Priority of claims

The net proceeds of liquidation must be distributed according to the rule of *absolute priority.* Under this rule each superior claim in the order of priority must be *fully* satisfied before the claim under it can receive anything. When the funds are to be exhausted, payments to the last class of creditors must be made on a pro rata basis.

The order of priorities under the Bankruptcy Reform Act of 1978 is as follows:

1. Secured creditors to the extent that their claims are covered by the proceeds of sale of the specific property pledged. If such proceeds do not fully satisfy their claims, the remaining balances become unsecured creditors' claims (Item 8, below).[6]
2. Court costs, including trustees' fees associated with conserving, administering, and liquidating the bankrupt estate.

[6]Notes payable to banks usually include the "right of offset." This provides that, in event of bankruptcy, the bank may retain any balance in the depository account of the borrower as partial payment of the note. In this sense, an unsecured note held by the bank is secured by the debtor's depository account. The remaining balance of the note is an unsecured creditors' claim (Item 8).

3. Claims reflecting expenses incurred after filing of a bankruptcy petition but before appointment of the trustee.
4. Wages, salaries, and commissions not exceeding $2,000 per person if incurred within 90 days prior to filing the bankruptcy petition.
5. Claims for contributions to employee benefit plans. These claims must have arisen within 180 days prior to filing of the petition or the debtor's cessation of operations, whichever comes first. These claims plus those under Item 4 may not exceed $2,000 per person.
6. Consumer claims not exceeding $900 each. These claims usually reflect customers' deposits.
7. Taxes due the United States or any political subdivision thereof.
8. Unsecured creditors. These include debentures, unsecured loans, trade credits, and any secured obligations not satisfied under Item 1 above. Subordinated creditors' claims are offset to the specific creditors to whom they are subordinated.
9. Preferred stock.
10. Common stock.

Table 24–1

NEWTON CORPORATION
Balance Sheet
($000s)

Assets		*Liabilities*	
Current assets	$3,000	Current liabilities:	
Fixed assets:		Notes payable—bank*	$ 500
Land and buildings (net)	2,000	Accounts payable—trade	2,000
Equipment (net)	1,000	Accrued wages	50
		Accrued pension fund payments	15
		Accrued taxes	35
		Total current liabilities	2,600
		Long-term, liabilities:	
		First mortgage bonds	1,400
		Debentures	500
		Subordinated debentures†	200
		Total long-term liabilities	2,100
		Equity Capital	
		Preferred stock	200
		Common stock	800
		Retained earnings	300
		Total equity	1,300
Total assets	$6,000	Total liabilities and equity capital	$6,000

*Secured by equipment.
†Subordinated to the debentures only.

To illustrate the distribution of proceeds from liquidation, begin with the balance sheet of Newton Corporation on the date of its filing in bankruptcy as shown in Table 24–1. Each liability and equity capital item becomes a class of claims in the bankruptcy proceeding. The net proceeds from liquidation of each type of assets were:

Current assets	$1,900,000
Land and buildings	1,700,000
Equipment	400,000
Total proceeds	$4,000,000

The distribution of this $4 million is shown in Table 24–2. The $1,400,000 in first mortgage bonds are secured by all the land and buildings, which were liquidated at $1,700,000. Therefore, these bonds are fully covered by security, and their holders receive the full amount of their claims, $1,400,000. The notes payable to banks are secured by all of the equipment, which was liquidated at $400,000. As these notes total $500,000, the bank receives $400,000 under its prior claim, and the unsatisfied portion of $100,000 becomes an unsecured claim. Court costs of $700,000 and wages, pension fund payments, and taxes totaling $100,000 all receive priority treatment and are paid in full. Thus, prior claims consume $2,600,000 of the total proceeds from sale of assets, leaving $1,400,000 available to the other unsecured creditors.

Calculation of the distributions to the various types of unsecured creditors is shown in the bottom portion of Table 24–2. As $1,400,000 is available to pay off total unsecured claims of $2,800,000, we begin by calculating 50 percent ($1,400,000/$2,800,000) of each claim in column 3. The bank will receive 50 percent of its $100,000 unsatisfied claim, or $50,000, in addition to the $400,000 received under its prior claim to proceed from the sale of equipment. Therefore, its total payments of $450,000 equal 90 percent of its total claim. Accounts payable to trade creditors are settled at 50 cents on the dollar, or $1,000,000.

As the subordinated debentures are subordinated only to the straight debentures, an adjustment is necessary. First, the straight debentures are entitled to 50 percent of their $500,000 claim, or $250,000. But the subordinated debentures, with a claim of $200,000 and entitled to $100,000 if they were not subordinated, must give up that $100,000 to the straight debenture holders in honoring the subordination agreement. Therefore, the entire $100,000 to which they would otherwise be entitled is transferred to the debenture holders who thereby receive $350,000, or 70 percent of their claim. The subordinated debenture holders receive nothing.

As all creditors' claims are not satisfied from the proceeds from liquidation, neither the preferred stockholders nor the common stockholders receive anything.

Table 24–2 Newton Corporation
Distribution of proceeds from liquidation ($000)

Proceeds from sale of assets		$4,000
Prior claims:		
First mortgage bonds (100%—from sale of land and buildings)	$1,400	
Bank (80%—from sale of equipment)	400	
Court costs, including trustee's fees and expenses	700	
Wages	50	
Pension fund payments	15	
Taxes	35	
Total prior claims		$2,600
Available to unsecured creditors		$1,400

Unsecured creditors:

(1) Type	(2) Claim	(3) 50 percent of claim	(4) After subordinated adjustment	(5) Percentage of claim received
Bank—unsatisfied portion of secured loan	$ 100	$ 50	$ 50	90%*
Accounts payable—trade	2,000	1,000	1,000	50
Debentures	500	250	350†	70
Subordinated debentures	200	100	0†	0
Total	$2,800	$1,400	$1,400	

*Includes $400,000 from sale of equipment and $50,000 from unsecured claim.
†Subordination adjustment transfers $100,000 from subordinated debentures to the straight debentures.

Terminal actions

When all claims have been paid according to their priorities as indicated above, the trustee furnishes an accounting to the creditors and the judge of the bankruptcy court. If the accounting is in order and the judge accepts it, he then issues a *discharge* order, which relieves the debtor of any remaining obligations. If the debtor is a corporation, as in the case illustrated, it becomes an empty corporate shell that probably will be dissolved.

Reorganization under Chapter 11

If the court had decided that Newton Corporation were worth more alive than dead, it would have proceeded with a Chapter 11 reorganization rather than the Chapter 7 liquidation described above. Under reorganization, the liabilities and equity of the firm would be restructured in such a way that claims would be honored according to their priorities, similar to those listed under liquidation. But many of the claimants would receive securities of the succeeding corporation rather than cash. Those claims of inferior priority that could not be satisfied by the going-concern value of the reorganized firm would be washed out and receive nothing.

If a reorganization is to be successful, the succeeding corporation must be economically viable. This requires that the operating causes of the failure be identified and corrected and that required new funds can be raised to provide sufficient working capital for operations. Fixed charges must be reduced and debt maturities lengthened under the reorganized capital structure so that the firm can live with its obligations. In simple terms, there is no sense in reorganizing a firm only to have it thrown back into bankruptcy at a later date.

Reorganization under Chapter 11 involves procedures somewhat different from those implemented under Chapter 7. The firm must be valued as a going concern and that value must compare favorably to the alternative liquidation value. Then a reorganization plan that is fair and equitable, and feasible must be developed. The proposed plan is submitted to a vote of each class of claimants and must be approved by the court. In the reorganization of a large corporation whose stock is publicly held, the SEC may enter the case as a friend of the court, and its opinion of the plan usually is given considerable weight. If approved by the court, the plan is executed by forming a new corporation and distributing its securities to the claimants.

Procedure

Under Chapter 11, if the petition is *voluntary*, management of the debtor firm may submit a reorganization plan. If the debtor fails to do this within 120 days, any claimant or committee of claimants may submit such a plan. If the petition is *involuntary*, that is, filed by creditors, a hearing is held, and the bankruptcy court determines whether the debtor is bankrupt according to essentially the same criteria as under Chapter 7. In either case, the claims are classified according to their priorities, each secured claim being a separate class. Any party to the proceeding may submit a reorganization plan. The court may either allow the present management to continue or approve a trustee elected by the unsecured creditors.

Valuation

Valuation is vital to reorganization because (1) the going-concern value must exceed liquidation value and (2) the fair and equitable distribution of securities of the succeeding corporation to the various claimants ultimately rests upon the value of those securities, which, in turn, reflect going-concern value. The theory of going-concern value previously has been discussed.

It is extremely difficult to estimate the value of a firm emerging from reorganization. The failed firm was not able to maintain its economic viability. What will be the sales, costs, and expenses of the succeeding firm? How risky is it? These are matters of conjecture; no one really knows whether or not it will succeed at all. From its selfish standpoint, each important class of claimants may submit and defend a going-concern valuation to give that particular class as large an interest as possible in the succeeding firm. Thus, the creditors with relatively high priority argue for a low valuation to give them the largest possible financial interest in the reorganized firm. Conversely, the stockholders argue for the highest possible valuation in an attempt to retain any interest at all. Therefore, the various reorganization plans submitted may be based upon widely varying going-concern valuations. In general, the larger the bankruptcy, the greater the diversity of valuation testimony and reorganization plans submitted on the basis of it.

To illustrate, let us assume that Newton Corporation is to be reorganized under Chapter 11. The court has approved this action because it agrees with testimony indicating that the going-concern value of a reorganized Newton Corporation would be \$4.7 million compared to its liquidation value of \$4 million.[7] Newton's prebankruptcy balance sheet is shown in Table 24–1, and the distribution which claimants would receive under liquidation is shown in Table 24–2. Once the trustee has accomplished the required restructuring of Newton's operations and management, a reorganization plan must be developed and approved. The plan will recapitalize Newton and distribute its securities in an equitable fashion to the claimants. For simplicity, we shall consider only one plan, although several might in fact be submitted.

The reorganization plan

Development of a reorganization plan requires that the existing liabilities and equity capital of the firm be recast into a new capital structure. This structure must be *feasible* by ensuring a high probability that the succeeding firm will be able to meet its obligations in the future and be sufficiently creditworthy that it can obtain the necessary trade and bank credit to finance its operating requirements. Distribution of the securities comprising this new capital structure also must be *fair and equitable* in settling the claims of the creditors and equity holders.

[7]Both of these are gross values before considering court costs, wages, pension fund payments, and taxes totaling \$800,000.

Fair and equitable Before January 1, 1979, when the Bankruptcy Reform Act became effective, "fair and equitable" meant in compliance with the rule of absolute priority. This required that each class of claimants receive either cash or securities equal in value to its claims before the class inferior to it could receive anything. This rule has been slightly modified under the 1978 Act to move in the direction of *relative priority*. The difference is that strict adherence to the absolute priority rule is no longer required if, and only if, (1) each class of claims superior to the class in question receives at least as much value as it would have under liquidation and (2) all secured claims receive cash or securities at least equal to the value of the specific collateral and the remaining portion (if any) of their claims is treated equally with those of other unsecured creditors. With these qualifications, settlements now held to be "fair and equitable" may allow some holders of claims inferior to those that would be honored under the absolute priority rule to receive some compensation in the form of stock of the reorganized corporation reflecting an excess of going-concern value over liquidation value.

To illustrate, let us examine the reorganization plan for Newton Corporation summarized in Table 24–3. The plan is based upon a going-concern

Table 24–3 Newton Corporation
Reorganization plan ($000)

Capital structure of reorganized firm:

12%, 20-year first mortgage bonds	$1,400
10% preferred stock (4,000 shares @ $100)*	400
Common stock (2,100,000 shares @ $1)	2,100
Total capital structure	$3,900

Distribution to claimants:

Claim	Amount	Securities received	Value	Percentage of claim
First mortgage bonds	$1,400	First mortgage bonds	$1,400	100%
Notes payable—bank	500	Preferred stock and common stock (70,000 shares)	400 70	94
Accounts payable	2,000	Common stock (1,400,000 shares)	1,400	70
Debentures	500	Common stock (490,000 shares)†	490	98
Subordinated debentures	200	Common stock (100,000 shares)	100	50
Preferred stock	200	Common stock (40,000 shares)	40	20
Common stock	1,100	None	0	0
Total			$3,900	

*Noncumulative for first three years.
†Includes 350,000 shares for straight debenture claim and 140,000 shares transferred from subordinated debenture claim.

value of $4,700,000 less court costs of $700,000 and a total of $100,000 in other priority claims for wages, pension fund payments, and taxes. These claims would be paid in cash. This leaves a new value of $3,900,000 to be capitalized by issuing $1,400,000 in first mortgage bonds, 4,000 shares of $100 par value preferred stock, and 2,100,000 shares of common stock valued at $1 per share.

Under this plan, the first mortgage bonds, secured by land and buildings worth $1,700,000, would simply be replaced dollar for dollar by first mortgage bonds of the new corporation. The $500,000 in notes payable to banks is secured by equipment valued at $400,000. The bank would receive the 4,000 shares of preferred stock, valued at $400,000, and 70,000 shares of common stock, valued at $1 each, for the unsatisfied portion of its claim. Trade creditors would receive 1,400,000 shares of common stock valued at $1 per share, representing 70 percent of their accounts payable claims. The straight debenture holders' original claims of $500,000 would be settled by their receiving 350,000 shares of common stock. Because the subordinated debentures are subordinated only to them, the debenture holders would receive another 140,000 shares of common stock, reflecting a 70 percent settlement honoring the subordination agreement.

At this point, the deviation from the rule of absolute priority under the Bankruptcy Reform Act comes into play. All of the superior claimants would receive securities of equal or greater value than if the corporation had been liquidated, and the value of the specific collateral pledged under the secured claims has been fully recognized. But the remaining 140,000 shares of common stock may now be distributed. Recognizing relative priority, the subordinated debenture holders might receive 100,000 shares of common stock, valued at 50 percent of their claims, and the preferred stockholders could receive the remaining 40,000 shares, valued at 20 percent of their claims. The common stockholders would receive nothing under this plan.

Perhaps the bank, the trade creditors, and/or the debenture holders might contest the plan as representing too much deviation from absolute priority. From the opposite standpoint, the common stockholders and perhaps the preferred stockholders might argue that the unsecured creditors will receive common stock valued at 70 percent of their claims whereas they would have received only 50 percent in cash if the firm had been liquidated.

This plan could be accepted by the court, but it illustrates the dilemma created by deviation from the absolute priority rule. How far should the court go in its deviation? Nobody knows; it is a matter of judgment. All parties to the proceeding must recognize that, depending upon the accuracy of the estimate of the going-concern value, Newton common stock may turn out to be worth more or less than $1 per share. The value of it and of the whole firm is far from definite.

Perhaps the SEC may render an opinion as to whether this plan is fair and equitable. The court must hear that opinion, but it may or may not abide by it in the final decision regarding the reorganization plan.

Feasible A feasible proposal, in the present context, is one that provides a high probability that the reorganized firm will survive. There are three aspects to establishing the feasibility of a reorganization. The first is to *restore* the firm's *earning power.* This is no small task because a bankrupt firm typically has suffered large and protracted operating losses. If these losses have resulted from extremely inept or fraudulent actions of management, rehabilitation of earning power may be accomplished by bringing in a competent management team. But often the task is more complex, involving elimination of unsuccessful product lines, establishing an effective control system, re-establishing satisfactory relations with disgruntled customers and suppliers, rebuilding employee morale, and so on.

The second aspect of feasibility is *financial.* The firm got into bankruptcy because it could not meet its maturing obligations. The reorganization plan must scale down fixed charges and lengthen maturity of debt so that the emerging firm *can meet its obligations.* Notice that Newton Corporation's reorganization plan reduced long-term liabilities from $2.1 million to $1.4 million and eliminated $2.5 million of defaulted current liabilities. Some of the latter were washed out, but most were replaced by stock. This eliminated fixed interest charges on the note payable to the bank and the immediate maturity of the accounts payable.

The third requirement is that the firm's *credit be re-established* so it can purchase required raw materials on competitive credit terms and obtain short-term bank loans necessary to finance its seasonal requirements. This usually results from the combined effects of reducing fixed charges, restoring an adequate equity cushion by converting debt to equity, and increasing operating cash flows to make the normal flow of funds—from inventories to receivables to cash—sufficient to service current obligations as they mature.

Now let us test the feasibility of the Newton Corporation reorganization plan. Assume that operating profitability has been restored. It is estimated that annual sales of $9,350,000 can be achieved and that an operating profit margin of 10 percent will yield earnings before interest and taxes of $935,000, as shown in its pro forma income statement, Table 24–4. Fixed interest charges of $168,000 (.12 × $1,400,000) are covered slightly more than 5.5 times by EBIT. This should be fully adequate, as EBIT could decline more than 80 percent and interest payments on the bonds would still be covered by earnings.

Preferred dividends of $40,000 are adequately covered. There is further protection in that the preferred stock is noncumulative during the first three years so that arrearages will not accumulate if the reorganized firm should encounter initial difficulties in getting on its feet.

If the estimates in Table 24–4 materialize, earnings per share of the new common stock will be 20 cents. Note that the basis for its valuation at $1 per share in developing the reorganization plan was the assumption that EPS would be 20 cents and that the market would value the stock at a price-earnings ratio of five times. This estimated PE ratio was based upon the current market prices and earnings of similar companies.

Table 24–4

NEWTON CORPORATION
Pro Forma Income Statement
($000)

Sales	$9,350
Operating costs and expenses	8,415
Earnings before interest and taxes	935
Interest (.12 × $1,400)	168
Net income before taxes	767
Income taxes (@40%)	307
Net income after taxes	460
Preferred dividends	40
Net income to common stock	$ 420
Number of common shares	2,100
Earnings per share	20¢

Would the succeeding firm have adequate credit to cover its operating needs? Newton would come out of the bankruptcy with total assets valued at $3,900,000, comprised of current assets totaling $1,800,000 and fixed assets of $2,100,000 (The fixed assets are given the liquidation values established earlier, and the current assets are valued at the residual estimated going-concern value of the firm. Thus, current assets might be somewhat overvalued here.) With no current liabilities at the outset, surely Newton could obtain trade and bank credit of at least $600,000 (based upon the current ratio of 3). Such current financing would appear to be adequate to cover its requirements. Thus this reorganization plan appears to be feasible.

Approval of the plan

The plan(s), accompanied by a disclosure statement, must be submitted to all claimants and the court. A hearing will be held by the bankruptcy court to approve the adequacy of the disclosure statement. In some cases, the SEC renders an opinion at this meeting as to the adequacy of disclosure, which must be such that a reasonable claimant may make an informed judgment regarding the plan.

After the judge has approved the disclosure statement, the vote of all members of each class of claimants is solicited. To indicate approval of the plan by a given class, a simple majority of the claimants in that class, representing at least two thirds of the dollar amount of claims, must vote in favor of it. The court is not bound by the acceptance or rejection by a given class so long as no class senior to a rejecting class receives securities of greater value than its priority share. This proviso is necessary because any class of creditors or stockholders whose claims will be washed out by the plan naturally will vote against it.

Finally, after the plan has been approved by the court, the new corporation is formed, assets are transferred to it, and payments of cash and securities of the succeeding corporation are made to the claimants as prescribed by the plan. The trustee (or management of the debtor if such is the case) furnishes an accounting to the claimants and court. When this is approved by the court, the trustee is dismissed.

Technically, under Chapter 11 there is no provision for discharge of the debtor from its remaining obligations. But this is effectively accomplished by leaving the debtor corporation an empty shell to be dissolved. All of the assets, liabilities, and capital relate to the newly formed corporation, which proceeds to do business without assuming any liability for the debt that has been eliminated by the reorganization.

Summary

This chapter dealt with the firm in serious financial difficulty. Understanding the various remedies available when a firm is in financial distress is valuable to its creditors and investors as well as the owners and managers of the failing firm. Many reasons for business failure may be cited, but in the vast majority of cases the ultimate cause is poor management.

There are various degrees of financial difficulty. A firm is illiquid (technically insolvent) when it cannot pay its obligations when due. It is insolvent when the real value of its assets is less than its liabilities. It is bankrupt when its affairs have been taken over by a federal bankruptcy court. Economic failure denotes inability of a firm to generate sufficient revenues to cover its costs, including the cost of capital.

Both management and creditors of a failing firm usually prefer informal remedies to formal bankruptcy because they are simpler, faster, and much less costly. Informal remedies are out-of-court arrangements developed by mutual agreement of the creditors and the debtor firm. The simplest is an extension that postpones the maturity of the overdue debt obligations. Extension is feasible when the debtor is temporarily illiquid but not insolvent or an economic failure.

If the firm is insolvent, perhaps a composition can be worked out under which the creditors accept a pro rata settlement of their claims. If it is highly probable that the debtor will recover if debt maturity is postponed and a portion of the debt is forgiven, a combination extension and composition might be agreeable. In many cases safeguards are provided to protect the creditors during the period of the extension. If the failure appears to be due to management incompetence or lack of integrity, the creditors may require assignment of the debtor's assets to an assignee (or trustee), who assumes control of the firm's affairs. The assignee may either liquidate the assets or install new management in an effort to rehabilitate the firm.

Attempts to develop informal remedies sometimes fail because agreement cannot be reached either among the creditors or between them and the debtor. Then the only alternative is to go to court. A firm that cannot meet its obligations may be filed into bankruptcy by its management or its creditors. The federal bankruptcy court may then either liquidate it under Chapter 7 or reorganize it under Chapter 11 of the Bankruptcy Reform Act of 1978. The remedy will depend upon whether the firm is worth more dead or alive.

If the debtor firm is to be liquidated, a trustee usually is selected by the creditors' committee and is responsible for conservation of the assets and the orderly liquidation of them. Proceeds of liquidation are distributed to the claimants in the order established by the Act according to the rule of absolute priority. Finally the debtor is discharged of any remaining obligations.

Reorganization requires that the operating causes of failure by identified and corrected and that the firm's liabilities and equity capital be restructured. One or more reorganization plans are developed and submitted to the vote of the various classes of claimants. To be approved by the court, a plan must be "fair and equitable" and "feasible". Under a plan that is fair and equitable, the value of cash or securities of the succeeding firm distributed to each class of claimants must be at least equal to the cash that would be received if the firm were liquidated. This allows some departure from the absolute priority rule.

For the plan to be feasible, there must be a high probability that the succeeding firm will survive. First, the earning power of the firm must be restored. Second, the plan must scale down the fixed charges and lengthen debt maturities so the firm can meet its financial obligations. Third, sufficient credit must be re-established that the firm can obtain working capital necessary for operations.

The approved plan is executed by forming of a new corporation, transferring the assets to it, and distributing cash and its securities to the claimants. Although there is no formal discharge, this is achieved by leaving the debtor corporation an empty shell to be dissolved.

Questions

1. If you and your firm are successful, why should you have any interest in failure, reorganization, and bankruptcy?

2. Define and identify the differences among:
   a. Illiquidity (technical insolvency).
   b. Insolvency (absolute insolvency).
   c. Bankruptcy, in the legal sense.
   d. Economic failure.

3. When a firm has failed, why might an informal remedy be preferable to filing in bankruptcy? Discuss from the standpoints of both the creditors and owners of the failed firm. What is the principal difficulty encountered in executing an informal remedy?

4. Define the following types of informal remedies:
   a. Extension.
   b. Composition.
   c. Combination extension and composition.
   d. Assignment.

5. When an assignment has been made, what are the functions of the assignee (or trustee)? What are the two alternative courses of action the assignee might pursue?

6. "One of the cornerstones of a competitive economic system is the free right to go broke." Discuss and evaluate this statement.

7. A firm may be filed into bankruptcy by a voluntary or an involuntary petition. What is the difference between the two? How does the acceptance of a petition in bankruptcy affect *(a)* the creditors and *(b)* the owners and managers of the firm?

8. What is the basic criterion governing the bankruptcy court's decision whether to liquidate the firm under Chapter 7 or to reorganize it under Chapter 11?

9. If a firm is liquidated in bankruptcy under Chapter 7, the net proceeds are distributed to claimants under the rule of absolute priority.

   a. What is the rule of absolute priority?

   b. In what *order* would the following claims be settled?

      (1) Claims of unsecured (general) creditors.
      (2) Tax claims.
      (3) Claims of preferred stockholders.
      (4) Claims of secured creditors covered by proceeds from sale of specific property pledged.
      (5) Court costs of administering the bankruptcy.
      (6) Consumer claims up to $900 each.
      (7) Claims of common stockholders.
      (8) Expenses incurred after filing but before appointment of the trustee.
      (9) Eligible wages and salaries.
      (10) Eligible contributions to employee benefit plans.

10. Who may file a reorganization plan in a Chapter 11 bankruptcy proceeding? Recognizing the practical difficulty of estimating the value of a reorganized firm, how would you go about valuing such a firm as the basis for developing a reorganization plan?

11. What constitutes a *fair and equitable* reorganization plan under Chapter 11? What deviation may be allowed from strict adherence to the rule of absolute priority? What criteria must be satisfied if the reorganization plan is to be *feasible*?

Problems

1. Classify as *illiquid, insolvent,* and/or as an *economic failure* each of the firms described below.

   a. The current value of firm A's assets is $400,000. Its total liabilities are $300,000, including $40,000 of overdue income tax payments and $75,000 of past-due accounts payable.

   b. The current value of firm B's assets is $200,000. Its total liabilities are $250,000, none of which are overdue. The firm has suffered losses during each of the past four years.

c. The current value of firm C's assets is $2 million, and its total liabilities are $1.8 million, none of which are past due. Company C has operated at an average annual net profit of $5,000 over the past seven years, last year's net profit being $2,000.

d. Company D has assets currently valued at $1 million and total liabilities of $2 million of which $500,000 are past due. The firm has operated at a loss for several years and recently had a $300,000 judgment for damages levied against it (included in the $500,000 past-due liabilities).

2. The Smith Corporation has encountered financial difficulties. At a meeting of its management and creditors, it was established that Smith has total liabilities (all current and most overdue) of $220,000. A creditors' committee was elected to seek an informal remedy. Indicate the amounts that will be paid and classify as an *extension,* a *composition,* a *combination extension-composition,* or an *assignment,* each of the following proposed remedies:

a. Each creditor will be paid 55 cents on the dollar in full settlement of the debt.

b. The claims of a group of small creditors, which total $10,000, will be paid in full immediately. Remaining claims will be paid in equal installments at the end of each of the next 12 months.

c. All of the assets of Smith will be transferred to a trustee selected by the creditors' committee. The trustee intends to liquidate the assets for about $160,000 and will incur costs of about $20,000 in doing so. The next proceeds will be distributed to all creditors on a ratable basis.

d. All creditors will be paid 80 percent of their claims in eight equal monthly installments, after which the debts will be considered fully satisfied.

3. Judson Corportaion has been admitted to bankruptcy. Its assets are estimated to have a liquidation value of about $840,000 after court costs and expenses of a Chapter 7 bankruptcy. The estimated average future annual earnings after taxes of a reorganized Judson Corporation are about $150,000, and a reasonable capitalization rate reflecting the uncertainty of these earnings is 15 percent. Court costs and expenses of a Chapter 11 reorganization would be about $100,000.

a. If you were the judge of the bankruptcy court, would you prefer that Judson be liquidated under Chapter 7 or reorganized under Chapter 11? Why?

b. If you were a banker holding a claim of $100,000 secured by the pledge of equipment with a liquidating value of $140,000, which course of action would you prefer? Why?

c. Assuming that creditors' claims total $1 million and that you are an unsecured trade creditor, which course of action would you prefer? Why?

(Note: Problems 4 and 5 are a series.)

4. The Rocking Table Company is liquidated under Chapter 7. Its balance sheet ($000) when filed into bankruptcy was as follows:

Assets		*Liabilities*	
Current assets	$10,000	Current liabilities	
Fixed assets		Notes payable—bank*	$ 3,000
Land and buildings (net)	4,500	Accounts payable—trade	7,000
Equipment (net)	5,500	Accrued wages†	1,400
		Accrued taxes	800
		Total current liabilities	$12,200
		Long-term liabilities:	
		12% first mortgage bonds‡	$ 2,600
		14% debentures	1,000
		Total long-term liabilities	3,600
		Equity capital	
		Common stock	$3,000
		Retained earnings	1,200
		Total equity capital	4,200
Total assets	$20,000	Total liabilities and equity capital	$20,000

*Unsecured.
†All eligible priority claims.
‡Secured by all land and buildings.

Proceeds from liquidation of the assets are:

	($000)
Current assets	$ 6,800
Land and buildings	2,100
Equipment	2,850
Total	$11,750

Court costs, including trustee's fees and expenses, total $550,000. What amount and percentage of claims will be received by each class of claimants?

5. Assume that the Rocking Table Company (Problem 4) is believed to be worth $14 million as a going concern and accordingly is being reorganized under Chapter 11. The going-concern value is based upon the forecast that its future annual earnings before taxes and interest (EBIT) will be $2 million and that the firm will be worth seven times its expected future annual EBIT.

(Assume that the $14 million valuation is after court costs, accrued taxes, and accured wages have been paid and that the tax rate will be 40 percent.)

a. Develop an unbiased reorganization plan.
b. Show why your plan is fair and equitable.
c. Show why it is feasible.

Part Seven
International Financial Management

25 International Financial Management

Chapter 25
International Financial Management

During the past two or three decades the outlook of many business executives has become increasingly international in scope. This development reflects tremendous improvements in transportation and communication, resulting in socio-political-economic involvement on a global basis. The world has become small. Therefore, financial managers must understand the added complexities of international finance.

Involvement in international finance may range all the way from that of a domestic firm importing some of its raw materials and/or exporting a portion of its products to that of a multinational firm producing and marketing its products throughout the world. An example of the former is Celestial Seasonings, which imports some of its herbs from various foreign countries, produces herbal teas in Boulder, Colorado, and markets its teas in the United States. Examples of major multinational corporations are Exxon, IBM, Coca-Cola, Gillette, and Ford. Although U.S.-based multinational firms are among the most prominent in the Western world, there also are many important foreign-based ones, for example Nestlé and Ciba-Geigy of Switzerland; ICL (Imperial Chemical, Limited) and British Petroleum of Great Britain; Volkswagen of West Germany; and Nissan, Toyota, and Sony of Japan. There are several intermediate degrees of involvement, such as selling through foreign branch sales offices, licensing processes and products to foreign manufacturers, or participating in joint ventures with foreign firms.

Participation of U.S. firms in foreign trade is indicated by 1980 total exports exceeding $220 billion, and imports of $245 billion. Direct investment by U.S. corporations in foreign assets amounted to $214 billion. Although these figures are huge, they may reflect only the beginning of much larger international business activity in the future.

The basic principles of financial management discussed throughout this book apply to international as well as domestic business activity. The fundamental considerations and analytical techniques relative to working capital management, capital allocation decisions, capital structure policy, dividend policy, and external expansion are essentially the same. But the environment of international business is more complex. Operating and financial transactions involve foreign currencies as well as the U.S. dollar. Relative values of these currencies are continually changing. The instruments and institutions through which financing may be arranged are more complex. The laws, tax structures, and customs, as well as the political and economic environment of each country, differ. In this chapter we shall focus upon the added dimensions that relate to financial policies and decisions in the international arena.

Foreign exchange markets will be introduced first. Then international transactions by domestic firms will be treated with respect to both the means by which foreign exchange risk may be managed and the instruments used to finance import-export transactions. Next, financial management of the multinational firm will be discussed, including unique risk and return considerations in capital investment abroad, accounting and tax influences, and monetary risk exposure management. Finally, institutions and instruments of multinational financing will be discussed.

Foreign exchange markets

A *foreign exchange rate* is the relationship between the values of two currencies. If you were planning a vacation in Switzerland, you would have to exchange your U.S. dollars for Swiss francs (S fr) to cover your expenses there. Likewise, a jewelry importer in New York must exchange U.S. dollars for Swiss francs to pay a Swiss exporter for watches purchased from it. On August 20, 1981, the exchange rate of the Swiss franc was $.4648, or approximately 46½ cents. Or the exchange rate may be quoted the other way around, $1 would buy 2.1575 Swiss francs.[1] Note that each rate is approximately the reciprocal of the other. The exchange rates of foreign currencies relative to the dollar are quoted daily in *The Wall Street Journal* and most other large daily newspapers. Spot exchange rates of several major trading currencies on August 20, 1981, are shown in Table 25–1. A *spot* exchange rate refers to a rate of exchange of two currencies for immediate delivery.

Foreign exchange rates change almost continuously, much the same as stock prices. The market is made by over-the-counter trading of dealers and

Table 25–1 Spot foreign exchange rates (August 20, 1981)

Country	Currency	U.S. dollar equivalent	Currency per $ U.S.
Belgium	franc	$ .0248	40.23
Britain	pound	1.8605	.5375
Canada	dollar	.8254	1.2115
France	franc	.1687	5.9250
Italy	lira	.000808	1237.00
Japan	yen	.00437	228.80
Netherlands	guilder	.3650	2.739
Switzerland	franc	.4648	2.1575
West Germany	mark	.4048	2.4700

Source: *The Wall Street Journal,* August 21, 1981.

[1]The rates quoted here and elsewhere in this chapter are New York foreign exchange rates, which apply to trading among banks in amounts of $1 million or more. Retail transactions, such as one to finance your Swiss vacation, will provide slightly fewer francs per dollar, say 2.10 rather than 2.1575.

major money-market banks in the various financial centers of the world, such as New York, London, Zurich, Frankfurt, and Tokyo. Since 1971, when the United States allowed the dollar to "float", exchange rates among major trading currencies have fluctuated widely, as demonstrated by Table 25–2.

Table 25–2 Exchange rates, 1976–1981
Cents per unit of foreign currency

Currency	1976	1977	1978	1979	1980	Aug. 20, 1981
British pound (£)	180.48	174.49	191.84	212.24	232.58	186.05
Canadian dollar (Can $)	101.41	94.11	87.73	85.39	85.53	82.54
French franc (F fr)	20.94	20.34	22.22	23.50	23.69	16.87
Japanese yen (Y)	.337	.373	.480	.458	.443	.437
Swiss franc (S fr)	40.01	41.71	56.28	60.12	59.70	46.48
West German mark (DM)	39.74	43.08	49.87	54.56	55.09	40.48

Sources: *Federal Reserve Bulletins* (Annual data, 1976–80); *The Wall Street Journal*, August 21, 1981 (August 20, 1981, data).

In general, the U.S. dollar was weak in relation to major trading currencies during the 70s. Note the rise of the British pound, French franc, Japanese yen, Swiss franc, and West German mark from 1976 to 1980. The exception was the Canadian dollar, which drifted lower against the U.S. dollar through this period. Then, beginning in the latter part of 1980, the U.S. dollar strengthened remarkably against the major trading currencies. Note the magnitude of the decline of the French franc, Swiss franc, and the West German mark in the brief period from 1980 to August 20, 1981. The point is that exchange rates, even those of relatively strong currencies, may fluctuate greatly. The data in Table 25–2 somewhat understate these fluctuations because annual average exchange rates are shown for 1976 through 1980. Intra-year fluctuations of considerable magnitude are now shown.

Exchange rates of currencies of less-developed countries tend to fluctuate much more violently than those of major trading currencies. This reflects their impoverished economies and high inflation rates and, often, their dependence for foreign exchange upon exports of one or a few agricultural crops or minerals.

Fluctuating exchange rates provide an added dimension to the risk entailed in conducting international business. Later we shall discuss the implications of this risk and various means of coping with it. But first the factors that influence exchange rates must be understood.

Factors influencing exchange rates

Any market price, in this case the rate of exchange between two currencies, is a function of supply and demand. We shall now examine the elements of supply and demand for a given currency, the British pound, relative to another currency, the U.S. dollar.

Immediate influences The *demand* for the pound (against the dollar) at any given time will arise largely from American importers of British goods who must make payment in pounds, such as an American clothing manufacturer requiring pounds to pay for a shipment of Harris tweed woolens. Additional demand arises from American tourist expenditures in Britain and the payment for services such as insurance placed through Lloyd's or transportation on British Airways. Investors buying British securities or multinational firms investing in real assets in Britain—say, Exxon investing in a North Sea oil drilling platform—also demand pounds. Remittances of dividends and interest to British investors on their investments in the United States create an additional demand for pounds. These elements of demand reflect normal commercial and financial transactions.

Another layer of demand, which may be much more volatile, reflects U.S. short-term investors (or speculators) depositing pounds in British banks or purchasing pound-denominated money-market securities such as British treasury bills. This so-called "hot money" may move in or out quickly depending upon relative interest rates and speculators' expectations of change in exchange rates.

A third layer of demand may be created by governmental activity to influence exchange rates. The central bank, the Bank of England, may buy pounds (or sell dollars) in an effort to stabilize a falling pound. Although foreign exchange rates generally are allowed to float in the market in response to normal supply and demand forces, central banks sometimes do enter the market in an effort to stabilize their currencies. For this reason, the current foreign exchange system is known as a "managed float" or "dirty float" system. As in any stabilizing effort, intervention by central banks is of limited effectiveness; it can hold back a wave but not a tide.

The *supply* of pounds in the foreign exchange market reflects the opposite factors. British importers, such as British Airways paying for aircraft purchased from Boeing, supply pounds to buy dollars. British tourists in the United States do the same. British investors or multinational firms, buying U.S. securities or properties, supply pounds to buy dollars. British firms remitting dividends and interest to American investors supply pounds to be exchanged into dollars. Short-term investors (or speculators), attracted by high U.S. interest rates or believing the pound will fall against the dollar, transfer accounts from British to U.S. banks or purchase U.S. dollar-dominated money-market securities. Or, if the pound is rising against the dollar, the Federal Reserve System may buy dollars and/or sell pounds.

These immediate factors determine foreign exchange rates, in this illustration the pound against the dollar, on an hour-to-hour, day-to-day basis. But more fundamental economic factors underlie the trends in foreign exchange rate movements.

Underlying influences The fundamental underlying factors that influence trends in foreign exchange rates are relative inflation, interest rates, and the policies of the respective governments.

Inflation The expectation of relative inflation in two given countries has a great effect upon the exchange rate of their currencies. For example, if inflation were expected to occur at an annual rate of 10 percent in the United States and 20 percent in France, the exchange rate of the French franc against the dollar would tend to be depressed. Assuming relatively free international trade and freedom to exchange currencies, exchange rates should tend toward *purchasing power parity*. Approximately the same amount of goods or services should be obtainable in either country for a given number of dollars or francs. To maintain that parity, the exchange rate of the French franc against the dollar would fall sufficiently to compensate for the inflation differential between the two countries. Note that the important factor is *expectation* of inflation rather than the past or present rate. Thus, when Mitterand, whose announced policies were highly inflationary, was elected president of France in mid-1981, the franc fell drastically against the U.S. dollar and the currencies of other countries such as West Germany and Switzerland that were pursuing anti-inflationary policies.

Interest rates Relative interest rates, particularly those on short-term securities and deposits, also have an important influence upon exchange rates. Other things being equal, international investors tend to sell securities in countries where interest rates are low and transfer their investments to countries in which higher interest rates are available. For example, if higher interest rates were available on money-market securities in the United States than in Germany, large amounts of funds would move from Germany to the United States, weakening the mark against the dollar. This happened in the first half of 1981, when extremely high short-term interest rates prevailed in the United States.

Relative interest rates and inflation rates tend to counterbalance each other in their influence upon exchange rates. High inflation rates (which tend to depress the exchange rate of a country's currency) usually are accompanied by high interest rates (which tend to increase the exchange rate). The net influence of these two factors is relative one to the other.

Governmental policies We do not live in a world of complete freedom of international trade or currency exchange. Various obstacles to trade among countries are established by national governments. Tariffs, quotas, and other import-export restrictions may inhibit the free flow of goods and services, thereby preventing full adjustment of exchange rates to purchasing power parity. In addition, governmental policy greatly influences such fundamental factors as inflation and interest rates.

Exchange of currencies is relatively free in most of the developed Western countries. However, even among these nations, foreign exchange rates are not completely free to seek their own levels because central banks intervene in attempts to stablize them. Many countries impose exchange restrictions that inhibit the conversion of their currencies to others. At the extreme, the Soviet Union and other countries of the communist bloc set exchange rates by government decree. Their fixed rates often bear no resemblance to those that would be established in a free market. Their international trade is conducted largely on the basis of specific barter arrangements rather than through the mechanisms of the international financial system.

Governmental policies and attitudes greatly influence exchange rates. Traders and investors are reluctant to enter into contracts or make investments in a country where there is doubt (risk) as to their ability to get their money out by converting it into their own currencies. Political stability of a country is another important factor. Even though the present government may allow relatively free trade and currency exchange, the risk of change to a government that will impose restrictions affects the rates of exchange of its currency.

International transactions by domestic firms

Here we consider international transactions, importing raw materials or parts and/or exporting products, by firms whose production facilities and primary marketing operations are located in the United States. Financial management is concerned with the risk of fluctuation in foreign exchange rates and the mechanisms that may be used to facilitate export or import credit transactions.

Foreign exchange risk management

Because distances are great and ocean transportation is slow, import or export transactions usually involve credit extended over a considerable period of time—60, 90, or even 180 days. Payment must be made in the currency of either the exporter or the importer, and therefore one of these parties must be concerned with the risk that the currency exchange rate will change during the credit period. This risk either may be assumed or it may be avoided at a cost. If the risk is to be assumed, the assuming party must weigh that risk and compensate for it in determining the acceptable transaction price. If the risk is to be avoided by hedging, the cost of the hedge must be considered in pricing the transaction.

Hedging *Hedging* is protecting oneself from loss by contracting with another party to counterbalance risk exposure. In connection with export-import transactions on a credit basis, a hedge may be accomplished either through the forward (futures) foreign exchange market or through short-term investment (or borrowing) denominated in the other party's currency.

The forward foreign exchange market To this point we have referred only to the *spot* foreign exchange market (Tables 25–1 and 25–2). Now we recognize the *forward* (futures) market, in which one may buy or sell foreign currency for delivery at a future date. The forward rate of exchange is a rate agreed upon today for delivery of currency, say 30, 60, 90, or 180 days hence. Bankers and other foreign exchange dealers agree to such contracts for future delivery in an over-the-counter market that operates in the same fashion as the spot market. Forward exchange rates of selected major trading currencies quoted on August 20, 1981, are compared to spot rates in Table 25–3. Forward rates may be either higher or lower than spot rates.

Table 25–3 Forward and spot exchange rates (August 20, 1981)

Currency	U.S. dollar equivalent
British pound (£)	
Spot	1.8605
30-day forward	1.8689
90-day forward	1.8822
180-day forward	1.9005
Canadian dollar (Can $)	
Spot	.8254
30-day forward	.8219
90-day forward	.8181
180-day forward	.8160
French franc (F fr)	
Spot	.1687
30-day forward	.1668
90-day forward	.1657
180-day forward	.1654
Japanese yen (Y)	
Spot	.00437
30-day forward	.004416
90-day forward	.004496
180-day forward	.004617
Swiss franc (S fr)	
Spot	.4648
30-day forward	.4690
90-day forward	.4762
180-day forward	.4863
West German mark (DM)	
Spot	.4048
30-day forward	.4071
90-day forward	.4112
180-day forward	.4172

Source: *The Wall Street Journal,* August 21, 1981.

Premiums (higher forward rates) reflect the market's expectation of strength of the foreign currency against the dollar and the implicit interest for the interval. Note the premiums of the pound, yen, Swiss franc, and mark in Table 25–3. Discounts (lower forward rates) indicate anticipated weakness of the currency against the dollar, at this time exemplified by the Canadian dollar and the French franc.

Foreign exchange *risk exposure* is the possibility of gain or loss resulting from change in foreign exchange rates. For example, the U.S. clothing manufacturer who buys Harris tweed woolens from a British exporter on 90-day credit terms will be obligated to pay the agreed price *in pounds* 90 days hence. If the price of this transaction is £53,750, its U.S. dollar equivalent in the spot market at the time of the transaction is $100,000 (53,750 × $1.8605). The American clothing manufacturer (the importer) may choose to bear the foreign exchange risk and do nothing at the time the order is placed. If the pound should rise against the dollar during the 90-day credit period to, say, $1.92, the importer will have to pay $103,200 (53,750 × $1.92) to purchase in the spot market at the due date the pounds required to pay the bill. If this happens, the importer will be sorry. On the other hand, if the pound should decline against the dollar during the period to, say, $1.81, then the required pounds could be purchased in the spot market at the due date for $97,288 (53,750 × $1.81); the importer would realize a gain resulting from the exchange risk exposure.

The American importer may choose to avoid the foreign exchange risk by hedging the transaction in the forward market. At the time the order is placed, the importer will buy £53,750 forward exchange for delivery in 90 days. These pounds will cost $1.8822 each, or a total of $101,168. Ninety days hence this forward contract will expire, paying the importer £53,750, which will be remitted by cable transfer to pay the British exporter. The American importer has avoided the foreign exchange risk by crystallizing the purchase price *in dollars* when the transaction was initiated.

There are several variations on this hedging theme. For example, if the price of the transaction had been agreed upon in dollars, the British exporter would be exposed to the foreign exchange risk. The transaction could be hedged by selling U.S. dollars for delivery in 90 days, receiving pounds at the time the sale was made. When the dollars were collected in 90 days, the British exporter would make delivery on the forward contract.[2]

[2]Investors in foreign short-term securities also use the forward exchange markets to hedge or "cover" their investments. For example, an American investor may buy 90-day British treasury bills. To pay for them, pounds are purchased with dollars in the spot market. By simultaneously executing a forward contract to exchange the principal and interest to be received in pounds in 90 days into dollars (at the 90-day forward rate), the investor is assured of the *fully hedged* or *covered* interest rate to be received. If the forward rate is a premium, the covered interest rate will be less than the uncovered rate. Conversely, if the forward rate is a discount, the covered rate will be higher.

Short-term foreign investment or borrowing Another method of hedging against foreign exchange risk is through investing (or borrowing) in the foreign country. Our American clothing manufacturer could buy 90-day British treasury bills (or other money-market securities such as CDs of British banks or commercial paper of British firms) at the time the order for the Harris tweeds is placed. These securities would be paid for by converting dollars to pounds at the spot exchange rate. The amount of British securities purchased would be such that the payment at par in 90 days would yield the pounds required to pay the exporter. The cost of this hedge would be the difference between the interest yield received on the investment in British securities and that which could have been obtained by investing the dollars in U.S. money-market securities of equal quality. If the American importer did not have the money available, the latter cost would be the interest paid to its bank to borrow the required funds.

Conversely, if the price of the woolens were fixed in dollars, the British exporter could hedge its risk by borrowing dollars, converting them to pounds in the spot market, and paying off the loan with the dollars received in 90 days from the American importer. Similarly an American exporter selling to a British importer in a transaction denominated in pounds could borrow pounds from a British bank and 90 days hence use the pounds collected from the customer to pay off the loan.

If an export-import transaction is to be hedged, the choice between using the forward foreign exchange market or investing (or borrowing) in the foreign country is strictly a matter of comparative costs. If the cost of the least expensive method appears to be unjustifiably high or the party exposed to foreign exchange risk feels that the probability of gain from bearing that risk exceeds the probability of loss, the transaction will not be hedged. The foreign exchange risk exposure simply may be chosen as a risk the firm wishes to take in quest of profit.

Facilitating import-export transactions

Most domestic credit transactions take place on open-book account; documentation other than the invoice is not considered necessary. Credit terms are relatively short, the buyer and seller usually are well known to each other, and the seller has adequate means of investigating the credit worthiness of the buyer. Some international transactions are conducted on the same basis, particularly when the buyer is a prominent firm of unquestioned credit standing. Thus, General Electric might be quite willing to sell electronic components to Phillips Electric of the Netherlands on open-book account.

But most international transactions are different. Credit terms are long and the seller may not know whether the foreign buyer is an excellent credit risk or a dead-beat. Mechanisms for ascertaining credit worthiness are either cumbersome or nonexistent. Therefore, the documentation and financing of international trade usually are formalized through documented trade drafts or bank letters of credit.

International trade drafts An international *trade draft* (also called a *bill of exchange*) is a written order to the *drawee* (the importer) to pay to the order of the *drawor* (the exporter) a specified amount of money. A *sight draft* is payable upon presentation to the drawee; a *time draft* is payable a stated number of days after sight.

If the exporter is unwilling to extend credit, but the importer wants to be assured that the goods have been shipped before paying for them, a *documentary* sight draft is used. The documents that accompany the draft are the *bill of lading* and other shipping documents, such as insurance papers and customs declarations. For example, assume that Norfolk Coal Company is exporting a shipload of coal to Italco of Genoa, Italy. Norfolk Coal will load the coal on the carrier, obtain a bill of lading and other required documentation, and write a sight draft. This draft and the accompanying documents will be forwarded through its Norfolk bank to a bank in Genoa designated by Italco for collection. If Italco pays the draft (in dollars or lira as prearranged), the Genoa bank gives Italco the documents, which will be required to obtain the coal when the ship arrives (the bill of lading documents title to the coal). In the unlikely event that Italco refuses to pay the draft, Norfolk Coal will be notified, the draft and accompanying documents will be returned to Norfolk, and the ship will be either recalled or rerouted to another customer.

Where credit is being granted, a time draft will be used in essentially the same way, except that Italco will *accept* the draft upon presentation by acknowledging in writing on the reverse side its obligation to pay the amount due at maturity. When so acknowledged, the time draft becomes a *trade acceptance*. Norfolk Coal may hold the acceptance until a few days before maturity, when it will forward it for collection to the Genoa bank. Or it may *discount* the trade acceptance at its bank in Norfolk. Norfolk Coal will be required to endorse the discounted acceptance, thus becoming liable for its payment if efforts to collect it from Italco fail.

If Italco's credit were not favorably known, Norfolk Coal would not be willing to go along with this arrangement. In such a case, Norfolk would insist upon a letter of credit issued by a major Italian bank.

Letters of credit. In essence, a *letter of credit* substitutes the issuing bank's credit for that of the importer (Italco). The letter of credit issued by the Italian bank authorizes Norfolk Coal to draw a draft *on the bank* for a stated or determinable amount when accompanied by designated documentation. Upon receipt of the letter of credit, Norfolk Coal proceeds as above, except that the Italian bank is obligated to honor the letter of credit by accepting the draft when it arrives in Genoa. The bank, of course, would not have issued the letter of credit unless it were fully satisfied that Italco's credit were worthy of the obligation. After the draft is accepted by the Italian bank, it becomes a *banker's acceptance*.

Norfolk Coal may either hold this banker's acceptance or discount it at its Norfolk bank. Banker's acceptances on major banks are recognized as high-quality money-market instruments and are traded among banks and other investors at discount rates reflecting the credit of the accepting bank. Therefore Norfolk Coal may discount this instrument at a rate very close to the prevailing Treasury bill rate. Its bank may either hold the instrument as an investment or sell it to another investor in the money market. Eventually, its holder will forward the banker's acceptance to Genoa (or to the Italian bank's New York correspondent) for collection at maturity. At that time the Italian bank will collect from Italco. The latter, of course, will pay a service charge for this accommodation by its bank.

Note how the use of the international banking system facilitates trade. In the first illustration of a documented trade draft, the Genoa bank acted as an intermediary in presenting the sight or time draft to Italco before the latter could obtain the documents required to gain possession of the goods. In the latter illustration, by issuing a letter of credit and accepting the banker's acceptance, the Genoa bank substituted its known credit for its customer's (Italco's) unknown credit, thus making the transaction possible. Throughout the credit period, Norfolk Coal was protected and, when the time draft (either trade acceptance or banker's acceptance) was used, Norfolk Coal's bank financed carrying the credit by discounting the acceptance.

Taxation

Normally, a domestic U.S. firm is subject to regular taxation on income resulting from export transactions. However, a tax shelter may be available through the formation of a domestic international sales corporation (DISC). The DISC is essentially a wholly-owned foreign marketing subsidiary of the U.S. corporation. At least 95 percent of its sales and assets must be connected with export business. The DISC is exempt from federal income taxes, but its stockholder, the parent company, is subject to normal tax on about 50 percent of the DISC's undistributed income when earned and is also subject to income tax on dividends received from it. The net effect on the parent company of using a DISC is to defer part of its current tax liabilities related to export business by retaining earnings within the DISC subsidiary.

Financial management of the multinational firm

The *multinational firm* is a breed apart. The term simply denotes a firm that is based in one country but owns assets and operates in one or more other nations. But there is more to it than that; the attitude and perspective of management are different. The true multinational firm views the world as its oyster: the vision of its top management is neither limited to nor focused upon the home country but rather is widely diffused to capitalize on opportunities and cope with risks on a global basis.

The capital investment process involves weighing of risks and returns available throughout the free world. Likewise, marketing strategy is developed on a global basis. Both short- and long-term financing may be arranged either in the home country or in any other nation in which the firm is commercially involved. Funds may be transferred frequently among various foreign subsidiaries or between them and the corporate headquarters.

Multinational capital investment

The feature that differentiates a multinational firm from a domestic one engaged in international trade is *direct capital investment* in foreign countries. We shall now consider the incentives and risks of such capital investment.

Incentives There are several reasons a firm may invest in capital assets abroad. In many cases, multinational investment has been motivated by the desire to broaden a firm's markets beyond its national borders. For example, after Coca-Cola achieved the largest share of the U.S. soft drink market, where could it go from there? The natural choice was to develop overseas markets. But in order to do this, it was necessary to invest in production facilities abroad. Higher rates of return were available from overseas operations, largely because these markets were less competitive. The net result is that nearly half of its assets in 1981 were located outside the United States, and almost two thirds of its operating income was derived from foreign sources.

Why not manufacture in the home country and export the products to broaden the market? Sometimes this alternative is ruled out by the high transportation costs. In other cases, tariffs or import quotas imposed by foreign nations make this course uneconomical. It is this type of deterrent to international trade that has led the major Japanese automobile companies to establish assembly plants in the United States.

Sometimes the capital investment motive is to obtain natural resources, exemplified by the huge overseas investments of the multinational energy and mining companies. In other instances, lower costs may be achieved by establishing production facilities in other countries. Notice how the major Japanese electronics firms first capitalized on relatively low labor costs in their home country; then, as Japan prospered and labor costs increased, they established production facilities in Taiwan, Hong Kong, South Korea, and in some cases the United States. Likewise, some multinationals based in the United States have established production facilities in the Far East.

Still another incentive to multinational investment is diversification to achieve a "portfolio effect." You may recall that we were somewhat skeptical regarding the advantages of diversification in domestic markets, such as that of the conglomerates in the United States, because the individual investor could achieve the same effect by investing in a diversified securities portfolio. But multinational diversification by a firm may have considerably greater merit. The reason is that there are substantial barriers to the creation of a globally diversified securities portfolio by the individual investor. How would you go about buying the stocks of nationally operating soft drink companies located in various countries throughout the world? This is a diversification that Coca-Cola can accomplish but you as an investor cannot. This portfolio advantage is illustrated by Coca-Cola's 1980 operating experience when sales and profits in the United States and most European, African, and Latin American countries increased, but those in Japan (its fourth largest market) were seriously depressed.

There are significant barriers to widespread international investment in securities by individual investors. Some of these are legal restrictions, lack of information, and, in some cases, currency restrictions. Therefore, capital markets among countries are somewhat segmented. Thus, the multinational firm may increase the value of its stock via the portfolio effect of multinational investment in real assets.

So far we have cited only incentives or advantages of multinational capital investment. Disadvantages result largely from the unique risks of investment in a foreign country. These are political risks, foreign exchange risks, remittance risks, and the operating risks of doing business in each foreign environment.

Political risk Political risk is an ever-present consideration in the appraisal and management of capital investments in foreign countries. This risk, like all others, is a matter of degree. On one end of the scale are the risks of war or expropriation (confiscation). At the other are the possibilities of changes in laws, tax rates, or government regulations that alter the profitability of the foreign subsidiary. Between these extremes are varying risks of special taxes on corporations controlled by foreigners as well as exchange controls that restrict the payment of dividends to the parent company or otherwise limit transferring funds out of the country. Other intermediate risks might be the requirement that a given percentage of the employees be nationals, regulation of wages and prices, requirements to invest in social projects, or regulations that unduly restrict production or operational flexibility. A socio-political risk that has recently become significant in some countries is the potential for local strife, riots, and terrorism, such as arson and kidnapping of management personnel, sometimes with the local government "looking the other way."

As in the appraisal of any risk, the view must be to the future. A multinational firm's relations with a foreign government might be excellent at the time a capital investment is made, only to be reversed when the government changes, perhaps by revolution. Witness Iran after the Shah was deposed or Chile when the Allende government came to power.

In general, the degree of political risk relates to the economic development of the country and the relative stability of political institutions. Presently, the lowest political risks probably are encountered in Switzerland, the United States, and West Germany, while the highest are encountered in some less-developed countries of Latin America, Africa, and Southeast Asia. Major multinational corporations, along with their consultants and international banks, devote considerable efforts to identifying, appraising, and classifying the political risks of all nations in which the multinational firms operate or are considering capital investments. These efforts reflect the importance of political risks in their managerial considerations.

How does management cope with political risk in considering foreign capital investments? One way, of course, is to stay out of countries where this risk is high. Another is to adjust the required rate of return to reflect this risk in appraising capital investment projects. Where political risk is high, the payback method (crude as it is) may be used in capital investment analysis rather than more sophisticated cash flow methods. Insistence upon a very short payback period may be a workable decision rule.

In connection with investments in some of the less-developed countries, approved projects may be insured through the Overseas Private Investment Corporation (OPIC), a U.S. government-owned corporation. Various programs of OPIC insure against expropriation, nationalization, losses due to war or revolution, and inconvertibility into dollars of amounts invested or income from those investments. Premiums, of course, are charged for such insurance, and OPIC is quite selective in insuring these risks.

Foreign exchange risk The foreign exchange risk of a multinational firm usually is greater than that of a domestic firm engaged in export transactions. The multinational firm is concerned not only with foreign exchange exposure of accounts or drafts receivable but with its earnings and all of its assets and liabilities denominated in foreign currencies. If, for example, Exxon has $400 million invested in monetary assets in France and owes $250 million in franc-denominated (monetary) liabilities, it has a net investment of $150 million exposed to changes in the exchange rate of the franc against the dollar. If the franc should drop, say from 18¢ to 16¢, Exxon would lose $16⅔ million as a result. For that reason, its financial managers will go to great lengths to hold neutral or short monetary positions in countries having weak currencies and to maintain neutral or long positions in countries having strong currencies.[3]

[3]Sometimes, when the currency of the home country is weak (as the U.S. dollar was during most of the 70s), management of a multinational firm may be criticized in the home country for "selling out" its currency by exchanging it for strong currencies (such as the Swiss franc, mark, or yen in the 70s). Remember the perspective of the multinational manager; this is simply good business, minimizing foreign exchange risk or capitalizing on exchange trends.

The degree of risk exposure depends upon the net monetary assets denominated in each foreign currency and the relative volatility of exchange rates of each of these currencies against the currency of the home country. Various means of adjusting or neutralizing foreign exchange risk exposure will be discussed later in this chapter.

Foreign exchange risk may be accounted for in the appraisal of capital investment projects either by adjusting the required rate of return to encompass this risk or by adjusting expected cash flows to include the cash outflows required to neutralize or hedge the risk exposure. Foreign exchange risk tends to be lowest in the major developed countries, which have relatively stable currencies, and highest in underdeveloped countries with vulnerable economies, high inflation rates, and/or unstable governments.

Remittance restrictions Remittance (sometimes called repatriation) restrictions constitute a special type of political risk. Some foreign countries limit the dividends that may be remitted to the home country to a given percentage of profits or net worth, or prohibit the remittance of dividends for a period of time, say the first five years. The remittance of depreciation cash flows often is restricted. The motive for such restrictions is to force the multnational firm to reinvest part or all of its profits in the country where those profits were made.

Such restrictions have a two-pronged effect upon the analysis of multinational capital investment projects. First, risk is increased because the forced reinvestment of earnings entails bearing political and foreign exchange risks for a longer period of time than if profits could be repatriated as earned. This added risk can be recognized in the capital investment analysis by increasing the required rate of return. The other influence relates to estimated cash flows. Future cash inflows expected to result from the investment may be considered in terms of the cash that can be repatriated in the currency of the home country. This requires conversion of net cash inflows expected to result from operations to the restricted remittances that can be made to the home country.

At the extreme, if no profits may be remitted until the end of, say, five years, then the forecasted net cash inflow will be nil until the end of the fifth year. Discounted at a relatively high rate reflecting consideration of political and foreign exchange risks, the net present value of expected cash inflow may be extremely low. Such restrictions, of course, greatly reduce the attractiveness of capital investment projects in countries that impose them.

Taxes and accounting—Foreign operations

The multinational corporation must consider the tax environment of each country in which it operates as well as that of the home country. Accounting procedures are complicated by the necessity of translating the earnings, balance sheets, and income statements of its foreign subsidiaries from foreign currencies into consolidated statements denominated in the currency of the home country. Although these matters are highly complicated, in practice requiring the services of international accounting firms, we shall present a brief digest of the basic principles.

Taxes First, a foreign subsidiary must pay income and other taxes levied by the country in which it operates. These vary widely both in magnitude and regulations regarding their computation (allowable exemptions, deductions, depreciation periods, capital gains versus current income, investment credits, and so on). Then, the multinational corporation may be taxed in its home country on dividends and royalties remitted to it by foreign subsidiaries.

However, a multinational firm incorporated in the United States receives a *tax credit* for the taxes paid to foreign governments. Computation of this tax credit is somewhat complicated, but the general principle is that the credit for taxes paid to a foreign government is limited to the tax rate to which the U.S. corporation would be subject on income earned in the United States. Thus, if a 54 percent tax rate were paid in the foreign country and the U.S. parent were subject to a 46 percent tax rate, the tax credit would be limited to the dollar equivalent of 46 percent of the foreign subsidiary's taxable income remitted to the United States. On the other hand, if foreign taxes were paid at a 30 percent rate, the U.S. parent would receive a tax credit of the full amount paid and would be subject to U.S. taxes equivalent to the additional 16 percent. (Note: This example assumes that 100 percent of the foreign subsidiary's net income was remitted in dividends to the U.S. parent.)

Many countries impose withholding taxes on dividends paid to foreign nationals. For example, Canada withholds 15 percent of such dividends. Dividend withholding taxes are considered in determination of the U.S. tax liability. The 85 percent exemption of dividends from a domestic corporation is not applicable to dividends received by a U.S. corporation from a foreign subsidiary. With some exceptions, no U.S. taxes are paid on income of a foreign subsidiary that is retained in the foreign country rather than remitted to its U.S. parent.

Accounting Accounting for assets, liabilities, and stockholders' equity of a U.S.-based multinational firm is greatly influenced by the *translation* of the accounts of foreign subsidiaries to its consolidated financial statements. This translation is now governed by Financial Accounting Standards Board (FASB) Statement No. 52.[4] The following standards apply:

[4]Financial Accounting Standards Board, *Statement of Financial Accounting Standards Board No. 52* was issued December 7, 1981. Use of it or the previous Statement No. 8 is optional for years ended 1981 and 1982. Beginning in 1983, Statement No. 52 is mandatory.

1. All assets and liabilities of the foreign subsidiary are translated at the *current* exchange rate, which is the rate prevailing at the end of the accounting period.
2. Accounts of subsidiaries in countries where inflation rates have been very high compared to that of the United States may be adjusted to reflect the difference in inflation.
3. Translation gains or losses resulting from foreign exchange rate fluctuations are reported as direct adjustments to stockholders' equity on the balance sheet rather than affecting reported current earnings by appearing in the income statement.[5]
4. Sales revenues and expenses on the income statement are translated at the average exchange rate during the period.

These standards have important implications regarding the foreign exchange risk exposure of the multinational firm.

Foreign exchange risk exposure management

Although FASB Statement No. 52 does not require that translation gains or losses be reflected on the income statement, the multinational firm still may be subject to *economic* gain or loss resulting from foreign exchange rate fluctuations. Therefore, its foreign exchange risk exposure must be controlled. Fixed assets by their nature are subject to little if any control in the short run, and inventories are not crystallized into definite values collectible in the foreign currency. The principal assets denominated in the foreign currency that can be controlled are cash, marketable securities, and notes and accounts receivable. These are called *monetary assets.* All liabilities denominated in the foreign currency are *monetary liabilities.*

Net monetary creditor or debtor position

The foreign subsidiary is a *net monetary creditor* if it holds monetary assets in excess of its monetary liabilities. A net monetary creditor is in a *long* position relative to the foreign currency—say, the Deutsche mark for its West German subsidiary. If the mark rises against the dollar, translation gains will result. Conversely, if the mark falls against the dollar, translation losses will be incurred.

A firm is a *net monetary debtor* when its position relative to a foreign currency is *short;* that is, its monetary liabilities exceed its monetary assets denominated in that currency. If a firm were in a short position relative to the mark, a rise in the mark against the dollar would result in translation losses.

[5]The prior FASB Statement, No. 8, issued in 1975, required that foreign-exchange gains or losses from balance sheet translations be reflected directly in the income statement for each period. This treatment was highly controversial because it tended to result in wide fluctuation of reported earnings of multinational firms.

Policy alternatives We shall now discuss the policy alternatives regarding foreign exchange risk exposure and the techniques by which that exposure may be controlled. From a policy standpoint, a firm might consciously *assume* this risk. For example, if it believes the probability is high that the mark will rise against the dollar, it may manage its German subsidiary to carry a long position in marks. Conversely, if management expects the mark to fall against the dollar, it may finance its German subsidiary in such a way as to place it in a short position in marks. In either case management would be consciously bearing foreign exchange risk in an attempt to increase the value of the firm. Gain or loss would depend on whether or not management's forecast were correct.

An opposite policy would be to *minimize* foreign exchange risk, foregoing the opportunity to gain from exchange rate fluctuation but also avoiding the possibility of suffering losses due to it. We shall first discuss the means of executing the risk minimizing policy.

Balancing monetary assets and liabilities The U.S.-based multinational firm may hedge its foreign exchange risk relative to the mark by attempting to balance the monetary assets of its German subsidiary with monetary liabilities owed within Germany in marks. In other words, management of the German subsidiary would try to maintain a quick or acid test ratio of one. This would tend to minimize the risk related to fluctuation of the mark against the dollar.

This policy of balancing monetary assets and liabilities, however, might be difficult to execute. If the monetary position were becoming long, the German subsidiary should borrow marks from its German bank to balance its position. But it might not have immediate operational needs for these funds. Conversely, if its position were becoming short, balance might be achieved by increasing its monetary assets in Germany or reducing its loans at the German bank. But this again might not be operationally or financially feasible at the time. Nonetheless, it may be desirable to attempt to balance monetary assets and liabilities of the foreign subsidiary while allowing minor variations related to operational requirements to occur.

The large multinational firm may attempt to control variations by borrowing in one currency to finance assets in another. Specialized financial managers at the multinational's headquarters constantly monitor financial positions of the various worldwide subsidiaries, frequently arranging such borrowings or repayment of loans, exchanging currencies and electronically transferring funds among subsidiaries to balance the monetary positions.

Use of forward foreign exchange markets The mechanics of using forward foreign exchange markets to hedge monetary risks of a multinational firm are essentially the same as those discussed earlier in connection with hedging export-import transactions of a domestic firm. The difference is in what is being hedged. In the earlier case we were concerned only with hedging the account or draft payable or receivable in connection with an export-import transaction. The multinational firm is concerned with hedging its foreign exchange risk exposure (its long or short position) resulting from imbalance of monetary assets and liabilities denominated in a foreign currency. For example, if the German subsidiary held monetary assets of DM 4,000,000 and owed DM 3,000,000, its long position of DM 1,000,000 may be hedged by selling DM 1,000,000 for future delivery. This balances the firm's obligations to pay a total of DM 4,000,000 with its holding of DM 4,000,000 of monetary assets. The cost of such hedging through the forward foreign exchange market must be weighted against that of using alternatives to balance the position and the risk of simply carrying the position.

Transfer payments among foreign subsidiaries Although not thereby securing an overall hedge against monetary risk exposure, a multinational firm may adjust its monetary position through transfer payments among foreign subsidiaries. For example, assume that a U.S.-based firm operates its principal European manufacturing facility in Germany and that plant sells parts to assembly plants in France and Italy. If the multinational's management feels that the mark is strong and the French franc and the lira are weakening, it might order the French and Italian subsidiaries to make large purchases of parts from the German subsidiary. Rather than utilizing the usual 60-day terms, payment would be made immediately. The French and Italian subsidiaries would borrow francs and lire, convert the proceeds to marks and remit the marks to the German subsidiary. These transactions would increase the monetary assets in marks (the strong currency) and increase the monetary liabilities denominated in francs and lire (the weak currencies). This would place the multinational firm in a long position on the mark and a short position relative to the franc and the lira, ready to gain from a strengthening of the exchange rate of the mark and a weakening of the franc and lira.

This is just one illustration of the use of transfer payments to adjust foreign exchange risk exposure positions. Another means of protecting against a decline in the French franc and the lira would be to order the French and Italian subsidiaries to pay as large dividends as possible to the U.S.-based parent company, thus converting their cash to U.S. dollars. Various other intracompany transfers are possible. The point is that when a multinational firm expects one or more foreign currencies to weaken, or at the extreme to be formally devalued, management will do everything possible to neutralize a long position in that currency or, preferably, establish a short position.

Carrying long or short monetary positions A multinational firm's management may assume an aggressive role relative to foreign exchange rate fluctuations by consciously carrying long monetary positions in strong currencies and, if possible, short positions in weak ones. Such a policy involves bearing foreign exchange risks and attempting to gain thereby. During the

70s, as the U.S. dollar tended to weaken, particularly against the mark, Swiss franc, and yen, some U.S.-based multinational firms profited greatly by carrying large long positions in the latter currencies. This, of course, is a risky policy in that all good things of this sort come to an end. When the U.S. dollar made a remarkable recovery in the latter part of 1980 and in 1981, some firms suffered substantial translation losses on these long monetary positions. Like playing the stock market, holding speculative positions in foreign exchange in a sense involves betting that your forecast of the future is better than the collective wisdom of the market.

As foreign exchange markets change, executing an aggressive foreign exchange risk exposure policy involves switching assets and liabilities from one country to another. As discussed earlier, such switches may be accomplished through transfer payments among subsidiaries and the parent company. They also may be accomplished by borrowing in one currency to finance assets in another. A similar technique is to lend funds denominated in a currency other than that of the lender.

Multinational financing

Sources of external financing of a multinational firm may be considerably broader than those of a domestic one. A multinational firm has not only the choice of short- or long-term debt or equity financing but also the choice of whether the financing will be done in its home country, the country in which the funds are to be utilized, or in some other country. Foreign borrowing may be denominated either in U.S. dollars or in various foreign currencies. In addition, foreign financial institutions having somewhat different structure and providing different services from their U.S. counterparts may be utilized.

International banking Much of the financing, both short- and long-term, of foreign subsidiaries is arranged through banks located in their respective countries. These may be foreign branches, subsidiaries, or affiliates of the major U.S.-based banks or local banks in the foreign countries. There are several important differences between U.S. banks and most major foreign banks, particularly those in Europe, in the ways in which business is conducted and the range of services offered.

Loans usually are made on an *overdraft* basis. Rather than signing a note for each borrowing and paying off these individual notes, as in the United States, the borrowing firm arranges a line of credit allowing it to overdraw its account up to a prearranged maximum amount. Interest on overdrafts may be charged either at a pre-established rate or more often at a floating rate based upon an agreed percentage over the lending rate of the country's central bank. For example, a British subsidiary may arrange overdrafts at Barclay's Bank up to £ 1 million at an interest rate of, say, 3 percent over the lending rate of the Bank of England.[6] A considerable portion of foreign banks' lending also is by discounting trade bills (acceptances), which are much more widely used in foreign countries than in the United States.

Many foreign banks accept deposits and make loans (overdrafts) in both their domestic currency and in the currencies of other major trading countries. Thus a Swiss subsidiary may have several deposit accounts in its Swiss bank, one denominated in French francs, another in marks, a third in Swiss francs, and a fourth in U.S. dollars. Likewise some of its borrowings might be denominated in Swiss francs and some in, say, U.S. dollars.

Although banking services vary according to laws and customs of each country, the service offerings of most major European and Japanese banks are much broader than those of the so-called full-service banks in the United States. Foreign banks make long-term loans as well as those for short and intermediate terms. Banks also perform the investment banking functions discussed in Chapter 16, underwriting and selling bonds and stock. Many of them also act as securities brokers, handling transactions in the secondary markets for their clients. Some also operate mutual funds and travel agencies, sell insurance, trade in precious metals, and even sell lottery tickets. These true "department stores of finance" provide the whole range of financial services that under stringent U.S. banking laws must be obtained from several different institutions.

Eurodollar financing A *Eurodollar* deposit is a deposit denominated in U.S. dollars held by a bank outside the United States.[7] The foreign bank (not necessarily located in Europe) may be either a local bank in the foreign country or a foreign branch of a U.S.-based bank. Examples of creation of Eurodollars are the deposit of U.S. dollars received by a German exporter from sale of goods to an American importer or the purchase of CDs of the London branch of the Chase Manhattan Bank by an American money-market fund. A foreign bank receiving these deposits may then lend these U.S. dollars to its customers. An active market in Eurodollar loans exists as long as the U.S. dollar is an acceptable currency for conducting trade throughout the world.

Eurodollar loans—in large amounts, usually multiples of $1 million—are made by foreign banks on an unsecured basis to customers of high credit standing. The interest rate on such borrowings is, of course, slightly higher than the rate paid by the foreign bank on the Eurodollar deposits. Rates on

[6] The lending rate of the central bank, the Bank of England, is the rate it charges operating banks on loans to them. It is essentially the counterpart of the discount rate of the Federal Reserve Banks in the United States.

[7] Interestingly, the Eurodollar was invented when the Soviet government deposited U.S. dollars in a Paris bank shortly after World War II for use in trading with Western countries. This was done because the Russians feared that if the dollars were deposited in the United States, they might be seized to make payments on defaulted Czarist bonds held by American investors. When the Paris bank began to lend these dollars, the Eurodollar market was born.

Eurodollar loans usually are quoted as, say, ½ or 1 percent over the London interbank offering (LIBO) rate. Since the LIBO rate fluctuates according to supply and demand for Eurodollars, it may at any given time be higher or lower than the U.S. prime rate.

The concept of the Eurodollar market has expanded to the *Eurocurrency* market. A Eurocurrency deposit is a deposit denominated in *any* currency other than that of the country in which the bank holding it is located. Thus a Frankfurt bank may hold Eurocurrency deposits denominated in pounds, from which loans, also denominated in pounds, can be made. Rather than only dollars being available, the Eurocurrency market provides loans denominated in the currencies of any of the major trading nations. The mechanisms of creation and lending of Eurocurrency are essentially the same as those pertaining to Eurodollars.

Eurobond financing A *Eurobond* is a bond denominated in a currency other than that of the country in which the issuer is located. International investment banking syndicates comprised of banks and investment bankers located throughout the free world underwrite and sell such bonds in many countries. Although Eurobonds usually are denominated in a single currency, in some cases individual bonds of a given issue may be denominated in the currencies of several different countries in which they are to be sold.

The Eurobond market facilitates the expansion of long-term debt sources to a truly international scope. Although bonds have long been sold in countries other than that of the borrower (the early development of American railroads in the 19th century was largely financed by sale of dollar-denominated bonds in Britain), Eurobonds provide the added dimension of allowing the bonds to be denominated in the currency of the foreign country in which they are to be sold. This enhances marketability because it eliminates foreign exchange risk of the bond investor. However, unless the proceeds from sale of Eurobonds are invested in that country (they usually are), then an added foreign exchange risk is borne by the issuer.

Governmental sources Many large foreign capital investment projects, particularly those in the less-developed countries, are financed through governmental or quasi-governmental sources. The principal U.S. governmental sources are the Export-Import Bank and the Agency for International Development. Many countries have established development banks, and some have banded together to establish quasi-governmental regional development banks. On a world-wide basis, the World Bank and its affiliate, the International Finance Corporation, provide financing to governments and private firms in various countries for capital investment purposes.

The Export-Import Bank (called the EXIM Bank) encourages exports from the United States by making loans, or participating with commercial banks in loans, to foreign firms to finance their purchases of goods and services from U.S. exporters. In some cases, EXIM guarantees payment of loans made by privately owned financial institutions to finance U.S. exports.

The Agency for International Development (AID) is involved in a wide range of U.S. foreign assistance programs, one of which is making long-term development loans to governments and private firms in underdeveloped countries. Its activities, which were quite prominent in the 60s and 70s, have been somewhat curtailed in recent years.

Numerous countries have established development banks that make long-term loans to finance economic developments either within the country or in other, less-developed nations. An example is Nacional Financiera, S.A., of Mexico. Regional development banks include the Inter-American Development Bank, in which the United States participates with a number of Latin American countries in making loans to both governments and private firms to finance economic development of the region.

The World Bank (officially titled the International Bank for Reconstruction and Development) is a quasi-governmental organization financed by its member nations and by sale of its own bonds. It makes loans to governments of less-developed countries and to privately owned firms in such countries when guaranteed by their governments. Most loans are made to finance large projects such as dams, power plants, irrigation projects, and the development of basic industries. An affiliate of the World Bank, the International Finance Corporation, participates with groups of private investors and/or financial institutions in investing in development banks and in making direct loans to private firms in developing countries.

Experience with loans by governmental and quasi-governmental organizations and the private investors and financial institutions that have participated with them has not been entirely favorable. In many cases, default has occurred and extensions on payment of interest and/or principal have had to be granted. Many such loans have been serviced properly, however, and the projects they financed have been successful.[8]

Summary

International business activities involve several financial considerations in addition to those common to domestic activities. The basic principles and analytical techniques are essentially the same as those pertinent to domestic

[8]Our treatment of international financial management and the many institutions associated with it has, of necessity, been brief. Readers interested in further elaboration of international finance may wish to take a course or refer to the following texts dealing exclusively with this subject: David K. Eiteman and Arthur I. Stonehill, *Multinational Business Finance,* 3d ed. (Reading, Mass.: Addison-Wesley Publishing, 1982); Charles N. Henning, William Pigott, and Robert H. Scott, *International Financial Management* (New York: McGraw-Hill, 1978); and Rita M. Rodriguez and E. Eugene Carter, *International Financial Management,* 2d ed. (Englewood Cliffs, N.J.: Prentice-Hall, 1979).

financial management but are complicated by unique risks and the use of additional financial instruments and institutions. International business involves conducting transactions, owning assets, and owing liabilities denominated in foreign currencies. Therefore, fluctuation of exchange rates of foreign currencies against the dollar entails risk.

A spot foreign exchange rate is the ratio at which one currency may be exchanged for another for current delivery. A forward rate applies to a specified future delivery. At any given time an exchange rate is determined by the relative supply and demand for the two currencies, which, in turn, are influenced by normal commercial and financial transactions, investment or speculation, and occasional trading by central banks. Trends in exchange rates are influenced by underlying factors including expectation of relative inflation, interest rates, and governmental policies.

Foreign exchange risk is a major concern in export-import transactions by domestic firms. As relatively long credit periods are common, one of the parties bears the risk that the exchange rate will change before payment is made. This risk may be either assumed or avoided by hedging. It may be hedged by a counterbalancing transaction in the forward exchange market or short-term investment (or borrowing) denominated in the currency in which the payment (or collection) is to be made. Export-import transactions usually are facilitated through documentary drafts, either trade acceptances or bankers' acceptances originated by letters of credit.

A multinational firm is one that owns assets and operates in several countries. Capital investments in foreign countries involve additional risks. These include political risk, remittance risk, and foreign exchange risk. Political risk ranges from war or expropriation to changes in laws, regulations, and taxes. Remittance risk relates to limitation or prohibition of transferring funds out of the foreign country. Some political and remittance risks related to investments in less-developed countries may be insured through OPIC.

Assets and liabilities denominated in foreign currencies are subject to foreign exchange risk. This risk particularly relates to the value of monetary assets and liabilities. A firm is a net monetary creditor when its monetary assets exceed its monetary liabilities denominated in a foreign currency. This long position results in translation gains if that currency rises against the dollar and losses if it falls. If it is a net monetary debtor, the firm is subject to risk of change in the exchange rate in the opposite direction. Monetary risk exposure may be managed by assuming it or by hedging. A hedge may be accomplished by balancing monetary assets and liabilities in the foreign country or by maintaining a counterbalancing position in the forward exchange market. Sometimes transfer payments among foreign subsidiaries may be used to adjust monetary positions.

Sources of financing of the multinational firm are broader than those of a domestic one. The firm may borrow or sell equity securities in its home country or in various foreign countries. Borrowing may be denominated in dollars or in foreign currencies. Foreign banks provide a much broader range of services than those in the United States. The Eurodollar or Eurocurrency markets are available to financially strong multinational firms for short-term borrowing and the Eurobond market for raising long-term funds. Some U.S. export transactions and foreign capital investment projects in less-developed countries are financed through governmental and quasi-governmental sources. These include the Export-Import Bank and the Agency for International Development in the United States, other national and regional development banks, and, on a world-wide scale, the World Bank and its affiliate, the International Finance Corporation.

Questions

1. What additional risks must be considered in international financial management (as compared to domestic)?

2. What is a foreign exchange rate? How are foreign exchange rates established?

3. What *immediate* market factors influence the exchange rate of a foreign currency, say the French franc, against the dollar? What *underlying* economic and political factors may influence the exchange rate?

4. What is *purchasing power parity*? How do foreign exchange rates tend to adjust to purchasing power parity? What factors may inhibit this adjustment?

5. Your U.S. firm is exporting products to England on 60-day credit terms. Explain two ways you could hedge your foreign exchange risk exposure related to these transactions?

6. What functions are performed by the following instruments in facilitating international trade transactions?
   a. An international trade draft (bill of exchange)?
   b. A bill of lading?
   c. A letter of credit?
   d. A banker's acceptance?

7. What is a DISC? How can a U.S. firm use a DISC to defer part of its income tax liabilities related to its export business? Is there any economic justification for this tax deferral?

8. Indicate some of the reasons a U.S.-based firm might consider making capital investments abroad.

9. What are some of the unique risks related to foreign capital investments? How can these additional risks be incorporated in the capital investment decision-making analysis?

10. Explain the foreign exchange risk exposure of a multinational firm. What policy alternatives are available relative to this risk exposure?

11. What constitutes a *net monetary creditor* position? How would the value of a firm in a net monetary creditor position relative to the French franc be changed if the exchange rate of the French franc against the dollar declined?

12. How can a multinational firm adjust its monetary position from long to short if it expects the exchange rate of the foreign currency to fall against the dollar?

13. What is a forward foreign exchange market? How can forward purchases or sales of foreign exchange be used to balance a multinational firm's monetary assets and liabilities denominated in a given foreign currency, say the French franc?

14. What is a Eurodollar? Explain how Eurodollars become available for making loans denominated in U.S. dollars by foreign banks.

15. What is a Eurobond? How could a U.S. firm issue Eurobonds for sale in Saudi Arabia, Japan, and West Germany?

16. What is the function of each of the following financial institutions?
   a. The Export-Import Bank (EXIM Bank)?
   b. The Overseas Private Investment Corporation (OPIC)?
   c. The World Bank?
   d. The Inter-American Development Bank?

Problems

1. *a.* Using the spot foreign exchange rates of August 20, 1981, shown in Table 25–1, compute the following:
   (1) How many French francs (F fr) could you buy with 100,000 U.S. dollars ?
   (2) How many U.S. dollars will 30,000 British pounds (£) buy?
   (3) How many French francs will £10,000 buy?
   (4) How many Japanese yen (Y) could you buy with $40,000 U.S.?
   (5) How many yen will $40,000 Canadian ($ Can) buy?

   b. Using the latest spot foreign exchange quotations, which you can obtain from *The Wall Street Journal* or other major daily newspaper, repeat the calculations required in *(a)*. How do your figures compare? Explain the differences.

2. A U.S. importer, Usimp Corporation, purchases £100,000 worth of machinery from a British exporter in Coventry on 90-day credit terms. On the

date of this transaction, the pound is quoted in the spot exchange market at $1.7675 and 90-day futures at $1.7814 in the forward exchange market.

a. If Usimp decides to hedge the transaction in the forward market, what will be its cost of the machinery in U.S. dollars?

b. If Usimp decides to bear the foreign exchange risk and the pound falls to $1.7590 at time of payment 90 days hence, how much will it have to pay in U.S. dollars at that time?

c. If Usimp bears the risk and the pound rises to $1.7930 ninety days hence, how much will it have to pay in U.S. dollars?

d. If Usimp considers its opportunity cost of funds to be 12 percent per year, would it be better off under alternative *(a)* or *(c)*? (Show your calculations)

3. A U.S. exporter, Usex, Inc., is selling 200,000 Swiss francs' worth of electronic equipment to a Swiss firm in Zurich on 60-day credit terms. The transaction is denominated in Swiss francs. The franc is quoted in the spot market at $0.5113 and 60-day futures at $0.5206 in the forward market.

a. If Usex hedges the transaction in the forward market, what will be the proceeds in U.S. dollars?

b. Alternatively, Usex could hedge the transaction by borrowing francs from a Swiss bank for 60 days at a 6 percent annual interest rate and use the francs collected from the Zurich firm to repay the principal and interest on the loan. How many francs would it borrow? What would be the net proceeds in dollars from this loan?

c. Which alternative should Usex choose, assuming that it wishes to hedge the foreign exchange risk?

4. The U.S. exporter, Usex, Inc., is selling 500,000 French francs' worth of equipment to a French firm in Lyon on 60-day credit terms. The transaction is denominated in French francs. The spot exchange rate of the franc is $0.1601 and the 60-day forward rate is $0.1564.

a. If Usex hedges the transaction in the forward market, what will be the proceeds in U.S. dollars?

b. Alternatively, Usex could hedge the transaction by borrowing francs from a Paris bank for 60 days at a 12 percent annual interest rate and use the francs collected from the Lyon firm to repay the principal and interest on the loan. How many francs would it borrow? What would be the net proceeds in dollars?

c. Which alternative should Usex choose, assuming that it wishes to hedge the foreign exchange risk?

5. In 1981, a Mexican firm borrowed $100,000 for one year from a U.S. bank at 16 percent interest, exchanging the proceeds for pesos at the spot exchange rate of 26 Mexican pesos to the dollar. When the loan was repaid after the devaluation of the peso in February 1982, the exchange rate was 45 pesos to the dollar.

a. Based on the pesos received and paid by the Mexican borrower, what was the effective rate of interest paid on this loan?

b. Largely because of the high Mexican inflation rate, the firm would have had to pay 85 percent interest to borrow pesos for one year in Mexico. Would it have been better or worse off to have done so?

6. The Global Corporation, a U.S.-based multinational firm, owns a 50 percent interest in a French affiliate, Global de France, S.A. The monetary assets of Global de France total 5 million francs and its total liabilities denominated in francs are 2 million francs.

a. If the exchange rate of the French francs declines from $0.16 to $0.14, what will be the net economic effect in dollars upon Global Corporation?

b. If the exchange rate of the franc were to rise from $0.16 to $0.17, what would be the effect in dollars upon the value of Global?

c. If Global de France were to borrow 3 million francs to finance additional inventories and fixed assets, how would Global Corporation's *immediate* foreign exchange risk exposure relative to the franc be affected?

7. Worldwide Industries, a U.S.-based multinational firm, wholly owns a West German subsidiary that holds monetary assets of DM 12 million and owes DM 8 million. Worldwide expects to balance the German subsidiary's monetary position in six months. The German subsidiary could borrow DM 4 million from its Frankfurt bank at a 12 percent annual interest rate. To balance its monetary position, the German subsidiary would convert the borrowed marks to dollars at the current spot exchange rate of $0.40 and remit the dollars to the United States. Worldwide would invest the dollars in U.S. Treasury bills for six months at an annual interest rate of 10 percent. At the end of six months, Worldwide would pay off the loan from the Frankfurt bank by converting the dollar proceeds from the maturing Treasury bills to marks at the then existing spot exchange rate.

a. What will be the cost in dollars to Worldwide to hedge its foreign exchange risk relative to the mark in this fashion?

b. Show how this hedge would work (1) if the mark should fall to $0.38 during the six-month period; (2) if the mark should rise to $0.42 during that period.

Appendix

Table A **Present value interest factors (PVIF)**

Present value of $1 to be received at the end of *n* periods discounted at *i* interest rate

$$PVIF\ (i, n) = \left[\frac{1}{(1 + i)^n}\right]$$

Period (*n*)	Discount rate (*i*) 1%	2%	3%	4%	5%	6%
1	0.990	0.980	0.971	0.962	0.952	0.943
2	0.980	0.961	0.943	0.925	0.907	0.890
3	0.971	0.942	0.915	0.889	0.864	0.840
4	0.961	0.924	0.888	0.855	0.823	0.792
5	0.951	0.906	0.863	0.822	0.784	0.747
6	0.942	0.888	0.837	0.790	0.746	0.705
7	0.933	0.871	0.813	0.760	0.711	0.665
8	0.923	0.853	0.789	0.731	0.677	0.627
9	0.914	0.837	0.766	0.703	0.645	0.592
10	0.905	0.820	0.744	0.676	0.614	0.558
11	0.896	0.804	0.722	0.650	0.585	0.527
12	0.887	0.788	0.701	0.625	0.557	0.497
13	0.879	0.773	0.681	0.601	0.530	0.469
14	0.870	0.758	0.661	0.577	0.505	0.442
15	0.861	0.743	0.642	0.555	0.481	0.417
16	0.853	0.728	0.623	0.534	0.458	0.394
17	0.844	0.714	0.605	0.513	0.436	0.371
18	0.836	0.700	0.587	0.494	0.416	0.350
19	0.828	0.686	0.570	0.475	0.396	0.331
20	0.820	0.673	0.554	0.456	0.377	0.312
25	0.780	0.610	0.478	0.375	0.295	0.233
30	0.742	0.552	0.412	0.308	0.231	0.174
40	0.672	0.453	0.307	0.208	0.142	0.097
50	0.608	0.372	0.228	0.141	0.087	0.054

Table A *(continued)*

Period (*n*)	Discount rate (*i*) 7%	8%	9%	10%	11%	12%	13%
1	0.935	0.926	0.917	0.909	0.901	0.893	0.885
2	0.873	0.857	0.842	0.826	0.812	0.797	0.783
3	0.816	0.794	0.772	0.751	0.731	0.712	0.693
4	0.763	0.735	0.708	0.683	0.659	0.636	0.613
5	0.713	0.681	0.650	0.621	0.593	0.567	0.543
6	0.666	0.630	0.596	0.564	0.535	0.507	0.480
7	0.623	0.583	0.547	0.513	0.482	0.452	0.425
8	0.582	0.540	0.502	0.467	0.434	0.404	0.376
9	0.544	0.500	0.460	0.424	0.391	0.361	0.333
10	0.508	0.463	0.422	0.386	0.352	0.322	0.295
11	0.475	0.429	0.388	0.350	0.317	0.287	0.261
12	0.444	0.397	0.356	0.319	0.286	0.257	0.231
13	0.415	0.368	0.326	0.290	0.258	0.229	0.204
14	0.388	0.340	0.299	0.263	0.232	0.205	0.181
15	0.362	0.315	0.275	0.239	0.209	0.183	0.160
16	0.339	0.292	0.252	0.218	0.188	0.163	0.141
17	0.317	0.270	0.231	0.198	0.170	0.146	0.125
18	0.296	0.250	0.212	0.180	0.153	0.130	0.111
19	0.277	0.232	0.194	0.164	0.138	0.116	0.098
20	0.258	0.215	0.178	0.149	0.124	0.104	0.087
25	0.184	0.146	0.116	0.092	0.074	0.059	0.047
30	0.131	0.099	0.075	0.057	0.044	0.033	0.026
40	0.067	0.046	0.032	0.022	0.015	0.011	0.008
50	0.034	0.021	0.013	0.009	0.005	0.003	0.002

Table A *(continued)*

Period (*n*)	Discount rate (*i*) 14%	15%	16%	17%	18%	19%
1	0.877	0.870	0.862	0.855	0.847	0.840
2	0.769	0.756	0.743	0.731	0.718	0.706
3	0.675	0.658	0.641	0.624	0.609	0.593
4	0.592	0.572	0.552	0.534	0.516	0.499
5	0.519	0.497	0.476	0.456	0.437	0.419
6	0.456	0.432	0.410	0.390	0.370	0.352
7	0.400	0.376	0.354	0.333	0.314	0.296
8	0.351	0.327	0.305	0.285	0.266	0.249
9	0.308	0.284	0.263	0.243	0.225	0.209
10	0.270	0.247	0.227	0.208	0.191	0.176
11	0.237	0.215	0.195	0.178	0.162	0.148
12	0.208	0.187	0.168	0.152	0.137	0.124
13	0.182	0.163	0.145	0.130	0.116	0.104
14	0.160	0.141	0.125	0.111	0.099	0.088
15	0.140	0.123	0.108	0.095	0.084	0.074
16	0.123	0.107	0.093	0.081	0.071	0.062
17	0.108	0.093	0.080	0.069	0.060	0.052
18	0.095	0.081	0.069	0.059	0.051	0.044
19	0.083	0.070	0.060	0.051	0.043	0.037
20	0.073	0.061	0.051	0.043	0.037	0.031
25	0.038	0.030	0.024	0.020	0.016	0.013
30	0.020	0.015	0.012	0.009	0.007	0.005
40	0.005	0.004	0.003	0.002	0.001	0.001
50	0.001	0.001	0.001	0	0	0

Table A *(concluded)*

Period (*n*)	Discount rate (*i*)					
	20%	*25%*	*30%*	*35%*	*40%*	*50%*
1	0.833	0.800	0.769	0.741	0.714	0.667
2	0.694	0.640	0.592	0.549	0.510	0.444
3	0.579	0.512	0.455	0.406	0.364	0.296
4	0.482	0.410	0.350	0.301	0.260	0.198
5	0.402	0.328	0.269	0.223	0.186	0.132
6	0.335	0.262	0.207	0.165	0.133	0.088
7	0.279	0.210	0.159	0.122	0.095	0.059
8	0.233	0.168	0.123	0.091	0.068	0.039
9	0.194	0.134	0.094	0.067	0.048	0.026
10	0.162	0.107	0.073	0.050	0.035	0.017
11	0.135	0.086	0.056	0.037	0.025	0.012
12	0.112	0.069	0.043	0.027	0.018	0.008
13	0.093	0.055	0.033	0.020	0.013	0.005
14	0.078	0.044	0.025	0.015	0.009	0.003
15	0.065	0.035	0.020	0.011	0.006	0.002
16	0.054	0.028	0.015	0.008	0.005	0.002
17	0.045	0.023	0.012	0.006	0.003	0.001
18	0.038	0.018	0.009	0.005	0.002	0.001
19	0.031	0.014	0.007	0.003	0.002	0
20	0.026	0.012	0.005	0.002	0.001	0
25	0.010	0.004	0.001	0.001	0	0
30	0.004	0.001	0	0	0	0
40	0.001	0	0	0	0	0
50	0	0	0	0	0	0

Source: Adapted from O. Maurice Joy, *Introduction to Financial Management*, rev. ed. (Homewood, Ill.: Richard D. Irwin, 1980), Appendix Table C, pp. 589–92. © 1980 by Richard D. Irwin, Inc.

Table B **Present value interest factors for an annuity (PVIFA)**
Present value of $1 to be received at the end of each of *n* periods discounted at *i* interest rate

$$PVIFA\ (i, n) = \sum_{t=1}^{n} \frac{1}{(1 + i)^t}$$

Period (*n*)	Discount rate (*i*) 1%	2%	3%	4%	5%	6%	7%
1	0.990	0.980	0.971	0.962	0.952	0.943	0.935
2	1.970	1.942	1.913	1.886	1.859	1.833	1.808
3	2.941	2.884	2.829	2.775	2.723	2.673	2.624
4	3.902	3.808	3.717	3.630	3.546	3.465	3.387
5	4.853	4.713	4.580	4.452	4.329	4.212	4.100
6	5.796	5.601	5.417	5.242	5.076	4.917	4.767
7	6.728	6.472	6.230	6.002	5.786	5.582	5.389
8	7.652	7.325	7.020	6.733	6.463	6.210	5.971
9	8.566	8.162	7.786	7.435	7.108	6.802	6.515
10	9.471	8.983	8.530	8.111	7.722	7.360	7.024
11	10.368	9.787	9.253	8.760	8.306	7.887	7.499
12	11.255	10.575	9.954	9.385	8.863	8.384	7.943
13	12.134	11.348	10.635	9.986	9.394	8.853	8.358
14	13.004	12.106	11.296	10.563	9.899	9.295	8.745
15	13.865	12.849	11.938	11.118	10.380	9.712	9.108
16	14.718	13.578	12.561	11.652	10.838	10.106	9.447
17	15.562	14.292	13.166	12.166	11.274	10.477	9.763
18	16.398	14.992	13.754	12.659	11.690	10.828	10.059
19	17.226	15.678	14.324	13.134	12.085	11.158	10.336
20	18.046	16.351	14.877	13.590	12.462	11.470	10.594
25	22.023	19.523	17.413	15.622	14.094	12.783	11.654
30	25.808	22.396	19.600	17.292	15.372	13.765	12.409
40	32.835	27.355	23.115	19.793	17.159	15.046	13.332
50	39.196	31.424	25.730	21.482	18.256	15.762	13.801

Table B *(continued)*

Period (*n*)	8%	9%	10%	11%	12%	13%
	Discount rate (*i*)					
1	0.926	0.917	0.909	0.901	0.893	0.885
2	1.783	1.759	1.736	1.713	1.690	1.668
3	2.577	2.531	2.487	2.444	2.402	2.361
4	3.312	3.240	3.170	3.102	3.037	2.974
5	3.993	3.890	3.791	3.696	3.605	3.517
6	4.623	4.486	4.355	4.231	4.111	3.998
7	5.206	5.033	4.868	4.712	4.564	4.423
8	5.747	5.535	5.335	5.146	4.968	4.799
9	6.247	5.995	5.759	5.537	5.328	5.132
10	6.710	6.418	6.145	5.889	5.650	5.426
11	7.139	6.805	6.495	6.207	5.938	5.687
12	7.536	7.161	6.814	6.492	6.194	5.918
13	7.904	7.487	7.103	6.750	6.424	6.122
14	8.244	7.786	7.367	6.982	6.628	6.302
15	8.559	8.061	7.606	7.191	6.811	6.462
16	8.851	8.313	7.824	7.379	6.974	6.604
17	9.122	8.544	8.022	7.549	7.120	6.729
18	9.372	8.756	8.201	7.702	7.250	6.840
19	9.604	8.950	8.365	7.839	7.366	6.938
20	9.818	9.129	8.514	7.963	7.469	7.025
25	10.675	9.823	9.077	8.422	7.843	7.330
30	11.258	10.274	9.427	8.694	8.055	7.496
40	11.925	10.757	9.779	8.951	8.244	7.634
50	12.233	10.962	9.915	9.042	8.304	7.675

Table B *(continued)*

Period (*n*)	Discount rate (*i*)					
	14%	*15%*	*16%*	*17%*	*18%*	*19%*
1	0.877	0.870	0.862	0.855	0.847	0.840
2	1.647	1.626	1.605	1.585	1.566	1.547
3	2.322	2.283	2.246	2.210	2.174	2.140
4	2.914	2.855	2.798	2.743	2.690	2.639
5	3.433	3.352	3.274	3.199	3.127	3.058
6	3.889	3.784	3.685	3.589	3.498	3.410
7	4.288	4.160	4.039	3.922	3.812	3.706
8	4.639	4.487	4.344	4.207	4.078	3.954
9	4.946	4.772	4.607	4.451	4.303	4.163
10	5.216	5.019	4.833	4.659	4.494	4.339
11	5.453	5.234	5.029	4.836	4.656	4.486
12	5.660	5.421	5.197	4.988	4.793	4.611
13	5.842	5.583	5.342	5.118	4.910	4.715
14	6.002	5.724	5.468	5.229	5.008	4.802
15	6.142	5.847	5.575	5.324	5.092	4.876
16	6.265	5.954	5.668	5.405	5.162	4.938
17	6.373	6.047	5.749	5.475	5.222	4.988
18	6.467	6.128	5.818	5.534	5.273	5.033
19	6.550	6.198	5.877	5.584	5.316	5.070
20	6.623	6.259	5.929	5.628	5.353	5.101
25	6.873	6.464	6.097	5.766	5.467	5.195
30	7.003	6.566	6.177	5.829	5.517	5.235
40	7.105	6.642	6.233	5.871	5.548	5.258
50	7.133	6.661	6.246	5.880	5.554	5.262

Table B *(concluded)*

Period (*n*)	Discount rate (*i*)					
	20%	*25%*	*30%*	*35%*	*40%*	*50%*
1	0.833	0.800	0.769	0.741	0.714	0.667
2	1.528	1.440	1.361	1.289	1.224	1.111
3	2.106	1.952	1.816	1.696	1.589	1.407
4	2.589	2.362	2.166	1.997	1.849	1.605
5	2.991	2.689	2.436	2.220	2.035	1.737
6	3.326	2.951	2.643	2.385	2.168	1.824
7	3.605	3.161	2.802	2.508	2.263	1.883
8	3.837	3.329	2.925	2.598	2.331	1.922
9	4.031	3.463	3.019	2.665	2.379	1.948
10	4.192	3.571	3.092	2.715	2.414	1.965
11	4.327	3.656	3.147	2.752	2.438	1.977
12	4.439	3.725	3.190	2.779	2.456	1.985
13	4.533	3.780	3.223	2.799	2.469	1.990
14	4.611	3.824	3.249	2.814	2.478	1.993
15	4.675	3.859	3.268	2.825	2.484	1.995
16	4.730	3.887	3.283	2.834	2.489	1.997
17	4.775	3.910	3.295	2.840	2.492	1.998
18	4.812	3.928	3.304	2.844	2.494	1.999
19	4.843	3.942	3.311	2.848	2.496	1.999
20	4.870	3.954	3.316	2.850	2.497	1.999
25	4.948	3.985	3.329	2.856	2.499	2.000
30	4.979	3.995	3.332	2.857	2.500	2.000
40	4.997	3.999	3.333	2.857	2.500	2.000
50	4.999	4.000	3.333	2.857	2.500	2.000

Source: Adapted from O. Maurice Joy, *Introduction to Financial Management*, rev. ed. (Homewood, Ill.: Richard D. Irwin, 1980), Appendix Table D, pp. 593–96. © 1980 by Richard D. Irwin, Inc.

Glossary

Accelerated cost recovery system (ACRS) A system of cost recovery (depreciation) for tax purposes under which property is classified by recovery periods and standard recovery percentages of eligible amounts may be charged against income each year.

Accounting rate of return A method of capital investment analysis under which the average accounting profit after taxes from a project is divided by the investment in the project. The investment may be either the initial outlay or the average book value of the capital asset.

Accrued liabilities Liabilities representing obligations of the firm for services that have been performed but not yet paid for. Accrued wages and salaries, rents, and taxes are the most common forms of accrued liabilities.

Aging of receivables Classification of a firm's receivables by the elapsed time since the sales were made. Aging is one method used to appraise the quality of aggregate receivables.

Analysis of balance sheet changes A crude analysis of sources and uses of funds achieved by catagorizing changes in balance sheet accounts between two dates as to sources and uses.

Annuity A series of cash flows of equal annual amounts for a specified number of years.

Arbitrage The simultaneous sale of one financial instrument and purchase of another that is exchangeable for the first. Arbitrage by traders tends to equate the market value of the exchangeable instruments.

Assignment Transfer of the assets of a failed firm to an assignee or trustee, who takes over the management and either liquidates the assets or attempts to rehabilitate the firm.

Average collection period A measure of the rate of cash inflow from the collection of receivables. Calculated by multiplying the reciprocal of the receivables turnover by the number of days in the accounting period.

Bankers' acceptances Short-term debt instruments usually created through international trade transactions. They are backed by the credit of both the importer and the accepting bank.

Bankruptcy A legal term indicating that a firm has been admitted to a proceeding under the Bankruptcy Reform Act of 1978, its assets are under the control of the bankruptcy court, and it will be either liquidated or reorganized.

"Best-efforts" distribution A securities offering in which the investment banker(s) agrees only to use its best efforts to distribute the securities rather than fully underwriting the offering.

Beta coefficient (β) The index of comovement of the rate of return on the individual investment relative to the rate of return on the market portfolio. Beta measures *nondiversifiable* risk. Beta of the market portfolio is 1. A higher beta indicates greater risk; a lower beta, less risk. A negative beta indicates returns from the asset are negatively correlated with those of the market portfolio.

Bond A long-term promise to pay interest periodically at a stated rate, to pay the principal at maturity, and to abide by other covenants of the indenture.

Bond indenture The detailed agreement covering the rights, privileges, and obligations of the bond issuer and the bondholders. It is executed between the issuer and the trustee. The trustee represents the bondholders in enforcing the provisions of the indenture.

Bond ratings Quality ratings of publicly issued bonds that reflect estimates of the probability of default (that the issuer will not fulfill the obligations of the bond). They are issued by investment services including Moody's and Standard & Poor's.

Bond refunding The refinancing of long-term debt by issuing new bonds to replace called or maturing bonds.

Book value The value at which an asset, liability, or equity is carried on the firm's balance sheet. Book value per share of common stock is the total of the common equity accounts, common stock, additional paid-in capital, and retained earnings, divided by the number of shares outstanding.

Break-even chart A graph depicting total operating revenues, fixed costs, variable costs, and total operating costs at various volumes of operations. The break-even point and net operating income (NOI) or loss may be read off the break-even chart.

Break-even point The volume of sales at which operating revenues are equal to operating costs. Net operating income (NOI) is zero at the break-even point.

Burden coverage ratio A ratio of approximate annual cash generation to fixed annual financial cash-flow requirements. May be extended to cover discretionary cash flows such as dividends or planned capital expenditures as well as fixed financial requirements.

Call equivalent The market price per common share at which the number of shares into which a convertible security may be exchanged is equal to the call price of the convertible security.

Call price The price at which a bond or preferred stock may be redeemed at the option of the issuer.

Call provision A provision under which a security may be repurchased by the issuer at a predetermined price.

Capital asset pricing model (CAPM) A model under which the required rate of return on an asset (K_j) is estimated as a function of the risk-free rate (R_F), the required rate of return on the market portfolio (K_M), and the beta coefficient (β_j). The CAPM is: $K_j = R_F + (K_M - R_F)\,\beta_j$.

Capital gain A gain from the sale of a fixed or capital asset at a price greater than its original cost. A long-term capital gain is realized if the asset has been held for longer than one year.

Capital investment An outlay (expenditure) that is expected to yield benefits over a period greater than one year. The term includes, but is not limited to, investment in capital or fixed assets.

Capital investment analysis (capital budgeting) The process of evaluating and selecting among proposed capital investment projects.

Capital loss A loss resulting from the sale of a fixed or capital asset at less than its unrecovered cost (depreciated book value).

Capital market A financial market dealing in long-term and/or equity securities. Primary capital markets relate to the issue of new securities. Secondary capital markets relate to the trading of outstanding securities among investors.

Capital rationing The allocation of a limited amount of funds to be invested in capital projects. Capital is rationed whenever proposed investments that would otherwise be acceptable under net present value or internal rate of return criteria are rejected.

Capital structure The long-term and permanent financing of the firm. It normally consists of long-term debt, preferred stock, common stock, paid-in or capital surplus, and retained earnings.

Carryback or carryforward For income tax purposes, losses that may be used to offset taxable income of previous years or future years to reduce taxes.

Cash break-even analysis Operating analysis that may include determination of the break-even point, the break-even chart, and the degree of operating leverage at various volumes of operations, considering only those costs requiring immediate cash outflows.

Cash discount A feature included in many credit terms under which the buyer is allowed to take a stated percentage discount from the net invoice amount if payment is made within a certain number of days after the beginning of the credit period.

Cash flow The payment or receipt of cash by the firm. Cash flow may not coincide with accounting income or expense because of the accrual method of accounting.

Cash forecast (cash budget) A forecast of the expected cash inflows and outflows in future periods, usually months or quarters. The cash forecast yields an estimate of future borrowing requirements and funds available for temporary investment.

Cash management Management and control of the liquid assets of a firm. It includes control of currency, bank depository accounts, and marketable securities investments.

Cash management model A mathematical model designed to determine the optimal average cash balance and maximum and minimum levels at which cash will be invested or replenished in predetermined amounts.

Cash position ratio A static liquidity ratio calculated by dividing cash and marketable securities by total current liabilities.

Certainty equivalent The minimum amount receivable with certainty at a given future date that the investor would exchange for the uncertain (risky) expectation of receiving whatever amount that might be generated at that future date. The certainty equivalent method of adjusting for project risk determines present value of the project by discounting certainty equivalents at the risk-free rate.

Certainty equivalent coefficient (CE_t) The ratio of the acceptable certain outcome to the uncertain (risky) expectation of future cash inflows from an investment. It may vary from 1, indicating certainty of outcome, to approach 0 as the uncertainty of outcome becomes extremely great.

Classified stock Any of two or more classes of common stock of a corporation that usually differ in voting rights and, in some cases, in rights to dividend distributions.

Clientele effect The tendency of a publicly held firm to attract stockholders whose dividend preferences correspond to the dividend policy of the firm.

Coefficient of correlation A statistical measure of the degree of correlation between series of numbers. It takes on values ranging from +1 for perfect positive correlation to −1 for perfect negative correlation. (*See* correlation.)

Coefficient of variation (CV) A statistical measure of dispersion of a probability distribution, calculated by dividing the standard deviation by the mean or expected value. It may be used to compare risk of projects of differing size and expected values.

Collateral Assets specifically pledged or assigned to secure a loan. The term is used synonomously with *security*.

Collateral trust bonds Bonds secured by common stock and/or other securities that have been deposited by the issuer with a trustee. They are issued primarily by holding companies.

Collection policy The policy and procedures of a creditor regarding efforts to collect overdue receivables. Means of inducing payment include collection letters, telephone calls, personal discussions, use of collection agencies, and legal action.

Comaker loan A loan evidenced by a note that is signed by someone in addition to the borrower. The cosigner or comaker usually is a party having higher credit standing than the borrower and becomes responsible for payment if the borrower defaults.

Commerical paper Short-term unsecured notes issued at a discount and payable to bearer at par. They are issued by corporations of high credit standing to mature in 1 to 270 days. Interest yields usually are lower than the prime bank lending rate.

Commercial paper dealer A financial institution that places open-market commercial paper for its issuer-clients. The issuer is charged a fee for this service.

Common stock The security held by the residual owners of a corporation. The common stockholders bear the residual risk of the firm and share directly through dividends or indirectly through retained earnings in the residual earnings.

Compensating balances Minimum or average deposit account balances required by commercial banks as compensation for maintaining lines of credit, making loans, or performing other services for their commercial customers.

Composition A settlement under which the creditors of a firm that cannot meet its obligations agree to accept a uniform percentage payment and absolve the debtor of the remaining debt.

Compound interest Interest earned (or paid) not only upon the original principal but also upon the reinvested (or retained) interest accumulated from previous periods.

Concentration banking The use of regional collection of accounts receivable, electronically transferring excess funds from the regional bank to the firm's concentration bank.

Conglomerate growth The combination of firms engaged in unrelated lines of business.

Consolidated financial statements Financial statements that combine the operating results and financial condition of several firms, such as a parent company and its subsidiaries.

Consolidated tax return An income tax return that combines the taxable income of several affiliated firms. To file a consolidated tax return, the parent must own 80 percent or more of the stock of the affiliated firms.

Consolidation Combination of two or more firms into a newly created corporation. Securities of the new corporation are exchanged for the assets of the acquired firm(s), and the liabilities usually are assumed.

Conversion feature A feature of a bond or a preferred stock that gives the holder the option of converting the security into a specified number of shares of common stock during a given period of time.

Conversion premium The amount or percentage by which the issue price of a convertible security exceeds the market value of the common stock into which it may be converted at the time of issue.

Conversion price The effective price paid per common share if the stock is obtained through conversion of a convertible bond or preferred stock. It may be stated or determined by dividing the par or face value of the convertible security by the conversion ratio.

Conversion ratio The number of shares of common stock into which a convertible bond or share of convertible preferred stock may be converted at the option of its holder.

Conversion value The market value of the common stock into which a convertible security may be exchanged, calculated by multiplying the market price of the common stock by the conversion ratio. It is sometimes called *stock value.*

Convertible security A bond or preferred stock that may, at the option of its owner, be exchanged for a predetermined number of shares of common stock.

Corporation A legal entity created by the state. Under this form of organization, the firm owns assets and owes creditors distinctly from its owners. Its stockholders' liability is limited.

Correlation A statistical relationship between two or more series of numbers. Series moving together are positively correlated; those moving in opposite directions are negatively correlated.

Cost of capital The cost of various types of capital to the firm. It includes cost of debt, preferred stock, new common stock, and retained earnings. The term often is used to refer to the overall, or weighted average, cost of capital of the firm. Overall cost of capital is the required rate of return of the firm.

Coupon rate The rate of interest stated on the face of a bond certificate.

Credit analysis Appraisal of a credit applicant or customer to decide whether to grant credit and, if so, in what amount.

Credit limit A maximum amount that will be charged to the account of a customer without reappraisal of the credit and approval by the responsible credit representative.

Credit period The period of time during which the customer is committed to pay for a purchase. If this period has expired, the account is past due.

Credit policy The policy of a firm relative to the management of accounts receivable. It includes standards for granting credit, terms of sale, and collection policy.

Credit rating A code classification established by Dun & Bradstreet or other credit agency that indicates the financial strength (equity capital) and credit quality appraisal of a business firm or individual.

Credit rating classification analysis Classification of a firm's accounts receivable balances by credit agency ratings of the debtors. This classification is a method used to appraise the quality of aggregate receivables.

Credit scoring system A simple method of credit analysis by which points are established for various credit-related characteristics of the applicant. Pre-established total numbers of points determine acceptance or rejection and credit limits.

Credit standards The criteria establishing the minimum credit worthiness of a customer to which credit will be granted.

Credit terms The payment terms under which credit is granted to a customer. These include the date the credit period begins, the cash discount and discount period, and the period within which the net amount is to be paid.

Coverage ratios A group of ratios that indicate the number of times EBIT or cash flows cover various financial service requirements, such as interest, preferred dividends, rental payments, and/or debt repayments.

Cumulative preferred stock A preferred stock providing that all dividends accumulated in arrears must be paid before any dividends may be paid on the common stock.

Cumulative voting A system of voting for the board of directors under which each share of stock is entitled to as many votes as the number of directors to be elected. Holders of a sufficient minority of the stock may elect one or more directors roughly in proportion to the shares held.

Current ratio A static liquidity ratio calculated by dividing the total current assets by total current liabilities.

Date of record The date on which the stockholders' record is closed regarding the issue of rights or payment of a dividend. The stock will begin trading ex-rights or ex-dividend four business days before the date of record.

Debentures Bonds that are not secured by the pledge of specific property. Their claim is that of a general creditor.

Debt ratios A group of financial ratios that relate total debt or certain types of debt to either tangible assets or equity capital. Debt ratios provide measures of solvency.

Debt to equity ratio A financial ratio calculated by dividing total liabilities by the owner's equity (usually less intangibles). It is sometimes called the debt to net worth ratio.

Debt to total assets ratio A ratio showing the percentage of tangible assets financed by creditors, calculated by dividing total liabilities by total tangible assets. It is sometimes simply called the debt ratio.

Degree of financial leverage (DFL) A measure of the percentage change in earnings per share (EPS) of the common stock relative to the percentage change in the firm's earnings before interest and taxes (EBIT) from a given EBIT level.

Degree of operating leverage (DOL) The measure of the percentage change in net operating income (NOI) relative to the percentage change in unit volume from a given level of operations.

Degree of total leverage (DTL) A measure of the percentage change in earnings per share (EPS) of the common stock relative to the percentage change in the firms unit volume of operations. DTL is equal to DOL times DFL.

Depreciation expense Recovery of that portion of capital outlays previously made that are attributable to operations of an accounting period. Depreciation expense is charged against income of the period.

Direct placement The private sale of a new issue of securities to one or a group of institutional investors, frequently used as an alternative to public offering of bonds or preferred stock.

Discounted cash flow (DCF) methods Methods of analyzing capital investment proposals that involve discounting estimated future cash flows to their values at the inception of the project. Both net present value (NPV) and internal rate of return (IRR) methods incorporate discounted cash flow.

Diversifiable risk The risk that relates to a specific asset but can be offset by combining a number of assets into a diversified portfolio. It is also called *unsystematic* or *avoidable* risk.

Dividend A payment made on a ratable basis by a corporation to its stockholders. Normally a dividend is a distribution of earnings and is paid in cash. A stock dividend is paid in stock, and a property dividend is paid in assets other than cash.

Dividend-growth model A common stock valuation or cost model based upon the dividends expected over the future, presumably infinite, life of the security. The simplest form of the general cost model is

$$K_e = \frac{d_1}{P} + g$$

Dividend reinvestment plan (DRP) A plan under which stockholders may elect to have their dividends withheld and used to purchase additional shares. The additional shares may be either newly issued or purchased in the secondary market.

Dividend yield The current annual dividend divided by the market price per share of stock.

Draft A written order to the drawee to pay to the order of the drawor a specified amount of money. If payment is to be made immediately, it is a *sight* draft; if to be paid at a future date, it is a *time* draft. When a time draft has been accepted by the drawee, it becomes an *acceptance.* A draft is often called a *bill of exchange* when used in foreign trade.

Dun & Bradstreet, Inc. The largest mercantile credit-reporting agency. It furnishes its subscribers credit rating books and individual credit reports and performs other credit-related services. It also publishes average ratios for a large variety of industries.

Du Pont system A model for relating a firm's operating rate of return (return on investment) to its operating profit margin and operating asset turnover. Margin and turnover are further broken down into their component elements.

EBIT Earnings before interest and taxes.

Economic order quantity (EOQ) model A model used to determine the optimum size of orders to replenish inventories. The EOQ minimizes inventory costs by minimizing the total of ordering costs and carrying costs.

Effective interest rate The true cost of a loan expressed as an annual percentage of funds usable by the borrower. It includes consideration of costs that may not be explicit in the quoted or nominal interest rate.

Efficient frontier In portfolio theory, the curve connecting the efficient portfolios included in the attainable set of possible portfolios.

Efficient market A market in which the fair price of an asset is determined. The efficient-markets hypothesis holds that, under a given set of assumptions, a market is in equilibrium and the price will neither under- nor overvalue an asset. The capital asset pricing model (CAPM) assumes an efficient market.

Efficient portfolio A portfolio of investments (assets) that provides the highest possible rate of return for a given level of risk or the minimum risk for a given rate of return.

Electronic funds transfer (EFT) Instantaneous transfer of funds from the payer's bank account to that of the payee by electronic telecommunications. EFT practically eliminates float in a collection system.

Equipment trust certificates Debt instruments used primarily by transportation companies to finance their equipment. The trustee issues the certificates, paying principal and interest from rentals received from the transportation firm.

Equity capital Long-term or permanent capital invested in the firm by or on behalf of its owners. It includes preferred stock, common stock, paid-in or capital surplus, and retained earnings in a corporation. Residual equity capital excludes preferred stock. Partners' or proprietors' accounts comprise the equity capital of unincorporated firms.

Ex-dividend A term indicating that stock is not entitled to a recently declared dividend. A stock begins trading ex-dividend four business days before the date of record of the dividend.

Exercise price The price at which a warrant holder may purchase a share of common stock by exercising the warrant. The exercise price is usually 10 to 20 percent above the market price of the common stock at the time warrants are issued.

Extension An informal arrangement under which the creditors of a firm that cannot meet its financial obligations agree to a postponement of maturity of debt obligations.

Eurobond A bond denominated in a currency other than that of the country in which the issuer is located.

Eurocurrency A deposit denominated in any currency other than that of the country in which the bank is located. A Eurocurrency loan is a loan denominated in the currency of another country.

Eurodollar A deposit denominated in U.S. dollars held by a bank outside the United States. A Eurodollar loan is a loan of such funds denominated in U.S. dollars made by a foreign bank.

Factoring receivables The sale of accounts receivable to a financial institution. The factor buys the receivables at a discount, assumes the responsibility of selecting, managing, collecting, and, except under recourse arrangements, absorbing bad debt losses. The firm may borrow the uncollected balance subject to a reserve.

Federal agency securities Notes or bonds issued by various agencies of the U.S. government, such as Federal Land Banks or the Federal National Mortgage Association. Although not direct obligations of the Treasury, they are of high quality.

Field warehousing arrangement A secured borrowing arrangement under which the pledged inventory is held in an independently administered warehouse on the borrower's premises. Inventories are controlled on behalf of the lender.

Financial Accounting Standards Board (FASB) The standard-setting board of the public accounting profession, successor to the Accounting Principles Board (APB).

Financial intermediary An institution that pools the savings of many economic units and reinvests these accumulated funds in debt or equity securities.

Financial (capital) lease A lease for a period approximately equal to expected life of the asset. The lease is noncancellable, and usually the lessee is responsible for maintenance, insurance, and taxes.

Financial leverage The magnification of the effect of change in net operating income upon the resulting change in return on owners' equity. It results from the existence of fixed financial costs.

Financial leverage chart A graph showing the earnings per share (EPS) on the common stock that would result from the use of two or more different capital structures. The financial *point of indifference* is indicated by the intersection of the lines depicting two different capital structures on this chart; at this EBIT level, the same EPS is produced by both capital structures.

Financial market Any place that suppliers and demanders of funds meet, create or exchange financial assets and liabilities, and establish prices of the financial instruments exchanged. They may be classified as *money markets,* dealing in short-term funds, or *capital markets,* dealing in long-term and/or equity securities.

Fixed charge coverage ratio A ratio calculated by dividing EBIT plus rental payments by combined interest and rental payment requirements.

Fixed costs Costs that do not fluctuate with changes in the volume of production or sales.

Float The amount of funds that have been paid by the drawer of a check but have not been collected by the payee's bank. Float results from the lapse of time in transporting, processing, and collection of the check through the clearing system.

Floating interest rate An interest rate on a loan under which the rate charged is adjusted periodically in relation to changes in the prime rate. Such a rate may be stated as "floating prime plus two percent."

Floating lien A pledge of all inventories owned by a firm under a security agreement providing no physical safeguard for protection of the lender.

Flotation costs The difference between the market price of a security at the time of issue and the net proceeds available to the issuer. Includes underpricing, investment bankers' fees, and out-of-pocket costs of preparing the issue.

Foreign exchange rate The relationship between the values of two currencies. A *spot* exchange rate refers to exchange of two currencies for immediate delivery. A *forward* exchange rate refers to purchase or sale of a foreign currency for delivery at a future date.

Going-concern value The theoretical value of the common stock of a firm that is expected to continue in operation indefinitely. It is the present value of expected future dividends discounted at a rate reflecting the riskless rate of return plus a premium for risk.

Gross profit margin The percentage of a sales dollar that is left after subtracting the cost of goods sold. It is calculated by dividing gross profit by net sales.

Holding company A corporation that owns controlling interest in the common stock of one or more other firms. A *pure* holding company owns only securities of other corporations; a *holding-operating* company both has operations of its own and holds controlling interest in other operating companies.

Horizontal integration The combination of firms engaged in the same line of business.

Illiquidity The financial state of a firm that is unable to meet its financial obligations as they become due. It is also called "technical insolvency."

Improper accumulation of earnings Retention of earnings by a corporation for the purpose of avoiding individual income taxes of its stockholders. Penalty taxes may be levied for such unjustifiable retention of earnings.

Income bonds Bonds (usually debentures) requiring payment of interest only when earned. Omitted interest usually is cumulative. Income bonds are typically issued in reorganization of a failed firm.

Independent projects Capital investment proposals where acceptance of one would not preclude acceptance of another.

Indifference curve A curve depicting the risk-return combinations that would equally satisfy an investor. A given investor has an infinite series of parallel, upward-sloping indifference curves reflecting that investor's utility functions.

Insolvency The financial state in which the liabilities of a firm exceed the real value of its assets; sometimes called *absolute insolvency. Technical* insolvency, in relation to bankruptcy, denotes inability to pay maturing financial obligations.

Integer programming A mathematical technique for optimizing an objective subject to specified constraints. It may be used to determine the optimal group of acceptable investment projects under capital rationing.

Interest The charge made by the lender to the borrower for the use of money. This charge usually is stated as an annual percentage of the principal amount owed, called an interest rate.

Interest coverage ratio A ratio calculated by dividing earnings before interest and taxes (EBIT) by the interest requirement (sometimes called "times interest earned").

Internal rate of return (IRR) A discounted cash flow method of analyzing capital investment proposals. The compound rate of return (discount rate) that equates the present values of the initial outlay and the future cash benefits from a capital investment project.

Inventory turnover ratio A dynamic liquidity ratio calculated by dividing cost of goods sold by average inventory.

Investment banker A financial middleman engaged in raising long-term funds for business firms and governmental bodies by arranging the sale of their securities to investors.

Investment tax credit A direct dollar-for-dollar reduction of tax liability for the year in which qualified assets are placed in service. The credit is a percentage of the cost of the asset that varies according to the recovery period.

Lease A contract under which the lessor, the owner of an asset, gives the lessee the right to use that asset for a stipulated period of time subject to the stated conditions of the contract. The lessee is obligated to make periodic rental payments to the lessor.

Legal capital The amount of equity capital that may not be impaired by the payment of dividends. Some states consider only the par or stated value of stock to be legal capital, others include additional paid-in capital.

Letter of credit A letter issued by a bank authorizing the drawing of a draft(s) on the bank up to a stated amount under specified conditions. Such letters are often used to facilitate foreign trade transactions.

Leverage The magnification of change. In finance the term is used to describe the effect of fixed costs in magnifying change in volume of operations upon change in net operating income (operating leverage) and change in operating income upon return on owners' equity (financial leverage).

Lien A legal claim against property owned by another party. A lien is obtained by a security agreement providing a security interest in designated property that is pledged as collateral on a loan.

Line of credit An expression of willingness on the part of a bank to lend on a specified basis up to a stated maximum amount at a given or determinable interest rate during a given future period. It is not a binding contract.

Liquid assets Those assets in the form of cash or forms almost immediately convertible to cash with negligible possibility of loss of value. Liquid assets include cash, demand deposits in banks, and marketable securities.

Liquidation The process of turning assets into cash. Liquidation value refers to the net proceeds that could be obtained from the sale of an asset after all costs of administering and selling it.

Liquidation value The net price at which an asset can be sold. As used in valuing common stock, it is the value at which all of the assets of the corporation could be sold less the liabilities and claims of preferred stockholders.

Liquidity The ability to pay financial obligations as they come due. It may also refer to the relative convertibility of an asset to cash.

Liquidity ratios A group of ratios that relate to the ability of a firm to pay financial obligations as they come due.

Lock-box system A collection system under which the customer mails the check to a post office box in a nearby city that may be far from the creditor's home office. A bank processes the check and usually remits collected balances daily by wire transfer to the concentration bank of the firm.

Long-term debt to equity ratio A static financial ratio calculated by dividing long-term debt by owner's equity (usually less intangibles).

Long-term debt to total capital structure ratio A static financial ratio calculated by dividing long-term debt by the total capital structure (usually less intangibles).

Majority voting A system of voting for the board of directors of a corporation under which each share of stock is entitled to one vote for each director. Holders of a simple majority of the shares may elect all of the directors.

Marginal (or incremental) analysis Analysis of the cost-benefit effects of a decision or strategy, such as the addition of a credit customer or class of customers of lower credit standing than those presently accepted. It is sometimes called cost-benefit analysis.

Market portfolio A portfolio theoretically consisting of all of the securities (assets) available in the market. A broadly-based index, such as the Standard & Poor's 500 Stock Composite Index, is used as a proxy for the common stock market portfolio.

Market premium The excess of the market price of a convertible security over the *theoretical value,* which is the higher of the straight security value or its conversion value. Market premium is often simply called the premium.

Market return (K_M) The required return on the market portfolio. This return includes the risk-free return (R_F) and compensation for bearing *diversifiable* risk of the market portfolio.

Market risk premium The difference between the return on the market portfolio (K_M) and the risk-free return (R_F) as used in the capital asset pricing model (CAPM).

Market value As applied to common stock, the value at which the stock is traded in the secondary market.

Marketable securities Short-term, high-quality, readily marketable debt securities held by a firm as temporary investments of excess funds.

Merger A combination of two firms in which the acquiring firm continues in operation and the acquired firm ceases to exist. This combination may be accomplished through a statutory merger or purchase of assets. The term is loosely applied to any acquisition of one firm by another.

Money market A financial market dealing in short-term funds. In a narrow sense, the term refers to the market for highest-quality short-term negotiable securities.

Money-market mutual fund An open-end investment company (mutual fund) that sells its shares to investors and, in turn, invests in a diversified portfolio of money-market instruments, such as T-bills, CDs, and commercial paper.

Mortgage bonds A bond issue secured by a lien on real property. The mortgage may be *closed-end* or *open-end.*

Multinational firm A firm based in one country but owning assets and operating in one or more other nations.

Municipal securities Notes or bonds issued by states, counties, school districts, and other governmental bodies below the federal level. Interest received on municipal securities is exempt from federal income tax.

Mutual fund A financial intermediary that sells its shares to investors and in turn invests in a diversified portfolio of securities.

Mutually exclusive projects Capital investment proposals that preclude acceptance of one another, such as the renovation of a machine versus its replacement by a new machine.

Negotiable certificate of deposit (CD) A transferable receipt for a large time deposit in a commercial bank. Firms often include CDs in their marketable securities portfolios.

Net present value (NPV) A discounted cash flow method of analyzing capital investment proposals. Net present value of a project is calculated by subtracting the initial investment from the present value of expected future net cash benefits, which, in turn, is determined by discounting those cash benefits at the required rate of return (RRR).

Net worth The owners' equity in the firm, usually consisting of common stock, paid-in or capital surplus, and retained earnings. For some purposes, proprietary reserves and/or preferred stock may be included.

Nondiversifiable risk Risk that affects all assets but will affect different assets in varying degrees. It cannot be diversified away by combining assets into a portfolio. It is also called *systematic* or *unavoidable* risk; it is measured by *beta* (β).

Note A written promise to pay a certain sum of money at a given time and place. A note (more formally called a *promissory note*) may be payable to bearer or to the order of a stated party.

Operating asset turnover The relationship obtained by dividing annual sales volume by net tangible operating assets.

Operating lease A lease for a short period compared to the estimated useful life of the asset. The lease is cancellable and usually provides that the lessor is responsible for maintenance, insurance, and taxes.

Operating leverage The magnification of the effect of a change in sales volume upon the resulting change in net operating income, computed by dividing the percentage change in net operating income by the percentage in sales. It results from the existence of fixed operating costs.

Operating profit margin The number of cents left from a dollar of sales after covering the operating costs and expenses, computed by dividing net operating income (before taxes) by sales (gross revenues), the result stated as a percentage.

Operating rate of return The relationship obtained by dividing net operating income by net tangible operating assets or by multiplying operating profit margin by operating asset turnover.

Opportunity cost The return that could be earned by investing in the next most favorable opportunity of similar risk. It is usually synonymous with the required rate of return on an investment.

Optimal portfolio In portfolio theory, the portfolio that is closest to the point of tangency of the investor's indifference curves and the efficient frontier. This portfolio embodies the best attainable set of risk-return relationships for that investor.

Order point The inventory level at which an order should be placed to replenish stocks.

Ordinary income For tax purposes, that income resulting from the normal operations of the business. Capital gains (and losses) are specifically excluded.

Overdraft The drawing of checks on a bank account in excess of the amount on deposit. In many foreign countries, banks authorize overdrafts up to a stated amount rather than making direct loans to their borrowing customers.

Overhanging convertible security A convertible security that has not been converted because the market price of the common stock into which it is convertible has not reached a sufficient level to induce voluntary conversion or to allow the issuer to force conversion by calling the security. It is also called a "hung" or "stuck" convertible.

Over-the-counter (OTC) market All securities trading that does not take place on an organized exchange. Securities dealers *make a market* by offering to buy a security at a *bid* price and to sell it at an *asked* price, communicating via a telecommunications network including NASDAQ.

Participating preferred stock A preferred stock providing that under certain conditions its holders may participate in dividend distributions beyond the regular preferred dividend.

Partnership Two or more persons engaging jointly in a business enterprise. General partners are jointly and severally liable to creditors of the firm.

Par value The face or stated value of a stock or a bond. Par value of a bond is its maturity value. Par value of a stock is determined by the firm's articles of incorporation.

Payback period The number of years required to recover the initial investment in a capital project. One method of capital investment analysis establishes a maximum payback period as the acceptance criterion.

Payout ratio The ratio of the dividends paid and the earnings available to common stock during the period. The same result may be computed by dividing the dividends per share by the earnings per share.

Perfection of a lien The degree of assurance a lender has that assets pledged as collateral under a security agreement will be available to it in event of default of a loan. It relates to both the legal claim and physical security.

Perpetuity An annuity of infinite duration. A series of cash flows of equal annual amounts for an infinite number of years.

"Pooling of interests" accounting A method of accounting for mergers under which the premerger book values of all accounts of the two firms are simply added to construct the postmerger balance sheet.

Portfolio An aggregation of assets, either financial assets (securities) or real assets, or both.

Portfolio effect The reduction of risk resulting from the combination of diversified assets in a portfolio.

Preemptive right The opportunity of a common stockholder to purchase on a proportionate basis new issues of common stock or securities convertible into common stock. This allows existing stockholders to maintain their proportionate share of ownership or be compensated for dilution by selling their rights.

Preferred stock A type of stock having a priority and limitation of its rights to dividends and distribution of assets in liquidation relative to the common stock. Often, it also has modified voting rights.

Present value The value at the present time (year 0) of a future sum or stream of cash flows, calculated by compound discounting at a specified discount rate.

Prime rate The announced rate of interest that a bank charges its most credit worthy customers for short-term loans in large amounts. The prime provides a *floor* or minimum rate upon which other lending rates are based.

Principal The amount of money borrowed under a debt instrument. Interest is paid on the basis of the principal amount owed.

Probability The percentage chance of occurrence of a given outcome.

Probability distribution A tabular or graphical representation of a set of possible outcomes and the percentage chance of occurrence of each outcome. A probability distribution may be *discrete* or *continuous* and may be subjectively or objectively determined.

Profitability Ability to earn a return on investment or business operations.

Profitability index (benefit/cost ratio) A ratio calculated by dividing the present value of future net cash benefits by the initial investment in a project. Used in analyzing capital investment proposals. It is a correlary to the NPV method.

Profitability ratios A group of ratios relating to the ability of a firm to earn in relation to sales, assets, or owners' equity.

Pro forma balance sheet A forecast of the asset, liability, and capital accounts at a future date. Pro forma balance sheets sometimes are also used to project past or present financial condition if capital structure were changed or if two firms were merged.

Pro forma financial statements Forecasted or projected balance sheets and income statements. May also be used to project past operating results or financial condition if two firms were merged.

Pro forma income statement A forecast of the revenues, costs, and expenses of a future period. May also be used to indicate operating results if two firms were merged.

Proprietorship A natural person engaged in business. There is no legal distinction between the business firm and its owner.

Prospectus A part of the SEC registration statement that is supplied to prospective purchasers of a new issue of securities. It must contain all material facts regarding the issue.

Proxy A temporary power of attorney giving another person the right to vote the shares of a stockholder in the election of directors and other matters coming before a stockholders' meeting.

Proxy fight A contest between management and an outside group of stockholders to garner sufficient votes to elect a majority of the board of directors of a corporation.

Proxy statement A statement furnished to stockholders by management in soliciting proxies to vote their shares at a stockholders' meeting. It summarizes the background of nominees to the board of directors and contains details regarding other matters to be voted upon.

"Purchase" accounting A method used in accounting for mergers under which the acquisition is treated as if the acquiring firm purchased the assets and assumed the liabilities of the acquired firm, making payment for the net assets at the current market value of the currency of exchange used.

PVIF Present value interest factor. The present value of $1 to be received at the end of a specific number of periods, discounted at a given interest rate.

PVIFA Present value interest factor of an annuity. The present value of one dollar to be received at the end of each period for a specified number of periods, discounted at a given interest rate.

Quick ratio A static liquidity ratio calculated by dividing total current assets less inventories by total current liabilities. Sometimes it is called the "acid test" ratio.

Range A simple and crude statistical measure of dispersion of a probability distribution, calculated by subtracting the lowest or most pessimistic outcome from the highest or most optimistic outcome.

Ratio of exchange In a merger, the number of shares (or fraction of a share) of stock of the acquiring company given for each share of the acquired firm. In foreign exchange, the number of units of one currency that may be exchanged for a unit of another currency.

Recapture of depreciation The excess of sale price above unrecovered cost (depreciated value) of a depreciable asset up to the asset's original cost. This amount is taxable as ordinary income.

Receivables turnover ratio A dynamic liquidity ratio calculated by dividing net credit sales by average accounts receivable.

Registration statement A document filed with the Securities and Exchange Commission by a prospective issuer of securities in interstate commerce. It must disclose all material facts regarding the security, the issuing corporation, and the underwriting arrangements.

Regression A statistical method of predicting the value of a dependent variable from the value of one or more independent variables. A *regression line* may be linear or curvilinear.

Relevant cash flows The incremental cash flows associated with a capital investment proposal. The test of relevance is that the cash flow would occur if the proposal were accepted but would not occur if it were rejected.

Reorganization The restructuring of liabilities and equity capital of a failed firm to reflect current values and provide an equitable settlement of claims. In bankruptcy, a reorganization is conducted under the provisions of Chapter 11 of the Bankruptcy Reform Act of 1978.

Repurchase agreement An instrument whereby a securities dealer sells U.S. Treasury or other money-market securities, agreeing to buy them back at a guaranteed price at the end of a stipulated short period of time.

Retained earnings The portion of earnings not paid out in dividends. On the balance sheet, this capital account is the accumulation of reinvested earnings over the life of the firm. It does not represent available funds, but rather is the capital account that "balances" the balance sheet.

Revolving credit agreement A contractual obligation of a bank to lend up to a stated maximum amount at any time during a specified future period. Usually the agreement is subject to certain conditions. A commitment fee is charged by the bank for the unused portion of the credit.

Right of offset A provision of a bank loan under which, in the event of bankruptcy or default, the bank has the right to transfer the borrower's depository account balance to make payment on the loan.

Rights offering The sale of additional shares of common stock by issuing *rights* to purchase the shares on a proportionate basis to the present stockholders. Stockholders receiving rights may either exercise them or sell them to others.

Risk The degree of potential variability of outcomes from forecasted values. The term is usually used interchangeably with *uncertainty*.

Risk-adjusted discount rates In capital investment analysis, discount rates that reflect risk differentials among projects or classes of projects. The adjustment may be with reference to either the risk-free rate or the firm's required rate of return (cost of capital), depending on the method used.

Risk-free rate of return (R_F) The rate of return, also called the *pure interest rate,* that can be earned on an investment entailing no risk. The rate of return on short-term Treasury obligations often is used as a proxy for the risk-free rate.

Risk premium The return in addition to the risk-free rate that investors require for bearing the risk of holding an asset. The CAPM defines the risk premium as $(K_M - R_F)\beta$, where K_M is the required return on the market portfolio, R_F is the risk-free rate, and β is the beta coefficient of the asset.

Robert Morris Associates The national association of bank credit and loan officers. It publishes *Statement Studies* containing average ratios for a large variety of industries.

Safety stock An amount of inventory in excess of predicted normal requirements held as a cushion to cover delays in receipt of orders and/or usage in excess of forecast.

Sale-leaseback An arrangement under which the user-firm sells a fixed asset and simultaneously leases that asset from the purchaser, usually for the approximate useful life of the asset.

Securities exchange An organized exchange in which members trade outstanding securities in a double-auction market. Members may trade listed securities as brokers representing investors or for their own accounts. The largest is the New York Stock Exchange (NYSE).

Securities and Exchange Commission (SEC) The federal agency that administers the Securities Act of 1933, regulating the sale of new securities, and the Securities Exchange Act of 1934, regulating the registered securities exchanges, their members, and the reporting requirements of firms whose securities are listed on them.

Security Assets specifically pledged or assigned to secure a loan. The term is used synonomously with *collateral.* The term is also used to denote a financial instrument such as a share of stock, a bond, or a note.

Security agreement A legal document, signed by the borrower, providing a security interest in designated property pledged or assigned to the lender to secure a loan. It gives the lender the right to seize that property in event of default of the loan.

Security interest The rights of a lender in relation to property pledged or assigned as collateral to secure a loan under a security agreement.

Security market line (SML) A graphical depiction of the capital asset pricing model (CAPM). An ascending straight line (the SML) is determined by the risk-free return (R_F) and the market return (K_M). With beta (β) plotted on the x-axis and required rate of return on the y-axis, the required rate of return (K_j) for an asset of any positive beta may be estimated from the SML.

Selling group A group of securities dealers organized by the managing underwriter to distribute an offering of securities to investors. Members of the selling group are compensated by a *selling concession* for each security sold.

Semivariable costs Costs that are fixed over a given range of volume, but that change in a stair-step pattern as volume increases to another range.

Serial bonds A bond issue in which individual bonds mature in consecutive years, used primarily in financing governmental bodies.

Sinking fund A means by which the issuer gradually repays all or a portion of the principal of a bond issue prior to its maturity date. The sinking fund is administered by the bond trustee.

Solvency The relative excess of value of assets over liabilities of a firm.

Sources and uses of funds statement A statement depicting in detail the sources and uses of cash or net working capital between two dates. It utilizes information drawn from both balance sheets and income statements.

Spontaneous liabilities Those liabilities that arise in the normal course of business and have no explicit cost. Examples are accounts payable, income tax liabilities, and other accruals.

Subchapter S corporation A corporation that has elected under Subchapter S of the Internal Revenue Code to be taxed as if it were a proprietorship or partnership.

Standard deviation (σ) A statistical measure of dispersion of a probability distribution, computed by taking the square root of the weighted average squared deviations of the individual outcomes from the expected (mean) value.

Standby underwriting An underwriting arrangement used in connection with a privileged subscription offering of a security to the present stockholders of the issuing firm. The underwriters agree to purchase at a stated price any of the securities not subscribed through the exercise of rights.

Stock dividend A payment by a corporation to its shareholders of additional shares of stock. A stock dividend capitalizes a portion of the firm's retained earnings.

Stock split The exchange of more than one new share of stock for each old share held. A reverse split is the exchange of less than one new share for each old share held.

Straight bond value The value at which a convertible bond would sell in the market in the absence of the conversion feature, based upon the future interest and principal payments discounted at a rate reflecting the risk-free interest rate and a premium for risk of the debt security. Sometimes it is called *investment value.*

Subordinated debentures Unsecured bonds having a claim inferior to the claims of other creditors stated in the indenture. They are ususally subordinated to straight debentures and/or unsecured bank debt.

Synergism Recognition that the value of a combination is greater than the sum of the values of its parts. This incremental value is the economic justification of most business combinations.

Target capital structure The proportions of various components of the capital structure that management seeks in the long run in an effort to minimize the firm's overall cost of capital. In practice, target proportions often are expressed in terms of ranges rather than finite percentages.

Target weights Capital structure proportions frequently used in weighting the costs of the various components in estimating the weighted average cost of capital (WACC) of the firm. Target weights reflect the target capital structure.

Tax anticipation bills or notes Short-term debt obligations of the U.S. Treasury that mature one week after income tax payment dates. They are accepted at par in payment of income taxes.

Tender offer An offer to securities holders to purchase a given number of the securities at a stated price. The securities holders receiving a tender offer may tender their securities to the offeror within a limited time period.

Terminal (salvage) value The expected value of a capital asset(s) upon termination of a capital investment project.

Term loan A loan maturing after more than one year. Term loans usually are made by financial institutions for periods from 2 to 20 years and are repaid in installments.

Total leverage The magnification of the effect of change in sales (revenues) upon the resulting change in earnings on the residual owners' equity (or earnings per share). The combined effect of operating and financial leverage.

Trade acceptance A negotiable instrument sometimes used in extending trade credit. The seller forwards to the buyer a time draft ordering the buyer to pay a certain amount of money to the seller or his order. When accepted by the buyer, the draft becomes a trade acceptance.

Trade credit Credit usually arising from open-account purchases. It may be evidenced by trade notes or trade acceptances. The buyer is obligated to pay the seller within a certain number of days after the invoice date.

Treasury bills Short-term debt obligations of a national government. U.S. Treasury bills are auctioned weekly at a discount and are payable at par. They are the premier instruments of the U.S. money market.

Treasury stock Shares of a firm's stock that have been repurchased by it and are held in its treasury.

Trust receipt A legal document entrusting to the borrower physical posession of goods held in title by the lender. The lender must release the title for the borrower to convey title to the goods. In some trades, this financing arrangement is known as *floor planning.*

Trustee (in bankruptcy) A party in a bankruptcy proceeding whose duty is to conserve the assets and either liquidate them (under Chapter 7) or reorganize the firm (under Chapter 11). The trustee is elected by the creditors' committee and is responsible to the court.

Uncertainty The degree of potential variability of outcomes from forecasted values. The term usually is used interchangeably with *risk*.

Underpricing The pricing of an additional issue of common stock at a discount from the current market value to account for dilution and the additional supply of the stock available to investors.

Underwriters' spread The difference between the price at which an issue of securities is offered to the public and the amount paid to the issuer by the investment bankers.

Underwriting Assumption of the risk that an offering of securities will be sold to investors. This function of the investment banking process usually is performed by an *underwriting syndicate* composed of a number of investment bankers. The term may be used broadly to denote the entire process of raising long-term funds by investment bankers.

Unrecovered cost The cost of a fixed asset that has not been recovered through depreciation. It usually refers to the tax status of the asset, the unrecovered cost being the base for calculation of gain or loss on sale of the asset.

Utility function A statistical expression of an investor's satisfaction obtained by various risk-return combinations embodied in investments.

Variable costs Costs that fluctuate directly with changes in the volume of production or sales.

Vertical integration The combination of functions along the chain of production and distribution between the raw materials and the ultimate consumer.

Warehouse receipt A document used in inventory financing. The borrower stores the pledged inventories in a public warehouse, furnishing the warehouse receipt to the lender. The warehouse receipt must be presented to the warehousing firm to withdraw the goods.

Warrant A long-term option, more specifically called a *stock purchase warrant*, to purchase a stated number of shares of common stock at a specified price. Warrants usually are issued in a "package" accompanying bonds, preferred stock, or common stock.

Warrant premium The amount or percentage by which the market price of a warrant exceeds its theoretical value, which, in turn, is based upon the market price of the common stock that can be purchased by exercising the warrant.

Weighted average cost of capital (WACC) A measure of the overall cost of capital of the firm, estimated by weighting the costs of the various types of capital by their proportions in the capital structure. Book value, market value, or target weights may be used.

Working capital The investment of the firm in current assets. Gross working capital refers to total current assets. Net working capital refers to total current assets less current liabilities, or that portion of current assets financed from long-term or permanent sources.

Working capital cycle (cash cycle) The cyclical flow of funds from cash to pay for inventories, which are sold to create receivables that are subsequently collected in cash. The term may refer to the period of time from the outlay of cash to its collection.

Yield The true rate of return received by an investor from holding a security. Yield to maturity refers to the return on a bond, taking into account the difference between purchase price and the principal amount as well as interest received.

Yield curve A graph, sometimes called a *term structure of interest rates* chart, comparing interest rates to the time to maturity of debt securities issued by the same issuer or issuers of the same risk class.

Index

A

B

Q–R

This book has been set Linotron 202, in 10 point Garamond Light, leaded 2 points. Part numbers and titles are 40 point Helvetica and chapter numbers and titles are 30 point Helvetica. The size of the type page is 34 by 45½ picas.